CCNA
200-301

Official Cert Guide, Volume 2

WENDELL ODOM, CCIE No. 1624 Emeritus

Cisco Press

CCNA 200-301 Official Cert Guide, Volume 2

Wendell Odom

Copyright © 2020 Pearson Education, Inc.

Published by: Cisco Press

11 2023

Library of Congress Control Number: 2019949625

ISBN-13: 978-1-58714-713-5
ISBN-10: 1-58714-713-0

Warning and Disclaimer

This book is designed to provide information about the Cisco CCNA 200-301 exam. Every effort has been made to make this book as complete and as accurate as possible, but no warranty or fitness is implied.

The information is provided on an "as is" basis. The authors, Cisco Press, and Cisco Systems, Inc. shall have neither liability nor responsibility to any person or entity with respect to any loss or damages arising from the information contained in this book or from the use of the discs or programs that may accompany it.

The opinions expressed in this book belong to the author and are not necessarily those of Cisco Systems, Inc.

Trademark Acknowledgments

All terms mentioned in this book that are known to be trademarks or service marks have been appropriately capitalized. Cisco Press or Cisco Systems, Inc., cannot attest to the accuracy of this information. Use of a term in this book should not be regarded as affecting the validity of any trademark or service mark.

Microsoft and/or its respective suppliers make no representations about the suitability of the information contained in the documents and related graphics published as part of the services for any purpose. All such documents and related graphics are provided "as is" without warranty of any kind. Microsoft and/ or its respective suppliers hereby disclaim all warranties and conditions with regard to this information, including all warranties and conditions of merchantability, whether express, implied or statutory, fitness for a particular purpose, title and non-infringement. In no event shall Microsoft and/or its respective suppliers be liable for any special, indirect or consequential damages or any damages whatsoever resulting from loss of use, data or profits, whether in an action of contract, negligence or other tortious action, arising out of or in connection with the use or performance of information available from the services.

The documents and related graphics contained herein could include technical inaccuracies or typographical errors. Changes are periodically added to the information herein. Microsoft and/or its respective suppliers may make improvements and/or changes in the product(s) and/or the program(s) described herein at any time. Partial screenshots may be viewed in full within the software version specified.

Microsoft® and Windows® are registered trademarks of the Microsoft Corporation in the U.S.A. and other countries. Screenshots and icons reprinted with permission from the Microsoft Corporation. This book is not sponsored or endorsed by or affiliated with the Microsoft Corporation.

Special Sales

For information about buying this title in bulk quantities, or for special sales opportunities (which may include electronic versions; custom cover designs; and content particular to your business, training goals, marketing focus, or branding interests), please contact our corporate sales department at corpsales@pearsoned.com or (800) 382-3419.

For government sales inquiries, please contact governmentsales@pearsoned.com.

For questions about sales outside the U.S., please contact intlcs@pearson.com.

Feedback Information

At Cisco Press, our goal is to create in-depth technical books of the highest quality and value. Each book is crafted with care and precision, undergoing rigorous development that involves the unique expertise of members from the professional technical community.

Readers' feedback is a natural continuation of this process. If you have any comments regarding how we could improve the quality of this book, or otherwise alter it to better suit your needs, you can contact us through email at feedback@ciscopress.com. Please make sure to include the book title and ISBN in your message.

We greatly appreciate your assistance.

Editor-in-Chief: Mark Taub	**Technical Editor:** Elan Beer
Business Operation Manager, Cisco Press: Ronald Fligge	**Editorial Assistant:** Cindy Teeters
Director, ITP Product Management: Brett Bartow	**Cover Designer:** Chuti Prasertsith
Managing Editor: Sandra Schroeder	**Composition:** Tricia Bronkella
Development Editor: Christopher Cleveland	**Indexer:** Ken Johnson
Senior Project Editor: Tonya Simpson	**Proofreader:** Debbie Williams
Copy Editor: Chuck Hutchinson	

CISCO.

Americas Headquarters	Asia Pacific Headquarters	Europe Headquarters
Cisco Systems, Inc.	Cisco Systems (USA) Pte. Ltd.	Cisco Systems International BV
San Jose, CA	Singapore	Amsterdam, The Netherlands

Cisco has more than 200 offices worldwide. Addresses, phone numbers, and fax numbers are listed on the Cisco Website at www.cisco.com/go/offices.

CCDE, CCENT, Cisco Eos, Cisco HealthPresence, the Cisco logo, Cisco Lumin, Cisco Nexus, Cisco StadiumVision, Cisco TelePresence, Cisco WebEx, DCE, and Welcome to the Human Network are trademarks; Changing the Way We Work, Live, Play, and Learn and Cisco Store are service marks; and Access Registrar, Aironet, AsyncOS, Bringing the Meeting To You, Catalyst, CCDA, CCDP, CCIE, CCIP, CCNA, CCNP, CCSP, CCVP, Cisco, the Cisco Certified Internetwork Expert logo, Cisco IOS, Cisco Press, Cisco Systems, Cisco Systems Capital, the Cisco Systems logo, Cisco Unity, Collaboration Without Limitation, EtherFast, EtherSwitch, Event Center, Fast Step, Follow Me Browsing, FormShare, GigaDrive, HomeLink, Internet Quotient, IOS, iPhone, iQuick Study, IronPort, the IronPort logo, LightStream, Linksys, MediaTone, MeetingPlace, MeetingPlace Chime Sound, MGX, Networkers, Networking Academy, Network Registrar, PCNow, PIX, PowerPanels, ProConnect, ScriptShare, SenderBase, SMARTnet, Spectrum Expert, StackWise, The Fastest Way to Increase Your Internet Quotient, TransPath, WebEx, and the WebEx logo are registered trademarks of Cisco Systems, Inc. and/or its affiliates in the United States and certain other countries.

All other trademarks mentioned in this document or website are the property of their respective owners. The use of the word partner does not imply a partnership relationship between Cisco and any other company. (0812R)

About the Author

Wendell Odom, CCIE No. 1624 Emeritus, has been in the networking industry since 1981. He has worked as a network engineer, consultant, systems engineer, instructor, and course developer; he currently works writing and creating certification study tools. This book is his 29th edition of some product for Pearson, and he is the author of all editions of the CCNA Cert Guides about Routing and Switching from Cisco Press. He has written books about topics from networking basics, certification guides throughout the years for CCENT, CCNA R&S, CCNA DC, CCNP ROUTE, CCNP QoS, and CCIE R&S. He maintains study tools, links to his blogs, and other resources at www.certskills.com.

About the Contributing Author

David Hucaby, CCIE No. 4594, CWNE No. 292, is a network engineer for University of Kentucky Healthcare. He has been authoring Cisco Press titles for 20 years, with a focus on wireless and LAN switching topics. David has bachelor of science and master of science degrees in electrical engineering. He lives in Kentucky with his wife, Marci, and two daughters.

About the Technical Reviewer

Elan Beer, CCIE No. 1837, is a senior consultant and Cisco instructor specializing in data center architecture and multiprotocol network design. For the past 27 years, Elan has designed networks and trained thousands of industry experts in data center architecture, routing, and switching. Elan has been instrumental in large-scale professional service efforts designing and troubleshooting internetworks, performing data center and network audits, and assisting clients with their short- and long-term design objectives. Elan has a global perspective of network architectures via his international clientele. Elan has used his expertise to design and troubleshoot data centers and internetworks in Malaysia, North America, Europe, Australia, Africa, China, and the Middle East. Most recently, Elan has been focused on data center design, configuration, and troubleshooting as well as service provider technologies. In 1993, Elan was among the first to obtain the Cisco Certified System Instructor (CCSI) certification, and in 1996, he was among the first to attain the Cisco System highest technical certification, the Cisco Certified Internetworking Expert. Since then, Elan has been involved in numerous large-scale data center and telecommunications networking projects worldwide.

Acknowledgments

Brett Bartow continues to be the backbone of the Cisco Press brand, guiding the entire author team through the big transition in 2019–2020 with all the changes Cisco introduced to its certifications. Simply the best! Thanks for all you do, Brett!

Dave Hucaby teamed up again to write this book, contributing one chapter here to go along with his four chapters in the CCNA Volume 1 book. It's such a joy to review his work and see such polished material from the first draft. It's been a joy to work with such a consummate professional—thanks, Dave!

Chris Cleveland developed the book—again—and made it much better—again—and did it with more juggling than ever before, I think. Five months, roughly 50 technology chapters and another 50 other book elements, and countless online elements, all done with apparent ease. Kudos to Chris, yet again!

I so look forward to reading Elan Beer's tech edits of the chapters. That may seem strange to hear, but Elan has truly amazing technical editing skills. His insights range from the details of technology, to the mind of the new learner, to wording and clarity, to holes in networking logic as compared to the wording, to tiny typos that impact the meaning. Thanks again Elan for improving the chapters so much!

Tonya Simpson managed this book, along with the CCNA Volume 1 book, all in that same compressed timeframe again. As usual, on both projects, Tonya has kept the production processes rolling along and getting through the idiosyncrasies of the content. Thanks for shepherding the book through the wild again, Tonya!

As always, thanks to the production team that works with Tonya. From fixing all my grammar and passive-voice sentences to pulling the design and layout together, they do it all; thanks for putting it all together and making it look easy. And Tonya got to juggle two books of mine at the same time (again)—thanks for managing the whole production process again.

Mike Tanamachi, illustrator and mind reader, did a great job on the figures again. Mike came through again with some beautiful finished products. Thanks again, Mike.

I could not have made the timeline for this book without Chris Burns of Certskills Professional. Chris owns much of the PTP question support and administration process, works on the labs we put on my blog, and then catches anything I need to toss over my shoulder so I can focus on the books. Chris, you are the man!

A special thank you to you readers who write in with suggestions and possible errors, and especially those of you who post online at the Cisco Learning Network and at my blog (https://blog.certskills.com). Without question, the comments I receive directly and overhear by participating at CLN made this edition a better book.

Thanks to my wonderful wife, Kris, who helps make this sometimes challenging work lifestyle a breeze. I love walking this journey with you, doll. Thanks to my daughter Hannah, who actually helped a bit with the book this summer before heading off to college (go Jackets!). And thanks to Jesus Christ, Lord of everything in my life.

Contents at a Glance

Reader Services

To access additional content for this book, simply register your product. To start the registration process, go to www.ciscopress.com/register and log in or create an account*. Enter the product ISBN 9781587147135 and click Submit. After the process is complete, you will find any available bonus content under Registered Products.

*Be sure to check the box that you would like to hear from us to receive exclusive discounts on future editions of this product.

Icons Used in This Book

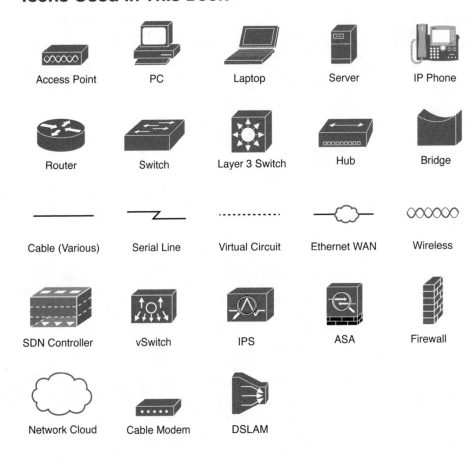

Command Syntax Conventions

The conventions used to present command syntax in this book are the same conventions used in the IOS Command Reference. The Command Reference describes these conventions as follows:

- **Boldface** indicates commands and keywords that are entered literally as shown. In actual configuration examples and output (not general command syntax), boldface indicates commands that are manually input by the user (such as a **show** command).

- *Italic* indicates arguments for which you supply actual values.

- Vertical bars (|) separate alternative, mutually exclusive elements.

- Square brackets ([ ]) indicate an optional element.

- Braces ({ }) indicate a required choice.

- Braces within brackets ([{ }]) indicate a required choice within an optional element.

Contents

Introduction

About Cisco Certifications and CCNA

Congratulations! If you're reading far enough to look at this book's Introduction, you've probably already decided to go for your Cisco certification, and the CCNA certification is the one place to begin that journey. If you want to succeed as a technical person in the networking industry at all, you need to know Cisco. Cisco has a ridiculously high market share in the router and switch marketplace, with more than 80 percent market share in some markets. In many geographies and markets around the world, networking equals Cisco. If you want to be taken seriously as a network engineer, Cisco certification makes perfect sense.

> **NOTE** This book discusses part of the content Cisco includes in the CCNA 200-301 exam, with the *CCNA 200-301 Official Cert Guide, Volume 1,* covering the rest. You will need both the Volume 1 and Volume 2 books to have all the content necessary for the exam.

The first few pages of this Introduction explain the core features of the Cisco Career Certification program, of which the Cisco Certified Network Associate (CCNA) serves as the foundation for all the other certifications in the program. This section begins with a comparison of the old to the new certifications due to some huge program changes in 2019. It then gives the key features of CCNA, how to get it, and what's on the exam.

The Big Changes to Cisco Certifications in 2019

Cisco announced sweeping changes to its career certification program around mid-year 2019. Because so many of you will have read and heard about the old versions of the CCNA certification, this Introduction begins with a few comparisons between the old and new CCNA as well as some of the other Cisco career certifications.

First, consider the Cisco career certifications before 2019, as shown in Figure I-1. At that time, Cisco offered 10 separate CCNA certifications in different technology tracks. Cisco also had eight Professional-level (CCNP, or Cisco Certified Network Professional) certifications.

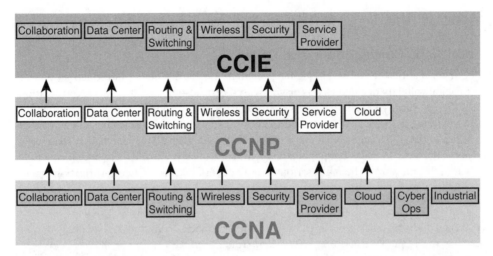

Figure I-1   *Old Cisco Certification Silo Concepts*

Why so many? Cisco began with one track—Routing and Switching—back in 1998. Over time, Cisco identified more and more technology areas that had grown to have enough content to justify another set of CCNA and CCNP certifications on those topics, so Cisco added more tracks. Many of those also grew to support expert-level topics with CCIE (Cisco Certified Internetwork Expert).

In 2019, Cisco consolidated the tracks and moved the topics around quite a bit, as shown in Figure I-2.

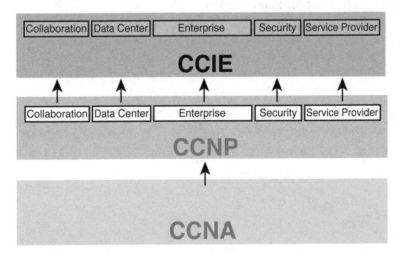

Figure I-2   *New Cisco Certification Tracks and Structure*

All the tracks now begin with the content in the one remaining CCNA certification. For CCNP, you now have a choice of five technology areas for your next steps, as shown in Figure I-2. (Note that Cisco replaced "Routing and Switching" with "Enterprise.")

Cisco made the following changes with the 2019 announcements:

CCENT: Retired the only entry-level certification (CCENT, or Cisco Certified Entry Network Technician), with no replacement.

CCNA: Retired all the CCNA certifications except what was then known as "CCNA Routing and Switching," which became simply "CCNA."

CCNP: Consolidated the professional-level (CCNP) certifications to five tracks, including merging CCNP Routing and Switching and CCNP Wireless into CCNP Enterprise.

CCIE: Achieved better alignment with CCNP tracks through the consolidations.

Cisco needed to move many of the individual exam topics from one exam to another because of the number of changes. For instance, Cisco announced the retirement of all the associate certifications—nine CCNA certifications plus the CCDA (Design Associate) certification—but those technologies didn't disappear! Cisco just moved the topics around to different exams in different certifications. (Note that Cisco later announced that CCNA Cyber Ops would remain, and not be retired, with details to be announced.)

Consider wireless LANs as an example. The 2019 announcements retired both CCNA Wireless and CCNP Wireless as certifications. Some of the old CCNA Wireless topics landed in the new CCNA, whereas others landed in the two CCNP Enterprise exams about wireless LANs.

For those of you who want to learn more about the transition, check out my blog (https://blog.certskills.com) and look for posts in the News category from around June 2019. Now on to the details about CCNA as it exists starting in 2019!

How to Get Your CCNA Certification

As you saw in Figure I-2, all career certification paths now begin with CCNA. So how do you get it? Today, you have one and only one option to achieve CCNA certification:

Take and pass one exam: the Cisco 200-301 CCNA exam.

To take the 200-301 exam, or any Cisco exam, you will use the services of Pearson VUE (vue.com). The process works something like this:

1. Establish a login at https://home.pearsonvue.com/ (or use your existing login).

2. Register for, schedule a time and place, and pay for the Cisco 200-301 exam, all from the VUE website.

3. Take the exam at the VUE testing center.

4. You will receive a notice of your score, and whether you passed, before you leave the testing center.

Types of Questions on the CCNA 200-301 Exam

The Cisco CCNA and CCNP exams all follow the same general format, with these types of questions:

- Multiple-choice, single-answer
- Multiple-choice, multiple-answer

- Testlet (one scenario with multiple multiple-choice questions)

- Drag-and-drop

- Simulated lab (sim)

- Simlet

Although the first four types of questions in the list should be somewhat familiar to you from other tests in school, the last two are more common to IT tests and Cisco exams in particular. Both use a network simulator to ask questions so that you control and use simulated Cisco devices. In particular:

Sim questions: You see a network topology and lab scenario, and can access the devices. Your job is to fix a problem with the configuration.

Simlet questions: This style combines sim and testlet question formats. As with a sim question, you see a network topology and lab scenario, and can access the devices. However, as with a testlet, you also see multiple multiple-choice questions. Instead of changing or fixing the configuration, you answer questions about the current state of the network.

These two question styles with the simulator give Cisco the ability to test your configuration skills with sim questions, and your verification and troubleshooting skills with simlet questions.

Before taking the test, learn the exam user interface by watching some videos Cisco provides about the interface. To find the videos, just go to www.cisco.com and search for "Cisco Certification Exam Tutorial Videos."

CCNA 200-301 Exam Content, Per Cisco

Ever since I was in grade school, whenever a teacher announced that we were having a test soon, someone would always ask, "What's on the test?" We all want to know, and we all want to study what matters and avoid studying what doesn't matter.

Cisco tells the world the topics on each of its exams. Cisco wants the public to know the variety of topics and get an idea about the kinds of knowledge and skills required for each topic for every Cisco certification exam. To find the details, go to www.cisco.com/go/certifications, look for the CCNA page, and navigate until you see the exam topics.

This book also lists those same exam topics in several places. From one perspective, every chapter sets about to explain a small set of exam topics, so each chapter begins with the list of exam topics covered in that chapter. However, you might want to also see the exam topics in one place, so Appendix G, "Exam Topics Cross-Reference," lists all the exam topics. You may want to download Appendix G in PDF form and keep it handy. The appendix lists the exam topics with two different cross-references:

- A list of exam topics and the chapter(s) that covers each topic

- A list of chapters and the exam topics covered in each chapter

Exam Topic Verbs and Depth

Reading and understanding the exam topics, especially deciding the depth of skills required for each exam topic, require some thought. Each exam topic mentions the name of some technology, but it also lists a verb that implies the depth to which you must master the topic. The primary exam topics each list one or more verbs that describe the skill level required. For example, consider the following exam topic:

Configure and **verify** IPv4 addressing and subnetting

Note that this one exam topic has two verbs (*configure* and *verify*). Per this exam topic, you should be able to not only configure IPv4 addresses and subnets, but you also should understand them well enough to verify that the configuration works. In contrast, the following exam topic asks you to describe a technology but does not ask you to configure it:

Describe the purpose of first hop redundancy protocol

The *describe* verb tells you to be ready to describe whatever a "first hop redundancy protocol" is. That exam topic also implies that you do not then need to be ready to configure or verify any first hop redundancy protocols (HSRP, VRRP, and GLBP).

Finally, note that the configure and verify exam topics imply that you should be able to describe and explain and otherwise master the concepts so that you understand what you have configured. The earlier "Configure and verify IPv4 addressing and subnetting" does not mean that you should know how to type commands but have no clue as to what you configured. You must first master the conceptual exam topic verbs. The progression runs something like this:

Describe, Identify, Explain, Compare/Contrast, Configure, Verify, Troubleshoot

For instance, an exam topic that lists "compare and contrast" means that you should be able to describe, identify, and explain the technology. Also, an exam topic with "configure and verify" tells you to also be ready to describe, explain, and compare/contrast.

The Context Surrounding the Exam Topics

Take a moment to navigate to www.cisco.com/go/certifications and find the list of exam topics for the CCNA 200-301 exam. Did your eyes go straight to the list of exam topics? Or did you take the time to read the paragraphs above the exam topics first?

That list of exam topics for the CCNA 200-301 exam includes a little over 50 primary exam topics and about 50 more secondary exam topics. The primary topics have those verbs as just discussed, which tell you something about the depth of skill required. The secondary topics list only the names of more technologies to know.

However, the top of the web page that lists the exam topics also lists some important information that tells us some important facts about the exam topics. In particular, that leading text, found at the beginning of Cisco exam topic pages of most every exam, tells us these important points:

■ The guidelines may change over time.

■ The exam topics are general guidelines about what may be on the exam.

■ The actual exam may include "other related topics."

Interpreting these three facts in order, I would not expect to see a change to the published list of exam topics for the exam. I've been writing the Cisco Press CCNA Cert Guides since Cisco announced CCNA back in 1998, and I've never seen Cisco change the official exam topics in the middle of an exam—not even to fix typos. But the introductory words say that they might change the exam topics, so it's worth checking.

As for the second item in the preceding list, even before you know what the acronyms mean, you can see that the exam topics give you a general but not detailed idea about each topic. The exam topics do not attempt to clarify every nook and cranny or to list every command and parameter; however, this book serves as a great tool in that it acts as a much more detailed interpretation of the exam topics. We examine every exam topic, and if we think a concept or command is possibly within an exam topic, we put it into the book. So, the exam topics give us general guidance, and these books give us much more detailed guidance.

The third item in the list uses literal wording that runs something like this: "However, other related topics may also appear on any specific delivery of the exam." That one statement can be a bit jarring to test takers, but what does it really mean? Unpacking the statement, it says that such questions may appear on any one exam but may not; in other words, they don't set about to ask every test taker some questions that include concepts not mentioned in the exam topics. Second, the phrase "...other **related** topics..." emphasizes that any such questions would be related to some exam topic, rather than being far afield—a fact that helps us in how we respond to this particular program policy.

For instance, the CCNA 200-301 exam includes configuring and verifying the OSPF routing protocol, but it does not mention the EIGRP routing protocol. I personally would be unsurprised to see an OSPF question that required a term or fact not specifically mentioned in the exam topics, but not one that's some feature that (in my opinion) ventures far away from the OSPF features in the exam topics. Also, I would not expect to see a question about how to configure and verify EIGRP.

And just as one final side point, note that Cisco does on occasion ask a test taker some unscored questions, and those may appear to be in this vein of questions from outside topics. When you sit down to take the exam, the small print mentions that you may see unscored questions and you won't know which ones are unscored. (These questions give Cisco a way to test possible new questions.) Yet some of these might be ones that fall into the "other related topics" category but then not affect your score.

You should prepare a little differently for any Cisco exam, in comparison to, say, an exam back in school, in light of Cisco's "other related questions" policy:

■ Do not approach an exam topic with an "I'll learn the core concepts and ignore the edges" approach.

■ Instead, approach each exam topic with a "pick up all the points I can" approach by mastering each exam topic, both in breadth and in depth.

■ Go beyond each exam topic when practicing configuration and verification by taking a little extra time to look for additional **show** commands and configuration options, and make sure you understand as much of the **show** command output that you can.

By mastering the known topics, and looking for places to go a little deeper, you will hopefully pick up the most points you can from questions about the exam topics. Then the extra practice you do with commands may happen to help you learn beyond the exam topics in a way that can help you pick up other points as well.

CCNA 200-301 Exam Content, Per This Book

When we created the Official Cert Guide content for the CCNA 200-301 exam, we considered a few options for how to package the content, and we landed on releasing a two-book set. Figure I-3 shows the setup of the content, with roughly 60 percent of the content in Volume 1 and the rest in Volume 2.

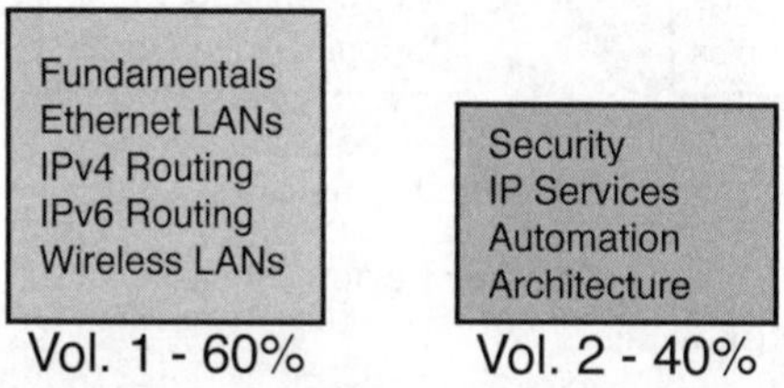

Fundamentals
Ethernet LANs
IPv4 Routing
IPv6 Routing
Wireless LANs

Security
IP Services
Automation
Architecture

Vol. 1 - 60%   Vol. 2 - 40%

Figure I-3 *Two Books for CCNA 200-301*

The two books together cover all the exam topics in the CCNA 200-301 exam. Each chapter in each book develops the concepts and commands related to an exam topic, with clear and detailed explanations, frequent figures, and many examples that build your understanding of how Cisco networks work.

As for choosing what content to put into the books, note that we begin and finish with Cisco's exam topics, but with an eye toward predicting as many of the "other related topics" as we can. We start with the list of exam topics and apply a fair amount of experience, discussion, and other secret sauce to come up with an interpretation of what specific concepts and commands are worthy of being in the books or not. At the end of the writing process, the books should cover all the published exam topics, with additional depth and breadth that I choose based on the analysis of the exam. As we have done from the very first edition of the *CCNA Official Cert Guide*, we intend to cover each and every topic in depth. But as you would expect, we cannot predict every single fact on the exam given the nature of the exam policies, but we do our best to cover all known topics.

Book Features

This book includes many study features beyond the core explanations and examples in each chapter. This section acts as a reference to the various features in the book.

Chapter Features and How to Use Each Chapter

Each chapter of this book is a self-contained short course about one small topic area, organized for reading and study, as follows:

"Do I Know This Already?" quizzes: Each chapter begins with a pre-chapter quiz.

Foundation Topics: This is the heading for the core content section of the chapter.

Chapter Review: This section includes a list of study tasks useful to help you remember concepts, connect ideas, and practice skills-based content in the chapter.

Figure I-4 shows how each chapter uses these three key elements. You start with the DIKTA quiz. You can use the score to determine whether you already know a lot, or not so much, and determine how to approach reading the Foundation Topics (that is, the technology content in the chapter). When finished, use the Chapter Review tasks to start working on mastering your memory of the facts and skills with configuration, verification, and troubleshooting.

Figure I-4 *Three Primary Tasks for a First Pass Through Each Chapter*

In addition to these three main chapter features, each "Chapter Review" section uses a variety of other book features, including the following:

■ **Review Key Topics:** Inside the "Foundation Topics" section, the Key Topic icon appears next to the most important items, for the purpose of later review and mastery. While all content matters, some is, of course, more important to learn, or needs more review to master, so these items are noted as key topics. The Chapter Review lists the key topics in a table. Scan the chapter for these items to review them. Or review the key topics interactively using the companion website.

■ **Complete Tables from Memory:** Instead of just rereading an important table of information, you will find some tables have been turned into memory tables, an interactive exercise found on the companion website. Memory tables repeat the table but with parts of the table removed. You can then fill in the table to exercise your memory and click to check your work.

■ **Key Terms You Should Know:** You do not need to be able to write a formal definition of all terms from scratch; however, you do need to understand each term well enough to understand exam questions and answers. The Chapter Review lists the key terminology from the chapter. Make sure you have a good understanding of each term and use the Glossary to cross-check your own mental definitions. You can also review key terms with the "Key Terms Flashcards" app on the companion website.

- **Labs:** Many exam topics use verbs such as *configure* and *verify*; all these refer to skills you should practice at the user interface (CLI) of a router or switch. The Chapter and Part Reviews refer you to these other tools. The upcoming section titled "About Building Hands-On Skills" discusses your options.

- **Command References:** Some book chapters cover a large number of router and switch commands. The Chapter Review includes reference tables for the commands used in that chapter, along with an explanation. Use these tables for reference, but also use them for study. Just cover one column of the table and see how much you can remember and complete mentally.

- **Review DIKTA Questions:** Although you have already seen the DIKTA questions from the chapters, re-answering those questions can prove a useful way to review facts. The Part Review suggests that you repeat the DIKTA questions but using the Pearson Test Prep (PTP) exam.

Part Features and How to Use the Part Review

The book organizes the chapters into parts for the purpose of helping you study for the exam. Each part groups a small number of related chapters together. Then the study process (described just before Chapter 1) suggests that you pause after each part to do a review of all chapters in the part. Figure I-5 lists the titles of the eight parts and the chapters in those parts (by chapter number) for this book.

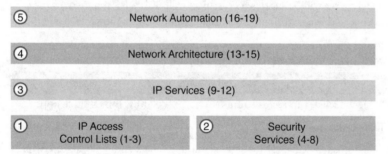

Figure I-5 *The Book Parts (by Title), and Chapter Numbers in Each Part*

The Part Review that ends each part acts as a tool to help you with spaced review sessions. Spaced reviews—that is, reviewing content several times over the course of your study—help improve retention. The Part Review activities include many of the same kinds of activities seen in the Chapter Review. Avoid skipping the Part Review, and take the time to do the review; it will help you in the long run.

The Companion Website for Online Content Review

We created an electronic version of every Chapter and Part Review task that could be improved though an interactive version of the tool. For instance, you can take a "Do I Know This Already?" quiz by reading the pages of the book, but you can also use our testing software. As another example, when you want to review the key topics from a chapter, you can find all those in electronic form as well.

All the electronic review elements, as well as other electronic components of the book, exist on this book's companion website. The companion website gives you a big advantage: you can do most of your Chapter and Part Review work from anywhere using the interactive tools on the site. The advantages include

- **Easier to use:** Instead of having to print out copies of the appendixes and do the work on paper, you can use these new apps, which provide you with an easy-to-use, interactive experience that you can easily run over and over.

- **Convenient:** When you have a spare 5–10 minutes, go to the book's website and review content from one of your recently finished chapters.

- **Untethered from the book:** You can access your review activities from anywhere—no need to have the book with you.

- **Good for tactile learners:** Sometimes looking at a static page after reading a chapter lets your mind wander. Tactile learners might do better by at least typing answers into an app, or clicking inside an app to navigate, to help keep you focused on the activity.

The interactive Chapter Review elements should improve your chances of passing as well. Our in-depth reader surveys over the years show that those who do the Chapter and Part Reviews learn more. Those who use the interactive versions of the review elements also tend to do more of the Chapter and Part Review work. So take advantage of the tools and maybe you will be more successful as well. Table I-1 summarizes these interactive applications and the traditional book features that cover the same content.

Table I-1 *Book Features with Both Traditional and App Options*

Feature	Traditional	App
Key Topic	Table with list; flip pages to find	Key Topics Table app
Config Checklist	Just one of many types of key topics	Config Checklist app
Key Terms	Listed in each "Chapter Review" section, with the Glossary in the back of the book	Glossary Flash Cards app

The companion website also includes links to download, navigate, or stream for these types of content:

- Pearson Sim Lite Desktop App

- Pearson Test Prep (PTP) Desktop App

- Pearson Test Prep (PTP) Web App

- Videos as mentioned in book chapters

How to Access the Companion Website

To access the companion website, which gives you access to the electronic content with this book, start by establishing a login at www.ciscopress.com and register your book. To do so, simply go to www.ciscopress.com/register and enter the ISBN of the print book: 9781587147135. After you have registered your book, go to your account page and click the **Registered Products** tab. From there, click the **Access Bonus Content** link to get access to the book's companion website.

Note that if you buy the *Premium Edition eBook and Practice Test* version of this book from Cisco Press, your book will automatically be registered on your account page. Simply go to your account page, click the **Registered Products** tab, and select **Access Bonus Content** to access the book's companion website.

How to Access the Pearson Test Prep (PTP) App

You have two options for installing and using the Pearson Test Prep application: a web app and a desktop app.

To use the Pearson Test Prep application, start by finding the registration code that comes with the book. You can find the code in these ways:

- **Print book:** Look in the cardboard sleeve in the back of the book for a piece of paper with your book's unique PTP code.

- **Premium Edition:** If you purchase the Premium Edition eBook and Practice Test directly from the Cisco Press website, the code will be populated on your account page after purchase. Just log in at www.ciscopress.com, click **account** to see details of your account, and click the **digital purchases** tab.

- **Amazon Kindle:** For those who purchase a Kindle edition from Amazon, the access code will be supplied directly from Amazon.

- **Other bookseller e-books:** Note that if you purchase an e-book version from any other source, the practice test is not included because other vendors to date have not chosen to vend the required unique access code.

NOTE Do not lose the activation code because it is the only means with which you can access the QA content with the book.

Once you have the access code, to find instructions about both the PTP web app and the desktop app, follow these steps:

Step 1. Open this book's companion website, as was shown earlier in this Introduction under the heading "How to Access the Companion Website."

Step 2. Click the **Practice Exams** button.

Step 3. Follow the instructions listed there both for installing the desktop app and for using the web app.

Note that if you want to use the web app only at this point, just navigate to www.pearsontestprep.com, establish a free login if you do not already have one, and register this book's practice tests using the registration code you just found. The process should take only a couple of minutes.

> **NOTE**   Amazon e-book (Kindle) customers: It is easy to miss Amazon's email that lists your PTP access code. Soon after you purchase the Kindle e-book, Amazon should send an email. However, the email uses very generic text and makes no specific mention of PTP or practice exams. To find your code, read every email from Amazon after you purchase the book. Also, do the usual checks (such as checking your spam folder) for ensuring your email arrives.

> **NOTE**   Other e-book customers: As of the time of publication, only the publisher and Amazon supply PTP access codes when you purchase their e-book editions of this book.

Feature Reference

The following list provides an easy reference to get the basic idea behind each book feature:

- **Practice exam:** The book gives you the rights to the Pearson Test Prep (PTP) testing software, available as a web app and desktop app. Use the access code on a piece of cardboard in the sleeve in the back of the book, and use the companion website to download the desktop app or navigate to the web app (or just go to www.pearsontestprep.com).

- **E-book:** Pearson offers an e-book version of this book that includes extra practice tests. If interested, look for the special offer on a coupon card inserted in the sleeve in the back of the book. This offer enables you to purchase the *CCNA 200-301 Official Cert Guide, Volume 2, Premium Edition eBook and Practice Test* at a 70 percent discount off the list price. The product includes three versions of the e-book: PDF (for reading on your computer), EPUB (for reading on your tablet, mobile device, or Nook or other e-reader), and Mobi (the native Kindle version). It also includes additional practice test questions and enhanced practice test features.

- **Mentoring videos:** The companion website also includes a number of videos about other topics as mentioned in individual chapters.

- **CCNA 200-301 Network Simulator Lite:** This lite version of the best-selling CCNA Network Simulator from Pearson provides you with a means, right now, to experience the Cisco command-line interface (CLI). No need to go buy real gear or buy a full simulator to start learning the CLI. Just install it from the companion website.

- **CCNA Simulator:** If you are looking for more hands-on practice, you might want to consider purchasing the CCNA Network Simulator. You can purchase a copy of this software from Pearson at http://pearsonitcertification.com/networksimulator or other retail outlets. To help you with your studies, Pearson has created a mapping guide that maps each of the labs in the simulator to the specific sections in each volume of the CCNA Cert Guide. You can get this mapping guide free on the Extras tab on the book product page: www.ciscopress.com/title/9781587147135.

- **PearsonITCertification.com:** The website www.pearsonitcertification.com is a great resource for all things IT-certification related. Check out the great CCNA articles, videos, blogs, and other certification preparation tools from the industry's best authors and trainers.

- **Author's website and blogs:** The author maintains a website that hosts tools and links useful when studying for CCNA. In particular, the site has a large number of free lab exercises about CCNA content, additional sample questions, and other exercises. Additionally, the site indexes all content so you can study based on the book chapters and parts. To find it, navigate to https://blog.certskills.com.

Book Organization, Chapters, and Appendixes

The *CCNA 200-301 Official Cert Guide, Volume 1*, contains 29 chapters, while this book has 19 core chapters. Each chapter covers a subset of the topics on the CCNA exam. The book organizes its chapters into parts of three to five chapters as follows:

- **Part I: IP Access Control Lists**

  - **Chapter 1, "Introduction to TCP/IP Transport and Applications,"** completes most of the detailed discussion of the upper two layers of the TCP/IP model (transport and application), focusing on TCP and applications.

  - **Chapter 2, "Basic IPv4 Access Control Lists,"** examines how standard IP ACLs can filter packets based on the source IP address so that a router will not forward the packet.

  - **Chapter 3, "Advanced IPv4 Access Control Lists,"** examines both named and numbered ACLs, and both standard and extended IP ACLs.

- **Part II: Security Services**

  - **Chapter 4, "Security Architectures,"** discusses a wide range of fundamental concepts in network security.

  - **Chapter 5, "Securing Network Devices,"** shows how to use the router and switch CLI and introduces the concepts behind firewalls and intrusion prevention systems (IPSs).

  - **Chapter 6, "Implementing Switch Port Security,"** explains the concepts as well as how to configure and verify switch port security, a switch feature that does basic MAC-based monitoring of the devices that send data into a switch.

  - **Chapter 7, "Implementing DHCP,"** discusses how hosts can be configured with their IPv4 settings and how they can learn those settings with DHCP.

  - **Chapter 8, "DHCP Snooping and ARP Inspection,"** shows how to implement two related switch security features, with one focusing on reacting to suspicious DHCP messages and the other reacting to suspicious ARP messages.

- Part III: IP Services

  - Chapter 9, "Device Management Protocols," discusses the concepts and configuration of some common network management tools: syslog, NTP, CDP, and LLDP.

  - Chapter 10, "Network Address Translation," works through the complete concept, configuration, verification, and troubleshooting sequence for the router NAT feature, including how it helps conserve public IPv4 addresses.

  - Chapter 11, "Quality of Service (QoS)," discusses a wide variety of concepts all related to the broad topic of QoS.

  - Chapter 12, "Miscellaneous IP Services," discusses several topics for which the exam requires conceptual knowledge but no configuration knowledge, including FHRPs (including HSRP), SNMP, TFTP, and FTP.

- Part IV: Network Architecture

  - Chapter 13, "LAN Architecture," examines various ways to design Ethernet LANs, discussing the pros and cons, and explains common design terminology, including Power over Ethernet (PoE).

  - Chapter 14, "WAN Architecture," discusses the concepts behind three WAN alternatives: Metro Ethernet, MPLS VPNs, and Internet VPNs.

  - Chapter 15, "Cloud Architecture," explains the basic concepts and then generally discusses the impact that cloud computing has on a typical enterprise network, including the foundational concepts of server virtualization.

- Part V: Network Automation

  - Chapter 16, "Introduction to Controller-Based Networking," discusses many concepts and terms related to how Software-Defined Networking (SDN) and network programmability are impacting typical enterprise networks.

  - Chapter 17, "Cisco Software-Defined Access (SDA)," discusses Cisco's Software-Defined Networking (SDN) offering for the enterprise, including the DNA Center controller.

  - Chapter 18, "Understanding REST and JSON," explains the foundational concepts of REST APIs, data structures, and how JSON can be useful for exchanging data using APIs.

  - Chapter 19, "Understanding Ansible, Puppet, and Chef," discusses the need for configuration management software and introduces the basics of each of these three configuration management tools.

- Part VI: Final Review

  - Chapter 20, "Final Review," suggests a plan for final preparation after you have finished the core parts of the book, in particular explaining the many study options available in the book.

- Part VII: Appendixes

  - Appendix A, "Numeric Reference Tables," lists several tables of numeric information, including a binary-to-decimal conversion table and a list of powers of 2.

- Appendix B, "CCNA 200-301 Volume 2 Exam Updates," is a place for the author to add book content mid-edition. Always check online for the latest PDF version of this appendix; the appendix lists download instructions.

- Appendix C, "Answers to the 'Do I Know This Already?' Quizzes," includes the explanations to all the "Do I Know This Already" quizzes.

- The **Glossary** contains definitions for many of the terms used in the book, including the terms listed in the "Key Terms You Should Know" sections at the conclusion of the chapters.

- Online Appendixes

  - Appendix D, "Topics from Previous Editions"

  - Appendix E, "Practice for Chapter 2: Basic IPv4 Access Control Lists"

  - Appendix F, "Previous Edition ICND1 Chapter 35: Managing IOS Files"

  - Appendix G, "Exam Topics Cross-Reference," provides some tables to help you find where each exam objective is covered in the book.

  - Appendix H, "Study Planner," is a spreadsheet with major study milestones, where you can track your progress through your study.

About Building Hands-On Skills

You need skills in using Cisco routers and switches, specifically the Cisco command-line interface (CLI). The Cisco CLI is a text-based command-and-response user interface: you type a command, and the device (a router or switch) displays messages in response. To answer sim and simlet questions on the exams, you need to know a lot of commands, and you need to be able to navigate to the right place in the CLI to use those commands.

This next section walks through the options of what is included in the book, with a brief description of lab options outside the book.

Config Lab Exercises

Some router and switch features require multiple configuration commands. Part of the skill you need to learn is to remember which configuration commands work together, which ones are required, and which ones are optional. So, the challenge level goes beyond just picking the right parameters on one command. You have to choose which commands to use, in which combination, typically on multiple devices. And getting good at that kind of task requires practice.

Each Config Lab lists details about a straightforward lab exercise for which you should create a small set of configuration commands for a few devices. Each lab presents a sample lab topology, with some requirements, and you have to decide what to configure on each device. The answer then shows a sample configuration. Your job is to create the configuration and then check your answer versus the supplied answer.

Config Lab content resides outside the book at the author's blog site (https://blog.certskills.com). You can navigate to the Config Lab in a couple of ways from the site, or just go directly to https://blog.certskills.com/category/hands-on/config-lab/ to reach a list of all Config Labs. Figure I-6 shows the logo that you will see with each Config Lab.

Figure I-6   *Config Lab Logo in the Author's Blogs*

These Config Labs have several benefits, including the following:

Untethered and responsive: Do them from anywhere, from any web browser, from your phone or tablet, untethered from the book.

Designed for idle moments: Each lab is designed as a 5- to 10-minute exercise if all you are doing is typing in a text editor or writing your answer on paper.

Two outcomes, both good: Practice getting better and faster with basic configuration, or if you get lost, you have discovered a topic that you can now go back and reread to complete your knowledge. Either way, you are a step closer to being ready for the exam!

Blog format: The format allows easy adds and changes by me and easy comments by you.

Self-assessment: As part of final review, you should be able to do all the Config Labs, without help, and with confidence.

Note that the blog organizes these Config Lab posts by book chapter, so you can easily use these at both Chapter Review and Part Review.

A Quick Start with Pearson Network Simulator Lite

The decision of how to get hands-on skills can be a little scary at first. The good news: You have a free and simple first step to experience the CLI: install and use the Pearson Network Simulator Lite (or NetSim Lite) that comes with this book.

This book comes with a lite version of the best-selling CCNA Network Simulator from Pearson, which provides you with a means, right now, to experience the Cisco CLI. No need to go buy real gear or buy a full simulator to start learning the CLI. Just install it from the companion website.

The CCNA 200-301 Network Simulator Lite Volume 2 software contains 13 labs covering ACL topics from Part I in the book. So, make sure to use the NetSim Lite to learn the basics of the CLI to get a good start.

Of course, one reason that you get access to the NetSim Lite is that the publisher hopes you will buy the full product. However, even if you do not use the full product, you can still learn from the labs that come with NetSim Lite while deciding about what options to pursue.

The Pearson Network Simulator

The Config Labs and the Pearson Network Simulator Lite both fill specific needs, and they both come with the book. However, you need more than those two tools.

The single best option for lab work to do along with this book is the paid version of the Pearson Network Simulator. This simulator product simulates Cisco routers and switches so that you can learn for CCNA certification. But more importantly, it focuses on learning for the exam by providing a large number of useful lab exercises. Reader surveys tell us that those people who use the Simulator along with the book love the learning process and rave about how the book and Simulator work well together.

Of course, you need to make a decision for yourself and consider all the options. Thankfully, you can get a great idea of how the full Simulator product works by using the Pearson Network Simulator Lite product included with the book. Both have the same base code, same user interface, and same types of labs. Try the Lite version to decide if you want to buy the full product.

Note that the Simulator and the books work on a different release schedule. For a time in 2020, the Simulator will be the one created for the previous versions of the exams (ICND1 100-101, ICND2 200-101, and CCNA 200-120). Interestingly, Cisco did not add a large number of new topics that require CLI skills to the CCNA 200-301 exam as compared with its predecessor, so the old Simulator covers most of the CCNA 200-301 CLI topics. So, during the interim before the products based on the 200-301 exam come out, the old Simulator products should be quite useful.

On a practical note, when you want to do labs when reading a chapter or doing Part Review, the Simulator organizes the labs to match the book. Just look for the Sort by Chapter tab in the Simulator's user interface. However, during the months in 2020 for which the Simulator is the older edition listing the older exams in the title, you will need to refer to a PDF that lists those labs versus this book's organization. You can find that PDF on the book product page under the Downloads tab here: www.ciscopress.com/title/9781587147135.

More Lab Options

If you decide against using the full Pearson Network Simulator, you still need hands-on experience. You should plan to use some lab environment to practice as much CLI as possible.

First, you can use real Cisco routers and switches. You can buy them, new or used, or borrow them at work. You can rent them for a fee. If you have the right mix of gear, you could even do the Config Lab exercises from my blog on that gear or try to re-create examples from the book.

Cisco also makes a simulator that works very well as a learning tool: Cisco Packet Tracer. Cisco now makes Packet Tracer available for free. However, unlike the Pearson Network Simulator, it does not include lab exercises that direct you as to how to go about learning each topic. If interested in more information about Packet Tracer, check out my series about using Packet Tracer at my blog (https://blog.certskills.com); just search for "Packet Tracer."

Cisco offers a virtualization product that lets you run router and switch operating system (OS) images in a virtual environment. This tool, the Virtual Internet Routing Lab (VIRL), lets you create a lab topology, start the topology, and connect to real router and switch OS images. Check out http://virl.cisco.com for more information.

You can even rent virtual Cisco router and switch lab pods from Cisco, in an offering called Cisco Learning Labs (https://learningnetworkstore.cisco.com/cisco-learning-labs).

This book does not tell you what option to use, but you should plan on getting some hands-on practice somehow. The important thing to know is that most people need to practice using the Cisco CLI to be ready to pass these exams.

For More Information

If you have any comments about the book, submit them via www.ciscopress.com. Just go to the website, select **Contact Us**, and type your message.

Cisco might make changes that affect the CCNA certification from time to time. You should always check www.cisco.com/go/ccna for the latest details.

The *CCNA 200-301 Official Cert Guide, Volume 2*, helps you attain CCNA certification. This is the CCNA certification book from the only Cisco-authorized publisher. We at Cisco Press believe that this book certainly can help you achieve CCNA certification, but the real work is up to you! I trust that your time will be well spent.

Figure Credits

Figure 7-9, screenshot of network connection details © Microsoft, 2019

Figure 7-10, screenshot(s) reprinted with permission from Apple, Inc.

Figure 7-11, screenshot of Linux © The Linux Foundation

Figure 12-16, screenshot of CS Blogfigs 2018 © FileZila

Figure 13-9, electric outlet © Mike McDonald/Shutterstock

Figure 15-10, screenshot of Set Up VM with Different CPU/RAM/OS © 2019, Amazon Web Services, Inc

Figure 16-13, illustration of man icon © AlexHliv/Shutterstock

Figure 17-1, illustration of man icon © AlexHliv/Shutterstock

Figure 17-11, illustration of man icon © AlexHliv/Shutterstock

Figure 18-9, screenshot of REST GET Request © 2019 Postman, Inc.

Figure 20-1, screenshot of PTP Grading © 2019 Pearson Education

Figure 20-2, screenshot of PTP Grading © 2019 Pearson Education

Figure D-1, ribbon set © petrnutil/123RF

The *CCNA Official Cert Guide, Volume 2* includes the topics that help you build an enterprise network so all devices can communicate with all other devices. Parts I and II of this book focus on how to secure that enterprise network so that only the appropriate devices and users can communicate.

Part I focuses on IP Version 4 (IPv4) access control lists (ACLs). ACLs are IPv4 packet filters that can be programmed to look at IPv4 packet headers, make choices, and either allow a packet through or discard the packet. Because you can implement IPv4 ACLs on any router, a network engineer has a large number of options of where to use ACLs, without adding additional hardware or software, making ACLs a very flexible and useful tool.

Chapter 1 begins this part with an introduction to the TCP/IP transport layer protocols TCP and UDP, along with an introduction to several TCP/IP applications. This chapter provides the necessary background to understand the ACL chapters and to better prepare you for upcoming discussions of additional security topics in Part II and IP services topics in Part III.

Chapters 2 and 3 get into details about ACLs. Chapter 2 discusses ACL basics, avoiding some of the detail to ensure that you master several key concepts. Chapter 3 then looks at the much wider array of ACL features to make you ready to take advantage of the power of ACLs and to be ready to better manage those ACLs.

Part I

IP Access Control Lists

Introduction to TCP/IP Transport and Applications

This chapter covers the following exam topics:

1.0 Network Fundamentals

1.5 Compare TCP to UDP

4.0 IP Services

4.3 Explain the role of DHCP and DNS in the network

The CCNA exam focuses mostly on functions at the lower layers of TCP/IP, which define how IP networks can send IP packets from host to host using LANs and WANs. This chapter explains the basics of a few topics that receive less attention on the exams: the TCP/IP transport layer and the TCP/IP application layer. The functions of these higher layers play a big role in real TCP/IP networks. Additionally, many of the security topics in Parts I and II of this book, and some of the IP services topics in Part III, require you to know the basics of how the transport and application layers of TCP/IP work. This chapter serves as that introduction.

This chapter begins by examining the functions of two transport layer protocols: Transmission Control Protocol (TCP) and User Datagram Protocol (UDP). The second major section of the chapter examines the TCP/IP application layer, including some discussion of how Domain Name System (DNS) name resolution works.

"Do I Know This Already?" Quiz

Take the quiz (either here or use the PTP software) if you want to use the score to help you decide how much time to spend on this chapter. The letter answers are listed at the bottom of the page following the quiz. Appendix C, found both at the end of the book as well as on the companion website, includes both the answers and explanations. You can also find both answers and explanations in the PTP testing software.

Table 1-1 "Do I Know This Already?" Foundation Topics Section-to-Question Mapping

Foundation Topics Section	Questions
TCP/IP Layer 4 Protocols: TCP and UDP	1–4
TCP/IP Applications	5–6

1. Which of the following header fields identify which TCP/IP application gets data received by the computer? (Choose two answers.)

   a. Ethernet Type

   b. SNAP Protocol Type

   c. IP Protocol

   d. TCP Port Number

   e. UDP Port Number

2. Which of the following are typical functions of TCP? (Choose four answers.)

   a. Flow control (windowing)

   b. Error recovery

   c. Multiplexing using port numbers

   d. Routing

   e. Encryption

   f. Ordered data transfer

3. Which of the following functions is performed by both TCP and UDP?

   a. Windowing

   b. Error recovery

   c. Multiplexing using port numbers

   d. Routing

   e. Encryption

   f. Ordered data transfer

4. What do you call data that includes the Layer 4 protocol header, and data given to Layer 4 by the upper layers, not including any headers and trailers from Layers 1 to 3? (Choose two answers.)

   a. L3PDU

   b. Chunk

   c. Segment

   d. Packet

   e. Frame

   f. L4PDU

5. In the URI http://blog.certskills.com/config-labs, which part identifies the web server?

   a. http

   b. blog.certskills.com

   c. certskills.com

   d. http://blog.certskills.com

   e. The file name.html includes the hostname.

6. Fred opens a web browser and connects to the www.certskills.com website. Which of the following are typically true about what happens between Fred's web browser and the web server? (Choose two answers.)

  a. Messages flowing toward the server use UDP destination port 80.

  b. Messages flowing from the server typically use RTP.

  c. Messages flowing to the client typically use a source TCP port number of 80.

  d. Messages flowing to the server typically use TCP.

Foundation Topics

TCP/IP Layer 4 Protocols: TCP and UDP

The OSI transport layer (Layer 4) defines several functions, the most important of which are error recovery and flow control. Likewise, the TCP/IP transport layer protocols also implement these same types of features. Note that both the OSI model and the TCP/IP model call this layer the transport layer. But as usual, when referring to the TCP/IP model, the layer name and number are based on OSI, so any TCP/IP transport layer protocols are considered Layer 4 protocols.

The key difference between TCP and UDP is that TCP provides a wide variety of services to applications, whereas UDP does not. For example, routers discard packets for many reasons, including bit errors, congestion, and instances in which no correct routes are known. As you have read already, most data-link protocols notice errors (a process called *error detection*) but then discard frames that have errors. TCP provides retransmission (error recovery) and helps to avoid congestion (flow control), whereas UDP does not. As a result, many application protocols choose to use TCP.

However, do not let UDP's lack of services make you think that UDP is worse than TCP. By providing fewer services, UDP needs fewer bytes in its header compared to TCP, resulting in fewer bytes of overhead in the network. UDP software does not slow down data transfer in cases where TCP can purposefully slow down. Also, some applications, notably today Voice over IP (VoIP) and video over IP, do not need error recovery, so they use UDP. So, UDP also has an important place in TCP/IP networks today.

Table 1-2 lists the main features supported by TCP/UDP. Note that only the first item listed in the table is supported by UDP, whereas all items in the table are supported by TCP.

Table 1-2 TCP/IP Transport Layer Features

Function	Description
Multiplexing using ports	Function that allows receiving hosts to choose the correct application for which the data is destined, based on the port number
Error recovery (reliability)	Process of numbering and acknowledging data with Sequence and Acknowledgment header fields
Flow control using windowing	Process that uses window sizes to protect buffer space and routing devices from being overloaded with traffic

Function	Description
Connection establishment and termination	Process used to initialize port numbers and Sequence and Acknowledgment fields
Ordered data transfer and data segmentation	Continuous stream of bytes from an upper-layer process that is "segmented" for transmission and delivered to upper-layer processes at the receiving device, with the bytes in the same order

Next, this section describes the features of TCP, followed by a brief comparison to UDP.

Transmission Control Protocol

Each TCP/IP application typically chooses to use either TCP or UDP based on the application's requirements. For example, TCP provides error recovery, but to do so, it consumes more bandwidth and uses more processing cycles. UDP does not perform error recovery, but it takes less bandwidth and uses fewer processing cycles. Regardless of which of these two TCP/IP transport layer protocols the application chooses to use, you should understand the basics of how each of these transport layer protocols works.

TCP, as defined in Request For Comments (RFC) 793, accomplishes the functions listed in Table 1-2 through mechanisms at the endpoint computers. TCP relies on IP for end-to-end delivery of the data, including routing issues. In other words, TCP performs only part of the functions necessary to deliver the data between applications. Also, the role that it plays is directed toward providing services for the applications that sit at the endpoint computers. Regardless of whether two computers are on the same Ethernet, or are separated by the entire Internet, TCP performs its functions the same way.

Figure 1-1 shows the fields in the TCP header. Although you don't need to memorize the names of the fields or their locations, the rest of this section refers to several of the fields, so the entire header is included here for reference.

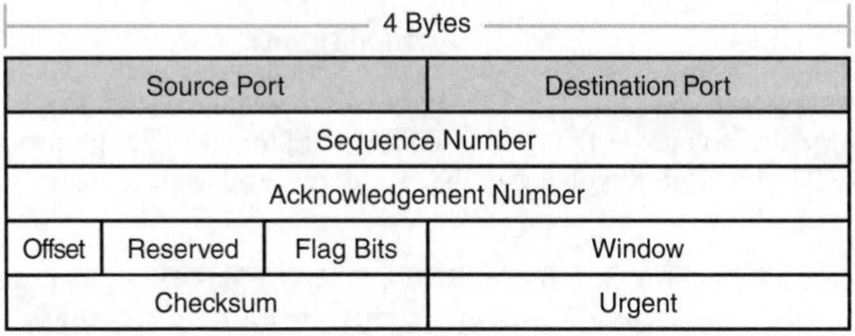

← 4 Bytes →	
Source Port	Destination Port
Sequence Number	
Acknowledgement Number	
Offset | Reserved | Flag Bits	Window
Checksum	Urgent

Figure 1-1 *TCP Header Fields*

The message created by TCP that begins with the TCP header, followed by any application data, is called a *TCP segment*. Alternatively, the more generic term *Layer 4 PDU*, or *L4PDU*, can also be used.

Multiplexing Using TCP Port Numbers

TCP and UDP both use a concept called *multiplexing*. Therefore, this section begins with an explanation of multiplexing with TCP and UDP. Afterward, the unique features of TCP are explored.

Multiplexing by TCP and UDP involves the process of how a computer thinks when receiving data. The computer might be running many applications, such as a web browser, an email package, or an Internet VoIP application (for example, Skype). TCP and UDP multiplexing tells the receiving computer to which application to give the received data.

Some examples will help make the need for multiplexing obvious. The sample network consists of two PCs, labeled Hannah and George. Hannah uses an application that she wrote to send advertisements that appear on George's screen. The application sends a new ad to George every 10 seconds. Hannah uses a second application, a wire-transfer application, to send George some money. Finally, Hannah uses a web browser to access the web server that runs on George's PC. The ad application and wire-transfer application are imaginary, just for this example. The web application works just like it would in real life.

Figure 1-2 shows the sample network, with George running three applications:

- A UDP-based advertisement application
- A TCP-based wire-transfer application
- A TCP web server application

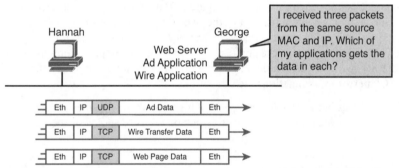

Figure 1-2 *Hannah Sending Packets to George, with Three Applications*

George needs to know which application to give the data to, but *all three packets are from the same Ethernet and IP address*. You might think that George could look at whether the packet contains a UDP or TCP header, but as you see in the figure, two applications (wire transfer and web) are using TCP.

TCP and UDP solve this problem by using a port number field in the TCP or UDP header, respectively. Each of Hannah's TCP and UDP segments uses a different *destination port number* so that George knows which application to give the data to. Figure 1-3 shows an example.

Multiplexing relies on a concept called a *socket*. A socket consists of three things:

- An IP address
- A transport protocol
- A port number

Answers to the "Do I Know This Already?" quiz:

1 D, E **2** A, B, C, F **3** C **4** C, F **5** B **6** C, D

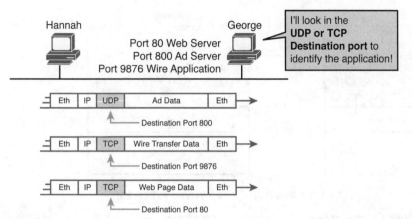

Figure 1-3   *Hannah Sending Packets to George, with Three Applications Using Port Numbers to Multiplex*

So, for a web server application on George, the socket would be (10.1.1.2, TCP, port 80) because, by default, web servers use the well-known port 80. When Hannah's web browser connects to the web server, Hannah uses a socket as well—possibly one like this: (10.1.1.1, TCP, 49160). Why 49160? Well, Hannah just needs a port number that is unique on Hannah, so Hannah sees that port 49160.

The Internet Assigned Numbers Authority (IANA), the same organization that manages IP address allocation worldwide, subdivides the port number ranges into three main ranges. The first two ranges reserve numbers that IANA can then allocate to specific application protocols through an application and review process, with the third category reserving ports to be dynamically allocated as used for clients, as with the port 49160 example in the previous paragraph. The names and ranges of port numbers (as detailed in RFC 6335) are

- **Well Known (System) Ports:** Numbers from 0 to 1023, assigned by IANA, with a stricter review process to assign new ports than user ports.
- **User (Registered) Ports:** Numbers from 1024 to 49151, assigned by IANA with a less strict process to assign new ports compared to well-known ports.
- **Ephemeral (Dynamic, Private) Ports:** Numbers from 49152 to 65535, not assigned and intended to be dynamically allocated and used temporarily for a client application while the app is running.

Figure 1-4 shows an example that uses three ephemeral ports on the user device on the left, with the server on the right using two well-known ports and one user port. The computers use three applications at the same time; hence, three socket connections are open. Because a socket on a single computer should be unique, a connection between two sockets should identify a unique connection between two computers. This uniqueness means that you can use multiple applications at the same time, talking to applications running on the same or different computers. Multiplexing, based on sockets, ensures that the data is delivered to the correct applications.

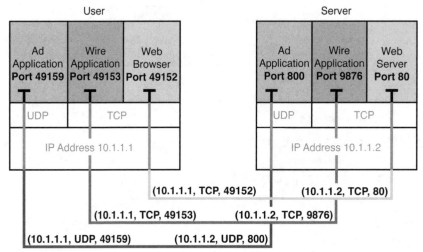

Figure 1-4 *Connections Between Sockets*

Port numbers are a vital part of the socket concept. Servers use well-known ports (or user ports), whereas clients use dynamic ports. Applications that provide a service, such as FTP, Telnet, and web servers, open a socket using a well-known port and listen for connection requests. Because these connection requests from clients are required to include both the source and destination port numbers, the port numbers used by the servers must be known beforehand. Therefore, each service uses a specific well-known port number or user port number. Both well-known and user ports are listed at www.iana.org/assignments/service-names-port-numbers/service-names-port-numbers.txt.

On client machines, where the requests originate, any locally unused port number can be allocated. The result is that each client on the same host uses a different port number, but a server uses the same port number for all connections. For example, 100 web browsers on the same host computer could each connect to a web server, but the web server with 100 clients connected to it would have only one socket and, therefore, only one port number (port 80, in this case). The server can tell which packets are sent from which of the 100 clients by looking at the source port of received TCP segments. The server can send data to the correct web client (browser) by sending data to that same port number listed as a destination port. The combination of source and destination sockets allows all participating hosts to distinguish between the data's source and destination. Although the example explains the concept using 100 TCP connections, the same port-numbering concept applies to UDP sessions in the same way.

NOTE You can find all RFCs online at www.rfc-editor.org/rfc/rfc*xxxx*.txt, where *xxxx* is the number of the RFC. If you do not know the number of the RFC, you can try searching by topic at www.rfc-editor.org.

Popular TCP/IP Applications

Throughout your preparation for the CCNA exam, you will come across a variety of TCP/IP applications. You should at least be aware of some of the applications that can be used to help manage and control a network.

The World Wide Web (WWW) application exists through web browsers accessing the content available on web servers. Although it is often thought of as an end-user application, you can actually use WWW to manage a router or switch. You enable a web server function in the router or switch and use a browser to access the router or switch.

The Domain Name System (DNS) allows users to use names to refer to computers, with DNS being used to find the corresponding IP addresses. DNS also uses a client/server model, with DNS servers being controlled by networking personnel and DNS client functions being part of most any device that uses TCP/IP today. The client simply asks the DNS server to supply the IP address that corresponds to a given name.

Simple Network Management Protocol (SNMP) is an application layer protocol used specifically for network device management. For example, Cisco supplies a large variety of network management products, many of them in the Cisco Prime network management software product family. They can be used to query, compile, store, and display information about a network's operation. To query the network devices, Cisco Prime software mainly uses SNMP protocols.

Traditionally, to move files to and from a router or switch, Cisco used Trivial File Transfer Protocol (TFTP). TFTP defines a protocol for basic file transfer—hence the word *trivial*. Alternatively, routers and switches can use File Transfer Protocol (FTP), which is a much more functional protocol, to transfer files. Both work well for moving files into and out of Cisco devices. FTP allows many more features, making it a good choice for the general end-user population. TFTP client and server applications are very simple, making them good tools as embedded parts of networking devices.

Some of these applications use TCP, and some use UDP. For example, Simple Mail Transfer Protocol (SMTP) and Post Office Protocol version 3 (POP3), both used for transferring mail, require guaranteed delivery, so they use TCP.

Regardless of which transport layer protocol is used, applications use a well-known port number so that clients know which port to attempt to connect to. Table 1-3 lists several popular applications and their well-known port numbers.

Table 1-3 Popular Applications and Their Well-Known Port Numbers

Port Number	Protocol	Application
20	TCP	FTP data
21	TCP	FTP control
22	TCP	SSH
23	TCP	Telnet
25	TCP	SMTP
53	UDP, TCP[1]	DNS
67	UDP	DHCP Server
68	UDP	DHCP Client
69	UDP	TFTP
80	TCP	HTTP (WWW)
110	TCP	POP3

Port Number	Protocol	Application
161	UDP	SNMP
443	TCP	SSL
514	UDP	Syslog

[1] DNS uses both UDP and TCP in different instances. It uses port 53 for both TCP and UDP.

Connection Establishment and Termination

TCP connection establishment occurs before any of the other TCP features can begin their work. Connection establishment refers to the process of initializing Sequence and Acknowledgment fields and agreeing on the port numbers used. Figure 1-5 shows an example of connection establishment flow.

Figure 1-5 *TCP Connection Establishment*

This three-way connection establishment flow (also called a three-way handshake) must complete before data transfer can begin. The connection exists between the two sockets, although the TCP header has no single socket field. Of the three parts of a socket, the IP addresses are implied based on the source and destination IP addresses in the IP header. TCP is implied because a TCP header is in use, as specified by the protocol field value in the IP header. Therefore, the only parts of the socket that need to be encoded in the TCP header are the port numbers.

TCP signals connection establishment using 2 bits inside the flag fields of the TCP header. Called the SYN and ACK flags, these bits have a particularly interesting meaning. SYN means "synchronize the sequence numbers," which is one necessary component in initialization for TCP.

Figure 1-6 shows TCP connection termination. This four-way termination sequence is straightforward and uses an additional flag, called the *FIN bit*. (FIN is short for "finished," as you might guess.) One interesting note: Before the device on the right sends the third TCP segment in the sequence, it notifies the application that the connection is coming down. It then waits on an acknowledgment from the application before sending the third segment in the figure. Just in case the application takes some time to reply, the PC on the right sends the second flow in the figure, acknowledging that the other PC wants to take down the connection. Otherwise, the PC on the left might resend the first segment repeatedly.

Figure 1-6 *TCP Connection Termination*

TCP establishes and terminates connections between the endpoints, whereas UDP does not. Many protocols operate under these same concepts, so the terms *connection-oriented* and *connectionless* are used to refer to the general idea of each. More formally, these terms can be defined as follows:

- **Connection-oriented protocol:** A protocol that requires an exchange of messages before data transfer begins, or that has a required pre-established correlation between two endpoints.

- **Connectionless protocol:** A protocol that does not require an exchange of messages and that does not require a pre-established correlation between two endpoints.

Error Recovery and Reliability

TCP provides for reliable data transfer, which is also called *reliability* or *error recovery*, depending on what document you read. To accomplish reliability, TCP numbers data bytes using the Sequence and Acknowledgment fields in the TCP header. TCP achieves reliability in both directions, using the Sequence Number field of one direction combined with the Acknowledgment field in the opposite direction.

Figure 1-7 shows an example of how the TCP Sequence and Acknowledgment fields allow the PC to send 3000 bytes of data to the server, with the server acknowledging receipt of the data. The TCP segments in the figure occur in order, from top to bottom. For simplicity's sake, all messages happen to have 1000 bytes of data in the data portion of the TCP segment. The first Sequence number is a nice round number (1000), again for simplicity's sake. The top of the figure shows three segments, with each sequence number being 1000 more than the previous, identifying the first of the 1000 bytes in the message. (That is, in this example, the first segment holds bytes 1000–1999; the second holds bytes 2000–2999; and the third holds bytes 3000–3999.)

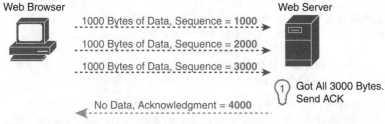

Figure 1-7 *TCP Acknowledgment Without Errors*

The fourth TCP segment in the figure—the only one flowing back from the server to the web browser—acknowledges the receipt of all three segments. How? The acknowledgment value of 4000 means "I received all data with sequence numbers up through one less than 4000, so I am ready to receive your byte 4000 next." (Note that this convention of acknowledging by listing the next expected byte, rather than the number of the last byte received, is called *forward acknowledgment.*)

This first example does not recover from any errors, however; it simply shows the basics of how the sending host uses the sequence number field to identify the data, with the receiving host using forward acknowledgments to acknowledge the data. The more interesting discussion revolves around how to use these same tools to do error recovery. TCP uses the Sequence and Acknowledgment fields so that the receiving host can notice lost data, ask the sending host to resend, and then acknowledge that the re-sent data arrived.

Many variations exist for how TCP does error recovery. Figure 1-8 shows just one such example, with similar details compared to the previous figure. The web browser again sends three TCP segments, again 1000 bytes each, again with easy-to-remember sequence numbers. However, in this example, the second TCP segment fails to cross the network.

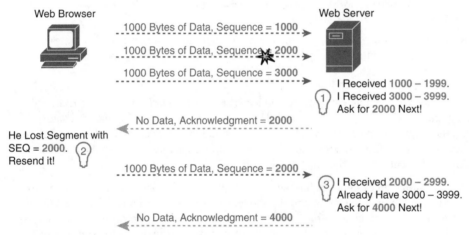

Figure 1-8 *TCP Acknowledgment with Errors*

The figure points out three sets of ideas behind how the two hosts think. First, on the right, the server realizes that it did not receive all the data. The two received TCP segments contain bytes numbered 1000–1999 and 3000–3999. Clearly, the server did not receive the bytes numbered in between. The server then decides to acknowledge all the data up to the lost data—that is, to send back a segment with the Acknowledgment field equal to 2000.

The receipt of an acknowledgment that does not acknowledge all the data sent so far tells the sending host to resend the data. The PC on the left may wait a few moments to make sure no other acknowledgments arrive (using a timer called the retransmission timer), but will soon decide that the server means "I really do need 2000 next—resend it." The PC on the left does so, as shown in the fifth of the six TCP segments in the figure.

Finally, note that the server can acknowledge not only the re-sent data, but any earlier data that had been received correctly. In this case, the server received the re-sent second TCP segment (the data with sequence numbers 2000–2999), but the server had already received the third TCP segment (the data numbered 3000–3999). The server's next Acknowledgment field acknowledges the data in both those segments, with an Acknowledgment field of 4000.

Flow Control Using Windowing

TCP implements flow control by using a window concept that is applied to the amount of data that can be outstanding and awaiting acknowledgment at any one point in time. The window concept lets the receiving host tell the sender how much data it can receive right now, giving the receiving host a way to make the sending host slow down or speed up. The receiver can slide the window size up and down—called a *sliding window* or *dynamic window*—to change how much data the sending host can send.

The sliding window mechanism makes much more sense with an example. The example, shown in Figure 1-9, uses the same basic rules as the examples in the previous few figures. In this case, none of the TCP segments have errors, and the discussion begins one TCP segment earlier than in the previous two figures.

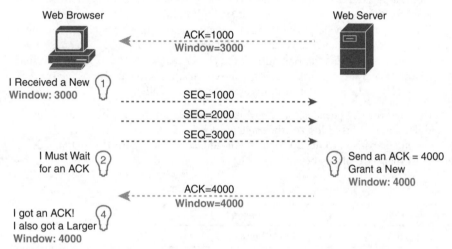

Figure 1-9   *TCP Windowing*

Begin with the first segment, sent by the server to the PC. The Acknowledgment field should be familiar by now: it tells the PC that the server expects a segment with sequence number 1000 next. The new field, the window field, is set to 3000. Because the segment flows to the PC, this value tells the PC that the PC can send no more than 3000 bytes over this connection before receiving an acknowledgment. So, as shown on the left, the PC realizes it can send only 3000 bytes, and it stops sending, waiting on an acknowledgment, after sending three 1000-byte TCP segments.

Continuing the example, the server not only acknowledges receiving the data (without any loss), but the server decides to slide the window size a little higher. Note that second message flowing right to left in the figure, this time with a window of 4000. Once the PC receives this TCP segment, the PC realizes it can send another 4000 bytes (a slightly larger window than the previous value).

Note that while the last few figures show examples for the purpose of explaining how the mechanisms work, the examples might give you the impression that TCP makes the hosts sit there and wait for acknowledgments a lot. TCP does not want to make the sending host have to wait to send data. For instance, if an acknowledgment is received before the window is exhausted, a new window begins, and the sender continues sending data until the current window is exhausted. Often times, in a network that has few problems, few lost segments, and little congestion, the TCP windows stay relatively large with hosts seldom waiting to send.

User Datagram Protocol

UDP provides a service for applications to exchange messages. Unlike TCP, UDP is connectionless and provides no reliability, no windowing, no reordering of the received data, and no segmentation of large chunks of data into the right size for transmission. However, UDP provides some functions of TCP, such as data transfer and multiplexing using port numbers, and it does so with fewer bytes of overhead and less processing required than TCP.

UDP data transfer differs from TCP data transfer in that no reordering or recovery is accomplished. Applications that use UDP are tolerant of the lost data, or they have some application mechanism to recover lost data. For example, VoIP uses UDP because if a voice packet is lost, by the time the loss could be noticed and the packet retransmitted, too much delay would have occurred, and the voice would be unintelligible. Also, DNS requests use UDP because the user will retry an operation if the DNS resolution fails. As another example, the Network File System (NFS), a remote file system application, performs recovery with application layer code, so UDP features are acceptable to NFS.

Figure 1-10 shows the UDP header format. Most importantly, note that the header includes source and destination port fields, for the same purpose as TCP. However, the UDP has only 8 bytes, in comparison to the 20-byte TCP header shown in Figure 1-1. UDP needs a shorter header than TCP simply because UDP has less work to do.

4 Bytes	
Source Port	Destination Port
Length	Checksum

Figure 1-10 *UDP Header*

TCP/IP Applications

The whole goal of building an enterprise network, or connecting a small home or office network to the Internet, is to use applications such as web browsing, text messaging, email, file downloads, voice, and video. This section examines one particular application—web browsing using Hypertext Transfer Protocol (HTTP).

The World Wide Web (WWW) consists of all the Internet-connected web servers in the world, plus all Internet-connected hosts with web browsers. *Web servers*, which consist of web server software running on a computer, store information (in the form of *web pages*) that might be useful to different people. A *web browser*, which is software installed on an end user's computer, provides the means to connect to a web server and display the web pages stored on the web server.

NOTE Although most people use the term *web browser*, or simply *browser*, web browsers are also called *web clients*, because they obtain a service from a web server.

For this process to work, several specific application layer functions must occur. The user must somehow identify the server, the specific web page, and the protocol used to get the data from the server. The client must find the server's IP address, based on the server's name, typically using DNS. The client must request the web page, which actually consists of multiple separate files, and the server must send the files to the web browser. Finally, for electronic commerce (e-commerce) applications, the transfer of data, particularly sensitive financial data, needs to be secure. The following sections address each of these functions.

Uniform Resource Identifiers

For a browser to display a web page, the browser must identify the server that has the web page, plus other information that identifies the particular web page. Most web servers have many web pages. For example, if you use a web browser to browse www.cisco.com and you click around that web page, you'll see another web page. Click again, and you'll see another web page. In each case, the clicking action identifies the server's IP address as well as the specific web page, with the details mostly hidden from you. (These clickable items on a web page, which in turn bring you to another web page, are called *links*.)

The browser user can identify a web page when you click something on a web page or when you enter a Uniform Resource Identifier (URI) in the browser's address area. Both options—clicking a link and typing a URI—refer to a URI, because when you click a link on a web page, that link actually refers to a URI.

> **NOTE** Most browsers support some way to view the hidden URI referenced by a link. In several browsers, hover the mouse pointer over a link, right-click, and select **Properties**. The pop-up window should display the URI to which the browser would be directed if you clicked that link.

In common speech, many people use the terms *web address* or the similar related terms *Universal Resource Locator* (or Uniform Resource Locator [URL]) instead of URI, but URI is indeed the correct formal term. In fact, URL had been more commonly used than URI for more than a few years. However, the IETF (the group that defines TCP/IP), along with the W3C consortium (W3.org, a consortium that develops web standards) has made a concerted effort to standardize the use of URI as the general term. See RFC 7595 for some commentary to that effect.

From a practical perspective, the URIs used to connect to a web server include three key components, as noted in Figure 1-11. The figure shows the formal names of the URI fields. More importantly to this discussion, note that the text before the :// identifies the protocol used to connect to the server, the text between the // and / identifies the server by name, and the text after the / identifies the web page.

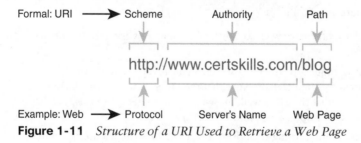

Figure 1-11 *Structure of a URI Used to Retrieve a Web Page*

In this case, the protocol is Hypertext Transfer Protocol (HTTP), the hostname is www.certskills.com, and the name of the web page is blog.

Finding the Web Server Using DNS

A host can use DNS to discover the IP address that corresponds to a particular hostname. URIs typically list the name of the server—a name that can be used to dynamically learn the IP address used by that same server. The web browser cannot send an IP packet to a destination name, but it can send a packet to a destination IP address. So, before the browser can send a packet to the web server, the browser typically needs to resolve the name inside the URI to that name's corresponding IP address.

To pull together several concepts, Figure 1-12 shows the DNS process as initiated by a web browser, as well as some other related information. From a basic perspective, the user enters the URI (in this case, http://www.cisco.com/go/learningnetwork), resolves the www.cisco.com name into the correct IP address, and starts sending packets to the web server.

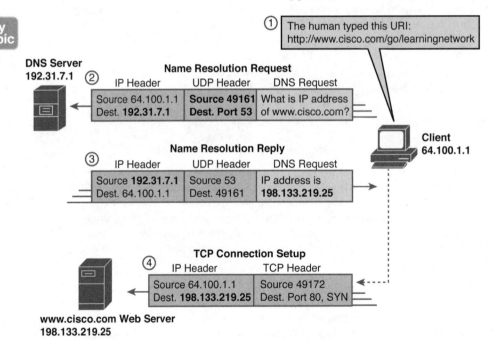

Figure 1-12 *DNS Resolution and Requesting a Web Page*

The steps shown in the figure are as follows:

1. The user enters the URI, http://www.cisco.com/go/learningnetwork, into the browser's address area.

2. The client sends a DNS request to the DNS server. Typically, the client learns the DNS server's IP address through DHCP. Note that the DNS request uses a UDP header, with a destination port of the DNS well-known port of 53. (See Table 1-3, earlier in this chapter, for a list of popular well-known ports.)

3. The DNS server sends a reply, listing IP address 198.133.219.25 as www.cisco.com's IP address. Note also that the reply shows a destination IP address of 64.100.1.1, the

client's IP address. It also shows a UDP header, with source port 53; the source port is 53 because the data is sourced, or sent, by the DNS server.

4. The client begins the process of establishing a new TCP connection to the web server. Note that the destination IP address is the just-learned IP address of the web server. The packet includes a TCP header, because HTTP uses TCP. Also note that the destination TCP port is 80, the well-known port for HTTP. Finally, the SYN bit is shown, as a reminder that the TCP connection establishment process begins with a TCP segment with the SYN bit turned on (binary 1).

The example in Figure 1-12 shows what happens when the client host does not know the IP address associated with the hostname but the enterprise does know the address. However, hosts can cache the results of DNS requests so that for a time the client does not need to ask the DNS to resolve the name. Also, the DNS server can cache the results of previous DNS requests; for instance, the enterprise DNS server in Figure 1-12 would not normally have configured information about hostnames in domains outside that enterprise, so that example relied on the DNS having cached the address associated with hostname www.cisco.com.

When the local DNS does not know the address associated with a hostname, it needs to ask for help. Figure 1-13 shows an example with the same client as in Figure 1-12. In this case, the enterprise DNS acts as a recursive DNS server, sending repeated DNS messages in an effort to identify the authoritative DNS server.

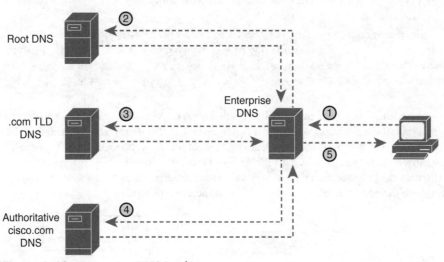

Figure 1-13 *Recursive DNS Lookup*

The steps shown in the figure are as follows:

1. The client sends a DNS request for www.cisco.com to the DNS server it knows, which is the enterprise DNS server.

2. The (recursive) enterprise DNS server does not know the answer yet, but it does not reject the client's DNS request. Instead, it follows a repetitive (recursive) process (shown as steps 2, 3, and 4), beginning with the DNS request sent to a root DNS server. The root does not supply the address either, but it supplies the IP address of another DNS server, one responsible for the .com top-level domain.

3. The recursive enterprise DNS sends the next DNS request to the DNS server learned at the previous step—this time the TLD DNS server for the .com domain. This DNS also does not know the address, but it knows the DNS server that should be the authoritative DNS server for domain cisco.com, so it supplies that DNS server's address.

4. The enterprise DNS sends another DNS request, to the DNS server whose address was learned in the previous step, again asking for resolution of the name www.cisco.com. This DNS server, the authoritative server for cisco.com, supplies the address.

5. The enterprise DNS server returns a DNS reply back to the client, supplying the IP address requested at step 1.

Transferring Files with HTTP

After a web client (browser) has created a TCP connection to a web server, the client can begin requesting the web page from the server. Most often, the protocol used to transfer the web page is HTTP. The HTTP application layer protocol, defined in RFC 7230, defines how files can be transferred between two computers. HTTP was specifically created for the purpose of transferring files between web servers and web clients.

HTTP defines several commands and responses, with the most frequently used being the HTTP GET request. To get a file from a web server, the client sends an HTTP GET request to the server, listing the filename. If the server decides to send the file, the server sends an HTTP GET response, with a return code of 200 (meaning OK), along with the file's contents.

NOTE Many return codes exist for HTTP requests. For example, when the server does not have the requested file, it issues a return code of 404, which means "file not found." Most web browsers do not show the specific numeric HTTP return codes, instead displaying a response such as "page not found" in reaction to receiving a return code of 404.

Web pages typically consist of multiple files, called *objects*. Most web pages contain text as well as several graphical images, animated advertisements, and possibly voice or video. Each of these components is stored as a different object (file) on the web server. To get them all, the web browser gets the first file. This file can (and typically does) include references to other URIs, so the browser then also requests the other objects. Figure 1-14 shows the general idea, with the browser getting the first file and then two others.

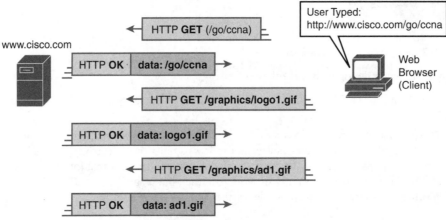

Figure 1-14 *Multiple HTTP GET Requests/Responses*

In this case, after the web browser gets the first file—the one called "/go/ccna" in the URI—the browser reads and interprets that file. Besides containing parts of the web page, the file refers to two other files, so the browser issues two additional HTTP GET requests. Note that, even though it isn't shown in the figure, all these commands flow over one (or possibly more) TCP connection between the client and the server. This means that TCP would provide error recovery, ensuring that the data was delivered.

How the Receiving Host Identifies the Correct Receiving Application

This chapter closes with a discussion of the process by which a host, when receiving any message over any network, can decide which of its many application programs should process the received data.

As an example, consider host A shown on the left side of Figure 1-15. The host happens to have three different web browser windows open, each using a unique TCP port. Host A also has an email client and a chat window open, both of which use TCP. Both the email and chat applications use a unique TCP port number on host A as shown in the figure.

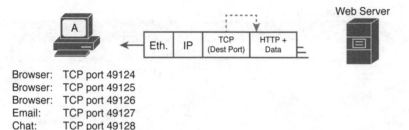

Browser:	TCP port 49124
Browser:	TCP port 49125
Browser:	TCP port 49126
Email:	TCP port 49127
Chat:	TCP port 49128

Figure 1-15 *Dilemma: How Host A Chooses the App That Should Receive This Data*

This chapter has shown several examples of how transport layer protocols use the destination port number field in the TCP or UDP header to identify the receiving application. For instance, if the destination TCP port value in Figure 1-15 is 49124, host A will know that the data is meant for the first of the three web browser windows.

Before a receiving host can even examine the TCP or UDP header, and find the destination port field, it must first process the outer headers in the message. If the incoming message is an Ethernet frame that encapsulates an IPv4 packet, the headers look like the details in Figure 1-16.

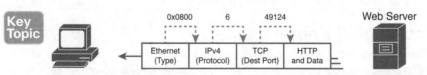

Figure 1-16 *Three Key Fields with Which to Identify the Next Header*

The receiving host needs to look at multiple fields, one per header, to identify the next header or field in the received message. For instance, host A uses an Ethernet NIC to connect to the network, so the received message is an Ethernet frame. The Ethernet Type field identifies the type of header that follows the Ethernet header—in this case, with a value of hex 0800, an IPv4 header.

The IPv4 header has a similar field called the IP Protocol field. The IPv4 Protocol field has a standard list of values that identify the next header, with decimal 6 used for TCP and decimal 17 used for UDP. In this case, the value of 6 identifies the TCP header that follows the IPv4 header. Once the receiving host realizes a TCP header exists, it can process the destination port field to determine which local application process should receive the data.

Chapter Review

One key to doing well on the exams is to perform repetitive spaced review sessions. Review this chapter's material using either the tools in the book or interactive tools for the same material found on the book's companion website. Refer to the "Your Study Plan" element for more details. Table 1-4 outlines the key review elements and where you can find them. To better track your study progress, record when you completed these activities in the second column.

Table 1-4 Chapter Review Tracking

Review Element	Review Date(s)	Resource Used
Review key topics		Book, website
Review key terms		Book, website
Repeat DIKTA questions		Book, PTP
Review memory tables		Book, website

Review All the Key Topics

Table 1-5 Key Topics for Chapter 1

Key Topic Element	Description	Page Number
Table 1-2	Functions of TCP and UDP	6
Table 1-3	Well-known TCP and UDP port numbers	11
Figure 1-5	Example of TCP connection establishment	12
List	Definitions of connection-oriented and connectionless	13
Figure 1-12	DNS name resolution	18
Figure 1-16	Header fields that identify the next header	21

Key Terms You Should Know

connection establishment, error detection, error recovery, flow control, forward acknowledgment, HTTP, ordered data transfer, port, segment, sliding windows, URI, web server, DNS server, recursive DNS server

CHAPTER 2

Basic IPv4 Access Control Lists

This chapter covers the following exam topics:

5.0 Security Fundamentals

5.6 Configure and verify access control lists

IPv4 access control lists (ACL) give network engineers the ability to program a filter into a router. Each router, on each interface, for both the inbound and outbound direction, can enable a different ACL with different rules. Each ACL's rules tell the router which packets to discard and which to allow through.

This chapter discusses the basics of IPv4 ACLs, and in particular, one type of IP ACL: standard numbered IP ACLs. Standard numbered ACLs use simple logic, matching on the source IP address field only, and use a configuration style that references the ACL using a number. This chapter sets out to help you learn this simpler type of ACL first. The next chapter, titled, "Advanced IPv4 Access Control Lists," completes the discussion by describing other types of IP ACLs. The other types of ACLs use features that build on the concepts you learn in this chapter, but with more complexity and additional configuration options.

"Do I Know This Already?" Quiz

Take the quiz (either here or use the PTP software) if you want to use the score to help you decide how much time to spend on this chapter. The letter answers are listed at the bottom of the page following the quiz. Appendix C, found both at the end of the book as well as on the companion website, includes both the answers and explanations. You can also find both answers and explanations in the PTP testing software.

Table 2-1   "Do I Know This Already?" Foundation Topics Section-to-Question Mapping

Foundation Topics Section	Questions
IP Access Control List Basics	1
Standard Numbered IPv4 ACLs	2–5
Practice Applying Standard IP ACLs	6

1. Barney is a host with IP address 10.1.1.1 in subnet 10.1.1.0/24. Which of the following are things that a standard IP ACL could be configured to do? (Choose two answers.)

   a. Match the exact source IP address.

   b. Match IP addresses 10.1.1.1 through 10.1.1.4 with one **access-list** command without matching other IP addresses.

   c. Match all IP addresses in Barney's subnet with one **access-list** command without matching other IP addresses.

   d. Match only the packet's destination IP address.

2. Which of the following answers list a valid number that can be used with standard numbered IP ACLs? (Choose two answers.)

   a. 1987

   b. 2187

   c. 187

   d. 87

3. Which of the following wildcard masks is most useful for matching all IP packets in subnet 10.1.128.0, mask 255.255.255.0?

   a. 0.0.0.0

   b. 0.0.0.31

   c. 0.0.0.240

   d. 0.0.0.255

   e. 0.0.15.0

   f. 0.0.248.255

4. Which of the following wildcard masks is most useful for matching all IP packets in subnet 10.1.128.0, mask 255.255.240.0?

   a. 0.0.0.0

   b. 0.0.0.31

   c. 0.0.0.240

   d. 0.0.0.255

   e. 0.0.15.255

   f. 0.0.248.255

5. ACL 1 has three statements, in the following order, with address and wildcard mask values as follows: 1.0.0.0 0.255.255.255, 1.1.0.0 0.0.255.255, and 1.1.1.0 0.0.0.255. If a router tried to match a packet sourced from IP address 1.1.1.1 using this ACL, which ACL statement does a router consider the packet to have matched?

   a. First

   b. Second

   c. Third

   d. Implied deny at the end of the ACL

6. Which of the following **access-list** commands matches all packets sent from hosts in subnet 172.16.4.0/23?

   a. access-list 1 permit 172.16.0.5 0.0.255.0

   b. access-list 1 permit 172.16.4.0 0.0.1.255

   c. access-list 1 permit 172.16.5.0

   d. access-list 1 permit 172.16.5.0 0.0.0.127

Foundation Topics

IPv4 Access Control List Basics

IPv4 access control lists (IP ACL) give network engineers a way to identify different types of packets. To do so, the ACL configuration lists values that the router can see in the IP, TCP, UDP, and other headers. For example, an ACL can match packets whose source IP address is 1.1.1.1, or packets whose destination IP address is some address in subnet 10.1.1.0/24, or packets with a destination port of TCP port 23 (Telnet).

IPv4 ACLs perform many functions in Cisco routers, with the most common use as a packet filter. Engineers can enable ACLs on a router so that the ACL sits in the forwarding path of packets as they pass through the router. After it is enabled, the router considers whether each IP packet will either be discarded or allowed to continue as if the ACL did not exist.

However, ACLs can be used for many other IOS features as well. As an example, ACLs can be used to match packets for applying Quality of Service (QoS) features. QoS allows a router to give some packets better service, and other packets worse service. For example, packets that hold digitized voice need to have very low delay, so ACLs can match voice packets, with QoS logic in turn forwarding voice packets more quickly than data packets.

This first section introduces IP ACLs as used for packet filtering, focusing on these aspects of ACLs: the locations and direction in which to enable ACLs, matching packets by examining headers, and taking action after a packet has been matched.

ACL Location and Direction

Cisco routers can apply ACL logic to packets at the point at which the IP packets enter an interface, or the point at which they exit an interface. In other words, the ACL becomes associated with an interface and for a direction of packet flow (either in or out). That is, the ACL can be applied inbound to the router, before the router makes its forwarding (routing) decision, or outbound, after the router makes its forwarding decision and has determined the exit interface to use.

The arrows in Figure 2-1 show the locations at which you could filter packets flowing left to right in the topology. For example, imagine that you wanted to allow packets sent by host A to server S1, but to discard packets sent by host B to server S1. Each arrowed line represents a location and direction at which a router could apply an ACL, filtering the packets sent by host B.

The four arrowed lines in the figure point out the location and direction for the router interfaces used to forward the packet from host B to server S1. In this particular example, those interfaces and direction are inbound on R1's F0/0 interface, outbound on R1's S0/0/0 interface, inbound on R2's S0/0/1 interface, and outbound on R2's F0/0 interface. If, for example, you enabled an ACL on R2's F0/1 interface, in either direction, that ACL could not possibly filter the packet sent from host B to server S1, because R2's F0/1 interface is not part of the route from B to S1.

Answers to the "Do I Know This Already?" quiz:

1 A, C **2** A, D **3** D **4** E **5** A **6** B

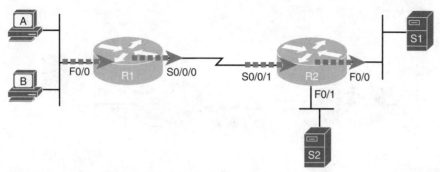

Figure 2-1 *Locations to Filter Packets from Hosts A and B Going Toward Server S1*

In short, to filter a packet, you must enable an ACL on an interface that processes the packet, in the same direction the packet flows through that interface.

When enabled, the router then processes every inbound or outbound IP packet using that ACL. For example, if enabled on R1 for packets inbound on interface F0/0, R1 would compare every inbound IP packet on F0/0 to the ACL to decide that packet's fate: to continue unchanged or to be discarded.

Matching Packets

When you think about the location and direction for an ACL, you must already be thinking about what packets you plan to filter (discard), and which ones you want to allow through. To tell the router those same ideas, you must configure the router with an IP ACL that matches packets. *Matching packets* refers to how to configure the ACL commands to look at each packet, listing how to identify which packets should be discarded and which should be allowed through.

Each IP ACL consists of one or more configuration commands, with each command listing details about values to look for inside a packet's headers. Generally, an ACL command uses logic like "look for these values in the packet header, and if found, discard the packet." (The action could instead be to allow the packet, rather than discard.) Specifically, the ACL looks for header fields you should already know well, including the source and destination IP addresses, plus TCP and UDP port numbers.

For example, consider an example with Figure 2-2, in which you want to allow packets from host A to server S1, but to discard packets from host B going to that same server. The hosts all now have IP addresses, and the figure shows pseudocode for an ACL on R2. Figure 2-2 also shows the chosen location to enable the ACL: inbound on R2's S0/0/1 interface.

Figure 2-2 shows a two-line ACL in a rectangle at the bottom, with simple matching logic: both statements just look to match the source IP address in the packet. When enabled, R2 looks at every inbound IP packet on that interface and compares each packet to those two ACL commands. Packets sent by host A (source IP address 10.1.1.1) are allowed through, and those sourced by host B (source IP address 10.1.1.2) are discarded.

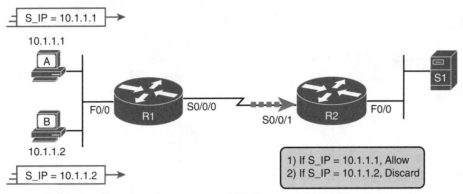

Figure 2-2 *Pseudocode to Demonstrate ACL Command-Matching Logic*

Taking Action When a Match Occurs

When using IP ACLs to filter packets, only one of two actions can be chosen. The configuration commands use the keywords **deny** and **permit**, and they mean (respectively) to discard the packet or to allow it to keep going as if the ACL did not exist.

This book focuses on using ACLs to filter packets, but IOS uses ACLs for many more features. Those features typically use the same matching logic. However, in other cases, the **deny** or **permit** keywords imply some other action.

Types of IP ACLs

Cisco IOS has supported IP ACLs since the early days of Cisco routers. Beginning with the original standard numbered IP ACLs in the early days of IOS, which could enable the logic shown earlier around Figure 2-2, Cisco has added many ACL features, including the following:

■ Standard numbered ACLs (1–99)

■ Extended numbered ACLs (100–199)

■ Additional ACL numbers (1300–1999 standard, 2000–2699 extended)

■ Named ACLs

■ Improved editing with sequence numbers

This chapter focuses solely on standard numbered IP ACLs, while the next chapter discusses the other three primary categories of IP ACLs. Briefly, IP ACLs will be either numbered or named in that the configuration identifies the ACL either using a number or a name. ACLs will also be either standard or extended, with extended ACLs having much more robust abilities in matching packets. Figure 2-3 summarizes the big ideas related to categories of IP ACLs.

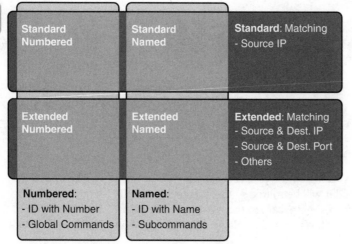

Figure 2-3 *Comparisons of IP ACL Types*

Standard Numbered IPv4 ACLs

The title of this section serves as a great introduction, if you can decode what Cisco means by each specific word. This section is about a type of Cisco filter (*ACL*) that matches only the source IP address of the packet (*standard*), is configured to identify the ACL using numbers rather than names (*numbered*), and looks at IPv4 packets.

This section examines the particulars of standard numbered IP ACLs. First, it examines the idea that one ACL is a list and what logic that list uses. Following that, the text closely looks at how to match the source IP address field in the packet header, including the syntax of the commands. This section ends with a complete look at the configuration and verification commands to implement standard ACLs.

List Logic with IP ACLs

A single ACL is both a single entity and, at the same time, a list of one or more configuration commands. As a single entity, the configuration enables the entire ACL on an interface, in a specific direction, as shown earlier in Figure 2-1. As a list of commands, each command has different matching logic that the router must apply to each packet when filtering using that ACL.

When doing ACL processing, the router processes the packet, compared to the ACL, as follows:

ACLs use first-match logic. Once a packet matches one line in the ACL, the router takes the action listed in that line of the ACL and stops looking further in the ACL.

To see exactly what that means, consider the example built around Figure 2-4. The figure shows an example ACL 1 with three lines of pseudocode. This example applies ACL 1 on R2's S0/0/1 interface, inbound (the same location as in earlier Figure 2-2).

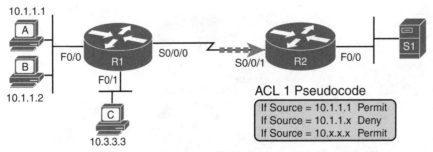

Figure 2-4 *Backdrop for Discussion of List Process with IP ACLs*

Consider the first-match ACL logic for a packet sent by host A to server S1. The source IP address will be 10.1.1.1, and it will be routed so that it enters R2's S0/0/1 interface, driving R2's ACL 1 logic. R2 compares this packet to the ACL, matching the first item in the list with a permit action. So this packet should be allowed through, as shown in Figure 2-5, on the left.

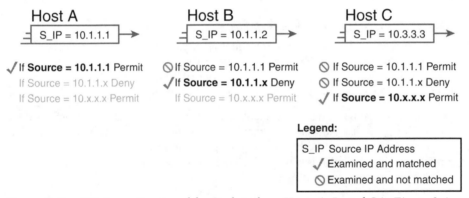

Figure 2-5 *ACL Items Compared for Packets from Hosts A, B, and C in Figure 2-4*

Next, consider a packet sent by host B, source IP address 10.1.1.2. When the packet enters R2's S0/0/1 interface, R2 compares the packet to ACL 1's first statement and does not make a match (10.1.1.1 is not equal to 10.1.1.2). R2 then moves to the second statement, which requires some clarification. The ACL pseudocode, back in Figure 2-4, shows 10.1.1.x, which is meant to be shorthand that any value can exist in the last octet. Comparing only the first three octets, R2 decides that this latest packet does have a source IP address that begins with the first three octets 10.1.1, so R2 considers that to be a match on the second statement. R2 takes the listed action (deny), discarding the packet. R2 also stops ACL processing on the packet, ignoring the third line in the ACL.

Finally, consider a packet sent by host C, again to server S1. The packet has source IP address 10.3.3.3, so when it enters R2's S0/0/1 interface and drives ACL processing on R2, R2 looks at the first command in ACL 1. R2 does not match the first ACL command (10.1.1.1 in the command is not equal to the packet's 10.3.3.3). R2 looks at the second command, compares the first three octets (10.1.1) to the packet source IP address (10.3.3), and still finds no match. R2 then looks at the third command. In this case, the wildcard means ignore the last three octets and just compare the first octet (10), so the packet matches. R2 then takes the listed action (permit), allowing the packet to keep going.

This sequence of processing an ACL as a list happens for any type of IOS ACL: IP, other protocols, standard or extended, named or numbered.

Finally, if a packet does not match any of the items in the ACL, the packet is discarded. The reason is that every IP ACL has a *deny all* statement implied at the end of the ACL. It does not exist in the configuration, but if a router keeps searching the list, and no match is made by the end of the list, IOS considers the packet to have matched an entry that has a **deny** action.

Matching Logic and Command Syntax

Standard numbered IP ACLs use the following global command:

```
access-list {1-99 | 1300-1999} {permit | deny} matching-parameters
```

Each standard numbered ACL has one or more **access-list** commands with the same number, any number from the ranges shown in the preceding line of syntax. (One number is no better than the other.) IOS refers to each line in an ACL as an Access Control Entry (ACE), but many engineers just call them ACL statements.

Besides the ACL number, each **access-list** command also lists the action (**permit** or **deny**), plus the matching logic. The rest of this section examines how to configure the matching parameters, which, for standard ACLs, means that you can only match the source IP address or portions of the source IP address using something called an ACL wildcard mask.

Matching the Exact IP Address

To match a specific source IP address, the entire IP address, all you have to do is type that IP address at the end of the command. For example, the previous example uses pseudocode for "permit if source = 10.1.1.1." The following command configures that logic with correct syntax using ACL number 1:

```
access-list 1 permit 10.1.1.1
```

Matching the exact full IP address is that simple.

In earlier IOS versions, the syntax included a **host** keyword. Instead of simply typing the full IP address, you first typed the **host** keyword and then the IP address. Note that in later IOS versions, if you use the **host** keyword, IOS accepts the command but then removes the keyword.

```
access-list 1 permit host 10.1.1.1
```

Matching a Subset of the Address with Wildcards

Often, the business goals you want to implement with an ACL do not match a single particular IP address, but rather a range of IP addresses. Maybe you want to match all IP addresses in a subnet. Maybe you want to match all IP addresses in a range of subnets. Regardless, you want to check for more than one IP address in a range of addresses.

IOS allows standard ACLs to match a range of addresses using a tool called a *wildcard mask*. Note that this is not a subnet mask. The wildcard mask (which this book abbreviates as *WC mask*) gives the engineer a way to tell IOS to ignore parts of the address when making comparisons, essentially treating those parts as wildcards, as if they already matched.

You can think about WC masks in decimal and in binary, and both have their uses. To begin, think about WC masks in decimal, using these rules:

Decimal 0: The router must compare this octet as normal.

Decimal 255: The router ignores this octet, considering it to already match.

Keeping these two rules in mind, consider Figure 2-6, which demonstrates this logic using three different but popular WC masks: one that tells the router to ignore the last octet, one that tells the router to ignore the last two octets, and one that tells the router to ignore the last three octets.

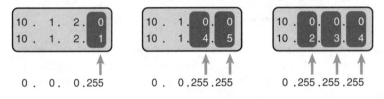

255 = Ignore

Figure 2-6 *Logic for WC Masks 0.0.0.255, 0.0.255.255, and 0.255.255.255*

All three examples in the boxes of Figure 2-6 show two numbers that are clearly different. The WC mask causes IOS to compare only some of the octets, while ignoring other octets. All three examples result in a match, because each wildcard mask tells IOS to ignore some octets. The example on the left shows WC mask 0.0.0.255, which tells the router to treat the last octet as a wildcard, essentially ignoring that octet for the comparison. Similarly, the middle example shows WC mask 0.0.255.255, which tells the router to ignore the two octets on the right. The rightmost case shows WC mask 0.255.255.255, telling the router to ignore the last three octets when comparing values.

To see the WC mask in action, think back to the earlier example related to Figure 2-4 and Figure 2-5. The pseudocode ACL in those two figures used logic that can be created using a WC mask. As a reminder, the logic in the pseudocode ACL in those two figures included the following:

Line 1: Match and permit all packets with a source address of exactly 10.1.1.1.

Line 2: Match and deny all packets with source addresses with first three octets 10.1.1.

Line 3: Match and permit all addresses with first single octet 10.

Figure 2-7 shows the updated version of Figure 2-4, but with the completed, correct syntax, including the WC masks. In particular, note the use of WC mask 0.0.0.255 in the second command, telling R2 to ignore the last octet of the number 10.1.1.0, and the WC mask 0.255.255.255 in the third command, telling R2 to ignore the last three octets in the value 10.0.0.0.

Finally, note that when using a WC mask, the **access-list** command's loosely defined *source* parameter should be a 0 in any octets where the WC mask is a 255. IOS will specify a source address to be 0 for the parts that will be ignored, even if nonzero values were configured.

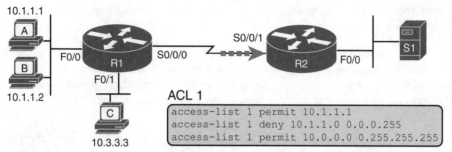

Figure 2-7 *Syntactically Correct ACL Replaces Pseudocode from Figure 2-4*

Binary Wildcard Masks

Wildcard masks, as dotted-decimal number (DDN) values, actually represent a 32-bit binary number. As a 32-bit number, the WC mask actually directs the router's logic bit by bit. In short, a WC mask bit of 0 means the comparison should be done as normal, but a binary 1 means that the bit is a wildcard and can be ignored when comparing the numbers.

Thankfully, for the purposes of CCNA study, and for most real-world applications, you can ignore the binary WC mask. Why? Well, we generally want to match a range of addresses that can be easily identified by a subnet number and mask, whether it be a real subnet, or a summary route that groups subnets together. If you can describe the range of addresses with a subnet number and mask, you can find the numbers to use in your ACL with some simple decimal math, as discussed next.

> **NOTE**   If you really want to know the binary mask logic, take the two DDN numbers the ACL will compare (one from the **access-list** command and the other from the packet header) and convert both to binary. Then, also convert the WC mask to binary. Compare the first two binary numbers bit by bit, but also ignore any bits for which the WC mask happens to list a binary 1, because that tells you to ignore the bit. If all the bits you checked are equal, it's a match!

Finding the Right Wildcard Mask to Match a Subnet

In many cases, an ACL needs to match all hosts in a particular subnet. To match a subnet with an ACL, you can use the following shortcut:

- Use the subnet number as the source value in the **access-list** command.
- Use a wildcard mask found by subtracting the subnet mask from 255.255.255.255.

For example, for subnet 172.16.8.0 255.255.252.0, use the subnet number (172.16.8.0) as the address parameter, and then do the following math to find the wildcard mask:

255.255.255.255
– 255.255.252.0
0. 0. 3.255

Continuing this example, a completed command for this same subnet would be as follows:

```
access-list 1 permit 172.16.8.0 0.0.3.255
```

The section "Practice Applying Standard IP ACLs" gives you a chance to practice matching subnets when configuring ACLs.

Matching Any/All Addresses

In some cases, you will want one ACL command to match any and all packets that reach that point in the ACL. First, you have to know the (simple) way to match all packets using the **any** keyword. More importantly, you need to think about when to match any and all packets.

First, to match any and all packets with an ACL command, just use the **any** keyword for the address. For example, to permit all packets:

```
access-list 1 permit any
```

So, when and where should you use such a command? Remember, all Cisco IP ACLs end with an implicit **deny any** concept at the end of each ACL. That is, if a router compares a packet to the ACL, and the packet matches none of the configured statements, the router discards the packet. Want to override that default behavior? Configure a **permit any** at the end of the ACL.

You might also want to explicitly configure a command to deny all traffic (for example, **access-list 1 deny any**) at the end of an ACL. Why, when the same logic already sits at the end of the ACL anyway? Well, the ACL **show** commands list counters for the number of packets matched by each command in the ACL, but there is no counter for that implicit **deny any** concept at the end of the ACL. So, if you want to see counters for how many packets are matched by the **deny any** logic at the end of the ACL, configure an explicit **deny any**.

Implementing Standard IP ACLs

This chapter has already introduced all the configuration steps in bits and pieces. This section summarizes those pieces as a configuration process. The process also refers to the **access-list** command, whose generic syntax is repeated here for reference:

```
access-list access-list-number {deny | permit} source [source-wildcard]
```

Step 1. Plan the location (router and interface) and direction (in or out) on that interface:

  A. Standard ACLs should be placed near to the destination of the packets so that they do not unintentionally discard packets that should not be discarded.

  B. Because standard ACLs can only match a packet's source IP address, identify the source IP addresses of packets as they go in the direction that the ACL is examining.

Step 2. Configure one or more **access-list** global configuration commands to create the ACL, keeping the following in mind:

  A. The list is searched sequentially, using first-match logic.

  B. The default action, if a packet does not match any of the **access-list** commands, is to **deny** (discard) the packet.

Step 3. Enable the ACL on the chosen router interface, in the correct direction, using the **ip access-group** *number* {**in** | **out**} interface subcommand.

The rest of this section shows a couple of examples.

Standard Numbered ACL Example 1

The first example shows the configuration for the same requirements demonstrated with Figure 2-4 and Figure 2-5. Restated, the requirements for this ACL are as follows:

1. Enable the ACL inbound on R2's S0/0/1 interface.

2. Permit packets coming from host A.

3. Deny packets coming from other hosts in host A's subnet.

4. Permit packets coming from any other address in Class A network 10.0.0.0.

5. The original example made no comment about what to do by default, so simply deny all other traffic.

Example 2-1 shows a completed correct configuration, starting with the configuration process, followed by output from the **show running-config** command.

Example 2-1 *Standard Numbered ACL Example 1 Configuration*

```
R2# configure terminal
Enter configuration commands, one per line. End with CNTL/Z.
R2(config)# access-list 1 permit 10.1.1.1
R2(config)# access-list 1 deny 10.1.1.0 0.0.0.255
R2(config)# access-list 1 permit 10.0.0.0 0.255.255.255
R2(config)# interface S0/0/1
R2(config-if)# ip access-group 1 in
R2(config-if)# ^Z
R2# show running-config
! Lines omitted for brevity

access-list 1 permit 10.1.1.1
access-list 1 deny 10.1.1.0 0.0.0.255
access-list 1 permit 10.0.0.0 0.255.255.255
```

First, pay close attention to the configuration process at the top of the example. Note that the **access-list** command does not change the command prompt from the global configuration mode prompt, because the **access-list** command is a global configuration command. Then, compare that to the output of the **show running-config** command: the details are identical compared to the commands that were added in configuration mode. Finally, make sure to note the **ip access-group 1 in** command, under R2's S0/0/1 interface, which enables the ACL logic (both location and direction).

Example 2-2 lists some output from Router R2 that shows information about this ACL. The **show ip access-lists** command lists details about IPv4 ACLs only, while the **show access-lists** command lists details about IPv4 ACLs plus any other types of ACLs that are currently configured; for example, IPv6 ACLs.

Example 2-2 *ACL show Commands on R2*

```
R2# show ip access-lists
Standard IP access list 1
    10 permit 10.1.1.1 (107 matches)
    20 deny   10.1.1.0, wildcard bits 0.0.0.255 (4 matches)
```

```
       30 permit 10.0.0.0, wildcard bits 0.255.255.255 (10 matches)
R2# show access-lists
Standard IP access list 1
    10 permit 10.1.1.1 (107 matches)
    20 deny   10.1.1.0, wildcard bits 0.0.0.255 (4 matches)
    30 permit 10.0.0.0, wildcard bits 0.255.255.255 (10 matches)
R2# show ip interface s0/0/1
Serial0/0/1 is up, line protocol is up
  Internet address is 10.1.2.2/24
  Broadcast address is 255.255.255.255
  Address determined by setup command
  MTU is 1500 bytes
  Helper address is not set
  Directed broadcast forwarding is disabled
  Multicast reserved groups joined: 224.0.0.9
  Outgoing access list is not set
  Inbound access list is 1
! Lines omitted for brevity
```

The output of these commands shows two items of note. The first line of output in this case notes the type (standard) and the number. If more than one ACL existed, you would see multiple stanzas of output, one per ACL, each with a heading line like this one. Next, these commands list packet counts for the number of packets that the router has matched with each command. For example, 107 packets so far have matched the first line in the ACL.

Finally, the end of the example lists the **show ip interface** command output. This command lists, among many other items, the number or name of any IP ACL enabled on the interface per the **ip access-group** interface subcommand.

Standard Numbered ACL Example 2

For the second example, use Figure 2-8, and imagine your boss gives you some requirements hurriedly in the hall. At first, he tells you he wants to filter packets going from the servers on the right toward the clients on the left. Then, he says he wants you to allow access for hosts A, B, and other hosts in their same subnet to server S1, but deny access to that server to the hosts in host C's subnet. Then, he tells you that, additionally, hosts in host A's subnet should be denied access to server S2, but hosts in host C's subnet should be allowed access to server S2—all by filtering packets going right to left only. He then tells you to put the ACL inbound on R2's F0/0 interface.

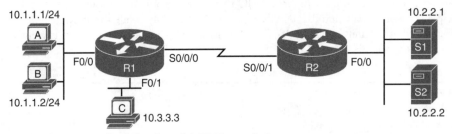

Figure 2-8 *Standard Numbered ACL Example 2*

If you cull through all the boss's comments, the requirements might be reduced to the following:

1. Enable the ACL inbound on R2's F0/0 interface.
2. Permit packets from server S1 going to hosts in A's subnet.
3. Deny packets from server S1 going to hosts in C's subnet.
4. Permit packets from server S2 going to hosts in C's subnet.
5. Deny packets from server S2 going to hosts in A's subnet.
6. (There was no comment about what to do by default; use the implied **deny all** default.)

As it turns out, you cannot do everything your boss asked with a standard ACL. For example, consider the obvious command for requirement number 2: **access-list 2 permit 10.2.2.1**. That permits all traffic whose source IP is 10.2.2.1 (server S1). The very next requirement asks you to filter (deny) packets sourced from that same IP address! Even if you added another command that checked for source IP address 10.2.2.1, the router would never get to it, because routers use first-match logic when searching the ACL. You cannot check both the destination and source IP address, because standard ACLs cannot check the destination IP address.

To solve this problem, you should get a new boss! No, seriously, you have to rethink the problem and change the rules. In real life, you would probably use an extended ACL instead, which lets you check both the source and destination IP address.

For the sake of practicing another standard ACL, imagine your boss lets you change the requirements. First, you will use two outbound ACLs, both on Router R1. Each ACL will permit traffic from a single server to be forwarded onto that connected LAN, with the following modified requirements:

1. Using an outbound ACL on R1's F0/0 interface, permit packets from server S1, and deny all other packets.
2. Using an outbound ACL on R1's F0/1 interface, permit packets from server S2, and deny all other packets.

Example 2-3 shows the configuration that completes these requirements.

Example 2-3 *Alternative Configuration in Router R1*

```
access-list 2 remark This ACL permits server S1 traffic to host A's subnet
access-list 2 permit 10.2.2.1
!
access-list 3 remark This ACL permits server S2 traffic to host C's subnet
access-list 3 permit 10.2.2.2
!
interface F0/0
 ip access-group 2 out
!
interface F0/1
 ip access-group 3 out
```

As highlighted in the example, the solution with ACL number 2 permits all traffic from server S1, with that logic enabled for packets exiting R1's F0/0 interface. All other traffic will be discarded because of the implied **deny any** at the end of the ACL. In addition, ACL 3 permits traffic from server S2, which is then permitted to exit R1's F0/1 interface. Also, note that the solution shows the use of the **access-list remark** parameter, which allows you to leave text documentation that stays with the ACL.

NOTE When routers apply an ACL to filter packets in the outbound direction, as shown in Example 2-3, the router checks packets that it routes against the ACL. However, a router does not filter packets that the router itself creates with an outbound ACL. Examples of those packets include routing protocol messages and packets sent by the **ping** and **traceroute** commands on that router.

Troubleshooting and Verification Tips

Troubleshooting IPv4 ACLs requires some attention to detail. In particular, you have to be ready to look at the address and wildcard mask and confidently predict the addresses matched by those two combined parameters. The upcoming practice problems a little later in this chapter can help prepare you for that part of the work. But a few other tips can help you verify and troubleshoot ACL problems on the exams as well.

First, you can tell if the router is matching packets or not with a couple of tools. Example 2-2 already showed that IOS keeps statistics about the packets matched by each line of an ACL. In addition, if you add the **log** keyword to the end of an **access-list** command, IOS then issues log messages with occasional statistics about matches of that particular line of the ACL. Both the statistics and the log messages can be helpful in deciding which line in the ACL is being matched by a packet.

For example, Example 2-4 shows an updated version of ACL 2 from Example 2-3, this time with the **log** keyword added. The bottom of the example then shows a typical log message, this one showing the resulting match based on a packet with source IP address 10.2.2.1 (as matched with the ACL), to destination address 10.1.1.1.

Example 2-4 *Creating Log Messages for ACL Statistics*

```
R1# show running-config
! lines removed for brevity
access-list 2 remark This ACL permits server S1 traffic to host A's subnet
access-list 2 permit 10.2.2.1 log
!
interface F0/0
 ip access-group 2 out

R1#
Feb 4 18:30:24.082: %SEC-6-IPACCESSLOGNP: list 2 permitted 0 10.2.2.1 -> 10.1.1.1, 1
packet
```

When you troubleshoot an ACL for the first time, before getting into the details of the matching logic, take the time to think about both the interface on which the ACL is enabled and the direction of packet flow. Sometimes, the matching logic is perfect—but the ACL has been enabled on the wrong interface, or for the wrong direction, to match the packets as configured for the ACL.

For example, Figure 2-9 repeats the same ACL shown earlier in Figure 2-7. The first line of that ACL matches the specific host address 10.1.1.1. If that ACL exists on Router R2, placing that ACL as an inbound ACL on R2's S0/0/1 interface can work, because packets sent by host 10.1.1.1—on the left side of the figure—can enter R2's S0/0/1 interface. However, if R2 enables ACL 1 on its F0/0 interface, for inbound packets, the ACL will never match a packet with source IP address 10.1.1.1, because packets sent by host 10.1.1.1 will never enter that interface. Packets sent by 10.1.1.1 will exit R2's F0/0 interface, but never enter it, just because of the network topology.

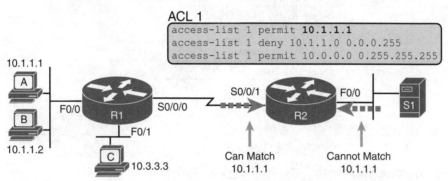

Figure 2-9 *Example of Checking the Interface and Direction for an ACL*

Practice Applying Standard IP ACLs

Some CCNA topics, like ACLs, simply require more drills and practice than others. ACLs require you to think of parameters to match ranges of numbers, and that of course requires some use of math and some use of processes.

This section provides some practice problems and tips, from two perspectives. First, this section asks you to build one-line standard ACLs to match some packets. Second, this section asks you to interpret existing ACL commands to describe what packets the ACL will match. Both skills are useful for the exams.

Practice Building access-list Commands

In this section, practice getting comfortable with the syntax of the **access-list** command, particularly with choosing the correct matching logic. These skills will be helpful when reading about extended and named ACLs in the next chapter.

First, the following list summarizes some important tips to consider when choosing matching parameters to any **access-list** command:

- To match a specific address, just list the address.
- To match any and all addresses, use the **any** keyword.
- To match based only on the first one, two, or three octets of an address, use the 0.255.255.255, 0.0.255.255, and 0.0.0.255 WC masks, respectively. Also, make the source (address) parameter have 0s in the wildcard octets (those octets with 255 in the wildcard mask).

- To match a subnet, use the subnet ID as the source, and find the WC mask by subtracting the DDN subnet mask from 255.255.255.255.

Table 2-2 lists the criteria for several practice problems. Your job: Create a one-line standard ACL that matches the packets. The answers are listed in the section "Answers to Earlier Practice Problems," later in this chapter.

Table 2-2 Building One-Line Standard ACLs: Practice

Problem	Criteria
1	Packets from 172.16.5.4
2	Packets from hosts with 192.168.6 as the first three octets
3	Packets from hosts with 192.168 as the first two octets
4	Packets from any host
5	Packets from subnet 10.1.200.0/21
6	Packets from subnet 10.1.200.0/27
7	Packets from subnet 172.20.112.0/23
8	Packets from subnet 172.20.112.0/26
9	Packets from subnet 192.168.9.64/28
10	Packets from subnet 192.168.9.64/30

Reverse Engineering from ACL to Address Range

In some cases, you may not be creating your own ACL. Instead, you may need to interpret some existing **access-list** commands. To answer these types of questions on the exams, you need to determine the range of IP addresses matched by a particular address/wildcard mask combination in each ACL statement.

Under certain assumptions that are reasonable for CCNA certifications, calculating the range of addresses matched by an ACL can be relatively simple. Basically, the range of addresses begins with the address configured in the ACL command. The range of addresses ends with the sum of the address field and the wildcard mask. That's it.

For example, with the command **access-list 1 permit 172.16.200.0 0.0.7.255**, the low end of the range is simply 172.16.200.0, taken directly from the command itself. Then, to find the high end of the range, just add this number to the WC mask, as follows:

172.16.200.0
+ 0. 0. 7.255
172.16.207.255

For this last bit of practice, look at the existing **access-list** commands in Table 2-3. In each case, make a notation about the exact IP address, or range of IP addresses, matched by the command.

Table 2-3 Finding IP Addresses/Ranges Matching by Existing ACLs

Problem	Commands for Which to Predict the Source Address Range
1	access-list 1 permit 10.7.6.5
2	access-list 2 permit 192.168.4.0 0.0.0.127
3	access-list 3 permit 192.168.6.0 0.0.0.31

Problem	Commands for Which to Predict the Source Address Range
4	access-list 4 permit 172.30.96.0 0.0.3.255
5	access-list 5 permit 172.30.96.0 0.0.0.63
6	access-list 6 permit 10.1.192.0 0.0.0.31
7	access-list 7 permit 10.1.192.0 0.0.1.255
8	access-list 8 permit 10.1.192.0 0.0.63.255

Interestingly, IOS lets the CLI user type an **access-list** command in configuration mode, and IOS will potentially change the address parameter before placing the command into the running-config file. This process of just finding the range of addresses matched by the **access-list** command expects that the **access-list** command came from the router, so that any such changes were complete.

The change IOS can make with an **access-list** command is to convert to 0 any octet of an address for which the wildcard mask's octet is 255. For example, with a wildcard mask of 0.0.255.255, IOS ignores the last two octets. IOS expects the address field to end with two 0s. If not, IOS still accepts the **access-list** command, but IOS changes the last two octets of the address to 0s. Example 2-5 shows an example, where the configuration shows address 10.1.1.1, but wildcard mask 0.0.255.255.

Example 2-5 *IOS Changing the Address Field in an* access-list *Command*

```
R2# configure terminal
Enter configuration commands, one per line. End with CNTL/Z.
R2(config)# access-list 21 permit 10.1.1.1 0.0.255.255
R2(config)# ^Z
R2#
R2# show ip access-lists
Standard IP access list 21
    10 permit 10.1.0.0, wildcard bits 0.0.255.255
```

The math to find the range of addresses relies on the fact that either the command is fully correct or that IOS has already set these address octets to 0, as shown in the example.

NOTE The most useful WC masks, in binary, do not interleave 0s and 1s. This book assumes the use of only these types of WC masks. However, Cisco IOS allows WC masks that interleave 0s and 1s, but using these WC masks breaks the simple method of calculating the range of addresses. As you progress through to CCIE studies, be ready to dig deeper to learn how to determine what an ACL matches.

Chapter Review

One key to doing well on the exams is to perform repetitive spaced review sessions. Review this chapter's material using either the tools in the book or interactive tools for the same material found on the book's companion website. Refer to the "Your Study Plan" element for more details. Table 2-4 outlines the key review elements and where you can find them. To better track your study progress, record when you completed these activities in the second column.

Table 2-4 Chapter Review Tracking

Review Element	Review Date(s)	Resource Used
Review key topics		Book, website
Review key terms		Book, website
Repeat DIKTA questions		Book, PTP
Review command tables		Book

Review All the Key Topics

Table 2-5 Key Topics for Chapter 2

Key Topic Element	Description	Page Number
Paragraph	Summary of the general rule of the location and direction for an ACL	27
Figure 2-3	Summary of four main categories of IPv4 ACLs in Cisco IOS	29
Paragraph	Summary of first-match logic used by all ACLs	29
List	Wildcard mask logic for decimal 0 and 255	32
List	Wildcard mask logic to match a subnet	33
List	Steps to plan and implement a standard IP ACL	34
List	Tips for creating matching logic for the source address field in the **access-list** command	39

Key Terms You Should Know

standard access list, wildcard mask

Additional Practice for This Chapter's Processes

For additional practice with analyzing subnets, you may do the same set of practice problems using your choice of tools:

Application: Use the two ACL practice exercise applications listed on the companion website.

PDF: Alternatively, practice the same problems found in these apps using online Appendix E, "Practice for Chapter 2: Basic IPv4 Access Control Lists."

Command References

Tables 2-6 and 2-7 list configuration and verification commands used in this chapter. As an easy review exercise, cover the left column in a table, read the right column, and try to recall the command without looking. Then repeat the exercise, covering the right column, and try to recall what the command does.

Table 2-6 Chapter 2 Configuration Command Reference

Command	Description
access-list *access-list-number* {**deny** | **permit**} *source* [*source-wildcard*] [**log**]	Global command for standard numbered access lists. Use a number between 1 and 99 or 1300 and 1999, inclusive.

Command	Description
access-list *access-list-number* **remark** *text*	Command that defines a remark to help you remember what the ACL is supposed to do.
ip access-group *number* {**in** | **out**}	Interface subcommand to enable access lists.

Table 2-7   Chapter 2 EXEC Command Reference

Command	Description
show ip interface [*type number*]	Includes a reference to the access lists enabled on the interface
show access-lists [*access-list-number* | *access-list-name*]	Shows details of configured access lists for all protocols
show ip access-lists [*access-list-number* | *access-list-name*]	Shows IP access lists

Answers to Earlier Practice Problems

Table 2-8 lists the answers to the problems listed earlier in Table 2-2.

Table 2-8   Building One-Line Standard ACLs: Answers

Problem	Answers
1	access-list 1 permit 172.16.5.4
2	access-list 2 permit 192.168.6.0 0.0.0.255
3	access-list 3 permit 192.168.0.0 0.0.255.255
4	access-list 4 permit any
5	access-list 5 permit 10.1.200.0 0.0.7.255
6	access-list 6 permit 10.1.200.0 0.0.0.31
7	access-list 7 permit 172.20.112.0 0.0.1.255
8	access-list 8 permit 172.20.112.0 0.0.0.63
9	access-list 9 permit 192.168.9.64 0.0.0.15
10	access-list 10 permit 192.168.9.64 0.0.0.3

Table 2-9 lists the answers to the problems listed earlier in Table 2-3.

Table 2-9   Address Ranges for Problems in Table 2-3: Answers

Problem	Address Range
1	One address: 10.7.6.5
2	192.168.4.0 – 192.168.4.127
3	192.168.6.0 – 192.168.6.31
4	172.30.96.0 – 172.30.99.255
5	172.30.96.0 – 172.30.96.63
6	10.1.192.0 – 10.1.192.31
7	10.1.192.0 – 10.1.193.255
8	10.1.192.0 – 10.1.255.255

Advanced IPv4 Access Control Lists

This chapter covers the following exam topics:

5.0 Security Fundamentals

5.6 Configure and verify access control lists

IPv4 ACLs are either standard or extended ACLs, with standard ACLs matching only the source IP address, and extended matching a variety of packet header fields. At the same time, IP ACLs are either numbered or named. Figure 3-1 shows the categories and the main features of each as introduced in the previous chapter.

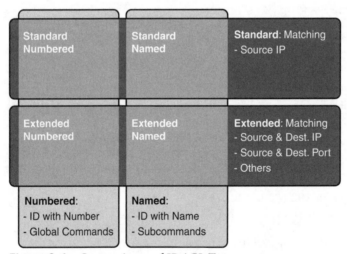

Figure 3-1 *Comparisons of IP ACL Types*

This chapter discusses the other three categories of ACLs beyond standard numbered IP ACLs and ends with a few miscellaneous features to secure Cisco routers and switches.

"Do I Know This Already?" Quiz

Take the quiz (either here or use the PTP software) if you want to use the score to help you decide how much time to spend on this chapter. The letter answers are listed at the bottom of the page following the quiz. Appendix C, found both at the end of the book as well as on the companion website, includes both the answers and explanations. You can also find both answers and explanations in the PTP testing software.

Table 3-1 "Do I Know This Already?" Foundation Topics Section-to-Question Mapping

Foundation Topics Section	Questions
Extended IP Access Control Lists	1–3
Named ACLs and ACL Editing	4–6

1. Which of the following fields cannot be compared based on an extended IP ACL? (Choose two answers.)

   a. Protocol

   b. Source IP address

   c. Destination IP address

   d. TOS byte

   e. URL

   f. Filename for FTP transfers

2. Which of the following **access-list** commands permit packets going from host 10.1.1.1 to all web servers whose IP addresses begin with 172.16.5? (Choose two answers.)

   a. access-list 101 permit tcp host 10.1.1.1 172.16.5.0 0.0.0.255 eq www

   b. access-list 1951 permit ip host 10.1.1.1 172.16.5.0 0.0.0.255 eq www

   c. access-list 2523 permit ip host 10.1.1.1 eq www 172.16.5.0 0.0.0.255

   d. access-list 2523 permit tcp host 10.1.1.1 eq www 172.16.5.0 0.0.0.255

   e. access-list 2523 permit tcp host 10.1.1.1 172.16.5.0 0.0.0.255 eq www

3. Which of the following **access-list** commands permits packets going to any web client from all web servers whose IP addresses begin with 172.16.5?

   a. access-list 101 permit tcp host 10.1.1.1 172.16.5.0 0.0.0.255 eq www

   b. access-list 1951 permit ip host 10.1.1.1 172.16.5.0 0.0.0.255 eq www

   c. access-list 2523 permit tcp any eq www 172.16.5.0 0.0.0.255

   d. access-list 2523 permit tcp 172.16.5.0 0.0.0.255 eq www 172.16.5.0 0.0.0.255

   e. access-list 2523 permit tcp 172.16.5.0 0.0.0.255 eq www any

4. In a router running a recent IOS version (at least version 15.0), an engineer needs to delete the second line in ACL 101, which currently has four commands configured. Which of the following options could be used? (Choose two answers.)

   a. Delete the entire ACL and reconfigure the three ACL statements that should remain in the ACL.

   b. Delete one line from the ACL using the **no access-list...** global command.

   c. Delete one line from the ACL by entering ACL configuration mode for the ACL and then deleting only the second line based on its sequence number.

   d. Delete the last three lines from the ACL from global configuration mode, and then add the last two statements back into the ACL.

5. Refer to the following command output, which details an ACL enabled on port G0/0 for the inbound direction. Which answers list a configuration mode and command that would result in the deletion of the line that matches subnet 172.16.1.0/24? (Choose two answers.)

```
show ip access-lists dikta-list
Standard IP access list dikta-list
    10 permit 172.16.1.0, wildcard bits 0.0.0.255
    20 permit 172.16.2.0, wildcard bits 0.0.0.255
    30 permit 172.16.3.0, wildcard bits 0.0.0.255
```

   a. In global config mode: **no 10**

   b. In interface G0/0 config mode: **no 10**

   c. In ACL dikta-list config mode: **no 10**

   d. In ACL dikta-list config mode: **no permit 172.16.1.0 0.0.0.255**

   e. In global config mode: **no permit 172.16.1.0 0.0.0.255**

6. An engineer configures an ACL but forgets to save the configuration. At that point, which of the following commands display the configuration of an IPv4 ACL, including line numbers? (Choose two answers.)

   a. show running-config

   b. show startup-config

   c. show ip access-lists

   d. show access-lists

Foundation Topics

Extended Numbered IP Access Control Lists

Extended IP access lists have many similarities compared to the standard numbered IP ACLs discussed in the previous chapter. Just like standard IP ACLs, you enable extended access lists on interfaces for packets either entering or exiting the interface. IOS searches the list sequentially. Extended ACLs also use first-match logic, because the router stops the search through the list as soon as the first statement is matched, taking the action defined in the first-matched statement. All these features are also true of standard numbered access lists (and named ACLs).

Extended ACLs differ from standard ACLs mostly because of the larger variety of packet header fields that can be used to match a packet. One extended ACE (ACL statement) can examine multiple parts of the packet headers, requiring that all the parameters be matched correctly to match that one ACE. That powerful matching logic makes extended access lists both more useful and more complex than standard IP ACLs.

Matching the Protocol, Source IP, and Destination IP

Like standard numbered IP ACLs, extended numbered IP ACLs also use the **access-list** global command. The syntax is identical, at least up through the **permit** or **deny** keyword. At that point, the command lists matching parameters, and those differ, of course. In particular, the extended ACL **access-list** command requires three matching parameters: the IP protocol type, the source IP address, and the destination IP address.

The IP header's Protocol field identifies the header that follows the IP header. Figure 3-2 shows the location of the IP Protocol field, the concept of it pointing to the type of header that follows, along with some details of the IP header for reference.

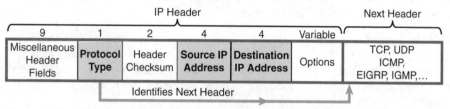

Figure 3-2 *IP Header, with Focus on Required Fields in Extended IP ACLs*

IOS requires that you configure parameters for the three highlighted parts of Figure 3-2. For the protocol type, you simply use a keyword, such as **tcp**, **udp**, or **icmp**, matching IP packets that happen to have a TCP, UDP, or ICMP header, respectively, following the IP header. Or you can use the keyword **ip**, which means "all IPv4 packets." You also must configure some values for the source and destination IP address fields that follow; these fields use the same syntax and options for matching the IP addresses as discussed in Chapter 2, "Basic IPv4 Access Control Lists." Figure 3-3 shows the syntax.

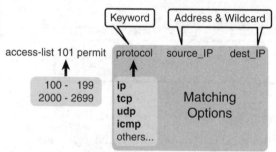

Figure 3-3 *Extended ACL Syntax, with Required Fields*

NOTE When matching IP addresses in the source and destination fields, there is one difference with standard ACLs: When matching a specific IP address, the extended ACL requires the use of the **host** keyword. You cannot simply list the IP address alone.

Table 3-2 lists several sample **access-list** commands that use only the required matching parameters. Feel free to cover the right side and use the table for an exercise, or just review the explanations to get an idea for the logic in some sample commands.

Table 3-2 Extended **access-list** Commands and Logic Explanations

access-list Statement	What It Matches
access-list 101 deny tcp any any	Any IP packet that has a TCP header
access-list 101 deny udp any any	Any IP packet that has a UDP header
access-list 101 deny icmp any any	Any IP packet that has an ICMP header
access-list 101 deny ip host 1.1.1.1 host 2.2.2.2	All IP packets from host 1.1.1.1 going to host 2.2.2.2, regardless of the header after the IP header
access-list 101 deny udp 1.1.1.0 0.0.0.255 any	All IP packets that have a UDP header following the IP header, from subnet 1.1.1.0/24, and going to any destination

The last entry in Table 3-2 helps make an important point about how IOS processes extended ACLs:

> In an extended ACL **access-list** command, all the matching parameters must match the packet for the packet to match the command.

For example, in that last example from Table 3-2, the command checks for UDP, a source IP address from subnet 1.1.1.0/24, and any destination IP address. If a packet with source IP address 1.1.1.1 were examined, it would match the source IP address check, but if it had a TCP header instead of UDP, it would not match this **access-list** command. All parameters must match.

Matching TCP and UDP Port Numbers

Extended ACLs can also examine parts of the TCP and UDP headers, particularly the source and destination port number fields. The port numbers identify the application that sends or receives the data.

The most useful ports to check are the well-known ports used by servers. For example, web servers use well-known port 80 by default. Figure 3-4 shows the location of the port numbers in the TCP header, following the IP header.

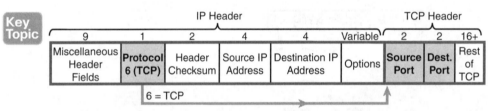

Figure 3-4 *IP Header, Followed by a TCP Header and Port Number Fields*

When an extended ACL command includes either the **tcp** or **udp** keyword, that command can optionally reference the source and/or destination port. To make these comparisons, the syntax uses keywords for equal, not equal, less than, greater than, and for a range of port numbers. In addition, the command can use either the literal decimal port numbers or more convenient keywords for some well-known application ports. Figure 3-5 shows the positions of the source and destination port fields in the **access-list** command and these port number keywords.

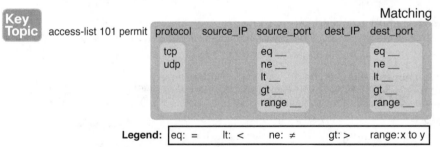

Figure 3-5 *Extended ACL Syntax with TCP and UDP Port Numbers Enabled*

For example, consider the simple network shown in Figure 3-6. The FTP server sits on the right, with the client on the left. The figure shows the syntax of an ACL that matches the following:

- Packets that include a TCP header
- Packets sent from the client subnet
- Packets sent to the server subnet
- Packets with TCP destination port 21 (FTP server control port)

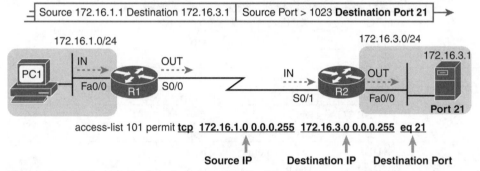

Figure 3-6 *Filtering Packets Based on Destination Port*

To fully appreciate the matching of the destination port with the **eq 21** parameters, consider packets moving from left to right, from PC1 to the server. Assuming the server uses well-known port 21 (FTP control port), the packet's TCP header has a destination port value of 21. The ACL syntax includes the **eq 21** parameters after the destination IP address. The position after the destination address parameters is important: that position identifies the fact that the **eq 21** parameters should be compared to the packet's destination port. As a result, the ACL statement shown in Figure 3-6 would match this packet and the destination port of 21 if used in any of the four locations implied by the four dashed arrowed lines in the figure.

Conversely, Figure 3-7 shows the reverse flow, with a packet sent by the server back toward PC1. In this case, the packet's TCP header has a source port of 21, so the ACL must check the source port value of 21, and the ACL must be located on different interfaces. In this case, the **eq 21** parameters follow the source address field but come before the destination address field.

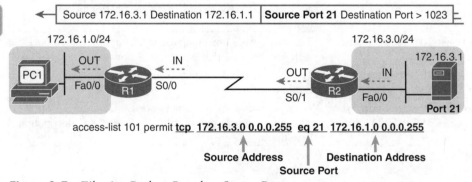

Figure 3-7 *Filtering Packets Based on Source Port*

When examining ACLs that match port numbers, first consider the location and direction in which the ACL will be applied. That direction determines whether the packet is being sent to the server or from the server. At that point, you can decide whether you need to check the source or destination port in the packet. For reference, Table 3-3 lists many of the popular port numbers and their transport layer protocols and applications. Note that the syntax of the **access-list** commands accepts both the port numbers and a shorthand version of the application name.

Table 3-3 Popular Applications and Their Well-Known Port Numbers

Port Number(s)	Protocol	Application	access-list Command Keyword
20	TCP	FTP data	**ftp-data**
21	TCP	FTP control	**ftp**
22	TCP	SSH	—
23	TCP	Telnet	**telnet**
25	TCP	SMTP	**smtp**
53	UDP, TCP	DNS	**domain**
67	UDP	DHCP Server	**bootps**
68	UDP	DHCP Client	**bootpc**
69	UDP	TFTP	**tftp**
80	TCP	HTTP (WWW)	**www**
110	TCP	POP3	**pop3**
161	UDP	SNMP	**snmp**
443	TCP	SSL	—
514	UDP	Syslog	—
16,384–32,767	UDP	RTP (voice, video)	—

Table 3-4 lists several sample **access-list** commands that match based on port numbers. Cover the right side of the table, and try to characterize the packets matched by each command. Then check the right side of the table to see if you agree with the assessment.

Table 3-4 Extended **access-list** Command Examples and Logic Explanations

access-list Statement	What It Matches
access-list 101 deny tcp any gt 49151 host 10.1.1.1 eq 23	Packets with a TCP header, any source IP address, with a source port greater than (gt) 49151, a destination IP address of exactly 10.1.1.1, and a destination port equal to (eq) 23.
access-list 101 deny tcp any host 10.1.1.1 eq 23	The same as the preceding example, but any source port matches, because that parameter is omitted in this case.
access-list 101 deny tcp any host 10.1.1.1 eq telnet	The same as the preceding example. The **telnet** keyword is used instead of port 23.
access-list 101 deny udp 1.0.0.0 0.255.255.255 lt 1023 any	A packet with a source in network 1.0.0.0/8, using UDP with a source port less than (lt) 1023, with any destination IP address.

Extended IP ACL Configuration

Because extended ACLs can match so many different fields in the various headers in an IP packet, the command syntax cannot be easily summarized in a single generic command. However, the two commands in Table 3-5 summarize the syntax options as covered in this book.

Table 3-5   Extended IP Access List Configuration Commands

Command	Configuration Mode and Description
access-list *access-list-number* {**deny** | **permit**} *protocol source source-wildcard destination destination-wildcard* [**log** | **log-input**]	Global command for extended numbered access lists. Use a number between 100 and 199 or 2000 and 2699, inclusive.
access-list *access-list-number* {**deny** | **permit**} {**tcp** | **udp**} *source source-wildcard* [*operator* [*port*]] *destination destination-wildcard* [*operator* [*port*]] [**established**] [**log**]	A version of the **access-list** command with parameters specific to TCP and/or UDP.

The configuration process for extended ACLs mostly matches the same process used for standard ACLs. You must choose the location and direction in which to enable the ACL, particularly the direction, so that you can characterize whether certain addresses and ports will be either the source or destination. Configure the ACL using **access-list** commands, and when complete, then enable the ACL using the same **ip access-group** command used with standard ACLs. All these steps mirror what you do with standard ACLs; however, when configuring, keep the following differences in mind:

- Place extended ACLs as close as possible to the source of the packets that will be filtered. Filtering close to the source of the packets saves some bandwidth.

- Remember that all fields in one **access-list** command must match a packet for the packet to be considered to match that **access-list** statement.

- Use numbers of 100–199 and 2000–2699 on the **access-list** commands; no one number is inherently better than another.

Extended IP Access Lists: Example 1

This example focuses on understanding basic syntax. In this case, the ACL denies Bob access to all FTP servers on R1's Ethernet, and it denies Larry access to Server1's web server. Figure 3-8 shows the network topology; Example 3-1 shows the configuration on R1.

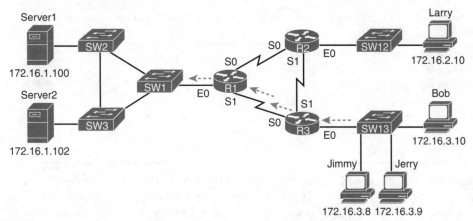

Figure 3-8   *Network Diagram for Extended Access List Example 1*

Example 3-1 *R1's Extended Access List: Example 1*

```
interface Serial0
 ip address 172.16.12.1 255.255.255.0
 ip access-group 101 in
!
interface Serial1
 ip address 172.16.13.1 255.255.255.0
 ip access-group 101 in
!
access-list 101 remark Stop Bob to FTP servers, and Larry to Server1 web
access-list 101 deny tcp host 172.16.3.10 172.16.1.0 0.0.0.255 eq ftp
access-list 101 deny tcp host 172.16.2.10 host 172.16.1.100 eq www
access-list 101 permit ip any any
```

The first ACL statement prevents Bob's access to FTP servers in subnet 172.16.1.0. The second statement prevents Larry's access to web services on Server1. The final statement permits all other traffic.

If we focus on the syntax for a moment, we can see several new items to review. First, the access-list number for extended access lists falls in the range of 100 to 199 or 2000 to 2699. Following the **permit** or **deny** action, the *protocol* parameter defines whether you want to check for all IP packets or specific headers, such as TCP or UDP headers. When you check for TCP or UDP port numbers, you must specify the TCP or UDP protocol. Both FTP and the web use TCP.

This example uses the **eq** parameter, meaning "equals," to check the destination port numbers for FTP control (keyword **ftp**) and HTTP traffic (keyword **www**). You can use the numeric values—or, for the more popular options, a more obvious text version is valid. (If you were to type **eq 80**, the config would show **eq www**.)

This example enables the ACL in two places on R1: inbound on each serial interface. These locations achieve the goal of the ACL. However, that initial placement was made to make the point that Cisco suggests that you locate them as close as possible to the source of the packet. Therefore, Example 3-2 achieves the same goal as Example 3-1 of stopping Bob's access to FTP servers at the main site, and it does so with an ACL on R3.

Example 3-2 *R3's Extended Access List Stopping Bob from Reaching FTP Servers Near R1*

```
interface Ethernet0
 ip address 172.16.3.1 255.255.255.0
 ip access-group 103 in

access-list 103 remark deny Bob to FTP servers in subnet 172.16.1.0/24
access-list 103 deny tcp host 172.16.3.10 172.16.1.0 0.0.0.255 eq ftp
access-list 103 permit ip any any
```

The new configuration on R3 meets the goals to filter Bob's traffic, while also meeting the overarching design goal of keeping the ACL close to the source of the packets. ACL 103 on R3 looks a lot like ACL 101 on R1 from Example 3-1, but this time, the ACL does not bother to check for the criteria to match Larry's traffic, because Larry's traffic will never enter R3's Ethernet 0 interface. ACL 103 filters Bob's FTP traffic to destinations in subnet 172.16.1.0/24, with all other traffic entering R3's E0 interface making it into the network.

Extended IP Access Lists: Example 2

Example 3-3, based on the network shown in Figure 3-9, shows another example of how to use extended IP access lists. This example uses the following criteria:

- Sam is not allowed access to the subnet of Bugs or Daffy.

- Hosts on the Seville Ethernet are not allowed access to hosts on the Yosemite Ethernet.

- All other combinations are allowed.

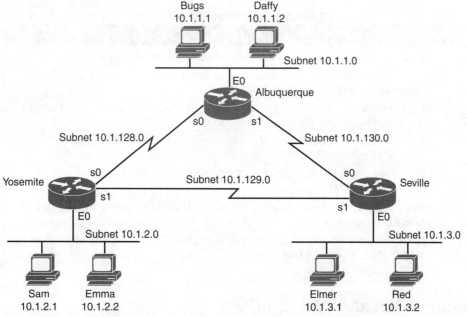

Figure 3-9 *Network Diagram for Extended Access List Example 2*

Example 3-3 *Yosemite Configuration for Extended Access List Example 2*

```
interface ethernet 0
 ip access-group 110 in
!
access-list 110 deny ip host 10.1.2.1 10.1.1.0 0.0.0.255
access-list 110 deny ip 10.1.2.0 0.0.0.255 10.1.3.0 0.0.0.255
access-list 110 permit ip any any
```

This configuration solves the problem with few statements while keeping to the Cisco design guideline of placing extended ACLs as close as possible to the source of the traffic. The ACL filters packets that enter Yosemite's E0 interface, which is the first router interface that packets sent by Sam enter. If the route between Yosemite and the other subnets changes over time, the ACL still applies. Also, the filtering mandated by the second requirement (to disallow Seville's LAN hosts from accessing Yosemite's) is met by the second **access-list** statement. Stopping packet flow from Yosemite's LAN subnet to Seville's LAN subnet stops effective communication between the two subnets. Alternatively, the opposite logic could have been configured at Seville.

Practice Building access-list Commands

Table 3-6 supplies a practice exercise to help you get comfortable with the syntax of the extended **access-list** command, particularly with choosing the correct matching logic. Your job: create a one-line extended ACL that matches the packets. The answers are in the section "Answers to Earlier Practice Problems," later in this chapter. Note that if the criteria mention a particular application protocol, for example, "web client," that means to specifically match for that application protocol.

Table 3-6   Building One-Line Extended ACLs: Practice

Problem	Criteria
1	From web client 10.1.1.1, sent to a web server in subnet 10.1.2.0/24.
2	From Telnet client 172.16.4.3/25, sent to a Telnet server in subnet 172.16.3.0/25. Match all hosts in the client's subnet as well.
3	ICMP messages from the subnet in which 192.168.7.200/26 resides to all hosts in the subnet where 192.168.7.14/29 resides.
4	From web server 10.2.3.4/23's subnet to clients in the same subnet as host 10.4.5.6/22.
5	From Telnet server 172.20.1.0/24's subnet, sent to any host in the same subnet as host 172.20.44.1/23.
6	From web client 192.168.99.99/28, sent to a web server in subnet 192.168.176.0/28. Match all hosts in the client's subnet as well.
7	ICMP messages from the subnet in which 10.55.66.77/25 resides to all hosts in the subnet where 10.66.55.44/26 resides.
8	Any and every IPv4 packet.

Named ACLs and ACL Editing

Now that you have a good understanding of the core concepts in IOS IP ACLs, this section examines a few enhancements to IOS support for ACLs: named ACLs and ACL editing with sequence numbers. Although both features are useful and important, neither adds any function as to what a router can and cannot filter. Instead, named ACLs and ACL sequence numbers make it easier to remember ACL names and edit existing ACLs when an ACL needs to change.

Named IP Access Lists

Named IP ACLs have many similarities with numbered IP ACLs. They can be used for filtering packets, plus for many other purposes. They can match the same fields as well: standard numbered ACLs can match the same fields as a standard named ACL, and extended numbered ACLs can match the same fields as an extended named ACL.

Of course, there are differences between named and numbered ACLs. Named ACLs originally had three big differences compared to numbered ACLs:

- Using names instead of numbers to identify the ACL, making it easier to remember the reason for the ACL

- Using ACL subcommands, not global commands, to define the action and matching parameters

- Using ACL editing features that allow the CLI user to delete individual lines from the ACL and insert new lines

You can easily learn named ACL configuration by just converting numbered ACLs to use the equivalent named ACL configuration. Figure 3-10 shows just such a conversion, using a simple three-line standard ACL number 1. To create the three **permit** subcommands for the named ACL, you literally copy parts of the three numbered ACL commands, beginning with the **permit** keyword.

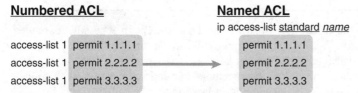

Figure 3-10 *Named ACL Versus Numbered ACL Configuration*

The only truly new part of the named ACL configuration is the **ip access-list** global configuration command. This command defines whether an ACL is a standard or extended ACL and defines the name. It also moves the user to ACL configuration mode, as shown in upcoming Example 3-4. Once in ACL configuration mode, you configure **permit**, **deny**, and **remark** commands that mirror the syntax of numbered ACL **access-list** commands. If you're configuring a standard named ACL, these commands match the syntax of standard numbered ACLs; if you're configuring extended named ACLs, they match the syntax of extended numbered ACLs.

Example 3-4 shows the configuration of a named extended ACL. Pay particular attention to the configuration mode prompts, which show ACL configuration mode.

Example 3-4 *Named Access List Configuration*

```
Router# configure terminal
Enter configuration commands, one per line. End with CNTL/Z.
Router(config)# ip access-list extended barney
Router(config-ext-nacl)# permit tcp host 10.1.1.2 eq www any
Router(config-ext-nacl)# deny udp host 10.1.1.1 10.1.2.0 0.0.0.255
Router(config-ext-nacl)# deny ip 10.1.3.0 0.0.0.255 10.1.2.0 0.0.0.255
Router(config-ext-nacl)# deny ip 10.1.2.0 0.0.0.255 10.2.3.0 0.0.0.255
Router(config-ext-nacl)# permit ip any any
Router(config-ext-nacl)# interface serial1
Router(config-if)# ip access-group barney out
Router(config-if)# ^Z
Router# show running-config
Building configuration...
```

```
Current configuration:

! lines omitted for brevity

interface serial 1
 ip access-group barney out
!
ip access-list extended barney
 permit tcp host 10.1.1.2 eq www any
 deny   udp host 10.1.1.1 10.1.2.0 0.0.0.255
 deny   ip 10.1.3.0 0.0.0.255 10.1.2.0 0.0.0.255
 deny   ip 10.1.2.0 0.0.0.255 10.2.3.0 0.0.0.255
 permit ip any any
```

Example 3-4 begins with the creation of an ACL named barney. The **ip access-list extended barney** command creates the ACL, naming it barney and placing the user in ACL configuration mode. This command also tells the IOS that barney is an extended ACL. Next, five different **permit** and **deny** statements define the matching logic and action to be taken upon a match. The **show running-config** command output lists the named ACL configuration before the single entry is deleted.

Named ACLs allow the user to delete and add new lines to the ACL from within ACL configuration mode. Example 3-5 shows how, with the **no deny ip…** command deleting a single entry from the ACL. Notice that the output of the **show access-list** command at the end of the example still lists the ACL, with four **permit** and **deny** commands instead of five.

Example 3-5 *Removing One Command from a Named ACL*

```
Router# configure terminal
Enter configuration commands, one per line. End with CNTL/Z.
Router(config)# ip access-list extended barney
Router(config-ext-nacl)# no deny ip 10.1.2.0 0.0.0.255 10.2.3.0 0.0.0.255
Router(config-ext-nacl)# ^Z
Router# show access-list

Extended IP access list barney
    10 permit tcp host 10.1.1.2 eq www any
    20 deny   udp host 10.1.1.1 10.1.2.0 0.0.0.255
    30 deny   ip 10.1.3.0 0.0.0.255 10.1.2.0 0.0.0.255
    50 permit ip any any
```

Editing ACLs Using Sequence Numbers

Numbered ACLs have existed in IOS since the early days of Cisco routers and IOS; however, for many years, through many IOS versions, the ability to edit a numbered IP ACL was poor. For example, to simply delete a line from the ACL, the user had to delete the entire ACL and then reconfigure it.

The ACL editing feature uses an ACL sequence number that is added to each ACL **permit** or **deny** statement, with the numbers representing the sequence of statements in the ACL.

ACL sequence numbers provide the following features for both numbered and named ACLs:

New configuration style for numbered: Numbered ACLs use a configuration style like named ACLs, as well as the traditional style, for the same ACL; the new style is required to perform advanced ACL editing.

Deleting single lines: An individual ACL **permit** or **deny** statement can be deleted with a **no** *sequence-number* subcommand.

Inserting new lines: Newly added **permit** and **deny** commands can be configured with a sequence number before the **deny** or **permit** command, dictating the location of the statement within the ACL.

Automatic sequence numbering: IOS adds sequence numbers to commands as you configure them, even if you do not include the sequence numbers.

To take advantage of the ability to delete and insert lines in an ACL, both numbered and named ACLs must use the same overall configuration style and commands used for named ACLs. The only difference in syntax is whether a name or number is used. Example 3-6 shows the configuration of a standard numbered IP ACL, using this alternative configuration style. The example shows the power of the ACL sequence number for editing. In this example, the following occurs:

Step 1. Numbered ACL 24 is configured using this new-style configuration, with three **permit** commands.

Step 2. The **show ip access-lists** command shows the three **permit** commands with sequence numbers 10, 20, and 30.

Step 3. The engineer deletes only the second **permit** command using the **no 20** ACL subcommand, which simply refers to sequence number 20.

Step 4. The **show ip access-lists** command confirms that the ACL now has only two lines (sequence numbers 10 and 30).

Step 5. The engineer adds a new **deny** command to the beginning of the ACL, using the **5 deny 10.1.1.1** ACL subcommand.

Step 6. The **show ip access-lists** command again confirms the changes, this time listing three commands, sequence numbers 5, 10, and 30.

NOTE   For this example, note that the user does not leave configuration mode, instead using the **do** command to tell IOS to issue the **show ip access-lists** EXEC command from configuration mode.

Example 3-6   *Editing ACLs Using Sequence Numbers*

```
! Step 1: The 3-line Standard Numbered IP ACL is configured.
R1# configure terminal
Enter configuration commands, one per line. End with CNTL/Z.
R1(config)# ip access-list standard 24
R1(config-std-nacl)# permit 10.1.1.0 0.0.0.255
R1(config-std-nacl)# permit 10.1.2.0 0.0.0.255
```

```
R1(config-std-nacl)# permit 10.1.3.0 0.0.0.255

! Step 2: Displaying the ACL's contents, without leaving configuration mode.
R1(config-std-nacl)# do show ip access-lists 24
Standard IP access list 24
    10 permit 10.1.1.0, wildcard bits 0.0.0.255
    20 permit 10.1.2.0, wildcard bits 0.0.0.255
    30 permit 10.1.3.0, wildcard bits 0.0.0.255

! Step 3: Still in ACL 24 configuration mode, the line with sequence number 20 is
deleted.
R1(config-std-nacl)# no 20

! Step 4: Displaying the ACL's contents again, without leaving configuration mode.
! Note that line number 20 is no longer listed.
R1(config-std-nacl)#do show ip access-lists 24
Standard IP access list 24
    10 permit 10.1.1.0, wildcard bits 0.0.0.255
    30 permit 10.1.3.0, wildcard bits 0.0.0.255

! Step 5: Inserting a new first line in the ACL.
R1(config-std-nacl)# 5 deny 10.1.1.1

! Step 6: Displaying the ACL's contents one last time, with the new statement
!(sequence number 5) listed first.
R1(config-std-nacl)# do show ip access-lists 24
Standard IP access list 24
     5 deny 10.1.1.1
    10 permit 10.1.1.0, wildcard bits 0.0.0.255
    30 permit 10.1.3.0, wildcard bits 0.0.0.255
```

Note that although Example 3-6 uses a numbered ACL, named ACLs use the same process to edit (add and remove) entries.

Numbered ACL Configuration Versus Named ACL Configuration

As a brief aside about numbered ACLs, note that IOS actually allows two ways to configure numbered ACLs in the more recent versions of IOS. First, IOS supports the traditional method, using the **access-list** global commands shown earlier in Examples 3-1, 3-2, and 3-3. IOS also supports the numbered ACL configuration with commands just like named ACLs, as shown in Example 3-6.

Oddly, IOS always stores numbered ACLs with the original style of configuration, as global **access-list** commands, no matter which method is used to configure the ACL. Example 3-7 demonstrates these facts, picking up where Example 3-6 ended, with the following additional steps:

Step 7.   The engineer lists the configuration (**show running-config**), which lists the old-style configuration commands—even though the ACL was created with the new-style commands.

Step 8.   The engineer adds a new statement to the end of the ACL using the old-style **access-list 24 permit 10.1.4.0 0.0.0.255** global configuration command.

Step 9.   The **show ip access-lists** command confirms that the old-style **access-list** command from the previous step followed the rule of being added only to the end of the ACL.

Step 10.   The engineer displays the configuration to confirm that the parts of ACL 24 configured with both new-style commands and old-style commands are all listed in the same old-style ACL (**show running-config**).

Example 3-7   *Adding to and Displaying a Numbered ACL Configuration*

```
! Step 7: A configuration snippet for ACL 24.

R1# show running-config
! The only lines shown are the lines from ACL 24
access-list 24 deny 10.1.1.1
access-list 24 permit 10.1.1.0 0.0.0.255
access-list 24 permit 10.1.3.0 0.0.0.255


! Step 8: Adding a new access-list 24 global command

R1# configure terminal
Enter configuration commands, one per line. End with CNTL/Z.
R1(config)# access-list 24 permit 10.1.4.0 0.0.0.255
R1(config)# ^Z


! Step 9: Displaying the ACL's contents again, with sequence numbers. Note that even
! the new statement has been automatically assigned a sequence number.

R1# show ip access-lists 24
Standard IP access list 24
    5 deny 10.1.1.1
    10 permit 10.1.1.0, wildcard bits 0.0.0.255
    30 permit 10.1.3.0, wildcard bits 0.0.0.255
    40 permit 10.1.4.0, wildcard bits 0.0.0.255


! Step 10: The numbered ACL config remains in old-style configuration commands.

R1# show running-config
! The only lines shown are the lines from ACL 24
access-list 24 deny    10.1.1.1
access-list 24 permit 10.1.1.0 0.0.0.255
access-list 24 permit 10.1.3.0 0.0.0.255
access-list 24 permit 10.1.4.0 0.0.0.255
```

ACL Implementation Considerations

ACLs can be a great tool to enhance the security of a network, but engineers should think about some broader issues before simply configuring an ACL to fix a problem. To help, Cisco makes the following general recommendations in the courses on which the CCNA exam is based:

- Place extended ACLs as close as possible to the source of the packet. This strategy allows ACLs to discard the packets early.

- Place standard ACLs as close as possible to the destination of the packet. This strategy avoids the mistake with standard ACLs (which match the source IPv4 address only) of unintentionally discarding packets that did not need to be discarded.

- Place more specific statements early in the ACL.

- Disable an ACL from its interface (using the **no ip access-group** interface subcommand) before making changes to the ACL.

The first point deals with the concept of where to locate your ACLs. If you intend to filter a packet, filtering closer to the packet's source means that the packet takes up less band-width in the network, which seems to be more efficient—and it is. Therefore, Cisco sug-gests locating extended ACLs as close to the source as possible.

However, the second point seems to contradict the first point, at least for standard ACLs, to locate them close to the destination. Why? Well, because standard ACLs look only at the source IP address, they tend to filter more than you want filtered when placed close to the source. For example, imagine that Fred and Barney are separated by four routers. If you filter Barney's traffic sent to Fred on the first router, Barney can't reach any hosts near the other three routers. So, the Cisco courses make a blanket recommendation to locate stan-dard ACLs closer to the destination to avoid filtering traffic you do not mean to filter.

For the third item in the list, by placing more specific matching parameters early in each list, you are less likely to make mistakes in the ACL. For example, imagine that the ACL first listed a command that permitted traffic going to 10.1.1.0/24, and the second command denied traffic going to host 10.1.1.1. Packets sent to host 10.1.1.1 would match the first command, and never match the more specific second command. Note that later IOS ver-sions prevent this mistake during configuration in some cases.

Finally, Cisco recommends that you disable the ACLs on the interfaces before you change the statements in the list. By doing so, you avoid issues with the ACL during an interim state. First, if you delete an entire ACL and leave the IP ACL enabled on an interface with the **ip access-group** command, IOS does not filter any packets (that was not always the case in far earlier IOS versions)! As soon as you add one ACL command to that enabled ACL, however, IOS starts filtering packets based on that ACL. Those interim ACL configurations could cause problems.

For example, suppose you have ACL 101 enabled on S0/0/0 for output packets. You delete list 101 so that all packets are allowed through. Then you enter a single **access-list 101** command. As soon as you press Enter, the list exists, and the router filters all packets exit-ing S0/0/0 based on the one-line list. If you want to enter a long ACL, you might temporari-ly filter packets you don't want to filter! Therefore, the better way is to disable the list from the interface, make the changes to the list, and then reenable it on the interface.

Additional Reading on ACLs

Cisco has long included IP ACLs in the CCNA exam. Preceding the current CCNA 200-301 exam, the CCNA R&S 200-125 exam included IP ACL troubleshooting. If you would like to learn more about ACLs, particularly about troubleshooting ACLs, as well as some unexpected behavior with ACLs and router-generated packets, refer to the section titled "Troubleshooting with IPv4 ACLs," in Appendix D, "Topics from Previous Editions."

Chapter Review

One key to doing well on the exams is to perform repetitive spaced review sessions. Review this chapter's material using either the tools in the book or interactive tools for the same material found on the book's companion website. Refer to the "Your Study Plan" element for more details. Table 3-7 outlines the key review elements and where you can find them. To better track your study progress, record when you completed these activities in the second column.

Table 3-7   Chapter Review Tracking

Review Element	Review Date(s)	Resource Used
Review key topics		Book, website
Review key terms		Book, website
Repeat DIKTA questions		Book, PTP
Review memory tables		Book, website
Review command tables		Book

Review All the Key Topics

Table 3-8   Key Topics for Chapter 3

Key Topic Element	Description	Page Number
Figure 3-3	Syntax and notes about the three required matching fields in the extended ACL **access-list** command	47
Paragraph	Summary of extended ACL logic that all parameters must match in a single **access-list** statement for a match to occur	48
Figure 3-4	Drawing of the IP header followed by a TCP header	48
Figure 3-5	Syntax and notes about matching TCP and UDP ports with extended ACL **access-list** commands	48
Figure 3-7	Logic and syntax to match TCP source ports	49
List	Guidelines for using extended numbered IP ACLs	51
List	Differences between named and numbered ACLs when named ACLs introduced	55
List	Features enabled by ACL sequence numbers	57
List	ACL implementation recommendations	60

Key Terms You Should Know

extended access list, named access list

Command References

Tables 3-9 and 3-10 list configuration and verification commands used in this chapter. As an easy review exercise, cover the left column in a table, read the right column, and try to recall the command without looking. Then repeat the exercise, covering the right column, and try to recall what the command does.

Table 3-9 Chapter 3 ACL Configuration Command Reference

Command	Description
access-list *access-list-number* {deny | permit} *protocol source source-wildcard destination destination-wildcard* [log]	Global command for extended numbered access lists. Use a number between 100 and 199 or 2000 and 2699, inclusive.
access-list *access-list-number* {deny | permit} tcp *source source-wildcard* [*operator* [*port*]] *destination destination-wildcard* [*operator* [*port*]] [log]	A version of the access-list command with TCP-specific parameters.
access-list *access-list-number* remark *text*	Command that defines a remark to help you remember what the ACL is supposed to do.
ip access-group {*number* | *name* [in | out]}	Interface subcommand to enable access lists.
access-class *number* | *name* [in | out]	Line subcommand to enable either standard or extended access lists on vty lines.
ip access-list {standard | extended} *name*	Global command to configure a named standard or extended ACL and enter ACL configuration mode.
{deny | permit} *source* [*source wildcard*] [log]	ACL mode subcommand to configure the matching details and action for a standard named ACL.
{deny | permit} *protocol source source-wildcard destination destination-wildcard* [log]	ACL mode subcommand to configure the matching details and action for an extended named ACL.
{deny | permit} tcp *source source-wildcard* [*operator* [*port*]] *destination destination-wildcard* [*operator* [*port*]] [log]	ACL mode subcommand to configure the matching details and action for a named ACL that matches TCP segments.
remark *text*	ACL mode subcommand to configure a description of a named ACL.

Table 3-10 Chapter 3 EXEC Command Reference

Command	Description
show ip *interface* [*type number*]	Includes a reference to the access lists enabled on the interface
show access-lists [*access-list-number* | *access-list-name*]	Shows details of configured access lists for all protocols
show ip access-lists [*access-list-number* | *access-list-name*]	Shows IP access lists

Answers to Earlier Practice Problems

Table 3-11 lists the answers to the practice problems listed in Table 3-6. Note that for any question that references a client, you might have chosen to match port numbers greater than 49151, matching all dynamic ports. The answers in this table mostly ignore that option, but just to show one sample, the answer to the first problem lists one with a reference to client ports greater than 49151 and one without. The remaining answers simply omit this part of the logic.

Table 3-11   Building One-Line Extended ACLs: Answers

	Criteria
1	access-list 101 permit tcp host 10.1.1.1 10.1.2.0 0.0.0.255 eq www or access-list 101 permit tcp host 10.1.1.1 gt 49151 10.1.2.0 0.0.0.255 eq www
2	access-list 102 permit tcp 172.16.4.0 0.0.0.127 172.16.3.0 0.0.0.127 eq telnet
3	access-list 103 permit icmp 192.168.7.192 0.0.0.63 192.168.7.8 0.0.0.7
4	access-list 104 permit tcp 10.2.2.0 0.0.1.255 eq www 10.4.4.0 0.0.3.255
5	access-list 105 permit tcp 172.20.1.0 0.0.0.255 eq 23 172.20.44.0 0.0.1.255
6	access-list 106 permit tcp 192.168.99.96 0.0.0.15 192.168.176.0 0.0.0.15 eq www
7	access-list 107 permit icmp 10.55.66.0 0.0.0.127 10.66.55.0 0.0.0.63
8	access-list 108 permit ip any any

3

Part I Review

Keep track of your part review progress with the checklist in Table P1-1. Details about each task follow the table.

Table P1-1 Part I Review Checklist

Activity	1st Date Completed	2nd Date Completed
Repeat All DIKTA Questions		
Answer Part Review Questions		
Review Key Topics		
Do Labs		

Repeat All DIKTA Questions

For this task, use the PTP software to answer the "Do I Know This Already?" questions again for the chapters in this part of the book.

Answer Part Review Questions

For this task, use PTP to answer the Part Review questions for this part of the book.

Review Key Topics

Review all key topics in all chapters in this part, either by browsing the chapters or by using the Key Topics application on the companion website.

Do Labs

Depending on your chosen lab tool, here are some suggestions for what to do in the lab:

Pearson Network Simulator: If you use the full Pearson CCNA simulator, focus more on the configuration scenario and troubleshooting scenario labs associated with the topics in this part of the book. These types of labs include a larger set of topics and work well as Part Review activities. (See the Introduction for some details about how to find which labs are about topics in this part of the book.)

Config Labs: In your idle moments, review and repeat any of the Config Labs for this book part in the author's blog; navigate to blog.certskills.com/config-labs for instructions on how to navigate to the labs.

Other: If you are using other lab tools, here are a few suggestions: when building ACL labs, you can test with Telnet (port 23), SSH (port 22), ping (ICMP), and traceroute (UDP) traffic as generated from an extra router. So, do not just configure the ACL; make an ACL that can match these types of traffic, denying some and permitting others, and then test.

With the introduction of the new CCNA certification in early 2020, Cisco expanded the number of security topics in comparison to the old CCNA Routing and Switching certification. Part II includes the majority of the new security topics added to the new CCNA 200-301 certification as well as a few of the classic topics found in previous CCNA R&S exams.

Chapter 4 kicks off Part II with a wide description of security threats, vulnerabilities, and exploits. This introductory chapter sets the stage to help you think more like a security engineer.

Chapters 5, 6, and 8 then focus on a wide range of short security topics. Those topics include Chapter 5's discussion of how to protect router and switch logins and passwords, along with an introduction to the functions and roles of firewalls or intrusion protection systems (IPSs). Chapters 6 and 8 then get into three separate security features built into Cisco switches: port security (Chapter 6), DHCP Snooping (Chapter 8), and Dynamic ARP Inspection (DAI). All three security features require a switch to examine frames as they enter the switch interface. This information enables port security, DHCP Snooping, and DAI to decide whether to allow the message to continue on its way.

Chapter 7 discusses the Dynamic Host Configuration Protocol (DHCP) as an end to itself. While this topic is actually an IP Service and would be a great fit for Part III (IP Services), the topics in Chapter 8 require that you know DHCP, so Chapter 7 sets that stage.

Part II

Security Services

CHAPTER 4

Security Architectures

This chapter covers the following exam topics:

5.0 Security Fundamentals

5.1 Define key security concepts (threats, vulnerabilities, exploits, and mitigation techniques)

5.2 Describe security program elements (user awareness, training, and physical access control)

5.4 Describe security password policies elements, such as management, complexity, and password alternatives (multifactor authentication, certificates, and biometrics)

5.8 Differentiate authentication, authorization, and accounting concepts

As you have learned about various networking technologies, your attention has probably been focused on using network devices to build functional networks. After all, networks should let data flow freely so that all connected users have a good experience, right? The unfortunate fact is that not all connected users can be trusted to obey the rules and be good network citizens. In this chapter, you will learn about many aspects of an enterprise network that can be exploited, as well as some ways you can protect them.

"Do I Know This Already?" Quiz

Take the quiz (either here or use the PTP software) if you want to use the score to help you decide how much time to spend on this chapter. The letter answers are listed at the bottom of the page following the quiz. Appendix C, found both at the end of the book as well as on the companion website, includes both the answers and explanations. You can also find both answers and explanations in the PTP testing software.

Table 4-1 "Do I Know This Already?" Section-to-Question Mapping

Foundation Topics Section	Questions
Security Terminology	1–2
Common Security Threats	3–7
Controlling and Monitoring User Access	8
Developing a Security Program to Educate Users	9

1. Which one of the following terms means anything that can be considered to be a weakness that can compromise security?

   a. Exploit

   b. Vulnerability

   c. Attack

   d. Threat

2. An actual potential to exploit a vulnerability is known as which one of the following terms?

   a. Vulnerability

   b. Attack

   c. Exploit

   d. Threat

3. In a spoofing attack, which of the following parameters are commonly spoofed? (Choose two answers.)

   a. MAC address

   b. Source IP address

   c. Destination IP address

   d. ARP address

4. Suppose an attacker sends a series of packets toward a destination IP address with the TCP SYN flag set but sends no other packet types. Which of the following attacks is likely taking place?

   a. Spoofing attack

   b. Reflection attack

   c. Reconnaissance attack

   d. Denial-of-service attack

   e. None of the choices are correct.

5. In a reflection attack, the source IP address in the attack packets is spoofed so that it contains which one of the following entities?

   a. The address of the attacker

   b. The address of the reflector

   c. The address of the victim

   d. The address of the router

6. During a successful man-in-the-middle attack, which two of the following actions is an attacker most likely to perform?

   a. Eavesdrop on traffic passing between hosts

   b. Induce a buffer overflow on multiple hosts

   c. Modify data passing between hosts

   d. Use ping sweeps and port scans to discover the network

7. Which one of the following is the goal of a brute-force attack?

   a. Try every possible TCP port until a service answers

   b. Try every possible combination of keyboard characters to guess a user's password

   c Initiate a denial-of-service operation on every possible host in a subnet

   d. Spoof every possible IP address in an organization

8. Which one of the following is an example of a AAA server?

   a. DHCP

   b. DNS

   c. SNMP

   d. ISE

9. Physical access control is important for which one of the following reasons?

   a. It prevents unauthorized people from sitting at a corporate user's desk and using their computer.

   b. It prevents users from getting angry and damaging computer equipment.

   c. It prevents unauthorized access to network closets.

   d. It prevents fires from destroying data centers.

Foundation Topics

Security Terminology

In a perfect world, you might build a network that supports every user in an enterprise, with the assumption that every user is known, every user is approved to access everything on the network, and every user will use the available resources exactly according to some corporate guidelines. The network shown in Figure 4-1 might represent such a scenario. Even this ideal, closed system is not completely secure because a user might decide to misbehave in order to pester a coworker or to view information on the corporate server that should be restricted or confidential.

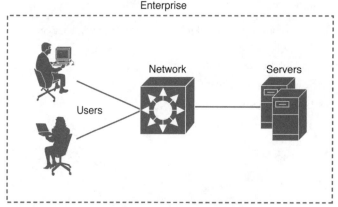

Figure 4-1 *An Example of an Enterprise Closed System*

Now consider that almost no enterprise uses such a limited, closed environment. After all, the enterprise will probably want to somehow connect itself to the public Internet and perhaps to some corporate partners. It will also probably want to allow its workers to be mobile and carry laptops, tablets, and smartphones in and out of the corporate boundaries for convenience. The enterprise might want to provide network access to guests who visit. If the enterprise offers wireless connectivity to its employees (and guests), it might also unknowingly offer its wireless access to people who are within range of the signals. And the list goes on and on. As the network and its connectivity expand, as Figure 4-2 shows, the enterprise will have more difficulty maintaining the safe, closed boundary around itself.

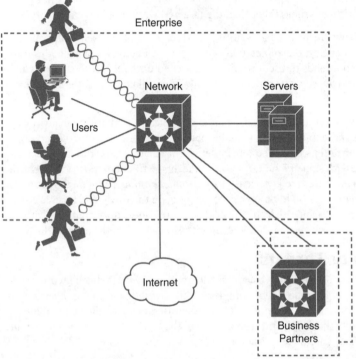

Figure 4-2   *An Example Enterprise Extends Beyond Its Own Boundary*

To begin securing a network, you first need to understand what might go wrong with it. Think of an enterprise network as a simple box-shaped facility, as shown in part A of Figure 4-3. When all of the walls, floor, and ceiling are made of a very strong material and are very thick, the contents inside the box will likely remain safe from harm or theft. The owner, however, might have a hard time getting in and out of the box.

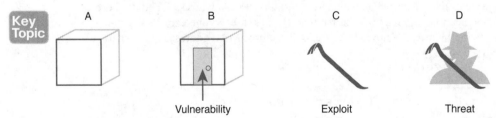

Figure 4-3   *Security Terminology Illustrated*

Suppose a door is introduced for convenience, as shown in part B of Figure 4-3. The owner can now come and go, but so might anyone else. Even if the door is locked, someone might find a way to get the door open and access the treasures inside. Because no door is impenetrable, the door becomes a *vulnerability*. In terms of security, a vulnerability is anything that can be considered to be a weakness that can compromise the security of something else, such as the integrity of data or how a system performs.

Just because a vulnerability exists, nothing is necessarily in jeopardy. In the locked door example, nobody but the trusted owner can open the door unless some sort of tool other than the key is used. Such a tool can be used to exploit a vulnerability. In fact, the tool itself is called an *exploit*, as shown by the pry bar in part C of Figure 4-3. An exploit is not very effective if it is used against anything other than the targeted weakness or vulnerability.

Technically, an exploit such as the pry bar is not very effective at all by itself. Someone must pick it up and use it against the vulnerability. In part D of Figure 4-3, a malicious user possesses the pry bar and intends to use it to open the locked door. Now there is an actual potential to break in, destroy, steal, or otherwise modify something without permission. This is known as a *threat*.

In the IT world of networks, systems, workstations, and applications, there are many, many different vulnerabilities and exploits that can be leveraged by malicious users to become threats to an organization and its data. The remainder of this chapter provides an overview of many of them, along with some techniques you can leverage to counteract or prevent the malicious activity. Such measures are known as *mitigation techniques*. You might be thinking of some ways the Figure 4-3 building owner could mitigate the threats he faces. Perhaps he could add stronger, more secure locks to the door, a more robust door frame to withstand prying forces, or an alarm system to detect an intrusion and alert the authorities.

Common Security Threats

Because modern enterprise networks are usually made up of many parts that all work together, securing them can become a very complex task. As with the simple box analogy, you cannot effectively try to secure it until you have identified many of the vulnerabilities, assessed the many exploits that exist, and realized where the threats might come from. Only then can the appropriate countermeasures and mitigations be put in place.

You should also consider some important attributes of enterprise resources that should be protected and preserved. As you work through the many threats that are discussed in this chapter, think about the vulnerability and exploit that makes the threat possible. Notice how many different parts of the enterprise network exhibit vulnerabilities and how the threats are crafted to take advantage of the weaknesses.

Attacks That Spoof Addresses

When systems behave normally, parameters and services can be trusted and used effectively. For example, when a machine sends an IP packet, everyone expects the source IP address to be the machine's own IP address. The source MAC address in the Ethernet frame

---

is expected to be the sender's own MAC address. Even services like DHCP and DNS should follow suit; if a machine sends a DHCP or DNS request, it expects any DHCP or DNS reply to come from a legitimate, trusted server.

Spoofing attacks focus on one vulnerability; addresses and services tend to be implicitly trusted. Attacks usually take place by replacing expected values with spoofed or fake values. Address spoofing attacks can be simple and straightforward, where one address value is substituted for another.

For example, an attacker can send packets with a spoofed source IP address instead of its own, as shown in Figure 4-4. When the target receives the packets, it will send return traffic to the spoofed address, rather than the attacker's actual address. If the spoofed address exists, then an unsuspecting host with that address will receive the packet. If the address does not exist, the packet will be forwarded and then dropped further out in the network.

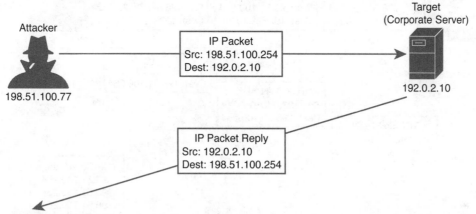

Figure 4-4 *A Sample Spoofing Attack*

An attacker can send spoofed MAC addresses too, to add false information to the forwarding tables used by Layer 2 switches or ARP tables used by other hosts and routers. DHCP requests with spoofed MAC addresses can also be sent to a legitimate DHCP server, filling its address lease table and leaving no free IP addresses for normal use.

Note that Chapter 6, "Implementing Switch Port Security," discusses a tool that can be used to help mitigate MAC address spoofing. In Chapter 8, "DHCP Snooping and ARP Inspection," you can learn more about Dynamic ARP Inspection (DAI) and how to use it to mitigate IP address spoofing using ARP.

Denial-of-Service Attacks

In the normal operation of a business application, clients open connections to corporate servers to exchange information. This might occur in the form of web-based sessions that are open to internal users as well as external users on the public Internet. The process is simple: users open a web browser to the corporate site, which then opens a TCP connection with the corporate web server; then some transaction can take place. If all the users are well behaved and conduct legitimate transactions, the corporate servers are (hopefully) not stressed and many clients can do business normally.

Now suppose a malicious user finds a way to open an abnormal connection to the same corporate server. The TCP connection begins with the malicious user sending a SYN flag to the server, but the source IP address is replaced with a fake address. The server adds the TCP connection to its table of client connections and replies to the fake address with a SYN-ACK. Because the fake address is not involved in the TCP connection, there is no ACK reply to complete the TCP three-way handshake. The incomplete connection stays in the server's table until it eventually times out and is removed. During this time, the attacker can try to open many, many more abnormal connections at such a rate that the server's connection table fills. At that point, the server is no longer able to maintain TCP connections with legitimate users, so their business transactions all halt. Figure 4-5 illustrates this process.

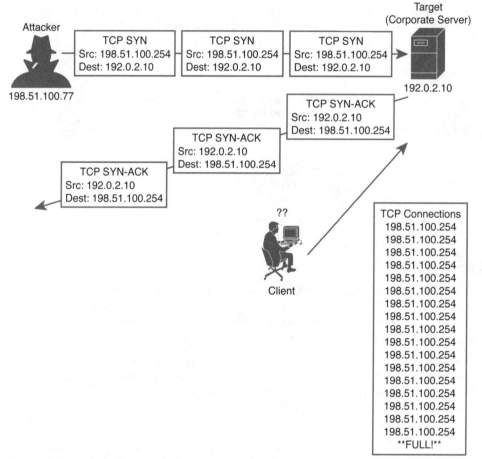

Figure 4-5 *A Sample Denial-of-Service Attack*

When an attacker is able to deplete a system resource, services and systems become unavailable or crash. This is called a *denial-of-service (DoS)* attack because it denies service to legitimate users or operations. DoS attacks can involve something as simple as ICMP echo (ping) packets, a flood of UDP packets, and TCP connections, such as the TCP SYN flood attack previously described. Such attacks can be successful provided a system has a vulnerability with the protocol or type of traffic that is exploited.

Attackers can carry the DoS idea even further by enlisting many other systems to partici-pate. To do this, the attacker sets up a master control computer somewhere on the Internet. Next, many computers must first be infected with malicious code or malware by leverag-ing vulnerabilities present in those machines. Each machine then silently becomes a "bot," appearing to operate normally, while awaiting commands from the master control. When the time comes for an attack to begin, the master control sends a command to every bot and tells it to initiate a denial-of-service attack against a single target host. This is called a *distributed denial-of-service* (DDoS) attack because the attack is distributed across a large number of bots, all flooding or attacking the same target.

Reflection and Amplification Attacks

Recall that in a spoofing attack, the attacker sends packets with a spoofed source address to a target. The goal is to force the target to deal with the spoofed traffic and send return traf-fic toward a nonexistent source. The attacker does not care where the return traffic goes or that it cannot be delivered successfully.

In a somewhat related attack, the attacker again sends packets with a spoofed source address toward a live host. However, the host is not the intended target; the goal is to get the host to reflect the exchange toward the spoofed address that is the target. This is known as a *reflection attack* as illustrated in Figure 4-6, and the host reflecting the traffic toward the target is called the reflector. The attacker might also send the spoofed packets to mul-tiple reflectors, causing the target to receive multiple copies of the unexpected traffic.

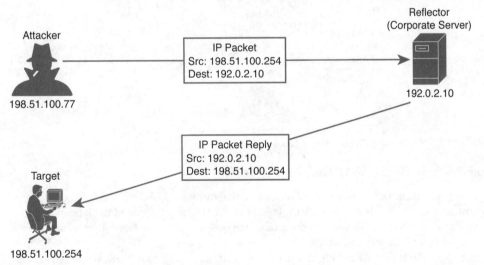

Figure 4-6 *A Sample Reflection Attack*

The impact of a reflection attack might seem limited because a single target host is the vic-tim, and the amount of traffic being reflected to the target is in proportion to the packets sent by the attacker. If an attacker is able to send a small amount of traffic to a reflector and leverage a protocol or service to generate a large volume of traffic toward a target, then an *amplification attack* has occurred. In effect, such an attack amplifies the attacker's efforts to disrupt the target. Another result is that large amounts of network bandwidth can be consumed forwarding the amplified traffic toward the target, especially if many reflectors are involved. Some mechanisms of DNS and NTP have been exploited in the past to set new records for enormous bandwidth consumption during an amplification attack.

Man-in-the-Middle Attacks

Many types of attacks are meant to disrupt or directly compromise targeted systems, often with noticeable results. Sometimes an attacker might want to eavesdrop on data that passes from one machine to another, avoiding detection. A *man-in-the-middle attack* does just that, by allowing the attacker to quietly wedge itself into the communication path as an intermediary between two target systems.

One type of man-in-the-middle attack exploits the ARP table that each host maintains to communicate with other hosts on its local network segment. Normally, if one host needs to send data to another, it looks for the destination host in its ARP table. If an entry is found, the Ethernet frame can be sent directly to the destination MAC address; otherwise, the sender must broadcast an ARP request containing the destination's IP address and wait for the destination to answer with an ARP reply and its own MAC address.

Figure 4-7 illustrates a successful man-in-the-middle attack.

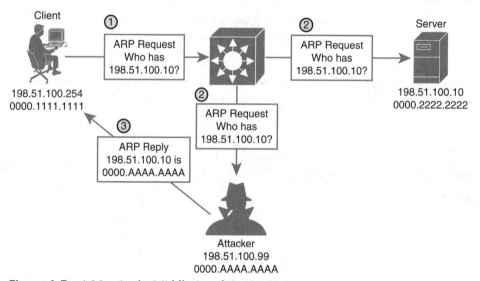

Figure 4-7 *A Man-in-the-Middle Attack Begins*

In step 1, a client broadcasts an ARP request to find out what MAC address is used by the host with IP address 198.51.100.10. In step 2, the ARP request is flooded to all hosts in the broadcast domain. This allows the attacker to overhear the ARP request and prepare to exploit the information learned. The legitimate owner of 198.51.100.10 may indeed respond with its own ARP reply and real MAC address, as expected. However, in step 3, the attacker simply waits a brief time and then sends a spoofed ARP reply containing its own MAC address, rather than that of the actual destination. The goal is for the attacker to send the last ARP reply so that any listening host will update its ARP table with the most recent information.

This process effectively poisons the ARP table entry in any system receiving the spoofed ARP reply. From that point on, a poisoned system will blindly forward traffic to the attacker's MAC address, which now masquerades as the destination. The attacker is able to know the real destination's MAC address because he received an earlier ARP reply from the destination host. Figure 4-8 depicts the end result. The attacker can repeat this process by poisoning the ARP entries on multiple hosts and then relaying traffic between them without easy detection.

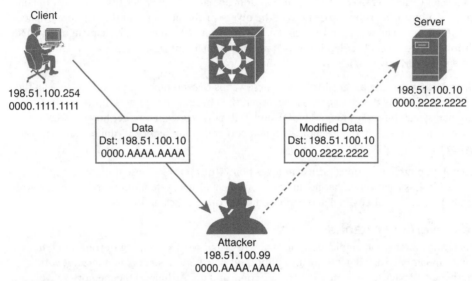

Figure 4-8   *A Man-in-the-Middle Attack Succeeds*

Once an attacker has inserted herself between two hosts, she can passively eavesdrop on and inspect all traffic passing between them. The attacker might also take an active role and modify the data passing through.

Address Spoofing Attack Summary

As you work through the various types of address spoofing attacks, remember that the attacker's goal is to disguise his identity and fool other systems in a malicious way. Use Table 4-2 to review the concepts and characteristics of each attack type.

Table 4-2   Summary of Address Spoofing Attacks

Goal	DoS/DDoS	Reflection	Amplification	Man-in-the-Middle
Exhaust a system service or resource; crash the target system	Yes	Yes	Yes	No
Trick an unwitting accomplice host to send traffic to target	No	Yes	Yes	No
Eavesdrop on traffic	No	No	No	Yes
Modify traffic passing through	No	No	No	Yes

Reconnaissance Attacks

When an attacker intends to launch an attack on a target, that attacker might want to identify some vulnerabilities so the attack can be focused and more effective. A *reconnaissance attack* can be used to discover more details about the target and its systems prior to an actual attack.

During a reconnaissance attack, the attacker can use some common tools to uncover public details like who owns a domain and what IP address ranges are used there. For example, the **nslookup** command exists in many operating systems and can perform a DNS lookup to resolve an IP address from a fully qualified domain name. If an attacker knows the domain name of a business, **nslookup** can reveal the owner of the domain and the IP address space registered to it. The **whois** and **dig** commands are complementary tools that can query DNS information to reveal detailed information about domain owners, contact information, mail servers, authoritative name servers, and so on.

Then the attacker can progress to using ping sweeps to send pings to each IP address in the target range. Hosts that answer the ping sweep then become live targets. Port scanning tools can then sweep through a range of UDP and TCP ports to see if a target host answers on any port numbers. Any replies indicate that a corresponding service is running on the target host.

Keep in mind that a reconnaissance attack is not a true attack because nothing is exploited as a result. It is used for gathering information about target systems and services so that vulnerabilities can be discovered and exploited using other types of attacks.

Buffer Overflow Attacks

Operating systems and applications normally read and write data using buffers and temporary memory space. Buffers are also important when one system communicates with another, as IP packets and Ethernet frames come and go. As long as the memory space is maintained properly and data is placed within the correct buffer boundaries, everything should work as expected.

However, some systems and applications have vulnerabilities that can allow buffers to overflow. This means some incoming data might be stored in unexpected memory locations if a buffer is allowed to fill beyond its limit. An attacker can exploit this condition by sending data that is larger than expected. If a vulnerability exists, the target system might store that data, overflowing its buffer into another area of memory, eventually crashing a service or the entire system. The attacker might also be able to specially craft the large message by inserting malicious code in it. If the target system stores that data as a result of a buffer overflow, then it can potentially run the malicious code without realizing.

Malware

Some types of security threats can come in the form of malicious software or *malware*. For example, a *trojan horse* is malicious software that is hidden and packaged inside other software that looks normal and legitimate. If a well-meaning user decides to install it, the trojan horse software is silently installed too. Then the malware can run attacks of its own on the local system or against other systems. Trojan horse malware can spread from one computer to another only through user interaction such as opening email attachments, downloading software from the Internet, and inserting a USB drive into a computer.

In contrast, *viruses* are malware that can propagate between systems more readily. To spread, virus software must inject itself into another application, then rely on users to transport the infected application software to other victims.

One other type of malware is able to propagate to and infect other systems on its own. An attacker develops *worm* software and deposits it on a system. From that point on, the worm replicates itself and spreads to other systems through their vulnerabilities, then replicates and spreads again and again.

To summarize, Table 4-3 lists the key ideas behind each type of malware described in this section.

Table 4-3   Summary of Malware Types

Characteristic	Trojan Horse	Virus	Worm
Packaged inside other software	Yes	No	No
Self-injected into other software	No	Yes	No
Propagates automatically	No	No	Yes

Human Vulnerabilities

Many types of attack must take advantage of a vulnerability in an operating system, service, or other types of application software. In other words, an attacker or the malware involved must find a weakness in the target computer system. There are still many other attacks that can succeed by exploiting weaknesses in the humans that use computer systems.

One rather straightforward attack is called *social engineering*, where human trust and social behaviors can become security vulnerabilities. For example, an attacker might pose as an IT staff member and attempt to contact actual end users through phone calls, emails, and social media. The end goal might be to convince the users to reveal their credentials or set their passwords to a "temporary" value due to some fictitious IT maintenance that will take place, allowing the attacker to gain easy access to secure systems. Attackers might also be physically present and secretly observe users as they enter their credentials.

Phishing is a technique that attackers use to lure victims into visiting malicious websites. The idea is to either disguise the invitation as something legitimate, frighten victims into following a link, or otherwise deceive users into browsing content that convinces them to enter their confidential information.

Phishing comes in many forms. *Spear phishing* targets a group of similar users who might work for the same company, shop at the same stores, and so on, who all receive the same convincing email with a link to a malicious site. *Whaling* is similar but targets high-profile individuals in corporations, governments, and organizations. Phishing can also occur over traditional communications, such as voice calls (*vishing*) and SMS text messages (*smishing*).

Pharming also attempts to send victims to a malicious website, but it takes a more drastic approach. Rather than enticing victims to follow a disguised link, pharming involves compromising the services that direct users toward a well-known or trusted website. For instance, an attacker can compromise a DNS service or edit local hosts files to change the entry for a legitimate site. When a victim tries to visit the site using its actual link, the altered name resolution returns the address of a malicious site instead.

In a *watering hole* attack, an attacker determines which users frequently visit a site; then that site is compromised and malware is deposited there. The malware infects only the target users who visit the site, while leaving other users unscathed.

You can refer to Table 4-4 to review the key ideas behind each type of human vulnerability that is commonly exploited.

4

Table 4-4 Summary of Human Security Vulnerabilities

Attack Type	Goal
Social engineering	Exploits human trust and social behavior
Phishing	Disguises a malicious invitation as something legitimate
Spear phishing	Targets group of similar users
Whaling	Targets high-profile individuals
Vishing	Uses voice calls
Smishing	Uses SMS text messages
Pharming	Uses legitimate services to send users to a compromised site
Watering hole	Targets specific victims who visit a compromised site

Password Vulnerabilities

Most systems in an enterprise network use some form of authentication to grant or deny user access. When users access a system, a username and password are usually involved. It might be fairly easy to guess someone's username based on that person's real name. If the user's password is set to some default value or to a word or text string that is easy to guess, an attacker might easily gain access to the system too.

Think like an attacker for a moment and see if you can make some guesses about passwords you might try if you wanted to log in to a random system. Perhaps you thought of pass-words like *password*, *password123*, *123456*, and so on. Perhaps you could try username *admin* and password *admin*.

An attacker can launch an online attack by actually entering each password guess as the system prompts for user credentials. In contrast, an offline attack occurs when the attacker is able to retrieve the encrypted or hashed passwords ahead of time, then goes offline to an external computer and uses software there to repeatedly attempt to recover the actual password.

Attackers can also use software to perform dictionary attacks to discover a user's password. The software will automatically attempt to log in with passwords taken from a dictionary or word list. It might have to go through thousands or millions of attempts before discover-ing the real password. In addition, the software can perform a brute-force attack by try-ing every possible combination of letter, number, and symbol strings. Brute-force attacks require very powerful computing resources and a large amount of time.

To mitigate password attacks, an enterprise should implement password policies for all users. Such a policy might include guidelines that require a long password string made up of a combination of upper- and lowercase characters along with numbers and some special characters. The goal is to require all passwords to be complex strings that are difficult to guess or reveal by a password attack. As well, password management should require all passwords to be changed periodically so that even lengthy brute-force attacks would not be able to recover a password before it is changed again.

Password Alternatives

A simple password string is the single factor that a user must enter to be authenticated. Because a password should be remembered and not written down anywhere, you might think of your password as "something you know." Hopefully nobody else knows it too; otherwise, they could use it to impersonate you when authenticating.

An enterprise might also consider using alternative credentials that bring more complexity and more security. Multifactor credentials require users to provide values or factors that come from different sources, reducing the chance that an attacker might possess all of the factors. An old saying describes two-factor credentials as "something you have" (a dynamic changing cryptographic key or a text message containing a time-limited code) and "something you know" (a password).

A digital certificate can serve as one alternative factor because it serves as a trusted form of identification, adheres to a standardized format, and contains encrypted information. If an enterprise supports certificate use, then a user must request and be granted a unique certificate to use for specific purposes. For example, certificates used for authenticating users must be approved for authentication. In order to be trusted, certificates must be granted and digitally signed by a trusted certificate authority (CA). As long as the services used by the enterprise know and trust the CA, then individual certificates signed by that CA can be trusted as well.

Digital certificates are also time sensitive, as each is approved for a specific time range. Once a certificate expires, any attempts to authenticate with it will be rejected. The user who possesses the certificate can request a new one prior to the expiration date or at any time afterward. Certificates can also be revoked, if the business decides to revoke privileges from a user, if the user separates from the business, and so on. Even if the user still possesses a revoked certificate, he will be refused access when he tries to authenticate with it.

Because digital certificates exist as files on a computer or device, you might think they can be freely copied and used to identify people other than the original owners. Each digital certificate must also carry proof of possession to show that it was truly granted to the user who presents it during authentication. This proof is built into the encrypted certificate content, as a result of combining public keys that the user's machine and the authentication server can publicly share, along with private keys that each party keeps private and secret. As long as the authentication server can verify that the certificate was created using the correct public and private keys, then the certificate must be possessed by the expected owner. If not, then authentication will be rejected to keep an imposter out.

Biometric credentials carry the scheme even further by providing a factor that represents "something you are." The idea is to use some physical attribute from a user's body to uniquely identify that person. Physical attributes are usually unique to each individual's body structure and cannot be easily stolen or duplicated. For example, a user's fingerprint can be scanned and used as an authentication factor. Other examples include face recognition, palm prints, voice recognition, iris recognition, and retinal scans. As you might expect, some methods can be trusted more than others. Sometimes facial recognition systems can be fooled when presented with photographs or masks of trusted individuals. Injuries and the aging process can also alter biometric patterns such as fingerprints, facial shapes, and iris patterns. To help mitigate potential weaknesses, multiple biometric credentials can be collected and used to authenticate users as well.

To summarize, Table 4-5 lists the key ideas used in each alternative to password authentication.

Table 4-5 Summary of Password Authentication and Alternatives

Characteristic	Password Only	Two-Factor	Digital Certificates	Biometric
Something you know	Yes	Yes		
Something you have		Yes	Yes	
Something you are				Yes

Controlling and Monitoring User Access

You can manage user activity to and through systems with authentication, authorization, and accounting (AAA, also pronounced "triple-A") mechanisms. AAA uses standardized methods to challenge users for their credentials before access is allowed or authorized. Accounting protocols also can record user activity on enterprise systems. AAA is commonly used to control and monitor access to network devices like routers, switches, firewalls, and so on.

In a nutshell, you can think of AAA in the following manner:

- **Authentication:** Who is the user?
- **Authorization:** What is the user allowed to do?
- **Accounting:** What did the user do?

As an example, a network administrator can have several methods to manage users who might try to log in to a switch to perform some operation. At the most basic level, you could authenticate users with simple passwords that are configured on the switch console and VTY lines. Authorization could be equally simple: when users successfully log in, they are authorized for EXEC level privileges. By entering the correct enable secret password, users could be authorized for a higher privilege level.

Under the simple scenario, if a user knows the correct password, he can connect to the switch. But who is that user? You might never know who actually logged in and changed the configuration or rebooted the switch! Instead, you could configure individual usernames and passwords on the switch. That would solve the user anonymity problem, but your network might consist of many administrative users and many switches, requiring quite a bit of username configuration and maintenance.

A more scalable solution is to leverage AAA functions that are centralized, standardized, resilient, and flexible. For example, a centralized authentication server can contain a database of all possible users and their passwords, as well as policies to authorize user activities. As users come and go, their accounts can be easily updated in one place. All switches and routers would query the AAA server to get up-to-date information about a user. For greater security, AAA servers can also support multifactor user credentials and more. Cisco implements AAA services in its Identity Services Engine (ISE) platform.

AAA servers usually support the following two protocols to communicate with enterprise resources:

- **TACACS+:** A Cisco proprietary protocol that separates each of the AAA functions. Communication is secure and encrypted over TCP port 49.
- **RADIUS:** A standards-based protocol that combines authentication and authorization into a single resource. Communication uses UDP ports 1812 and 1813 (accounting) but is not completely encrypted.

Both TACACS+ and RADIUS are arranged as a client/server model, where an authenticating device acts as a client talking to a AAA server. Figure 4-9 shows a simplified view of the process, where a user is attempting to connect to a switch for management purposes. In the AAA client role, the switch is often called Network Access Device (NAD) or Network Access Server (NAS). When a user tries to connect to the switch, the switch challenges the user for credentials, then passes the credentials along to the AAA server. In simple terms, if the user passes authentication, the AAA server returns an "accept" message to the switch. If the AAA server requires additional credentials, as in multifactor authentication, it returns a "challenge" message to the switch. Otherwise, a "reject" message is returned, denying access to the user.

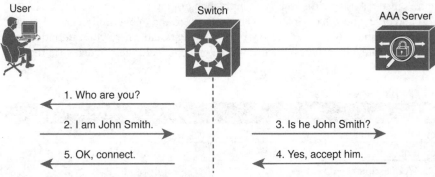

Figure 4-9   *A Simplified View of AAA*

Developing a Security Program to Educate Users

One effective approach an enterprise can take to improve information security is to educate its user community through a corporate security program. Most users may not have an IT background, so they might not recognize vulnerabilities or realize the consequences of their own actions. For example, if corporate users receive an email message that contains a message concerning a legal warrant for their arrest or a threat to expose some supposed illegal behavior, they might be tempted to follow a link to a malicious site. Such an action might infect a user's computer and then open a back door or introduce malware or a worm that could then impact the business operations.

An effective security program should have the following basic elements:

- **User awareness:** All users should be made aware of the need for data confidentiality to protect corporate information, as well as their own credentials and personal information. They should also be made aware of potential threats, schemes to mislead, and proper procedures to report security incidents. Users should also be instructed to follow strict guidelines regarding data loss. For example, users should not include sensitive information in emails or attachments, should not keep or transmit that information from a smartphone, or store it on cloud services or removable storage drives.

- **User training:** All users should be required to participate in periodic formal training so that they become familiar with all corporate security policies. (This also implies that the enterprise should develop and publish formal security policies for its employees, users, and business partners to follow.)

■ **Physical access control:** Infrastructure locations, such as network closets and data centers, should remain securely locked. Badge access to sensitive locations is a scalable solution, offering an audit trail of identities and timestamps when access is granted. Administrators can control access on a granular basis and quickly remove access when an employee is dismissed.

Chapter Review

One key to doing well on the exams is to perform repetitive spaced review sessions. Review this chapter's material using either the tools in the book or interactive tools for the same material found on the book's companion website. Refer to the "Your Study Plan" element for more details. Table 4-6 outlines the key review elements and where you can find them. To better track your study progress, record when you completed these activities in the second column.

Table 4-6 Chapter Review Tracking

Review Element	Review Date(s)	Resource Used
Review key topics		Book, website
Review key terms		Book, website
Answer DIKTA questions		Book, PTP
Review memory tables		Website

Review All the Key Topics

Table 4-7 Key Topics for Chapter 4

Key Topic Element	Description	Page Number
Figure 4-3	Security terminology	71
Section	Common Security Threats	72
Table 4-3	Types of malware	79
Table 4-4	Human security vulnerabilities	80
Paragraph	Password vulnerabilities	80
List	AAA functions	82
List	User education	83

Key Terms You Should Know

AAA, amplification attack, brute-force attack, buffer overflow attack, denial-of-service (DoS) attack, dictionary attack, distributed denial-of-service (DDoS) attack, exploit, malware, man-in-the-middle attack, mitigation technique, multifactor authentication, password guessing, pharming, phishing, reconnaissance attack, reflection attack, social engineering, spear phishing, spoofing attack, threat, trojan horse, virus, vulnerability, watering hole attack, whaling, worm

CHAPTER 5

Securing Network Devices

This chapter covers the following exam topics:

1.0 Network Fundamentals

    1.1 Explain the Role of Network Components

        1.1.c Next-generation Firewalls and IPS

4.0 IP Services

    4.8 Configure network devices for remote access using SSH

5.0 Security Fundamentals

    5.3 Configure device access control using local passwords

All devices in the network—endpoints, servers, and infrastructure devices like routers and switches—include some methods for the devices to legitimately communicate using the network. To protect those devices, the security plan will include a wide variety of tools and mitigation techniques, with the chapters in Part II of this book discussing a large variety of those tools and techniques.

This chapter focuses on two particular security needs in an enterprise network. First, access to the CLI of the network devices needs to be protected. The network engineering team needs to be able to access the devices remotely, so the devices need to allow remote SSH (and possibly Telnet) access. The first half of this chapter discusses how to configure passwords to keep them safe and how to filter login attempts at the devices themselves.

The second half of the chapter turns to two different security functions most often implemented with purpose-built appliances: firewalls and IPSs. These devices together monitor traffic in transit to determine if the traffic is legitimate or if it might be part of some exploit. If considered to be part of an exploit, or if contrary to the rules defined by the devices, they can discard the messages, stopping any attack before it gets started.

"Do I Know This Already?" Quiz

Take the quiz (either here or use the PTP software) if you want to use the score to help you decide how much time to spend on this chapter. The letter answers are listed at the bottom of the page following the quiz. Appendix C, found both at the end of the book as well as on the companion website, includes both the answers and explanations. You can also find both answers and explanations in the PTP testing software.

Table 5-1   "Do I Know This Already?" Foundation Topics Section-to-Question Mapping

Foundation Topics Section	Questions
Securing IOS Passwords	1–4
Firewalls and Intrusion Prevention Systems	5, 6

1. Imagine that you have configured the **enable secret** command, followed by the **enable password** command, from the console. You log out of the switch and log back in at the console. Which command defines the password that you had to enter to access privileged mode?

   a. **enable password**

   b. **enable secret**

   c. Neither

   d. The **password** command, if it's configured

2. Some IOS commands store passwords as clear text, but you can then encrypt the passwords with the **service password-encryption** global command. By comparison, other commands store a computed hash of the password instead of storing the password. Comparing the two options, which one answer is the *most accurate* about why one method is better than the other?

   a. Using hashes is preferred because encrypted IOS passwords can be easily decrypted.

   b. Using hashes is preferred because of the large CPU effort required for encryption.

   c. Using encryption is preferred because it provides stronger password protection.

   d. Using encryption is preferred because of the large CPU effort required for hashes.

3. A network engineer issues a **show running-config** command and sees only one line of output that mentions the **enable secret** command, as follows:

   ```
   enable secret 5 $1$ZGMA$e8cmvkz4UjiJhVp7.maLE1
   ```

   Which of the following is true about users of this router?

   a. A user must type **1ZGMA$e8cmvkz4UjiJhVp7.maLE1** to reach enable mode.

   b. The router will hash the clear-text password that the user types to compare to the hashed password.

   c. A **no service password-encryption** configuration command would decrypt this password.

   d. The router will decrypt the password in the configuration to compare to the clear-text password typed by the user.

4. A single-line ACL has been added to a router configuration using the command **ip access-list 1 permit 172.16.4.0 0.0.1.255**. The configuration also includes the **access-class 1 in** command in VTY configuration mode. Which answer accurately describes how the router uses ACL 1?

   a. Hosts in subnet 172.16.4.0/23 alone can telnet into the router.

   b. CLI users cannot telnet from the router to hosts in subnet 172.16.4.0/23 alone.

   c. Hosts in subnet 172.16.4.0/23 alone can log in but cannot reach enable mode of the router.

   d. The router will only forward packets with source addresses in subnet 172.16.4.0/23.

5. A next-generation firewall sits at the edge of a company's connection to the Internet. It has been configured to prevent Telnet clients residing in the Internet from accessing Telnet servers inside the company. Which of the following might a next-generation firewall use that a traditional firewall would not?

   a. Match message destination well-known port 23

   b. Match message application data

   c. Match message IP protocol 23

   d. Match message source TCP ports greater than 49152

6. Which actions show a behavior typically supported by a Cisco next-generation IPS (NGIPS) beyond the capabilities of a traditional IPS? (Choose two answers)

   a. Gather and use host-based information for context

   b. Comparisons between messages and a database of exploit signatures

   c. Logging events for later review by the security team

   d. Filter URIs using reputation scores

Foundation Topics

Securing IOS Passwords

The ultimate way to protect passwords in Cisco IOS devices is to not store passwords in IOS devices. That is, for any functions that can use an external authentication, authorization, and accounting (AAA) server, use it. However, it is common to store some passwords in a router or switch configuration, and this first section of the chapter discusses some of the ways to protect those passwords.

As a brief review, Figure 5-1 summarizes some typical login security configuration on a router or switch. On the lower left, you see Telnet support configured, with the use of a password only (no username required). On the right, the configuration adds support for login with both username and password, supporting both Telnet and SSH users. The upper left shows the one command required to define an enable password in a secure manner.

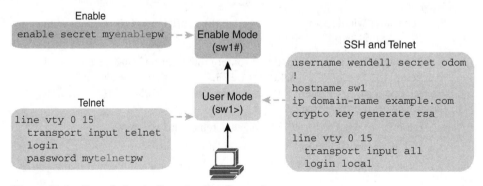

Figure 5-1 *Sample Login Security Configuration*

NOTE The configuration on the far right of the figure supports both SSH and Telnet, but consider allowing SSH only by instead using the **transport input ssh** command. The Telnet protocol sends all data unencrypted, so any attacker who copies the message with a Telnet login will have a copy of the password.

The rest of this first section discusses how to make these passwords secure. In particular, this section looks at ways to avoid keeping clear-text passwords in the configuration and storing the passwords in ways that make it difficult for attackers to learn the password.

Encrypting Older IOS Passwords with service password-encryption

Some older-style IOS passwords create a security exposure because the passwords exist in the configuration file as clear text. These clear-text passwords might be seen in printed versions of the configuration files, in a backup copy of the configuration file stored on a server, or as displayed on a network engineer's display.

Cisco attempted to solve this clear-text problem by adding a command to encrypt those passwords: the **service password-encryption** global configuration command. This command encrypts passwords that are normally held as clear text, specifically the passwords for these commands:

password *password* (console or vty mode)

username *name* **password** *password* (global)

enable password *password* (global)

To see how it works, Example 5-1 shows how the **service password-encryption** command encrypts the clear-text console password. The example uses the **show running-config | section line con 0** command both before and after the encryption; this command lists only the section of the configuration about the console.

Example 5-1 *Encryption and the* **service password-encryption** *Command*

```
Switch3# show running-config | section line con 0
line con 0
 password cisco
 login


Switch3# configure terminal
Enter configuration commands, one per line.    End with CNTL/Z.
Switch3(config)# service password-encryption
Switch3(config)# ^Z


Switch3# show running-config | section line con 0
line con 0
 password 7 070C285F4D06
 login
```

A close examination of the before and after **show running-config** command output reveals both the obvious effect and a new concept. The encryption process now hides the original clear-text password. Also, IOS needs a way to signal that the value in the **password** command lists an encrypted password rather than the clear text. IOS adds the encryption or encoding type of "7" to the command, which specifically refers to passwords encrypted with the **service password-encryption** command. (IOS considers the clear-text passwords to be type 0; some commands list the 0, and some do not.)

While the **service password-encryption** global command encrypts passwords, the **no service password-encryption** global command does not immediately decrypt the passwords back to their clear-text state. Instead, the process works as shown in Figure 5-2. Basically, after you enter the **no service password-encryption** command, the passwords remain encrypted until you change a password.

Figure 5-2 *Encryption Is Immediate; Decryption Awaits Next Password Change*

Unfortunately, the **service password-encryption** command does not protect the passwords very well. Armed with the encrypted value, you can search the Internet and find sites with tools to decrypt these passwords. In fact, you can take the encrypted password from this example, plug it into one of these sites, and it decrypts to "cisco." So, the **service password-encryption** command will slow down the curious, but it will not stop a knowledgeable attacker.

Encoding the Enable Passwords with Hashes

In the earliest days of IOS, Cisco used the **enable password** *password* global command to define the password that users had to use to reach enable mode (after using the **enable** EXEC command). However, as just noted, the **enable password** *password* command stored the password as clear text, and the **service password-encryption** command encrypted the password in a way that was easily decrypted.

Cisco solved the problem of only weak ways to store the password of the **enable password** *password* global command by making a more secure replacement: the **enable secret** *password* global command. However, both these commands exist in IOS even today. The next few pages look at these two commands from a couple of angles, including interactions between these two commands, why the **enable secret** command is more secure, along with a note about some advancements in how IOS secures the **enable secret** password.

Interactions Between Enable Password and Enable Secret

First, for real life: use the **enable secret** *password* global command, and ignore the **enable password** *password* global command. That has been true for around 20 years.

However, to be complete, Cisco has never removed the much weaker **enable password** command from IOS. So, on a single switch (or router), you can configure one or the other, both, or neither. What, then, does the switch expect us to type as the password to reach enable mode? It boils down to these rules:

Both commands configured: Users must use the password in the **enable secret** *password* command (and ignore the **enable password** *password* command).

Only one command configured: Use the password in that one command.

Neither command configured (default): Console users move directly to enable mode without a password prompt; Telnet and SSH users are rejected with no option to supply an enable password.

Making the Enable Secret Truly Secret with a Hash

The Cisco **enable secret** command protects the password value by never even storing the clear-text password in the configuration. However, that one sentence may cause you a bit of confusion: If the router or switch does not remember the clear-text password, how can the switch know that the user typed the right password after using the **enable** command? This section works through a few basics to show you how and appreciate why the password's value is secret.

First, by default, IOS uses a hash function called Message Digest 5 (MD5) to store an alternative value in the configuration, rather than the clear-text password. Think of MD5 as a rather complex mathematical formula. In addition, this formula is chosen so that even if you know the exact result of the formula—that is, the result after feeding the clear-text password through the formula as input—it is computationally difficult to compute the original clear-text password. Figure 5-3 shows the main ideas:

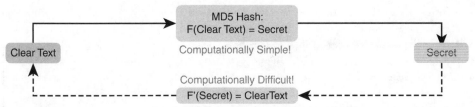

Figure 5-3 *One-Way Nature of MD5 Hash to Create Secret*

> **NOTE** "Computationally difficult" is almost a code phrase, meaning that the designers of the function hope that no one is willing to take the time to compute the original clear text.

So, if the original clear-text password cannot be re-created, how can a switch or router use it to compare to the clear-text password typed by the user? The answer depends on another fact about these security hashes like MD5: each clear-text input results in a unique result from the math formula.

The **enable secret fred** command generates an MD5 hash. If a user types **fred** when trying to enter enable mode, IOS will run MD5 against that value and get the same MD5 hash as is listed in the **enable secret** command, so IOS allows the user to access enable mode. If the user typed any other value besides **fred**, IOS would compute a different MD5 hash than the value stored with the **enable secret** command, and IOS would reject that user's attempt to reach enable mode.

Knowing that fact, the switch can make a comparison when a user types a password after using the **enable** EXEC command as follows:

Step 1. IOS computes the MD5 hash of the password in the **enable secret** command and stores the hash of the password in the configuration.

Step 2. When the user types the **enable** command to reach enable mode, a password that needs to be checked against that configuration command, IOS hashes the clear-text password as typed by the user.

Step 3. IOS compares the two hashed values: if they are the same, the user-typed password must be the same as the configured password.

As a result, IOS can store the hash of the password but never store the clear-text password; however, it can still determine whether the user typed the same password.

Switches and routers already use the logic described here, but you can see the evidence by looking at the switch configuration. Example 5-2 shows the creation of the **enable secret** command, with a few related details. This example shows the stored (hashed) value as revealed in the **show running-configuration** command output. That output also shows that IOS changed the **enable secret fred** command to list the encryption type 5 (which means the listed password is actually an MD5 hash of the clear-text password). The gobbledygook long text string is the hash, preventing others from reading the password.

Example 5-2 *Cisco IOS Encoding Password "fred" as Type 5 (MD5)*

```
Switch3(config)# enable secret fred
Switch3(config)# ^Z
Switch3# show running-config | include enable secret

enable secret 5 $1$ZGMA$e8cmvkz4UjiJhVp7.maLE1

Switch3# configure terminal
Enter configuration commands, one per line.    End with CNTL/Z.
Switch3(config)# no enable secret
Switch3(config)# ^Z
```

The end of the example also shows an important side point about deleting the **enable secret** password: after you are in enable mode, you can delete the enable secret password using the **no enable secret** command, without even having to enter the password value. You can also overwrite the old password by just repeating the **enable secret** command. But you cannot view the original clear-text password.

NOTE Example 5-2 shows another shortcut illustrating how to work through long **show** command output, this time using the pipe to the **include** command. The **| include enable secret** part of the command processes the output from **show running-config** to include only the lines with the case-sensitive text "enable secret."

Improved Hashes for Cisco's Enable Secret

The use of any hash function to encode passwords relies on several key features of the particular hash function. In particular, every possible input value must result in a single hashed value, so that when users type a password, only one password value matches each hashed value. Also, the hash algorithm must result in computationally difficult math (in other words, a pain in the neck) to compute the clear-text password based on the hashed value to discourage attackers.

The MD5 hash algorithm has been around 30 years. Over those years, computers have gotten much faster, and researchers have found creative ways to attack the MD5 algorithm, making MD5 less challenging to crack. That is, someone who saw your running configuration would have an easier time re-creating your clear-text secret passwords than in the early years of MD5.

These facts are not meant to say that MD5 is bad, but like many cryptographic functions before MD5, progress has been made, and new functions were needed. To provide more recent options that would create a much greater challenge to attackers, Cisco added two additional hashes in the 2010s, as noted in Figure 5-4.

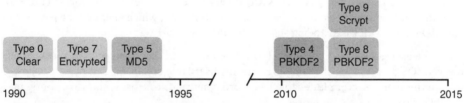

Figure 5-4 *Timeline of Encryptions/Hashes of Cisco IOS Passwords*

IOS now supports two alternative algorithm types in the more recent router and switch IOS images. Both use an SHA-256 hash instead of MD5, but with two newer options, each of which has some differences in the particulars of how each algorithm uses SHA-256. Table 5-2 shows the configuration of all three algorithm types on the **enable secret** command.

Table 5-2 Commands and Encoding Types for the **enable secret** Command

Command	Type	Algorithm
enable [algorithm-type md5] secret *password*	5	MD5
enable algorithm-type sha256 secret *password*	8	SHA-256
enable algorithm-type scrypt secret *password*	9	SHA-256

Example 5-3 shows the **enable secret** command being changed from MD5 to the scrypt algorithm. Of note, the example shows that only one **enable secret** command should exist between those three commands in Table 5-2. Basically, if you configure another **enable secret** command with a different algorithm type, that command replaces any existing **enable secret** command.

Example 5-3 *Cisco IOS Encoding Password "mypass1" as Type 9 (SHA-256)*

```
R1# show running-config | include enable
enable secret 5 $1$ZSYj$725dBZmLUJ0nx8gFPTtTv0
R1# configure terminal
Enter configuration commands, one per line. End with CNTL/Z.
R1(config)# enable algorithm-type scrypt secret mypass1
R1(config)# ^Z
```

```
R1#
R1# show running-config | include enable
enable secret 9 $9$II/EeKiRW91uxE$fwYuOE5EHoii16AWv2wSywkLJ/KNeGj8uK/24B0TVU6
R1#
```

Following the process shown in the example, the first command confirms that the current **enable secret** command uses encoding type 5, meaning it uses MD5. Second, the user configures the password using algorithm type scrypt. The last command confirms that only one **enable secret** command exists in the configuration, now with encoding type 9.

Encoding the Passwords for Local Usernames

Cisco added the **enable secret** command back in the 1990s to overcome the problems with the **enable password** command. The **username password** and **username secret** commands have a similar history. Originally, IOS supported the **username** *user* **password** *password* command—a command that had those same issues of being a clear-text password or a poorly encrypted value (with the **service password-encryption** feature). Many years later, Cisco added the **username** *user* **secret** *password* global command, which encoded the password as an MD5 hash, with Cisco adding support for the newer SHA-256 hashes later.

Today, the **username secret** command is preferred over the **username password** command; however, IOS does not use the same logic for the **username** command as it does for allowing both the **enable secret** plus **enable password** commands to exist in the same configuration. IOS allows

- Only one **username** command for a given username—either a **username** *name* **password** *password* command or a **username** *name* **secret** *password* command
- A mix of commands (**username password** and **username secret**) in the same router or switch (for different usernames)

You should use the **username secret** command instead of the **username password** command when possible. However, note that some IOS features require that the router knows a clear-text password via the **username** command (for instance, when performing some common authentication methods for serial links called PAP and CHAP). In those cases, you still need to use the **username password** command.

As mentioned, the more recent IOS versions on both switches and routers use the additional encoding options beyond MD5, just as supported with the **enable secret** command. Table 5-3 shows the syntax of those three options in the **username** command, with the MD5 option shown as an option because it is the default used with the **username secret** command.

Table 5-3 Commands and Encoding Types for the **username secret** Command

Command	Type	Algorithm
username *name* [algorithm-type md5] secret *password*	5	MD5
username *name* algorithm-type sha256 secret *password*	8	SHA-256
username *name* algorithm-type scrypt secret *password*	9	SHA-256

Controlling Password Attacks with ACLs

Attackers can repeatedly try to log in to your network devices to gain access, but IOS has a feature that uses ACLs to prevent the attacker from even seeing a password prompt. When an external user connects to a router or switch using Telnet or SSH, IOS uses a vty line to represent that user connection. IOS can apply an ACL to the vty lines, filtering the addresses that can telnet or SSH into the router or switch. If filtered, the user never sees a login prompt.

For example, imagine that all the network engineering staff's devices connect into subnet 10.1.1.0/24. The security policy states that only the network engineering staff should be allowed to telnet or SSH into any of the Cisco routers in a network. In such a case, the configuration shown in Example 5-4 could be used on each router to deny access from IP addresses not in that subnet.

Example 5-4 *vty Access Control Using the* **access-class** *Command*

```
line vty 0 4
 login
 password cisco
 access-class 3 in
!
! Next command is a global command that matches IPv4 packets with
! a source address that begins with 10.1.1.
 access-list 3 permit 10.1.1.0 0.0.0.255
```

The **access-class** command refers to the matching logic in **access-list 3**. The keyword **in** refers to Telnet and SSH connections into this router—in other words, people telnetting into this router. As configured, ACL 3 checks the source IP address of packets for incoming Telnet connections.

IOS also supports using ACLs to filter outbound Telnet and SSH connections. For example, consider a user who first uses Telnet or SSH to connect to the CLI and now sits in user or enable mode. With an outbound vty filter, IOS will apply ACL logic if the user tries the **telnet** or **ssh** commands to connect *out of the local device* to another device.

To configure an outbound VTY ACL, use the **access-class** *acl* **out** command in VTY configuration mode. Once configured, the router filters any attempts made by current vty users to use the **telnet** and **ssh** commands to initiate new connections to other devices.

Of the two options—to protect inbound and outbound connections—protecting inbound connections is by far the more important and more common. However, to be complete, outbound VTY ACLs have a surprisingly odd feature in how they use the ACL. When the **out** keyword is used, the standard IP ACL listed in the **access-class** command actually looks at the *destination IP address*, and not the source. That is, it filters based on the device to which the **telnet** or **ssh** command is trying to connect.

Firewalls and Intrusion Prevention Systems

The next topic examines the roles of a couple of different kinds of networking devices: firewalls and intrusion prevention systems (IPSs). Both devices work to secure networks but with slightly different goals and approaches.

This second major section of the chapter takes a look at each. This section first discusses the core traditional features of both firewalls and IPSs. The section closes with a description of the newer features in the current generation of these products, called next-generation products, which improves the functions of each.

Traditional Firewalls

Traditionally, a firewall sits in the forwarding path of all packets so that the firewall can then choose which packets to discard and which to allow through. By doing so, the firewall protects the network from different kinds of issues by allowing only the intended types of traffic to flow in and out of the network. In fact, in its most basic form, firewalls do the same kinds of work that routers do with ACLs, but firewalls can perform that packet-filtering function with many more options, as well as perform other security tasks.

Figure 5-5 shows a typical network design for a site that uses a physical firewall. The figure shows a firewall, like the Cisco Adaptive Security Appliance (ASA) firewall, connected to a Cisco router, which in turn connects to the Internet. All enterprise traffic going to or from the Internet would be sent through the firewall. The firewall would consider its rules and make a choice for each packet, whether the packet should be allowed through.

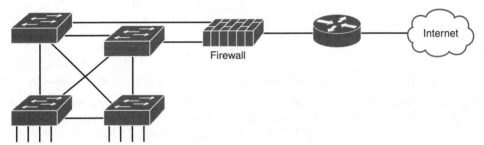

Firewall

Figure 5-5 *Firewall as Positioned in the Packet Forwarding Path*

Although firewalls have some router-like features (such as packet forwarding and packet filtering), they provide much more advanced security features than a traditional router. For example, most firewalls can use the following kinds of logic to make the choice of whether to discard or allow a packet:

- Like router IP ACLs, match the source and destination IP addresses

- Like router IP ACLs, identify applications by matching their static well-known TCP and UDP ports

- Watch application-layer flows to know what additional TCP and UDP ports are used by a particular flow, and filter based on those ports

- Match the text in the URI of an HTTP request—that is, look at and compare the contents of what is often called the web address—and match patterns to decide whether to allow or deny the download of the web page identified by that URI

- Keep state information by storing information about each packet, and make decisions about filtering future packets based on the historical state information (called *stateful inspection*, or being a stateful firewall)

The stateful firewall feature provides the means to prevent a variety of attacks and is one of the more obvious differences between the ACL processing of a router versus security filtering by a firewall. Routers must spend as little time as possible processing each packet so that the packets experience little delay passing through the router. The router cannot take the time to gather information about a packet, and then for future packets, consider some saved state information about earlier packets when making a filtering decision. Because they focus on network security, firewalls do save some information about packets and can consider that information for future filtering decisions.

As an example of the benefits of using a stateful firewall, consider a simple denial of service (DoS) attack. An attacker can make this type of attack against a web server by using tools that create (or start to create) a large volume of TCP connections to the server. The firewall might allow TCP connections to that server normally, but imagine that the server might typically receive 10 new TCP connections per second under normal conditions and 100 per second at the busiest times. A DoS attack might attempt thousands or more TCP connections per second, driving up CPU and RAM use on the server and eventually overloading the server to the point that it cannot serve legitimate users.

A stateful firewall could be tracking the number of TCP connections per second—that is, recording state information based on earlier packets—including the number of TCP connection requests from each client IP address to each server address. The stateful firewall could notice a large number of TCP connections, check its state information, and then notice that the number of requests is very large from a small number of clients to that particular server, which is typical of some kinds of DoS attacks. The stateful firewall could then start filtering those packets, helping the web server survive the attack, whereas a stateless firewall or a router ACL would not have had the historical state information to realize that a DoS attack was occurring.

Security Zones

Firewalls not only filter packets, they also pay close attention to which host initiates communications. That concept is most obvious with TCP as the transport layer protocol, where the client initiates the TCP connection by sending a TCP segment that sets the SYN bit only (as seen in Figure 1-5 in Chapter 1, "Introduction to TCP/IP Transport and Applications").

Firewalls use logic that considers which host initiated a TCP connection by watching these initial TCP segments. To see the importance of who initiates the connections, think about a typical enterprise network with a connection to the Internet, as shown in Figure 5-6. The company has users inside the company who open web browsers, initiating connections to web servers across the Internet. However, by having a working Internet connection, that same company opens up the possibility that an attacker might try to create a TCP connection to the company's internal web servers used for payroll processing. Of course, the company does not want random Internet users or attackers to be able to connect to their payroll server.

Firewalls use the concept of *security zones* (also called a *zone* for short) when defining which hosts can initiate new connections. The firewall has rules, and those rules define which host can initiate connections from one zone to another zone. Also, by using zones, a firewall can place multiple interfaces into the same zone, in cases for which multiple interfaces should have the same security rules applied. Figure 5-7 depicts the idea with the inside part of the enterprise considered to be in a separate zone compared to the interfaces connected toward the Internet.

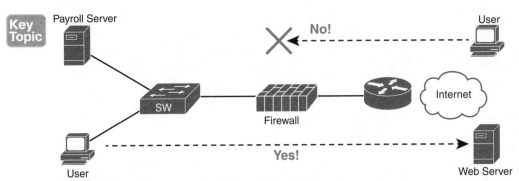

Figure 5-6 *Allowing Outbound Connections and Preventing Inbound Connections*

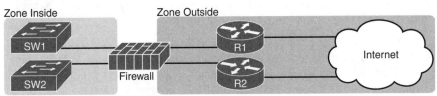

Figure 5-7 *Using Security Zones with Firewalls*

The most basic firewall rule when using two zones like Figure 5-7 reduces to this logic:

> Allow hosts from zone inside to initiate connections to hosts in zone outside, for a pre-defined set of safe well-known ports (like HTTP port 80, for instance).

Note that with this one simple rule, the correct traffic is allowed while filtering the unwanted traffic by default. Firewalls typically disallow all traffic unless a rule specifically allows the packet. So, with this simple rule to allow inside users to initiate connections to the outside zone, and that alone, the firewall also prevents outside users from initiating connections to inside hosts.

Most companies have an inside and outside zone, as well as a special zone called the *demilitarized zone (DMZ)*. Although the DMZ name comes from the real world, it has been used in IT for decades to refer to a firewall security zone used to place servers that need to be available for use by users in the public Internet. For example, Figure 5-8 shows a typical Internet edge design, with the addition of a couple of web servers in its DMZ connected through the firewall. The firewall then needs another rule that enables users in the zone outside—that is, users in the Internet—to initiate connections to those web servers in the DMZ. By separating those web servers into the DMZ, away from the rest of the enterprise, the enterprise can prevent Internet users from attempting to connect to the internal devices in the inside zone, preventing many types of attacks.

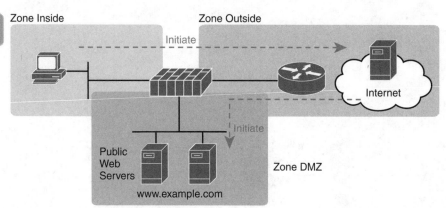

Figure 5-8   *Using a DMZ for Enterprise Servers That Need to Be Accessible from the Internet*

Intrusion Prevention Systems (IPS)

Traditionally, a firewall works with a set of user-configured rules about where packets should be allowed to flow in a network. The firewall needs to sit in the path of the packets so it can filter the packets, redirect them for collection and later analysis, or let them continue toward their destination.

A traditional intrusion prevention system (IPS) can sit in the path packets take through the network, and it can filter packets, but it makes its decisions with different logic. The IPS first downloads a database of exploit signatures. Each signature defines different header field values found in sequences of packets used by different exploits. Then the IPS can examine packets, compare them to the known exploit signatures, and notice when packets may be part of a known exploit. Once identified, the IPS can log the event, discard packets, or even redirect the packets to another security application for further examination.

A traditional IPS differs from firewalls in that instead of an engineer at the company defining rules for that company based on applications (by port number) and zones, the IPS applies the logic based on signatures supplied mostly by the IPS vendor. Those signatures look for these kinds of attacks:

- DoS
- DDoS
- Worms
- Viruses

To accomplish its mission, the IPS needs to download and keep updating its signature database. Security experts work to create the signatures. The IPS must then download the exploit signature database and keep downloading updates over time, as shown in Figure 5-9.

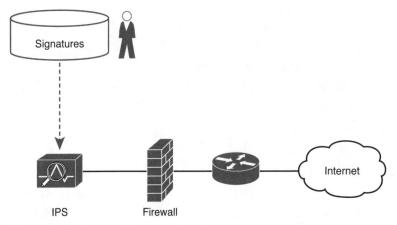

Figure 5-9 *IPS and Signature Database*

For example, think about what happens when an entirely new computer virus has been created. Host-based security products, like antivirus software, should be installed on the computers inside the company. These tools use a similar model as the IPS, keeping an updated database of virus signatures. The signatures might look for patterns in how a computer virus could be stored inside files on the computer, or in files sent to the computer via email or web browsers. But there will be some time lag between the day when the virus has been discovered (called zero-day attacks) and when researchers have developed a virus signature, changed their database, and allowed time for all the hosts to update their antivirus software. The hosts are at risk during this time lag.

The IPS provides a complimentary service to prevent viruses. Researchers will look for ways an IPS could recognize the same virus while in flight through the network with new IPS signatures—for instance, looking for packets with a particular port and a particular hex string in the application payload. Once developed, the IPS devices in the network need to be updated with the new signature database, protecting against that virus. Both the host-based and IPS-based protections play an important role, but the fact that one IPS protects sections of a network means that the IPS can sometimes more quickly react to new threats to protect hosts.

Cisco Next-Generation Firewalls

The CCNA 200-301 exam topics mention the terms *firewall* and *IPS* but prefaced with the term *next-generation*. Around the mid 2010s, Cisco and some of their competitors started using the term *next generation* when discussing their security products to emphasize some of the newer features. In short, a next-generation firewall (NGFW) and a next-generation IPS (NGIPS) are the now-current firewall and IPS products from Cisco.

However, the use of the term *next generation* goes far beyond just a marketing label: the term emphasizes some major shifts and improvements over the years. The security industry sees endless cycles of new attacks followed by new solutions, with some solutions requiring new product features or even new products. Some of the changes that have required new security features include the proliferation of mobile devices—devices that leave the enterprise, connect to the Internet, and return to the Enterprise—creating a whole new level of risk. Also, no single security function or appliance (firewall, IPS, antimalware) can hope to stop some threats, so the next-generation tools must be able to work better together to provide solutions. In short, the next-generation products have real useful features not found in their predecessor products.

As for Cisco products, for many years Cisco branded its firewalls as the Cisco Adaptive Security Appliance (ASA). Around 2013, Cisco acquired Sourcefire, a security product company. Many of the next-generation firewall (and IPS) features come from software acquired through that acquisition. As of 2019 (when this chapter was written), all of Cisco's currently sold firewalls have names that evoke memories of the Sourcefire acquisition, with most of the firewall product line being called Cisco Firepower firewalls (www.cisco.com/go/firewalls).

An NGFW still does the traditional functions of a firewall, of course, like stateful filtering by comparing fields in the IP, TCP, and UDP headers, and using security zones when defining firewall rules. To provide some insight into some of the newer next-generation features, consider the challenge of matching packets with ports:

1. Each IP-based application should use a well-known port.
2. Attackers know that firewalls will filter most well-known ports from sessions initiated from the outside zone to the inside zone (see Figure 5-8).
3. Attackers use port scanning to find any port that a company's firewall will allow through right now.
4. Attackers attempt to use a protocol of their choosing (for example, HTTP) but with the nonstandard port found through port scanning as a way to attempt to connect to hosts inside the enterprise.

The sequence lists a summary of some of the steps attackers need to take but does not list every single task. However, even to this depth, you can see how attackers can find a way to send packets past the corporate firewall.

The solution? A next-generation firewall that looks at the application layer data to identify the application instead of relying on the TCP and UDP port numbers used. Cisco performs their deep packet inspection using a feature called Application Visibility and Control (AVC). Cisco AVC can identify many applications based on the data sent (application layer headers plus application data structures far past the TCP and UDP headers). When used with a Cisco NGFW, instead of matching port numbers, the firewall matches the application, defeating attacks like the one just described.

The following list mentions a few of the features of an NGFW. Note that while *NGFW* is a useful term, the line between a traditional firewall and a next-generation firewall can be a bit blurry, as the terms describe products that have gone through repeated changes over long periods of time. This list does summarize a few of the key points, however:

- **Traditional firewall:** An NGFW performs traditional firewall features, like stateful firewall filtering, NAT/PAT, and VPN termination.
- **Application Visibility and Control (AVC):** This feature looks deep into the application layer data to identify the application. For instance, it can identify the application based on the data, rather than port number, to defend against attacks that use random port numbers.
- **Advanced Malware Protection:** NGFW platforms run multiple security services, not just as a platform to run a separate service, but for better integration of functions. A network-based antimalware function can run on the firewall itself, blocking file transfers that would install malware, and saving copies of files for later analysis.

- **URL Filtering:** This feature examines the URLs in each web request, categorizes the URLs, and either filters or rate limits the traffic based on rules. The Cisco Talos security group monitors and creates reputation scores for each domain known in the Internet, with URL filtering being able to use those scores in its decision to categorize, filter, or rate limit.
- **NGIPS:** The Cisco NGFW products can also run their NGIPS feature along with the firewall.

Note that for any of the services that benefit from being in the same path that packets traverse, like a firewall, it makes sense that over time those functions could migrate to run on the same product. So, when the design needs both a firewall and IPS at the same location in the network, these NGFW products can run the NGIPS feature as shown in the combined device in Figure 5-10.

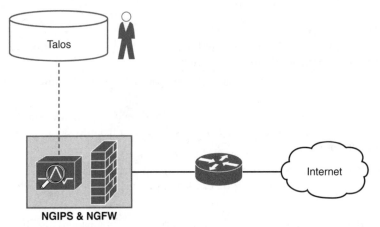

Figure 5-10 *Next-Generation Firewall with Next-Generation IPS Module*

Cisco Next-Generation IPS

The Cisco next-generation IPS (NGIPS) products have followed a similar path as the Cisco NGFW products. Cisco first added NGIPS features primarily through its Sourcefire acquisition, with the now-current (in 2019) Cisco IPS products also using the Firepower name. In fact, as a product line, the hardware NGFW and NGIPS products are the same products, with the ability to run both the NGFW and NGIPS.

As with the NGFW, the NGIPS adds features to a traditional IPS. For instance, one of the biggest issues with a traditional IPS comes with the volume of security events logged by the IPS. For instance:

1. An IPS compares the signature database, which lists all known exploits, to all messages.
2. It generates events, often far more than the security staff can read.
3. The staff must mentally filter events to find the proverbial needle in the haystack, possible only through hard work, vast experience, and a willingness to dig.

An NGIPS helps with this issue in a couple of ways. First, an NGIPS examines the context by gathering data from all the hosts and the users of those hosts. The NGIPS will know the OS, software revision levels, what apps are running, open ports, the transport protocols and port numbers in use, and so on. Armed with that data, the NGIPS can make much more intelligent choices about what events to log.

For instance, consider an NGIPS placed into a network to protect a campus LAN where end users connect, but no data center exists in that part of the network. Also, all PCs happen to be running Windows, and possibly the same version, by corporate policy. The signature database includes signatures for exploits of Linux hosts, Macs, Windows version nonexistent in that part of the network, and exploits that apply to server applications that are not running on those hosts. After gathering those facts, an NGIPS can suggest de-emphasizing checks for exploits that do not apply to those endpoints, spending more time and focus on events that could occur, greatly reducing the number of events logged.

The following list mentions a few of the Cisco NGIPS features:

- **Traditional IPS:** An NGIPS performs traditional IPS features, like using exploit signatures to compare packet flows, creating a log of events, and possibly discarding and/or redirecting packets.

- **Application Visibility and Control (AVC):** As with NGFWs, an NGIPS has the ability to look deep into the application layer data to identify the application.

- **Contextual Awareness:** NGFW platforms gather data from hosts—OS, software version/level, patches applied, applications running, open ports, applications currently sending data, and so on. Those facts inform the NGIPS as to the often more limited vulnerabilities in a portion of the network so that the NGIPS can focus on actual vulnerabilities while greatly reducing the number of logged events.

- **Reputation-Based Filtering:** The Cisco Talos security intelligence group researches security threats daily, building the data used by the Cisco security portfolio. Part of that data identifies known bad actors, based on IP address, domain, name, or even specific URL, with a reputation score for each. A Cisco NGIPS can perform reputation-based filtering, taking the scores into account.

- **Event Impact Level:** Security personnel need to assess the logged events, so an NGIPS provides an assessment based on impact levels, with characterizations as to the impact if an event is indeed some kind of attack.

If you want to learn a little more about these topics for your own interest, let me refer you to a couple of resources. First, check out articles and blog posts from the Cisco Talos Intelligence Group (www.talosintelligence.com). The Cisco Talos organization researches security issues around the globe across the entire spectrum of security products. Additionally, one Cisco Press book has some great information about both next-generation firewalls and IPSs, written at a level appropriate as a next step. If you want to read more, check out this book with the long name: *Integrated Security Technologies and Solutions, Volume I: Cisco Security Solutions for Advanced Threat Protection with Next Generation Firewall, Intrusion Prevention, AMP, and Content Security* (or just use its ISBN, 9781587147067), with one chapter each on NGFW and NGIPS.

Chapter Review

One key to doing well on the exams is to perform repetitive spaced review sessions. Review this chapter's material using either the tools in the book or interactive tools for the same material found on the book's companion website. Refer to the "Your Study Plan" element for more details. Table 5-4 outlines the key review elements and where you can find them. To better track your study progress, record when you completed these activities in the second column.

Table 5-4 Chapter Review Tracking

Review Element	Review Date(s)	Resource Used
Review key topics		Book, website
Review key terms		Book, website
Repeat DIKTA questions		Book, PTP
Do labs		Blog
Review command tables		Book

Review All the Key Topics

Table 5-5 Key Topics for Chapter 5

Key Topic Element	Description	Page Number
List	Commands whose passwords are encrypted by **service password-encryption**	89
List	Rules for when IOS uses the password set with the **enable password** versus **enable secret** commands	91
List	Logic by which IOS can use the **enable secret** hash when a user types a clear-text password to reach enable mode	92
List	Rule for combinations of the **username** command	94
Figure 5-6	Typical client filtering by firewall at Internet edge	98
Figure 5-8	Firewall security zones with DMZ	99
List	Features of next-generation firewalls	101
List	Features of next-generation IPSs	103

Key Terms You Should Know

enable secret, local username, MD5 hash, username secret, firewall, IPS, next-generation firewall (NGFW), next-generation IPS (NGIPS), Application Visibility and Control

Do Labs

The Sim Lite software is a version of Pearson's full simulator learning product with a subset of the labs, included free with this book. The Sim Lite with this book includes a couple of labs about various password-related topics. Also, check the author's blog site pages for configuration exercises (Config Labs) at https://blog.certskills.com/config-labs.

Command References

Tables 5-6 and 5-7 list configuration and verification commands used in this chapter. As an easy review exercise, cover the left column in a table, read the right column, and try to recall the command without looking. Then repeat the exercise, covering the right column, and try to recall what the command does.

Table 5-6 Chapter 5 Configuration Commands

Command	Mode/Purpose/Description
line console 0	Command that changes the context to console configuration mode.
line vty *1st-vty last-vty*	Command that changes the context to vty configuration mode for the range of vty lines listed in the command.
login	Console and vty configuration mode. Tells IOS to prompt for a password.
password *pass-value*	Console and vty configuration mode. Lists the password required if the **login** command is configured.
login local	Console and vty configuration mode. Tells IOS to prompt for a username and password, to be checked against locally configured **username** global configuration commands.
username *name* [algorithm-type md5 | sha256 | scrypt] secret *pass-value*	Global command. Defines one of possibly multiple usernames and associated passwords, stored as a hashed value (default MD5), with other hash options as well.
username *name* password *pass-value*	Global command. Defines a username and password, stored in clear text in the configuration by default.
crypto key generate rsa [modulus 512 | 768 | 1024]	Global command. Creates and stores (in a hidden location in flash memory) the keys required by SSH.
transport input {telnet | ssh | all | none}	vty line configuration mode. Defines whether Telnet and/or SSH access is allowed into this switch.
[no] service password-encryption	Global command that encrypts all clear-text passwords in the running-config. The **no** version of the command disables the encryption of passwords when the password is set.
enable password *pass-value*	Global command to create the enable password, stored as a clear text instead of a hashed value.
enable [algorithm-type md5 | sha256 | scrypt] secret *pass-value*	Global command to create the enable password, stored as a hashed value instead of clear text, with the hash defined by the algorithm type.
no enable secret no enable password	Global command to delete the **enable secret** or **enable password** commands, respectively.
access-class *number* | *name* in	A vty mode command that enables inbound ACL checks against Telnet and SSH clients connecting to the router.

Table 5-7 Chapter 5 EXEC Command Reference

Command	Purpose
show running-config | section vty	Lists the vty lines and subcommands from the configuration.
show running-config | section con	Lists the console and subcommands from the configuration.
show running-config | include enable	Lists all lines in the configuration with the word *enable*.

CHAPTER 6

Implementing Switch Port Security

This chapter covers the following exam topics:

5.0 Security Fundamentals

5.7 Configure Layer 2 security features (DHCP snooping, dynamic ARP inspection, and port security)

In modern networks, security must be implemented in depth. The security architecture should use firewalls and intrusion prevention systems (IPS) at strategic locations, and hosts should use antivirus and antimalware tools. Routers, which already need to exist throughout the enterprise at the edge between local-area networks and wide-area networks, can be configured with IP access control lists to filter packets related to different IP address ranges in that enterprise.

LAN switches have a unique opportunity as a security enforcement point, particularly LAN switches connected to endpoint devices. Attackers often launch attacks from the endpoints connected to an enterprise LAN switch. The attacker might gain physical access to the endpoint or first infect the device to then launch an attack. Additionally, a mobile device can become infected while outside the company network and then later connect to the company network, with the attack launching at that point.

Engineers should assume that attacks might be launched from end-user devices connected directly to access ports on the enterprise's LAN switches, so Cisco switches include a number of useful tools to help prevent several types of attacks. This chapter discusses one such tool: port security. Chapter 8, "DHCP Snooping and ARP Inspection," discusses two other switch security tools that take advantage of the switch's access layer role, with Chapter 7, "Implementing DHCP," providing the background details needed to understand the tools in Chapter 8.

This short chapter takes a straightforward approach to the port security feature. The first section discusses the concepts, configuration, and verification, using the primary port security operational mode: shutdown mode. The second section then discusses some of the intricacies of the three operational modes: shutdown, protect, and restrict.

"Do I Know This Already?" Quiz

Take the quiz (either here or use the PTP software) if you want to use the score to help you decide how much time to spend on this chapter. The letter answers are listed at the bottom of the page following the quiz. Appendix C, found both at the end of the book as well as on the companion website, includes both the answers and explanations. You can also find both answers and explanations in the PTP testing software.

Table 6-1 "Do I Know This Already?" Foundation Topics Section-to-Question Mapping

Foundation Topics Section	Questions
Port Security Concepts and Configuration	1–3
Port Security Violation Modes	4, 5

1. Which of the following is required when configuring port security with sticky learning?

   a. Setting the maximum number of allowed MAC addresses on the interface with the **switchport port-security maximum** interface subcommand.

   b. Enabling port security with the **switchport port-security** interface subcommand.

   c. Defining the specific allowed MAC addresses using the **switchport port-security mac-address** interface subcommand.

   d. All the other answers list required commands.

2. A Cisco Catalyst switch connects to what should be individual user PCs. Each port has the same port security configuration, configured as follows:

   ```
   interface range gigabitethernet 0/1 - 24
    switchport mode access
    switchport port-security
    switchport port-security mac-address sticky
   ```

   Which of the following answers describe the result of the port security configuration created with these commands? (Choose two answers.)

   a. Prevents unknown devices with unknown MAC addresses from sending data through the switch ports.

   b. If a user connects a switch to the cable, prevents multiple devices from sending data through the port.

   c. Will allow any one device to connect to each port and *will* save that device's MAC address into the startup-config.

   d. Will allow any one device to connect to each port but *will not* save that device's MAC address into the startup-config.

3. Which of the following commands list the MAC address table entries for MAC addresses configured by port security? (Choose two answers.)

   a. show mac address-table dynamic

   b. show mac address-table

   c. show mac address-table static

   d. show mac address-table port-security

4. The **show port-security interface f0/1** command lists a port status of secure-shutdown. Which one of the following answers must be true about this interface at this time?

   a. The **show interface status** command lists the interface status as connected.

   b. The **show interface status** command lists the interface status as err-disabled.

   c. The **show port-security interface** command could list a mode of shutdown or restrict, but not protect.

   d. The **show port-security interface** command violation counter can increase while in the secure-down port state.

5. A switch's port Gi0/1 has been correctly enabled with port security. The configuration sets the violation mode to restrict. A frame that violates the port security policy enters the interface, followed by a frame that does not. Which of the following answers correctly describe what happens in this scenario? (Choose two answers.)

   a. The switch puts the interface into an err-disabled state when the first frame arrives.

   b. The switch generates syslog messages about the violating traffic for the first frame.

   c. The switch increments the violation counter for Gi0/1 by 1.

   d. The switch discards both the first and second frame.

Foundation Topics

Port Security Concepts and Configuration

If the network engineer knows what devices should be cabled and connected to particular interfaces on a switch, the engineer can use *port security* to restrict that interface so that only the expected devices can use it. This reduces exposure to attacks in which the attacker connects a laptop to some unused switch port. When that inappropriate device attempts to send frames to the switch interface, the switch can take different actions, ranging from simply issuing informational messages to effectively shutting down the interface.

Port security identifies devices based on the source MAC address of Ethernet frames that the devices send. For example, in Figure 6-1, PC1 sends a frame, with PC1's MAC address as the source address. SW1's F0/1 interface can be configured with port security, and if so, SW1 would examine PC1's MAC address and decide whether PC1 was allowed to send frames into port F0/1.

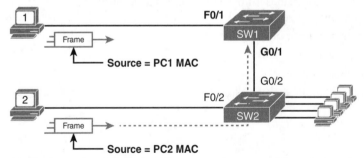

Figure 6-1 *Source MAC Addresses in Frames as They Enter a Switch*

Port security also has no restrictions on whether the frame came from a local device or was forwarded through other switches. For example, switch SW1 could use port security on its G0/1 interface, checking the source MAC address of the frame from PC2, when forwarded up to SW1 from SW2.

Port security has several flexible options, but all operate with the same core concepts. First, switches enable port security per port, with different settings available per port. Each port has a maximum number of allowed MAC addresses, meaning that for all frames entering that port, only that number of *different* source MAC addresses can be used before port security thinks a violation has occurred. When a frame with a new source MAC address arrives, pushing the number of MAC addresses past the allowed maximum, a port security violation occurs. At that point, the switch takes action—by default, discarding all future incoming traffic on that port.

The following list summarizes these ideas common to all variations of port security:

- It examines frames received on the interface to determine if a violation has occurred.
- It defines a maximum number of unique source MAC addresses allowed for all frames coming in the interface.
- It keeps a list and counter of all unique source MAC addresses on the interface.
- It monitors newly learned MAC addresses, considering those MAC addresses to cause a violation if the newly learned MAC address would push the total number of MAC table entries for the interface past the configured maximum allowed MAC addresses for that port.
- It takes action to discard frames from the violating MAC addresses, plus other actions depending on the configured violation mode.

Those rules define the basics, but port security allows other options as well, including options like these:

- Define a maximum of three MAC addresses, defining all three specific MAC addresses.
- Define a maximum of three MAC addresses but allow those addresses to be dynamically learned, allowing the first three MAC addresses learned.
- Define a maximum of three MAC addresses, predefining one specific MAC address, and allowing two more to be dynamically learned.

You might like the idea of predefining the MAC addresses for port security, but finding the MAC address of each device can be a bother. Port security provides a useful compromise using a feature called *sticky secure MAC addresses*. With this feature, port security learns the MAC addresses off each port so that you do not have to preconfigure the values. It also adds the learned MAC addresses to the port security configuration (in the running-config file). This feature helps reduce the big effort of finding out the MAC address of each device.

As you can see, port security has a lot of detailed options. The next few sections walk you through these options to pull the ideas together.

Configuring Port Security

Port security configuration involves several steps. First, port security works on both access ports and trunk ports, but it requires you to statically configure the port as a trunk or an access port, rather than let the switch dynamically decide whether to use trunking. The following configuration checklist details how to enable port security, set the maximum allowed MAC addresses per port, and configure the actual MAC addresses:

Step 1.   Use the **switchport mode access** or the **switchport mode trunk** interface subcommands, respectively, to make the switch interface either a static access or trunk interface.

Step 2.   Use the **switchport port-security** interface subcommand to enable port security on the interface.

Step 3.   (Optional) Use the **switchport port-security maximum** *number* interface subcommand to override the default maximum number of allowed MAC addresses associated with the interface (1).

Step 4.   (Optional) Use the **switchport port-security violation** {**protect** | **restrict** | **shutdown**} interface subcommand to override the default action to take upon a security violation (shutdown).

Step 5.   (Optional) Use the **switchport port-security mac-address** *mac-address* interface subcommand to predefine any allowed source MAC addresses for this interface. Use the command multiple times to define more than one MAC address.

Step 6.   (Optional) Use the **switchport port-security mac-address sticky** interface subcommand to tell the switch to "sticky learn" dynamically learned MAC addresses.

To demonstrate how to configure this variety of the settings, Figure 6-2 and Example 6-1 show four examples of port security. Three ports operate as access ports, while port F0/4, connected to another switch, operates as a trunk.

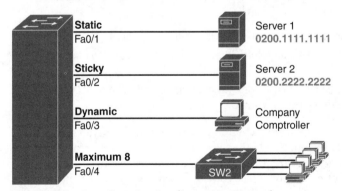

Figure 6-2 *Port Security Configuration Example*

Example 6-1 *Variations on Port Security Configuration*

```
SW1# show running-config
(Lines omitted for brevity)


interface FastEthernet0/1
 switchport mode access
 switchport port-security
 switchport port-security mac-address 0200.1111.1111
!
interface FastEthernet0/2
 switchport mode access
 switchport port-security
 switchport port-security mac-address sticky
!
interface FastEthernet0/3
 switchport mode access
 switchport port-security
!
interface FastEthernet0/4
 switchport mode trunk
 switchport port-security
 switchport port-security maximum 8
```

First, scan the configuration for all four interfaces in Example 6-1, focusing on the first two interface subcommands in each case. Note that the first three interfaces in the example use the same first two interface subcommands, matching the first two configuration steps noted before Figure 6-2. The **switchport port-security** command enables port security, with all defaults, with the **switchport mode access** command meeting the requirement to configure the port as either an access or trunk port. The final port, F0/4, has a similar configuration, except that it has been configured as a trunk rather than as an access port.

Next, scan all four interfaces again, and note that the configuration differs on each interface after those first two interface subcommands. Each interface simply shows a different example for perspective.

The first interface, FastEthernet 0/1, adds one optional port security subcommand: **switchport port-security mac-address 0200.1111.1111**, which defines a specific source MAC address. With the default maximum source address setting of 1, only frames with source MAC 0200.1111.1111 will be allowed in this port. When a frame with a source other than 0200.1111.1111 enters F0/1, the switch would normally perform MAC address learning and want to add the new source MAC address to the MAC address table. Port security will see that action as learning one too many MAC addresses on the port, taking the default violation action to disable the interface.

As a second example, FastEthernet 0/2 uses the same logic as FastEthernet 0/1, except that it uses the sticky learning feature. For port F0/2, the configuration of the **switchport port-security mac-address sticky** command tells the switch to dynamically learn source MAC addresses and add **port-security** commands to the running-config. Example 6-2 shows the running-config file that lists the sticky-learned MAC address in this case.

Example 6-2 *Configuration Added by the Port Security Sticky Feature*

```
SW1# show running-config interface f0/2
Building configuration...
Current configuration : 188 bytes
!
interface FastEthernet0/2
 switchport mode access
 switchport port-security
 switchport port-security mac-address sticky
 switchport port-security mac-address sticky 0200.2222.2222
```

Port security does not save the configuration of the sticky addresses, so use the **copy running-config startup-config** command if desired.

The other two interfaces in Example 6-1 do not predefine MAC addresses, nor do they sticky-learn the MAC addresses. The only difference between these two interfaces' port security configuration is that FastEthernet 0/4 supports eight MAC addresses because it connects to another switch and should receive frames with multiple source MAC addresses. Interface F0/3 uses the default maximum of one MAC address.

NOTE Switches can also use port security on voice ports and EtherChannels. For voice ports, make sure to configure the maximum MAC address to at least two (one for the phone, or for a PC connected to the phone). On EtherChannels, the port security configuration should be placed on the port-channel interface, rather than the individual physical interfaces in the channel.

Verifying Port Security

The **show port-security interface** command provides the most insight to how port security operates, as shown in Example 6-3. This command lists the configuration settings for port security on an interface; plus it lists several important facts about the current operation of port security, including information about any security violations. The two commands in the example show interfaces F0/1 and F0/2, based on Example 6-1's configuration.

Example 6-3 *Using Port Security to Define Correct MAC Addresses of Particular Interfaces*

```
SW1# show port-security interface fastEthernet 0/1
Port Security                : Enabled
Port Status                  : Secure-shutdown
Violation Mode               : Shutdown
Aging Time                   : 0 mins
Aging Type                   : Absolute
SecureStatic Address Aging   : Disabled
Maximum MAC Addresses        : 1
Total MAC Addresses          : 1
Configured MAC Addresses     : 1
Sticky MAC Addresses         : 0
Last Source Address:Vlan     : 0013.197b.5004:1
```

```
Security Violation Count   : 1

SW1# show port-security interface fastEthernet 0/2
Port Security              : Enabled
Port Status                : Secure-up
Violation Mode             : Shutdown
Aging Time                 : 0 mins
Aging Type                 : Absolute
SecureStatic Address Aging : Disabled
Maximum MAC Addresses      : 1
Total MAC Addresses        : 1
Configured MAC Addresses   : 1
Sticky MAC Addresses       : 1
Last Source Address:Vlan   : 0200.2222.2222:1
Security Violation Count   : 0
```

The two commands in Example 6-3 confirm that a security violation has occurred on FastEthernet 0/1, but no violations have occurred on FastEthernet 0/2. The **show port- security interface fastethernet 0/1** command shows that the interface is in a *secure-shutdown* state, which means that the interface has been disabled because of port security. In this case, another device connected to port F0/1, sending a frame with a source MAC address other than 0200.1111.1111, is causing a violation. However, port Fa0/2, which used sticky learning, simply learned the MAC address used by Server 2.

Port Security MAC Addresses

To complete this chapter, take a moment to think about Layer 2 switching, along with all those examples of output from the **show mac address-table dynamic** EXEC command.

Once a switch port has been configured with port security, the switch no longer considers MAC addresses associated with that port as being dynamic entries as listed with the **show mac address-table dynamic** EXEC command. Even if the MAC addresses are dynamically learned, once port security has been enabled, you need to use one of these options to see the MAC table entries associated with ports using port security:

■ **show mac address-table secure:** Lists MAC addresses associated with ports that use port security

■ **show mac address-table static:** Lists MAC addresses associated with ports that use port security, as well as any other statically defined MAC addresses

Example 6-4 proves the point. It shows two commands about interface F0/2 from the port security example shown in Figure 6-2 and Example 6-1. In that example, port security was configured on F0/2 with sticky learning, so from a literal sense, the switch learned a MAC address off that port (0200.2222.2222). However, the **show mac address-table dynamic** command does not list the address and port because IOS considers that MAC table entry to be a static entry. The **show mac address-table secure** command does list the address and port.

Example 6-4 *Using the* secure *Keyword to See MAC Table Entries When Using Port Security*

```
SW1# show mac address-table secure interface F0/2
          Mac Address Table
-------------------------------------------

Vlan    Mac Address      Type        Ports
----    -----------      --------    -----
  1     0200.2222.2222   STATIC      Fa0/2
Total Mac Addresses for this criterion: 1

SW1# show mac address-table dynamic interface f0/2
          Mac Address Table
-------------------------------------------

Vlan    Mac Address      Type        Ports
----    -----------      --------    -----
SW1#
```

Port Security Violation Modes

The first half of the chapter discussed many details of port security, but it mostly ignored one major feature: the port security violation mode. The violation mode defines how port security should react when a violation occurs.

First, to review, what is a port security violation? Any received frame that breaks the port security rules on an interface. For example:

■ For an interface that allows any two MAC addresses, a violation occurs when the total of preconfigured and learned MAC addresses on the interface exceeds the configured maximum of two.

■ For an interface that predefines all the specific MAC addresses allowed on the interface, a violation occurs when the switch receives a frame whose source MAC is not one of those configured addresses.

With port security, each switch port can be configured to use one of three violation modes that defines the actions to take when a violation occurs. All three options cause the switch to discard the offending frame (a frame whose source MAC address would push the number of learned MAC addresses over the limit). However, the modes vary in how many other steps they take. For instance, some modes include the action of the switch generating syslog messages and SNMP Trap messages, while some define the action to disable the interface. Table 6-2 lists the three modes, their actions, along with the keywords that enable each mode on the **switchport port-security violation {protect | restrict | shutdown}** interface subcommand.

Table 6-2 Actions When Port Security Violation Occurs

Option on the switchport port-security violation Command	Protect	Restrict	Shutdown
Discards offending traffic	Yes	Yes	Yes
Sends log and SNMP messages	No	Yes	Yes
Disables the interface by putting it in an err-disabled state, discarding all traffic	No	No	Yes

Because IOS reacts so differently with shutdown mode as compared to restrict and protect modes, the next few pages explain the differences—first for shutdown mode, then for the other two modes.

Port Security Shutdown Mode

When the (default) shutdown violation mode is used and a port security violation occurs on a port, port security stops all frame forwarding on the interface, both in and out of the port. In effect, it acts as if port security has shut down the port; however, it does not literally configure the port with the **shutdown** interface subcommand. Instead, port security uses the err-disabled feature. Cisco switches use the err-disabled state for a wide range of purposes, but when using port security shutdown mode and a violation occurs, the following happens:

- The switch interface state (per **show interfaces** and **show interfaces status**) changes to an err-disabled state.
- The switch interface port security state (per **show port-security**) changes to a secure-shutdown state.
- The switch stops sending and receiving frames on the interface.

Once port security has placed a port in err-disabled state, by default the port remains in an err-disabled state until someone takes action. To recover from an err-disabled state, the interface must be shut down with the **shutdown** command and then enabled with the **no shutdown** command. Alternately, the switch can be configured to automatically recover from the err-disabled state, when caused by port security, with these commands:

- **errdisable recovery cause psecure-violation:** A global command to enable automatic recovery for interfaces in an err-disabled state caused by port security
- **errdisable recovery interval** *seconds***:** A global command to set the time to wait before recovering the interface

To take a closer look at shutdown mode, start by checking the configuration state of the switch. You can check the port security configuration on any interface with the **show port-security interface** *type number* command, as seen back in Example 6-2, but the **show port-security** command (as listed in Example 6-5) shows briefer output, with one line per enabled interface.

6

Example 6-5 *Confirming the Port Security Violation Mode*

```
SW1# show port-security
Secure Port  MaxSecureAddr  CurrentAddr  SecurityViolation  Security Action
             (Count)        (Count)      (Count)
----------------------------------------------------------------------------
   Fa0/13            1            1                  1            Shutdown
----------------------------------------------------------------------------
Total Addresses in System (excluding one mac per port) : 0
Max Addresses limit in System (excluding one mac per port) : 8192
```

Note that for these next examples, a switch has configured port security on port Fa0/13 only. In this case, the switch appears to be configured to support one MAC address, has already reached that total, and has a security violation action of "shutdown."

Next, Example 6-6 shows the results after a port security violation has already occurred on port F0/13. The first command confirms the err-disabled state (per the **show interfaces status** command) and the secure-shutdown state (per the **show port-security** command).

Example 6-6 *Port Security Status in Shutdown Mode After a Violation*

```
! The next lines show the log message generated when the violation occurred.
Jul 31 18:00:22.810: %PORT_SECURITY-2-PSECURE_VIOLATION: Security violation occurred,
caused by MAC address 0200.3333.3333 on port FastEthernet0/13

! The next command shows the err-disabled state, implying a security violation.
SW1# show interfaces Fa0/13 status

Port    Name                    Status       Vlan   Duplex  Speed  Type
Fa0/13                          err-disabled 1      auto    auto   10/100BaseTX
!
! The next command's output has shading for several of the most important facts.
SW1# show port-security interface Fa0/13
Port Security              : Enabled
Port Status                : Secure-shutdown
Violation Mode             : Shutdown
Aging Time                 : 0 mins
Aging Type                 : Absolute
SecureStatic Address Aging : Disabled
Maximum MAC Addresses      : 1
Total MAC Addresses        : 1
Configured MAC Addresses   : 1
Sticky MAC Addresses       : 0
Last Source Address:Vlan   : 0200.3333.3333:2
Security Violation Count   : 1
```

The output of the **show port-security interface** command lists the current port-security status (secure-shutdown) as well as the configured mode (shutdown). The last line of output lists the number of violations that caused the interface to fail to an err-disabled state, while the second-to-last line identifies the MAC address and VLAN of the device that caused the violation.

Figure 6-3 summarizes these behaviors, assuming the same scenario shown in the example.

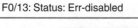

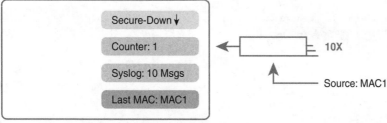

Figure 6-3 *Summary of Actions: Port Security Violation Mode Shutdown*

Note that the violations counter notes the number of times the interface has been moved to the err-disabled (secure-shutdown) state. For instance, the first time it fails, the counter increments to 1; while err-disabled, many frames can arrive, but the counter remains at 1. IOS will reset the counter to 0 when you recover the interface using a **shutdown/no shutdown** command combination, so that the next violation will cause the counter to increment to 1.

Port Security Protect and Restrict Modes

The restrict and protect violation modes take a much different approach to securing ports. These modes still discard offending traffic, but the interface remains in a connected (up/up) state and in a port security state of secure-up. As a result, the port continues to forward good traffic but discards offending traffic.

Having a port in a seemingly good state that also discards traffic can be a challenge when troubleshooting. Basically, you have to know about the feature and then know how to tell when port security is discarding some traffic on a port even though the interface status looks good.

With protect mode, the only action the switch takes for a frame that violates the port security rules is to discard the frame. The switch does not change the port to an err-disabled state, does not generate messages, and does not even increment the violations counter.

Example 6-7 shows a sample with protect mode after several violations have occurred. Note that the **show** command confirms the mode (protect) as configured in the top part of the example, with a port security state of secure-up—a state that will not change in protect mode. Also, note that the counter at the bottom shows 0, even though several violations have occurred, because protect mode does not count the violating frames.

Example 6-7 *Port Security Using Protect Mode*

```
SW1# show running-config
! Lines omitted for brevity
interface FastEthernet0/13
  switchport mode access
  switchport port-security
```

```
  switchport port-security mac-address 0200.1111.1111
  switchport port-security violation protect
! Lines omitted for brevity

SW1# show port-security interface Fa0/13
Port Security                 : Enabled
Port Status                   : Secure-up
Violation Mode                : Protect
Aging Time                    : 0 mins
Aging Type                    : Absolute
SecureStatic Address Aging    : Disabled
Maximum MAC Addresses         : 1
Total MAC Addresses           : 1
Configured MAC Addresses      : 1
Sticky MAC Addresses          : 0
Last Source Address:Vlan      : 0000.0000.0000:0
Security Violation Count      : 0
```

NOTE The small particulars of the violation counters and last source address might be slightly different with some older switch models and IOS versions. Note that this edition's testing is based on 2960XR switches running IOS 15.2.(6)E2.

While shutdown mode disables the interface, and protect mode does nothing more than discard the offending traffic, restrict mode provides a compromise between the other two modes. If Example 6-7 had used the restrict violation mode instead of protect, the port status would have also remained in a secure-up state; however, IOS would show some indication of port security activity, such as an accurate incrementing violation counter, as well as syslog messages. Example 6-8 shows an example of the violation counter and ends with an example port security syslog message. In this case, 97 incoming frames so far violated the rules, with the most recent frame having a source MAC address of 0200.3333.3333 in VLAN 1.

Example 6-8 *Port Security Using Violation Mode Restrict*

```
SW1# show port-security interface fa0/13
Port Security                 : Enabled
Port Status                   : Secure-up
Violation Mode                : Restrict
Aging Time                    : 0 mins
Aging Type                    : Absolute
SecureStatic Address Aging    : Disabled
Maximum MAC Addresses         : 1
Total MAC Addresses           : 1
Configured MAC Addresses      : 1
Sticky MAC Addresses          : 0
Last Source Address:Vlan      : 0200.3333.3333:1
Security Violation Count      : 97
```

```
!
! The following log message also points to a port security issue.
!
01:46:58: %PORT_SECURITY-2-PSECURE_VIOLATION: Security violation occurred, caused by
MAC address 0200.3333.3333 on port FastEthernet0/13.
```

Figure 6-4 summarizes the key points about the restrict mode for port security. In this case, the figure matches the same scenario as the example again, with 97 total violating frames arriving so far, with the most recent being from source MAC address MAC3.

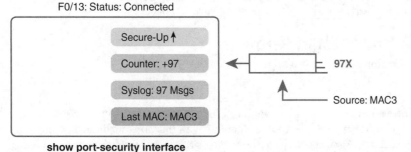

Figure 6-4 *Summary of Actions: Port Security Violation Mode Restrict*

Chapter Review

One key to doing well on the exams is to perform repetitive spaced review sessions. Review this chapter's material using either the tools in the book or interactive tools for the same material found on the book's companion website. Refer to the "Your Study Plan" element for more details. Table 6-3 outlines the key review elements and where you can find them. To better track your study progress, record when you completed these activities in the second column.

Table 6-3 Chapter Review Tracking

Review Element	Review Date(s)	Resource Used
Review key topics		Book, website
Review key terms		Book, website
Answer DIKTA questions		Book, PTP
Review command tables		Book
Review memory tables		Book, website
Review config checklists		Book, website
Do labs		Sim Lite, blog
Watch Video		Website

Review All the Key Topics

Table 6-4 Key Topics for Chapter 6

Key Topic Element	Description	Page Number
List	Summary of port security concepts	109
List	Port security configuration checklist	110
Example 6-1	Port security configuration samples	111
Table 6-2	Port security actions and the results of each action	115
List	Switch actions when a port security violation occurs	115

Key Terms You Should Know

port security, violation mode, error disabled (err-disable)

Do Labs

The Sim Lite software is a version of Pearson's full simulator learning product with a subset of the labs, included free with this book. The Sim Lite with this book includes a couple of labs about port security. Also, check the author's blog site pages for configuration exercises (Config Labs) at https://blog.certskills.com/config-labs.

Command References

Tables 6-5 and 6-6 list configuration and verification commands used in this chapter. As an easy review exercise, cover the left column in a table, read the right column, and try to recall the command without looking. Then repeat the exercise, covering the right column, and try to recall what the command does.

Table 6-5 Chapter 6 Configuration Command Reference

Command	Mode/Purpose/Description
**switchport mode {access	trunk}**	Interface configuration mode command that tells the switch to always be an access port, or always be a trunk port
switchport port-security mac-address *mac-address*	Interface configuration mode command that statically adds a specific MAC address as an allowed MAC address on the interface
switchport port-security mac-address sticky	Interface subcommand that tells the switch to learn MAC addresses on the interface and add them to the configuration for the interface as secure MAC addresses
switchport port-security maximum *value*	Interface subcommand that sets the maximum number of static secure MAC addresses that can be assigned to a single interface
**switchport port-security violation {protect	restrict	shutdown}**	Interface subcommand that tells the switch what to do if an inappropriate MAC address tries to access the network through a secure switch port

Command	Mode/Purpose/Description
errdisable recovery cause psecure-violation	Global command that enables the automatic recovery from err-disabled state for ports that reach that state due to port security violations
errdisable recovery interval *seconds*	Global command that sets the delay, in seconds, before a switch attempts to recover an interface in err-disabled mode, regardless of the reason for that interface being in that state
shutdown no shutdown	Interface subcommands that administratively disable and enable an interface, respectively

Table 6-6   Chapter 6 EXEC Command Reference

Command	Purpose
show running-config	Lists the currently used configuration
show running-config | interface *type number*	Displays the running-configuration excerpt of the listed interface and its subcommands only
show mac address-table dynamic [interface *type number*]	Lists the dynamically learned entries in the switch's address (forwarding) table
show mac address-table secure [interface *type number*]	Lists MAC addresses defined or learned on ports configured with port security
show mac address-table static [interface *type number*]	Lists static MAC addresses and MAC addresses learned or defined with port security
show interfaces [interface *type number*] status	Lists one output line per interface (or for only the listed interface if included), noting the description, operating state, and settings for duplex and speed on each interface
show port-security interface *type number*	Lists an interface's port security configuration settings and security operational status
show port-security	Lists one line per interface that summarizes the port security settings for any interface on which it is enabled

6

CHAPTER 7

Implementing DHCP

This chapter covers the following exam topics:

1.0 Network Fundamentals

  1.10 Identify IP parameters for Client OS (Windows, Mac OS, Linux)

4.0 IP Services

  4.3 Explain the role of DHCP and DNS within the network

  4.6 Configure and verify DHCP client and relay

In the world of TCP/IP, the word *host* refers to any device with an IP address: your phone, your tablet, a PC, a server, a router, a switch—any device that uses IP to provide a service or just needs an IP address to be managed. The term *host* includes some less-obvious devices as well: the electronic advertising video screen at the mall, your electrical power meter that uses the same technology as mobile phones to submit your electrical usage information for billing, your new car.

No matter the type of host, any host that uses IPv4 needs four IPv4 settings to work properly:

- IP address
- Subnet mask
- Default routers
- DNS server IP addresses

This chapter discusses these basic IP settings on hosts. The chapter begins by discussing how a host can dynamically learn these four settings using the Dynamic Host Configuration Protocol (DHCP). The second half of this chapter then shows how to find the settings on hosts and the key facts to look for when displaying the settings.

Just a note about the overall flow of the chapters: This chapter does not discuss security topics, although it sits inside Part II, "Security Services." I located this DHCP-focused chapter here because Chapter 8, "DHCP Snooping and ARP Inspection," relies heavily on knowledge of DHCP.

"Do I Know This Already?" Quiz

Take the quiz (either here or use the PTP software) if you want to use the score to help you decide how much time to spend on this chapter. The letter answers are listed at the bottom of the page following the quiz. Appendix C, found both at the end of the book as well as on the companion website, includes both the answers and explanations. You can also find both answers and explanations in the PTP testing software.

Table 7-1 "Do I Know This Already?" Foundation Topics Section-to-Question Mapping

Foundation Topics Section	Questions
Dynamic Host Configuration Protocol	1–4
Identifying Host IPv4 Settings	5, 6

1. A PC connects to a LAN and uses DHCP to lease an IP address for the first time. Of the usual four DHCP messages that flow between the PC and the DHCP server, which ones do the client send? (Choose two answers.)

   a. Acknowledgment

   b. Discover

   c. Offer

   d. Request

2. Which of the following kinds of information are part of a DHCP server configuration? (Choose two answers.)

   a. Ranges of IP addresses in subnets that the server should lease

   b. Ranges of IP addresses to not lease per subnet

   c. DNS server hostnames

   d. The default router IP and MAC address in each subnet

3. Which answers list a criterion for choosing which router interfaces need to be configured as a DHCP relay agent? (Choose two answers.)

   a. If the subnet off the interface does not include a DHCP server

   b. If the subnet off the interface does include a DHCP server

   c. If the subnet off the interface contains DHCP clients

   d. If the router interface already has an **ip address dhcp** command

4. A router connects to an Internet Service Provider (ISP) using its G0/0/0 interface, with the **ip address dhcp** command configured. What does the router do with the DHCP-learned default gateway information?

   a. The router ignores the default gateway value learned from the DHCP server.

   b. The router uses the default gateway just like a host, ignoring its routing table.

   c. The router forwards received packets based on its routing table but uses its default gateway setting to forward packets it generates itself.

   d. The router adds a default route based on the default gateway to its IP routing table.

5. In the following excerpt from a command on a Mac, which of the following parts of the output represent information learned from a DHCP server? (Choose two answers.)

```
Macprompt$ ifconfig en0

En1: flags=8863<UP,BROADCAST,SMART,RUNNING,SIMPLEX,MULTICAST> mtu 1500
        options=10b<RXCSUM,TXCSUM,VLAN_HWTAGGING,AV>
        ether 00:6d:e7:b1:9a:11
        inet 172.16.4.2 netmask 0xffffff00 broadcast 172.16.4.255
```

   a. 00:6d:e7:b1:9a:11
   b. 172.16.4.2
   c. 0xffffff00
   d. 172.16.4.255

6. Which of the following commands on a Windows OS should list both the IP address and DNS servers as learned with DHCP?

   a. ifconfig
   b. ipconfig
   c. ifconfig /all
   d. ipconfig /all

Foundation Topics

Dynamic Host Configuration Protocol

Dynamic Host Configuration Protocol (DHCP) provides one of the most commonly used services in a TCP/IP network. The vast majority of hosts in a TCP/IP network are user devices, and the vast majority of user devices learn their IPv4 settings using DHCP.

Using DHCP has several advantages over the other option of manually configuring IPv4 settings. The configuration of host IP settings sits in a DHCP server, with each client learning these settings using DHCP messages. As a result, the host IP configuration is controlled by the IT staff, rather than on local configuration on each host, resulting in fewer user errors. DHCP allows both the permanent assignment of host addresses, but more commonly, DHCP assigns a temporary lease of IP addresses. With these leases, the DHCP server can reclaim IP addresses when a device is removed from the network, making better use of the available addresses.

DHCP also enables mobility. For example, every time a user moves to a new location with a tablet computer—to a coffee shop, a client location, or back at the office—the user's device can connect to another wireless LAN, use DHCP to lease a new IP address in that LAN, and begin working on the new network. Without DHCP, the user would have to ask for information about the local network and configure settings manually, with more than a few users making mistakes.

Although DHCP works automatically for user hosts, it does require some preparation from the network, with some configuration on routers. In some enterprise networks, that router configuration can be a single command on many of the router's LAN interfaces (**ip helper-address** *server-ip*), which identifies the DHCP server by its IP address. In other cases, the router acts as the DHCP server. Regardless, the routers have some role to play.

This first major section of the chapter takes a tour of DHCP, including concepts and the router configuration to enable the routers to work well with a separate DHCP server.

DHCP Concepts

Sit back for a moment and think about the role of DHCP for a host computer. The host acts as a DHCP client. As a DHCP client, the host begins with no IPv4 settings—no IPv4 address, no mask, no default router, and no DNS server IP addresses. But a DHCP client does have knowledge of the DHCP protocol, so the client can use that protocol to (a) discover a DHCP server and (b) request to lease an IPv4 address.

DHCP uses the following four messages between the client and server. (Also, as a way to help remember the messages, note that the first letters spell DORA):

Discover: Sent by the DHCP client to find a willing DHCP server

Offer: Sent by a DHCP server to offer to lease to that client a specific IP address (and inform the client of its other parameters)

Request: Sent by the DHCP client to ask the server to lease the IPv4 address listed in the Offer message

Acknowledgment: Sent by the DHCP server to assign the address and to list the mask, default router, and DNS server IP addresses

DHCP clients, however, have a somewhat unique problem: they do not have an IP address yet, but they need to send these DHCP messages inside IP packets. To make that work, DHCP messages make use of two special IPv4 addresses that allow a host that has no IP address to still be able to send and receive messages on the local subnet:

0.0.0.0: An address reserved for use as a source IPv4 address for hosts that do not yet have an IP address.

255.255.255.255: The local broadcast IP address. Packets sent to this destination address are broadcast on the local data link, but routers do not forward them.

To see how these addresses work, Figure 7-1 shows an example of the IP addresses used between a host (A) and a DHCP server on the same LAN. Host A, a client, sends a Discover message, with source IP address of 0.0.0.0 because host A does not have an IP address to use yet. Host A sends the packet to destination 255.255.255.255, which is sent in a LAN broadcast frame, reaching all hosts in the subnet. The client hopes that there is a DHCP server on the local subnet. Why? Packets sent to 255.255.255.255 only go to hosts in the local subnet; router R1 will not forward this packet.

NOTE Figure 7-1 shows one example of the addresses that can be used in a DHCP request. This example shows details assuming the DHCP client chooses to use a DHCP option called the *broadcast flag*; all examples in this book assume the broadcast flag is used.

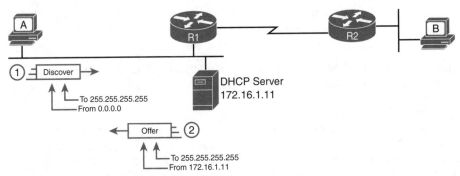

Figure 7-1 *DHCP Discover and Offer*

Now look at the Offer message sent back by the DHCP server. The server sets the destination IP address to 255.255.255.255 again. Why? Host A still does not have an IP address, so the server cannot send a packet directly to host A. So, the server sends the packet to "all local hosts in the subnet" address (255.255.255.255). (The packet is also encapsulated in an Ethernet broadcast frame.)

Note that all hosts in the subnet receive the Offer message. However, the original Discover message lists a number called the client ID, which includes the host's MAC address, that identifies the original host (host A in this case). As a result, host A knows that the Offer message is meant for host A. The rest of the hosts will receive the Offer message, but notice that the message lists another device's DHCP client ID, so the rest of the hosts ignore the Offer message.

Supporting DHCP for Remote Subnets with DHCP Relay

Network engineers have a major design choice to make with DHCP: Do they put a DHCP server in every LAN subnet or locate a DHCP server in a central site? The question is legitimate. Cisco routers can act as the DHCP server, so a distributed design could use the router at each site as the DHCP server. With a DHCP server in every subnet, as shown in Figure 7-1, the protocol flows stay local to each LAN.

However, a centralized DHCP server approach has advantages as well. In fact, some Cisco design documents suggest a centralized design as a best practice, in part because it allows for centralized control and configuration of all the IPv4 addresses assigned throughout the enterprise.

With a centralized DHCP server, those DHCP messages that flowed only on the local subnet in Figure 7-1 somehow need to flow over the IP network to the centralized DHCP server and back. To make that work, the routers connected to the remote LAN subnets need an interface subcommand: the **ip helper-address** *server-ip* command.

The **ip helper-address** *server-ip* subcommand tells the router to do the following for the messages coming in an interface, from a DHCP client:

Answers to the "Do I Know This Already?" quiz:

1 B, D **2** A, B **3** A, C **4** D **5** B, C **6** D

1. Watch for incoming DHCP messages, with destination IP address 255.255.255.255.
2. Change that packet's source IP address to the router's incoming interface IP address.
3. Change that packet's destination IP address to the address of the DHCP server (as configured in the **ip helper-address** command).
4. Route the packet to the DHCP server.

This command gets around the "do not route packets sent to 255.255.255.255" rule by changing the destination IP address. Once the destination has been set to match the DHCP server's IP address, the network can route the packet to the server.

> **NOTE** This feature, by which a router relays DHCP messages by changing the IP addresses in the packet header, is called *DHCP relay*.

Figure 7-2 shows an example of the process. Host A sits on the left, as a DHCP client. The DHCP server (172.16.2.11) sits on the right. R1 has an **ip helper-address 172.16.2.11** command configured, under its G0/0 interface. At step 1, router R1 notices the incoming DHCP packet destined for 255.255.255.255. Step 2 shows the results of changing both the source and destination IP address, with R1 routing the packet.

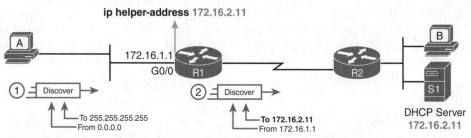

Figure 7-2 *IP Helper Address Effect*

The router uses a similar process for the return DHCP messages from the server. First, for the return packet from the DHCP server, the server simply reverses the source and destination IP address of the packet received from the router (relay agent). For example, in Figure 7-2, the Discover message lists source IP address 172.16.1.1, so the server sends the Offer message back to destination IP address 172.16.1.1.

When a router receives a DHCP message, addressed to one of the router's own IP addresses, the router realizes the packet might be part of the DHCP relay feature. When that happens, the DHCP relay agent (router R1) needs to change the destination IP address, so that the real DHCP client (host A), which does not have an IP address yet, can receive and process the packet.

Figure 7-3 shows one example of how these addresses work, when R1 receives the DHCP Offer message sent to R1's own 172.16.1.1 address. R1 changes the packet's destination to 255.255.255.255 and forwards it out G0/0, because the packet was destined to G0/0's 172.16.1.1 IP address. As a result, all hosts in that LAN (including the DHCP client A) will receive the message.

Many enterprise networks use a centralized DHCP server, so the normal router configuration includes an **ip helper-address** command on every LAN interface/subinterface. With that standard configuration, user hosts off any router LAN interface can always reach the DHCP server and lease an IP address.

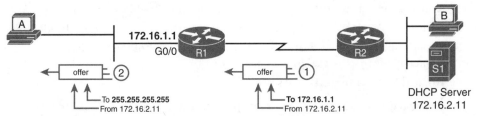

Figure 7-3 *IP Helper Address for the Offer Message Returned from the DHCP Server*

Information Stored at the DHCP Server

A DHCP server might sound like some large piece of hardware, sitting in a big locked room with lots of air conditioning to keep the hardware cool. However, like most servers, the server is actually software, running on some server OS. The DHCP server could be a piece of software downloaded for free and installed on an old PC. However, because the server needs to be available all the time, to support new DHCP clients, most companies install the software on a very stable and highly available data center, with high availability features. The DHCP service is still created by software, however.

To be ready to answer DHCP clients and to supply them with an IPv4 address and other information, the DHCP server (software) needs configuration. DHCP servers typically organize these IPv4 settings per subnet, because the information the server tells the client is usually the same for all hosts in the same subnet, but slightly different for hosts in different subnets. For example, IP addressing rules tell us that all hosts on the same subnet should use the same mask but hosts in different subnets would have a different default gateway setting.

The following list shows the types of settings the DHCP server needs to know to support DHCP clients:

Subnet ID and mask: The DHCP server can use this information to know all addresses in the subnet. (The DHCP server knows to not lease the subnet ID or subnet broadcast address.)

Reserved (excluded) addresses: The server needs to know which addresses in the subnet to *not* lease. This list allows the engineer to reserve addresses to be used as static IP addresses. For example, most router and switch IP addresses, server addresses, and addresses of most anything other than user devices use a statically assigned IP address. Most of the time, engineers use the same convention for all subnets, either reserving the lowest IP addresses in all subnets or reserving the highest IP addresses in all subnets.

Default router(s): This is the IP address of the router on that subnet.

DNS IP address(es): This is a list of DNS server IP addresses.

Figure 7-4 shows the concept behind the preconfiguration on a DHCP server for two LAN-based subnets, 172.16.1.0/24 and 172.16.2.0/24. The DHCP server sits on the right. For each subnet, the server defines all the items in the list. In this case, the configuration reserves the lowest IP addresses in the subnet to be used as static addresses.

The configuration can list other parameters as well. For example, it can set the time limit for leasing an IP address. The server leases an address for a time (usually a number of days), and then the client can ask to renew the lease. If the client does not renew, the server can reclaim the IP address and put it back in the pool of available IP addresses. The server configuration sets the maximum time for the lease.

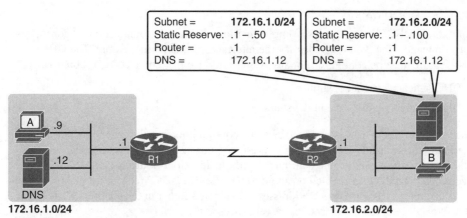

Subnet =	**172.16.1.0/24**	Subnet =	**172.16.2.0/24**
Static Reserve:	.1 – .50	Static Reserve:	.1 – .100
Router =	.1	Router =	.1
DNS =	172.16.1.12	DNS =	172.16.1.12

A   .9

.1 R1   R2 .1

.12

B

DNS

172.16.1.0/24   **172.16.2.0/24**

Figure 7-4 *Preconfiguration on a DHCP Server*

DHCP uses three allocation modes, based on small differences in the configuration at the DHCP server. *Dynamic allocation* refers to the DHCP mechanisms and configuration described throughout this chapter. Another method, *automatic allocation*, sets the DHCP lease time to infinite. As a result, once the server chooses an address from the pool and assigns the IP address to a client, the IP address remains with that same client indefinitely. A third mode, *static allocation*, preconfigures the specific IP address for a client based on the client's MAC address. That specific client is the only client that then uses the IP address. (Note that this chapter shows examples and configuration for dynamic allocation only.)

Additionally, the DHCP server can be configured to supply some other useful configuration settings. For instance, a server can supply the IP address of a Trivial File Transfer Protocol (TFTP) server. TFTP servers provide a basic means of storing files that can then be trans-ferred to a client host. As it turns out, Cisco IP phones rely on TFTP to retrieve several configuration files when the phone initializes. DHCP plays a key role by supplying the IP address of the TFTP server that the phones should use.

Configuring DHCP Features on Routers and Switches

Cisco routers and switches support a variety of features. Routers can be configured to act as a DHCP server with just a few straightforward commands—a feature useful in the lab and in some limited cases. More commonly, the enterprise uses a centralized DHCP server (that does not run on a router) but with the router DHCP relay feature on most every router interface. Finally, Cisco routers and switches can also act as DHCP clients, learning their IP addresses from a DHCP server.

This section discusses the DHCP configuration topics mentioned for the current exam top-ics. Those include the router DHCP relay feature and the configuration to enable DHCP cli-ent services on both switches and routers.

> **NOTE** The CCNA 200-301 exam blueprint does not mention the DHCP server function, but many people like to use the IOS DHCP server in the lab for testing with DHCP. If you are interested in how to configure a DHCP server on a router, refer to Appendix D, "Topics from Previous Editions."

7

Configuring DHCP Relay

Configuring DHCP relay requires a simple decision and a single straightforward configuration command. First, you must identify the interfaces that need the feature. The DHCP relay feature must be configured for any router interface that connects to a subnet where

- DHCP clients exist in the subnet
- DHCP servers do not exist in the subnet

Once such interfaces have been identified, the configuration requires the **ip helper-address** interface subcommand on each of those interfaces. For instance, with earlier Figure 7-3, R1's G0/0 interface needs to be configured with the **ip helper-address 172.16.2.11** interface subcommand. Once enabled on an interface, the IOS DHCP relay agent makes changes in the incoming DHCP messages' addresses as described earlier in the chapter. Without the DHCP relay agent, the DHCP request never arrives at the server.

To verify the relay agent, you can use the **show running-config** command and look for the single configuration command or use the **show ip interface g0/0** command as shown in Example 7-1. The highlighted line confirms the configured setting. Note that if there were no **ip helper-address** commands configured on the interface, the text would instead read "Helper address is not set."

Example 7-1 *Listing the Current Helper Address Setting with* show ip interface

```
R1# show ip interface g0/0
GigabitEthernet0/0 is up, line protocol is up
  Internet address is 172.16.1.1/24
  Broadcast address is 255.255.255.255
  Address determined by non-volatile memory
  MTU is 1500 bytes
  Helper address is 172.16.2.11
! Lines omitted for brevity (about 20 lineSc
```

Configuring a Switch as DHCP Client

A switch can act as a DHCP client to lease its IP address. In most cases, you will want to instead use a static IP address so that the staff can more easily identify the switch's address for remote management. However, as an example of how a DHCP client can work, this next topic shows how to configure and verify DHCP client operations on a switch.

NOTE Chapter 6, "Configuring Basic Switch Management," in *CCNA 200-301 Official Cert Guide, Volume 1,* also shows this same example of how to configure a switch to be a DHCP client. This chapter repeats the example here so you can see all the related DHCP configuration details in a single place in this volume.

To configure a switch to use DHCP to lease an address, configure a switch's IP address as normal, but with the **ip address dhcp** interface subcommand. Example 7-2 shows a sample.

Example 7-2 *Switch Dynamic IP Address Configuration with DHCP*

```
Emma# configure terminal
Enter configuration commands, one per line. End with CNTL/Z.
Emma(config)# interface vlan 1
Emma(config-if)# ip address dhcp
Emma(config-if)# no shutdown
Emma(config-if)# ^Z
Emma#
00:38:20: %LINK-3-UPDOWN: Interface Vlan1, changed state to up
00:38:21: %LINEPROTO-5-UPDOWN: Line protocol on Interface Vlan1, changed state to up
```

To verify that DHCP worked, start with the traditional way to check IP addresses on switch VLAN interfaces: the **show interfaces vlan** *x* command as demonstrated in Example 7-3. First, check the interface state, because the switch does not attempt DHCP until the VLAN interface reaches an up/up state. Notably, if you forget to issue the **no shutdown** command, the VLAN 1 interface will remain in a shutdown state and listed as "administratively down" in the **show** command output.

Example 7-3 *Verifying DHCP-Learned IP Address on a Switch*

```
Emma# show interfaces vlan 1
Vlan1 is up, line protocol is up
  Hardware is EtherSVI, address is 0019.e86a.6fc0 (bia 0019.e86a.6fc0)
  Internet address is 192.168.1.101/24
  MTU 1500 bytes, BW 1000000 Kbit, DLY 10 usec,
     reliability 255/255, txload 1/255, rxload 1/255
! lines omitted for brevity
```

The second half of Example 7-3 shows the **show interfaces vlan** *x* command output, which lists the interface's IP address on the third line. If you statically configure the IP address, the IP address will always be listed; however, when using DHCP, this line only exists if DHCP succeeded. Also, note that when present, the output does not state whether the address was statically configured or learned with DHCP. The output lists 192.168.1.101 as the address, but with no information to identify whether the IP address is a static or DHCP-learned IP address.

To see more details specific to DHCP, instead use the **show dhcp lease** command to see the (temporarily) leased IP address and other parameters. (Note that the switch does not store the DHCP-learned IP configuration in the running-config file.) Example 7-4 shows sample output. Note also that the switch learns its default-gateway setting using DHCP as well.

Key Topic

Example 7-4 *Verifying DHCP-Learned Information on a Switch*

```
Emma# show dhcp lease
Temp IP addr: 192.168.1.101    for peer on Interface: Vlan1
Temp sub net mask: 255.255.255.0
   DHCP Lease server: 192.168.1.1, state: 3 Bound
   DHCP transaction id: 1966
   Lease: 86400 secs,  Renewal: 43200 secs,  Rebind: 75600 secs
Temp default-gateway addr: 192.168.1.1
```

```
    Next timer fires after: 11:59:45
    Retry count: 0    Client-ID: cisco-0019.e86a.6fc0-Vl1
    Hostname: Emma

Emma# show ip default-gateway
192.168.1.1
```

Configuring a Router as DHCP Client

Just as with switches, you can configure router interfaces to lease an IP address using DHCP rather than using a static IP address, although those cases will be rare. In most every case it makes more sense to statically configure router interface IP addresses with the address listed in the **ip address** *address mask* interface subcommand. However, configuring a router to lease an address using DHCP makes sense in some cases with a router connected to the Internet; in fact, most every home-based router does just that.

A router with a link to the Internet can learn its IP address and mask with DHCP and also learn the neighboring ISP router's address as the default gateway. Figure 7-5 shows an example, with three routers on the left at one enterprise site. Router R1 uses DHCP to learn its IP address (192.0.2.2) from the ISP router over a connection to the Internet.

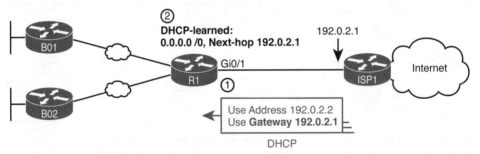

Figure 7-5 *Enterprise Router Building and Advertising Default Routes with DHCP Client*

The DHCP process supplies a default gateway IP address to router R1, but routers do not normally use a default gateway setting; only hosts use a default gateway setting. However, the router takes advantage of that information by turning that default gateway IP address into the basis for a default route. For instance, in Figure 7-5, router R1 dynamically adds a default route to its routing table with the default gateway IP address from the DHCP message—which is the ISP router's IP address—as the next-hop address. At that point, R1 has a good route to use to forward packets into the Internet.

Additionally, router R1 can distribute that default route to the rest of the routers using an interior routing protocol like OSPF. See the section titled "OSPF Default Routes" in Chapter 20 of the *CCNA 200-301 Official Cert Guide, Volume 1,* for more information.

Example 7-5 shows the configuration on router R1 to match Figure 7-5. Note that it begins with R1 configuring its G0/1 interface to use DHCP to learn the IP address to use on the interface, using the **ip address dhcp** command.

Example 7-5 *Learning an Address and Default Static Route with DHCP*

```
R1# configure terminal
R1(config)# interface gigabitethernet0/1
R1(config-if)# ip address dhcp
R1(config-if)# end
R1#
R1# show ip route static
! Legend omitted
Gateway of last resort is 192.0.2.1 to network 0.0.0.0

S*    0.0.0.0/0 [254/0] via 192.0.2.1
```

The end of the example shows the default route added to R1's routing table as a result of learning a default gateway address of 192.0.2.1 from DHCP. Oddly, IOS displays this route as a static route (destination 0.0.0.0/0), although the route is learned dynamically based on the DHCP-learned default gateway. To recognize this route as a DHCP-learned default route, look to the administrative distance value of 254. IOS uses a default administrative distance of 1 for static routes configured with the **ip route** configuration command but a default of 254 for default routes added because of DHCP.

Identifying Host IPv4 Settings

Whether learned using DHCP or not, every host that uses IP version 4 needs to have some settings to work correctly. This second major division of the chapter examines those settings and shows examples of those settings on Windows, Linux, and macOS.

Host Settings for IPv4

To work correctly, an IPv4 host needs to know these values:

- DNS server IP addresses
- Default gateway (router) IP address
- Device's own IP address
- Device's own subnet mask

To review the basics, the host must know the IP address of one or more DNS servers to send the servers' name resolution requests. For enterprises, the servers may reside in the enterprise, as shown in Figure 7-6. The host on the left (sometimes called an endpoint) typically knows the addresses of at least two DNS servers for redundancy. If the first DNS fails to respond, the endpoint can then attempt name resolution with the next DNS server.

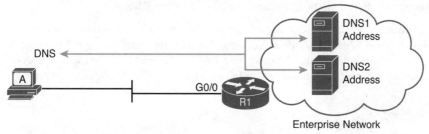

Figure 7-6 *Host A Needs to Know the IP Address of the DNS Servers*

Each endpoint needs to know the IP address of a router that resides in the same subnet. The endpoint uses that router as its default router or default gateway, as shown in Figure 7-7. From a host logic perspective, the host can then forward packets destined for addresses outside the subnet to the default router, with that router then forwarding the packet based on its routing table.

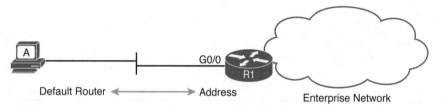

Figure 7-7 *Host Default Router Setting Should Equal Router Interface Address*

Of course, each device needs its own IP address and subnet mask. Equally as important, note that the host and the default router need to agree as to the addresses inside the subnet. The host will use the address and mask to do the math to determine which addresses are in the same subnet and which are in other subnets. For routing to work correctly, the default router's interface address and mask should result in the same definition of the subnet with the same addresses, as shown in Figure 7-8.

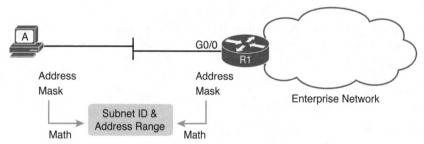

Figure 7-8 *The Need for Subnet Agreement Between Host and Default Router*

The rest of this section shows examples of the display of these settings in the graphical user interface (GUI) and command-line interface (CLI) of three different host operating systems.

Host IP Settings on Windows

Most every OS in the world—certainly the more common OSs people work with every day—have a fairly easy-to-reach settings window that lists most if not all the IPv4 settings in one place. For example, Figure 7-9 shows the Network configuration screen from a Windows 10 host from the network area of the Windows Control Panel. This particular example shows the big four settings: address, mask, router, and DNS.

However, beyond the GUI, most OSs have a variety of networking commands available from a command line. With all Windows versions, the **ipconfig** and **ipconfig /all** commands supply the most direct help, as shown in Example 7-6. As you can see, both list the address, mask, and default gateway, with the **ipconfig /all** command also listing the DNS server settings.

Figure 7-9 *IP Address, Mask, and Default Router Settings on Windows*

Example 7-6 ipconfig *and* ipconfig /all *(Windows)*

```
C:\DOCUME1\OWNER> ipconfig


Windows IP Configuration


Ethernet adapter Ethernet3:

   Connection-specific DNS Suffix  . :
   IPv4 Address. . . . . . . . . . . : 192.168.1.172
   Subnet Mask . . . . . . . . . . . : 255.255.255.0
   Default Gateway . . . . . . . . . : 192.168.1.1

C:\DOCUME1\OWNER> ipconfig /all
! Lines omitted for brevity
Ethernet adapter Ethernet 3:

   Connection-specific DNS Suffix  . :
   Description . . . . . . . . . . . : ASIX AX88179 USB 3.0 to Gigabit Ethernet
Adapter
   Physical Address. . . . . . . . . : 00-05-1B-A3-5D-D0
   DHCP Enabled. . . . . . . . . . . : Yes
   Autoconfiguration Enabled . . . . : Yes
   IPv4 Address. . . . . . . . . . . : 192.168.1.172(Preferred)
```

```
   Subnet Mask . . . . . . . . . . : 255.255.255.0
   Lease Obtained. . . . . . . . . : Friday, August 2, 2019 12:55:50 PM
   Lease Expires . . . . . . . . . : Saturday, August 3, 2019 1:01:45 AM
   Default Gateway . . . . . . . . : 192.168.1.1
   DHCP Server . . . . . . . . . . : 192.168.1.1
   DNS Servers . . . . . . . . . . : 208.67.222.222
                                     208.67.220.220
   NetBIOS over Tcpip. . . . . . . : Enabled
```

Another common command on most user host OSs is the **netstat -rn** command. This command lists the host's IP routing table. Of interest, the top of the table lists a route based on the default gateway, with the destination subnet and mask listed as 0.0.0.0 and 0.0.0.0. The top of the output also lists several other routes related to having a working interface, like a route to the subnet connected to the interface. Example 7-7 lists an excerpt from the **netstat -rn** command from the same Windows host, with the default route and the route to the local subnet (192.168.1.0) listed. Note that a gateway of "on-link" means that the PC thinks the destination is on the local subnet (link).

Example 7-7 netstat -rn *Command (Windows)*

```
C:\DOCUME1\OWNER> netstat -rn

IPv4 Route Table
===========================================================================
Active Routes:
Network Destination        Netmask          Gateway       Interface  Metric
          0.0.0.0          0.0.0.0      192.168.1.1    192.168.1.172     25
        127.0.0.0        255.0.0.0         On-link        127.0.0.1    331
        127.0.0.1  255.255.255.255         On-link        127.0.0.1    331
  127.255.255.255  255.255.255.255         On-link        127.0.0.1    331
      169.254.0.0      255.255.0.0         On-link  169.254.244.178    291
  169.254.244.178  255.255.255.255         On-link  169.254.244.178    291
  169.254.255.255  255.255.255.255         On-link  169.254.244.178    291
      192.168.1.0    255.255.255.0         On-link    192.168.1.172    281
    192.168.1.172  255.255.255.255         On-link    192.168.1.172    281
    192.168.1.255  255.255.255.255         On-link    192.168.1.172    281
! Lines omitted for brevity
```

Host IP Settings on macOS

Although the particulars vary, like Windows, macOS has both a graphical interface to see network settings and a variety of network commands. This section shows examples of each, beginning with Figure 7-10. It shows the network settings in macOS for an Ethernet interface, with the address, mask, default router, and DNS server addresses. Also note the setting states that the interface is using DHCP.

Figure 7-10 *IP Address, Mask, and Default Router Settings on macOS*

macOS and Linux both support the **ifconfig** command to list information similar to the Windows **ipconfig /all** command. (Note that **ifconfig** does not have an **/all** option.) Of note, the **ifconfig** command does not list the default gateway or DNS servers, so Example 7-8 includes two other macOS commands that supply those details.

Example 7-8 ifconfig, networksetup -getinfo, *and* networksetup -getdnsservers *(macOS)*

```
Wendell-Odoms-iMac:~ wendellodom$ ifconfig en0
en0: flags=8863<UP,BROADCAST,SMART,RUNNING,SIMPLEX,MULTICAST> mtu 1500
        options=10b<RXCSUM,TXCSUM,VLAN_HWTAGGING,AV>
        ether 0c:4d:e9:a9:9c:41
        inet 192.168.1.102 netmask 0xffffff00 broadcast 192.168.1.255
! IPv6 details omitted for brevity
        media: autoselect (1000baseT <full-duplex,flow-control,energy-efficient-
ethernet>)
        status: active


Wendell-Odoms-iMac:~ wendellodom$ networksetup -getinfo Ethernet
DHCP Configuration
IP address: 192.168.1.102
Subnet mask: 255.255.255.0
Router: 192.168.1.1
Client ID:
IPv6: Automatic
```

```
IPv6 IP address: none

IPv6 Router: none

Ethernet Address: 0c:4d:e9:a9:9c:41


Wendell-Odoms-iMac:~ wendellodom$ networksetup -getdnsservers Ethernet
8.8.8.4
8.8.8.8
```

Like Windows, macOS adds a default route to its host routing table based on the default gateway, as well as a route to the local subnet calculated based on the IP address and mask learned with DHCP. And like Windows, macOS uses the **netstat -rn** command to list those routes—but with several differences in the output. Of note in the macOS sample shown in Example 7-9, the output represents the default route using the word *default* rather than the paired numbers 0.0.0.0 and 0.0.0.0 for the destination subnet and mask.

Example 7-9 netstat -rn *Command (macOS)*

```
C:\DOCUME1\OWNER> netstat -rn
Routing tables


Internet:
Destination        Gateway              Flags      Refs      Use   Netif Expire
default            192.168.1.1          UGSc         92        0     en0
127                127.0.0.1            UCS           0        0     lo0
127.0.0.1          127.0.0.1            UH            4     1950     lo0
169.254            link#5               UCS           2        0     en0      !
169.254.210.104    0:5:1b:a3:5d:d0      UHLSW         0        0     en0      !
192.168.1          link#5               UCS           9        0     en0      !
192.168.1.1/32     link#5               UCS           1        0     en0      !
192.168.1.1        60:e3:27:fb:70:97    UHLWIir      12     2502     en0   1140
192.168.1.102/32   link#5               UCS           0        0     en0      !
! lines omitted for brevity
```

Host IP Settings on Linux

On Linux, the graphical windows to display network settings differ for many reasons. First, the Linux world includes a large number of different Linux versions or distributions. Additionally, Linux separates the OS from the desktop (the graphical interface) so that a user of one Linux distribution can choose between different desktop interfaces. As a result, you will see different GUI screens to display the Linux network settings.

For perspective, this section shows a few examples from the MATE desktop included in the Ubuntu MATE Linux distribution (www.ubuntu-mate.org). First, the image in Figure 7-11 shows details for a wireless LAN adapter and includes the IPv4 address, mask, default router, and primary DNS IP address.

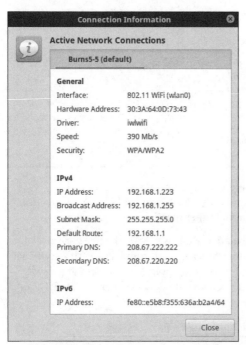

Figure 7-11 *IP Address, Mask, and Default Router Settings on Linux*

From the command line, Linux hosts will often support a large set of commands. However, an older set of commands, referenced together as *net-tools*, has been deprecated in Linux, to the point that some Linux distributions do not include net-tools. (You can easily add net-tools to most Linux distributions.) The net-tools library includes **ifconfig** and **netstat -rn**. To replace those tools, Linux uses the iproute library, which includes a set of replacement commands and functions, many performed with the **ip** command and some parameters.

NOTE   Check out this link for a broader comparison of the commands: https://access.red-hat.com/sites/default/files/attachments/rh_ip_command_cheatsheet_1214_jcs_print.pdf.

Example 7-10 shows a sample of the **ifconfig** command for the same interface detailed in Figure 7-11. Note that it lists the Ethernet MAC and IPv4 addresses, along with the subnet mask, similar to the macOS version of the command. However, on Linux, it also shows some interface counters.

Example 7-10 ifconfig *and* ip address *Commands (Linux)*

```
chris@LL ~ $ ifconfig wlan0
wlan0     Link encap:Ethernet  HWaddr 30:3a:64:0d:73:43
          inet addr:192.168.1.223  Bcast:192.168.1.255  Mask:255.255.255.0
          inet6 addr: fe80::e5b8:f355:636a:b2a4/64 Scope:Link
          UP BROADCAST RUNNING MULTICAST  MTU:1500  Metric:1
          RX packets:2041153 errors:0 dropped:0 overruns:0 frame:0
          TX packets:712814 errors:0 dropped:0 overruns:0 carrier:0
          collisions:0 txqueuelen:1000
```

```
          RX bytes:2677874115 (2.6 GB)   TX bytes:134076542 (134.0 MB)

chris@LL ~ $ ip address
3: wlan0: <BROADCAST,MULTICAST,UP,LOWER_UP> mtu 1500 qdisc mq state UP group default
qlen 1000
    link/ether 30:3a:64:0d:73:43 brd ff:ff:ff:ff:ff:ff
    inet 192.168.1.223/24 brd 192.168.1.255 scope global wlan0
       valid_lft forever preferred_lft forever
    inet6 fe80::e5b8:f355:636a:b2a4/64 scope link
       valid_lft forever preferred_lft forever
```

The bottom of the example shows the command from the iproute package that replaces **ifconfig**, namely the **ip address**. Note that it shows the same basic addressing information, just with the subnet mask shown in prefix notation rather than in dotted decimal.

Linux has long supported the **netstat -rn** command as well, as part of the net-tools package, with a sample shown in Example 7-11. The output lists a default route, but with a style that shows the destination as 0.0.0.0. As usual, the default route points to the default gateway as learned with DHCP: 192.168.1.1. It also lists a route to the local subnet (192.168.1.0 as highlighted toward the bottom of the output).

Example 7-11 netstat -rn *and* ip route *Commands (Linux)*

```
chris@LL ~ $ netstat -rn
Kernel IP routing table
Destination     Gateway         Genmask         Flags   MSS Window  irtt Iface
0.0.0.0         192.168.1.1     0.0.0.0         UG        0 0        0 wlan0
169.254.0.0     0.0.0.0         255.255.0.0     U         0 0        0 wlan0
192.168.1.0     0.0.0.0         255.255.255.0   U         0 0        0 wlan0

chris@LL ~ $ ip route
default via 192.168.1.1 dev wlan0  proto static  metric 600
169.254.0.0/16 dev wlan0  scope link  metric 1000
192.168.1.0/24 dev wlan0  proto kernel  scope link  src 192.168.1.223  metric 600
chris@LL ~ $
```

The bottom of the example shows the command meant to replace **netstat -rn: ip route**. Note that it also shows a default route that references the default router, along with a route for the local subnet.

Chapter Review

One key to doing well on the exams is to perform repetitive spaced review sessions. Review this chapter's material using either the tools in the book or interactive tools for the same material found on the book's companion website. Refer to the "Your Study Plan" element for more details. Table 7-2 outlines the key review elements and where you can find them. To better track your study progress, record when you completed these activities in the second column.

Table 7-2   Chapter Review Tracking

Review Element	Review Date(s)	Resource Used
Review key topics		Book, website
Review key terms		Book, website
Repeat DIKTA questions		Book, PTP
Review command tables		Book

Review All the Key Topics

Table 7-3   Key Topics for Chapter 7

Key Topic Element	Description	Page Number
List	Definitions of special IPv4 addresses 0.0.0.0 and 255.255.255.255	125
List	Four logic steps created by the **ip helper-address** command	127
Figure 7-2	What the **ip helper-address** command changes in a DHCP Discover message	127
List	The two facts that must be true about a subnet for a router to need to be a DHCP relay agent for that subnet	130
Example 7-4	Switch commands that confirm the details of DHCP client operations based on the **ip address dhcp** interface subcommand	131
List	The IPv4 settings expected on an end-user host	133
Example 7-6	Output from a Windows **ipconfig /all** command	135
Example 7-8	Output from a macOS **ifconfig** command plus two **networksetup** commands	137

Key Terms You Should Know

DHCP client, DHCP server, DHCP relay agent, default gateway, DNS server

Command References

Tables 7-4, 7-5, and 7-6 list configuration and verification commands used in this chapter. As an easy review exercise, cover the left column in a table, read the right column, and try to recall the command without looking. Then repeat the exercise, covering the right column, and try to recall what the command does.

Table 7-4   Chapter 7 Configuration Command Reference

Command	Description
ip helper-address *IP-address*	An interface subcommand that tells the router to notice local subnet broadcasts (to 255.255.255.255) that use UDP, and change the source and destination IP address, enabling DHCP servers to sit on a remote subnet
ip address dhcp	An interface subcommand that tells the router or switch to use DHCP to attempt to lease a DHCP address from a DHCP server

7

Table 7-5 Chapter 7 EXEC Command Reference

Command	Description
show arp, show ip arp	Command that lists the router's IPv4 ARP table
show dhcp lease	Switch command that lists information about addresses leased because of the configuration of the **ip address dhcp** command
show ip default-gateway	Switch command that lists the switch's default gateway setting, no matter whether learned by DHCP or statically configured

Table 7-6 Chapter 7 Generic Host Networking Command Reference

Command	Description
ipconfig /all	(Windows) Lists IP address, mask, gateway, and DNS servers
ifconfig	(Mac, Linux) Lists IP address and mask for an interface
networksetup -getinfo *interface*	(Mac) Lists IP settings including default router
networksetup -getdnsservers *interface*	(Mac) Lists DNS servers used
netstat -rn	(Windows, Mac, Linux) Lists the host's routing table, including a default route that uses the DHCP-learned default gateway
arp -a	(Windows, Mac, Linux) Lists the host's ARP table
ip address	(Linux) Lists IP address and mask information for interfaces; the Linux replacement for **ifconfig**
ip route	(Linux) Lists routes, including the default route and a route to the local subnet; the Linux replacement for **netstat -rn**

CHAPTER 8

DHCP Snooping and ARP Inspection

This chapter covers the following exam topics:

5.0 Security Fundamentals

5.7 Configure Layer 2 security features (DHCP snooping, dynamic ARP inspection, and port security)

To understand the kinds of risks that exist in modern networks, you have to first understand the rules. Then you have to think about how an attacker might take advantage of those rules in different ways. Some attacks might cause harm as part of a denial-of-service (DoS) attack, while a reconnaissance attack may gather more data to prepare for some other attack. For every protocol and function you learn in networking, there are possible methods to take advantage of those features to give an attacker an advantage.

This chapter discusses two switch features that help prevent some types of attacks that can result in the attacker getting copies of packets sent to/from a legitimate host. One of these features, DHCP Snooping, notices DHCP messages that fall outside the normal use of DHCP—messages that may be part of an attack—and discards those messages. It also watches the DHCP messages that flow through a LAN switch, building a table that lists the details of legitimate DHCP flows, so that other switch features can know what legitimate DHCP leases exist for devices connected to the switch.

The second such feature, Dynamic ARP Inspection (DAI), also helps prevent packets being redirected to an attacking host. Some ARP attacks try to convince hosts to send packets to the attacker's device instead of the true destination. The switch watches ARP messages as they flow through the switch. The switch checks incoming ARP messages, checking those against normal ARP operation as well as checking the details against other data sources, including the DHCP Snooping binding table. When the ARP message does not match the known information about the legitimate addresses in the network, the switch filters the ARP message.

This chapter examines DHCP Snooping concepts and configuration in the first major section and DAI in the second.

"Do I Know This Already?" Quiz

Take the quiz (either here or use the PTP software) if you want to use the score to help you decide how much time to spend on this chapter. The letter answers are listed at the bottom of the page following the quiz. Appendix C, found both at the end of the book as well as on the companion website, includes both the answers and explanations. You can also find both answers and explanations in the PTP testing software.

Table 8-1 "Do I Know This Already?" Foundation Topics Section-to-Question Mapping

Foundation Topics Section	Questions
DHCP Snooping	1–4
Dynamic ARP Inspection	5–7

1. An engineer hears about DHCP Snooping and decides to implement it. Which of the following are the devices on which DHCP Snooping could be implemented? (Choose two answers.)

   a. Layer 2 switches

   b. Routers

   c. Multilayer switches

   d. End-user hosts

2. Layer 2 switch SW2 connects a Layer 2 switch (SW1), a router (R1), a DHCP server (S1), and three PCs (PC1, PC2, and PC3). All PCs are DHCP clients. Which of the following are the most likely DHCP Snooping trust state configurations on SW2 for the ports connected to the listed devices? (Choose two answers.)

   a. The port connected to the router is untrusted.

   b. The port connected to switch SW1 is trusted.

   c. The port connected to PC1 is untrusted.

   d. The port connected to PC3 is trusted.

3. Switch SW1 needs to be configured to use DHCP Snooping in VLAN 5 and only VLAN 5. Which commands must be included, assuming at least one switch port in VLAN 5 must be an untrusted port? (Choose two answers.)

   a. no ip dhcp snooping trust

   b. ip dhcp snooping untrust

   c. ip dhcp snooping

   d. ip dhcp snooping vlan 5

4. On a multilayer switch, a switch needs to be configured to perform DHCP Snooping on some Layer 2 ports in VLAN 3. Which command may or may not be needed depending on whether the switch also acts as a DHCP relay agent?

   a. no ip dhcp snooping information option

   b. ip dhcp snooping limit rate 5

   c. errdisable recovery cause dhcp-rate-limit

   d. ip dhcp snooping vlan 3

5. Switch SW1 has been configured to use Dynamic ARP Inspection with DHCP Snooping in VLAN 5. An ARP request arrives on port G0/1. Which answer describes two items DAI always compares regardless of the configuration?

    a. The message's ARP origin hardware address and the message's Ethernet header source MAC address

    b. The message's ARP origin hardware address and the DHCP Snooping binding table

    c. The message's ARP target IP address and the DHCP Snooping binding table

    d. The message's ARP target IP address and the switch's ARP table

6. Switch SW1 needs to be configured to use Dynamic ARP Inspection along with DHCP Snooping in VLAN 6 and only VLAN 6. Which commands must be included, assuming at least one switch port in VLAN 6 must be a trusted port? (Choose two answers.)

    a. no ip arp inspection untrust

    b. ip arp inspection trust

    c. ip arp inspection

    d. ip arp inspection vlan 6

7. A Layer 2 switch needs to be configured to use Dynamic ARP Inspection along with DHCP Snooping. Which command would make DAI monitor ARP message rates on an interface at an average rate of 4 received ARP messages per second? (Choose two answers.)

    a. ip arp inspection limit rate 4 burst interval 2

    b. ip arp inspection limit rate 10 burst interval 2

    c. ip arp inspection limit rate 16 burst interval 4

    d. ip arp inspection limit rate 4

Foundation Topics

DHCP Snooping

DHCP servers play a vital role in most every network today, with almost every user endpoint using DHCP to learn its IP address, mask, default gateway, and DNS server IP addresses. Chapter 7, "Implementing DHCP," shows how DHCP should work under normal circumstances. This section now examines how attackers might use DHCP for their own ends and how two specific tools—DHCP Snooping and Dynamic ARP Inspection (DAI)—help defeat those attacks.

This section begins with an examination of the need for DHCP Snooping concepts including the types of attacks it can try to prevent, followed by details of how to configure DHCP Snooping.

DHCP Snooping Concepts

DHCP Snooping on a switch acts like a firewall or an ACL in many ways. It analyzes incoming messages on the specified subset of ports in a VLAN. DHCP Snooping never filters non-DHCP messages, but it may choose to filter DHCP messages, applying logic to make a choice—allow the incoming DHCP message or discard the message.

While DHCP itself provides a Layer 3 service, DHCP Snooping operates on LAN switches and is commonly used on Layer 2 LAN switches and enabled on Layer 2 ports. The reason to put DHCP Snooping on the switch is that the function needs to be performed between a typical end-user device—the type of device that acts as a DHCP client—and DHCP servers or DHCP relay agents.

Figure 8-1 shows a sample network that provides a good backdrop to discuss DHCP Snooping. First, all devices connect to Layer 2 switch SW2, with all ports as Layer 2 switch-ports, all in the same VLAN. The typical DHCP clients sit on the right of the figure. The left shows other devices that could be the path through which to reach a DHCP server.

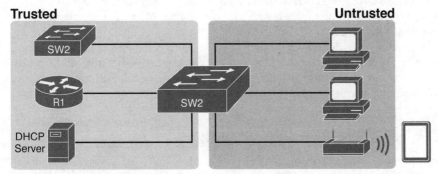

Figure 8-1   *DHCP Snooping Basics: Client Ports Are Untrusted*

DHCP Snooping works first on all ports in a VLAN, but with each port being trusted or untrusted by DHCP Snooping. To understand why, consider this summary of the general rules used by DHCP Snooping. Note that the rules differentiate between messages normally sent by servers (like DHCPOFFER and DHCPACK) versus those normally sent by DHCP clients:

- DHCP messages received on an untrusted port, for messages normally sent by a server, will always be discarded.

- DHCP messages received on an untrusted port, as normally sent by a DHCP client, may be filtered if they appear to be part of an attack.

- DHCP messages received on a trusted port will be forwarded; trusted ports do not filter (discard) any DHCP messages.

A Sample Attack: A Spurious DHCP Server

To give you some perspective, Figure 8-2 shows a legitimate user's PC on the far right and the legitimate DHCP server on the far left. However, an attacker has connected his laptop to the LAN and started his DHCP attack by acting like a DHCP server. Following the steps in the figure, assume PC1 is attempting to lease an IP address while the attacker is making his attack:

1. PC1 sends a LAN broadcast with PC1's first DHCP message (DHCPDISCOVER).

2. The attacker's PC—acting as a spurious DHCP server—replies to the DHCPDISCOVER with a DHCPOFFER.

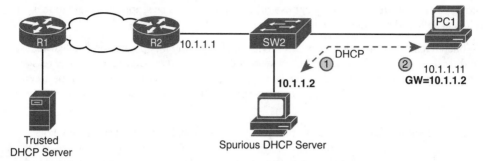

Figure 8-2 *DHCP Attack Supplies Good IP Address but Wrong Default Gateway*

In this example, the DHCP server created and used by the attacker actually leases a useful IP address to PC1, in the correct subnet, with the correct mask. Why? The attacker wants PC1 to function, but with one twist. Notice the default gateway assigned to PC1: 10.1.1.2, which is the attacker's PC address, rather than 10.1.1.1, which is router R1's address. Now PC1 thinks it has all it needs to connect to the network, and it does—but now all the packets sent by PC1 to what it thinks is its default router flow first through the attacker's PC, creating a man-in-the-middle attack, as shown in Figure 8-3.

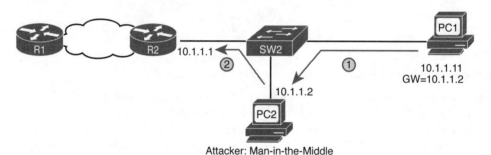

Figure 8-3 *Unfortunate Result: DHCP Attack Leads to Man-in-the-Middle*

Note that the legitimate DHCP also returns a DHCPOFFER message to host PC1, but most hosts use the first received DHCPOFFER, and the attacker will likely be first in this scenario.

The two steps in the figure show data flow once DHCP has completed. For any traffic destined to leave the subnet, PC1 sends its packets to its default gateway, 10.1.1.2, which happens to be the attacker. The attacker forwards the packets to R1. The PC1 user can connect to any and all applications just like normal, but now the attacker can keep a copy of anything sent by PC1.

DHCP Snooping Logic

The preceding example shows just one attack in which the attacker acts like a DHCP server (spurious DHCP server). DHCP Snooping defeats such attacks by making most ports untrusted, which by definition would filter the DHCP server messages that arrive on the untrusted ports. For instance, in Figures 8-2 and 8-3, making the port connected to the attacker, a DHCP Snooping untrusted port defeats the attack.

To appreciate the broader set of DHCP Snooping rules and logic, it helps to have a handy reference of some of the more common DHCP messages and processes. For a quick review, the normal message flow includes this sequence: DISCOVER, OFFER, REQUEST, ACK (DORA). In particular:

■ Clients send DISCOVER and REQUEST.

■ Servers send OFFER and ACK.

Additionally, DHCP clients also use the DHCP RELEASE and DHCP DECLINE messages. When a client has a working lease for an address but no longer wants to use the address, the DHCP client can tell the DHCP server it no longer needs the address, releasing it back to the DHCP server, with the DHCP RELEASE message. Similarly, a client can send a DHCP DECLINE message to turn down the use of an IP address during the normal DORA flow on messages.

Now to the logic for DHCP Snooping untrusted ports. Figure 8-4 summarizes the ideas, with two switch ports. On the left, the switch port connects to a DHCP server, so it should be trusted; otherwise DHCP would not work, because the switch would filter all DHCP messages sent by the DHCP server. On the right, PC1 connects to an untrusted port with a DHCP client.

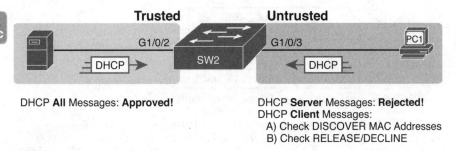

Figure 8-4 *Summary of Rules for DHCP Snooping*

The following list summarizes the DHCP Snooping rules:

1. Examine all incoming DHCP messages.

2. If normally sent by servers, discard the message.

3. If normally sent by clients, filter as follows:

    a. For DISCOVER and REQUEST messages, check for MAC address consistency between the Ethernet frame and the DHCP message.

    b. For RELEASE or DECLINE messages, check the incoming interface plus IP address versus the DHCP Snooping binding table.

4. For messages not filtered that result in a DHCP lease, build a new entry to the DHCP Snooping binding table.

The next few pages complete the discussion of concepts by explaining a little more about steps 3 and 4 in the list.

Filtering DISCOVER Messages Based on MAC Address

DHCP Snooping does one straightforward check for the most common client-sent messages: DISCOVER and REQUEST. First, note that DHCP messages define the chaddr (client hardware address) field to identify the client. Hosts on LANs include the device's MAC address as part of chaddr. As usual, Ethernet hosts encapsulate the DHCP messages inside Ethernet frames, and those frames of course include a source MAC address—an address that should be the same MAC address used in the DHCP chaddr field. DHCP Snooping does a simple check to make sure those values match.

Figure 8-5 shows how an attacker could attempt to overload the DHCP server and lease all the addresses in the subnet. The attacker's PC uses pseudo MAC address A, so all three DISCOVER messages in the figure show a source Ethernet address of "A." However, each message (in the DHCP data) identifies a different MAC address in the chaddr value (shown as MAC1, MAC2, and MAC3 in the figure for brevity), so from a DHCP perspective, each message appears to be a different DHCP request. The attacker can attempt to lease every IP address in the subnet so that no other hosts could obtain a lease.

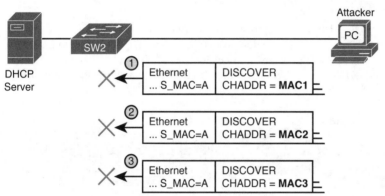

Figure 8-5 *DHCP Snooping Checks chaddr and Ethernet Source MAC*

The core feature of DHCP Snooping defeats this type of attack on untrusted ports. It checks the Ethernet header source MAC address and compares that address to the MAC address in the DHCP header, and if the values do not match, DHCP Snooping discards the message.

Filtering Messages that Release IP Addresses

Before looking at the next bit of logic, you need to first understand the DHCP Snooping binding table.

DHCP Snooping builds the DHCP Snooping binding table for all the DHCP flows it sees that it allows to complete. That is, for any working legitimate DHCP flows, it keeps a list of some of the important facts. Then DHCP Snooping, and other features like Dynamic ARP Inspection, can use the table to make decisions.

As an example, consider Figure 8-6, which repeats the same topology as Figure 8-4, now with one entry in its DHCP Snooping binding table.

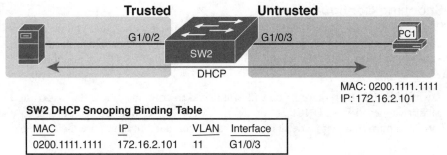

Figure 8-6 *Legitimate DHCP Client with DHCP Binding Entry Built by DHCP Snooping*

In this simple network, the DHCP client on the right leases IP address 172.16.2.101 from the DHCP server on the left. The switch's DHCP Snooping feature combines the information from the DHCP messages, with information about the port (interface G1/0/3, assigned to VLAN 11 by the switch), and puts that in the DHCP Snooping binding table.

DHCP Snooping then applies additional filtering logic that uses the DHCP Snooping binding table: it checks client-sent messages like RELEASE and DECLINE that would cause the DHCP server to be allowed to release an address. For instance, a legitimate user might lease address 172.16.2.101, and at some point release the address back to the server; however, before the client has finished with its lease, an attacker could send DHCP RELEASE message to release that address back into the pool. The attacker could then immediately try to lease that address, hoping the DHCP server assigns that same 172.16.2.101 address to the attacker.

Figure 8-7 shows an example. PC1 already has a DHCP address (172.16.2.101), with SW2 listing an entry in the DHCP Snooping binding table. The figure shows the action by which the attacker off port G1/0/5 attempts to release PC1's address. DHCP Snooping compares the incoming message, incoming interface, and matching table entry:

1. The incoming message is a DHCP RELEASE message in port G1/0/5 listing address 172.16.2.101.

2. The DHCP Snooping binding table lists 172.16.2.101 as being originally leased via messages arriving on port G1/0/3.

3. DHCP Snooping discards the DHCP RELEASE message.

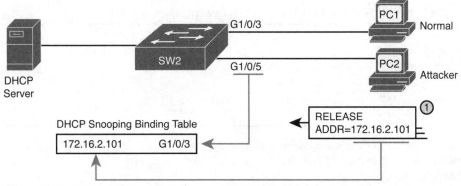

Figure 8-7 *DHCP Snooping Defeats a DHCP RELEASE from Another Port*

DHCP Snooping Configuration

DHCP Snooping requires several configuration steps to make it work. First, you need to use a pair of associated global commands: one to enable DHCP Snooping and another to list the VLANs on which to use DHCP Snooping. Both must be included for DHCP Snooping to operate.

Second, while not literally required, you will often need to configure a few ports as trusted ports. Most switches that use DHCP Snooping for a VLAN have some trusted ports and some untrusted ports, and with a default of untrusted, you need to configure the trusted ports.

This section begins with an example that shows how to configure a typical Layer 2 switch to use DHCP Snooping, with required commands as just described, and with other optional commands.

Configuring DHCP Snooping on a Layer 2 Switch

The upcoming examples all rely on the topology illustrated in Figure 8-8, with Layer 2 switch SW2 as the switch on which to enable DHCP Snooping. The DHCP server sits on the other side of the WAN, on the left of the figure. As a result, SW2's port connected to router R2 (a DHCP relay agent) needs to be trusted. On the right, two sample PCs can use the default untrusted setting.

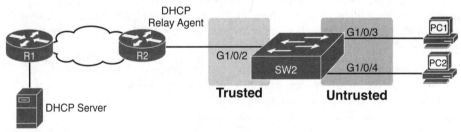

Figure 8-8 *Sample Network Used in DHCP Snooping Configuration Examples*

Switch SW2 places all the ports in the figure in VLAN 11, so to enable DHCP Snooping in VLAN 11, SW2 requires two commands, as shown near the top of Example 8-1: **ip dhcp snooping** and **ip dhcp snooping vlan 11**. Then, to change the logic on port G1/0/2 (connected to the router) to be trusted, the configuration includes the **ip dhcp snooping trust** interface subcommand.

Example 8-1 *DHCP Snooping Configuration to Match Figure 8-8*

```
ip dhcp snooping
ip dhcp snooping vlan 11
no ip dhcp snooping information option
!
interface GigabitEthernet1/0/2
 ip dhcp snooping trust
```

Note that the **no ip dhcp snooping information option** command in Example 8-1 will be explained in a better context just after Example 8-2 but is listed in Example 8-1 to make the example complete.

With this configuration, the switch follows the logic steps detailed in the earlier section titled "DHCP Snooping Logic." To see some support for that claim, look at Example 8-2, which shows the output from the **show ip dhcp snooping** command on switch SW2.

Example 8-2 *SW2 DHCP Snooping Status*

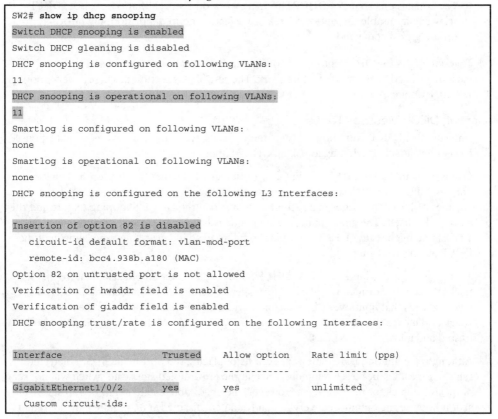

```
SW2# show ip dhcp snooping
Switch DHCP snooping is enabled
Switch DHCP gleaning is disabled
DHCP snooping is configured on following VLANs:
11
DHCP snooping is operational on following VLANs:
11
Smartlog is configured on following VLANs:
none
Smartlog is operational on following VLANs:
none
DHCP snooping is configured on the following L3 Interfaces:

Insertion of option 82 is disabled
   circuit-id default format: vlan-mod-port
   remote-id: bcc4.938b.a180 (MAC)
Option 82 on untrusted port is not allowed
Verification of hwaddr field is enabled
Verification of giaddr field is enabled
DHCP snooping trust/rate is configured on the following Interfaces:

Interface                Trusted    Allow option    Rate limit (pps)
-----------------------  -------    ------------    ----------------
GigabitEthernet1/0/2     yes        yes             unlimited
  Custom circuit-ids:
```

The highlighted lines in the example point out a few of the key configuration settings. Starting at the top, the first two confirm the configuration of the **ip dhcp snooping** and **ip dhcp snooping vlan 11** commands, respectively. Also, the highlighted lines at the bottom of the output show a section that lists trusted ports—in this case, only port G1/0/2.

Also, you might have noticed that highlighted line in the middle that states **Insertion of option 82 is disabled**. That line confirms the addition of the **no ip dhcp information option** command to the configuration back in Example 8-1. To understand why the example includes this command, consider these facts about DHCP relay agents:

■ DHCP relay agents add new fields to DHCP requests—defined as option 82 DHCP header fields (in RFC 3046).

■ DHCP Snooping uses default settings that work well if the switch acts as a Layer 3 switch and as a DHCP relay agent, meaning that the switch should insert the DHCP option 82 fields into DHCP messages. In effect, the switch defaults to use **ip dhcp snooping information option**.

8

- When the switch does not also act as a DHCP relay agent, the default setting stops DHCP from working for end users. The switch sets fields in the DHCP messages as if it were a DHCP relay agent, but the changes to those messages cause most DHCP servers (and most DHCP relay agents) to ignore the received DHCP messages.

- The conclusion: To make DHCP Snooping work on a switch that is not also a DHCP relay agent, disable the option 82 feature using the **no ip dhcp snooping information option** global command.

That concludes the DHCP Snooping configuration that is both required and that you will most often need to make the feature work. The rest of this section discusses a few optional DHCP Snooping features.

Limiting DHCP Message Rates

Knowing that DHCP Snooping prevents their attacks, what might attackers do in response? Devise new attacks, including attacking DHCP Snooping itself.

One way to attack DHCP Snooping takes advantage of the fact that it uses the general-purpose CPU in a switch. Knowing that, attackers can devise attacks to generate large volumes of DHCP messages in an attempt to overload the DHCP Snooping feature and the switch CPU itself. The goal can be as a simple denial-of-service attack or a combination of attacks that might cause DHCP Snooping to fail to examine every message, allowing other DHCP attacks to then work.

To help prevent this kind of attack, DHCP Snooping includes an optional feature that tracks the number of incoming DHCP messages. If the number of incoming DHCP messages exceeds that limit over a one-second period, DHCP Snooping treats the event as an attack and moves the port to an err-disabled state. Also, the feature can be enabled both on trusted and untrusted interfaces.

Although rate limiting DHCP messages can help, placing the port in an err-disabled state can itself create issues. As a reminder, once in the err-disabled state, the switch will not send or receive frames for the interface. However, the err-disabled state might be too severe an action because the default recovery action for an err-disabled state requires the configuration of a **shutdown** and then a **no shutdown** subcommand on the interface.

To help strike a better balance, you can enable DHCP Snooping rate limiting and then also configure the switch to automatically recover from the port's err-disabled state, without the need for a **shutdown** and then **no shutdown** command.

Example 8-3 shows how to enable DHCP Snooping rate limits and err-disabled recovery. First, look at the lower half of the configuration, to the interfaces, to see the straightforward setting of the per-interface limits using the **ip dhcp snooping rate limit** *number* interface subcommands. The top of the configuration uses two global commands to tell IOS to recover from an err-disabled state if it is caused by DHCP Snooping, and to use a nondefault number of seconds to wait before recovering the interface. Note that the configuration in Example 8-3 would rely on the core configuration for DHCP Snooping as shown in Example 8-1.

Example 8-3 *Configuring DHCP Snooping Message Rate Limits*

```
errdisable recovery cause dhcp-rate-limit
errdisable recovery interval 30
!
interface GigabitEthernet1/0/2
 ip dhcp snooping limit rate 10
!
interface GigabitEthernet1/0/3
 ip dhcp snooping limit rate 2
```

A repeat of the **show ip dhcp snooping** command now shows the rate limits near the end of the output, as noted in Example 8-4.

Example 8-4 *Confirming DHCP Snooping Rate Limits*

```
SW2# show ip dhcp snooping
! Lines omitted for brevity

Interface                Trusted   Allow option   Rate limit (pps)
-----------------------  -------   ------------   ----------------
GigabitEthernet1/0/2     yes       yes            10
  Custom circuit-ids:
GigabitEthernet1/0/3     no        no             2
  Custom circuit-ids:
```

DHCP Snooping Configuration Summary

The following configuration checklist summarizes the commands included in this section about how to configure DHCP Snooping.

Step 1. Configure this pair of commands (both required):

A. Use the **ip dhcp snooping** global command to enable DHCP Snooping on the switch.

B. Use the **ip dhcp snooping vlan** *vlan-list* global command to identify the VLANs on which to use DHCP Snooping.

Step 2. (Optional): Use the **no ip dhcp snooping information option** global command on Layer 2 switches to disable the insertion of DHCP Option 82 data into DHCP messages, specifically on switches that do not act as a DHCP relay agent.

Step 3. Configure the **ip dhcp snooping trust** interface subcommand to override the default setting of not trusted.

Step 4. (Optional): Configure DHCP Snooping rate limits and err-disabled recovery:

Step A. (Optional): Configure the **ip dhcp snooping limit rate** *number* interface subcommand to set a limit of DHCP messages per second.

Step B. (Optional): Configure the **no ip dhcp snooping limit rate** *number* interface subcommand to remove an existing limit and reset the interface to use the default of no rate limit.

Step C. (Optional): Configure the **errdisable recovery cause dhcp-rate-limit** global command to enable the feature of automatic recovery from err-disabled mode, assuming the switch placed the port in err-disabled state because of exceeding DHCP Snooping rate limits.

Step D. (Optional): Configure the **errdisable recovery interval** *seconds* global commands to set the time to wait before recovering from an interface err-disabled state (regardless of the cause of the err-disabled state).

Dynamic ARP Inspection

The Dynamic ARP Inspection (DAI) feature on a switch examines incoming ARP messages on untrusted ports to filter those it believes to be part of an attack. DAI's core feature compares incoming ARP messages with two sources of data: the DHCP Snooping binding table and any configured ARP ACLs. If the incoming ARP message does not match the tables in the switch, the switch discards the ARP message.

This section follows the same sequence as with the DHCP Snooping section, first examining the concepts behind DAI and ARP attacks, and then showing how to configure DAI with both required and optional features.

DAI Concepts

To understand the attacks DAI can prevent, you need to be ready to compare normal ARP operations with the abnormal use of ARP used in some types of attacks. This section uses that same flow, first reviewing a few important ARP details, and then showing how an attacker can just send an ARP reply—called a gratuitous ARP—triggering hosts to add incorrect ARP entries to their ARP tables.

Review of Normal IP ARP

If all you care about is how ARP works normally, with no concern about attacks, you can think of ARP to the depth shown in Figure 8-9. The figure shows a typical sequence. Host PC1 needs to send an IP packet to its default router (R2), so PC1 first sends an ARP request message in an attempt to learn the MAC address associated with R2's 172.16.2.2 address. Router R2 sends back an ARP reply, listing R2's MAC address (note the figure shows pseudo MAC addresses to save space).

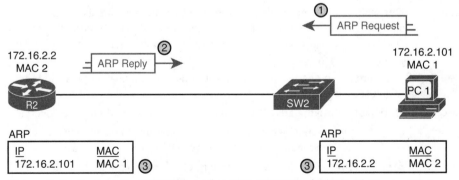

Figure 8-9 *Legitimate ARP Tables After PC1 DHCP and ARP with Router R2*

The ARP tables at bottom of the figure imply an important fact: both hosts learn the other host's MAC address with this two-message flow. Not only does PC1 learn R2's MAC address based on the ARP reply (message 2), but router R2 learns PC1's IP and MAC address because of the ARP request (message 1). To see why, take a look at the more detailed view of those messages as shown in Figure 8-10.

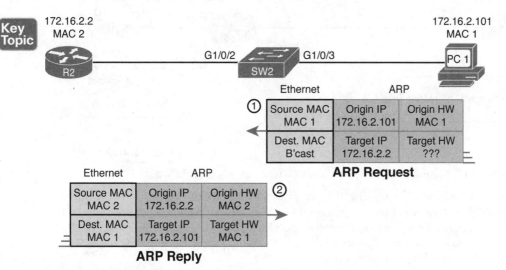

Figure 8-10   *A Detailed Look at ARP Request and Reply*

The ARP messages define origin IP and hardware (MAC) address fields as well as target IP and hardware address fields. The origin should list the sending device's IP address and MAC, no matter whether the message is an ARP reply or ARP request. For instance, message 1 in the figure, sent by PC1, lists PC1's IP and MAC addresses in the origin fields, which is why router R2 could learn that information. PC1 likewise learns of R2's MAC address per the origin address fields in the ARP reply.

Gratuitous ARP as an Attack Vector

Normally, a host uses ARP when it knows the IP address of another host and wants to learn that host's MAC address. However, for legitimate reasons, a host might also want to inform all the hosts in the subnet about its MAC address. That might be useful when a host changes its MAC address, for instance. So, ARP supports the idea of a gratuitous ARP message with these features:

- It is an ARP reply.
- It is sent without having first received an ARP request.
- It is sent to an Ethernet destination broadcast address so that all hosts in the subnet receive the message.

For instance, if a host's MAC address is MAC A, and it changes to MAC B, to cause all the other hosts to update their ARP tables, the host could send a gratuitous ARP that lists an origin MAC of MAC B.

Attackers can take advantage of gratuitous ARPs because they let the sending host make other hosts change their ARP tables. Figure 8-11 shows just such an example initiated by PC A (an attacker) with a gratuitous ARP. However, this ARP lists PC1's IP address but a different device's MAC address (PC A) at step 1, causing the router to update its ARP table (step 2).

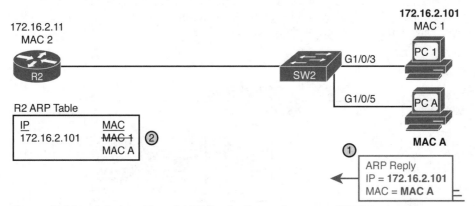

Figure 8-11 *Nefarious Use of ARP Reply Causes Incorrect ARP Data on R2*

At this point, when R2 forwards IP packets to PC1's IP address (172.16.2.101), R2 will encapsulate them in an Ethernet frame with PC A as the destination rather than with PC1's MAC address. At first, this might seem to stop PC1 from working, but instead it could be part of a man-in-the-middle attack so that PC A can copy every message. Figure 8-12 shows the idea of what happens at this point:

1. PC1 sends messages to some server on the left side of router R2.
2. The server replies to PC1's IP address, but R2 forwards that packet to PC A's MAC address, rather than to PC1.
3. PC A copies the packet for later processing.
4. PC A forwards the packet inside a new frame to PC1 so that PC1 still works.

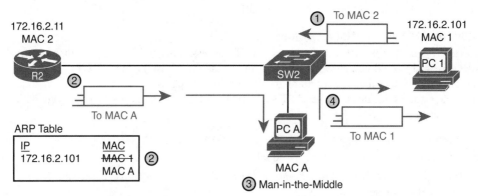

Figure 8-12 *Man-in-the-Middle Attack Resulting from Gratuitous ARP*

Dynamic ARP Inspection Logic

DAI has a variety of features that can prevent these kinds of ARP attacks. To understand how, consider the sequence of a typical client host with regards to both DHCP and ARP. When a host does not have an IP address yet—that is, before the DHCP process completes—it does not need to use ARP. Once the host leases an IP address and learns its subnet mask, it needs ARP to learn the MAC addresses of other hosts or the default router in the subnet, so it sends some ARP messages. In short, DHCP happens first, then ARP.

DAI takes an approach for untrusted interfaces that confirms an ARP's correctness based on DHCP Snooping's data about the earlier DHCP messages. The correct normal DHCP messages list the IP address leased to a host as well as that host's MAC address. The DHCP Snooping feature also records those facts into the switch's DHCP Snooping binding table.

For any DAI untrusted ports, DAI compares the ARP message's origin IP and origin MAC address fields to the DHCP Snooping binding table. If found in the table, DAI allows the ARP through, but if not, DAI discards the ARP. For instance, Figure 8-13 shows step 1 in which the attacker at PC A attempts the gratuitous ARP shown earlier in Figure 8-11. At step 2, DAI makes a comparison to the DHCP Snooping binding table, not finding a match with MAC A along with IP address 172.16.2.101, so DAI would discard the message.

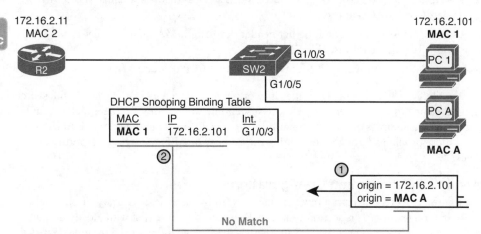

Figure 8-13 *DAI Filtering ARP Based on DHCP Snooping Binding Table*

DAI works with the idea of trusted and untrusted ports with the same general rules as DHCP Snooping. Access ports connected to end-user devices are often untrusted by both DHCP Snooping and DAI. Ports connected to other switches, routers, the DHCP server—anything other than links to end-user devices—should be trusted by DAI.

Note that although DAI can use the DHCP Snooping table as shown here, it can also use similar statically configured data that lists correct pairs of IP and MAC addresses via a tool called *ARP ACLs*. Using ARP ACLs with DAI becomes useful for ports connected to devices that use static IP addresses rather than DHCP. Note that DAI looks for both the DCHP Snooping binding data and ARP ACLs.

Beyond that core feature, note that DAI can optionally perform other checks as well. For instance, the Ethernet header that encapsulates the ARP should have addresses that match the ARP origin and target MAC addresses. Figure 8-14 shows an example of the comparison of the Ethernet source MAC address and the ARP message origin hardware field.

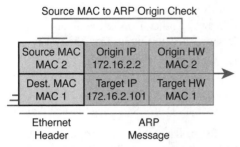

Figure 8-14 *DAI Filtering Checks for Source MAC Addresses*

DAI can be enabled to make the comparisons shown in the figure, discarding these messages:

- Messages with an Ethernet header source MAC address that is not equal to the ARP origin hardware (MAC) address

- ARP reply messages with an Ethernet header destination MAC address that is not equal to the ARP target hardware (MAC) address

- Messages with unexpected IP addresses in the two ARP IP address fields

Finally, like DHCP Snooping, DAI does its work in the switch CPU rather than in the switch ASIC, meaning that DAI itself can be more susceptible to DoS attacks. The attacker could generate large numbers of ARP messages, driving up CPU usage in the switch. DAI can avoid these problems through rate limiting the number of ARP messages on a port over time.

Dynamic ARP Inspection Configuration

Configuring DAI requires just a few commands, with the usual larger variety of optional configuration settings. This section examines DAI configuration, first with mostly default settings and with reliance on DHCP Snooping. It then shows a few of the optional features, like rate limits, automatic recovery from err-disabled state, and how to enable additional checks of incoming ARP messages.

Configuring ARP Inspection on a Layer 2 Switch

Before configuring DAI, you need to think about the feature and make a few decisions based on your goals, topology, and device roles. The decisions include the following:

- Choose whether to rely on DHCP Snooping, ARP ACLs, or both.

- If using DHCP Snooping, configure it and make the correct ports trusted for DHCP Snooping.

- Choose the VLAN(s) on which to enable DAI.

- Make DAI trusted (rather than the default setting of untrusted) on select ports in those VLANs, typically for the same ports you trusted for DHCP Snooping.

All the configuration examples in this section use the same sample network used in the DHCP Snooping configuration topics, repeated here as Figure 8-15. Just as with DHCP Snooping, switch SW2 on the right should be configured to trust the port connected to the router (G1/0/2), but not trust the two ports connected to the PCs.

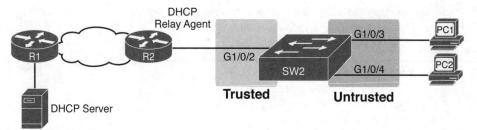

Figure 8-15 *Sample Network Used in ARP Inspection Configuration Examples*

Example 8-5 shows the required configuration to enable DAI on switch SW2 in Figure 8-15—a configuration that follows a similar progression compared to DHCP Snooping. All ports in the figure connect to VLAN 11, so to enable DAI in VLAN 11, just add the **ip arp inspection vlan 11** global command. Then, to change the logic on port G1/0/2 (connected to the router) to be trusted by DAI, add the **ip arp inspection trust** interface subcommand.

Example 8-5 *IP ARP Inspection Configuration to Match Figure 8-15*

```
ip arp inspection vlan 11
!
interface GigabitEthernet1/0/2
 ip arp inspection trust
```

Example 8-5 configures DAI, but it omits both DHCP Snooping and ARP ACLs. (If you were to configure a switch only with commands shown in Example 8-5, the switch would filter all ARPs entering all untrusted ports in VLAN 11.) Example 8-6 shows a complete and working DAI configuration that adds the DHCP Snooping configuration to match the DAI configuration in Example 8-5. Note that Example 8-6 combines Example 8-1's earlier DHCP Snooping configuration for this same topology to the DAI configuration just shown in Example 8-5, with highlights for the DAI-specific configuration lines.

Example 8-6 *IP DHCP Snooping Configuration Added to Support DAI*

```
ip arp inspection vlan 11
ip dhcp snooping
ip dhcp snooping vlan 11
no ip dhcp snooping information option
!
interface GigabitEthernet1/0/2
 ip dhcp snooping trust
 ip arp inspection trust
```

Remember, DHCP occurs first with DHCP clients, and then they send ARP messages. With the configuration in Example 8-6, the switch builds its DHCP Snooping binding table by analyzing incoming DHCP messages. Next, any incoming ARP messages on DAI untrusted ports must have matching information in that binding table.

Example 8-7 confirms the key facts about correct DAI operation in this sample network based on the configuration in Example 8-6. The **show ip arp inspection** command gives both configuration settings along with status variables and counters. For instance, the highlighted lines show the total ARP messages received on untrusted ports in that VLAN and the number of dropped ARP messages (currently 0).

Example 8-7 *SW2 IP ARP Inspection Status*

```
SW2# show ip arp inspection

Source Mac Validation     : Disabled
Destination Mac Validation : Disabled
IP Address Validation     : Disabled

Vlan     Configuration    Operation    ACL Match         Static ACL
----     -------------    ---------    ---------         ----------
  11     Enabled          Active

Vlan     ACL Logging      DHCP Logging     Probe Logging
----     -----------      ------------     -------------
  11     Deny             Deny             Off

Vlan     Forwarded        Dropped      DHCP Drops       ACL Drops
----     ---------        -------      ----------       ---------
  11          59                0               0               0

Vlan     DHCP Permits    ACL Permits  Probe Permits  Source MAC Failures
----     ------------    -----------  -------------  -------------------
  11          7               0            49                   0

Vlan     Dest MAC Failures  IP Validation Failures  Invalid Protocol Data
----     -----------------  ----------------------  ---------------------

Vlan     Dest MAC Failures  IP Validation Failures  Invalid Protocol Data
----     -----------------  ----------------------  ---------------------
  11             0                     0                       0
SW2# show ip dhcp snooping binding
MacAddress          IpAddress      Lease(sec) Type           VLAN  Interface
-----------------   -------------  ---------- ------------   ----  -------------------
02:00:11:11:11:11   172.16.2.101   86110      dhcp-snooping   11   GigabitEthernet1/0/3
02:00:22:22:22:22   172.16.2.102   86399      dhcp-snooping   11   GigabitEthernet1/0/4
Total number of bindings: 2
```

The end of Example 8-7 shows an example of the **show ip dhcp snooping binding** command on switch SW2. Note that the first two columns list a MAC and IP address as learned from the DHCP messages. Then, imagine an ARP message arrives from PC1, a message that should list PC1's 0200.1111.1111 MAC address and 172.16.2.101 as the origin MAC and IP address, respectively. Per this output, the switch would find that matching data and allow the ARP message.

Example 8-8 shows some detail of what happens when switch SW2 receives an invalid ARP message on port G1/0/4 in Figure 8-15. In this case, to create the invalid ARP message,

PC2 in the figure was configured with a static IP address of 172.16.2.101 (which is PC1's DHCP-leased IP address). The highlights in the log message at the top of the example show PC2's claimed origin MAC and origin IP addresses in the ARP message. If you refer back to the bottom of Example 8-7, you can see that this origin MAC/IP pair does not exist in the DHCP Snooping binding table, so DAI rejects the ARP message.

Example 8-8 *Sample Results from an ARP Attack*

```
Jul 25 14:28:20.763: %SW_DAI-4-DHCP_SNOOPING_DENY: 1 Invalid ARPs (Req) on Gi1/0/4,
vlan 11.([0200.2222.2222/172.16.2.101/0000.0000.0000/172.16.2.1/09:28:20 EST Thu Jul
25 2019])

SW2# show ip arp inspection statistics

 Vlan       Forwarded         Dropped     DHCP Drops     ACL Drops
 ----       ---------         -------     ----------     ---------
   11              59              17             17             0


 Vlan    DHCP Permits    ACL Permits   Probe Permits   Source MAC Failures
 ----    ------------    -----------   -------------   -------------------
   11               7              0              49                     0


 Vlan   Dest MAC Failures    IP Validation Failures   Invalid Protocol Data
 ----   -----------------    ----------------------   ---------------------
   11                   0                         0                       0
```

The statistics from the **show ip arp inspection** command also confirms that the switch has dropped some ARP messages. The highlighted lines in the middle of the table show 17 total dropped ARP messages in VLAN 11. That same highlighted line confirms that it dropped all 17 because of the DHCP Snooping binding table ("DHCP Drops"), with zero dropped due to an ARP ACL ("ACL Drops").

Limiting DAI Message Rates

Like DHCP Snooping, DAI can also be the focus of a DoS attack with the attacker generating a large number of ARP messages. Like DHCP Snooping, DAI supports the configuration of rate limits to help prevent those attacks, with a reaction to place the port in an err-disabled state, and with the ability to configure automatic recovery from that err-disabled state.

The DHCP Snooping and DAI rate limits do have some small differences in operation, defaults, and in configuration, as follows:

■ DAI defaults to use rate limits for all interfaces (trusted and untrusted), with DHCP Snooping defaulting to not use rate limits.

■ DAI allows the configuration of a burst interval (a number of seconds), so that the rate limit can have logic like "*x* ARP messages over *y* seconds" (DHCP Snooping does not define a burst setting).

It helps to look at DAI and DHCP Snooping rate limit configuration together to make comparisons, so Example 8-9 shows both. The example repeats the exact same DHCP Snooping

8

commands in earlier Example 8-3 but adds the DAI configuration (highlighted). The configuration in Example 8-7 could be added to the configuration shown in Example 8-6 for a complete DHCP Snooping and DAI configuration.

Example 8-9 *Configuring ARP Inspection Message Rate Limits*

```
errdisable recovery cause dhcp-rate-limit
errdisable recovery cause arp-inspection
errdisable recovery interval 30
!
interface GigabitEthernet1/0/2
 ip dhcp snooping limit rate 10
 ip arp inspection limit rate 8
!
interface GigabitEthernet1/0/3
 ip dhcp snooping limit rate 2
 ip arp inspection limit rate 8 burst interval 4
```

Example 8-10 lists output that confirms the configuration settings. For instance, Example 8-9 configures port G1/0/2 with a rate of 8 messages for each (default) burst of 1 second; the output in Example 8-10 for interface G1/0/2 also lists a rate of 8 and burst interval of 1. Similarly, Example 8-9 configures port G1/0/3 with a rate of 8 over a burst of 4 seconds, with Example 8-10 confirming those same values for port G1/0/3. Note that the other two interfaces in Example 8-10 show the default settings of a rate of 15 messages over a one-second burst.

Example 8-10 *Confirming ARP Inspection Rate Limits*

```
SW2# show ip arp inspection interfaces
 Interface        Trust State      Rate (pps)    Burst Interval
 ---------------  -----------      ----------    --------------
 Gi1/0/1          Untrusted               15                 1
 Gi1/0/2          Trusted                  8                 1
 Gi1/0/3          Untrusted                8                 4
 Gi1/0/4          Untrusted               15                 1
! Lines omitted for brevity
```

Configuring Optional DAI Message Checks

As mentioned in the section titled "Dynamic ARP Inspection Logic," DAI always checks the ARP message's origin MAC and origin IP address fields versus some table in the switch, but it can also perform other checks. Those checks require more CPU, but they also help prevent other types of attacks.

Example 8-11 shows how to configure those three additional checks. Note that you can configure one, two, or all three of the options: just configure the **ip arp inspection validate** command again with all the options you want in one command, and it replaces the previous global configuration command. The example shows the three options, with the **src-mac** (source mac) option configured.

Example 8-11 *Confirming ARP Inspection Rate Limits*

```
SW2# configure terminal
Enter configuration commands, one per line.  End with CNTL/Z.

SW2(config)# ip arp inspection validate ?
  dst-mac  Validate destination MAC address
  ip       Validate IP addresses
  src-mac  Validate source MAC address

SW2(config)# ip arp inspection validate src-mac
SW2(config)# ^Z
SW2#
SW2# show ip arp inspection

Source Mac Validation      : Enabled
Destination Mac Validation : Disabled
IP Address Validation      : Disabled
```

IP ARP Inspection Configuration Summary

The following configuration checklist summarizes the commands included in this section about how to configure Dynamic IP ARP Inspection:

Step 1.   Use the **ip arp inspection vlan** *vlan-list* global command to enable Dynamic ARP Inspection (DAI) on the switch for the specified VLANs.

Step 2.   Separate from the DAI configuration, also configure DHCP Snooping and/or ARP ACLs for use by DAI.

Step 3.   Configure the **ip arp inspection trust** interface subcommand to override the default setting of not trusted.

Step 4.   (Optional): Configure DAI rate limits and err-disabled recovery:

    Step A.   (Optional): Configure the **ip arp inspection limit rate** *number* [**burst interval** *seconds*] interface subcommand to set a limit of ARP messages per second, or ARP messages for each configured interval.

    Step B.   (Optional): Configure the **ip arp inspection limit rate none** interface subcommand to disable rate limits.

    Step C.   (Optional): Configure the **errdisable recovery cause arp-inspection** global command to enable the feature of automatic recovery from err-disabled mode, assuming the switch placed the port in err-disabled state because of exceeding DAI rate limits.

    Step D.   (Optional): Configure the **errdisable recovery interval** *seconds* global commands to set the time to wait before recovering from an interface err-disabled state (regardless of the cause of the err-disabled state).

Step 5.   (Optional): Configure the **ip arp inspection validate** {[**dst-mac**] [**src-mac**] [**ip**]} global command to add DAI validation steps.

8

Chapter Review

One key to doing well on the exams is to perform repetitive spaced review sessions. Review this chapter's material using either the tools in the book or interactive tools for the same material found on the book's companion website. Refer to the "Your Study Plan" element for more details. Table 8-2 outlines the key review elements and where you can find them. To better track your study progress, record when you completed these activities in the second column.

Table 8-2 Chapter Review Tracking

Review Element	Review Date(s)	Resource Used
Review key topics		Book, website
Review key terms		Book, website
Answer DIKTA questions		Book, PTP
Review config checklists		Book, website

Review All the Key Topics

Table 8-3 Key Topics for Chapter 8

Key Topic Element	Description	Page Number
Figure 8-4	DHCP filtering actions on trusted and untrusted ports	149
List	DHCP Snooping logic	149
Figure 8-6	DHCP Snooping binding table concept	151
Example 8-1	DHCP Snooping configuration	152
List	DHCP Snooping configuration checklist	155
Figure 8-10	Detail inside ARP messages with origin and target	157
List	Gratuitous ARP details	157
Figure 8-13	Core Dynamic ARP Inspection logic	159
Example 8-6	Dynamic ARP Inspection configuration with associated DHCP Snooping configuration	161
List	Dynamic ARP Inspection checklist	165

Key Terms You Should Know

DHCP Snooping, trusted port, untrusted port, DHCP Snooping binding table, Dynamic ARP Inspection, (ARP) origin IP address, (ARP) origin hardware address, ARP reply, gratuitous ARP

Command References

Tables 8-4 and 8-5 list the configuration and verification commands used in this chapter. As an easy review exercise, cover the left column in a table, read the right column, and try to recall the command without looking. Then repeat the exercise, covering the right column, and try to recall what the command does.

Table 8-4   Chapter 8 Configuration Command Reference

Command	Mode/Purpose/Description
ip dhcp snooping	Global command that enables DHCP Snooping if combined with enabling it on one or more VLANs
ip dhcp snooping vlan *vlan-list*	Global command that lists VLANs on which to enable DHCP Snooping, assuming the **ip dhcp snooping** command is also configured
[no] ip dhcp snooping information option	Command that enables (or disables with **no** option) the feature of inserting DHCP option 82 parameters by the switch when also using DHCP Snooping
[no] ip dhcp snooping trust	Interface subcommand that sets the DHCP Snooping trust state for an interface (default **no**, or untrusted)
ip dhcp snooping limit rate *number*	Interface subcommand that sets a limit to the number of incoming DHCP messages processed on an interface, per second, before DHCP Snooping discards all other incoming DHCP messages in that same second
err-disable recovery cause dhcp-rate-limit	Global command that enables the switch to automatically recover an err-disabled interface if set to that state because of exceeding a DHCP rate limit setting
err-disable recovery interval *seconds*	Global command that sets the number of seconds IOS waits before recovering any err-disabled interfaces which, per various configuration settings, should be recovered automatically
err-disable recovery cause arp-inspection	Global command that enables the switch to automatically recover an err-disabled interface if set to that state because of an ARP Inspection violation

Table 8-5   Chapter 8 EXEC Command Reference

Command	Purpose
show ip dhcp snooping	Lists a large variety of DHCP Snooping configuration settings
show ip dhcp snooping statistics	Lists counters regarding DHCP Snooping behavior on the switch
show ip dhcp snooping binding	Displays the contents of the dynamically created DHCP Snooping binding table
show ip arp inspection	Lists both configuration settings for Dynamic ARP Inspection (DAI) as well as counters for ARP messages processed and filtered
show ip arp inspection statistics	Lists the subset of the **show ip arp inspection** command output that includes counters

8

Part II Review

Keep track of your part review progress with the checklist shown in Table P2-1. Details on each task follow the table.

Table P2-1 Part II Review Checklist

Activity	1st Date Completed	2nd Date Completed
Repeat All DIKTA Questions		
Answer Part Review Questions		
Review Key Topics		
Do Labs		
Review Videos		

Repeat All DIKTA Questions

For this task, use the PTP software to answer the "Do I Know This Already?" questions again for the chapters in this part of the book.

Answer Part Review Questions

For this task, use PTP to answer the Part Review questions for this part of the book.

Review Key Topics

Review all key topics in all chapters in this part, either by browsing the chapters or by using the Key Topics application on the companion website.

Use Per-Chapter Interactive Review Elements

Using the companion website, browse through the interactive review elements, such as memory tables and key term flashcards, to review the content from each chapter.

Labs

Depending on your chosen lab tool, here are some suggestions for what to do in the lab:

Pearson Network Simulator: If you use the full Pearson CCNA simulator, focus more on the configuration scenario and troubleshooting scenario labs associated with the topics in this part of the book. These types of labs include a larger set of topics and work well as Part Review activities. (See the Introduction for some details about how to find which labs are about topics in this part of the book.)

Blog Config Labs: The author's blog (https://blog.certskills.com) includes a series of configuration-focused labs that you can do on paper, each in 10–15 minutes. Review and perform the labs for this part of the book by using the menus to navigate to the per-chapter content and then finding all config labs related to that chapter. (You can see more detailed instructions at https://blog.certskills.com/config-labs.)

Other: If using other lab tools, here are a few suggestions: make sure to experiment with the variety of configuration topics in this part, including router and switch passwords, switch port security, Dynamic ARP Inspection, and DHCP Snooping.

Watch Videos

Two chapters in this part mention videos included as extra material related to those chapters. Check out the reference in Chapter 4 to a video about using RADIUS protocol, as well as Chapter 6's reference to a video about troubleshooting switch port security.

Part III shifts to a variety of topics that can be found in most every network. None are required for a network to work, but many happen to be useful services. Most happen to use IP or support the IP network in some way, so Part III groups the topics together as IP Services.

Part III begins and ends with chapters that examine a series of smaller topics. First, Chapter 9 examines several IP services for which the CCNA exam requires you to develop configuration and verification skills. Those services include logging and syslog, the Network Time Protocol (NTP), as well as two related services: CDP and LLDP.

Chapter 12, at the end of Part III, closes with another series of smaller topics—although the CCNA 200-301 exam topics require only conceptual knowledge, not configuration skills for these topics. This chapter includes First Hop Redundancy Protocols (FHRPs), Simple Network Management Protocol (SNMP), and two related protocols: TFTP and FTP.

The two middle chapters in Part III also focus on IP-based services, beginning with Chapter 10's examination of Network Address Translation (NAT). Almost every network uses NAT with IPv4, although in many cases, the firewall implements NAT. This chapter shows how to configure and verify NAT in a Cisco router.

Chapter 11 at first may give the appearance of a large chapter about one topic—Quality of Service—and it does focus on QoS; however, QoS by nature includes a wide variety of individual QoS tools. This chapter walks you through the basic concepts of the primary QoS features.

Part III

IP Services

CHAPTER 9

Device Management Protocols

This chapter covers the following exam topics:

2.0 Network Access

2.3 Configure and verify Layer 2 discovery protocols (Cisco Discovery Protocol and LLDP)

4.0 IP Services

4.2 Configure and verify NTP operating in a client and server mode

4.5 Describe the use of syslog features including facilities and levels

This chapter begins Part III with a discussion of the concepts, configuration, and verification of three functions found on Cisco routers and switches. These functions focus more on managing the network devices themselves than on managing the network that devices create.

The first major section of this chapter focuses on log messages and syslog. Most computing devices have a need to notify the administrator of any significant issue; generally, across the world of computing, messages of this type are called log messages. Cisco devices generate log messages as well. The first section shows how a Cisco device handles those messages and how you can configure routers and switches to ignore the messages or save them in different ways.

Next, different router and switch functions benefit from synchronizing their time-of-day clocks. Like most every computing device, routers and switches have an internal clock function to keep time. Network Time Protocol (NTP) provides a means for devices to synchronize their time, as discussed in the second section.

The final major section focuses on two protocols that do the same kinds of work: Cisco Discovery Protocol (CDP) and Link Layer Discovery Protocol (LLDP). Both provide a means for network devices to learn about neighboring devices, without requiring that IPv4 or IPv6 be working at the time.

"Do I Know This Already?" Quiz

Take the quiz (either here or use the PTP software) if you want to use the score to help you decide how much time to spend on this chapter. The letter answers are listed at the bottom of the page following the quiz. Appendix C, found both at the end of the book as well as on the companion website, includes both the answers and explanations. You can also find both answers and explanations in the PTP testing software.

Table 9-1 "Do I Know This Already?" Foundation Topics Section-to-Question Mapping

Foundation Topics Section	Questions
System Message Logging (Syslog)	1–2
Network Time Protocol (NTP)	3–4
Analyzing Topology Using CDP and LLDP	5–6

1. What level of logging to the console is the default for a Cisco device?

   a. Informational

   b. Errors

   c. Warnings

   d. Debugging

2. What command limits the messages sent to a syslog server to levels 4 through 0?

   a. **logging trap 0-4**

   b. **logging trap 0,1,2,3,4**

   c. **logging trap 4**

   d. **logging trap through 4**

3. Which of the following is accurate about the NTP client function on a Cisco router?

   a. The client synchronizes its time-of-day clock based on the NTP server.

   b. It counts CPU cycles of the local router CPU to more accurately keep time.

   c. The client synchronizes its serial line clock rate based on the NTP server.

   d. The client must be connected to the same subnet as an NTP server.

4. The only NTP configuration on router R1 is the **ntp server 10.1.1.1** command. Which answers describe how NTP works on the router?

   a. As an NTP server only

   b. As an NTP client only

   c. As an NTP server only after the NTP client synchronizes with NTP server 10.1.1.1

   d. As an NTP server regardless of whether the NTP client synchronizes with NTP server 10.1.1.1

5. Imagine that a switch connects through an Ethernet cable to a router, and the router's host name is Hannah. Which of the following commands could tell you information about the IOS version on Hannah without establishing a Telnet connection to Hannah? (Choose two answers.)

   a. **show neighbors Hannah**

   b. **show cdp**

   c. **show cdp neighbors**

   d. **show cdp neighbors Hannah**

   e. **show cdp entry Hannah**

   f. **show cdp neighbors detail**

6. A switch is cabled to a router whose host name is Hannah. Which of the following LLDP commands could identify Hannah's enabled capabilities? (Choose two answers.)

   a. show neighbors

   b. show neighbors Hannah

   c. show lldp

   d. show lldp interface

   e. show lldp neighbors

   f. show lldp entry Hannah

Foundation Topics

System Message Logging (Syslog)

It is amazing just how helpful Cisco devices try to be to their administrators. When major (and even not-so-major) events take place, these Cisco devices attempt to notify administrators with detailed system messages. As you learn in this section, these messages vary from the very mundane to those that are incredibly important. Thankfully, administrators have a large variety of options for storing these messages and being alerted to those that could have the largest impact on the network infrastructure.

When an event happens that the device's OS thinks is interesting, how does the OS notify us humans? Cisco IOS can send the messages to anyone currently logged in to the device. It can also store the message so that a user can later look at the messages. The next few pages examine both topics.

> **NOTE** The CCNA 200-301 exam topics list one exam topic about logging and syslog: "Describe the use of syslog features including facilities and levels." This exam topic does not require you to understand the related configuration. However, the configuration reveals many of the core concepts, so this section includes the configuration details as a means to help you understand how logging and syslog work.

Sending Messages in Real Time to Current Users

Cisco IOS running on a device at least tries to allow current users to see log messages when they happen. Not every router or switch may have users connected, but if some user is logged in, the router or switch benefits by making the network engineer aware of any issues.

By default, IOS shows log messages to console users for all severity levels of messages. That default happens because of the default **logging console** global configuration command. In fact, if you have been using a console port throughout your time reading this book, you likely have already noticed many syslog messages, like messages about interfaces coming up or going down.

For other users (that is, Telnet and SSH users), the device requires a two-step process before the user sees the messages. First, IOS has another global configuration setting—**logging monitor**—that tells IOS to enable the sending of log messages to all logged users. However, that default configuration is not enough to allow the user to see the log messages. The user must also issue the **terminal monitor** EXEC command during the login session, which tells IOS that this terminal session would like to receive log messages.

Figure 9-1 summarizes these key points about how IOS on a Cisco router or switch processes log messages for currently connected users. In the figure, user A sits at the console and always receives log messages. On the right, the fact that user B sees messages (because user B issued the **terminal monitor** command after login), and user C does not, shows that each user can control whether or not she receives log messages.

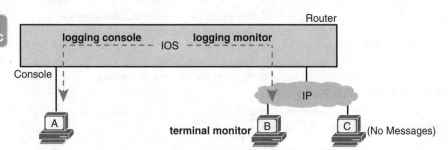

Figure 9-1 *IOS Processing for Log Messages to Current Users*

Storing Log Messages for Later Review

With logging to the console and to terminals, an event happens, IOS sends the messages to the console and terminal sessions, and then IOS can discard the message. However, clearly, it would be useful to keep a copy of the log messages for later review, so IOS provides two primary means to keep a copy.

IOS can store copies of the log messages in RAM by virtue of the **logging buffered** global configuration command. Then any user can come back later and see the old log messages by using the **show logging** EXEC command.

As a second option—an option used frequently in production networks—all devices store their log messages centrally to a syslog server. RFC 5424 defines the syslog protocol, which provides the means by which a device like a switch or router can use a UDP protocol to send messages to a syslog server for storage. All devices can send their log messages to the server. Later, a user can connect to the server (typically with a graphical user interface) and browse the log messages from various devices. To configure a router or switch to send log messages to a syslog server, add the **logging host** {*address* | *hostname*} global command, referencing the IP address or host name of the syslog server.

Figure 9-2 shows the ideas behind the buffered logging and syslog logging.

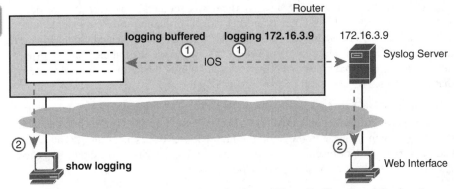

Figure 9-2 *IOS Storing Log Messages for Later View: Buffered and Syslog Server*

Log Message Format

IOS defines the format of log messages. The message begins with some data fields about the message, followed by some text more easily read by humans. For example, take a close look at this sample message:

```
*Dec 18 17:10:15.079: %LINEPROTO-5-UPDOWN: Line protocol on Interface
FastEthernet0/0, changed state to down
```

Notice that by default on this particular device, we see the following:

A timestamp: *Dec 18 17:10:15.079

The facility on the router that generated the message: %LINEPROTO

The severity level: 5

A mnemonic for the message: UPDOWN

The description of the message: Line protocol on Interface FastEthernet0/0, changed state to down

IOS dictates most of the contents of the messages, but you can at least toggle on and off the use of the timestamp (which is included by default) and a log message sequence number (which is not enabled by default). Example 9-1 reverses those defaults by turning off time-stamps and turning on sequence numbers.

Example 9-1 *Disabling Timestamps and Enabling Sequence Numbers in Log Messages*

```
R1(config)# no service timestamps
R1(config)# service sequence-numbers
R1(config)# end
R1#
000011: %SYS-5-CONFIG_I: Configured from console by console
```

To see the change in format, look at the log message at the end of the example. As usual, when you exit configuration mode, the device issues yet another log message. Comparing

---

Answers to the "Do I Know This Already?" quiz:

1 D **2** C **3** A **4** C **5** E, F **6** E, F

this message to the previous example, you can see it now no longer lists the time of day but does list a sequence number.

Log Message Severity Levels

Log messages may just tell you about some mundane event, or they may tell you of some critical event. To help you make sense of the importance of each message, IOS assigns each message a severity level (as noted in the same messages in the preceding page or so). Figure 9-3 shows the severity levels: the lower the number, the more severe the event that caused the message. (Note that the values on the left and center are used in IOS commands.)

Keyword	Numeral	Description	
Emergency	0	System unusable	Severe
Alert	1	Immediate action required	
Critical	2	Critical Event (Highest of 3)	
Error	3	Error Event (Middle of 3)	Impactful
Warning	4	Warning Event (Lowest of 3)	
Notification	5	Normal, More Important	Normal
Informational	6	Normal, Less Important	
Debug	7	Requested by User Debug	Debug

Figure 9-3 *Syslog Message Severity Levels by Keyword and Numeral*

Figure 9-3 breaks the eight severity levels into four sections just to make a little more sense of the meaning. The two top levels in the figure are the most severe. Messages from this level mean a serious and immediate issue exists. The next three levels, called Critical, Error, and Warning, also tell about events that impact the device, but they are not as immediate and severe. For instance, one common log message about an interface failing to a physically down state shows as a severity level 3 message.

Continuing down the figure, IOS uses the next two levels (5 and 6) for messages that are more about notifying the user rather than identifying errors. Finally, the last level in the figure is used for messages requested by the **debug** command, as shown in an example later in this chapter.

Table 9-2 summarizes the configuration commands used to enable logging and to set the severity level for each type. When the severity level is set, IOS will send messages of that severity level and more severe ones (lower severity numbers) to the service identified in the command. For example, the command **logging console 4** causes IOS to send severity level 0–4 messages to the console. Also, note that the command to disable each service is the **no** version of the command, with *no* in front of the command (**no logging console**, **no logging monitor**, and so on).

Table 9-2 How to Configure Logging Message Levels for Each Log Service

Service	To Enable Logging	To Set Message Levels
Console	**logging console**	**logging console** *level-name* | *level-number*
Monitor	**logging monitor**	**logging monitor** *level-name* | *level-number*
Buffered	**logging buffered**	**logging buffered** *level-name* | *level-number*
Syslog	**logging host** *address* | *hostname*	**logging trap** *level-name* | *level-number*

9

Configuring and Verifying System Logging

With the information in Table 9-2, configuring syslog in a Cisco IOS router or switch should be relatively straightforward. Example 9-2 shows a sample, based on Figure 9-4. The figure shows a syslog server at IP address 172.16.3.9. Both switches and both routers will use the same configuration shown in Example 9-2, although the example shows the configuration process on a single device, router R1.

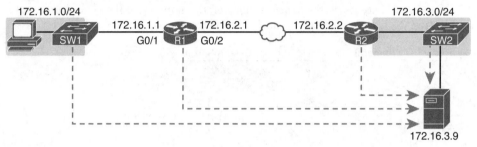

172.16.1.0/24

172.16.1.1
G0/1

172.16.2.1
G0/2

172.16.2.2

172.16.3.0/24

172.16.3.9

Figure 9-4 *Sample Network Used in Logging Examples*

Example 9-2 *Syslog Configuration on R1*

```
logging console 7
logging monitor debug
logging buffered 4
logging host 172.16.3.9
logging trap warning
```

First, note that the example configures the same message level at the console and for terminal monitoring (level 7, or debug), and the same level for both buffered and logging to the syslog server (level 4, or warning). The levels may be set using the numeric severity level or the name as shown earlier in Figure 9-3.

The **show logging** command confirms those same configuration settings and also lists the log messages per the logging buffered configuration. Example 9-3 shows a sample, with the configuration settings to match Example 9-2 highlighted in gray.

Example 9-3 *Viewing the Configured Log Settings per the Earlier Example*

```
R1# show logging
Syslog logging: enabled (0 messages dropped, 3 messages rate-limited, 0 flushes, 0
overruns, xml disabled, filtering disabled)


No Active Message Discriminator.


No Inactive Message Discriminator.

    Console logging: level debugging, 45 messages logged, xml disabled,
                    filtering disabled
    Monitor logging: level debugging, 0 messages logged, xml disabled,
                    filtering disabled
    Buffer logging: level warnings, 0 messages logged, xml disabled,
                    filtering disabled
```

```
    Exception Logging: size (8192 bytes)
    Count and timestamp logging messages: disabled
    Persistent logging: disabled

No active filter modules.

    Trap logging: level warnings, 0 message lines logged
        Logging to 172.16.3.9 (udp port 514, audit disabled,
            link up),
            0 message lines logged,
            0 message lines rate-limited,
            0 message lines dropped-by-MD,
        xml disabled, sequence number disabled
        filtering disabled
    Logging Source-Interface: VRF Name:

Log Buffer (8192 bytes):
```

You might notice by now that knowing the names of all eight log message levels can be handy if you want to understand the output of the commands. Most of the **show** commands list the log message levels by name, not by number. As you can see in the gray highlights in this example, two levels list "debug," and two list "warning," even though some of the configuration commands referred to those levels by number.

Also, you cannot know this from the output, but in Example 9-3, router R1 has no buffered log messages. (Note the counter value of 0 for buffered logging messages.) If any log messages had been buffered, the actual log messages would be listed at the end of the command. In this case, I had just booted the router, and no messages had been buffered yet. (You could also clear out the old messages from the log with the **clear logging** EXEC command.)

The next example shows the difference between the current severity levels. This example shows the user disabling interface G0/1 on R1 with the **shutdown** command and then re-enabling it with the **no shutdown** command. If you look closely at the highlighted messages, you will see several severity 5 messages and one severity 3 message. The **logging buffered 4** global configuration command on R1 (see Example 9-2) means that R1 will not buffer the severity level 5 log messages, but it will buffer the severity level 3 message. Example 9-4 ends by showing that log message at the end of the output of the **show logging** command.

Example 9-4 *Seeing Severity 3 and 5 Messages at the Console, and Severity 3 Only in the Buffer*

```
R1# configure terminal
Enter configuration commands, one per line. End with CNTL/Z.
R1(config)# interface g0/1
R1(config-if)# shutdown
R1(config-if)#
*Oct 21 20:07:07.244: %LINK-5-CHANGED: Interface GigabitEthernet0/1, changed state to
administratively down
*Oct 21 20:07:08.244: %LINEPROTO-5-UPDOWN: Line protocol on Interface GigabitEther-
```

9

```
net0/1, changed state to down
R1(config-if)# no shutdown
R1(config-if)#
*Oct 21 20:07:24.312: %LINK-3-UPDOWN: Interface GigabitEthernet0/1, changed state to
up
*Oct 21 20:07:25.312: %LINEPROTO-5-UPDOWN: Line protocol on Interface GigabitEther-
net0/1, changed state to up
R1(config-if)# ^Z
R1#
*Oct 21 20:07:36.546: %SYS-5-CONFIG_I: Configured from console by console
R1# show logging
! Skipping about 20 lines, the same lines in Example 9-3, until the last few lines


Log Buffer (8192 bytes):


*Oct 21 20:07:24.312: %LINK-3-UPDOWN: Interface GigabitEthernet0/1, changed state to
up
```

The debug Command and Log Messages

Of the eight log message severity levels, one level, debug level (7), has a special purpose: for messages generated as a result of a user logged in to the router or switch who issues a **debug** command.

The **debug** EXEC command gives the network engineer a way to ask IOS to monitor for certain internal events, with that monitoring process continuing over time, so that IOS can issue log messages when those events occur. The engineer can log in, issue the **debug** command, and move on to other work. The user can even log out of the device, and the debug remains enabled. IOS continues to monitor the request in that **debug** command and generate log messages about any related events. The debug remains active until some user issues the **no debug** command with the same parameters, disabling the debug.

> **NOTE** While the **debug** command is just one command, it has a huge number of options, much like the **show** command may be one command, but it also has many, many options.

The best way to see how the **debug** command works, and how it uses log messages, is to see an example. Example 9-5 shows a sample debug of OSPF Hello messages for router R1 in Figure 9-4. The router (R1) enables OSPF on two interfaces and has established one OSPF neighbor relationship with router R2 (RID 2.2.2.2). The debug output shows one log message for the sent Hello, as well as log messages for received Hello messages.

Example 9-5 *Using* debug ip ospf hello *from R1's Console*

```
R1# debug ip ospf hello
OSPF hello debugging is on
R1#
*Aug 10 13:38:19.863: OSPF-1 HELLO Gi0/1: Send hello to 224.0.0.5 area 0 from
172.16.1.1
*Aug 10 13:38:21.199: OSPF-1 HELLO Gi0/2: Rcv hello from 2.2.2.2 area 0 172.16.2.2
```

```
*Aug 10 13:38:22.843: OSPF-1 HELLO Gi0/2: Send hello to 224.0.0.5 area 0 from
172.16.2.1
R1#
```

The console user sees the log messages created on behalf of that **debug** command after the debug command completes. Per the earlier configuration in Example 9-2, R1's **logging console 7** command tells us that the console user will receive severity levels 0–7, which includes level 7 debug messages. Note that with the current settings, these debug messages would not be in the local log message buffer (because of the level in the **logging buffered warning** command), nor would they be sent to the syslog server (because of the level in the **logging trap 4** command).

Note that the console user automatically sees the log messages as shown in Example 9-4. However, as noted in the text describing Figure 9-1, a user who connects to R1 would need to also issue the **terminal monitor** command to see those debug messages. For instance, anyone logged in with SSH at the time Example 9-4's output was gathered would not have seen the output, even with the **logging monitor debug** command configured on router R1, without first issuing a **terminal monitor** command.

Note that all enabled debug options use router CPU, which can cause problems for the router. You can monitor CPU use with the **show process cpu** command, but you should use caution when using **debug** commands carefully on production devices. Also, note the more CLI users that receive debug messages, the more CPU that is consumed. So, some installations choose to not include debug-level log messages for console and terminal logging, requiring users to look at the logging buffer or syslog for those messages, just to reduce router CPU load.

Network Time Protocol (NTP)

Each networking device has some concept of a date and a time-of-day clock. For instance, the log messages discussed in the first major section of this chapter had a timestamp with the date and time of day listed. Now imagine looking at all the log messages from all routers and switches stored at a syslog server. All those messages have a date and timestamp, but how do you make sure the timestamps are consistent? How do you make sure that all devices synchronize their time-of-day clocks so that you can make sense of all the log messages at the syslog server? How could you make sense of the messages for an event that impacted devices in three different time zones?

For example, consider the messages on two routers, R1 and R2, as shown in Example 9-6. Routers R1 and R2 do not synchronize their clocks. A problem keeps happening on the serial link between the two routers. A network engineer looks at all the log messages as stored on the syslog server. However, when the engineer sees some messages from R1, at 13:38:39 (around 1:40 p.m.), he does not think to look for messages from R2 that have a timestamp of around 9:45 a.m.

Example 9-6   *Log Messages from Routers R1 and R2, Compared*

```
*Oct 19 13:38:37.568: %OSPF-5-ADJCHG: Process 1, Nbr 2.2.2.2 on Serial0/0/0 from FULL
to DOWN, Neighbor Down: Interface down or detached
*Oct 19 13:38:40.568: %LINEPROTO-5-UPDOWN: Line protocol on Interface Serial0/0/0,
changed state to down
! These messages happened on router R2
Oct 19 09:44:09.027: %LINK-3-UPDOWN: Interface Serial0/0/1, changed state to down
Oct 19 09:44:09.027: %OSPF-5-ADJCHG: Process 1, Nbr 1.1.1.1 on Serial0/0/1 from FULL
to DOWN, Neighbor Down: Interface down or detached
```

In reality, the messages in both parts of Example 9-6 happened within 0.5 seconds of each other because I issued a **shutdown** command on one of the routers. However, the two routers' time-of-day clocks were not synchronized, which makes the messages on the two routers look unrelated. With synchronized clocks, the two routers would have listed practically identical timestamps of almost the exact same time when these messages occurred, making it much easier to read and correlate messages.

Routers, switches, other networking devices, and pretty much every device known in the IT world has a time-of-day clock. For a variety of reasons, it makes sense to synchronize those clocks so that all devices have the same time of day, other than differences in time zone. The Network Time Protocol (NTP) provides the means to do just that.

NTP gives any device a way to synchronize their time-of-day clocks. NTP provides protocol messages that devices use to learn the timestamp of other devices. Devices send timestamps to each other with NTP messages, continually exchanging messages, with one device changing its clock to match the other, eventually synchronizing the clocks. As a result, actions that benefit from synchronized timing, like the timestamps on log messages, work much better.

This section works through a progression of topics that leads to the more common types of NTP configurations seen in real networks. The section begins with basic settings, like the timezone and initial configured time on a router or switch, followed by basic NTP configuration. The text then examines some NTP internals regarding how NTP defines the sources of time data (reference clocks) and how good each time source is (stratum). The section closes with more configuration that explains typical enterprise configurations, with multiple **ntp** commands for redundancy and the use of loopback interfaces for high availability.

Setting the Time and Timezone

NTP's job is to synchronize clocks, but NTP works best if you set the device clock to a reasonably close time before enabling the NTP client function with the **ntp server** command. For instance, my wristwatch says 8:52 p.m. right now. Before starting NTP on a new router or switch so that it synchronizes with another device, I should set the time to 8:52 p.m., set the correct date and timezone, and even tell the device to adjust for daylight savings time—and then enable NTP. Setting the time correctly gives NTP a good start toward synchronizing.

Example 9-7 shows how to set the date, time, timezone, and daylight savings time. Oddly, it uses two configuration commands (for the timezone and daylight savings time) and one EXEC command to set the date and time on the router.

Example 9-7 *Setting the Date/Time with* clock set, *Plus Timezone/DST*

```
R1# configure terminal
Enter configuration commands, one per line. End with CNTL/Z.
R1(config)# clock timezone EST -5
R1(config)# clock summer-time EDT recurring
R1(config)# ^Z
R1#
R1# clock set 20:52:49 21 October 2015
*Oct 21 20:52:49.000: %SYS-6-CLOCKUPDATE: System clock has been updated from 00:36:38
UTC Thu Oct 22 2015 to 20:52:49 UTC Wed Oct 21 2015, configured from console by
```

```
console.
R1# show clock
20:52:55.051 EDT Wed Oct 21 2015
```

Focus on the two configuration commands first. You should set the first two commands before setting the time of day with the **clock set** EXEC command because the two configuration commands impact the time that is set. In the first command, the **clock timezone** part defines the command and a keyword. The next parameter, "EST" in this case, is any value you choose, but choose the name of the timezone of the device. This value shows up in **show** commands, so although you make up the value, the value needs to be meaningful to all. I chose EST, the acronym for US Eastern Standard Time. The "-5" parameter means that this device is 5 hours behind Universal Time Coordinated (UTC).

The **clock summer-time** part of the second command defines what to do, again with the "EDT" being a field in which you could have used any value. However, you should use a meaningful value. This is the value shown with the time in **show** commands when daylight savings time is in effect, so I chose EDT because it is the acronym for daylight savings time in that same EST time zone. Finally, the **recurring** keyword tells the router to spring forward an hour and fall back an hour automatically over the years.

The **clock set** EXEC command then sets the time, day of the month, month, and year. However, note that IOS interprets the time as typed in the command in the context of the time zone and daylight savings time. In the example, the **clock set** command lists a time of 20:52:49 (the command uses a time syntax with a 24-hour format, not with a 12-hour format plus a.m./p.m.). As a result of that time plus the two earlier configuration commands, the **show clock** command (issued seconds later) lists that time, but also notes the time as EDT, rather than UTC time.

Basic NTP Configuration

With NTP, servers supply information about the time of day to clients, and clients react by adjusting their clocks to match. The process requires repeated small adjustments over time to maintain that synchronization. The configuration itself can be simple, or it can be extensive once you add security configuration and redundancy.

Cisco supplies two **ntp** configuration commands that dictate how NTP works on a router or switch, as follows:

- **ntp master** {*stratum-level*}: NTP server mode—the device acts only as an NTP server, and not as an NTP client. The device gets its time information from the internal clock on the device.

- **ntp server** {*address* | *hostname*}: NTP client/server mode—the device acts as both client and server. First, it acts as an NTP client, to synchronize time with a server. Once synchronized, the device can then act as an NTP server, to supply time to other NTP clients.

For an example showing the basic configuration syntax and **show** commands, consider Figure 9-5. With this simple configuration:

- R3 acts as an NTP server only.
- R2 acts in client/server mode—first as an NTP client to synchronize time with NTP server R3, then as a server to supply time to NTP client R1.

9

■ R1 acts in client/server mode—first as an NTP client to synchronize time with NTP server R2. (R1 will be willing to act as a server, but no devices happen to reference R1 as an NTP server in this example.)

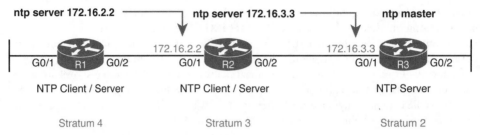

Figure 9-5 *R1 as NTP Client, R2 as Client/Server, R3 as Server*

As you can see, NTP requires little configuration to make it work with a single configuration command on each device. Example 9-8 collects the configuration from the devices shown in the figure for easy reference.

Example 9-8 *NTP Client/Server Configuration*

```
! Configuration on R1:
ntp server 172.16.2.2
! Configuration on R2:
ntp server 172.16.3.3
! Configuration on R3:
ntp master 2
```

Example 9-9 lists the output from the **show ntp status** command on R1, with the first line of output including a few important status items. First, it lists a status of synchronized, which confirms the NTP client has completed the process of changing its time to match the server's time. Any router acting as an NTP client will list "unsynchronized" in that first line until the NTP synchronization process completes with at least one server. It also confirms the IP address of the server—this device's *reference clock*—with the IP address configured in Example 9-8 (172.16.2.2).

Example 9-9 *Verifying NTP Client Status on R1*

```
R1# show ntp status
Clock is synchronized, stratum 4, reference is 172.16.2.2
nominal freq is 250.0000 Hz, actual freq is 250.0000 Hz, precision is 2**21
ntp uptime is 1553800 (1/100 of seconds), resolution is 4000
reference time is DA5E7147.56CADEA7 (19:54:31.339 EST Thu Feb 4 2016)
clock offset is 0.0986 msec, root delay is 2.46 msec
root dispersion is 22.19 msec, peer dispersion is 5.33 msec
loopfilter state is 'CTRL' (Normal Controlled Loop), drift is 0.000000009 s/s
system poll interval is 64, last update was 530 sec ago.
```

Next, look at the **show ntp associations** command output from both R1 and R2 as shown in Example 9-10. This command lists all the NTP servers that the local device can attempt to use, with status information about the association between the local device (client) and the various NTP servers. Beginning with R1, note that it has one association (that is, relationship with an NTP server), based on the one **ntp server 172.16.2.2** configuration command on R1. The * means that R1 has successfully contacted the server. You will see similar data from the same command output taken from router R2.

Example 9-10   *Verifying NTP Client Status on R1 and R2*

```
R1# show ntp associations
! This output is taken from router R1, acting in client/server mode
   address     ref clock      st  when poll  reach  delay  offset  disp
*~172.16.2.2  172.16.3.3      3   50   64    377    1.223  0.090   4.469
 * sys.peer, # selected, + candidate, - outlyer, x falseticker, ~ configured
```

```
R2# show ntp associations
! This output is taken from router R2, acting in client/server mode
   address     ref clock      st  when poll  reach  delay  offset  disp
*~172.16.3.3  127.127.1.1     2   49   64    377    1.220  -7.758  3.695
 * sys.peer, # selected, + candidate, - outlyer, x falseticker, ~ configured
```

NTP Reference Clock and Stratum

NTP servers must learn the time from some device. For devices acting in NTP client/server mode, the device uses the NTP client function to learn the time. However, devices that act solely as an NTP server get their time from either internal device hardware or from some external clock using mechanisms other than NTP.

For instance, when configured with the **ntp master** command, a Cisco router/switch uses its internal device hardware to determine the time. All computers, networking devices included, need some means to keep time for a myriad of reasons, so they include both hardware components and software processes to keep time even over periods in which the device loses power.

Additionally, NTP servers and clients use a number to show the perceived accuracy of their reference clock data based on stratum level. The lower the stratum level, the more accurate the reference clock is considered to be. An NTP server that uses its internal hardware or external reference clock sets its own stratum level. Then, an NTP client adds 1 to the stratum level it learns from its NTP server, so that the stratum level increases the more hops away from the original clock source.

For instance, back in Figure 9-5, you can see the NTP primary server (R3) with a stratum of 2. R2, which references R3, adds 1 so it has a stratum of 3. R1 uses R2 as its NTP server, so R1 adds 1 to have a stratum of 4. These increasing stratum levels allow devices to refer to several NTP servers and then use time information from the best NTP server, best being the server with the lowest stratum level.

Routers and switches use the default stratum level of 8 for their internal reference clock based on the default setting of 8 for the stratum level in the **ntp master** [*stratum-level*] command. The command allows you to set a value from 1 through 15; in Example 9-8, the **ntp master 2** command set router R3's stratum level to 2.

9

> **NOTE** NTP considers 15 to be the highest useful stratum level, so any devices that calculate their stratum as 16 consider the time data unusable and do not trust the time. So, avoid setting higher stratum values on the **ntp master** command.

To see the evidence, refer back to Example 9-10, which shows two commands based on the same configuration in Example 9-8 and Figure 9-5. The output highlights details about reference clocks and stratum levels, as follows:

R1: Per the configured **ntp server 172.16.2.2** command, the **show** command lists the same address (which is router R2's address). The ref clock (reference clock) and st (stratum) fields represent R2's reference clock as 172.16.3.3—in other words, R2's NTP server, which is R3 in this case. The st field value of 3 shows R2's stratum.

R2: Per the configured **ntp server 172.16.3.3** command, the **show** command lists 172,16,3,3, which is an address on router R3. The output notes R3's ref clock as 127.127.1.1—an indication that the server (R3) gets its clock internally. It lists R3's st (stratum) value of 2—consistent with the configured **ntp master 2** command on R3 (per Example 9-8).

On the NTP primary server itself (R3 in this case), the output has more markers indicating the use of the internal clock. Example 9-11 shows output from R3, with a reference clock of the 127.127.1.1 loopback address, used to refer to the fact that this router gets its clock data internally. Also, in the **show ntp associations** command output at the bottom, note that same address, along with a reference clock value of ".LOCL." In effect, R3, per the **ntp master** configuration command, has an association with its internal clock.

Example 9-11 *Examining NTP Server, Reference Clock, and Stratum Data*

```
R3# show ntp status
Clock is synchronized, stratum 2, reference is 127.127.1.1
nominal freq is 250.0000 Hz, actual freq is 250.0000 Hz, precision is 2**20
ntp uptime is 595300 (1/100 of seconds), resolution is 4000
reference time is E0F9174C.87277EBB (16:13:32.527 daylight Sat Aug 10 2019)
clock offset is 0.0000 msec, root delay is 0.00 msec
root dispersion is 0.33 msec, peer dispersion is 0.23 msec
loopfilter state is 'CTRL' (Normal Controlled Loop), drift is 0.000000000 s/s
system poll interval is 16, last update was 8 sec ago.


R3# show ntp associations
  address          ref clock       st   when   poll reach  delay  offset    disp
*~127.127.1.1      .LOCL.           1     15     16   377  0.000   0.000   0.232
 * sys.peer, # selected, + candidate, - outlyer, x falseticker, ~ configured
```

Redundant NTP Configuration

Instead of using a networking device as the reference clock for the enterprise, you can instead reference better time sources in the Internet or purchase a purpose-built NTP server that has better clocking hardware. For instance, an enterprise could use NTP to reference NTP servers that use an atomic clock as their reference source, like the NTP primary servers in Figure 9-6, which happen to be run by the US National Institute of Standards and Technology (NIST) (see tf.nist.gov).

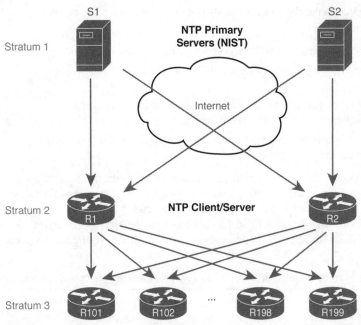

Figure 9-6 *Stratum Levels When Using an Internet-based Stratum 1 NTP Server*

> **NOTE**   While the common terms *NTP server mode* and *NTP client/server mode* are use-
> ful, the NTP RFCs (1305 and 5905) also use two other specific terms for similar ideas: *NTP
> primary server* and *NTP secondary server*. An NTP primary server acts only as a server,
> with a reference clock external to the device, and has a stratum level of 1, like the two NTP
> primary servers shown in Figure 9-6. NTP secondary servers are servers that use client/server
> mode as described throughout this section, relying on synchronization with some other
> NTP server.

For good design, the enterprise NTP configuration ought to refer to at least two external
NTP servers for redundancy. Additionally, just a few enterprise devices should refer to
those external NTP servers and then act as both NTP client and server. The majority of the
devices in the enterprise, like those shown at the bottom of the figure, would act as NTP
clients. Example 9-12 shows the configuration on router R1 and R2 in the figure to accomplish this design.

Example 9-12 *NTP Configuration on R1, R2 per Figure 9-6*

```
ntp server time-a-b-nist.gov
ntp server time-a-g.nist.gov
```

In addition to referencing redundant NTP primary servers, some routers in the enterprise
need to be ready to supply clock data if those NTP primary servers become unreachable.
An exposure exists with the configuration in Example 9-12 because if router R1 and R2 no
longer hear NTP messages from the NTP servers in the Internet they will lose their only reference clock. After losing their reference clock, R1 and R2 could no longer be useful NTP
servers to the rest of the enterprise.

To overcome this potential issue, the routers can also be configured with the **ntp master** command, resulting in this logic:

1. Establish an association with the NTP servers per the **ntp server** command.

2. Establish an association with your internal clock using the **ntp master** *stratum* command.

3. Set the stratum level of the internal clock (per the **ntp master** {*stratum-level*} command) to a higher (worse) stratum level than the Internet-based NTP servers.

4. Synchronize with the best (lowest) known time source, which will be one of the Internet NTP servers in this scenario

The logic has a few steps, but the configuration itself is simple, as shown in Example 9-13. Compared to Example 9-12, just add the **ntp master** command. The NTP servers used in this example have a stratum level of 1, so the use of the **ntp master 7** command, with a much higher stratum, will cause routers R1 and R2 to use one of the NIST NTP servers when available and use the internal clock source only when connectivity to the NIST servers is lost.

Example 9-13 *NTP Configuration on R1 and R2 to Protect Against Internet Failures*

```
ntp server time-a-b-nist.gov
ntp server time-a-g.nist.gov
ntp master 7
```

NTP Using a Loopback Interface for Better Availability

An NTP server will accept NTP messages arriving to any of its IPv4 addresses by default. However, the clients reference a specific IP address on the NTP server. That creates an availability issue.

For instance, consider the topology in Figure 9-7, with router R4 on the right acting as NTP server and the other routers acting as clients. R4 has three IP addresses that the clients could put in their **ntp server** *address* commands. Now consider what happens when one interface on R4 fails, but only one. No matter which of the three interfaces fails, that IP address on that interface cannot be used to send and receive packets. In that case, for any NTP clients that had referred to that specific IP address

■ There would likely still be a route to reach R4 itself.

■ The NTP client would not be able to send packets to the configured address because that interface is down.

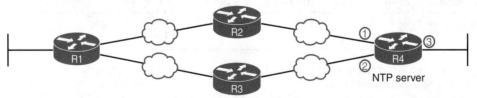

Figure 9-7 *The Availability Issue of Referencing an NTP Server's Physical Interface IP Address*

What is needed is a way to send a packet to R4, a way that is not tied to the state of any one interface. That is, as long as there is some path to send packets to R4 itself, allow NTP to keep working. The goal is to avoid the case in which a single interface failure on router R4 also causes NTP to fail.

Cisco uses the router loopback interface to meet that exact need. Loopback interfaces are virtual interfaces internal to Cisco IOS, created via the command **interface loopback** *number*, where the number is an integer. Once configured, that loopback interface exists inside that router and is not tied to any physical interface. A loopback interface can be assigned an IP address, routing protocols can advertise about the subnet, and you can ping/ traceroute to that address. It acts like other physical interfaces in many ways, but once configured, it remains in an up/up state as long as

- The router remains up.
- You do not issue a **shutdown** command on that loopback interface.

> **NOTE**   This discussion is not about the special IPv4 loopback address 127.0.0.1. The loop-back interface discussed in this section is a different concept altogether.

Example 9-14 shows the small configuration change that adds the loopback interface to the NTP configuration, which is based on Figure 9-5. In this case, the Example 9-14 configu-ration slightly changes the configuration shown earlier in Example 9-8. R1, still acting as client, now points to R2's new loopback interface IP address of 172.16.9.9. R2 now has con-figuration for a new loopback interface (loopback 0). R2 also has a command that tells it to use that loopback 0 interface's IP address as the source address when sending NTP packets.

Example 9-14   *NTP Client/Server Configuration on R1 and R2 Using a Loopback Interface*

```
! Configuration on R1, a client
ntp server 172.16.9.9
! Configuration on R2 for its server function
interface loopback 0
   ip address 172.16.9.9 255.255.255.0
!
ntp master 4
ntp source loopback 0
! Verification on router R2
R2# show interfaces loopback 0
Loopback0 is up, line protocol is up
   Hardware is Loopback
     Internet address is 172.16.9.9/24
! lines omitted for brevity
```

Loopback interfaces have a wide range of uses across IOS features. They are mentioned here with NTP because NTP is a feature that can benefit from using loopback interfaces. (As a reminder, OSPF happens to use loopback interfaces with OSPF configuration for a completely different purpose.)

Analyzing Topology Using CDP and LLDP

The first two major sections of this chapter showed two features—syslog and NTP—that work the same way on both routers and switches. This final section shows yet another feature common to both routers and switches, with two similar protocols: the Cisco Discovery Protocol (CDP) and the Link Layer Discovery Protocol (LLDP). This section focuses on CDP, followed by LLDP.

Examining Information Learned by CDP

CDP discovers basic information about neighboring routers and switches without needing to know the passwords for the neighboring devices. To discover information, routers and switches send CDP messages out each of their interfaces. The messages essentially announce information about the device that sent the CDP message. Devices that support CDP learn information about others by listening for the advertisements sent by other devices.

CDP discovers several useful details from the neighboring Cisco devices:

- **Device identifier:** Typically the host name
- **Address list:** Network and data-link addresses
- **Port identifier:** The interface on the remote router or switch on the other end of the link that sent the CDP advertisement
- **Capabilities list:** Information on what type of device it is (for example, a router or a switch)
- **Platform:** The model and OS level running on the device

CDP plays two general roles: to provide information to the devices to support some function and to provide information to the network engineers that manage the devices. For example, Cisco IP Phones use CDP to learn the data and voice VLAN IDs as configured on the access switch. For that second role, CDP has **show** commands that list information about neighboring devices, as well as information about how CDP is working. Table 9-3 describes the three **show** commands that list the most important CDP information.

Table 9-3 show cdp Commands That List Information About Neighbors

Command	Description
show cdp neighbors [*type number*]	Lists one summary line of information about each neighbor or just the neighbor found on a specific interface if an interface was listed
show cdp neighbors detail	Lists one large set (approximately 15 lines) of information, one set for every neighbor
show cdp entry *name*	Lists the same information as the **show cdp neighbors detail** command, but only for the named neighbor (case sensitive)

> **NOTE** Cisco routers and switches support the same CDP commands, with the same parameters and same types of output.

The next example shows the power of the information in CDP commands. The example uses the network shown in Figure 9-8, with Example 9-15 listing the output of several **show cdp** commands.

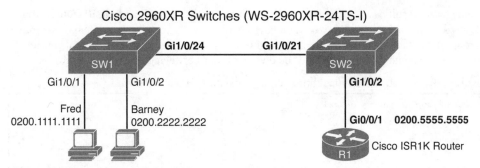

Figure 9-8 *Small Network Used in CDP Examples*

Example 9-15 show cdp neighbors *Command Examples: SW2*

```
SW2# show cdp neighbors
Capability Codes: R - Router, T - Trans Bridge, B - Source Route Bridge
                  S - Switch, H - Host, I - IGMP, r - Repeater, P - Phone,
                  D - Remote, C - CVTA, M - Two-port Mac Relay


Device ID          Local Intrfce      Holdtme    Capability  Platform  Port ID
SW1                Gig 1/0/21         155                S I  WS-C2960X Gig 1/0/24
R1                 Gig 1/0/2          131              R S I  C1111-8P  Gig 0/0/1


Total cdp entries displayed : 2
```

The **show cdp neighbors** command lists one line per neighbor. (Look for the Device ID column and the list that includes SW1 and R1.) Each of those two lines lists the most important topology information about each neighbor: the neighbor's host name (Device ID), the local device's interface, and the neighboring device's interface (under the Port heading).

Pay close attention to the local device's interface and the neighboring device's interface, comparing the example to the figure. For example, SW2's **show cdp neighbors** command lists an entry for SW1, with SW2's local interface of Gi1/0/21 and SW1's interface of Gi1/0/24 under the heading "Port ID."

This command also lists the platform, identifying the specific model of the neighboring router or switch. So, even using this basic information, you could either construct a figure like Figure 9-8 or confirm that the details in the figure are correct.

Figure 9-8 and Example 9-15 provide a good backdrop as to why devices learn about direct neighbors with CDP, but not other neighbors. First, CDP defines encapsulation that uses the data-link header, but no IP header. To ensure all devices receive a CDP message, the Ethernet header uses a multicast destination MAC address (0100.0CCC.CCCC). However, when any device that supports CDP receives a CP message, the device processes the message and then discards it, rather than forwarding it. So, for instance, when router R1 sends a CDP message to Ethernet multicast address 0100.0CCC.CCCC, switch SW2 receives it, processes it, but does not forward it to switch SW1—so SW1 will not list router R1 as a CDP neighbor.

Next, consider the **show cdp neighbors detail** command as shown in Example 9-16, again taken from switch SW2. This command lists more detail, as you might have guessed. The detail lists the full name of the switch model (WS-2960XR-24TS-I) and the IP address configured on the neighboring device. You have to look closely, but the example has one long group of messages for each of the two neighbors; the example includes one comment line with gray highlight to help you find the dividing point between groups of messages.

Example 9-16 show cdp neighbors detail *Command on SW2*

```
SW2# show cdp neighbors detail
-------------------------
Device ID: SW1
Entry address(es):
  IP address: 1.1.1.1
Platform: cisco WS-C2960XR-24TS-I,  Capabilities: Switch IGMP
Interface: GigabitEthernet1/0/21,  Port ID (outgoing port): GigabitEthernet1/0/24
Holdtime : 144 sec

Version :
Cisco IOS Software, C2960X Software (C2960X-UNIVERSALK9-M), Version 15.2(6)E2, RELEASE
SOFTWARE (fc4)
Technical Support: http://www.cisco.com/techsupport
Copyright (c) 1986-2018 by Cisco Systems, Inc.
Compiled Thu 13-Sep-18 03:43 by prod_rel_team

advertisement version: 2
Protocol Hello:  OUI=0x00000C, Protocol ID=0x0112; payload len=27, value=00000000FFFFF
FFF0102250100000000000BCC4938BA180FF0000
VTP Management Domain: 'fred'
Native VLAN: 1
Duplex: full
Management address(es):
  IP address: 1.1.1.1

-------------------------
Device ID: R1
Entry address(es):
  IP address: 10.12.25.5
Platform: cisco C1111-8P,  Capabilities: Router Switch IGMP
Interface: GigabitEthernet1/0/2,  Port ID (outgoing port): GigabitEthernet0/0/1
Holdtime : 151 sec

Version :
Cisco IOS Software [Fuji], ISR Software (ARMV8EB_LINUX_IOSD-UNIVERSALK9_IAS-M), Ver-
sion 16.8.1, RELEASE SOFTWARE (fc3)
Technical Support: http://www.cisco.com/techsupport
Copyright (c) 1986-2018 by Cisco Systems, Inc.
Compiled Tue 27-Mar-18 10:56 by mcpre

advertisement version: 2
```

```
VTP Management Domain: ''
Duplex: full
Management address(es):
  IP address: 10.12.25.5

Total cdp entries displayed : 2
```

NOTE The **show cdp entry** *name* command lists the exact same details shown in the output of the **show cdp neighbors detail** command, but for only the one neighbor listed in the command.

As you can see, you can sit on one device and discover a lot of information about a neighboring device—a fact that actually creates a security exposure. Cisco recommends that CDP be disabled on any interface that might not have a need for CDP. For switches, any switch port connected to another switch, a router, or to an IP phone should use CDP.

Finally, note that CDP shows information about directly connected neighbors. For instance, **show cdp neighbors** on SW1 would list an entry for SW2 in this case, but not R1, because R1 is not directly connected to SW1.

Configuring and Verifying CDP

Most of the work you do with CDP relates to what CDP can tell you with **show** commands. However, it is an IOS feature, so you can configure CDP and use some **show** commands to examine the status of CDP itself.

IOS typically enables CDP globally and on each interface by default. You can then disable CDP per interface with the **no cdp enable** interface subcommand and later re-enable it with the **cdp enable** interface subcommand. To disable and re-enable CDP globally on the device, use the **no cdp run** and **cdp run** global commands, respectively.

To examine the status of CDP itself, use the commands in Table 9-4.

Table 9-4 Commands Used to Verify CDP Operations

Command	Description
show cdp	States whether CDP is enabled globally and lists the default update and holdtime timers
show cdp interface [*type number*]	States whether CDP is enabled on each interface, or a single interface if the interface is listed, and states update and holdtime timers on those interfaces
show cdp traffic	Lists global statistics for the number of CDP advertisements sent and received

Example 9-17 lists sample output from each of the commands in Table 9-4, based on switch SW2 in Figure 9-8.

9

Example 9-17 show cdp *Commands That Show CDP Status*

```
SW2# show cdp
Global CDP information:
        Sending CDP packets every 60 seconds
        Sending a holdtime value of 180 seconds
        Sending CDPv2 advertisements is enabled


SW2# show cdp interface GigabitEthernet1/0/2
GigabitEthernet1/0/2 is up, line protocol is up
  Encapsulation ARPA
  Sending CDP packets every 60 seconds
  Holdtime is 180 seconds


SW2# show cdp traffic
CDP counters :
        Total packets output: 304, Input: 305
        Hdr syntax: 0, Chksum error: 0, Encaps failed: 0
        No memory: 0, Invalid packet: 0,
        CDP version 1 advertisements output: 0, Input: 0
        CDP version 2 advertisements output: 304, Input: 305
```

The first two commands in the example list two related settings about how CDP works: the send time and the hold time. CDP sends messages every 60 seconds by default, with a hold time of 180 seconds. The hold time tells the device how long to wait after no longer hearing from a device before removing those details from the CDP tables. You can override the defaults with the **cdp timer** *seconds* and **cdp holdtime** *seconds* global commands, respectively.

Examining Information Learned by LLDP

Cisco created the Cisco-proprietary CDP before any standard existed for a similar protocol. CDP has many benefits. As a Layer 2 protocol, sitting on top of Ethernet, it does not rely on a working Layer 3 protocol. It provides device information that can be useful in a variety of ways. Cisco had a need but did not see a standard that met the need, so Cisco made up a protocol, as has been the case many times over history with many companies and protocols.

Link Layer Discovery Protocol (LLDP), defined in IEEE standard 802.1AB, provides a standardized protocol that provides the same general features as CDP. LLDP has similar configuration and practically identical **show** commands as compared with CDP.

The LLDP examples all use the same topology used in the CDP examples per Figure 9-8 (the same figure used in the CDP examples). Example 9-18 lists switch SW2's LLDP neighbors as learned after LLDP was enabled on all devices and ports in that figure. The example highlights the items that match the similar output from the **show cdp neighbors** command listed at the end of the example, also from switch SW2.

Example 9-18 show lldp neighbors *on SW2 with Similarities to CDP Highlighted*

```
SW2# show lldp neighbors
Capability codes:
    (R) Router, (B) Bridge, (T) Telephone, (C) DOCSIS Cable Device
    (W) WLAN Access Point, (P) Repeater, (S) Station, (O) Other

Device ID           Local Intf     Hold-time  Capability     Port ID
R1                  Gi1/0/2        120        R              Gi0/0/1
SW1                 Gi1/0/21       120        B              Gi1/0/24


Total entries displayed: 2


SW2# show cdp neighbors
Capability Codes: R - Router, T - Trans Bridge, B - Source Route Bridge
                  S - Switch, H - Host, I - IGMP, r - Repeater, P - Phone,
                  D - Remote, C - CVTA, M - Two-port Mac Relay


Device ID          Local Intrfce   Holdtme   Capability  Platform  Port ID
SW1                Gig 1/0/21      155             S I   WS-C2960X Gig 1/0/24
R1                 Gig 1/0/2       131           R S I   C1111-8P  Gig 0/0/1
Total entries displayed: 2
```

The most important take-away from the output is the consistency between CDP and LLDP in how they refer to the interfaces. Both the **show cdp neighbors** and **show lldp neighbors** commands have "local intf" (interface) and "port ID" columns. These columns refer to the local device's interface and the neighboring device's interface, respectively.

However, the LLDP output in the example does differ from CDP in a few important ways:

- LLDP uses **B** as the capability code for switching, referring to **bridge**, a term for the device type that existed before switches that performed the same basic functions.

- LLDP does not identify IGMP as a capability, while CDP does (**I**).

- CDP lists the neighbor's **platform**, a code that defines the device type, while LLDP does not.

- LLDP lists capabilities with different conventions (see upcoming Example 9-19).

The first three items in the list are relatively straightforward, but that last item in the list requires a closer look with more detail. Interestingly, CDP lists all the capabilities of the neighbor in the **show cdp neighbors** command output, no matter whether the device currently enables all those features. LLDP instead lists the enables (configured) capabilities, rather than all supported capabilities, in the output from **show lldp neighbors** command.

LLDP makes the difference in a neighbor's total capabilities and configured capabilities with the **show lldp neighbors detail** and **show lldp entry** *hostname* commands. These commands provide identical detailed output, with the first command providing detail for all neighbors, and the second providing detail for the single listed neighbor. Example 9-19 shows the detail for neighbor R1.

Example 9-19 show lldp entry r2 *Command on SW2*

```
SW2# show lldp entry R1


Capability codes:
    (R) Router, (B) Bridge, (T) Telephone, (C) DOCSIS Cable Device
    (W) WLAN Access Point, (P) Repeater, (S) Station, (O) Other
------------------------------------------------
Local Intf: Gi1/0/2
Chassis id: 70ea.1a9a.d300
Port id: Gi0/0/1
Port Description: GigabitEthernet0/0/1
System Name: R1

System Description:
Cisco IOS Software [Fuji], ISR Software (ARMV8EB_LINUX_IOSD-UNIVERSALK9_IAS-M),
Version 16.8.1, RELEASE SOFTWARE (fc3)
Technical Support: http://www.cisco.com/techsupport
Copyright (c) 1986-2018 by Cisco Systems, Inc.
Compiled Tue 27-Mar-18 10:56 by mcpre
Time remaining: 100 seconds
System Capabilities: B,R
Enabled Capabilities: R
Management Addresses:
    IP: 10.12.25.5
Auto Negotiation - not supported
Physical media capabilities - not advertised
Media Attachment Unit type - not advertised
Vlan ID: - not advertised


Total entries displayed: 1
```

First, regarding the device capabilities, note that the LLDP command output lists two lines about the neighbor's capabilities:

System Capabilities: What the device can do

Enabled Capabilities: What the device does now with its current configuration

For instance, in Example 9-19, the neighboring R1 claims the ability to perform routing and switching (codes **R** and **B**) but also claims to currently be using only its routing capability, as noted in the "enabled capabilities" line.

Also, take a moment to look at the output for the similarities to CDP. For instance, this output lists detail for neighbor, R1, which uses its local port G0/0/1, with a host name of R1. The output also notes the IOS name and version, from which an experienced person can infer the model number, but there is no explicit mention of the model.

> **NOTE**   LLDP uses the same messaging concepts as CDP, encapsulating messages directly in data-link headers. Devices do not forward LLDP messages so that LLDP learns only of directly connected neighbors. LLDP does use a different multicast MAC address (0180. C200.000E).

Configuring and Verifying LLDP

LLDP uses a similar configuration model as CDP, but with a few key differences. First, Cisco devices default to disable LLDP. Additionally, LLDP separates the sending and receiving of LLDP messages as separate functions. For instance, LLDP support processing receives LLDP messages on an interface so that the switch or router learns about the neighboring device while not transmitting LLDP messages to the neighboring device. To support that model, the commands include options to toggle on|off the transmission of LLDP messages separately from the processing of received messages.

The three LLDP configuration commands are as follows:

- **[no] lldp run:** A global configuration command that sets the default mode of LLDP operation for any interface that does not have more specific LLDP subcommands (**lldp transmit, lldp receive**). The **lldp run** global command enables LLDP in both directions on those interfaces, while **no lldp run** disables LLDP.

- **[no] lldp transmit:** An interface subcommand that defines the operation of LLDP on the interface regardless of the global **[no] lldp run** command. The **lldp transmit** interface subcommand causes the device to transmit LLDP messages, while **no lldp transmit** causes it to not transmit LLDP messages.

- **[no] lldp receive:** An interface subcommand that defines the operation of LLDP on the interface regardless of the global **[no] lldp run** command. The **lldp receive** interface subcommand causes the device to process received LLDP messages, while **no lldp receive** causes it to not process received LLDP messages.

For example, consider a switch that has no LLDP configuration commands at all. Example 9-20 adds a configuration that first enables LLDP for all interfaces (in both directions) with the **lldp run** global command. It then shows how to disable LLDP in both directions on Gi1/0/17 and how to disable LLDP in one direction on Gi1/0/18.

Example 9-20   *Enabling LLDP on All Ports, Disabling on a Few Ports*

```
lldp run
!
interface gigabitEthernet1/0/17
 no lldp transmit
 no lldp receive
!
interface gigabitEthernet1/0/18
 no lldp receive
```

Example 9-21 adds another example that again begins with a switch with all default settings. In this case, the configuration does not enable LLDP for all interfaces with the **lldp run** command, meaning that all interfaces default to not transmit and not receive LLDP messages. The example does show how to then enable LLDP for both directions on one interface and in one direction for a second interface.

Example 9-21 *Enabling LLDP on Limited Ports, Leaving Disabled on Most*

```
interface gigabitEthernet1/0/19
 lldp transmit
 lldp receive
!
interface gigabitEthernet1/0/20
 lldp receive
```

Finally, checking LLDP status uses the exact same commands as CDP as listed in Table 9-4, other than the fact that you use the **lldp** keyword instead of **cdp**. For instance, **show lldp interface** lists the interfaces on which LLDP is enabled. Example 9-22 shows some examples from switch SW2 based on earlier Figure 9-8 (the same figure used in the CDP examples), with LLDP enabled in both directions on all interfaces with the **cdp run** global command.

Example 9-22 show lldp *Commands That Show LLDP Status*

```
SW2# show lldp
Global LLDP Information:
    Status: ACTIVE
    LLDP advertisements are sent every 30 seconds
    LLDP hold time advertised is 120 seconds
    LLDP interface reinitialisation delay is 2 seconds

SW2# show lldp interface g1/0/2

GigabitEthernet1/0/2:
    Tx: enabled
    Rx: enabled
    Tx state: IDLE
    Rx state: WAIT FOR FRAME

SW2# show lldp traffic

LLDP traffic statistics:
    Total frames out: 259
    Total entries aged: 0
    Total frames in: 257
    Total frames received in error: 0
    Total frames discarded: 0
    Total TLVs discarded: 0
    Total TLVs unrecognized: 0
```

Also, note that like CDP, LLDP uses a send timer and hold timer for the same purposes as CDP. The example shows the default settings of 30 seconds for the send timer and 120 seconds for the hold timer. You can override the defaults with the **lldp timer** *seconds* and **lldp holdtime** *seconds* global commands, respectively.

Chapter Review

One key to doing well on the exams is to perform repetitive spaced review sessions. Review this chapter's material using either the tools in the book or interactive tools for the same material found on the book's companion website. Refer to the "Your Study Plan" element for more details. Table 9-5 outlines the key review elements and where you can find them. To better track your study progress, record when you completed these activities in the second column.

Table 9-5 Chapter Review Tracking

Review Element	Review Date(s)	Resource Used
Review key topics		Book, website
Review key terms		Book, website
Answer DIKTA questions		Book, PTP
Review memory tables		Book, app
Do labs		Blog
Review command references		Book

Review All the Key Topics

Table 9-6 Key Topics for Chapter 9

Key Topic Element	Description	Page Number
Figure 9-1	Logging to console and terminal	175
Figure 9-2	Logging to syslog and buffer	176
Figure 9-3	Log message levels	177
Table 9-2	Logging configuration commands	177
List	The **ntp master** and **ntp server** commands	183
List	Sequence for NTP client to choose a reference clock	188
List	Key facts about loopback interfaces	189
List	Information gathered by CDP	190
Table 9-3	Three CDP **show** commands that list information about neighbors	190
List	Differences between LLDP and CDP	195
List	LLDP configuration commands and logic	197

Key Terms You Should Know

log message, syslog server, Network Time Protocol (NTP), NTP client, NTP client/server mode, NTP server, NTP synchronization, CDP, LLDP

Command References

Tables 9-7 and 9-8 list configuration and verification commands used in this chapter. As an easy review exercise, cover the left column in a table, read the right column, and try to recall the command without looking. Then repeat the exercise, covering the right column, and try to recall what the command does.

Table 9-7 Configuration Command Reference

Command	Description
[no] logging console	Global command that enables (or disables with the **no** option) logging to the console device.
[no] logging monitor	Global command that enables (or disables with the **no** option) logging to users connected to the device with SSH or Telnet.
[no] logging buffered	Global command that enables (or disables with the **no** option) logging to an internal buffer.
logging [host] *ip-address* | *hostname*	Global command that enables logging to a syslog server.
logging console *level-name* | *level-number*	Global command that sets the log message level for console log messages.
logging monitor *level-name* | *level-number*	Global command that sets the log message level for log messages sent to SSH and Telnet users.
logging buffered *level-name* | *level-number*	Global command that sets the log message level for buffered log messages displayed later by the **show logging** command.
logging trap *level-name* | *level-number*	Global command that sets the log message level for messages sent to syslog servers.
[no] service sequence-numbers	Global command to enable or disable (with the **no** option) the use of sequence numbers in log messages.
clock timezone *name* *+-number*	Global command that names a timezone and defines the +/– offset versus UTC.
clock summertime *name* recurring	Global command that names a daylight savings time for a timezone and tells IOS to adjust the clock automatically.
ntp server *address* | *hostname*	Global command that configures the device as an NTP client by referring to the address or name of an NTP server.
ntp master *stratum-level*	Global command that configures the device as an NTP server and assigns its local clock stratum level.
ntp source *name/number*	Global command that tells NTP to use the listed interface (by name/number) for the source IP address for NTP messages.
interface loopback *number*	Global command that, at first use, creates a loopback interface. At all uses, it also moves the user into interface configuration mode for that interface.
[no] cdp run	Global command that enables and disables (with the **no** option) CDP for the entire switch or router.
[no] cdp enable	Interface subcommand to enable and disable (with the **no** option) CDP for a particular interface.
cdp timer *seconds*	Global command that changes the CDP send timer (the frequency at which CDP sends messages).
cdp holdtime *seconds*	Global command that changes how long CDP waits since the last received message from a neighbor before believing the neighbor has failed, removing the neighbor's information from the CDP table.

Command	Description
[no] lldp run	Global command to enable and disable (with the **no** option) LLDP for the entire switch or router.
[no] lldp transmit	Interface subcommand to enable and disable (with the **no** option) the transmission of LLDP messages on the interface.
[no] lldp receive	Interface subcommand to enable and disable (with the **no** option) the processing of received LLDP messages on the interface.
lldp timer *seconds*	Global command that changes the LLDP send timer (the frequency at which LLDP sends messages).
lldp holdtime *seconds*	Global command that changes how long LLDP waits since the last received message from a neighbor before believing the neighbor has failed, removing the neighbor's information from the LLDP table.

Table 9-8   Chapter 9 EXEC Command Reference

Command	Description
show logging	Lists the current logging configuration and lists buffered log messages at the end
terminal monitor terminal no monitor	For a user (SSH or Telnet) session, toggles on (**terminal monitor**) or off (**terminal no monitor**) the receipt of log messages, for that one session, if **logging monitor** is also configured
[no] debug {*various*}	EXEC command to enable or disable (with the **no** option) one of a multitude of debug options
show clock	Lists the time-of-day and the date per the local device
show ntp associations	Shows all NTP clients and servers with which the local device is attempting to synchronize with NTP
show ntp status	Shows current NTP client status in detail
show interfaces loopback *number*	Shows the current status of the listed loopback interface
show cdp | lldp neighbors [*type number*]	Lists one summary line of information about each neighbor; optionally, lists neighbors off the listed interface
show cdp | lldp neighbors detail	Lists one large set of information (approximately 15 lines) for every neighbor
show cdp | lldp entry *name*	Displays the same information as **show cdp|lldp neighbors detail** but only for the named neighbor
show cdp | lldp	States whether CDP or LLDP is enabled globally and lists the default update and holdtime timers
show cdp | lldp interface [*type number*]	States whether CDP or LDP is enabled on each interface or a single interface if the interface is listed
show cdp | lldp traffic	Displays global statistics for the number of CDP or LDP advertisements sent and received

9

CHAPTER 10

Network Address Translation

This chapter covers the following exam topics:

4.0 IP Services

4.1 Configure and verify inside source NAT using static and pools

This chapter examines a very popular and very important part of both enterprise and small office/home office (SOHO) networks: Network Address Translation, or NAT. NAT helped solve a big problem with IPv4: the IPv4 address space would have been completely consumed by the mid-1990s. After it was consumed, the Internet could not continue to grow, which would have significantly slowed the development of the Internet.

This chapter breaks the topics into three major sections. The first section explains the challenges to the IPv4 address space caused by the Internet revolution of the 1990s. The second section explains the basic concept behind NAT, how several variations of NAT work, and how the Port Address Translation (PAT) option conserves the IPv4 address space. The final section shows how to configure NAT from the Cisco IOS Software command-line interface (CLI) and how to troubleshoot NAT.

"Do I Know This Already?" Quiz

Take the quiz (either here or use the PTP software) if you want to use the score to help you decide how much time to spend on this chapter. The letter answers are listed at the bottom of the page following the quiz. Appendix C, found both at the end of the book as well as on the companion website, includes both the answers and explanations. You can also find both answers and explanations in the PTP testing software.

Table 10-1 "Do I Know This Already?" Foundation Topics Section-to-Question Mapping

Foundation Topics Section	Questions
Perspectives on IPv4 Address Scalability	1–2
Network Address Translation Concepts	3–4
NAT Configuration and Troubleshooting	5–7

1. Which of the following summarized subnets represent routes that could have been created for CIDR's goal to reduce the size of Internet routing tables?

   a. 10.0.0.0 255.255.255.0

   b. 10.1.0.0 255.255.0.0

   c. 200.1.1.0 255.255.255.0

   d. 200.1.0.0 255.255.0.0

2. Which of the following are not private addresses according to RFC 1918? (Choose two answers.)

    a. 172.31.1.1

    b. 172.33.1.1

    c. 10.255.1.1

    d. 10.1.255.1

    e. 191.168.1.1

3. With static NAT, performing translation for inside addresses only, what causes NAT table entries to be created?

    a. The first packet from the inside network to the outside network

    b. The first packet from the outside network to the inside network

    c. Configuration using the **ip nat inside source** command

    d. Configuration using the **ip nat outside source** command

4. With dynamic NAT, performing translation for inside addresses only, what causes NAT table entries to be created?

    a. The first packet from the inside network to the outside network

    b. The first packet from the outside network to the inside network

    c. Configuration using the **ip nat inside source** command

    d. Configuration using the **ip nat outside source** command

5. NAT has been configured to translate source addresses of packets for the inside part of the network, but only for some hosts as identified by an access control list. Which of the following commands indirectly identifies the hosts?

    a. ip nat inside source list 1 pool barney

    b. ip nat pool barney 200.1.1.1 200.1.1.254 netmask 255.255.255.0

    c. ip nat inside

    d. ip nat inside 200.1.1.1 200.1.1.2

6. Examine the following configuration commands:

```
interface Ethernet0/0
 ip address 10.1.1.1 255.255.255.0
 ip nat inside
interface Serial0/0
 ip address 200.1.1.249 255.255.255.252
ip nat inside source list 1 interface Serial0/0
access-list 1 permit 10.1.1.0 0.0.0.255
```

If the configuration is intended to enable source NAT overload, which of the following commands could be useful to complete the configuration? (Choose two answers.)

a. The **ip nat outside** command

b. The **ip nat pat** command

c. The **overload** keyword

d. The **ip nat pool** command

7. Examine the following **show** command output on a router configured for dynamic NAT:

```
-- Inside Source
access-list 1 pool fred refcount 2288
 pool fred: netmask 255.255.255.240
 start 200.1.1.1 end 200.1.1.7
 type generic, total addresses 7, allocated 7 (100%), misses 965
```

Users are complaining about not being able to reach the Internet. Which of the following is the most likely cause?

a. The problem is not related to NAT, based on the information in the command output.

b. The NAT pool does not have enough entries to satisfy all requests.

c. Standard ACL 1 cannot be used; an extended ACL must be used.

d. The command output does not supply enough information to identify the problem.

Foundation Topics

Perspectives on IPv4 Address Scalability

The original design for the Internet required every organization to ask for, and receive, one or more registered classful IPv4 network numbers. The people administering the program ensured that none of the IP networks were reused. As long as every organization used only IP addresses inside its own registered network numbers, IP addresses would never be duplicated, and IP routing could work well.

Connecting to the Internet using only a registered network number, or several registered network numbers, worked well for a while. In the early to mid-1990s, it became apparent that the Internet was growing so fast that all IP network numbers would be assigned by the mid-1990s! Concern arose that the available networks would be completely assigned, and some organizations would not be able to connect to the Internet.

The main long-term solution to the IPv4 address scalability problem was to increase the size of the IP address. This one fact was the most compelling reason for the advent of IP version 6 (IPv6). (Version 5 was defined much earlier but was never deployed, so the next attempt was labeled as version 6.) IPv6 uses a 128-bit address, instead of the 32-bit address in IPv4. With the same or improved process of assigning unique address ranges to every organization connected to the Internet, IPv6 can easily support every organization and individual on the planet, with the number of IPv6 addresses theoretically reaching above 10^{38}.

Many short-term solutions to the addressing problem were suggested, but three standards worked together to solve the problem. Two of the standards work closely together: Network Address Translation (NAT) and private addressing. These features together allow many organizations to use the same unregistered IPv4 network numbers internally—and still communicate well with the Internet. The third standard, classless interdomain routing (CIDR), allows ISPs to reduce the wasting of IPv4 addresses by assigning a company a subset of a network number rather than the entire network. CIDR also can allow Internet service providers (ISP) to summarize routes such that multiple Class A, B, or C networks match a single route, which helps reduce the size of Internet routing tables.

> **NOTE**   These tools have worked well. Estimates in the early 1990s predicted that the world would run out of IPv4 addresses by the mid-1990s, but IANA did not exhaust the IPv4 address space until February 2011, and ARIN (the RIR for North America) did not exhaust its supply of public IPv4 addresses until September 2015.

CIDR

CIDR is a global address assignment convention that defines how the Internet Assigned Numbers Authority (IANA), its member agencies, and ISPs should assign the globally unique IPv4 address space to individual organizations.

CIDR, defined in RFC 4632, has two main goals. First, CIDR defines a way to assign public IP addresses, worldwide, to allow route aggregation or route summarization. These route summaries greatly reduce the size of routing tables in Internet routers.

Figure 10-1 shows a typical case of CIDR route aggregation and how CIDR could be used to replace more than 65,000 routes with one route. First, imagine that ISP 1 owns Class C networks 198.0.0.0 through 198.255.255.0—not by accident, but by purposeful and thoughtful design to make this route aggregation example possible. In other words, IANA allocated all addresses that begin with 198 to one of the five Regional Internet Registries (RIR), and that RIR assigned this entire range to one big ISP in that part of the world.

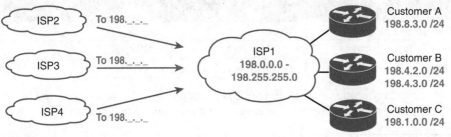

Figure 10-1   *Typical Use of CIDR*

The assignment of all addresses that begin with 198 to one ISP lets other ISPs use one route—a route for 198.0.0.0/8—to match all those addresses, forwarding packets for those addresses to ISP1. Figure 10-1 shows the ISPs on the left each with one route to 198.0.0.0/8—in other words, a route to all hosts whose IP address begins with 198. This one summary route will match packets sent to all addresses in the 65,536 Class C IP networks that begin with 198.

The second major CIDR feature allows RIRs and ISPs to reduce waste by assigning a subset of a classful network to a single customer. For example, imagine that ISP1's customer A needs only 10 IP addresses and that customer C needs 25 IP addresses. ISP1 does something like this:

■ Assign customer A CIDR block 198.8.3.16/28, with 14 assignable addresses (198.8.3.17 to 198.8.3.30).

■ Assign customer B CIDR block 198.8.3.32/27, with 30 assignable addresses (198.8.3.33 to 198.8.3.62).

These *CIDR blocks* act very much like a public IP network; in particular, they give each company a consecutive set of public IPv4 addresses to use. The public address assignment process has much less waste than before as well. In fact, most public address assignments for the last 20 years have been a CIDR block rather than an entire class A, B, or C network.

Private Addressing

Some computers might never be connected to the Internet. These computers' IP addresses could be duplicates of registered IP addresses in the Internet. When designing the IP addressing convention for such a network, an organization could pick and use any network number(s) it wanted, and all would be well. For example, you can buy a few routers, connect them in your office, and configure IP addresses in network 1.0.0.0, and it would work. The IP addresses you use might be duplicates of real IP addresses in the Internet, but if all you want to do is learn on the lab in your office, everything will be fine.

When building a private network that will have no Internet connectivity, you can use IP network numbers called *private internets*, as defined in RFC 1918, "Address Allocation for Private Internets." This RFC defines a set of networks that will never be assigned to any organization as a registered network number. Instead of using someone else's registered network numbers, you can use numbers in a range that are not used by anyone else in the public Internet. Table 10-2 shows the private address space defined by RFC 1918.

Table 10-2 RFC 1918 Private Address Space

Range of IP Addresses	Network(s)	Class of Networks	Number of Networks
10.0.0.0 to 10.255.255.255	10.0.0.0	A	1
172.16.0.0 to 172.31.255.255	172.16.0.0 – 172.31.0.0	B	16
192.168.0.0 to 192.168.255.255	192.168.0.0 – 192.168.255.0	C	256

In other words, any organization can use these network numbers. However, no organization is allowed to advertise these networks using a routing protocol on the Internet.

Answers to the "Do I Know This Already?" quiz:
1 D **2** B, E **3** C **4** A **5** A **6** A, C **7** B

Table 10-3 summarizes these important features that have helped extend the life of IPv4 by decades.

Table 10-3   Three Important Functions That Extended the Life of IPv4

Feature	RFC(s)	Main Benefits
CIDR*	4632	Assign more-specific public IPv4 address blocks to companies than Class A, B, and C networks. Aggregate routes to public IPv4 addresses based on worldwide address allocation plan.
NAT*	3022	Enable approximately 65,000 TCP/UDP sessions to be supported by a single public IPv4 address.
Private Networks	1918	Enable the use of NAT for enterprise Internet connections, with private addresses used inside the enterprise.

*CIDR and NAT may be better known for their original RFCs (1518, 1519 for CIDR; 1631 for NAT).

Network Address Translation Concepts

NAT, defined in RFC 3022, allows a host that does not have a valid, registered, globally unique IP address to communicate with other hosts through the Internet. The hosts might be using private addresses or addresses assigned to another organization. In either case, NAT allows these addresses that are not Internet ready to continue to be used and still allows communication with hosts across the Internet.

NAT achieves its goal by using a valid registered IP address to represent the private address to the rest of the Internet. The NAT function changes the private IP addresses to publicly registered IP addresses inside each IP packet, as shown in Figure 10-2.

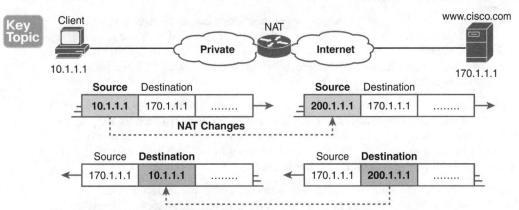

Figure 10-2   *NAT IP Address Swapping: Private Addressing*

Notice that the router, performing NAT, changes the packet's source IP address when the packet leaves the private organization. The router performing NAT also changes the destination address in each packet that is forwarded back into the private network. (Network 200.1.1.0 is a registered network in Figure 10-2.) The NAT feature, configured in the router labeled NAT, performs the translation.

This book discusses *source NAT*, which is the type of NAT that allows enterprises to use private addresses and still communicate with hosts in the Internet. Within source NAT, Cisco IOS supports several different ways to configure NAT. The next few pages cover the concepts behind several of these variations.

Static NAT

Static NAT works just like the example shown in Figure 10-2, but with the IP addresses statically mapped to each other. To help you understand the implications of static NAT and to explain several key terms, Figure 10-3 shows a similar example with more information.

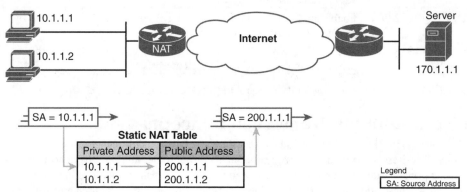

Figure 10-3 *Static NAT Showing Inside Local and Global Addresses*

First, the concepts: The company's ISP has assigned it registered network 200.1.1.0. Therefore, the NAT router must make the private IP addresses look like they are in network 200.1.1.0. To do so, the NAT router changes the source IP addresses in the packets going from left to right in the figure.

In this example, the NAT router changes the source address (SA in the figure) of 10.1.1.1 to 200.1.1.1. With static NAT, the NAT router simply configures a one-to-one mapping between the private address and the registered address that is used on its behalf. The NAT router has statically configured a mapping between private address 10.1.1.1 and public, registered address 200.1.1.1.

Supporting a second IP host with static NAT requires a second static one-to-one mapping using a second IP address in the public address range. For example, to support 10.1.1.2, the router statically maps 10.1.1.2 to 200.1.1.2. Because the enterprise has a single registered Class C network, it can support at most 254 private IP addresses with NAT, with the usual two reserved numbers (the network number and network broadcast address).

The terminology used with NAT, particularly with configuration, can be a little confusing. Notice in Figure 10-3 that the NAT table lists the private IP addresses as "private" and the public, registered addresses from network 200.1.1.0 as "public." Cisco uses the term *inside local* for the private IP addresses in this example and *inside global* for the public IP addresses.

Using NAT terminology, the enterprise network that uses private addresses, and therefore needs NAT, is the "inside" part of the network. The Internet side of the NAT function is the "outside" part of the network. A host that needs NAT (such as 10.1.1.1 in the example) has the IP address it uses inside the network, and it needs an IP address to represent it in the outside network. So, because the host essentially needs two different addresses to represent it, you need two terms. Cisco calls the private IP address used in the inside network the *inside local* address and the address used to represent the host to the rest of the Internet the *inside global* address. Figure 10-4 repeats the same example, with some of the terminology shown.

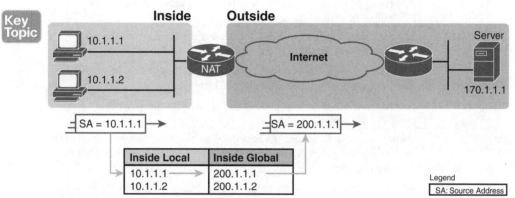

Figure 10-4   *Static NAT Terminology*

Source NAT changes only the IP address of inside hosts. Therefore, the current NAT table shown in Figure 10-4 shows the inside local and corresponding inside global registered addresses. The term *inside local* refers to the address used for the host inside the enterprise, the address used locally versus globally, which means in the enterprise instead of the global Internet. Conversely, the term *inside global* still refers to an address used for the host inside the enterprise, but it is the global address used while the packet flows through the Internet.

Note that the NAT feature called *destination NAT*, not covered in this book, uses similar terms *outside local* and *outside global*. However, with source NAT, one of the terms, *outside global*, is used. This term refers to the host that resides outside the enterprise. Because source NAT does not change that address, the term *outside global* applies at all times.

Table 10-4 summarizes these four similar terms and refers to the IPv4 addresses used as samples in the last three figures as examples.

Table 10-4 NAT Addressing Terms

Term	Values in Figures	Meaning
Inside local	10.1.1.1	**Inside:** Refers to the permanent location of the host, from the enterprise's perspective: it is inside the enterprise.
		Local: Means not global; that is, local. It is the address used for that host while the packet flows in the local enterprise rather than the global Internet.
		Alternative: Think of it as inside private, because this address is typically a private address.
Inside global	200.1.1.1	**Inside:** Refers to the permanent location of the host, from the enterprise's perspective.
		Global: Means global as in the global Internet. It is the address used for that host while the packet flows in the Internet.
		Alternative: Think of it as inside public, because the address is typically a public IPv4 address.
Outside global	170.1.1.1	With source NAT, the one address used by the host that resides outside the enterprise, which NAT does not change, so there is no need for a contrasting term.
		Alternative: Think of it as outside public, because the address is typically a public IPv4 address.
Outside local	—	This term is not used with source NAT. With destination NAT, the address would represent a host that resides outside the enterprise, but the address used to represent that host as packets pass through the local enterprise.

Dynamic NAT

Dynamic NAT has some similarities and differences compared to static NAT. Like static NAT, the NAT router creates a one-to-one mapping between an inside local and inside global address, and changes the IP addresses in packets as they exit and enter the inside network. However, the mapping of an inside local address to an inside global address happens dynamically.

Dynamic NAT sets up a pool of possible inside global addresses and defines matching criteria to determine which inside local IP addresses should be translated with NAT. For example, in Figure 10-5, a pool of five inside global IP addresses has been established: 200.1.1.1 through 200.1.1.5. NAT has also been configured to translate any inside local addresses that start with 10.1.1.

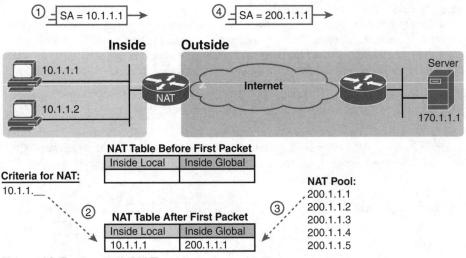

Figure 10-5 *Dynamic NAT*

The numbers 1, 2, 3, and 4 in the figure refer to the following sequence of events:

1. Host 10.1.1.1 sends its first packet to the server at 170.1.1.1.

2. As the packet enters the NAT router, the router applies some matching logic to decide whether the packet should have NAT applied. Because the logic has been configured to match source IP addresses that begin with 10.1.1, the router adds an entry in the NAT table for 10.1.1.1 as an inside local address.

3. The NAT router needs to allocate an IP address from the pool of valid inside global addresses. It picks the first one available (200.1.1.1, in this case) and adds it to the NAT table to complete the entry.

4. The NAT router translates the source IP address and forwards the packet.

The dynamic entry stays in the table as long as traffic flows occasionally. You can configure a timeout value that defines how long the router should wait, having not translated any packets with that address, before removing the dynamic entry. You can also manually clear the dynamic entries from the table using the **clear ip nat translation** * command.

NAT can be configured with more IP addresses in the inside local address list than in the inside global address pool. The router allocates addresses from the pool until all are allocated. If a new packet arrives from yet another inside host, and it needs a NAT entry, but all the pooled IP addresses are in use, the router simply discards the packet. The user must try again until a NAT entry times out, at which point the NAT function works for the next host that sends a packet. Essentially, the inside global pool of addresses needs to be as large as the maximum number of concurrent hosts that need to use the Internet at the same time—unless you use PAT, as is explained in the next section.

Overloading NAT with Port Address Translation

Some networks need to have most, if not all, IP hosts reach the Internet. If that network uses private IP addresses, the NAT router needs a very large set of registered IP addresses. With static NAT, for each private IP host that needs Internet access, you need a publicly registered IP address, completely defeating the goal of reducing the number of public IPv4

10

addresses needed for that organization. Dynamic NAT lessens the problem to some degree, because every single host in an internetwork should seldom need to communicate with the Internet at the same time. However, if a large percentage of the IP hosts in a network will need Internet access throughout that company's normal business hours, NAT still requires a large number of registered IP addresses, again failing to reduce IPv4 address consumption.

The NAT Overload feature, also called Port Address Translation (PAT), solves this problem. Overloading allows NAT to scale to support many clients with only a few public IP addresses.

The key to understanding how overloading works is to recall how hosts use TCP and User Datagram Protocol (UDP) ports. To see why, first consider the idea of three separate TCP connections to a web server, from three different hosts, as shown in Figure 10-6.

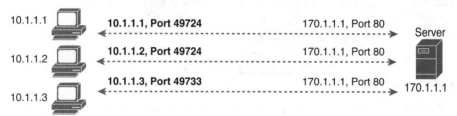

Figure 10-6 *Three TCP Connections from Three PCs*

Next, compare those three TCP connections in Figure 10-6 to three similar TCP connections, now with all three TCP connections from one client, as shown in Figure 10-7. The server does realize a difference because the server sees the IP address and TCP port number used by the clients in both figures. However, the server really does not care whether the TCP connections come from different hosts or the same host; the server just sends and receives data over each connection.

Figure 10-7 *Three TCP Connections from One PC*

NAT takes advantage of the fact that, from a transport layer perspective, the server doesn't care whether it has one connection each to three different hosts or three connections to a single host IP address. NAT overload (PAT) translates not only the address, but the port number when necessary, making what looks like many TCP or UDP flows from different hosts look like the same number of flows from one host. Figure 10-8 outlines the logic.

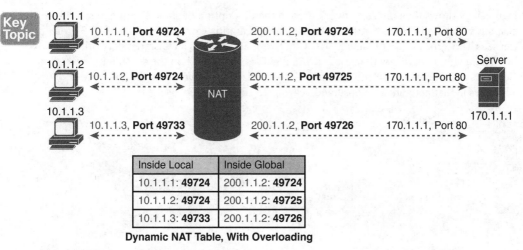

Dynamic NAT Table, With Overloading

Figure 10-8 *NAT Overload (PAT)*

When PAT creates the dynamic mapping, it selects not only an inside global IP address but also a unique port number to use with that address. The NAT router keeps a NAT table entry for every unique combination of inside local IP address and port, with translation to the inside global address and a unique port number associated with the inside global address. And because the port number field has 16 bits, NAT overload can use more than 65,000 port numbers, allowing it to scale well without needing many registered IP addresses—in many cases, needing only one inside global IP address.

Of the three types of NAT covered in this chapter so far, PAT is by far the most popular option. Static NAT and Dynamic NAT both require a one-to-one mapping from the inside local to the inside global address. PAT significantly reduces the number of required registered IP addresses compared to these other NAT alternatives.

NAT Configuration and Troubleshooting

The following sections describe how to configure the three most common variations of NAT: static NAT, dynamic NAT, and PAT, along with the **show** and **debug** commands used to troubleshoot NAT.

Static NAT Configuration

Static NAT configuration requires only a few configuration steps. Each static mapping between a local (private) address and a global (public) address must be configured. In addition, because NAT may be used on a subset of interfaces, the router must be told on which interfaces it should use NAT. Those same interface subcommands tell NAT whether the interface is inside or outside. The specific steps are as follows:

Step 1.   Use the **ip nat inside** command in interface configuration mode to configure interfaces to be in the inside part of the NAT design.

Step 2.   Use the **ip nat outside** command in interface configuration mode to configure interfaces to be in the outside part of the NAT design.

Step 3.   Use the **ip nat inside source static** *inside-local inside-global* command in global configuration mode to configure the static mappings.

Figure 10-9 shows the familiar network used in the description of static NAT earlier in this chapter, which is also used for the first several configuration examples. In Figure 10-9, you can see that Certskills has obtained Class C network 200.1.1.0 as a registered network number. That entire network, with mask 255.255.255.0, is configured on the serial link between Certskills and the Internet. With a point-to-point serial link, only two of the 254 valid IP addresses in that network are consumed, leaving 252 addresses.

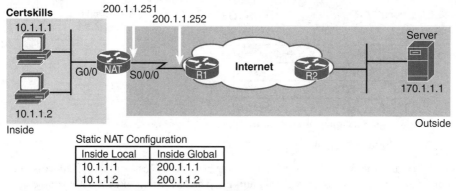

Static NAT Configuration

Inside Local	Inside Global
10.1.1.1	200.1.1.1
10.1.1.2	200.1.1.2

Figure 10-9 *Sample Network for NAT Examples, with Public Class C 200.1.1.0/24*

When planning a NAT configuration, you must find some IP addresses to use as inside global IP addresses. Because these addresses must be part of some registered IP address range, it is common to use the extra addresses in the subnet connecting the enterprise to the Internet—for example, the extra 252 IP addresses in network 200.1.1.0 in this case. The router can also be configured with a loopback interface and assigned an IP address that is part of a globally unique range of registered IP addresses.

Example 10-1 lists the NAT configuration, using 200.1.1.1 and 200.1.1.2 for the two static NAT mappings.

Example 10-1 *Static NAT Configuration*

```
NAT# show running-config
!
! Lines omitted for brevity
!
interface GigabitEthernet0/0
 ip address 10.1.1.3 255.255.255.0
 ip nat inside
!
interface Serial0/0/0
 ip address 200.1.1.251 255.255.255.0
 ip nat outside
!
ip nat inside source static 10.1.1.2 200.1.1.2
ip nat inside source static 10.1.1.1 200.1.1.1

NAT# show ip nat translations
Pro Inside global     Inside local     Outside local      Outside global
```

```
---  200.1.1.1          10.1.1.1          ---                ---
---  200.1.1.2          10.1.1.2          ---                ---

NAT# show ip nat statistics
Total active translations: 2 (2 static, 0 dynamic; 0 extended)
Outside interfaces:
  Serial0/0/0
Inside interfaces:
  GigabitEthernet0/0
Hits: 100 Misses: 0
Expired translations: 0
Dynamic mappings:
```

The static mappings are created using the **ip nat inside source static** command. The **inside** keyword means that NAT translates addresses for hosts on the inside part of the network. The **source** keyword means that NAT translates the source IP address of packets coming into its inside interfaces. The **static** keyword means that the parameters define a static entry, which should never be removed from the NAT table because of timeout. Because the design calls for two hosts—10.1.1.1 and 10.1.1.2—to have Internet access, two **ip nat inside** commands are needed.

After creating the static NAT entries, the router needs to know which interfaces are "inside" and which are "outside." The **ip nat inside** and **ip nat outside** interface subcommands identify each interface appropriately.

A couple of **show** commands list the most important information about NAT. The **show ip nat translations** command lists the two static NAT entries created in the configuration. The **show ip nat statistics** command lists statistics, listing things such as the number of currently active translation table entries. The statistics also include the number of hits, which increments for every packet for which NAT must translate addresses.

Dynamic NAT Configuration

As you might imagine, dynamic NAT configuration differs in some ways from static NAT, but it has some similarities as well. Dynamic NAT still requires that each interface be identified as either an inside or outside interface, and of course static mapping is no longer required. Dynamic NAT uses an access control list (ACL) to identify which inside local (private) IP addresses need to have their addresses translated, and it defines a pool of registered public IP addresses to allocate. The specific steps are as follows:

Step 1.   Use the **ip nat inside** command in interface configuration mode to configure interfaces to be in the inside part of the NAT design (just like with static NAT).

Step 2.   Use the **ip nat outside** command in interface configuration mode to configure interfaces to be in the outside part of the NAT design (just like with static NAT).

Step 3.   Configure an ACL that matches the packets entering inside interfaces for which NAT should be performed.

Step 4.   Use the **ip nat pool** *name first-address last-address* **netmask** *subnet-mask* command in global configuration mode to configure the pool of public registered IP addresses.

10

Step 5. Use the **ip nat inside source list** *acl-number* **pool** *pool-name* command in global configuration mode to enable dynamic NAT. Note the command references the ACL (step 3) and pool (step 4) per previous steps.

The next example shows a sample dynamic NAT configuration using the same network topology as the previous example (see Figure 10-9). In this case, the same two inside local addresses—10.1.1.1 and 10.1.1.2—need translation. However, unlike the previous static NAT example, the configuration in Example 10-2 places the public IP addresses (200.1.1.1 and 200.1.1.2) into a pool of dynamically assignable inside global addresses.

Example 10-2 *Dynamic NAT Configuration*

```
NAT# show running-config
!
! Lines omitted for brevity
!
interface GigabitEthernet0/0
 ip address 10.1.1.3 255.255.255.0
 ip nat inside
!
interface Serial0/0/0
 ip address 200.1.1.251 255.255.255.0
 ip nat outside
!
ip nat pool fred 200.1.1.1 200.1.1.2 netmask 255.255.255.252
ip nat inside source list 1 pool fred
!
access-list 1 permit 10.1.1.2
access-list 1 permit 10.1.1.1
```

Dynamic NAT configures the pool of public (global) addresses with the **ip nat pool** command listing the first and last numbers in an inclusive range of inside global addresses. For example, if the pool needed 10 addresses, the command might have listed 200.1.1.1 and 200.1.1.10, which means that NAT can use 200.1.1.1 through 200.1.1.10.

Dynamic NAT also performs a verification check on the **ip nat pool** command with the required **netmask** parameter. If the address range would not be in the same subnet, assuming the configured **netmask** was used on the addresses in the configured range, then IOS will reject the **ip nat pool** command. For example, as configured with the low end of 200.1.1.1, high end of 200.1.1.2, and a mask of 255.255.255.252, IOS would use the following checks, to ensure that both calculations put 200.1.1.1 and 200.1.1.2 in the same subnet:

- 200.1.1.1 with mask 255.255.255.252 implies subnet 200.1.1.0, broadcast address 200.1.1.3.
- 200.1.1.2 with mask 255.255.255.252 implies subnet 200.1.1.0, broadcast address 200.1.1.3.

If the command had instead showed low and high end values of 200.1.1.1 and 200.1.1.6, again with mask 255.255.255.252, IOS would reject the command. IOS would do the math spelled out in the following list, realizing that the numbers were in different subnets:

- 200.1.1.1 with mask 255.255.255.252 implies subnet 200.1.1.0, broadcast address 200.1.1.3.
- 200.1.1.6 with mask 255.255.255.252 implies subnet 200.1.1.4, broadcast address 200.1.1.7.

One other big difference between the dynamic NAT and static NAT configuration in Example 10-1 has to do with two options in the **ip nat inside source** command. The dynamic NAT version of this command refers to the name of the NAT pool it wants to use for inside global addresses—in this case, fred. It also refers to an IP ACL, which defines the matching logic for inside local IP addresses. So, the logic for the **ip nat inside source list 1 pool fred** command in this example is as follows:

> Create NAT table entries that map between hosts matched by ACL 1, for packets entering any inside interface, allocating an inside global address from the pool called fred.

Dynamic NAT Verification

Examples 10-3 and 10-4 show the evidence that dynamic NAT begins with no NAT table entries, but the router reacts after user traffic correctly drives the NAT function. Example 10-3 shows the output of the **show ip nat translations** and **show ip nat statistics** commands before any users generate traffic that makes NAT do some work. The **show ip nat translations** command, which lists the NAT table entries, lists a blank line; the **show ip nat statistics** command, which shows how many times NAT has created a NAT table entry, shows 0 active translations.

Example 10-3 *Dynamic NAT Verifications Before Generating Traffic*

```
! The next command lists one empty line because no entries have been dynamically
! created yet.
NAT# show ip nat translations

NAT# show ip nat statistics
Total active translations: 0 (0 static, 0 dynamic; 0 extended)
Peak translations: 8, occurred 00:02:44 ago
Outside interfaces:
  Serial0/0/0
Inside interfaces:
  GigabitEthernet0/0
Hits: 0 Misses: 0
CEF Translated packets: 0, CEF Punted packets: 0
Expired translations: 0
Dynamic mappings:
-- Inside Source
[id 1] access-list 1 pool fred refcount 0
 pool fred: netmask 255.255.255.252
    start 200.1.1.1 end 200.1.1.2
    type generic, total addresses 2, allocated 0 (0%), misses 0

Total doors: 0
Appl doors: 0
Normal doors: 0
Queued Packets: 0
```

The **show ip nat statistics** command at the end of the example lists some particularly interesting troubleshooting information with two different counters labeled "misses," as highlighted in the example. The first occurrence of this counter counts the number of times a new packet comes along, needing a NAT entry, and not finding one. At that point, dynamic NAT reacts and builds an entry. The second misses counter toward the end of the command output lists the number of misses in the pool. This counter increments only when dynamic NAT tries to allocate a new NAT table entry and finds no available addresses, so the packet cannot be translated—probably resulting in an end user not getting to the application.

Next, Example 10-4 updates the output of both commands after the user of the host at 10.1.1.1 telnets to host 170.1.1.1.

Example 10-4 *Dynamic NAT Verifications After Generating Traffic*

```
NAT# show ip nat translations
Pro Inside global       Inside local      Outside local       Outside global
--- 200.1.1.1           10.1.1.1          ---                 ---


NAT# show ip nat statistics
Total active translations: 1 (0 static, 1 dynamic; 0 extended)
Peak translations: 11, occurred 00:04:32 ago
Outside interfaces:
  Serial0/0/0
Inside interfaces:
  GigabitEthernet0/0
Hits: 69 Misses: 1
Expired translations: 0
Dynamic mappings:
-- Inside Source
access-list 1 pool fred refcount 1
[eml fred: netmask 255.255.255.252
    start 200.1.1.1 end 200.1.1.2
    type generic, total addresses 2, allocated 1 (50%), misses 0
```

The example begins with host 10.1.1.1 telnetting to 170.1.1.1 (not shown), with the NAT router creating a NAT entry. The NAT table shows a single entry, mapping 10.1.1.1 to 200.1.1.1. And, the first line in the output of the **show ip nat statistics** command lists a counter for 1 active translation, as shown in the NAT table at the top of the example.

Take an extra moment to consider the highlighted line, where the **show ip nat statistics** command lists 1 miss and 69 hits. The first miss counter, now at 1, means that one packet arrived that needed NAT, but there was no NAT table entry. NAT reacted and added a NAT table entry, so the hit counter of 69 means that the next 69 packets used the newly added NAT table entry. The second misses counter, still at 0, did not increment because the NAT pool had enough available inside global IP addresses to use to allocate the new NAT table entry. Also note that the last line lists statistics on the number of pool members allocated (1) and the percentage of the pool currently in use (50%).

The dynamic NAT table entries time out after a period of inactivity, putting those inside global addresses back in the pool for future use. Example 10-5 shows a sequence in which two different hosts make use of inside global address 200.1.1.1. Host 10.1.1.1 uses inside global address 200.1.1.1 at the beginning of the example. Then, instead of just waiting on the NAT entry to time out, the example clears the NAT table entry with the **clear ip nat translation** * command. At that point, the user at 10.1.1.2 telnets to 170.1.1.1, and the new NAT table entry appears, using the same 200.1.1.1 inside global address.

Example 10-5   *Example of Reuse of a Dynamic Inside Global IP Address*

```
! Host 10.1.1.1 currently uses inside global 200.1.1.1
NAT# show ip nat translations
Pro Inside global     Inside local      Outside local      Outside global
--- 200.1.1.1         10.1.1.1          ---                ---
NAT# clear ip nat translation *

!
! telnet from 10.1.1.2 to 170.1.1.1 happened next; not shown
!
! Now host 10.1.1.2 uses inside global 200.1.1.1

NAT# show ip nat translations
Pro Inside global     Inside local      Outside local      Outside global
--- 200.1.1.1         10.1.1.2          ---                ---
!
! Telnet from 10.1.1.1 to 170.1.1.1 happened next; not shown
!
NAT# debug ip nat
IP NAT debugging is on

Oct 20 19:23:03.263: NAT*: s=10.1.1.1->200.1.1.2, d=170.1.1.1 [348]
Oct 20 19:23:03.267: NAT*: s=170.1.1.1, d=200.1.1.2->10.1.1.1 [348]
Oct 20 19:23:03.464: NAT*: s=10.1.1.1->200.1.1.2, d=170.1.1.1 [349]
Oct 20 19:23:03.568: NAT*: s=170.1.1.1, d=200.1.1.2->10.1.1.1 [349]
```

Finally, at the end of Example 10-5, you see that host 10.1.1.1 has telnetted to another host in the Internet, plus the output from the **debug ip nat** command. This **debug** command causes the router to issue a message every time a packet has its address translated for NAT. You generate the output results by entering a few lines from the Telnet connection from 10.1.1.1 to 170.1.1.1. The debug output tells you that host 10.1.1.1 now uses inside global address 200.1.1.2 for this new connection.

NAT Overload (PAT) Configuration

The static and dynamic NAT configurations matter, but the NAT overload (PAT) configuration in this section matters more. This is the feature that saves public IPv4 addresses and prolonged IPv4's life.

NAT overload, as mentioned earlier, allows NAT to support many inside local IP addresses with only one or a few inside global IP addresses. By essentially translating the private IP address and port number to a single inside global address, but with a unique port number, NAT can support many (more than 65,000) private hosts with only a single public, global address.

10

Two variations of PAT configuration exist in IOS. If PAT uses a pool of inside global addresses, the configuration looks exactly like dynamic NAT, except the **ip nat inside source list** global command has an **overload** keyword added to the end. If PAT just needs to use one inside global IP address, the router can use one of its interface IP addresses. Because NAT can support over 65,000 concurrent flows with a single inside global address, a single public IP address can support an entire organization's NAT needs.

The following statement details the configuration difference between NAT overload and 1:1 NAT when using a NAT pool:

Use the same steps for configuring dynamic NAT, as outlined in the previous section, but include the **overload** keyword at the end of the **ip nat inside source list** global command.

The following checklist details the configuration when using an interface IP address as the sole inside global IP address:

Step 1. As with dynamic and static NAT, configure the **ip nat inside** interface subcommand to identify inside interfaces.

Step 2. As with dynamic and static NAT, configure the **ip nat outside** interface subcommand to identify outside interfaces.

Step 3. As with dynamic NAT, configure an ACL that matches the packets entering inside interfaces.

Step 4. Configure the **ip nat inside source list** *acl-number* **interface** *type/number* **overload** global configuration command, referring to the ACL created in step 3 and to the interface whose IP address will be used for translations.

Example 10-2 demonstrated a dynamic NAT configuration. To convert it to a PAT configuration, you would use the **ip nat inside source list 1 pool fred overload** command instead, simply adding the **overload** keyword.

The next example shows PAT configuration using a single interface IP address. Figure 10-10 shows the same familiar network, with a few changes. In this case, the ISP has given Certskills a subset of network 200.1.1.0: CIDR subnet 200.1.1.248/30. In other words, this subnet has two usable addresses: 200.1.1.249 and 200.1.1.250. These addresses are used on either end of the serial link between Certskills and its ISP. The NAT feature on the Certskills router translates all NAT addresses to its serial IP address, 200.1.1.249.

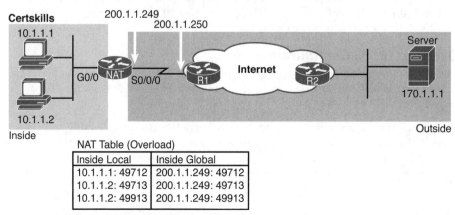

Figure 10-10 *NAT Overload and PAT*

In Example 10-6, which shows the NAT overload configuration, NAT translates using inside global address 200.1.1.249 only, so the NAT pool is not required. In the example, host 10.1.1.2 creates two Telnet connections, and host 10.1.1.1 creates one Telnet connection, causing three dynamic NAT entries, each using inside global address 200.1.1.249, but each with a unique port number.

Example 10-6 *NAT Overload Configuration*

```
NAT# show running-config
!
! Lines Omitted for Brevity
!
interface GigabitEthernet0/0
 ip address 10.1.1.3 255.255.255.0
 ip nat inside
!
interface Serial0/0/0
 ip address 200.1.1.249 255.255.255.252
 ip nat outside
!
ip nat inside source list 1 interface Serial0/0/0 overload
!
access-list 1 permit 10.1.1.2
access-list 1 permit 10.1.1.1
!

NAT# show ip nat translations
Pro  Inside global      Inside local      Outside local      Outside global
tcp  200.1.1.249:49712  10.1.1.1:49712    170.1.1.1:23       170.1.1.1:23
tcp  200.1.1.249:49713  10.1.1.2:49713    170.1.1.1:23       170.1.1.1:23
tcp  200.1.1.249:49913  10.1.1.2:49913    170.1.1.1:23       170.1.1.1:23
NAT# show ip nat statistics
Total active translations: 3 (0 static, 3 dynamic; 3 extended)
Peak translations: 12, occurred 00:01:11 ago
Outside interfaces:
  Serial0/0/0
Inside interfaces:
  GigabitEthernet0/0
Hits: 103 Misses: 3
Expired translations: 0
Dynamic mappings:
-- Inside Source
access-list 1 interface Serial0/0/0 refcount 3
```

The **ip nat inside source list 1 interface serial 0/0/0 overload** command has several parameters, but if you understand the dynamic NAT configuration, the new parameters shouldn't be too hard to grasp. The **list 1** parameter means the same thing as it does for dynamic NAT: inside local IP addresses matching ACL 1 have their addresses translated. The **interface serial 0/0/0** parameter means that the only inside global IP address available is the IP address of the NAT router's interface serial 0/0/0. Finally, the **overload** parameter means that overload is enabled. Without this parameter, the router does not perform overload, just dynamic NAT.

As you can see in the output of the **show ip nat translations** command, three translations have been added to the NAT table. Before this command, host 10.1.1.1 creates one Telnet connection to 170.1.1.1, and host 10.1.1.2 creates two Telnet connections. The router creates one NAT table entry for each unique combination of inside local IP address and port.

NAT Troubleshooting

The majority of NAT troubleshooting issues relate to getting the configuration correct. Source NAT has several configuration options—static, dynamic, PAT—with several configuration commands for each. You should work hard at building skills with the configuration so that you can quickly recognize configuration mistakes. The following troubleshooting checklist summarizes the most common source NAT issues, most of which relate to incorrect configuration.

■ **Reversed inside and outside:** Ensure that the configuration includes the **ip nat inside** and **ip nat outside** interface subcommands and that the commands are not reversed (the **ip nat inside** command on outside interfaces, and vice versa). With source NAT, only the inside interface triggers IOS to add new translations, so designating the correct inside interfaces is particularly important.

■ **Static NAT:** Check the **ip nat inside source static** command to ensure it lists the inside local address first and the inside global IP address second.

■ **Dynamic NAT (ACL):** Ensure that the ACL configured to match packets sent by the inside hosts match that host's packets before any NAT translation has occurred. For example, if an inside local address of 10.1.1.1 should be translated to 200.1.1.1, ensure that the ACL matches source address 10.1.1.1, not 200.1.1.1.

■ **Dynamic NAT (pool):** For dynamic NAT without PAT, ensure that the pool has enough IP addresses. When not using PAT, each inside host consumes one IP address from the pool. A large or growing value in the second misses counter in the **show ip nat statistics** command output can indicate this problem. Also, compare the configured pool to the list of addresses in the NAT translation table (**show ip nat translations**). Finally, if the pool is small, the problem may be that the configuration intended to use PAT and is missing the **overload** keyword (see the next item).

■ **PAT:** It is easy to forget to add the **overload** option on the end of the **ip nat inside source list** command. PAT configuration is identical to a valid dynamic NAT configuration except that PAT requires the **overload** keyword. Without it, dynamic NAT works, but the pool of addresses is typically consumed very quickly. The NAT router will not translate nor forward traffic for hosts if there is not an available pool IP address for their traffic, so some hosts experience an outage.

■ **ACL:** As mentioned in Chapter 3, "Advanced IPv4 Access Control Lists," you can always add a check for ACLs that cause a problem. Perhaps NAT has been configured correctly, but an ACL exists on one of the interfaces, discarding the packets. Note that the order of operations inside the router matters in this case. For packets entering an interface, IOS processes ACLs before NAT. For packets exiting an interface, IOS processes any outbound ACL after translating the addresses with NAT.

- **User traffic required:** NAT reacts to user traffic. If you configure NAT in a lab, NAT does not act to create translations (**show ip nat translations**) until some user traffic enters the NAT router on an inside interface, triggering NAT to do a translation. The NAT configuration can be perfect, but if no inbound traffic occurs that matches the NAT configuration, NAT does nothing.

- **IPv4 routing:** IPv4 routing could prevent packets from arriving on either side of the NAT router. Note that the routing must work for the destination IP addresses used in the packets.

With source NAT, the user sits at some user device like a PC. She attempts to connect to some server, using that server's DNS name. After DNS resolution, the client (the inside host) sends an IP packet with a destination address of the server. For instance, as shown in Figure 10-11, PC1 sends an IP packet with destination IP address 170.1.1.1, some server in the Internet. PC1 is an inside host, the server is an outside host, and 170.1.1.1 is the outside global address. (Note that these addresses match the previous example, which referenced Figure 10-10.)

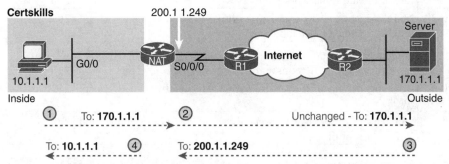

Figure 10-11 *Destination Address Changes on Outside to Inside (Only) with Source NAT*

Note that with source NAT in what should be a familiar design, the destination IP address of the packet does not change during the entire trip. So, troubleshooting of IPv4 routing toward the outside network will be based on the same IP address throughout.

Now look at steps 3 and 4 in the figure, which reminds you that the return packet will first flow to the NAT inside global address (200.1.1.249 in this case) as shown at step 3. Then NAT converts the destination address to 10.1.1.1 in this case. So, to troubleshoot packets flowing right to left in this case, you have to troubleshoot based on two different destination IP addresses.

Chapter Review

One key to doing well on the exams is to perform repetitive spaced review sessions. Review this chapter's material using either the tools in the book or interactive tools for the same material found on the book's companion website. Refer to the "Your Study Plan" element for more details. Table 10-5 outlines the key review elements and where you can find them. To better track your study progress, record when you completed these activities in the second column.

Table 10-5 Chapter Review Tracking

Review Element	Review Date(s)	Resource Used
Review key topics		Book, website
Review key terms		Book, website
Repeat DIKTA questions		Book, PTP
Review memory tables		Book, website
Review command tables		Book
Do labs		Blog

Review All the Key Topics

Table 10-6 Key Topics for Chapter 10

Key Topic Element	Description	Page Number
Table 10-2	List of private IP network numbers	206
Figure 10-2	Main concept of NAT translating private IP addresses into publicly unique global addresses	207
Figure 10-4	Typical NAT network diagram with key NAT terms listed	209
Table 10-4	List of four key NAT terms and their meanings	210
Figure 10-8	Concepts behind address conservation achieved by NAT overload (PAT)	213
Paragraph	Summary of differences between dynamic NAT configuration and PAT using a pool	220

Key Terms You Should Know

CIDR, inside global, inside local, NAT overload, outside global, Port Address Translation, private IP network, source NAT

Command References

Tables 10-7 and 10-8 list configuration and verification commands used in this chapter. As an easy review exercise, cover the left column in a table, read the right column, and try to recall the command without looking. Then repeat the exercise, covering the right column, and try to recall what the command does.

Table 10-7   Chapter 10 Configuration Command Reference

Command	Description
ip nat {inside	outside}	Interface subcommand to enable NAT and identify whether the interface is in the inside or outside of the network
ip nat inside source {list {*access-list-number*	*access-list-name*}} {interface *type number*	pool *pool-name*} [overload]	Global command that enables NAT globally, referencing the ACL that defines which source addresses to NAT, and the interface or pool from which to find global addresses
ip nat pool *name start-ip end-ip* {netmask *netmask*	prefix-length *prefix-length*}	Global command to define a pool of NAT addresses
ip nat inside source *inside-local inside-global*	Global command that lists the inside and outside address (or, an outside interface whose IP address should be used) to be paired and added to the NAT translation table

Table 10-8   Chapter 10 EXEC Command Reference

Command	Description
show ip nat statistics	Lists counters for packets and NAT table entries, as well as basic configuration information
show ip nat translations [verbose]	Displays the NAT table
clear ip nat translation {*	[inside *global-ip local-ip*] [outside *local-ip global-ip*]}	Clears all or some of the dynamic entries in the NAT table, depending on which parameters are used
clear ip nat translation *protocol* inside *global-ip global-port local-ip local-port* [outside *local-ip global-ip*]	Clears some of the dynamic entries in the NAT table, depending on which parameters are used
debug ip nat	Issues a log message describing each packet whose IP address is translated with NAT

10

CHAPTER 11

Quality of Service (QoS)

This chapter covers the following exam topics:

4.0 IP Services

4.7 Explain the forwarding per-hop behavior (PHB) for QoS such as classification, marking, queuing, congestion, policing, shaping

Quality of Service (QoS) refers to tools that network devices can use to manage several related characteristics of what happens to a packet while it flows through a network. Specifically, these tools manage the bandwidth made available to that type of packet, the delay the packet experiences, the jitter (variation in delay) between successive packets in the same flow, and the percentage of packet loss for packets of each class. These tools balance the trade-offs of which types of traffic receive network resources and when, giving more preference to some traffic and less preference to others.

QoS tools define actions a device can apply to a message between the time it enters the device until it exits the device. QoS defines these actions as *per-hop behaviors* (PHBs), which is a formal term to refer to actions other than storing and forwarding a message. These actions can delay the message, discard it, or even change header fields. The device can choose different PHBs for different kinds of messages, improving the QoS behavior for some messages, while worsening the QoS behavior for others.

This chapter works through the QoS tools listed in the single QoS exam topic: "Explain the forwarding per-hop behavior (PHB) for QoS such as classification, marking, queuing, congestion, policing, shaping." Each topic emphasizes the problems each tool solves and how each tool manages bandwidth, delay, jitter, and loss.

"Do I Know This Already?" Quiz

Take the quiz (either here or use the PTP software) if you want to use the score to help you decide how much time to spend on this chapter. The letter answers are listed at the bottom of the page following the quiz. Appendix C, found both at the end of the book as well as on the companion website, includes both the answers and explanations. You can also find both answers and explanations in the PTP testing software.

Table 11-1 "Do I Know This Already?" Foundation Topics Section-to-Question Mapping

Foundation Topics Section	Questions
Introduction to QoS	1
Classification and Marking	2, 3
Queuing	4
Shaping and Policing	5
Congestion Avoidance	6

1. Which of the following attributes do QoS tools manage? (Choose three answers.)
    a. Bandwidth
    b. Delay
    c. Load
    d. MTU
    e. Loss

2. Which of the following QoS marking fields could remain with a packet while being sent through four different routers, over different LAN and WAN links? (Choose two answers.)
    a. CoS
    b. IPP
    c. DSCP
    d. MPLS EXP

3. Which of the following are available methods of classifying packets in DiffServ on Cisco routers? (Choose three answers.)
    a. Matching the IP DSCP field
    b. Matching the 802.1p CoS field
    c. Matching fields with an extended IP ACL
    d. Matching the SNMP Location variable

4. Which of the following behaviors are applied to a low latency queue in a Cisco router or switch? (Choose two answers.)
    a. Shaping
    b. Policing
    c. Priority scheduling
    d. Round-robin scheduling

5. Think about a policing function that is currently working, and also think about a shaping function that is also currently working. That is, the current bit rate of traffic exceeds the respective policing and shaping rates. Which statements are true about these features? (Choose two answers.)
    a. The policer may or may not be discarding packets.
    b. The policer is definitely discarding packets.
    c. The shaper may or may not be queuing packets to slow down the sending rate.
    d. The shaper is definitely queuing packets to slow down the sending rate.

6. A queuing system has three queues serviced with round-robin scheduling and one low latency queue that holds all voice traffic. Round-robin queue 1 holds predominantly UDP traffic, while round-robin queues 2 and 3 hold predominantly TCP traffic. The packets in each queue happen to have a variety of DSCP markings per the QoS design. In which queues would it make sense to use a congestion avoidance (drop management) tool? (Choose two answers.)

   a. The LLQ
   b. Queue 1
   c. Queue 2
   d. Queue 3

Foundation Topics

Introduction to QoS

Routers typically sit at the WAN edge, with both WAN interfaces and LAN interfaces. Those LAN interfaces typically run at much faster speeds, while the WAN interfaces run at slower speeds. While that slower WAN interface is busy sending the packets waiting in the router, hundreds or even thousands more IP packets could arrive in the LAN interfaces, all needing to be forwarded out that same WAN interface. What should the router do? Send them all, in the same order in which they arrived? Prioritize the packets, to send some earlier than others, preferring one type of traffic over another? Discard some of the packets when the number of packets waiting to exit the router gets too large?

That first paragraph described some of the many classic Quality of Service (QoS) questions in networking. QoS refers to the tools that networking devices use to apply some different treatment to packets in the network as they pass through the device. For instance, the WAN edge router would queue packets waiting for the WAN interface to be available. The router could also use a queue scheduling algorithm to determine which packets should be sent next, using some other order than the arrival order—giving some packets better service and some worse service.

QoS: Managing Bandwidth, Delay, Jitter, and Loss

Cisco offers a wide range of QoS tools on both routers and switches. All these tools give you the means to manage four characteristics of network traffic:

- Bandwidth
- Delay
- Jitter
- Loss

Bandwidth refers to the speed of a link, in bits per second (bps). But while we think of bandwidth as speed, it helps to also think of bandwidth as the capacity of the link, in terms of how many bits can be sent over the link per second. The networking device's QoS tools determine what packet is sent over the link next, so the networking device is in control of which messages get access to the bandwidth next and how much of that bandwidth (capacity) each type of traffic gets over time.

For example, consider that typical WAN edge router that has hundreds of packets waiting to exit the WAN link. An engineer might configure a queuing tool to reserve 10 percent of the bandwidth for voice traffic, 50 percent for mission-critical data applications, and leave the rest of the bandwidth for all other types of traffic. The queuing tool could then use those settings to make the choice about which packets to send next.

Delay can be described as one-way delay or round-trip delay. *One-way delay* refers to the time between sending one packet and that same packet arriving at the destination host. *Round-trip delay* counts the one-way delay plus the time for the receiver of the first packet to send back a packet—in other words, the time it takes to send one packet between two hosts and receive one back. Many different individual actions impact delay; this chapter will discuss a few of those, including queuing and shaping delay.

Jitter refers to the variation in one-way delay between consecutive packets sent by the same application. For example, imagine an application sends a few hundred packets to one particular host. The first packet's one-way delay is 300 milliseconds (300 ms, or .3 seconds). The next packet's one-way delay is 300 ms; so is the third's; and so on. In that case, there is no jitter. However, if instead the first packet has a one-way delay of 300 ms, the next has a one-way delay of 310 ms, and the next has 325 ms, then there is some variation in the delay; 10 ms between packets 1 and 2, and another 15 ms between packets 2 and 3. That difference is called jitter.

Finally, *loss* refers to the number of lost messages, usually as a percentage of packets sent. The comparison is simple: if the sender for some application sends 100 packets, and only 98 arrive at the destination, that particular application flow experienced 2 percent loss. Loss can be caused by many factors, but often, people think of loss as something caused by faulty cabling or poor WAN services. That is one cause. However, more loss happens because of the normal operation of the networking devices, in which the devices' queues get too full, so the device has nowhere to put new packets, and it discards the packet. Several QoS tools manage queuing systems to help control and avoid loss.

Types of Traffic

With QoS, a network engineer sets about to prefer one type of traffic over another in regard to bandwidth, delay, jitter, and loss. Sometimes, that choice relates to the specific business. For example, if all the mission-critical applications sit on servers in three known subnets, then the QoS plan could be set up to match packets going to/from that subnet and give that traffic better treatment compared to other traffic. However, in other cases, the choice of how to apply QoS tools relates to the nature of different kinds of applications. Some applications have different QoS needs than others. This next topic compares the basic differences in QoS needs based on the type of traffic.

Data Applications

First, consider a basic web application, with a user at a PC or tablet. The user types in a URI to request a web page. That request may require a single packet going to the web server, but it may result in hundreds or thousands of packets coming back to the web client, as shown in Figure 11-1.

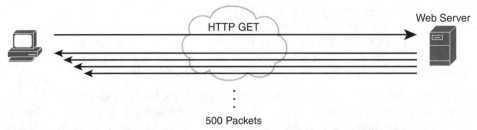

Figure 11-1 *Concept of Disproportionate Packet/Byte Volumes with HTTP Traffic*

> **NOTE** If you wonder how one web page might require thousands of packets, consider this math: with a 1500-byte IP maximum transmission unit (MTU), the data part of a TCP segment could be at most 1460 bytes (1500 bytes minus 20 bytes each for the IP and TCP header). In this example, 1000 such packets total to 1,460,000 bytes, or about 1.5 MB. It is easy to imagine a web page with just a few graphics that totals more than 1.5 MB in size.

So, what is the impact of bandwidth, delay, jitter, and loss on an interactive web-based application? First, the packets require a certain amount of bandwidth capacity. As for delay, each of those packets from the server to the client takes some amount of one-way delay, with some jitter as well. Of the 500 packets shown in Figure 11-1, if some are lost (transmission errors, discarded by devices, or other reasons), then the server's TCP logic will retransmit, but parts of the web page may not show up right away.

While QoS tools focus on managing bandwidth, delay, jitter, and loss, the user mainly cares about the quality of the overall experience. For instance, with a web application, how long after clicking do you see something useful in your web browser? So, as a user, you care about the *Quality of Experience* (QoE), which is a term referring to users' perception of their use of the application on the network. QoS tools directly impact bandwidth, delay, jitter, and loss, which then should have some overall good effect to influence the users' QoE. And you can use QoS tools to create a better QoE for more important traffic; for instance, you might give certain business-critical applications better QoS treatment, which improves QoE for users of those apps.

In contrast, a noninteractive data application (historically called *batch* traffic)—for instance, data backup or file transfers—has different QoS requirements than interactive data applications. Batch applications typically send more data than interactive applications, but because no one is sitting there waiting to see something pop on the screen, the delay and jitter do not matter much. Much more important for these applications is meeting the need to complete the larger task (transferring files) within a larger time window. QoS tools can be used to provide enough bandwidth to meet the capacity needs of these applications and manage loss to reduce the number of retransmissions.

Voice and Video Applications

Voice and video applications each have a similar breakdown of interactive and noninteractive flows. To make the main points about both voice and video, this section looks more deeply at voice traffic.

Answers to the "Do I Know This Already?" quiz:

1 A, B, E **2** B, C **3** A, B, C **4** B, C **5** A, D **6** C, D

Before looking at voice, though, first think about the use of the term *flow* in networking. A flow is all the data moving from one application to another over the network, with one flow for each direction. For example, if you open a website and connect to a web server, the web page content that moves from the server to the client is one flow. Listen to some music with a music app on your phone, and that creates a flow from your app to the music app's server and a flow from the server back to your phone. From a voice perspective, a phone call between two IP phones would create a flow for each direction. For video, it could be the traffic from one video surveillance camera collected by security software.

Now on to voice, specifically Voice over IP (VoIP). VoIP defines the means to take the sound made at one telephone and send it inside IP packets over an IP network, playing the sound back on the other telephone. Figure 11-2 shows the general idea. The steps in the figure include

Step 1. The phone user makes a phone call and begins speaking.

Step 2. A chip called a *codec* processes (digitizes) the sound to create a binary code (160 bytes with the G.711 codec, for example) for a certain time period (usually 20 ms).

Step 3. The phone places the data into an IP packet.

Step 4. The phone sends the packet to the destination IP phone.

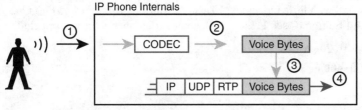

Figure 11-2 *Creating VoIP Packets with an IP Phone and a G.711 Codec*

If you work through the math a bit, this single call, with the G.711 codec, requires about 80 Kbps of bandwidth (ignoring the data-link header and trailer overhead). Counting the headers and VoIP payload as shown in the figure, each of the IP packets has 200 bytes. Each holds 20 ms of digitized voice, so the phone sends 50 packets per second. These 50 packets at 200 bytes each equal 10,000 bytes per second, or 80,000 bits per second, which is 80 Kbps. Other voice codecs require even less bandwidth, with the commonly used G.729 taking about 24 Kbps (again ignoring data-link overhead).

At first, it may look like VoIP calls require little in regard to QoS. For bandwidth, a single voice call or flow requires only a little bandwidth in comparison to many data applications. However, interactive voice does require a much better level of quality for delay, jitter, and loss.

For instance, think about making a phone call with high one-way delay. You finish speaking and pause for the other person to respond. And he does not, so you speak again—and hear the other person's voice overlaid on your own. The problem: too much delay. Or, consider calls for which the sound breaks up. The problem? It could have been packet loss, or it could have been jitter.

11

You can achieve good-quality voice traffic over an IP network, but you must implement QoS to do so. QoS tools set about to give different types of traffic the QoS behavior they need. Cisco's *Enterprise QoS Solution Reference Network Design Guide*, which itself quotes other sources in addition to relying on Cisco's long experience in implementing QoS, suggests the following guidelines for interactive voice:

- **Delay (one-way):** 150 ms or less
- **Jitter:** 30 ms or less
- **Loss:** 1% or less

In comparison, interactive voice requires more attention than interactive data applications for QoS features. Data applications generally tolerate more delay, jitter, and loss than voice (and video). A single voice call does generally take less bandwidth than a typical data application, but that bandwidth requirement is consistent. Data applications tend to be bursty, with data bursts in reaction to the user doing something with the application.

Video has a much more varied set of QoS requirements. Generally, think of video like voice, but with a much higher bandwidth requirement than voice (per flow) and similar requirements for low delay, jitter, and loss. As for bandwidth, video can use a variety of codecs that impact the amount of data sent, but many other technical features impact the amount of bandwidth required for a single video flow. (For instance, a sporting event with lots of movement on screen takes more bandwidth than a news anchor reading the news in front of a solid background with little movement.) This time quoting from *End-to-End QoS Network Design*, Second Edition (Cisco Press, 2013), some requirements for video include

- **Bandwidth:** 384 Kbps to 20+ Mbps
- **Delay (one-way):** 200–400 ms
- **Jitter:** 30–50 ms
- **Loss:** 0.1%–1%

> **NOTE** *End-to-End QoS Network Design* is written by some of the same people who created the Cisco *Enterprise QoS Solution Reference Network Design Guide* (available at Cisco.com). If you are looking for a book to dig into more depth on QoS, this book is an excellent reference for Cisco QoS.

QoS as Mentioned in This Book

QoS tools change the QoS characteristics of certain flows in the network. The rest of the chapter focuses on the specific tools mentioned in the lone CCNA 200-301 exam topic about QoS, presented in the following major sections:

- "Classification and Marking" is about the marking of packets and the definition of trust boundaries.
- "Queuing" describes the scheduling of packets to give one type of packet priority over another.
- "Shaping and Policing" explains these two tools together because they are often used on opposite ends of a link.
- "Congestion Avoidance" addresses how to manage the packet loss that occurs when network devices get too busy.

QoS on Switches and Routers

Before moving on to several sections of the chapter about specific QoS tools, let me make a point about the terms *packet* and *frame* as used in this chapter.

The QoS tools discussed in this chapter can be used on both switches and routers. There are some differences in the features and differences in implementation, due to the differences of internal architecture between routers and switches. However, to the depth discussed here, the descriptions apply equally to both LAN switches and IP routers.

This chapter uses the word *packet* in a general way, to refer to any message being processed by a networking device, just for convenience. Normally, the term *packet* refers to the IP header and encapsulated headers and data, but without the data-link header and trailer. The term *frame* refers to the data-link header/trailer with its encapsulated headers and data. For this chapter, those differences do not matter to the discussion, but at the same time, the discussion often shows a message that sometimes is literally a packet (without the data-link header/trailer) and sometimes a frame.

Throughout the chapter, the text uses *packet* for all messages, because the fact of whether or not the message happens to have a data-link header/trailer at that point is immaterial to the basic discussion of features.

Additionally, note that all the examples in the chapter refer to routers, just to be consistent.

Classification and Marking

The first QoS tool discussed in this chapter, classification and marking, or simply marking, refers to a type of QoS tool that classifies packets based on their header contents, and then marks the message by changing some bits in specific header fields. This section looks first at the role of classification across all QoS tools, and then it examines the marking feature.

Classification Basics

QoS tools sit in the path that packets take when being forwarded through a router or switch, much like the positioning of ACLs. Like ACLs, QoS tools are enabled on an interface. Also like ACLs, QoS tools are enabled for a direction: packets entering the interface (before the forwarding decision) or for messages exiting the interface (after the forwarding decision).

The term *classification* refers to the process of matching the fields in a message to make a choice to take some QoS action. So, again comparing QoS tools to ACLs, ACLs perform classification and filtering; that is, ACLs match (classify) packet headers. ACLs can have the purpose (action) of choosing which packets to discard. QoS tools perform classification (matching of header fields) to decide which packets to take certain QoS actions against. Those actions include the other types of QoS tools discussed in this chapter, such as queuing, shaping, policing, and so on.

For example, consider the internal processing done by a router as shown in Figure 11-3. In this case, an output queuing tool has been enabled on an interface. Routers use queuing tools to place some packets in one output queue, other packets in another, and so on, when the outgoing interface happens to be busy. Then, when the outgoing interface becomes available to send another message, the queuing tool's scheduler algorithm can pick the next message from any one of the queues, prioritizing traffic based on the rules configured by the network engineer.

11

Router Internals

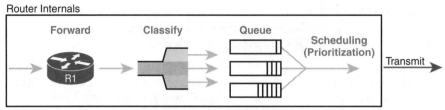

Figure 11-3 *Big Idea: Classification for Queuing in a Router*

The figure shows the internals of a router and what happens to the packet during part of that internal processing, moving left to right inside the router, as follows:

Step 1.   The router makes a forwarding (routing) decision.

Step 2.   The output queuing tool uses classification logic to determine which packets go into which output queue.

Step 3.   The router holds the packets in the output queue waiting for the outgoing interface to be available to send the next message.

Step 4.   The queuing tool's scheduling logic chooses the next packet, effectively prioritizing one packet over another.

While the example shows a queuing tool, note that the queuing tool requires the ability to classify messages by comparing the messages to the configuration, much like ACLs.

Matching (Classification) Basics

Now think about classification from an enterprise-wide perspective, which helps us appreciate the need for marking. Every QoS tool can examine various headers to make comparisons to classify packets. However, you might apply QoS tools on most every device in the network, sometimes at both ingress and egress on most of the interfaces. Using complex matching of many header fields in every device and on most interfaces requires lots of configuration. The work to match packets can even degrade device performance of some devices. So, while you could have every device use complex packet matching, doing so is a poor strategy.

A better strategy, one recommended both by Cisco and by RFCs, suggests doing complex matching early in the life of a packet and then marking the packet. *Marking* means that the QoS tool changes one or more header fields, setting a value in the header. Several header fields have been designed for the purpose of marking the packets for QoS processing. Then, devices that process the packet later in its life can use much simpler classification logic.

Figure 11-4 shows an example, with a PC on the left sending an IP packet to some host off the right side of the figure (not shown). Switch SW1, the first networking device to forward the packet, does some complex comparisons and marks the packet's Differentiated Services Code Point (DSCP) field, a 6-bit field in the IP header meant for QoS marking. The next three devices that process this message—SW2, R1, and R2—then use simpler matching to classify the packet by comparing the packet's DSCP value, placing packets with one DSCP value in class 1, and packets with another DSCP value in class 2.

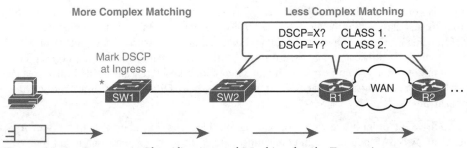

Figure 11-4 *Systematic Classification and Marking for the Enterprise*

Classification on Routers with ACLs and NBAR

Now that you know the basics of what classification and marking do together, this section takes the discussion a little deeper with a closer look at classification on routers, which is followed by a closer look at the marking function.

First, QoS classification sounds a lot like what ACLs do, and it should. In fact, many QoS tools support the ability to simply refer to an IP ACL, with this kind of logic:

For any packet matched by the ACL with a permit action, consider that packet a match for QoS, so do a particular QoS action.

As a reminder, Figure 11-5 shows the IP and TCP header. All these fields are matchable for QoS classification.

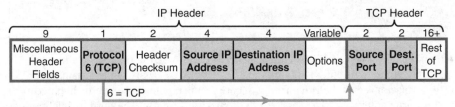

Figure 11-5 *Classification with Five Fields Used by Extended ACLs*

Now think about the enterprise's QoS plan for a moment. That plan should list details such as which types of traffic should be classified as being in the same class for queuing purposes, for shaping, and for any other QoS tool. That plan should detail the fields in the header that can be matched. For instance, if all the IP phones sit in subnets within the range of addresses 10.3.0.0/16, then the QoS plan should state that. Then the network engineer could configure an extended ACL to match all packets to/from IP addresses inside 10.3.0.0/16 and apply appropriate QoS actions to that voice traffic.

However, not every classification can be easily made by matching with an ACL. In more challenging cases, Cisco Network Based Application Recognition (NBAR) can be used. NBAR is basically in its second major version, called NBAR2, or next-generation NBAR. In short, NBAR2 matches packets for classification in a large variety of ways that are very useful for QoS.

NBAR2 looks far beyond what an ACL can examine in a message. Many applications cannot be identified based on well-known port alone. NBAR solves those problems.

Cisco also organizes what NBAR can match in ways that make it easy to separate the traffic into different classes. For instance, the Cisco WebEx application provides audio and video conferencing on the web. In a QoS plan, you might want to classify WebEx differently than other video traffic and classify it differently than voice calls between IP phones. That is, you might classify WebEx traffic and give it a unique DSCP marking. NBAR provides easy built-in matching ability for WebEx, plus more than 1000 different subcategories of applications.

Just to drive the point home with NBAR, Example 11-1 lists four lines of help output for one of many NBAR configuration commands. I chose a variety of items that might be more memorable. With the use of the keywords on the left in the correct configuration command, you could match the following: entertainment video from Amazon, video from Cisco's video surveillance camera products, voice from Cisco IP Phones, and video from sports channel ESPN. (NBAR refers to this idea of defining the characteristics of different applications as *application signatures*.)

Example 11-1 *Example of the Many NBAR2 Matchable Applications*

```
R1#(config)# class-map matchingexample
R1(config-cmap)# match protocol attribute category voice-and-video ?
! output heavily edited for length
    amazon-instant-video        VOD service by Amazon
    cisco-ip-camera             Cisco video surveillance camera
    cisco-phone                 Cisco IP Phones and PC-based Unified Communicators
    espn-video                  ESPN related websites and mobile applications video
    facetime                    Facetime video calling software
! Output snipped.
```

To wrap up the discussion of NBAR for classification, compare the first two highlighted entries in the output. Without NBAR, it would be difficult to classify an entertainment video from Amazon versus the video from a security camera, but those two highlighted entries show how you easily have classified that traffic differently. The third highlighted item shows how to match traffic for Cisco IP Phones (and PC-based equivalents), again making for an easier match of packets of a particular type.

Marking IP DSCP and Ethernet CoS

The QoS plan for an enterprise centers on creating classes of traffic that should receive certain types of QoS treatment. That plan would note how to classify packets into each classification and the values that should be marked on the packets, basically labeling each packet with a number to associate it with that class. For example, that plan might state the following:

- Classify all voice payload traffic that is used for business purposes as IP DSCP EF and CoS 5.

- Classify all video conferencing and other interactive video for business purposes as IP DSCP AF41 and CoS 4.

- Classify all business-critical data application traffic as IP DSCP AF21 and CoS 2.

This next topic takes a closer look at the specific fields that can be marked, defining the DSCP and CoS marking fields.

Marking the IP Header

Marking a QoS field in the IP header works well with QoS because the IP header exists for the entire trip from the source host to the destination host. When a host sends data, the host sends a data-link frame that encapsulates an IP packet. Each router that forwards the IP packet discards the old data-link header and adds a new header. Because the routers do not discard and reinsert IP headers, marking fields in the IP header stay with the data from the first place it is marked until it reaches the destination host.

IPv4 defines a Type of Service (ToS) byte in the IPv4 header, as shown in Figure 11-6. The original RFC defined a 3-bit IP Precedence (IPP) field for QoS marking. That field gave us eight separate values—binary 000, 001, 010, and so on, through 111—which when converted to decimal are decimals 0 through 7.

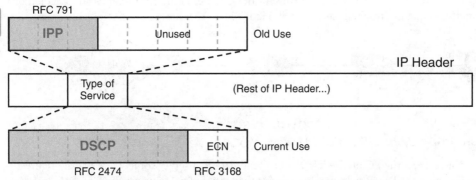

Figure 11-6 *IP Precedence and Differentiated Services Code Point Fields*

NOTE Those last 5 bits of the ToS byte per RFC 791 were mostly defined for some purpose but were not used in practice to any significant extent.

While a great idea, IPP gave us only eight different values to mark, so later RFCs redefined the ToS byte with the DSCP field. DSCP increased the number of marking bits to 6 bits, allowing for 64 unique values that can be marked. The DiffServ RFCs, which became RFCs back in the late 1990s, have become accepted as the most common method to use when doing QoS, and using the DSCP field for marking has become quite common.

IPv6 has a similar field to mark as well. The 6-bit field also goes by the name DSCP, with the byte in the IPv6 header being called the IPv6 *Traffic Class* byte. Otherwise, think of IPv4 and IPv6 being equivalent in terms of marking.

IPP and DSCP fields can be referenced by their decimal values as well as some convenient text names. The later section titled "DiffServ Suggested Marking Values" details some of the names.

Marking the Ethernet 802.1Q Header

Another useful marking field exists in the 802.1Q header, in a field originally defined by the IEEE 802.1p standard. This field sits in the third byte of the 4-byte 802.1Q header, as a 3-bit field, supplying eight possible values to mark (see Figure 11-7). It goes by two different names: *Class of Service*, or CoS, and *Priority Code Point*, or PCP.

11

Ethernet Frame

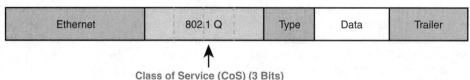

Figure 11-7 *Class of Service Field in 802.1Q/p Header*

The figure uses two slightly different shades of gray (in print) for the Ethernet header and trailer fields versus the 802.1Q header, as a reminder: the 802.1Q header is not included in all Ethernet frames. The 802.1Q header only exists when 802.1Q trunking is used on a link. As a result, QoS tools can make use of the CoS field only for QoS features enabled on interfaces that use trunking, as shown in Figure 11-8.

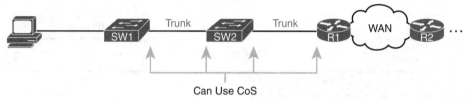

Figure 11-8 *Useful Life of CoS Marking*

For instance, if the PC on the left were to send data to a server somewhere off the figure to the right, the DSCP field would exist for that entire trip. However, the CoS field would exist over the two trunks only and would be useful mainly on the four interfaces noted with the arrow lines.

Other Marking Fields

Other marking fields also exist in other headers. Table 11-2 lists those fields for reference.

Table 11-2 Marking Fields

Field Name	Header(s)	Length (bits)	Where Used
DSCP	IPv4, IPv6	6	End-to-end packet
IPP	IPv4, IPv6	3	End-to-end packet
CoS	802.1Q	3	Over VLAN trunk
TID	802.11	3	Over Wi-Fi
EXP	MPLS Label	3	Over MPLS WAN

Defining Trust Boundaries

The end-user device can mark the DSCP field—and even the CoS field if trunking is used on the link. Would you, as the network engineer, trust those settings and let your networking devices trust and react to those markings for their various QoS actions?

Most of us would not, because anything the end user controls might be used inappropriately at times. For instance, a PC user could know enough about DiffServ and DSCPs to know that most voice traffic is marked with a DSCP called Expedited Forwarding (EF), which has a decimal value of 46. Voice traffic gets great QoS treatment, so PC users could mark all their traffic as DSCP 46, hoping to get great QoS treatment.

The people creating a QoS plan for an enterprise have to choose where to place the trust boundary for the network. The *trust boundary* refers to the point in the path of a packet flowing through the network at which the networking devices can trust the current QoS markings. That boundary typically sits in a device under the control of the IT staff.

For instance, a typical trust boundary could be set in the middle of the first ingress switch in the network, as shown in Figure 11-9. The markings on the message as sent by the PC cannot be trusted. However, because SW1 performed classification and marking as the packets entered the switch, the markings can be trusted at that point.

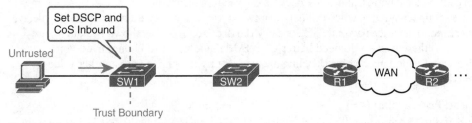

Figure 11-9 *Trusting Devices—PC*

Interestingly, when the access layer includes an IP Phone, the phone is typically the trust boundary, instead of the access layer switch. IP Phones can set the CoS and DSCP fields of the messages created by the phone, as well as those forwarded from the PC through the phone. The specific marking values are actually configured on the attached access switch. Figure 11-10 shows the typical trust boundary in this case, with notation of what the phone's marking logic usually is: mark all of the PC's traffic with a particular DSCP and/or CoS, and the phone's traffic with different values.

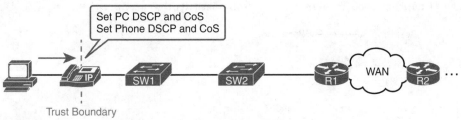

Figure 11-10 *Trusting Devices—IP Phone*

DiffServ Suggested Marking Values

Everything in this chapter follows the DiffServ architecture as defined originally by RFC 2475, plus many other DiffServ RFCs. In particular, DiffServ goes beyond theory in several areas, including making suggestions about the specific DSCP values to use when marking IP packets. By suggesting specific markings for specific types of traffic, DiffServ hoped to create a consistent use of DSCP values in all networks. By doing so, product vendors could provide good default settings for their QoS features, QoS could work better between an enterprise and service provider, and many other benefits could be realized.

The next two topics outline three sets of DSCP values as used in DiffServ.

Expedited Forwarding (EF)

DiffServ defines the *Expedited Forwarding* (EF) DSCP value—a single value—as suggested for use for packets that need low latency (delay), low jitter, and low loss. The Expedited Forwarding RFC (RFC 3246) defines the specific DSCP value (decimal 46) and an equivalent text name (Expedited Forwarding). QoS configuration commands allow the use of the decimal value or text name, but one purpose of having a text acronym to use is to make the value more memorable, so many QoS configurations refer to the text names.

Most often QoS plans use EF to mark voice payload packets. With voice calls, some packets carry voice payload, and other packets carry call signaling messages. Call signaling messages set up (create) the voice call between two devices, and they do not require low delay, jitter, and loss. Voice payload packets carry the digitized voice, as shown back in Figure 11-2, and these packets do need better QoS. By default, Cisco IP Phones mark voice payload with EF, and mark voice signaling packets sent by the phone with another value called CS3.

Assured Forwarding (AF)

The Assured Forwarding (AF) DiffServ RFC (2597) defines a set of 12 DSCP values meant to be used in concert with each other. First, it defines the concept of four separate queues in a queuing system. Additionally, it defines three levels of drop priority within each queue for use with congestion avoidance tools. With four queues, and three drop priority classes per queue, you need 12 different DSCP markings, one for each combination of queue and drop priority. (Queuing and congestion avoidance mechanisms are discussed later in this chapter.)

Assured Forwarding defines the specific AF DSCP text names and equivalent decimal values as listed in Figure 11-11. The text names follow a format of AFXY, with X referring to the queue (1 through 4) and Y referring to the drop priority (1 through 3).

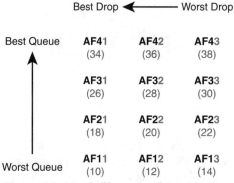

Figure 11-11 *Differentiated Services Assured Forwarding Values and Meaning*

For example, if you marked packets with all 12 values, those with AF11, AF12, and AF13 would all go into one queue; those with AF21, AF22, and AF23 would go into another queue; and so on. Inside the queue with all the AF2y traffic, you would treat the AF21, AF22, and AF23 each differently in regard to drop actions (congestion avoidance), with AF21 getting the preferred treatment and AF23 the worst treatment.

Class Selector (CS)

Originally, the ToS byte was defined with a 3-bit IP Precedence (IPP) field. When DiffServ redefined the ToS byte, it made sense to create eight DSCP values for backward compatibility with IPP values. The Class Selector (CS) DSCP values are those settings.

Figure 11-12 shows the main idea along with the eight CS values, both in name and in decimal value. Basically, the DSCP values have the same first 3 bits as the IPP field, and with binary 0s for the last 3 bits, as shown on the left side of the figure. CSx represents the text names, where x is the matching IPP value (0 through 7).

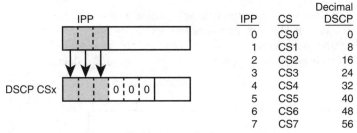

IPP	CS	Decimal DSCP
0	CS0	0
1	CS1	8
2	CS2	16
3	CS3	24
4	CS4	32
5	CS5	40
6	CS6	48
7	CS7	56

Figure 11-12 *Class Selector*

This section on classification and marking has provided a solid foundation for understanding the tools explored in the next three major sections of this chapter: queuing, shaping/policing, and congestion avoidance.

Guidelines for DSCP Marking Values

Even with this introduction to the various DSCP marking values, you could imagine that an enterprise needs to follow a convention for how to use the markings. With so many different values, having different uses of different DSCP values by different devices in the same enterprise would make deploying QoS quite difficult at best.

Among its many efforts to standardize QoS, Cisco helped to develop RFC 4594, an RFC that defines several conventions for how to use the DSCP field. The RFC provides alternative plans with different levels of detail. Each plan defines a type of traffic and the DSCP value to use when marking data. Without getting into the depth of any one plan, the plans all specify some variation for how all devices should mark data as follows:

- DSCP EF: Voice payload
- AF4x: Interactive video (for example, videoconferencing)
- AF3x: Streaming video
- AF2x: High priority (low latency) data
- CS0: Standard data

Cisco not only worked to develop the RFC standards but also uses those standards. Cisco uses default marking conventions based on the marking data in RFC 4594, with some small exceptions. If you want to read more about these QoS marking plans, refer to a couple of sources. First, look for the Cisco QoS Design Guides at Cisco.com. Also refer to RFC 4594.

11

Queuing

All networking devices use queues. Network devices receive messages, make a forwarding decision, and then send the message—but sometimes the outgoing interface is busy. So, the device keeps the outgoing message in a queue, waiting for the outgoing interface to be available—simple enough.

The term *queuing* refers to the QoS toolset for managing the queues that hold packets while they wait their turn to exit an interface (and in other cases in which a router holds packets waiting for some resource). But queuing refers to more than one idea, so you have to look inside devices to think about how they work. For instance, consider Figure 11-13, which shows the internals of a router. The router, of course, makes a forwarding decision, and it needs to be ready to queue packets for transmission once the outgoing interface is available. At the same time, the router may take a variety of other actions as well—ingress ACL, ingress NAT (on the inside interface), egress ACLs after the forwarding decision is made, and so on.

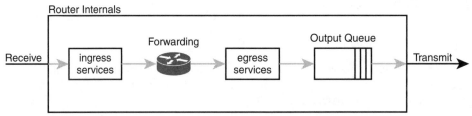

Figure 11-13 *Output Queuing in a Router: Last Output Action Before Transmission*

The figure shows *output queuing* in which the device holds messages until the output interface is available. The queuing system may use a single output queue, with a first-in, first-out (FIFO) scheduler. (In other words, it's like ordering lunch at the sandwich shop that has a single ordering line.)

Next, think a little more deeply about the queuing system. Most networking devices can have a queuing system with multiple queues. To use multiple queues, the queuing system needs a classifier function to choose which packets are placed into which queue. (The classifier can react to previously marked values or do a more extensive match.) The queuing system needs a scheduler as well, to decide which message to take next when the interface becomes available, as shown in Figure 11-14.

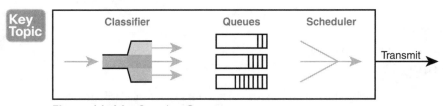

Figure 11-14 *Queuing Components*

Of all these components of the queuing system, the scheduler can be the most interesting part because it can perform prioritization. *Prioritization* refers to the concept of giving priority to one queue over another in some way.

Round-Robin Scheduling (Prioritization)

One scheduling algorithm used by Cisco routers and switches uses round-robin logic. In its most basic form, round robin cycles through the queues in order, taking turns with each queue. In each cycle, the scheduler either takes one message or takes a number of bytes from each queue by taking enough messages to total that number of bytes. Take some messages from queue 1, move on and take some from queue 2, then take some from queue 3, and so on, starting back at queue 1 after finishing a complete pass through the queues.

Round-robin scheduling also includes the concept of *weighting* (generally called *weighted round robin*). Basically, the scheduler takes a different number of packets (or bytes) from each queue, giving more preference to one queue over another.

For example, routers use a popular tool called *Class-Based Weighted Fair Queuing* (CBWFQ) to guarantee a minimum amount of bandwidth to each class. That is, each class receives at least the amount of bandwidth configured during times of congestion, but maybe more. Internally, CBWFQ uses a weighted round-robin scheduling algorithm, while letting the network engineer define the weightings as a percentage of link bandwidth. Figure 11-15 shows an example in which the three queues in the system have been given 20, 30, and 50 percent of the bandwidth each, respectively.

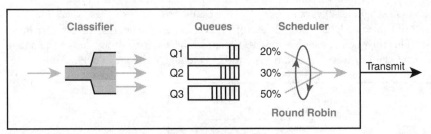

Figure 11-15   *CBWFQ Round-Robin Scheduling*

With the queuing system shown in the figure, if the outgoing link is congested, the scheduler guarantees the percentage bandwidth shown in the figure to each queue. That is, queue 1 gets 20 percent of the link even during busy times.

Low Latency Queuing

Earlier in the chapter, the section titled "Voice and Video Applications" discussed the reasons why voice and video, particularly interactive voice and video like phone calls and videoconferencing, need low latency (low delay), low jitter, and low loss. Unfortunately, a round-robin scheduler does not provide low enough delay, jitter, or loss. The solution: add Low Latency Queuing (LLQ) to the scheduler.

First, for a quick review, Table 11-3 lists the QoS requirements for a voice call. The numbers come from the *Enterprise QoS Solution Reference Network Design Guide*, referenced earlier in the chapter. The amount of bandwidth required per call varies based on the codec used by the call. However, the delay, jitter, and loss requirements remain the same for all voice calls. (Interactive video has similar requirements for delay, jitter, and loss.)

Table 11-3   QoS Requirements for a VoIP Call per Cisco Voice Design Guide

Bandwidth/call	One-way Delay (max)	Jitter (max)	Loss (max)
30–320 Kbps	150 ms	30 ms	<1%

11

A round-robin queuing system adds too much delay for these voice and video packets. To see why, imagine a voice packet arrives and is routed to be sent out some interface with the queuing system shown in Figure 11-16. However, that next voice packet arrives just as the round-robin scheduler moves on to service the queue labeled "data 1." Even though the voice queue has been given 50 percent of the link bandwidth, the scheduler does not send that voice message until it sends some messages from the other three queues—adding delay and jitter.

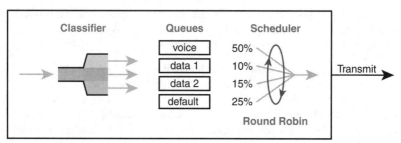

Figure 11-16 *Round Robin Not Good for Voice Delay (Latency) and Jitter*

The solution, LLQ, tells the scheduler to treat one or more queues as special *priority queues*. The LLQ scheduler always takes the next message from one of these special priority queues. Problem solved: very little delay for packets in that queue, resulting in very little jitter as well. Plus the queue never has time to fill up, so there are no drops due to the queue filling up. Figure 11-17 shows the addition of the LLQ logic for the voice queue.

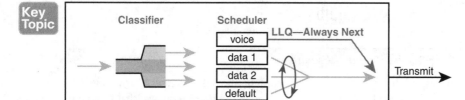

Figure 11-17 *LLQ Always Schedules Voice Packet Next*

Using LLQ, or a priority queue, provides the needed low delay, jitter, and loss for the traffic in that queue. However, think about those other queues. Do you see the problem? What happens if the speed of the interface is X bits per second, but more than X bits per second come into the voice queue? The scheduler never services the other queues (called *queue starvation*).

As you might guess, there is a solution: limit the amount of traffic placed into the priority queue, using a feature called policing. The next section talks about policers in more detail, but for now, think of it as a cap on the bandwidth used by the priority queue. For instance, you could reserve 20 percent of the link's bandwidth for the voice queue and make it a priority queue. However, in this case, instead of 20 percent being the minimum bandwidth, it is the maximum for that queue. If more than 20 percent of the link's worth of bits shows up in that queue, the router will discard the excess.

Limiting the amount of bandwidth in the priority queue protects the other queues, but it causes yet another problem. Voice and video need low loss, and with LLQ, we put the voice and video into a priority queue that will discard the excess messages beyond the bandwidth limit. The solution? Find a way to limit the amount of voice and video that the network routes out this link, so that the policer never discards any of the traffic. There are QoS tools to help you do just that, called Call Admission Control (CAC) tools. However, CAC tools did not get a mention in the exam topics, so this chapter leaves those tools at a brief mention.

A Prioritization Strategy for Data, Voice, and Video

This section about queuing introduces several connected ideas, so before leaving the discussion of queuing, think about this strategy for how most enterprises approach queuing in their QoS plans:

1. Use a round-robin queuing method like CBWFQ for data classes and for noninteractive voice and video.

2. If faced with too little bandwidth compared to the typical amount of traffic, give data classes that support business-critical applications much more guaranteed bandwidth than is given to less important data classes.

3. Use a priority queue with LLQ scheduling for interactive voice and video, to achieve low delay, jitter, and loss.

4. Put voice in a separate queue from video so that the policing function applies separately to each.

5. Define enough bandwidth for each priority queue so that the built-in policer should not discard any messages from the priority queues.

6. Use Call Admission Control (CAC) tools to avoid adding too much voice or video to the network, which would trigger the policer function.

Shaping and Policing

This section introduces two related QoS tools—shaping and policing. These tools have a more specialized use and are not found in as many locations in a typical enterprise. These tools are most often used at the WAN edge in an enterprise network design.

Both policing and shaping monitor the bit rate of the combined messages that flow through a device. Once enabled, the policer or shaper notes each packet that passes and measures the number of bits per second over time. Both attempt to keep the bit rate at or below the configured speed, but by using two different actions: policers discard packets, and shapers hold packets in queues to delay the packets.

Shapers and policers monitor the traffic rate (the bits per second that move through the shaper or policer) versus a configured shaping rate or policing rate, respectively. The basic question that both ask is listed below, with the actions based on the answers:

1. Does this next packet push the measured rate past the configured shaping rate or policing rate?

2. If no:

   a. Let the packet keep moving through the normal path and do nothing extra to the packet.

3. If yes:

   a. If shaping, delay the message by queuing it.

   b. If policing, either discard the message or mark it differently.

11

This section first explains policing, which discards or re-marks messages that exceed the policing rate, followed by shaping, which slows down messages that exceed the shaping rate.

Policing

Focus on the traffic rate versus the configured policing rate for a moment, and the policing action of discarding messages. Those concepts sit at the core of what the policing function does.

Traffic arrives at networking devices at a varying rate, with valleys and spikes. That is, if you graph the bit rate of the collective bits that enter or exit any interface, the graph would look something like the one on the left side of Figure 11-18. The policer would measure that rate and make a similar measurement. Still on the left side of the figure, the horizontal dashed line represents the policing rate, which is the rate configured for the policer. So, the policer has some awareness of the measured bit rate over time, which can be compared to the configured rate.

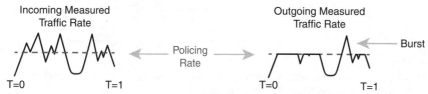

Figure 11-18 *Effect of a Policer and Shaper on an Offered Traffic Load*

The right side of the figure shows a graph of what happens to the traffic when a policer discards any messages that would have otherwise pushed the rate over the configured policing rate. In effect, the policer chops off the top of the graph at the policing rate.

The graph on the right also shows one example of a policer allowing a burst of traffic. Policers allow for a burst beyond the policing rate for a short time, after a period of low activity. So, that one peak that exceeds the policing rate on the graph on the right side allows for the nature of bursty data applications.

Where to Use Policing

Now that you understand the basics of policing, take a moment to ponder. Policers monitor messages, measure a rate, and discard some messages. How does that help a network in regard to QoS? At first glance, it seems to hurt the network, discarding messages, many of which the transport or application layer will have to resend. How does that improve bandwidth, delay, jitter, or loss?

Policing makes sense only in certain cases, and as a general tool, it can be best used at the edge between two networks. For instance, consider a typical point-to-point metro Ethernet WAN connection between two enterprise routers, R1 and R2. Usually, the enterprise network engineers just view the WAN as a cloud, with Ethernet interfaces on the routers, as shown at the top of Figure 11-19.

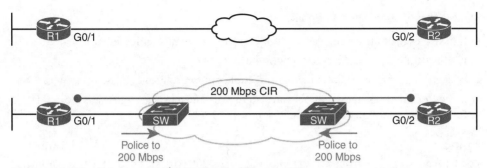

Figure 11-19   *Ethernet WAN: Link Speed Versus CIR*

Now think about the contract for this MetroE connection, as shown at the bottom of Figure 11-19. In this case, this connection uses Gigabit Ethernet for the access links, and a 200-Mbps *committed information rate* (CIR). That is, the SP providing the WAN service agrees to allow the enterprise to send 200 Mbps of traffic in each direction. However, remember that the enterprise routers transmit the data at the speed of the access link, or 1 Gbps in this case.

Think like the SP for a moment, and think about supporting tens of thousands of Gigabit Ethernet links into your WAN service, all with 200-Mbps CIRs. What would happen if you just let all those customers send data that, over time, averaged close to 1000 Mbps (1 Gbps)? That is, if all customers kept sending data far beyond their contracted CIR, that much traffic could cause congestion in the WAN service. Also, those customers might choose to pay for a lower CIR, knowing that the SP would send the data anyway. And customers who were well behaved and did not send more data than their CIR might suffer from the congestion just as much as the customers who send far too much data.

Figure 11-19 also notes the solution to the problem: The SP can police incoming packets, setting the policing rate to match the CIR that the customer chooses for that link. By doing so, the SP protects all customers from the negative effects of the customers who send too much traffic. Customers receive what they paid for. And the SP can provide reports of actual traffic rates, so the enterprise knows when to buy a faster CIR for each link.

Policers can discard excess traffic, but they can also re-mark packets. Think again about what an SP does with an ingress policer, as shown in Figure 11-19: they are discarding their customers' messages. So, the SP might want to make a compromise that works better for its customers, while still protecting the SP's network. The SP could mark the messages with a new marking value, with this strategy:

1. Re-mark packets that exceed the policing rate, but let them into the SP's network.

2. If other SP network devices are experiencing congestion when they process the packet, the different marking means that device can discard the packet. However…

3. …if no other SP network devices are experiencing congestion when forwarding that re-marked packet, it gets through the SP network anyway.

With this strategy, the SP can treat their customers a little better by discarding less traffic, while still protecting the SP's network during times of stress.

Summarizing the key features of policing:

- It measures the traffic rate over time for comparison to the configured policing rate.
- It allows for a burst of data after a period of inactivity.
- It is enabled on an interface, in either direction, but typically at ingress.
- It can discard excess messages but can also re-mark the message so that it is a candidate for more aggressive discard later in its journey.

Shaping

You have a 1-Gbps link from a router into a SP, but a 200-Mbps CIR for traffic to another site, as seen in Figure 11-19. The SP has told you that it always discards incoming traffic that exceeds the CIR. The solution? Use a shaper to slow down the traffic—in this case to a 200-Mbps shaping rate.

That scenario—shaping before sending data to an SP that is policing—is one of the typical uses of a shaper. Shapers can be useful in other cases as well, but generally speaking, shapers make sense when a device can send at a certain speed, but there is a benefit to slowing down the rate.

The shaper slows messages down by queuing the messages. The shaper then services the shaping queues, but not based on when the physical interface is available. Instead, the shaper schedules messages from the shaping queues based on the shaping rate, as shown in Figure 11-20. Following the left-to-right flow in the figure, for a router, the packet is routed out an interface; the shaper queues packets so that the sending rate through the shaper does not exceed the shaping rate; and then output queuing works as normal, if needed.

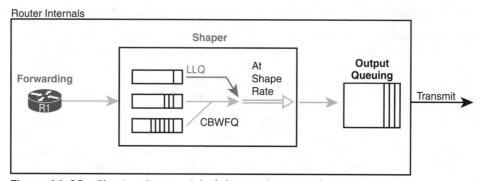

Figure 11-20 *Shaping Queues: Scheduling with LLQ and CBWFQ*

Note that in some cases, the output queuing function has little to do. For instance, in the earlier example shown in Figure 11-19, the SP is policing incoming messages at 200 Mbps. If the router (R1, for instance) were to shape all traffic exiting toward the SP to 200 Mbps as well, with that 1-Gbps interface, the output queue would seldom if ever be congested.

Because shapers create queues where messages wait, you should apply a queuing tool to those queues. It is perfectly normal to apply the round-robin and priority queuing features of CBWFQ and LLQ, respectively, to the shaping queues, as noted in the figure.

Setting a Good Shaping Time Interval for Voice and Video

Once again, a QoS tool has attempted to solve one QoS problem but introduces another. The unfortunate side effect of a shaper is that it slows down packets, which then creates more delay and probably more jitter. The delay occurs in part because of the message simply waiting in a queue, but partly because of the mechanisms used by a shaper. Thankfully, you can (and should) configure a shaper's setting that changes the internal operation of the shaper, which then reduces the delay and jitter caused to voice and video traffic.

A shaper's *time interval* refers to its internal logic and how a shaper averages, over time, sending at a particular rate. A shaper basically sends as fast as it can and then waits; sends and waits; sends and waits. For instance, the policing and shaping example in this section suggests shaping at 200 Mbps on a router that has a 1000-Mbps (1-Gbps) outgoing interface. In that case, the shaper would result in the interface sending data 20 percent of the time and being silent 80 percent of the time.

Figure 11-21 shows a graph of the shaping time interval concept, assuming a time interval of 1 second. To average 200 million bits per second, the shaper would allow 200 million bits to exit its shaping queues and exit the interface each second. Because the interface transmits bits at 1 Gbps, it takes just .2 seconds, or 200 ms, to send all 200 million bits. Then the shaper must wait for the rest of the time interval, another 800 ms, before beginning the next time interval.

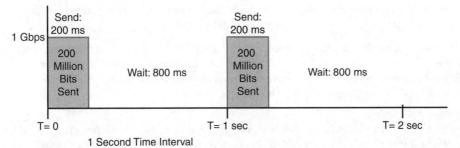

Figure 11-21 *One Second (1000 ms) Shaping Time Interval, Shaping at 20 Percent of Line Rate*

Now think about a voice or video packet that needs very low delay and jitter—and unfortunately, it arrives just as the shaper finishes sending data for a time interval. Even if that voice or video packet is in a priority shaping queue, the packet will wait 800 ms before the shaper schedules the next packet—far too long compared to the 150-ms one-way delay goal for voice.

The solution to this problem: configure a short time interval. For example, consider the following time intervals (abbreviated Tc), and their effects, for this same example (1-Gbps link, shaping to 200 Mbps), but with shorter and shorter time intervals:

Tc = 1 second (1000 ms): Send at 1 Gbps for 200 ms, rest for 800 ms

Tc = .1 second (100 ms): Send at 1 Gbps for 20 ms, rest for 80 ms

Tc = .01 second (10 ms): Send at 1 Gbps for 2 ms, rest for 8 ms

When shaping, use a short time interval. By recommendation, use a 10-ms time interval to support voice and video. With that setting, a voice or video packet should wait no more than 10 ms while waiting for the next shaping time interval, at which point the priority queue scheduling should take all the voice and video messages next.

11

Summarizing the key features of shapers:

- Shapers measure the traffic rate over time for comparison to the configured shaping rate.
- Shapers allow for bursting after a period of inactivity.
- Shapers are enabled on an interface for egress (outgoing packets).
- Shapers slow down packets by queuing them and over time releasing them from the queue at the shaping rate.
- Shapers use queuing tools to create and schedule the shaping queues, which is very important for the same reasons discussed for output queuing.

Congestion Avoidance

The QoS feature called congestion avoidance attempts to reduce overall packet loss by preemptively discarding some packets used in TCP connections. To see how it works, you first need to look at how TCP works in regard to windowing and then look at how congestion avoidance features work.

TCP Windowing Basics

TCP uses a flow control mechanism called *windowing*. Each TCP receiver grants a window to the sender. The window, which is a number, defines the number of bytes the sender can send over the TCP connection before receiving a TCP acknowledgment for at least some of those bytes. More exactly, the window size is the number of unacknowledged bytes that the sender can send before the sender must simply stop and wait.

The TCP window mechanism gives the receiver control of the sender's rate of sending data. Each new segment sent by the receiver back to the sender grants a new window, which can be smaller or larger than the previous window. By raising and lowering the window, the receiver can make the sender wait more or wait less.

> **NOTE** Each TCP connection has two senders and two receivers; that is, each host sends and receives data. For this discussion, focus on one direction, with one host as the sender and the other as the receiver. If calling one host the "sender" and one the "receiver," note that the receiver then acknowledges data in TCP segments sent back to the sender by the receiver.

By choice, when all is well, the receiver keeps increasing the granted window, doubling it every time the receiver acknowledges data. Eventually, the window grows to the point that the sender never has to stop sending: the sender keeps receiving TCP acknowledgments before sending all the data in the previous window. Each new acknowledgment (as listed in a TCP segment and TCP header) grants a new window to the sender.

Also by choice, when a TCP receiver senses the loss of a TCP segment, he shrinks the window with the next window size listed in the next TCP segment the receiver sends back to the sender. For each TCP segment lost, the window can shrink by one-half, with multiple segment losses causing the window to shrink by half multiple times, slowing down the sender's rate significantly.

Now think about router queues for a moment. Without a congestion avoidance tool, an event called a *tail drop* causes the most drops in a network. Figure 11-22 shows the idea, showing the same queuing system, but in three separate conditions—little congestion, medium congestion, and much congestion. On the left, with little congestion, the output queues on an interface have not yet filled. In the middle, the queues have started to fill, with one queue being totally full. Any new packets that arrive for that queue right now will be dropped because there is no room at the tail of the queue (tail drop).

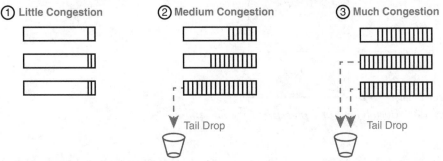

Figure 11-22   *Tail Drop Concepts with Three Different Scenarios*

The worse the congestion in the queues, the more likely tail drop will occur, as shown with the most congested case on the right side of the figure. The more congestion, the bigger the negative impact on traffic—both in terms of loss and in terms of increasing delay in TCP connections.

Congestion Avoidance Tools

Congestion avoidance tools attempt to avoid the congestion, primarily through using TCP's own windowing mechanisms. These tools discard some TCP segments before the queues fill, hoping that enough TCP connections will slow down, reducing congestion, and avoiding a much worse problem: the effects of many more packets being dropped due to tail drop. The strategy is simple: discard some now in hopes that the device discards far fewer in the long term.

Congestion avoidance tools monitor the average queue depth over time, triggering more severe actions the deeper the queue, as shown in Figure 11-23. The height of the box represents the queue depth, or the number of packets in the queue. When the queue depth is low, below the minimum threshold values, the congestion avoidance tool does nothing. When the queue depth is between the minimum and maximum thresholds, the congestion avoidance tool discards a percentage of the packets—usually a small percentage, like 5, 10, or 20 percent. If the queue depth passes the maximum threshold, the tool drops all packets, in an action called *full drop*.

Of course, like all the QoS tools mentioned in this chapter, congestion avoidance tools can classify messages to treat some packets better than others. In the same queue, packets with one marking might be dropped more aggressively, and those with better DSCP markings dropped less aggressively.

11

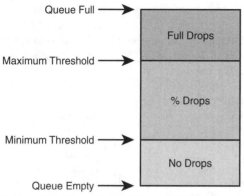

Figure 11-23 *Mechanisms of Congestion Avoidance*

Chapter Review

One key to doing well on the exams is to perform repetitive spaced review sessions. Review this chapter's material using either the tools in the book or interactive tools for the same material found on the book's companion website. Refer to the "Your Study Plan" element for more details. Table 11-4 outlines the key review elements and where you can find them. To better track your study progress, record when you completed these activities in the second column.

Table 11-4 Chapter Review Tracking

Review Element	Review Date(s)	Resource Used
Review key topics		Book, website
Review key terms		Book, website
Answer DIKTA questions		Book, PTP
Review memory tables		Book, website
Watch video		website

Review All the Key Topics

Table 11-5 Key Topics for Chapter 11

Key Topic Element	Description	Page Number
List	Four QoS characteristics	228
List	Voice call QoS requirements	232
List	Video QoS requirements	232
Figure 11-6	IP Precedence and IP DSCP marking fields	237
Figure 11-7	802.1Q CoS marking field	238
Figure 11-10	Trust boundary with IP Phones	239
Figure 11-14	Queuing components	242
Figure 11-17	LLQ scheduling logic with a priority queue	244

Key Topic Element	Description	Page Number
List	A strategy for using queuing (congestion management) to prioritize traffic	245
List	Logic steps for shapers and policers	245
List	Key features of policers	248
List	Key features of shapers	250

Key Terms You Should Know

per-hop behavior (PHB), marking, classification, Quality of Service (QoS), IP Precedence (IPP), Differentiated Services Code Point (DSCP), Class of Service (CoS), bandwidth, delay, jitter, loss, queuing, priority queue, round robin, policing, shaping, Differentiated Services (DiffServ), policing rate, shaping rate

11

CHAPTER 12

Miscellaneous IP Services

This chapter covers the following exam topics:

3.0 IP Connectivity

3.5 Describe the purpose of First Hop Redundancy Protocol

4.0 Infrastructure Services

4.4 Explain the function of SNMP in network operations

4.9 Describe the capabilities and function of TFTP/FTP in the network

When reading this chapter, think of it as three separate small topics rather than one large topic. The content just happens to include a few IP-based services that have little to do with each other, but the length of coverage of each topic is too short to justify a separate chapter. The result: Chapter 12, "Miscellaneous IP Services." So when reading, feel free to treat each of the three major headings as a separate study event.

First Hop Redundancy Protocols (FHRPs), which provides redundancy for the function of the default router in any subnet, begins the chapter. The term *FHRP* refers to a class of solutions, with three options, and with the examples showing the most popular option, Hot Standby Router Protocol (HSRP).

Simple Network Management Protocol (SNMP) follows in the second major section. As per the associated exam topic, this section focuses on SNMP concepts rather than configuration, including how managed devices—SNMP agents—can be interrogated by network management systems—SNMP clients—to find the current status of each device.

File Transfer Protocol (FTP) and Trivial File Transfer Protocol (TFTP) star in the third major section. The first branch of this section focuses on a few practical uses of TFTP and FTP, specifically how to use these protocols on Cisco routers to upgrade the IOS. Armed with that practical knowledge, you then look at the protocol details of both FTP and TFTP in the rest of the section.

"Do I Know This Already?" Quiz

Take the quiz (either here or use the PTP software) if you want to use the score to help you decide how much time to spend on this chapter. The letter answers are listed at the bottom of the page following the quiz. Appendix C, found both at the end of the book as well as on the companion website, includes both the answers and explanations. You can also find both answers and explanations in the PTP testing software.

Table 12-1 "Do I Know This Already?" Foundation Topics Section-to-Question Mapping

Foundation Topics Section	Questions
First Hop Redundancy Protocol	1–3
Simple Network Management Protocol	4, 5
FTP and TFTP	6, 7

1. R1 and R2 attach to the same Ethernet VLAN, with subnet 10.1.19.0/25, with addresses 10.1.19.1 and 10.1.19.2, respectively, configured with the **ip address** interface subcommand. Host A refers to 10.1.19.1 as its default router, and host B refers to 10.1.19.2 as its default router. The routers do not use an FHRP. Which of the following is a problem for this LAN?

   a. The design breaks IPv4 addressing rules because two routers cannot connect to the same LAN subnet.

   b. If one router fails, neither host can send packets off-subnet.

   c. If one router fails, both hosts will use the one remaining router as a default router.

   d. If one router fails, the host that uses that router as a default router cannot send packets off-subnet.

2. R1 and R2 attach to the same Ethernet VLAN, with subnet 10.1.19.0/25, with addresses 10.1.19.1 and 10.1.19.2, respectively, configured with the **ip address** interface subcommand. The routers use an FHRP. Host A and host B attach to the same LAN and have correct default router settings per the FHRP configuration. Which of the following statements is true for this LAN?

   a. The design breaks IPv4 addressing rules because two routers cannot connect to the same LAN subnet.

   b. If one router fails, neither host can send packets off-subnet.

   c. If one router fails, both hosts will use the one remaining router as a default router.

   d. If one router fails, only one of the two hosts will still be able to send packets off-subnet.

3. R1 and R2 attach to the same Ethernet VLAN, with subnet 10.1.19.0/25, with addresses 10.1.19.1 and 10.1.19.2, respectively, configured with the **ip address** interface subcommand. The routers use HSRP. The network engineer prefers to have R1 be the default router when both R1 and R2 are up. Which of the following is the likely default router setting for hosts in this subnet?

   a. 10.1.19.1

   b. 10.1.19.2

   c. Another IP address in subnet 10.1.19.0/25 other than 10.1.19.1 and 10.1.19.2

   d. A host name that the FHRP mini-DNS will initially point to 10.1.19.1

4. A Network Management Station (NMS) is using SNMP to manage some Cisco routers and switches with SNMPv2c. Which of the following answers most accurately describes how the SNMP agent on a router authenticates any SNMP Get requests received from the NMS?

    a. Using a username and hashed version of a password

    b. Using either the read-write or read-only community string

    c. Using only the read-write community string

    d. Using only the read-only community string

5. Which of the following SNMP messages are typically sent by an SNMP agent?

    a. Trap

    b. Get Request

    c. Inform

    d. Set Request

6. An FTP client connects to an FTP server using active mode and retrieves a copy of a file from the server. Which of the answers describes a TCP connection initiated by the FTP client?

    a. The FTP control connection

    b. The FTP data connection

    c. The FTP TLS connection

    d. None of the other answers are correct.

7. Which of the following functions are supported by FTP but not by TFTP? (Choose two answers.)

    a. Transferring files from client to server

    b. Changing the current directory on the server

    c. Transferring files from server to client

    d. Listing directory contents of a server's directory

Foundation Topics

First Hop Redundancy Protocol

When networks use a design that includes redundant routers, switches, LAN links, and WAN links, in some cases other protocols are required to take advantage of that redundancy and to prevent problems caused by it.

For instance, imagine a WAN with many remote branch offices. If each remote branch has two WAN links connecting it to the rest of the network, those routers can use an IP routing protocol to pick the best routes. The routing protocol learns routes over both WAN links, adding the best route into the routing table. When the better WAN link fails, the routing protocol adds the alternate route to the IP routing table, taking advantage of the redundant link.

As another example, consider a LAN with redundant links and switches. Those LANs have problems unless the switches use Spanning Tree Protocol (STP) or Rapid STP (RSTP). STP/RSTP prevents the problems created by frames that loop through those extra redundant paths in the LAN.

This section examines yet another type of protocol that helps when a network uses some redundancy, this time with redundant default routers. When two or more routers connect to the same LAN subnet, all those routers could be used as the default router for the hosts in the subnet. However, to make the best use of the redundant default routers, another protocol is needed. The term *First Hop Redundancy Protocol* (FHRP) refers to the category of protocols that can be used so that the hosts take advantage of redundant routers in a subnet.

This first major section of the chapter discusses the major concepts behind how different FHRPs work. This section begins by discussing a network's need for redundancy in general and the need for redundant default routers. It then shows how the three available FHRP options can each solve the problems that occur when using redundant default routers.

The Need for Redundancy in Networks

Networks need redundant links to improve the availability of those networks. Eventually, something in a network will fail. A router power supply might fail, or a cable might break, or a switch might lose power. And those WAN links, shown as simple lines in most drawings in this book, are actually the most complicated physical parts of the network, with many individual parts that can fail as well.

Depending on the design of the network, the failure of a single component might mean an outage that affects at least some part of the user population. Network engineers refer to any one component that, if it fails, brings down that part of the network as a *single point of failure*. For instance, in Figure 12-1, the LANs appear to have some redundancy, whereas the WAN does not. If most of the traffic flows between sites, many single points of failure exist, as shown in the figure.

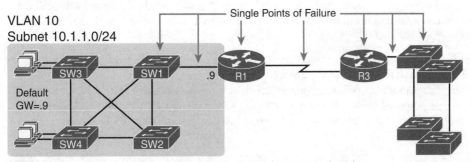

Figure 12-1   *R1 and the One WAN Link as Single Points of Failure*

The figure notes several components as a single point of failure. If any one of the noted parts of the network fails, packets cannot flow from the left side of the network to the right.

Generally speaking, to improve availability, the network engineer first looks at a design and finds the single points of failure. Then the engineer chooses where to add to the network so

12

that one (or more) single point of failure now has redundant options, increasing availability. In particular, the engineer

■ Adds redundant devices and links

■ Implements any necessary functions that take advantage of the redundant device or link

For instance, of all the single points of failure in Figure 12-1, the most expensive over the long term would likely be the WAN link because of the ongoing monthly charge. However, statistically, the WAN links are the most likely component to fail. So, a reasonable upgrade from the network in Figure 12-1 would be to add a WAN link and possibly even connect to another router on the right side of the network, as shown in Figure 12-2.

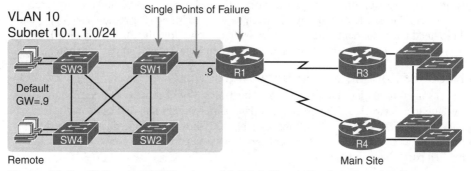

Figure 12-2 *Higher Availability but with R1 Still as a Single Point of Failure*

Many real enterprise networks follow designs like Figure 12-2, with one router at each remote site, two WAN links connecting back to the main site, and redundant routers at the main site (on the right side of the figure). Compared to Figure 12-1, the design in Figure 12-2 has fewer single points of failure. Of the remaining single points of failure, a risk remains, but it is a calculated risk. For many outages, a reload of the router solves the problem, and the outage is short. But the risk still exists that the switch or router hardware fails completely and requires time to deliver a replacement device on-site before that site can work again.

For enterprises that can justify more expense, the next step in higher availability for that remote site is to protect against those catastrophic router and switch failures. In this particular design, adding one router on the left side of the network in Figure 12-2 removes all the single points of failure that had been noted earlier. Figure 12-3 shows the design with a second router, which connects to a different LAN switch so that SW1 is also no longer a single point of failure.

NOTE Medium to large enterprise networks work hard at striking a balance of high-availability features versus the available budget dollars. Cisco.com has many design documents that discuss trade-offs in high-availability design. If interested in learning more, search Cisco.com for "high availability campus network design."

Answers to the "Do I Know This Already?" quiz:

1 D **2** C **3** C **4** B **5** A, C **6** A **7** B, D

VLAN 10
Subnet 10.1.1.0/24

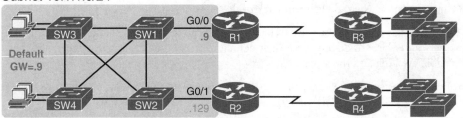

Figure 12-3 *Removing All Single Points of Failure from the Network Design*

The Need for a First Hop Redundancy Protocol

Of the designs shown so far in this chapter, only Figure 12-3's design has two routers to support the LAN on the left side of the figure, specifically the same VLAN and subnet. While having the redundant routers on the same subnet helps, the network needs to use an FHRP when these redundant routers exist.

To see the need and benefit of using an FHRP, first think about how these redundant routers could be used as default routers by the hosts in VLAN 10/subnet 10.1.1.0/24, as shown in Figure 12-4. The host logic will remain unchanged, so each host has a single default router setting. So, some design options for default router settings include the following:

■ All hosts in the subnet use R1 (10.1.1.9) as their default router, and they statically reconfigure their default router setting to R2's 10.1.1.129 if R1 fails.

■ All hosts in the subnet use R2 (10.1.1.129) as their default router, and they statically reconfigure their default router setting to R1's 10.1.1.9 if R2 fails.

■ Half the hosts use R1, and half use R2, as their default router, and if either router fails, that half of the users statically reconfigure their default router setting.

To make sure the concept is clear, Figure 12-4 shows this third option, with half the hosts using R1 and the other half using R2. The figure removes all the LAN switches just to unclutter the figure. Hosts A and B use R1 as their default router, and hosts C and D use R2 as their default router.

VLAN10, Subnet 10.1.1.0/24

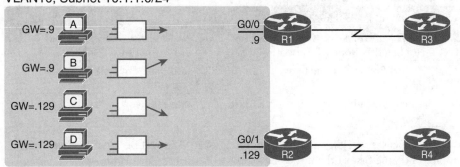

Figure 12-4 *Balancing Traffic by Assigning Different Default Routers to Different Clients*

12

All of these options have a problem: the users have to take action. They have to know an outage occurred. They have to know how to reconfigure their default router setting. And they have to know when to change it back to the original setting.

FHRPs make this design work better. The two routers appear to be a single default router. The users never have to do anything: their default router setting remains the same, and their ARP table even remains the same.

To allow the hosts to remain unchanged, the routers have to do some more work, as defined by one of the FHRP protocols. Generically, each FHRP makes the following happen:

1. All hosts act like they always have, with one default router setting that never has to change.

2. The default routers share a virtual IP address in the subnet, defined by the FHRP.

3. Hosts use the FHRP virtual IP address as their default router address.

4. The routers exchange FHRP protocol messages so that both agree as to which router does what work at any point in time.

5. When a router fails or has some other problem, the routers use the FHRP to choose which router takes over responsibilities from the failed router.

The Three Solutions for First-Hop Redundancy

The term *First Hop Redundancy Protocol* does not name any one protocol. Instead, it names a family of protocols that fill the same role. For a given network, like the left side of Figure 12-4, the engineer would pick one of the protocols from the FHRP family.

> **NOTE** *First Hop* is a reference to the default router being the first router, or first router hop, through which a packet must pass.

Table 12-2 lists the three FHRP protocols in chronological order, based on when these were first used. Cisco first introduced the proprietary Hot Standby Router Protocol (HSRP), and it worked well for many of its customers. Later, the IETF developed an RFC for a similar protocol, Virtual Router Redundancy Protocol (VRRP). Finally, Cisco developed a more robust option, Gateway Load Balancing Protocol (GLBP).

Table 12-2 Three FHRP Options

Acronym	Full Name	Origin	Redundancy Approach	Load Balancing Per...
HSRP	Hot Standby Router Protocol	Cisco	active/standby	subnet
VRRP	Virtual Router Redundancy Protocol	RFC 5798	active/standby	subnet
GLBP	Gateway Load Balancing Protocol	Cisco	active/active	host

This chapter focuses on HSRP and does not discuss VRRP and GLBP other than this brief mention. HSRP, the first of the three FHRP protocols to enter the market, remains a popular option in many networks. The current CCNA 200-301 exam requires you to know the functions of an FHRP, so the example of HSRP meets that need, with the next few pages walking through the concepts of how HSRP works. (Note that Appendix D, "Topics from

Previous Editions," contains a section with more depth about GLBP, copied from an earlier edition of the book, as well as a section on HSRP configuration if you are interested in reading more that goes beyond the current exam's topics.)

HSRP Concepts

HSRP operates with an active/standby model (also more generally called *active/passive*). HSRP allows two (or more) routers to cooperate, all being willing to act as the default router. However, at any one time, only one router actively supports the end-user traffic. The packets sent by hosts to their default router flow to that one active router. Then the other routers, with an HSRP standby state, sit there patiently waiting to take over should the active HSRP router have a problem.

The HSRP active router implements a virtual IP address and matching virtual MAC address. This virtual IP address exists as part of the HSRP configuration, which is an additional con-figuration item compared to the usual **ip address** interface subcommand. This virtual IP address is in the same subnet as the interface IP address, but it is a different IP address. The router then automatically creates the virtual MAC address. All the cooperating HSRP rout-ers know these virtual addresses, but only the HSRP active router uses these addresses at any one point in time.

Hosts refer to the virtual IP address as their default router address, instead of any one router's interface IP address. For instance, in Figure 12-5, R1 and R2 use HSRP. The HSRP virtual IP address is 10.1.1.1, with the virtual MAC address referenced as VMAC1 for sim-plicity's sake.

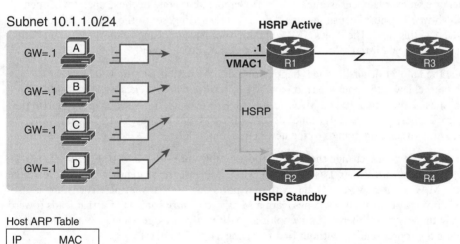

Figure 12-5 *All Traffic Goes to .1 (R1, Which Is Active); R2 Is Standby*

HSRP Failover

HSRP on each router has some work to do to make the network function as shown in Figure 12-5. The two routers need HSRP configuration, including the virtual IP address. The two routers send HSRP messages to each other to negotiate and decide which router should currently be active and which should be standby. Then the two routers continue to send messages to each other so that the standby router knows when the active router fails so that it can take over as the new active router.

Figure 12-6 shows the result when R1, the HSRP active router in Figure 12-5, fails. R1 quits using the virtual IP and MAC address, while R2, the new active router, starts using these addresses. The hosts do not need to change their default router settings at all, with traffic now flowing to R2 instead of R1.

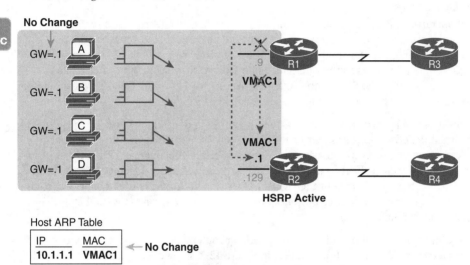

Figure 12-6 *Packets Sent Through R2 (New Active) Once It Takes Over for Failed R1*

When the failover happens, some changes do happen, but none of those changes happen on the hosts. The host keeps the same default router setting, set to the virtual IP address (10.1.1.1 in this case). The host's ARP table does not have to change either, with the HSRP virtual MAC being listed as the MAC address of the virtual router.

When the failover occurs, changes happen on both the routers and the LAN switches. Clearly, the new active router has to be ready to receive packets (encapsulated inside frames) using the virtual IP and MAC addresses. However, the LAN switches, hidden in the last few figures, formerly sent frames destined for VMAC1 to router R1. Now the switches must know to send the frames to the new active router, R2.

To make the switches change their MAC address table entries for VMAC1, R2 sends an Ethernet frame with VMAC1 as the source MAC address. The switches, as normal, learn the source MAC address (VMAC1), but with new ports that point toward R2. The frame is also a LAN broadcast, so all the switches learn a MAC table entry for VMAC1 that leads toward R2. (By the way, this Ethernet frame holds an ARP Reply message, called a gratuitous ARP, because the router sends it without first receiving an ARP Request.)

HSRP Load Balancing

The active/standby model of HSRP means that in one subnet all hosts send their off-subnet packets through only one router. In other words, the routers do not share the workload, with one router handling all the packets. For instance, back in Figure 12-5, R1 was the active router, so all hosts in the subnet sent their packets through R1, and none of the hosts in the subnet sent their packets through R2.

HSRP does support load balancing by preferring different routers to be the active router in different subnets. Most sites that require a second router for redundancy are also big enough to use several VLANs and subnets at the site. The two routers will likely connect to all the VLANs, acting as the default router in each VLAN. HSRP then can be configured to prefer one router as active in one VLAN and another router as active in another VLAN, balancing the traffic. Or you can configure multiple instances of HSRP in the same subnet (called multiple HSRP groups), preferring one router to be active in one group and the other router to be preferred as active in another.

For instance, Figure 12-7 shows a redesigned LAN, now with two hosts in VLAN 1 and two hosts in VLAN 2. Both R1 and R2 connect to the LAN, and both use a VLAN trunking and router-on-a-stick (ROAS) configuration. Both routers use HSRP in each of the two subnets, supporting each other. However, on purpose, R1 has been configured so that it wins the negotiation to become HSRP active in VLAN 1, and R2 has been configured to win in VLAN 2.

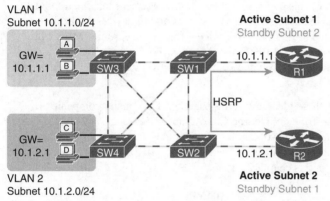

Figure 12-7 *Load Balancing with HSRP by Using Different Active Routers per Subnet*

Note that by having each router act as the HSRP active router in some subnets, the design makes use of both routers and both WAN links.

FHRPs are needed on any device that acts as a default router, which of course includes both traditional routers and Layer 3 switches. HSRP can be configured on routers and Layer 3 switches on interfaces that have IP addresses configured. However, in most cases, HSRP is used on interfaces to subnets that have hosts that need to use a default router. Those interfaces include router physical interfaces, router trunk subinterfaces, and Layer 3 switched virtual interfaces (SVI).

Simple Network Management Protocol

In 1988, RFC 1065, "Structure and Identification of Management Information for TCP/IP-based Internets," was published. The idea behind this document was the fact that information about devices on a TCP/IP-based network—configuration settings, status information, counters, and so on—could be broken down into a database of variables. Those variables could then be collected by management software to monitor and manage the IP-based network. After all, the elements of any IP-based machines would have commonalities. For example, a PC, a network printer, and a router would all have commonalities such as interfaces, IP addresses, and buffers. Why not create a standardized database of these variables and a simple system for monitoring and managing them? This idea was brilliant, caught on, and became what we know today as *Simple Network Management Protocol* (SNMP).

12

This second of three major sections of the chapter now turns our attention to SNMP by looking at the major concepts along with the two common versions used today: SNMPv2c and SNMPv3.

SNMP is an application layer protocol that provides a message format for communication between what are termed *managers* and *agents*. An SNMP manager is a network management application running on a PC or server, with that host typically being called a Network Management Station (NMS). Many SNMP agents exist in the network, one per device that is managed. The SNMP agent is software running inside each device (router, switch, and so on), with knowledge of all the variables on that device that describe the device's configuration, status, and counters. The SNMP manager uses SNMP protocols to communicate with each SNMP agent.

Each agent keeps a database of variables that make up the parameters, status, and counters for the operations of the device. This database, called the Management Information Base (MIB), has some core elements in common across most networking devices. It also has a large number of variables unique to that type of device—for instance, router MIBs will include variables not needed on switch MIBs, and vice versa. (For perspective, I did a quick check on a router when writing this section and found a little over 7000 MIB variables on a router.)

Figure 12-8 connects a few of these ideas and terms together. First, many companies sell SNMP management products—for example, the Cisco Prime series of management products (www.cisco.com/go/prime) use SNMP (and other protocols) to manage networks. IOS on routers and switches include an SNMP agent, with built-in MIB, that can be enabled with the configuration shown later in this chapter.

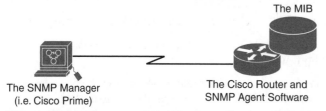

The MIB

The SNMP Manager
(i.e. Cisco Prime)

The Cisco Router and
SNMP Agent Software

Figure 12-8 *Elements of Simple Network Management Protocol*

SNMP Variable Reading and Writing: SNMP Get and Set

The NMS typically polls the SNMP agent on each device. The NMS can notify the human user in front of the PC or send emails, texts, and so on to notify the network operations staff of any issues identified by the data found by polling the devices. You can even reconfigure the device through these SNMP variables in the MIB if you permit this level of control.

Specifically, the NMS uses the SNMP Get, GetNext, and GetBulk messages (together referenced simply as Get messages) to ask for information from an agent. The NMS sends an SNMP Set message to write variables on the SNMP agent as a means to change the configuration of the device. These messages come in pairs, with, for instance, a Get Request asking the agent for the contents of a variable, and the Get Response supplying that information. Figure 12-9 shows an example of a typical flow, with the NMS using an SNMP Get to ask for the MIB variable that describes the status of a particular router interface.

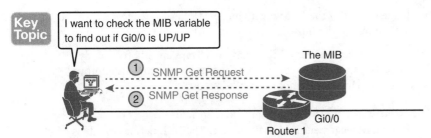

Figure 12-9 *SNMP Get Request and Get Response Message Flow*

SNMP permits much flexibility in how you monitor variables in the MIB. Most commonly, a network administrator gathers and stores statistics over time using the NMS. The NMS, with the stored data, can then analyze various statistical facts such as averages, minimums, and maximums. To be proactive, administrators can set thresholds for certain key variables, telling the NMS to send a notification (email, text, and so on) when a threshold is passed.

SNMP Notifications: Traps and Informs

In addition to asking for information with Get commands and setting variables on agents with the Set command, SNMP agents can initiate communications to the NMS. These messages, generally called notifications, use two specific SNMP messages: Trap and Inform. SNMP agents send a Trap or Inform SNMP message to the NMS to list the state of certain MIB variables when those variables reach a certain state.

As an example of a Trap, suppose that Router 1's G0/0 interface fails, as shown at step 1 of Figure 12-10. With Traps configured, the router would send an SNMP Trap message to the NMS, with that Trap message noting the down state of the G0/0 interface. Then, the NMS software can send a text message to the network support staff, pop up a window on the NMS screen, change the color of the correct router icon to red on the graphical interface, and so on.

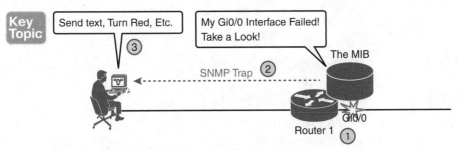

Figure 12-10 *SNMP Trap Notification Process*

SNMP Traps and Inform messages have the exact same purpose but differ in the protocol mechanisms. SNMP Traps, available since the first version of SNMP from the late 1980s (SNMP Version 1, or SNMPv1), use a fire-and-forget process. The SNMP agent sends the Trap to the IP address of the NMS, with UDP as the transport protocol as with all SNMP messages, and with no application layer error recovery. If the Trap arrives, great; if it is lost in transit, it is lost.

Inform messages are like Trap messages but with reliability added. Added to the protocol with SNMP Version 2 (SNMPv2), Informs still use UDP but add application layer reliability.

12

The NMS must acknowledge receipt of the Inform with an SNMP Response message, or the SNMP agent will time out and resend the Inform.

Note that Traps and Informs both have a useful role today, and Traps are still frequently used. Both inform the NMS. Traps use less overhead on the agent, while Informs improve reliability of the messages but require a little more overhead effort.

The Management Information Base

Every SNMP agent has its own Management Information Base. The MIB defines variables whose values are set and updated by the agent. The MIB variables on the devices in the network enable the management software to monitor/control the network device.

More formally, the MIB defines each variable as an *object ID* (OID). On most devices, the MIB then organizes the OIDs based in part on RFC standards, and in part with vendor-proprietary variables. The MIB organizes all the variables into a hierarchy of OIDs, usually shown as a tree. Each node in the tree can be described based on the tree structure sequence, either by name or by number. Figure 12-11 shows a small part of the tree structure of an MIB that happens to be part of the Cisco-proprietary part of the MIB.

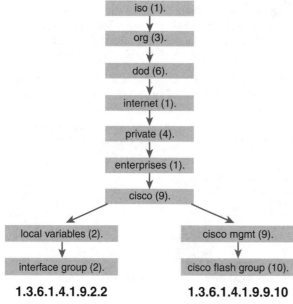

Figure 12-11 *Management Information Base (MIB)*

Working directly with an MIB, with long variable names and numbers, can be a bit of a challenge, so NMS software typically hides the complexity of the MIB variable numbering and names. However, to get a sense for the variable names, Figure 12-11 shows the tree structure for two variables, with the variable names being the long string of numbers shown at the bottom of the figure. Working with those numbers and the tree structure can be difficult at best. As a result, most people manage their networks using an NMS such as Cisco Prime. For perspective, you could use an SNMP manager and type MIB variable 1.3.6.1.4.1.9.2.1.58.0 and click a button to get that variable, to see the current CPU usage percentage from a Cisco router. However, most users of an NMS would much prefer to ignore those details and have a simple graphical interface to ask for the same information, never having to know that 1.3.6.1.4.9.2.1.58.0 represents the router CPU utilization MIB variable.

Securing SNMP

SNMP supports a few security mechanisms, depending in part on the particular version. This section works through the options.

First, one strong method to secure SNMP is to use ACLs to limit SNMP messages to those from known servers only. SNMP agents on Cisco routers and switches support SNMP messages that flow in both IPv4 and IPv6 packets. The SNMP agent can configure an IPv4 ACL to filter incoming SNMP messages that arrive in IPv4 packets and an IPv6 ACL to filter SNMP messages that arrive in IPv6 packets.

Using an IPv4 and IPv6 ACL to secure an agent makes good sense. The only hosts that should be sending SNMP messages to the SNMP agent in a router or switch are the NMS hosts. Those NMS hosts seldom move and their IP addresses should be well known to the networking staff. It makes good sense to configure an ACL that permits packets sourced from the IP addresses of all NMS hosts, but no others.

As for the SNMP protocol messages, all versions of SNMP support a basic clear-text password mechanism, although none of those versions refer to the mechanism as using a password. SNMP Version 3 (SNMPv3) adds more modern security as well.

SNMPv1 defined clear-text passwords called SNMP *communities*. Basically, both the SNMP agent and the SNMP manager need prior knowledge of the same SNMP community value (called a *community string*). The SNMP Get messages and the Set message include the appropriate community string value, in clear text. If the NMS sends a Get or Set with the correct community string, as configured on the SNMP agent, the agent processes the message.

SNMPv1 defines both a read-only community and a read-write community. The *read-only (RO) community* allows Get messages, and the *read-write (RW) community* allows both reads and writes (Gets and Sets). Figure 12-12 shows the concepts. At steps 1 and 2, the agent is configured with particular RO and RW community strings, and the NMS configures the matching values. At step 3, the SNMP Get can flow with either community, but at Step 4, the Set Request must use the RW community.

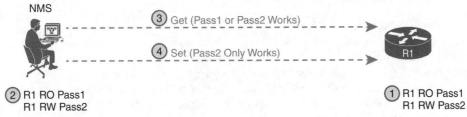

Figure 12-12 *RO and RW Communities with the Get and Set Commands*

SNMPv2, and the related Community-based SNMP Version 2 (SNMPv2c), added a wrinkle in naming but basically kept the same community security feature as SNMPv1 once the standards process completed. The original specifications for SNMPv2 did not include SNMPv1 communities; however, the marketplace still wanted communities, so an additional

RFC added the SNMPv1 communities mechanism back to SNMPv2. This updated RFC, "Community-based SNMPv2," came to be known simply as SNMPv2c. Vendors (including Cisco) implemented SNMPv2c; however, security was still relatively weak.

SNMPv3 arrived with much celebration among network administrators. Finally, security had arrived with the powerful network management protocol. SNMPv3 does away with communities and replaces them with the following features:

- **Message integrity:** This mechanism, applied to all SNMPv3 messages, confirms whether or not each message has been changed during transit.

- **Authentication:** This optional feature adds authentication with both a username and password, with the password never sent as clear text. Instead, it uses a hashing method like many other modern authentication processes.

- **Encryption (privacy):** This optional feature encrypts the contents of SNMPv3 messages so that attackers who intercept the messages cannot read their contents.

> **NOTE** The CCNA 200-301 exam blueprint lists SNMP in one exam topic, with that exam topic reduced to "explain SNMP," with no requirement for configuration or verification skills. However, the previous version of the CCNA R&S certification did include SNMP configuration. Refer to Appendix D if interested in learning about SNMP configuration and verification.

FTP and TFTP

This final of three major sections of the chapter focuses on two topics: File Transfer Protocol (FTP) and Trivial File Transfer Protocol (TFTP). Both exist as TCP/IP protocols defined in RFCs. Both use a client and server model, in which the client connects to a server and then the client can copy files to the server or from the server. Both exist as a myriad of implementations of both client and server code, from command-line clients to apps with graphical interfaces, using the respective FTP or TFTP protocols behind the scenes.

This section discusses FTP and TFTP with two branches. The first section takes a practical view of the most common use of TFTP and FTP by network engineers while on the job: the job of updating IOS images. The process can make use of TFTP and FTP, so this section provides the basics. The second branch of this final major section then moves on to talk about FTP and TFTP in a much broader sense, with details about each protocol, their capabilities, and what capabilities each provides to any user.

Managing Cisco IOS Images with FTP/TFTP

IOS exists as a file—a single file—that the router then loads into RAM to use as its operating system. To better understand the process, you must understand a few more details about how IOS works. In particular, you need to understand the IO file system (IFS), which defines how IOS stores files (including the IOS file). The IOS image upgrade process occurs by copying new IOS files into the router and then booting the router with that new IOS.

The IOS File System

Every OS creates file systems to store files. A computer needs some type of permanent storage, but it needs more than just a place to store bytes. The OS organizes the storage into a file system, which includes directories, structure, and filenames, with the associated rules. By using a file system, the OS can keep data organized so the user and the applications can find the data later.

Every OS defines its own file system conventions. Windows OSs, for instance, use a left-leaning slash (\) in directory structures, like \Desktop\Applications. Linux and macOS use a right-leaning slash, for example, /Desktop. Each OS refers to physical disks slightly differently as well, and IOS is no different.

As for the physical storage, Cisco routers typically use flash memory, with no hard disk drive. Flash memory is rewriteable, permanent storage, which is ideal for storing files that need to be retained when the router loses power. Cisco purposefully uses flash memory rather than hard disk drives in its products because there are no moving parts in flash memory, so there is a smaller chance of failure as compared with disk drives. Some routers have flash memory on the motherboard. Others have flash memory slots that allow easy removal and replacement of the flash card, but with the intent that the card remain in the device most of the time. Also, many devices have USB slots that support USB flash drives.

For each physical memory device in the router, IOS creates a simple IOS file system and gives that device a name. Example 12-1 lists the surprisingly long list of IOS file systems. Note that entries of type *disk* and *usbflash* are the physical storage devices in that router. In this case, the router has one of two of the 2901's compact flash slots populated with a 256-MB flash card and one of the two USB flash slots populated with an 8-GB USB flash drive. Look at the size column and prefixes column in the output to find these devices, based on their types as *disk* and *usbflash*.

Example 12-1   *Cisco IOS File Systems on a Router*

```
R2# show file systems
File Systems:


     Size(b)       Free(b)       Type    Flags    Prefixes
           -             -      opaque      rw     archive:
           -             -      opaque      rw     system:
           -             -      opaque      rw     tmpsys:
           -             -      opaque      rw     null:
           -             -     network      rw     tftp:
*  256487424      49238016        disk      rw     flash0: flash:#
           -             -        disk      rw     flash1:
      262136        253220       nvram      rw     nvram:
           -             -      opaque      wo     syslog:
           -             -      opaque      rw     xmodem:
           -             -      opaque      rw     ymodem:
           -             -     network      rw     rcp:
           -             -     network      rw     pram:
           -             -     network      rw     http:
           -             -     network      rw     ftp:
           -             -     network      rw     scp:
           -             -      opaque      ro     tar:
           -             -     network      rw     https:
           -             -      opaque      ro     cns:
  7794737152    7483719680    usbflash      rw     usbflash0:
74503236 bytes copied in 187.876 secs (396555 bytes/sec)
```

12

The example lists 20 different IOS file systems in this case, but the router does not have 20 different physical storage devices. Instead, IOS uses these file systems for other purposes as well, with these types:

- **Opaque:** To represent logical internal file systems for the convenience of internal functions and commands
- **Network:** To represent external file systems found on different types of servers for the convenience of reference in different IOS commands
- **Disk:** For flash
- **Usbflash:** For USB flash
- **NVRAM:** A special type for NVRAM memory, the default location of the startup-config file

Many IOS commands refer to files in an IFS, but only some commands refer directly to the files by their formal names. The formal names use the prefix as seen in the far right column of Example 12-1. For instance, the command **more flash0:/wotemp/fred** would display the contents of file *fred* in directory */wotemp* in the first flash memory slot in the router. (The **more** command itself displays the contents of a file.) However, many commands use a keyword that indirectly refers to a formal filename, to reduce typing. For example:

- **show running-config** command: Refers to file system:running-config
- **show startup-config** command: Refers to file nvram:startup-config
- **show flash** command: Refers to default flash IFS (usually flash0:)

Upgrading IOS Images

One of the first steps to upgrade a router's IOS to a new version is to obtain the new IOS image and put it in the right location. Typically, Cisco routers have their IOS in one of the local physical file systems, most often in permanent flash. The only requirement is that the IOS be in some reachable file system—even if the file sits on an external server and the device loads the OS over the network. However, the best practice is to store each device's IOS file in flash that will remain with the device permanently.

Figure 12-13 illustrates the process to upgrade an IOS image into flash memory, using the following steps:

Step 1. Obtain the IOS image from Cisco, usually by downloading the IOS image from Cisco.com using HTTP or FTP.

Step 2. Place the IOS image someplace that the router can reach. Locations include TFTP or FTP servers in the network or a USB flash drive that is then inserted into the router.

Step 3. Issue the **copy** command from the router, copying the file into the flash memory that usually remains with the router on a permanent basis. (Routers usually cannot boot from the IOS image in a USB flash drive.)

Figure 12-13 *Copying an IOS Image as Part of the Cisco IOS Software Upgrade Process*

Copying a New IOS Image to a Local IOS File System Using TFTP

Example 12-2 provides an example of step 3 from Figure 12-13, copying the IOS image into flash memory. In this case, router R2, a 2901, copies an IOS image from a TFTP server at IP address 2.2.2.1.

Example 12-2   copy tftp flash *Command Copies the IOS Image to Flash Memory*

```
R2# copy tftp flash
Address or name of remote host []? 2.2.2.1
Source filename []? c2900-universalk9-mz.SPA.152-4.M1.bin
Destination filename [c2900-universalk9-mz.SPA.152-4.M1.bin ]?
Accessing tftp://2.2.2.1/c2900-universalk9-mz.SPA.152-4.M1.bin ...
Loading c2900-universalk9-mz.SPA.152-4.M1.bin from 2.2.2.1 (via GigabitEthernet0/1):
!!!!!!!!!!!!!!!!!!!!!!!!!!!!!!!!!!!!!!!!!!!!!!!!!!!!!!!!!!!!!!!!!!!!!!!!!!!!!!!!!!!!!!!!!
!!!!!!!!!!!!!!!!!!!!!!!!!!!!!!!!!!!!!!!!!!!!!!!!!!!!!!!!!!!!!!!!!!!!!!!!!!!!!!!!!!!!!!!!!
!!!!!!!!!!!!!!!!!!!!!!!!!!!!!!!!!!!!!!!!!!!!!!!!!!!!!!!!!!!!!!!!!!!!!!!!!!!!!!!!!!!!!!!!!
!!!!!!!!!!!!!!!!!!!!!!!!!!!!!!!!!!!!!!
[OK - 97794040 bytes]

97794040 bytes copied in 187.876 secs (396555 bytes/sec)
R2#
```

The **copy** command does a simple task—copy a file—but the command also has several small items to check. It needs a few pieces of information from the user, so the command prompts the user for that information by showing the user some text and waiting for the user's input. The bold items in the example show the user's input. The router then has to check to make sure the copy will work. The command works through these kinds of questions:

1. What is the IP address or host name of the TFTP server?
2. What is the name of the file?
3. Ask the server to learn the size of the file, and then check the local router's flash to ask whether enough space is available for this file in flash memory.
4. Does the server actually have a file by that name?
5. Do you want the router to erase any old files in flash?

The router prompts you for answers to some of these questions, as necessary. For each question, you should either type an answer or press **Enter** if the default answer (shown in square brackets at the end of the question) is acceptable. Afterward, the router erases flash memory if directed, copies the file, and then verifies that the checksum for the file shows that no errors occurred in transmission.

NOTE   Most people use the IOS filenames that Cisco supplies because these names embed information about the IOS image, like the version. Also, if you want to use the same destination filename as the source, avoid the mistake of typing "y" or "yes" to confirm the selection; instead, you would be setting the destination filename to "y" or "yes." Simply press **Enter** to confirm the selection listed in brackets.

You can view the contents of the flash file system to see the IOS file that was just copied by using a couple of commands. The **show flash** command shows the files in the default flash file system (flash0:), as seen at the top of Example 12-3. Below it, the more general **dir flash0:** command lists the contents of that same file system, with similar information. (You can use the **dir** command to display the contents of any local IFS.)

Example 12-3 *Command Copies the IOS Image to Flash Memory*

```
R4# show flash
-#- --length-- -----date/time------ path
1    104193476 Jul 21 2015 13:38:06 +00:00  c2900-universalk9-mz.SPA.154-3.M3.bin
3      3000320 Jul 10 2012 00:05:44 +00:00  cpexpress.tar
4         1038 Jul 10 2012 00:05:52 +00:00  home.shtml
5       122880 Jul 10 2012 00:06:02 +00:00  home.tar
6      1697952 Jul 10 2012 00:06:16 +00:00  securedesktop-ios-3.1.1.45-k9.pkg
7       415956 Jul 10 2012 00:06:28 +00:00  sslclient-win-1.1.4.176.pkg
8         1153 Aug 16 2012 18:20:56 +00:00  wo-lic-1
9     97794040 Oct 10 2014 21:06:38 +00:00  c2900-universalk9-mz.SPA.152-4.M1.bin

49238016 bytes available (207249408 bytes used)


R4# dir flash0:
Directory of flash0:/

    1  -rw-  104193476  Jul 21 2015 13:38:06 +00:00  c2900-universalk9-mz.SPA.154-3.
M3.bin
    3  -rw-    3000320  Jul 10 2012 00:05:44 +00:00  cpexpress.tar
    4  -rw-       1038  Jul 10 2012 00:05:52 +00:00  home.shtml
    5  -rw-     122880  Jul 10 2012 00:06:02 +00:00  home.tar
    6  -rw-    1697952  Jul 10 2012 00:06:16 +00:00  securedesktop-ios-3.1.1.45-k9.
pkg
    7  -rw-     415956  Jul 10 2012 00:06:28 +00:00  sslclient-win-1.1.4.176.pkg
    8  -rw-       1153  Aug 16 2012 18:20:56 +00:00  wo-lic-1
    9  -rw-   97794040  Oct 10 2014 21:06:38 +00:00  c2900-universalk9-mz.SPA.152-4.
M1.bin

256487424 bytes total (49238016 bytes free)
```

Pay close attention to the memory usage per file and for the IFS as shown in the example. The output lists the size in bytes for each file. Note that the size of the final IOS file in the output matches the size shown earlier in the TFTP transfer in Example 12-2. The end of each of the commands then lists the amount of space available for new files to be added to flash (one lists it as "bytes available"; the other as "bytes free"). However, that same ending line of each command shows slightly different information about usage: **show flash** lists the bytes used, whereas the **dir** command lists the total bytes (bytes used plus bytes free). Play around with the numbers in this example to make sure you know which command lists which particular total.

Verifying IOS Code Integrity with MD5

You download the IOS from Cisco, copy it to your router, and run it. Is it really the code from Cisco? Or did some nefarious attacker somehow get you to download a fake IOS that has a virus?

Cisco provides a means to check the integrity of the IOS file to prevent this type of problem. Figure 12-14 shows the basic mechanics of the process. First, when Cisco builds a new IOS image, it calculates and publishes an MD5 hash value for that specific IOS file. That is, Cisco uses as input the IOS file itself, runs the MD5 math algorithm against that file, producing a hex code. Cisco places that code at the download site for all to see. Then, you run that same MD5 math on your router against the IOS file on the router, using the IOS **verify** command. That command will list the MD5 hash as recalculated on your router. If both MD5 hashes are equal, the file has not changed.

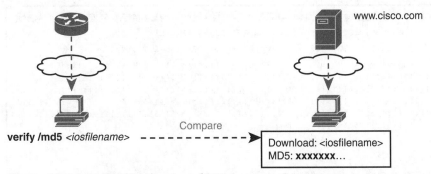

Figure 12-14 *MD5 Verification of IOS Images—Concepts*

The **verify /md5** command generates the MD5 hash on your router, as shown in Example 12-4. Note that you can include the hash value computed by Cisco as the last parameter (as shown in the example), or leave it off. If you include it, IOS will tell you if the locally computed value matches what you copied into the command. If you leave it out, the **verify** command lists the locally computed MD5 hash, and you have to do the picky character-by-character check of the values yourself.

Example 12-4 *Verifying Flash Memory Contents with the* **show flash** *Command*

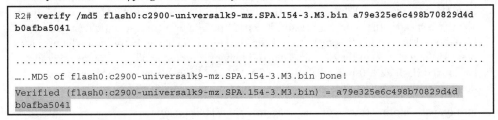

```
R2# verify /md5 flash0:c2900-universalk9-mz.SPA.154-3.M3.bin a79e325e6c498b70829d4d
b0afba5041
.........................................................................................
.........................................................................................
.....MD5 of flash0:c2900-universalk9-mz.SPA.154-3.M3.bin Done!
Verified (flash0:c2900-universalk9-mz.SPA.154-3.M3.bin) = a79e325e6c498b70829d4d
b0afba5041
```

Copying Images with FTP

The networking world has many options for file transfer, several of which IOS supports for the transfer of files into and out of the IOS file systems that reside on the router. TFTP and FTP have been supported for the longest time, with more recent support added for protocols like Secure Copy Protocol (SCP), which uses the SSH File Transfer Protocol (SFTP). Table 12-3 lists some of the names of file transfer protocols that you might come across when working with routers.

12

Table 12-3 Common Methods to Copy Files Outside a Router

Method	Method (Full Name)	Encrypted?
TFTP	Trivial File Transfer Protocol	No
FTP	File Transfer Protocol	No
SCP	Secure Copy Protocol	Yes

To copy files with FTP, you follow the same kind of process you use with TFTP (see Example 12-5). You can follow the interactive prompts after using an EXEC command like **copy ftp flash**. However, the **copy** command allows you to use a URI for the source and/or destination, which lets you put most or all of the information in the command line itself. Each URI refers to the formal name of a file in the IFS.

Example 12-5 *Installing a New IOS with FTP*

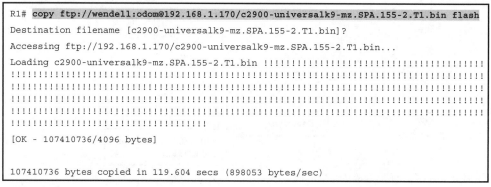

```
R1# copy ftp://wendell:odom@192.168.1.170/c2900-universalk9-mz.SPA.155-2.T1.bin flash
Destination filename [c2900-universalk9-mz.SPA.155-2.T1.bin]?
Accessing ftp://192.168.1.170/c2900-universalk9-mz.SPA.155-2.T1.bin...
Loading c2900-universalk9-mz.SPA.155-2.T1.bin !!!!!!!!!!!!!!!!!!!!!!!!!!!!!!!!!!!!!!
!!!!!!!!!!!!!!!!!!!!!!!!!!!!!!!!!!!!!!!!!!!!!!!!!!!!!!!!!!!!!!!!!!!!!!!!!!!!!!!!!!!!!!!!
!!!!!!!!!!!!!!!!!!!!!!!!!!!!!!!!!!!!!!!!!!!!!!!!!!!!!!!!!!!!!!!!!!!!!!!!!!!!!!!!!!!!!!!!
!!!!!!!!!!!!!!!!!!!!!!!!!!!!!!!!!!!!!!!!!!!!!!!!!!!!!!!!!!!!!!!!!!!!!!!!!!!!!!!!!!!!!!!!
!!!!!!!!!!!!!!!!!!!!!!!!!!!!!!!!!!!!!!!!!!!!!!!!!!!!!!!!!!!!!!!!!!!!!!!!!!!!!!!!!!!!!!!!
!!!!!!!!!!!!!!!!!!!!!!!!!!!!!!!!!!!!!!!!
[OK - 107410736/4096 bytes]

107410736 bytes copied in 119.604 secs (898053 bytes/sec)
```

First, take a close look at the long URI in the command that begins with "ftp." The "ftp" part identifies the protocol, of course. After the //, the text references the username (wendell) and password (odom), as well as the FTP server's IP address. After the single / comes the filename on the server.

Although the command is long, it has only two parameters, with the long first parameter and the short keyword **flash** as the second parameter. The **copy** command lists the source location as the first parameter and the destination as the second. The destination in this case, **flash**, is a keyword that refers to the default flash, typically flash0:, but it does not identify a specific filename. As a result, IOS prompts the user for a specific destination filename, with a default (in brackets) to keep the source filename. In this case, the user just pressed Enter to accept the default. To avoid being prompted at all, the command could have listed **flash:c2900-universalk9-mz.SPA.155-2.T1.bin** as that second parameter, fully defining the destination file.

Finally, with another twist, you can configure the FTP username and password on the router so that you do not have to include them in the **copy** command. For instance, the global configuration commands **ip ftp username wendell** and **ip ftp password odom** would have configured those values. Then the **copy** command would have begun with **copy ftp://192.168.1.170/...**, omitting the username:password in the command, without needing to then prompt the user for the username and password.

That completes the examples of showing how to copy IOS files into a router using TFTP and FTP. The exam topics happen to mention TFTP and FTP, but not the IOS upgrade process, so the text now turns away from the IOS upgrade process to focus more on TFTP and FTP. However, there are a few more steps to complete to upgrade IOS, such as configuring the boot system command and reloading the router. If you want to read about the rest of the IOS upgrade process or other related tasks like managing configuration files and performing password recovery, refer to this book's Appendix F, "Previous Edition ICND1 Chapter 35: Managing IOS Files."

However, to complete the IOS upgrade process, you need to finish a few more required steps.

The FTP and TFTP Protocols

The IOS **copy** command, when using the **tftp** or **ftp** keyword, makes the command act as a client. The client connects to a TFTP or FTP server and then attempts to transfer the file. In the examples from the IOS, that **copy** command copied the file from the server into the client device (a router).

The rest of this section examines what happens behind the scenes in that process, with a closer look at both FTP and TFTP as protocols and tools.

FTP Protocol Basics

FTP has long been a core Internet protocol, serving as the primary file transfer protocol for several decades. RFC 959, which standardizes FTP, dates back to 1985. FTP uses TCP as its transport protocol, relying on TCP to provide an error-free in-order deliver of data so that the FTP application knows that each file transfer creates an exact copy of the file with no omissions. FTP uses well-known TCP port 21 and in some cases also well-known port 20.

As for normal operation, FTP uses a client/server model for file transfer, as shown in the example in Figure 12-15. The figure shows the major steps but not every message. For instance, step 1 shows host A creating a TCP connection to the server (which takes the usual three TCP messages). Step 2 represents the exchange that allows the server to authenticate the client. Step 3 shows the idea that, once authenticated, the client and server can send FTP commands over the connection to tell the other device what to do.

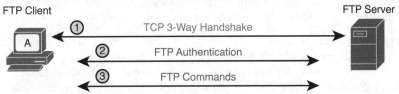

Figure 12-15   *Major Concepts with FTP Clients and Servers*

The commands that flow over this initial TCP connection—called the FTP control connection—define the kinds of functions supported by FTP. Those commands allow the client to navigate around the directory structures of the server, list files, and then transfer files from the server (FTP GET) or to the server (FTP PUT). Following is a summary of some of the FTP actions:

12

- **Navigate directories:** List the current directory, change the current directory to a new directory, go back to the home directory, all on both the server and client side of the connection.

- **Add/remove directories:** Create new directories and remove existing directories on both the client and server.

- **List files:** List files on both the client and server.

- **File transfer:** Get (client gets a copy of the file from the server), Put (client takes a file that exists on the client and puts a copy of the FTP server).

While many OSs support command-line FTP clients, which require you to learn the various FTP commands and use those from the command line, most users instead use an FTP client app that issues the FTP commands behind the scenes. Clients typically display files on the local system as well as the server with a user interface similar to a typical file browser on a desktop OS (for instance, Windows Explorer, macOS Finder). Figure 12-16 shows a sample user interface from the Filezilla FTP client (Filezilla-project.org).

Local Files   Server Files

Filename ∧	Filesize	Filetype	L	Filename ∧	Filesize	Filetype	Last modif
..				CL114-1.png	107,905	png-file	12/13/201
2019-Cert-announcements		Direct...	0	CL114-2.png	111,682	png-file	12/13/201
ACL Drills		Direct...	0	CL115_Trunk_puzzle_1.jpg	31,156	jpg-file	12/13/201
CCNA Anniversary		Direct...	0	CL116.png	67,020	png-file	12/13/201
CLUS 2018		Direct...	0	CL117-IP-Addr-2-V2.png	163,004	png-file	12/13/201
CML-VIRL		Direct...	0	CL117-IP-Addr-2.jpg	60,182	jpg-file	12/13/201
Config_Museum		Direct...	1	CL118.png	77,867	png-file	12/13/201
FR_Drills		Direct...	0	CL120.jpg	23,741	jpg-file	12/13/201
IPv6		Direct...	0	CL122.png	90,784	png-file	12/13/201
Labs		Direct...	0	CL123.png	109,179	png-file	12/13/201
				CL124.jpg	26,147	jpg-file	12/13/201

22 files and 16 directories. Total size: 8,482,143 bytes   793 files. Total size: 240,932,609 bytes

Figure 12-16 *FTP Client Example with Filezilla*

The client application in Figure 12-16 lists the client computer's local file system on the left and the FTP server's file system on the right. The user can click on the right to change directories, much like using any app that browses a file system, with FTP performing the commands behind the scenes. The user can also drag and drop files from the left to the right to put a file on the server, or vice versa to get a file from the server.

The FTP server can be a server application installed and managed by others, or you can install or enable an FTP server for your own use. For instance, a network engineer might install an FTP server application on her laptop for use in upgrading IOS files, while the IT staff may keep an FTP server available 24/7 for all employees of the company to use. A simple Internet search can show a variety of FTP server applications that run on the common desktop OSs. Additionally, both Windows 10 and macOS come with an FTP or FTPS (FTP Secure) server option built into the OS; all you have to do is enable it. (The Linux distributions all have FTP servers available via simple downloads.)

Once installed, the server can be configured with a variety of settings. For instance, the server needs to specify which users can access the server, so it can use the same login credentials allowed for the host where it resides or specify other credentials. It can specify the directories that each user can access, and whether the user has read-only or read-write access.

FTP Active and Passive Modes

FTP can operate in either active or passive mode. The choice of mode may impact whether the TCP client can or cannot connect to the server and perform normal functions. The user at the FTP client can choose which mode to use, so this section works through the underlying details to explain why FTP passive mode may be the more likely option to work.

First, note that FTP uses two types of TCP connections:

- **Control Connection:** Used to exchange FTP commands
- **Data Connection:** Used for sending and receiving data, both for file transfers and for output to display to a user

Given the two roles, when a client connects to an FTP server, the client first creates the FTP control connection as shown in Figure 12-17. The server listens for new control connections on its well-known port 21; the client allocates any new dynamic port (49222 in this case) and creates a TCP connection to the server.

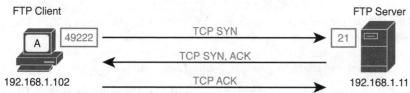

Figure 12-17 *FTP Client Creates an FTP Control Connection*

After creating the TCP connection, the user authenticates to the FTP server and takes some actions. Some of those actions require only the control connection, but eventually the user will take an action (like getting a file) that requires a data connection. When that happens, to create the FTP data connection, the client will either use active mode or passive mode, as shown in the next two examples.

Figure 12-18 shows an example of what happens in active mode. Following the steps in the figure:

1. The FTP client allocates a currently unused dynamic port and starts listening on that port.
2. The client identifies that port (and its IP address) to the FTP server by sending an FTP **PORT** command to the server.
3. The server, because it also operates in active mode, expects the **PORT** command; the server reacts and initiates the FTP data connection to the client's address (192.168.1.102) and port (49333).

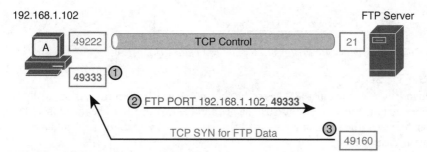

Figure 12-18 *FTP Active Mode Process to Create the Data Connection*

12

Active mode works well with both the FTP client and server sitting inside the same enterprise network. When within the same network, typically no NAT function and no firewall sits between the two. However, if the FTP client sits in an enterprise network, and the FTP server resides somewhere in the Internet, an active mode connection typically fails. Most firewalls do not allow Internet-based hosts to initiate TCP connections to hosts inside the enterprise without a specific firewall rule allowing connections to a known port, and in this case, the FTP client allocates any available port number. For instance, in Figure 12-18, the TCP connection (step 3) would be discarded by a firewall.

> **NOTE** FTP reserves two well-known ports: port 21 for control connections and port 20 for data connections. However, due to changes to FTP over the years, FTP often uses other TCP ports for the TCP data connection, as seen in the examples in this chapter.

Passive mode helps solve the firewall restrictions by having the FTP client initiate the FTP data connection to the server. However, passive mode does not simply cause the FTP client to connect to a well-known port on the server; it requires more exchanges of port numbers to use between the server and client, as shown in Figure 12-19, with these steps:

1. The FTP client changes to use FTP passive mode, notifying the server using the FTP **PASV** command.

2. The server chooses a port to listen on for the upcoming new TCP connection, in this case TCP port 49444.

3. The FTP notifies the FTP client of its IP address and chosen port with the FTP **PORT** command.

4. The FTP client opens the TCP data connection to the IP address and port learned at the previous step.

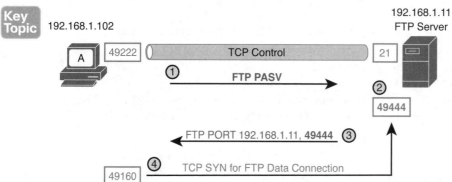

Figure 12-19 *FTP Passive Mode Process to Create the Data Connection*

FTP over TLS (FTP Secure)

FTP, defined in RFC 959 back in 1985, has some shortcomings with security. As originally defined, it does include the ability to use usernames and passwords for authentication and authorization; however, the username/password flows as clear text. Additionally, all data transfers flow as clear text.

Over the years, several RFCs defined security improvements for FTP. Those new features include using digital certificates for authentication as well as using Transport Layer Security (TLS) to encrypt all data (including usernames/passwords). Fast forward to today and many of those features converge into what most FTP clients and servers support as FTP over TLS or as FTP Secure (FTPS).

With FTPS, the client and server still use FTP commands and still use both a control and data connection. However, FTPS encrypts both the control and data connections with TLS, including the exchange of the usernames and passwords. FTPS includes a few variations, including the FTPS explicit mode process shown in Figure 12-20:

1. The client creates the FTP control TCP connection to server well-known port 21.

2. The client initiates the use of TLS in the control connection with the FTP **AUTH** command.

3. When the user takes an action that requires an FTP data connection, the client creates an FTP data TCP connection to server well-known port 21.

4. The client initiates the use of TLS in the data connection with the FTP **AUTH** command.

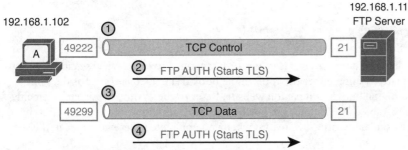

Figure 12-20 *FTPS Explicit Mode Control and Data Connection Establishment*

In contrast, the implicit mode process begins with a required TLS connection, with no need for an FTP AUTH command, using well-known ports 990 (for the control connection) and 989 (for the data connection).

> **NOTE** SSH File Transfer Protocol (SFTP) is a different protocol than FTPS. SFTP uses SSH to encrypt file transfers over an SSH connection. However, the acronym SFTP does not refer to a secure version of FTP.

TFTP Protocol Basics

FTP has a role as a general file transfer tool for any user, with a good number of FTP client application options available. TFTP plays a much smaller role as a tool for the average user, but it does play a more useful role for IT support staff.

For the basics, Trivial File Transfer Protocol uses UDP well-known port 69. Because it uses UDP, TFTP adds a feature to check each file for transmission errors by using a checksum process on each file after the transfer completes.

The word *trivial* in the name refers to its relatively small number of features, meant to be an advantage by making the tool lightweight. For instance, it supports far fewer commands than FTP (fewer functions), meaning that the code requires less space to install, which can be useful for devices with limited memory. TFTP can Get and Put files, but it includes no commands to change directories, create/remove directories, or even to list files on the

Key Topic

12

server. TFTP does not support even simple clear-text authentication. In effect, if a TFTP server is running, it should accept requests from any TFTP client.

Ideally, TFTP has its best use as a temporary tool for quick file transfers in a controlled environment, particularly when the data itself does not have to be secure. For instance, imagine this scenario:

1. A network engineer keeps all router and switch IOS images in a folder.

2. The engineer enables a TFTP server on her laptop as needed; otherwise, the TFTP server remains disabled.

3. The engineer connects her laptop to a LAN and enables the TFTP server long enough to transfer IOS images into or out of a few devices.

4. If the engineer forgets to disable TFTP, the only risk is that someone may copy an IOS image—an image that is already available from Cisco.com to any customer.

Chapter Review

One key to doing well on the exams is to perform repetitive spaced review sessions. Review this chapter's material using either the tools in the book or interactive tools for the same material found on the book's companion website. Refer to the "Your Study Plan" element for more details. Table 12-4 outlines the key review elements and where you can find them. To better track your study progress, record when you completed these activities in the second column.

Table 12-4 Chapter Review Tracking

Review Element	Review Date(s)	Resource Used
Review key topics		Book, website
Review key terms		Book, website
Answer DIKTA questions		Book, PTP
Review Command Tables		Book

Review All the Key Topics

Table 12-5 Key Topics for Chapter 12

Key Topic Element	Description	Page Number
List	Common characteristics of all FHRPs	260
Table 12-2	Comparisons of HSRP, VRRP, GLBP	260
Figure 12-5	HSRP concepts	261
Figure 12-6	HSRP failover results	262
Figure 12-9	The SNMP Get Request and Get Response message flow	265
Figure 12-10	SNMP notification with SNMP Trap messages	265
Figure 12-12	The use of SNMP RO and RW communities with SNMP Get and Set	267

Key Topic Element	Description	Page Number
List	SNMP security benefits	268
Figure 12-13	Process of upgrading IOS using TFTP	270
Example 12-2	Example of using TFTP to load new IOS	271
Example 12-5	Example of using FTP to load new IOS	274
List	FTP functions	276
List	FTP data and control connections	277
Figure 12-17	FTP Control connection establishment	277
Figure 12-19	FTP data connection establishment in passive mode	278
Paragraph	Description of limited functions of TFTP	279

Key Terms You Should Know

First Hop Redundancy Protocol (FHRP), Hot Standby Router Protocol (HSRP), Virtual Router Redundancy Protocol (VRRP), Gateway Load Balancing Protocol (GLBP), virtual IP address, virtual MAC address, HSRP active, HSRP standby, Simple Network Management Protocol (SNMP), SNMP community, read-only community, read-write community, notification community, SNMP Get, SNMP Set, SNMP Trap, SNMP Inform, Management Information Base (MIB), SNMPv2c, SNMPv3, Network Management System (NMS), SNMP manager, SNMP agent, IOS image, flash memory, IOS file system, code integrity, TFTP, FTP, FTP control connection, FTP data connection, FTP over TLS

Command References

Tables 12-6 and 12-7 list configuration and verification commands used in this chapter. As an easy review exercise, cover the left column in a table, read the right column, and try to recall the command without looking. Then repeat the exercise, covering the right column, and try to recall what the command does.

Table 12-6   Chapter 12 Configuration Command Reference

Command	Description
boot system flash [*flash-fs:*] [*filename*]	Global command that identifies the location of an IOS image in flash memory
boot system {**tftp** | **ftp**} *filename* [*ip-address*]	Global command that identifies an external server, protocol, and filename to use to load an IOS from an external server
ip ftp username *name*	Global command to define the username used when referencing the **ftp:** IOS file system but not supplying a username
ip ftp password *pass*	Global command to define the password used when referencing the **ftp:** IOS file system but not supplying a password

12

Table 12-7 Chapter 12 EXEC Command Reference

Command	Description
copy *from-location to-location*	Enable mode EXEC command that copies files from one file location to another. Locations include the startup-config and running-config files, files on TFTP and RPC servers, and flash memory.
show flash	Lists the names and size of the files in flash memory, and notes the amount of flash memory consumed and available.
dir *filesystem:* dir *filesystem:directory*	Lists the files in the referenced file system or file system directory.
verify /md5 *filesystem:name* [MD5-hash]	Performs an MD5 hash of the referenced file and displays the results. If listed, the command compares the MD5 hash in the command with the results of performing MD5 on the local file.

Part III Review

Keep track of your part review progress with the checklist shown in Table P3-1. Details on each task follow the table.

Table P3-1   Part III Review Checklist

Activity	1st Date Completed	2nd Date Completed
Repeat All DIKTA Questions		
Answer Part Review Questions		
Review Key Topics		
Do Labs		
Review Videos		

Repeat All DIKTA Questions

For this task, use the PTP software to answer the "Do I Know This Already?" questions again for the chapters in this part of the book.

Answer Part Review Questions

For this task, use PTP to answer the Part Review questions for this part of the book.

Review Key Topics

Review all key topics in all chapters in this part, either by browsing the chapters or by using the Key Topics application on the companion website.

Use Per-Chapter Interactive Review Elements

Using the companion website, browse through the interactive review elements, such as memory tables and key term flashcards, to review the content from each chapter.

Labs

Depending on your chosen lab tool, here are some suggestions for what to do in the lab:

Pearson Network Simulator: If you use the full Pearson CCNA simulator, focus more on the configuration scenario and troubleshooting scenario labs associated with the topics in this part of the book. These types of labs include a larger set of topics and work well as Part Review activities. (See the Introduction for some details about how to find which labs are about topics in this part of the book.)

Blog Config Labs: The author's blog (https://blog.certskills.com) includes a series of configuration-focused labs that you can do on paper, each in 10–15 minutes. Review and perform the labs for this part of the book by using the menus to navigate to the per-chapter content and then finding all config labs related to that chapter. (You can see more detailed instructions at https://blog.certskills.com/config-labs.)

Other: If using other lab tools, here are a few suggestions: All the exam topics in Part III that include the word *configure* exist in Chapters 9 and 10, so focus on those chapters. Those chapters touch on CDP/LLDP, NTP, syslog, and NAT/PAT.

Watch Videos

Part III's Chapter 11 includes a mention of a video about QoS Classification and Marking. You can find a link to view that video in the section for videos in the companion website for this book.

Part IV turns the attention away from the concept-configure-verify approach needed for many of the topics seen earlier in this book and in *CCNA 200-301 Official Cert Guide, Volume 1*. Instead, this part collects topics that will be presented more from an architecture and design perspective. In fact, the CCNA 200-301 exam organizes six exam topics with this same approach, all listed under exam topic 1.2 "Describe characteristics of network topology architectures." The chapters in this part examine most of those topics.

First, Chapter 13 revisits LAN switching, which was covered to some depth in Volume 1. This chapter discusses campus LAN design concepts and terminology, like the *2 tier* and *3 tier* terms listed in the exam topics. This chapter also discusses how to supply power over that LAN infrastructure using Power over Ethernet (PoE), as well as the term *small office/home office* (SOHO).

CCNA 200-301 mentions WAN as an end to itself in one exam topic within the context of topology and architecture. Chapter 14 takes that thread and presents three major WAN architectures, going beyond the concepts you need to know to support the simple WAN cases used in the examples throughout both books so far. Those topics include MPLS VPN WANs, Ethernet WANs, and Internet VPNs.

Chapter 15 completes the architecture-focused chapters with a discussion of cloud architectures. This chapter begins by defining basic concepts and terms related to data centers and cloud and closes with design discussions that show packet flows in a public cloud environment.

Part IV

Network Architecture

CHAPTER 13

LAN Architecture

This chapter covers the following exam topics:

1.0 Network Fundamentals

1.2 Describe characteristics of network topology architectures

1.2.a 2 tier

1.2.b 3 tier

1.2.e Small office/home office (SOHO)

1.3 Compare physical interface and cabling types

1.3.c Concepts of PoE

By now you have learned a lot about Ethernet and Ethernet switches. You have learned how individual links work, with cabling and duplex settings as well as framing. You know how addresses work and how switches forward frames based on those addresses. You have seen how switches deal with redundancy, using STP/RSTP and collecting links into EtherChannels. And here in Volume 2, you have learned about a variety of security features available for switches, including Dynamic ARP Inspection, DHCP Snooping, and ARP Inspection.

What the earlier discussions of individual features do not do to any great extent is discuss architecture and design. You now know how switches work, but why would you connect switches in one topology versus another? If you could connect switches in two different topologies, why would you prefer one over the other? This chapter examines a few such design questions, specifically the topic areas mentioned in the CCNA 200-301 exam topics. (Note that the CCNA 200-301 exam does not include a comprehensive look at LAN design issues, but one of the current CCNP Enterprise exams does.)

This chapter covers three specific topics that have design-related considerations. The first section looks at the topology of a wired Ethernet LAN and the design terms *two tier* and *three tier*, which describe how many switch layers exist between the endpoints and the devices that lead out of the campus to some other site. Following that, the second section examines small office/home office (SOHO) LANs and how they differ from enterprise LANs. The final section introduces the concepts behind Power over Ethernet (PoE), along with the reasons why LAN design activities need to consider PoE.

"Do I Know This Already?" Quiz

Take the quiz (either here or use the PTP software) if you want to use the score to help you decide how much time to spend on this chapter. The letter answers are listed at the bottom of the page following the quiz. Appendix C, found both at the end of the book as well as on the companion website, includes both the answers and explanations. You can also find both answers and explanations in the PTP testing software.

Table 13-1 "Do I Know This Already?" Foundation Topics Section-to-Question Mapping

Foundation Topics Section	Questions
Analyzing Campus LAN Topologies	1–3
Small Office/Home Office	4
Power over Ethernet	5–6

1. In a two-tier campus LAN design, which of the following are typically true of the topology design? (Choose two answers.)

   a. The design uses a full mesh of links between access and distribution switches.

   b. The design uses a partial mesh of links between access and distribution switches.

   c. The design uses a partial mesh of links between the distribution and core switches.

   d. The end-user and server devices connect directly to access layer switches.

2. In a three-tier campus LAN design, which of the following are typically true of the topology design? (Choose two answers.)

   a. The design uses a partial mesh of links between access and distribution switches.

   b. The design uses a full mesh of links between access and distribution switches.

   c. The design uses a partial mesh of links between the distribution and core switches.

   d. The end-user and server devices connect directly to distribution layer switches.

3. Which one answer gives the strongest match between one part of a typical three-tier design with the idea behind the listed generic topology design term?

   a. The access layer looks like a partial mesh.

   b. The distribution layer looks like a full mesh.

   c. The distribution layer looks like a hybrid design.

   d. The access layer looks like a star design.

4. Which answers list criteria typical of a SOHO network? (Choose two answers.)

   a. The AP functions using standalone mode.

   b. The AP functions using a split-MAC architecture using a WLC.

   c. A single networking device implements the router, switch, AP, and firewall functions.

   d. A separate networking device implements each function (router, switch, AP, and firewall).

5. Which answer describes how a LAN switch dynamically chooses the initial power level to apply to a UTP cable with PoE?

   a. Autonegotiation

   b. CDP

   c. LLDP

   d. Preconfigured values

6. Which of the following refer to standards that deliver power over all four pairs in a UTP cable? (Choose two answers.)

  a. PoE

  b. UPoE

  c. PoE+

  d. UPoE+

Analyzing Campus LAN Topologies

The term *campus LAN* refers to the LAN created to support the devices in a building or in multiple buildings in somewhat close proximity to one another. For example, a company might lease office space in several buildings in the same office park. The network engineers can then build a campus LAN that includes switches in each building, plus Ethernet links between the switches in the buildings, to create a larger campus LAN.

When planning and designing a campus LAN, the engineers must consider the types of Ethernet available and the cabling lengths supported by each type. The engineers also need to choose the speeds required for each Ethernet segment. In addition, some thought needs to be given to the idea that some switches should be used to connect directly to end-user devices, whereas other switches might need to simply connect to a large number of these end-user switches. Finally, most projects require that the engineer consider the type of equipment that is already installed and whether an increase in speed on some segments is worth the cost of buying new equipment.

This first of three major sections of the chapter discusses the topology of a campus LAN design. Network designers do not just plug in devices to any port and connect switches to each other in an arbitrary way, like you might do with a few devices on the same table in a lab. Instead, there are known better ways to design the topology of a campus LAN, and this section introduces some of the key points and terms

Two-Tier Campus Design (Collapsed Core)

To sift through all the requirements for a campus LAN, and then have a reasonable conversation about it with peers, most Cisco-oriented LAN designs use some common terminology to refer to the design. For this book's purposes, you should be aware of some of the key campus LAN design terminology.

The Two-Tier Campus Design

Figure 13-1 shows a typical design of a large campus LAN, with the terminology included in the figure. This LAN has around 1000 PCs connected to switches that support around 25 ports each. Explanations of the terminology follow the figure.

Cisco uses three terms to describe the role of each switch in a campus design: *access*, *distribution*, and *core*. The roles differ based on whether the switch forwards traffic from user devices and the rest of the LAN (access), or whether the switch forwards traffic between other LAN switches (distribution and core).

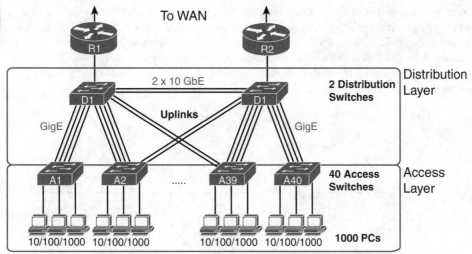

Figure 13-1 *Campus LAN with Design Terminology Listed*

Access switches connect directly to end users, providing user device access to the LAN. Access switches normally send traffic to and from the end-user devices to which they are connected and sit at the edge of the LAN.

Distribution switches provide a path through which the access switches can forward traffic to each other. By design, each of the access switches connects to at least one distribution switch, typically to two distribution switches for redundancy. The distribution switches provide the service of forwarding traffic to other parts of the LAN. Note that most designs use at least two uplinks to two different distribution switches (as shown in Figure 13-1) for redundancy.

The figure shows a two-tier design, with the tiers being the access tier (or layer) and the distribution tier (or layer). A two-tier design solves two major design needs:

- Provides a place to connect end-user devices (the access layer, with access switches)
- Connects the switches with a reasonable number of cables and switch ports by connecting all 40 access switches to two distribution switches

NOTE   The terms two-tier and 2-tier are synonyms, as are the terms three-tier and 3-tier. Cisco happens to use the versions of these terms with numerals in the exam topics.

Topology Terminology Seen Within a Two-Tier Design

The networking world uses several common terms about LAN and WAN topology and design including these:

Star: A design in which one central device connects to several others, so that if you drew the links out in all directions, the design would look like a star with light shining in all directions.

Full mesh: For any set of network nodes, a design that connects a link between each pair of nodes.

Partial mesh: For any set of network nodes, a design that connects a link between some pairs of nodes, but not all. In other words, a mesh that is not a full mesh.

Hybrid: A design that combines topology design concepts into a larger (typically more complex) design.

13

Armed with those formal definitions, note that the two-tier design is indeed a hybrid design that uses both a star topology at the access layer and a partial mesh at the distribution layer. To see why, consider Figure 13-2. It redraws a typical access layer switch, but instead of putting the PCs all below the switch, it spreads them around the switch. Then on the right, a similar version of the same drawing shows why the term *star* might be used—the topology looks a little like a child's drawing of a star.

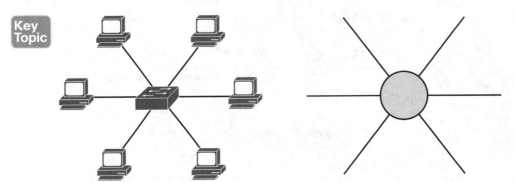

Figure 13-2 *The Star Topology Design Concept in Networking*

The distribution layer creates a partial mesh. If you view the access and distribution switches as nodes in a design, some nodes have a link between them, and some do not. Just refer to Figure 13-1 and note that, by design, none of the access layer switches connect to each other.

Finally, a design could use a full mesh. However, for a variety of reasons beyond the scope of the design discussion here, a campus design typically does not need to use the number of links and ports required by a full mesh design. However, just to make the point, first consider how many links and switch ports would be required for a single link between nodes in a full mesh, with six nodes, as shown in Figure 13-3.

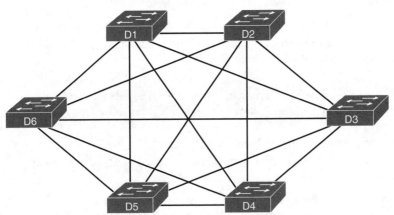

Figure 13-3 *Using a Full Mesh at the Distribution Layer, 6 Switches, 15 Links*

Answers to the "Do I Know This Already?" quiz:

1 B, D **2** A, C **3** D **4** A, C **5** A **6** B, D

Even with only six switches, a full mesh would consume 15 links (and 30 switch ports—two per link).

Now think about a full mesh at the distribution layer for a design like Figure 13-1, with 40 access switches and two distribution switches. Rather than drawing it and counting it, the number of links is calculated with this old math formula from high school: $N(N - 1) / 2$, or in this case, $42 * 41 / 2 = 861$ links, and 1722 switch ports consumed among all switches.

For comparison's sake, the partial mesh design of Figure 13-1, with a pair of links from each access switch to each distribution switch, requires only 160 links and a total of 320 ports among all switches.

Three-Tier Campus Design (Core)

The two-tier design of Figure 13-1, with a partial mesh of links at the distribution layer, happens to be the most common campus LAN design. It also goes by two common names: a two-tier design (for obvious reasons) and a collapsed core (for less obvious reasons). The term *collapsed core* refers to the fact that the two-tier design does not have a third tier, the core tier. This next topic examines a three-tier design that does have a core, for perspective.

Imagine your campus has just two or three buildings. Each building has a two-tier design inside the building, with a pair of distribution switches in each building and access switches spread around the building as needed. How would you connect the LANs in each building? Well, with just a few buildings, it makes sense to simply cable the distribution switches together, as shown in Figure 13-4.

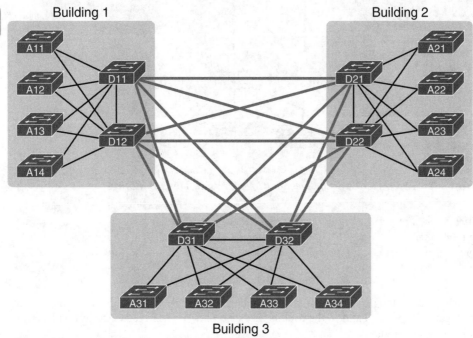

Figure 13-4 *Two-Tier Building Design, No Core, Three Buildings*

The design in Figure 13-4 works well, and many companies use this design. Sometimes the center of the network uses a full mesh, sometimes a partial mesh, depending on the availability of cables between the buildings.

However, a design with a third tier (a core tier) saves on switch ports and on cables in larger designs. And note that with the links between buildings, the cables run outside, are often more expensive to install, and are almost always fiber cabling with more expensive switch ports, so conserving the number of cables used between buildings can help reduce costs.

A three-tier core design, unsurprisingly at this point, adds a few more switches (core switches), which provide one function: to connect the distribution switches. Figure 13-5 shows the migration of the Figure 13-4 collapsed core (that is, a design without a core) to a three-tier core design.

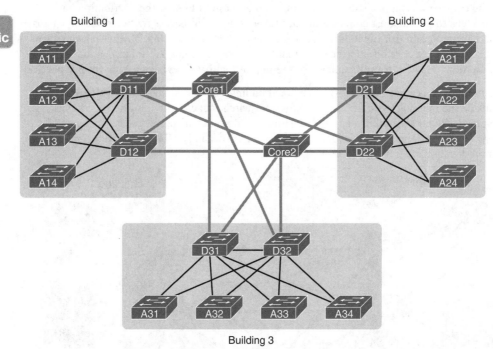

Figure 13-5 *Three-Tier Building Design (Core Design), Three Buildings*

NOTE The core switches sit in the middle of the figure. In the physical world, they often sit in the same room as one of the distribution switches, rather than in some purpose-built room in the middle of the office park. The figure focuses more on the topology rather than the physical location.

By using a core design, with a partial mesh of links in the core, you still provide connectivity to all parts of the LAN and to the routers that send packets over the WAN, just with fewer links between buildings.

The following list summarizes the terms that describe the roles of campus switches:

- **Access:** Provides a connection point (access) for end-user devices. Does not forward frames between two other access switches under normal circumstances.

- **Distribution:** Provides an aggregation point for access switches, providing connectivity to the rest of the devices in the LAN, forwarding frames between switches, but not connecting directly to end-user devices.

- **Core:** Aggregates distribution switches in very large campus LANs, providing very high forwarding rates for the larger volume of traffic due to the size of the network.

Topology Design Terminology

To close the discussion of Enterprise LAN topology, the next topic applies some of the generic topology terms to a typical two-tier design.

Consider Figure 13-6, which shows a few of the terms. First, on the left, drawings often show access switches with a series of cables, parallel to each other. However, the combinations of an access switch and its access links is often called a *star topology*. Why? Look at the redrawn access switch in the center of the figure, with the cables radiating out from the center. It does not look like a real star, but it looks a little like a child's drawing of a star, hence the term *star topology*.

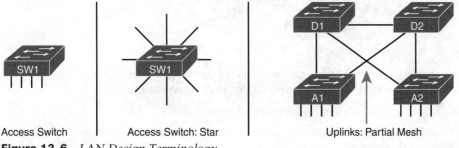

Access Switch   Access Switch: Star   Uplinks: Partial Mesh

Figure 13-6   *LAN Design Terminology*

The right side of the figure repeats a typical two-tier design, focusing on the mesh of links between the access and distribution switches. Any group of nodes that connect with more links than a star topology is typically called a *mesh*. In this case, the mesh is a *partial mesh*, because not all nodes have a direct link between each other. A design that connects all nodes with a link would be a *full mesh*.

Real networks make use of these topology ideas, but often a network combines the ideas together. For instance, the right side of Figure 13-6 combines the star topology of the access layer with the partial mesh of the distribution layer. So you might hear these designs that combine concepts called a *hybrid design*.

Small Office/Home Office

Now that you know more about design choices and terms for an enterprise LAN, this next section examines one particular type of smaller LAN: the small office/home office (SOHO) LAN. SOHO refers to designs and implementations that have such a small volume of requirements—few switch ports, few APs, few routers and WAN links—that the design differs significantly. The term itself refers to the two most common cases: a user who works

13

from home or a small office with a small number of workers and devices. This next short topic points out a few of the highlights that make a SOHO network different from an enterprise network.

First, as a reminder, the IEEE defines both Ethernet LANs and wireless LANs (WLANs). In case it was not obvious yet, all Ethernet standards use cables—that is, Ethernet defines wired LANs. The IEEE 802.11 working group defines wireless LANs, also called Wi-Fi per a trademarked term from the Wi-Fi Alliance (www.wi-fi.org), a consortium that helps encourage wireless LAN development in the marketplace.

Most of you have used Wi-Fi, and may use it daily. Some of you may have set it up at home, with a basic setup as shown in Figure 13-7. In a home, you probably used a single consumer device called a *wireless router*. One side of the device connects to the Internet, while the other side connects to the devices in the home. In the home, the devices can connect either with Wi-Fi or with a wired Ethernet cable.

SOHO

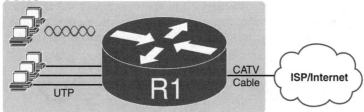

Figure 13-7 *A Typical Home Wired and Wireless LAN*

While the figure shows the hardware as a single router icon, internally, that one wireless router acts like separate devices you would find in an enterprise campus:

- An Ethernet switch, for the wired Ethernet connections
- A wireless access point (AP), to communicate with the wireless devices and forward the frames to/from the wired network
- A router, to route IP packets to/from the LAN and WAN (Internet) interfaces
- A firewall, which often defaults to allow only clients to connect to servers in the Internet, but not vice versa

Figure 13-8 repeats the previous figure, breaking out the internal components as if they were separate physical devices, just to make the point that a single consumer wireless router acts like several different devices.

SOHO

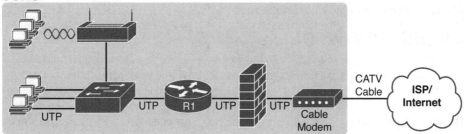

Figure 13-8 *A Representation of the Functions Inside a Consumer Wireless Routing Product*

In a SOHO wireless LAN, the wireless AP acts autonomously, rather than with a WLC, doing all the work required to create and control the WLAN. In other words, the autonomous AP communicates with the various wireless devices using 802.11 protocols and radio waves. It uses Ethernet protocols on the wired side. It converts between the differences in header formats between 802.11 and 802.3 frames before forwarding to/from 802.3 Ethernet and 802.11 wireless frames. But it does not encapsulate frames in CAPWAP, because the AP will not send the frames to a WLC.

For the Internet connection, the router (combo) device connects with any available Internet access technology, including cable Internet, DSL, 4G/5G wireless, or fiber Ethernet. Note that Chapter 14, "WAN Architecture," introduces those technologies.

Power over Ethernet (PoE)

Just walk around any building and you see electrical power outlets everywhere. When finishing the interior of a building, electricians run electrical cables and install electrical outlets to any and every location that might need power. They also run power cables so that devices such as light fixtures can be wired to power as well. And when network engineers thought about electrical power, they thought in terms of making sure the electricians had run enough power to the wiring closets and other locations to power the networking devices.

Power over Ethernet (PoE) changes that thinking so that the responsibility to provide electrical power to some devices can fall to the network engineering team. Some classes of device types have been built to be able to receive their power over the Ethernet cable, rather than using a separate power cord. To make that work, the LAN switch connected to the cable must supply that power over the cable. By using PoE, companies can gain several advantages, including reduced cost by requiring fewer cable runs and better power management capabilities as compared with using a traditional electrical power cable run and power outlet. This final section of the chapter examines PoE.

PoE Basics

The family of standards that supply power goes by the general name *Power over Ethernet* (PoE). With PoE, some device, typically a LAN switch, acts as the Power Sourcing Equipment (PSE)—that is, the device that supplies DC power over the Ethernet UTP cable (as shown in Figure 13-9). A device that has the capability to be powered over the Ethernet cable, rather than by some other power connector on the device, is called the Powered Device (PD).

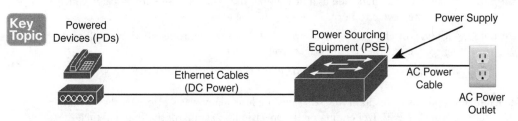

Figure 13-9 *Power over Ethernet Terminology*

13

PoE has a great advantage for devices installed to locations that often do not have a pre-installed power cable or power output. For instance, wireless design places APs in a wide range across the ceiling of a floor (or story) in a building. Also, IP video cameras might be placed in the ceiling corners inside or at various outside locations. Instead of running new power and new network cables to support each device, a single Ethernet cable run can supply power to the device while allowing normal Ethernet communications over the same cable and same wire pairs.

PoE also helps in some less obvious practical ways because it supplies DC power over the Ethernet cable, so the device does not need an AC/DC converter. For instance, devices like laptops and IP phones use a power cord that includes a power brick—an AC-to-DC converter—which converts the AC power from the power outlet to the DC power needed by the device. PoE supplies DC current over the Ethernet cable. So, for an IP Phone, for instance, no more power cable and no more power brick cluttering the desk or taking up a power outlet.

PoE Operation

PoE must have a means to avoid harming the devices on the end of the circuit. Every electrical device can be harmed by receiving too much current into the device, which is why electricians install circuit breakers and why we use surge protectors. Applying power over an Ethernet cable could have the same effect, harming the device on the other end, if the device does not support PoE. So PoE must (and does) have processes in place to determine if PoE is needed, and for how much power, before applying any potentially harmful power levels to the circuit.

PoE, standardized by the IEEE, extends the same IEEE autonegotiation mechanisms. In fact, the mechanisms need to work before the PD has booted, because the PD needs power before it can boot and initialize. By using these IEEE autonegotiation messages and watching for the return signal levels, PoE can determine whether the device on the end of the cable requires power (that is, it is a PD) and how much power to supply. This list details the major steps:

Step 1. Do not supply power on a PoE-capable port unless negotiation identifies that the device needs power.

Step 2. Use Ethernet autonegotiation techniques, sending low power signals and monitoring the return signal, to determine the PoE power class, which determines how much power to supply to the device.

Step 3. If the device is identified as a PD, supply the power per the power class, which allows the device to boot.

Step 4. Monitor for changes to the power class, both with autonegotiation and listening for CDP and LLDP messages from the PD.

Step 5. If a new power class is identified, adjust the power level per that class.

The negotiation processes result in the PDs signaling how many watts of power they would like to receive from the PSE. Depending on the specific PoE standard, the PSE will then supply the power, either over two pairs or four pairs, as noted in Table 13-2.

Table 13-2   Power over Ethernet Standards

Name	Standard	Watts at PSE	Powered Wire Pairs
Cisco Inline Power	Cisco	7	2
PoE	802.3af	15	2
PoE+	802.3at	30	2
UPoE	802.3bt	60	4
UpoE+	802.3bt	100	4

Cisco has been developing products to use some form of PoE since around 2000. Cisco has often developed prestandard power capabilities, like its original Cisco Inline Power (ILP) feature. Over time, the IEEE has produced standards similar to Cisco's power features, with Cisco supporting the standard version once completed. However, for the most part, the Cisco literature refers to the more common names in the first column of the table.

PoE and LAN Design

Most of the LAN switch features discussed in this book (and in *CCNA 200-301 Official Cert Guide, Volume 1*) exist as software features. Once you learn about a software feature, in some cases all you have to do is configure the feature and start using it. (In some cases, you might need to research and license the feature first.) Regardless, adding the feature takes little or no prior planning.

PoE does require some planning and engineering effort when designing a LAN, both when planning for the cable plant (both Ethernet and electrical), as well as when planning for new networking hardware. Planning with PoE in mind prepares the network to supply power to network devices, rather than reacting and missing opportunities to save money and time.

The following list includes some of the key points to consider when planning a LAN design that includes PoE:

■ **Powered Devices:** Determine the types of devices and specific models, along with their power requirements.

■ **Power Requirements:** Plan the numbers of different types of PDs to connect into each wiring closet to build a power budget. That power budget can then be processed to determine the amount of PoE power to make available through each switch.

■ **Switch Ports:** Some switches support PoE standards on all ports, some on no ports, some on a subset of ports. Research the various switch models so that you purchase enough PoE-capable ports for the switches planned for each wiring closet.

■ **Switch Power Supplies:** Without PoE, when purchasing a switch, you choose a power supply so that it delivers enough power to power the switch itself. With PoE, the switch acts as a distributor of electrical power, so the switch power supply must deliver many more watts than it needs to run the switch itself. You will need to create a power budget per switch, based on the number of connected PDs, and purchase power supplies to match those requirements.

■ **PoE Standards versus Actual:** Consider the number of PoE switch ports needed, the standards they support, the standards supported by the PDs, and how much power they consume. For instance, a PD and a switch port may both support PoE+, which supports up to 30 watts supplied by the PSE. However, that powered device may need at most 9 watts to operate, so your power budget needs to reserve less power than the maximum for those devices.

13

Chapter Review

One key to doing well on the exams is to perform repetitive spaced review sessions. Review this chapter's material using either the tools in the book or interactive tools for the same material found on the book's companion website. Refer to the "Your Study Plan" element for more details. Table 13-3 outlines the key review elements and where you can find them. To better track your study progress, record when you completed these activities in the second column.

Table 13-3 Chapter Review Tracking

Review Element	Review Date(s)	Resource Used
Review key topics		Book, app
Review key terms		Book, app
Answer DIKTA questions		Book, PTP
Review memory tables		Book, app

Review All the Key Topics

Table 13-4 Key Topics for Chapter 13

Key Topic Element	Description	Page Number
Figure 13-1	Campus LAN design terms	291
Figure 13-2	Star topology	292
Figure 13-4	A two-tier (collapsed core) LAN topology	293
Figure 13-5	A three-tier (core) LAN topology	294
List	Definitions for LAN core, distribution, and access layers	295
List	Components in an integrated SOHO network device	296
Figure 13-9	PoE roles and terms	297
List	Typical steps to discover power requirements with PoE	298

Key Terms You Should Know

star topology, full mesh, partial mesh, collapsed core design, core design, access layer, distribution layer, core layer, SOHO, powered device (PD), power sourcing equipment (PSE), PoE, UPoE

CHAPTER 14

WAN Architecture

This chapter covers the following exam topics:

1.0 Network Fundamentals

1.2 Describe the characteristics of network topology architecture

1.2.d WAN

5.0 Security Fundamentals

5.5 Describe remote access and site-to-site VPNs

The CCNA 200-301 exam topics include only brief mentions of WAN topics. Because of that sparse attention to WANs, the *CCNA 200-301 Official Cert Guide, Volume 1*, introduced just enough detail about two types of WAN links—point-to-point serial and point-to-point Ethernet WAN links—so that you could understand IP routing, which is a major focus in CCNA.

This chapter now turns our attention to WAN topics for a deeper look at three branches of WAN technology. As usual for this book's discussion of WAN services, the service is viewed mostly from the perspective of the enterprise, as the customer of some WAN service provider (SP). That means the discussion focuses on what the enterprise receives from the service, rather than how the service provider implements the service inside its network. (Note that Cisco's Service Provider certification track explores the details of how an SP implements its network.)

This chapter begins with a discussion of Metro Ethernet, a technology that defines how to use Ethernet links between a customer site and the SP. The second section then examines MPLS VPNs, even though MPLS VPNs came before Metro Ethernet historically. The chapter introduces Metro Ethernet first because the many similarities between using Ethernet in the LAN and using Ethernet in the WAN make this topic easier to learn.

The chapter closes with a third section about how to use the Internet as a private WAN service by using virtual private network (VPN) technology. The Internet does not inherently provide a private service in that any attacker who gets a copy of your packets as they pass through the Internet can read the contents. VPN servers secure the data sent over the Internet, effectively creating a private WAN service over the public Internet.

"Do I Know This Already?" Quiz

Take the quiz (either here or use the PTP software) if you want to use the score to help you decide how much time to spend on this chapter. The letter answers are listed at the bottom of the page following the quiz. Appendix C, found both at the end of the book as well as on the companion website, includes both the answers and explanations. You can also find both answers and explanations in the PTP testing software.

Table 14-1 "Do I Know This Already?" Foundation Topics Section-to-Question Mapping

Foundation Topics Section	Questions
Metro Ethernet	1–3
Multiprotocol Label Switching (MPLS)	4–6
Internet VPNs	7

1. Which of the following topology terms most closely describe the topology created by a Metro Ethernet Tree (E-Tree) service? (Choose two answers.)

   a. Full mesh

   b. Partial mesh

   c. Hub and spoke

   d. Point-to-point

2. Which of the following is the most likely technology used for an access link to a Metro Ethernet service?

   a. 100BASE-LX10

   b. High-speed TDM (for example, T3, E3)

   c. MPLS

   d. 100BASE-T

3. An enterprise uses a Metro Ethernet WAN with an Ethernet LAN (E-LAN) service, with the company headquarters plus 10 remote sites connected to the service. The enterprise uses OSPF at all sites, with one router connected to the service from each site. Which of the following are true about the Layer 3 details most likely used with this service and design? (Choose two answers.)

   a. The WAN uses one IP subnet.

   b. The WAN uses 10 or more IP subnets.

   c. A remote site router would have one OSPF neighbor.

   d. A remote site router would have 10 OSPF neighbors.

4. An enterprise uses an MPLS Layer 3 VPN with the company headquarters connected plus 10 remote sites connected to the service. The enterprise uses OSPF at all sites, with one router connected to the service from each site. Which of the following are true about the Layer 3 details most likely used with this service and design? (Choose two answers.)

   a. The WAN uses one IP subnet.

   b. The WAN uses 10 or more IP subnets.

   c. A remote site router would have one OSPF neighbor.

   d. A remote site router would have 10 or more OSPF neighbors.

5. Which of the following answers is most accurate about access link options for an MPLS network?

    a. Uses only TDM (T1, T3, E1, E3, etc.)

    b. Uses only Ethernet

    c. Uses only DSL and cable

    d. Uses a wide variety of Layer 1 and Layer 2 networking technologies

6. An enterprise connects 20 sites into an MPLS VPN WAN. The enterprise uses OSPF for IPv4 routes at all sites. Consider the OSPF area design options and the PE-CE links. Which of the following answers is most accurate about OSPF areas and the PE-CE links?

    a. The PE-CE link may or may not be chosen to be in backbone area 0.

    b. The PE-CE link must not be in the backbone area 0.

    c. The PE-CE link must be in the backbone area 0.

    d. The PE-CE link will not be in any OSPF area.

7. A colleague mentions using a remote access VPN. Which of the following protocols or technologies would you expect your colleague to have used?

    a. TLS

    b. IPsec

    c. GRE

    d. FTPS

Foundation Topics

Metro Ethernet

Metro Ethernet (MetroE) includes a variety of WAN services with some common features. Each MetroE service uses Ethernet physical links to connect the customer's device to the service provider's device. Second, the service is a Layer 2 service in that the WAN provider forwards Ethernet frames from one customer device to another.

To begin the conversation with a basic view, Metro Ethernet acts much as if the WAN service were created by one Ethernet switch, as shown in Figure 14-1. The figure shows four sites in the same company, each with a router. Each router is connected to the WAN service with an Ethernet link of some kind; those Ethernet links typically use one of the fiber Ethernet standards due to the distances involved. From the customer's perspective (that is, from the perspective of the enterprise that is the customer of the WAN SP), the WAN service acts like a LAN switch in that it forwards Ethernet frames.

NOTE Throughout this chapter, the word *customer* refers to the customer of the service provider—that is, the enterprise that is purchasing the WAN service.

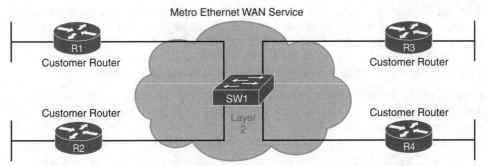

Figure 14-1   *Metro Ethernet Concept as a Large Ethernet Switch*

Although the main concept makes a Metro Ethernet service act like a big LAN switch, there are many options, and you should understand the basics of each. Additionally, many customers connect to a Metro Ethernet service with either routers or Layer 3 switches, which brings up some Layer 3 issues with IP addressing and routing protocols. This section closes with a discussion of the Layer 3 issues.

Metro Ethernet Physical Design and Topology

From an enterprise perspective, to use a Metro Ethernet service, each site needs to connect to the service with (at least) one Ethernet link. There is no need to connect each enterprise router to each other enterprise router directly with a physical link. For instance, in Figure 14-1 in the previous section, each of the four enterprise routers connects to the SP's MetroE service with one physical Ethernet link, rather than connecting directly to the other enterprise routers.

From the SP perspective, the SP needs to build a network to create the Metro Ethernet service. To keep costs lower the SP puts a device (typically an Ethernet switch) physically near to as many customer sites as possible, in an SP facility called a *point of presence* (PoP). Those SP switches need to be near enough to many customer locations so that some Ethernet standard supports the distance from the SP's PoP to each customer site. Figure 14-2 collects some of these terms and ideas together.

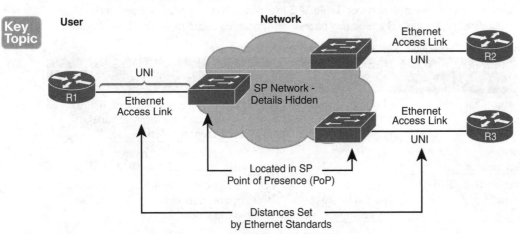

Figure 14-2   *Ethernet Access Links into a Metro Ethernet Service*

Working through the details in the figure, the physical link between the customer and the SP is called an *access link* or, when using Ethernet specifically, an *Ethernet access link*. Everything that happens on that link falls within the definition of the *user network interface*, or UNI. Breaking down the term UNI, the word *network* refers to the SP's network, while the SP's customer (the enterprise) is known as the *user* of the network.

Focusing on the center of Figure 14-2, the SP's network remains hidden to a great extent. The SP promises to deliver Ethernet frames across the WAN. To do that, the access links connect to an Ethernet switch. As you can imagine, the switch will look at the Ethernet header's MAC address fields and at 802.1Q trunking headers for VLAN tags, but the details inside the network remain hidden.

The UNI references a variety of standards, including the fact that any IEEE Ethernet standard can be used for the access link. Table 14-2 lists some of the standards you might expect to see used as Ethernet access links, given their support of longer distances than the standards that use UTP cabling.

Table 14-2 IEEE Ethernet Standards Useful for Metro Ethernet Access

Name	Speed	Distance
100BASE-LX10	100 Mbps	10 Km
1000BASE-LX	1 Gbps	5 Km
1000BASE-LX10	1 Gbps	10 Km
1000BASE-ZX	1 Gbps	100 Km
10GBASE-LR	10 Gbps	10 Km
10GBASE-ER	10 Gbps	40 Km

Ethernet WAN Services and Topologies

Beyond adding a physical Ethernet connection from each site into the SP's Metro Ethernet WAN service, the enterprise must choose between several possible variations of MetroE services. Those variations use different topologies that meet different customer needs.

MEF (www.mef.net) defines the standards for Metro Ethernet, including the specifications for different kinds of MetroE services. Table 14-3 lists three service types described in this chapter and their topologies. The next few pages after the table go into more depth about each.

Table 14-3 Three MEF Service Types and Their Topologies

MEF Service Name	MEF Short Name	Topology Terms	Description
Ethernet Line Service	E-Line	Point-to-point	Two customer premise equipment (CPE) devices can exchange Ethernet frames, similar in concept to a leased line.
Ethernet LAN Service	E-LAN	Full mesh	This service acts like a LAN, in that all devices can send frames to all other devices.
Ethernet Tree Service	E-Tree	Hub and spoke; partial mesh; point-to-multipoint	A central site can communicate to a defined set of remote sites, but the remote sites cannot communicate directly.

Answers to the "Do I Know This Already?" quiz:

1 B, C **2** A **3** A, D **4** B, C **5** D **6** A **7** A

NOTE You might see the term *Virtual Private Wire Service* (VPWS) used for what MEF defines as E-Line service, and *Virtual Private LAN Service* (VPLS) used for what MEF defines as E-LAN service. You might also see the term *Ethernet over MPLS* (EoMPLS). All these terms refer to cases in which the SP uses MPLS internally to create what the customer sees as an Ethernet WAN service.

Ethernet Line Service (Point-to-Point)

The Ethernet Line Service, or E-Line, is the simplest of the Metro Ethernet services. The customer connects two sites with access links. Then the MetroE service allows the two customer devices to send Ethernet frames to each other. Figure 14-3 shows an example, with routers as the CPE devices.

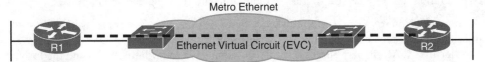

Figure 14-3 *Point-to-Point Topology in Metro Ethernet E-Line Service Between Routers*

As with all MetroE services, the promise made by the service is to deliver Ethernet frames across the service, as if the two customer routers had a rather long crossover cable connected between them. In fact, the E-Line service is the same Ethernet WAN service you have already seen in many examples throughout this book and *CCNA 200-301 Official Cert Guide, Volume 1*. For instance, in this case:

■ The routers would use physical Ethernet interfaces.

■ The routers would configure IP addresses in the same subnet as each other.

■ Their routing protocols would become neighbors and exchange routes.

The MetroE specifications define the concept of an *Ethernet Virtual Connection*, or EVC, to define which user (customer) devices can communicate with which. By definition, an E-Line service (as shown in Figure 14-4) creates a point-to-point EVC, meaning that the service allows two endpoints to communicate.

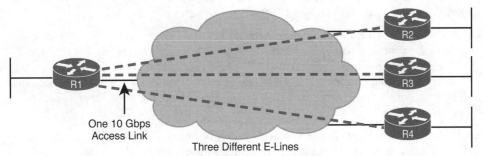

Figure 14-4 *Using Multiple E-Lines, One for Each Remote Site*

It may be that an enterprise wants to implement a network exactly as shown in Figure 14-3, with two sites and two routers, with MetroE WAN connectivity using an E-Line service. Other variations exist, even other variations using an E-Line.

For example, think of a common enterprise WAN topology with a central site and 100 remote sites. As shown so far, with an E-Line service, the central site router would need 100 physical Ethernet interfaces to connect to those 100 remote sites. That could be expensive. As an alternative, the enterprise could use the design partially shown in Figure 14-4 (just three remote sites shown). In this case:

- The central site router uses a single 10-Gbps access link.
- The central site connects to 100 E-Lines (only three shown).
- All the E-Lines send and receive frames over the same access link.

Note that this chapter does not get into the configuration details for WAN services. However, designs like Figure 14-4, with multiple E-Line services on a single access link, use 802.1Q trunking, with a different VLAN ID for each E-Line service. As a result, the router configuration can use a typical router configuration with trunking and subinterfaces.

Before moving on to the next MetroE service, note that the customer could use switches instead of routers to connect to the WAN. Historically, enterprise engineers place routers at the edge of a WAN, in part because that device connected to both the WAN and the LAN, and the LAN and WAN used different types of physical interfaces and different data-link protocols. As a result of how routing works, routers served as the perfect device to sit at the edge between LAN and WAN (called the WAN edge). With MetroE, the LAN and WAN are both Ethernet, so an Ethernet switch becomes an option.

Ethernet LAN Service (Full Mesh)

Imagine an enterprise needs to connect several sites to a WAN, and the goal is to allow every site to send frames directly to every other site. You could do that with E-Lines, but you would need possibly lots of E-Lines. For instance, to connect three sites with E-Lines so that each site could send frames directly to each other, you only need three E-Lines. But with four, five, and six sites, you would need 6, 10, and 15 E-Lines, respectively. Get up to 20 sites for which all could send frames directly to each other, and you would need 190 E-Lines. (The formula is $N(N - 1) / 2$.)

The people who created MetroE anticipated the need for designs that allow a full mesh— that is, for each pair of nodes in the service to send frames to each other directly. In fact, allowing all devices to send directly to every other device sounds a lot like an Ethernet LAN, so the MetroE service is called an *Ethernet LAN service*, or E-LAN.

One E-LAN service allows all devices connected to that service to send Ethernet frames directly to every other device, just as if the Ethernet WAN service were one big Ethernet switch. Figure 14-5 shows a representation of a single E-LAN EVC. In this case, the one EVC connects to four customer sites, creating one E-LAN. Routers R1, R2, R3, and R4 can all send frames directly to each other. They would also all be in the same Layer 3 subnet on the WAN.

An E-LAN service connects the sites in a full mesh. The term *full mesh* refers to a design that, for a set of devices, creates a direct communication path for each pair. In contrast, a partial mesh refers to a design in which only some of the pairs can communicate directly. The Ethernet Tree service (E-Tree), as discussed in the next topic, creates a partial mesh design.

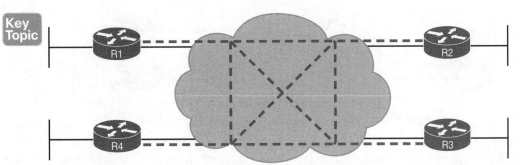

Figure 14-5 *MetroE Ethernet LAN Service—Any-to-Any Forwarding over the Service*

Ethernet Tree Service (Hub and Spoke)

The Ethernet Tree service (E-Tree) creates a WAN topology in which the central site device can send Ethernet frames directly to each remote (leaf) site, but the remote (leaf) sites can send only to the central site. Figure 14-6 shows the topology, again with a single EVC. In this case, router R1 is the root site, and can send to all three remote sites. Routers R2, R3, and R4 can send only to R1.

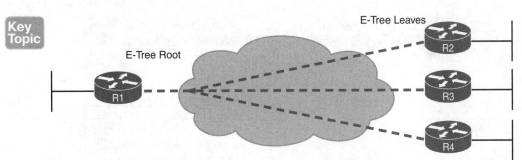

Figure 14-6 *E-Tree Service Creates a Hub-and-Spoke Topology*

With an E-Tree, the central site serves as the root of a tree and each remote site as one of the leaves. The topology goes by many names: partial mesh, hub and spoke, and point-to-multipoint. Regardless of the term you use, an E-Tree service creates a service that works well for designs with a central site plus many remote sites.

Layer 3 Design Using Metro Ethernet

Now that you know the basics of the E-Line (point-to-point), E-LAN (full mesh), and E-Tree (point-to-multipoint, hub and spoke) services, this next topic reviews some Layer 3 design details when using E-Line and E-Tree services. That is, if the enterprise uses routers or Layer 3 switches as its WAN edge devices, how should the engineer plan for IP addresses and subnets? What is the impact on routing protocols? This section answers those questions.

Note that this section uses routers as the enterprise's devices, but the concepts apply to Layer 3 switches as well.

Layer 3 Design with E-Line Service

Every E-Line uses a point-to-point topology. As a result, the two routers on the ends of an E-Line need to be in the same subnet. Similarly, when an enterprise uses multiple E-Lines, each should be in a different subnet. As an example, consider Figure 14-7, which shows two E-Lines, both of which connect to router R1 on the left.

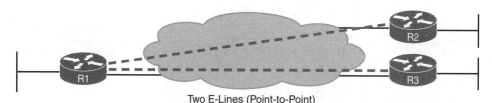

Two E-Lines (Point-to-Point)

Figure 14-7 *Routing Protocol Neighbor Relationships over Metro Ethernet E-Line*

Focusing on the E-Lines and ignoring the access links for the most part, think of each E-Line as a subnet. Each router needs an IP address in each subnet, and the subnets need to be unique. All the addresses come from the enterprise's IP address space. Figure 14-8 shows an example of the addresses, subnets, and three OSPF-learned routes in the routing table of R3.

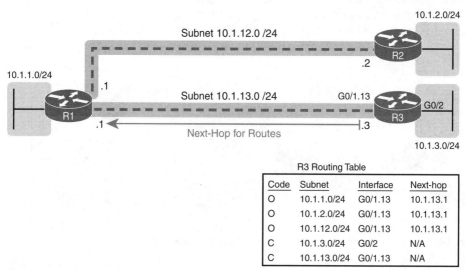

R3 Routing Table

Code	Subnet	Interface	Next-hop
O	10.1.1.0/24	G0/1.13	10.1.13.1
O	10.1.2.0/24	G0/1.13	10.1.13.1
O	10.1.12.0/24	G0/1.13	10.1.13.1
C	10.1.3.0/24	G0/2	N/A
C	10.1.13.0/24	G0/1.13	N/A

Figure 14-8 *Layer 3 Forwarding Between Remote Sites—Through Central Site*

Examine the IP routing table in the lower right of the figure, first focusing on the route to subnet 10.1.1.0/24, which is the LAN subnet off router R1. R3's route points to a next-hop router IP address that is R1's IP address on the Ethernet WAN, specifically the address on the other side of the E-Line that connects R1 and R3. This route should not be a surprise: for R3 to send packets to a subnet connected to R1, R3 sends the packets to R1. Also, it happens to use a subinterface (G0/1.13), which means that the design is using 802.1Q trunking on the link.

Next, look at R3's route for subnet 10.1.2.0/24, which supports the fact that R3 cannot send packets directly to R2 with the current WAN design. R3 does not have an E-Line that allows R3 to send frames directly to R2. R3 will not become routing protocol neighbors with R2 either. So, R3 will learn its route for subnet 10.1.2.0/24 from R1, with R1's 10.1.13.1 address as the next-hop address. As a result, when forwarding packets, R3 will forward packets to R1, which will then forward them over the other E-Line to R2.

Layer 3 Design with E-LAN Service

If you connected four routers to one LAN switch, all in the same VLAN, what would you expect for the IP addresses on those routers? And if all four routers used the same routing protocol, which would become neighbors? Typically, with four routers connected to the same switch, on the same VLAN, using the same routing protocol, normally all four routers would have IP addresses in the same subnet, and all would become neighbors.

On an E-LAN service, the same IP addressing design is used, with the same kinds of routing protocol neighbor relationships. Figure 14-9 shows an example that includes subnets and addresses, plus one route as an example. Note that the four routers connected to the E-LAN service in the center all have addresses in subnet 10.1.99.0/24.

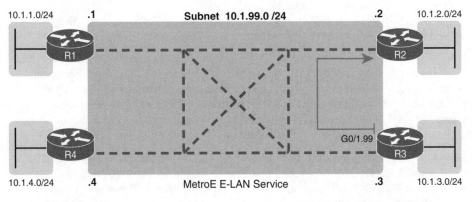

R3 Routing Table (OSPF Routes Only)

Subnet	Interface	Next-hop
10.1.2.0/24	G0/1.99	**10.1.99.2**
10.1.1.0/24	G0/1.99	10.1.99.1
10.1.4.0/24	G0/1.99	10.1.99.4

Figure 14-9   *Layer 3 Forwarding Between Sites with E-LAN Service*

Look at R3's routing table in the figure, the route from R3 to R2's LAN subnet (10.1.2.0/24). In this case, R3's next-hop address is the WAN address on R2 (10.1.99.2), and R3 will send packets (encapsulated in Ethernet frames) directly to R2. Note also that the other two routes in the routing table list the next-hop addresses of R1 (10.1.99.1) and R4 (10.1.99.4).

The details in this first section of the chapter should provide plenty of perspective on how enterprise routers use Ethernet WANs for connectivity. However, if you want a little more detail, the section titled "Ethernet Virtual Circuit Bandwidth Profiles" in Appendix D, "Topics from Previous Editions," discusses the logic behind how Ethernet WANs use physical links at one speed while supporting services that run at a variety of slower speeds.

Multiprotocol Label Switching (MPLS)

From your CCNA preparation so far, you already understand a lot about the Layer 3 routing, as represented by the packet flowing left to right in Figure 14-10. Each router makes a separate forwarding decision to forward the packet, as shown as steps 1, 2, and 3 in the figure. Each router makes a comparison between the packet's destination IP address and that router's IP routing table; the matching IP routing table entry tells the router where to forward the packet next. To learn those routes, the routers typically run some routing protocol.

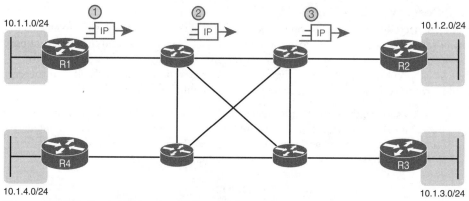

Figure 14-10 *Basic IP Routing of IP Packets*

MPLS creates a WAN service that routes IP packets between customer sites. The enterprise deploys routers and switches as usual. The SP then creates its own IP network, spanning a large geographic area. The customer can then connect to the MPLS network, with a link from each site, with the SP routing IP packets from one customer site to the other. For instance, in Figure 14-10, the middle four routers could represent the SP's MPLS network, with the numbered routers on the edges being routers owned by one company.

However, an SP cannot just build a large IP network and connect all its customers to that same IP network because of some issues that arise to support multiple customers at the same time. For instance, many customers will use the same private IP network (for instance, network 10.0.0.0), so the SP's IP network would learn large numbers of routes to overlapping subnets.

To overcome this and other issues, the SP builds its IP network to also use Multiprotocol Label Switching (MPLS), in particular MPLS VPNs. MPLS VPNs allow the SP to build one large MPLS network, which also creates a private IP-based WAN for each of its customers. With MPLS VPNs, the SP can separate the routes learned from one customer from the routes learned for the next customer; consequently, the SP can support each customer while preventing packets from leaking from one customer to the next.

To give you a little insight as to why MPLS is not just an IP network with routers, internally, the devices in an MPLS network use label switching—hence, the name MPLS. The routers on the edge of the MPLS network add and remove an MPLS header to packets as they enter and exit the MPLS network. The devices inside the MPLS network then use the label field inside that MPLS header when forwarding data across the MPLS network. The choices of the labels to use, along with other related logic, allow the MPLS VPN to create separate VPNs to keep different customers' traffic separate.

NOTE While MPLS VPNs provide a Layer 3 service to customers, MPLS itself is sometimes called a Layer 2.5 protocol because it adds the MPLS header between the data-link header (Layer 2) and the IP header (Layer 3).

As usual, the discussion of WAN services in this book ignores as much of the SP's network as possible. For instance, you do not need to know how MPLS labels work. However, because MPLS VPNs create a Layer 3 service, the customer must be more aware of what the SP does than with other WAN servers, so you need to know a few facts about how an MPLS network approaches some Layer 3 functions. In particular, the SP's MPLS VPN network

- Will use a routing protocol to build routing protocol neighbor relationships with customer routers
- Will learn customer subnets/routes with those routing protocols
- Will advertise a customer's routes with a routing protocol so that all routers that customer connects to the MPLS VPN can learn all routes as advertised through the MPLS VPN network
- Will make decisions about MPLS VPN forwarding, including what MPLS labels to add and remove, based on the customer's IP address space and customer IP routes

As an aside, MPLS VPNs create a private network by keeping customer data separate, but not by encrypting the data. Some VPN services encrypt the data, expecting that attackers might be able to receive copies of the packets. With MPLS, even though the packets for two customers may pass through the same devices and links inside the MPLS network, MPLS logic can keep the packets separate for each customer.

This second of two major sections of the chapter works through the basics of MPLS, specifically MPLS VPNs. This section first looks at the design, topology, and terminology related to building the customer-facing parts of an MPLS network. It then looks at the impact and issues created by the fact that the MPLS network provides a Layer 3 service.

MPLS VPN Physical Design and Topology

MetroE provides a Layer 2 service by forwarding Layer 2 Ethernet frames. To do that, the SP often uses Ethernet switches at the edge of its network. Those switches are configured to do more than what you learn about Ethernet LAN switches for CCNA, but a LAN switch's most fundamental job is to forward an Ethernet frame, so it makes sense for MetroE to use an Ethernet switch at the edge of the SP's MetroE network.

MPLS provides a Layer 3 service in that it promises to forward Layer 3 packets (IPv4 and IPv6). To support that service, MPLS SPs typically use routers at the edge of the MPLS networks because routers provide the function of forwarding Layer 3 packets.

As usual, each WAN technology has its own set of terms and acronyms, so Figure 14-11 shows two important MPLS terms in context: customer edge (CE) and provider edge (PE). Because MPLS requires so much discussion about the devices on the edge of the customer and SP network, MPLS uses specific terms for each. The *customer edge* device is typically a router, and it sits at a customer site—that is, at a site in the company that is buying the MPLS service. The *provider edge* devices sit at the edge of the SP's network, on the other end of the access link.

Next, to appreciate what MPLS does, think back to how routers use their different kinds of physical interfaces and different kinds of data-link protocols. When routing a packet, routers discard an incoming data-link frame's data-link header and trailer and then build a new data-link header/trailer. That action allows the incoming packet to arrive inside a frame of one data-link protocol and leave out an interface with another data-link protocol.

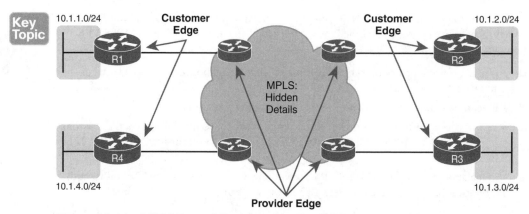

Figure 14-11 *MPLS Layer 3 Design, with PE and CE Routers*

With MPLS, the fact that the devices are routers, discarding and adding new data-link headers, means that MPLS networks support a variety of access links. The fact that MPLS acts as a Layer 3 service, discarding incoming data-link headers, means that any data-link protocol could in theory be used on MPLS access links. In reality, MPLS does support many types of access links, as shown in Figure 14-12.

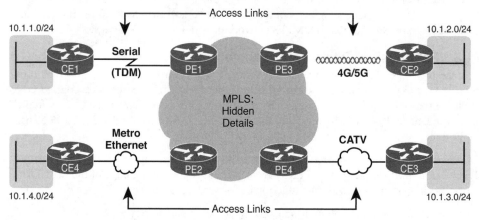

Figure 14-12 *Popular MPLS Access Link Technologies*

The variety of access links available for MPLS networks makes MPLS a great option for building large enterprise networks. For sites that are near MetroE services, especially for sites that need at least 10 Mbps of bandwidth, using MetroE as an access link makes great sense. Then, for sites that are more remote, the carrier may not offer MetroE services to that area, but many carriers can install a serial link to remote sites. Or, common Internet access technologies, like cable and wireless 4G/5G services, can also be used to access an MPLS network.

MPLS and Quality of Service

MPLS stands apart from other WAN services as the first WAN service for which the SP provided effective Quality of Service (QoS) features. You should be able to get a general idea of an MPLS QoS benefit with the following basic example.

IP networks can and often do forward voice traffic in IP packets, called Voice over IP (VoIP). If a WAN service does not provide QoS, that means that the WAN service does not treat one packet any differently than any other packet. With QoS, the SP's network can treat packets differently, giving some packets (like VoIP) better treatment. For a voice call to sound good, each voice packet must have low loss (that is, few packets are discarded); low one-way delay through the network; and low variation in delay (called jitter). Without QoS, a voice call over an IP network will not sound good.

With a QoS-capable WAN, the customer can mark VoIP packets so that the MPLS network can recognize VoIP packets and treat them better, resulting in better voice call quality. But to make it work correctly, the customer and MPLS provider need to cooperate.

For instance, for VoIP packets traveling left to right in Figure 14-13, router CE1 could be configured with QoS marking tools. Marking tools could recognize VoIP packets and place a specific value in the IP header of VoIP packets (a value called DSCP EF, per the figure). The MPLS WAN provider would then configure its QoS tools to react for packets that have that marking, typically sending that packet as soon as possible. The result: low delay, low jitter, low loss, and a better call quality.

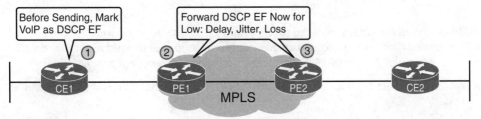

Figure 14-13 *MPLS VPN QoS Marking and Reaction in the MPLS WAN*

Summarizing the ideas so far, MPLS supports a variety of access links. An enterprise would select the type and speed of access link for each site based on the capacity (bandwidth) required for each site. Beyond that basic connectivity, the enterprise will want to work with the SP to define other features of the service. The customer and SP will need to work through the details of some Layer 3 design choices (as discussed in more depth in the next section). The customer will also likely want to ask for QoS services from the MPLS provider and define those details.

Layer 3 with MPLS VPN

Because MetroE provides a Layer 2 service, the SP has no need to understand anything about the customer's Layer 3 design. The SP knows nothing about the customer's IP addressing plan and has no need to participate with routing protocols.

MPLS VPNs take the complete opposite approach. As a Layer 3 service, MPLS must be aware of the customer IP addressing. The SP will even use routing protocols and advertise those customer routes across the WAN. This section takes a closer look at what that means.

First, keep the primary goals in mind. The customer pays good money for a WAN service to deliver data between sites, with certain levels of availability and quality (for instance, low delay, jitter, and loss for VoIP). But to support that base function of allowing packet delivery from each WAN site to the other, the CE routers need to exchange routes with the PE routers in the MPLS network. Additionally, all the CE routers need to learn routes from the other CE routers—a process that relies on the PE routers.

First, the CE routers and the PE router on the ends of the same access link need to exchange routes, as shown in Figure 14-14. The figure shows the CE-PE routing protocol neighbor relationships (as lines with circles on the ends). In this case, the customer chose to use OSPF. However, MPLS allows for many familiar routing protocols on the edge of the MPLS network: RIPv2, EIGRP, OSPF, and even eBGP.

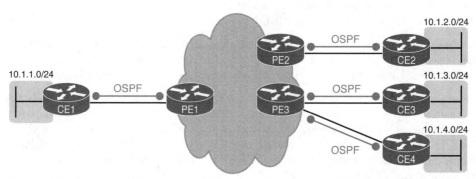

Figure 14-14 *Routing Protocol Neighbor Relationships with MPLS Customer Edge Routers*

Additionally, all the CE routers need to learn routes from the other CE routers. However, a CE router does not form routing protocol neighbor relationships directly with the other CE routers, as noted in Figure 14-14. Summarizing what does and does not happen:

- A CE router does become neighbors with the PE router on the other end of the access link.

- A CE router does not become neighbors with other CE routers.

- The MPLS network does advertise the customer's routes between the various PE routers so that the CE routers can learn all customer routes through their PE-CE routing protocol neighbor relationship.

To advertise the customer routes between the PE routers, the PE routers use another routing protocol along with a process called *route redistribution*. Route redistribution happens inside one router, taking routes from one routing protocol process and injecting them into another. MPLS does route redistribution in the PE routers between the routing protocol used by the customer and a variation of BGP called Multiprotocol BGP (MPBGP). (Redistribution is needed when the PE-CE routing protocol is not BGP.) Figure 14-15 shows the idea.

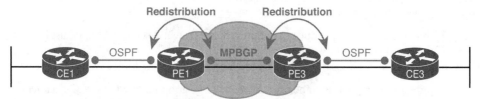

Figure 14-15 *MPLS VPN Using Redistribution with MPBGP at PE Router*

Just as a quick aside about MPBGP, MPLS VPNs use MPBGP (as opposed to other routing protocols) because MPBGP can advertise routes from multiple customers while keeping the routes logically separated. For instance, continuing the example in Figure 14-15, router PE1 might sit in one PoP but connect to dozens of different customers. Likewise, router PE3 might connect to many of those same customers. MPBGP can advertise routes for all those customers and mark which routes are from which customers so that only the correct routes are advertised to each CE router for different customers.

At the end of the process, for all single enterprises, all the routers can learn routes to all the subnets reachable over the MPLS VPN WAN. WAN routes on the CE routers refer to the neighboring PE router as the *next-hop router*. Each CE router becomes a routing protocol neighbor with the SP's PE router on the other end of the access link. Plus, MPLS provides the flexibility to use whatever type of physical access link makes sense for the location at each site, while still connecting to the same MPLS network.

Internet VPNs

To build the Internet, Internet service providers (ISP) need links to other ISPs as well as links to the ISPs' customers. The Internet core connects ISPs to each other using a variety of high-speed technologies. Additionally, Internet access links connect an ISP to each customer, again with a wide variety of technologies. The combination of ISP networks and customer networks that connect to the ISPs together create the worldwide Internet.

For these customer access links, the technologies need to be inexpensive so that a typical consumer can afford to pay for the service. But businesses can use many of these same technologies to connect to the Internet. Some WAN technologies happen to work particularly well as Internet access technologies. For example, several use the same telephone line installed into most homes by the phone company so that the ISPs do not have to install additional cabling. Some use the TV cabling, whereas others use wireless.

While consumers typically connect to the Internet to reach destinations on the Internet, businesses can also use the Internet as a WAN service. First, the enterprise can connect each business site to the Internet. Then, using virtual private network (VPN) technology, the enterprise can create an Internet VPN. An Internet VPN can keep the enterprise's packet private through encryption and other means, even while sending the data over the Internet.

This final major section of the chapter discusses some of the basics of Internet access links. The section then details how an enterprise can communicate securely over the Internet, making the public Internet act like a private network, by creating an Internet VPN.

Internet Access

Private WAN technology may be used to access an ISP's network, including the Ethernet WAN and MPLS technologies discussed earlier in this chapter. Figure 14-16 shows a few of these, just as a visual reminder of these options.

In addition to the traditional services shown in the figure, enterprises can also use Internet access technologies more commonly used by consumers, including DSL, cable, 4G/5G, and fiber Ethernet. The chapter includes this information about Internet access technologies to provide useful background information before getting into Internet VPN topics.

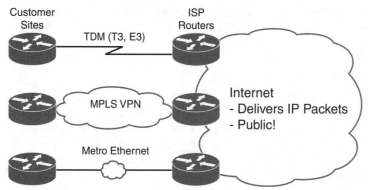

Figure 14-16 *Three Examples of Internet Access Links for Companies*

Digital Subscriber Line

In the consumer Internet access space, one big speed breakthrough happened with the introduction of the digital subscriber line (DSL). It represented a big technological breakthrough
in terms of raw speed in comparison to some older technologies, such as analog modems.
These faster speeds available through DSL also changed how people could use the Internet
because many of today's common applications would be unusable with the earlier Internet
access technologies (analog modems and Integrated Services Digital Network, or ISDN).

Telephone companies (telcos) greatly influenced the creation of DSL. As a technology, DSL
gave telcos a way to offer much faster Internet access speeds. As a business opportunity,
DSL gave telcos a way to offer a valuable high-speed Internet service to many of their existing telephone customers, over the same physical phone line already installed, which created
a great way for telcos to make money.

Figure 14-17 shows some of the details of how DSL works on a home phone line. The
phone can do what it has always done: plug into a phone jack and send analog signals.
For the data, a DSL modem connects to a spare phone outlet. The DSL modem sends and
receives the data, as digital signals, at higher frequencies, over the same local loop, even at
the same time as a telephone call. (Note that the physical installation often uses frequency
filters that are not shown in the figure or discussed here.)

Because DSL sends analog (voice) and digital (data) signals on the same line, the telco has
to somehow split those signals on the telco side of the connection. To do so, the local loop
must be connected to a *DSL access multiplexer* (DSLAM) located in the nearby telco central office (CO). The DSLAM splits out the digital data over to the router on the lower right
in Figure 14-17, which completes the connection to the Internet. The DSLAM also splits out
the analog voice signals over to the voice switch on the upper right.

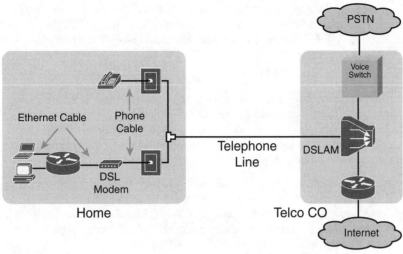

Figure 14-17 *Wiring and Devices for a Home DSL Link*

Cable Internet

DSL uses the local link (telephone line) from the local telco. Cable Internet instead uses the cabling from what has become the primary competitor to the telco in most markets: the cable company.

Cable Internet creates an Internet access service that, when viewed generally rather than specifically, has many similarities to DSL. Like DSL, cable Internet takes full advantage of existing cabling, using the existing cable TV (CATV) cable to send data. Like DSL, cable Internet uses asymmetric speeds, sending data faster downstream than upstream, which works well for most consumer locations. And cable Internet still allows the normal service on the cable (cable TV), at the same time as the Internet access service is working.

Cable Internet also uses the same general idea for in-home cabling as DSL, just using CATV cabling instead of telephone cabling. The left side of Figure 14-18 shows a TV connected to the CATV cabling, just as it would normally connect. At another cable outlet, a cable modem connects to the same cable. The Internet service flows over one frequency, like yet another TV channel, just reserved for Internet service.

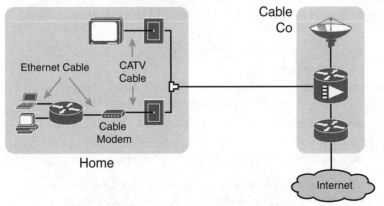

Figure 14-18 *Wiring and Devices for a Home Cable Internet Link*

Similar to DSL, on the CATV company side of the connection (on the right side of the figure), the CATV company must split out the data and video traffic. Data flows to the lower right, through a router, to the Internet. The video comes in from video dishes for distribution out to the TVs in people's homes.

Wireless WAN (3G, 4G, LTE, 5G)

Many of you reading this book have a mobile phone that has Internet access. That is, you can check your email, surf the Web, download apps, and watch videos. Many of us today rely on our mobile phones, and the Internet access built in to those phones, for most of our tweets and the like. This section touches on the big concepts behind the Internet access technology connecting those mobile phones.

Mobile phones use radio waves to communicate through a nearby mobile phone tower. The phone has a small radio antenna, and the provider has a much larger antenna sitting at the top of a tower somewhere within miles of you and your phone. Phones, tablet computers, laptops, and even routers (with the correct interface cards) can communicate through to the Internet using this technology, as represented in Figure 14-19.

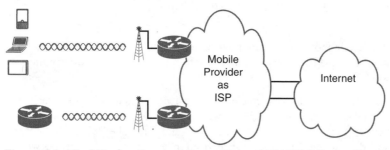

Figure 14-19 *Wireless Internet Access Using 3G/4G/5G Technology*

The mobile phone radio towers also have cabling and equipment, including routers. The mobile provider builds its own IP network, much like an ISP builds out an IP network. The customer IP packets pass through the IP router at the tower into the mobile provider's IP network and then out to the Internet.

The market for mobile phones and wireless Internet access for other devices is both large and competitive. As a result, the mobile providers spend a lot of money advertising their services, with lots of names for one service or the other. Frankly, it can be difficult to tell what all the marketing jargon means, but a few terms tend to be used throughout the industry:

Wireless Internet: This general term refers to Internet services from a mobile phone or from any device that uses the same technology.

3G/4G Wireless: Short for third generation and fourth generation, these terms refer to the major changes over time to the mobile phone companies' wireless networks.

LTE: Long-Term Evolution is a newer and faster technology considered to be part of fourth generation (4G) technology.

5G Wireless: This is the fifth major generation of wireless phone technology.

The takeaway from all this jargon is this: when you hear about wireless Internet services with a mobile phone tower in the picture—whether the device is a phone, tablet, or PC—it is probably a 3G, 4G, or LTE wireless Internet connection, with newer services offering 5G capabilities by 2020 and beyond.

Enterprises can use this same wireless technology to connect to the Internet. For instance, a network engineer can install a 4G wireless card in a router. ISPs team with wireless operators to create contracts for wireless and Internet service.

Fiber (Ethernet) Internet Access

The consumer-focused Internet access technologies discussed in this section use a couple of different physical media. DSL uses the copper wiring installed between the telco CO and the home. Cable uses the copper CATV cabling installed from the cable company to the home. And, of course, wireless WAN technologies do not use cables for Internet access.

The cabling used by DSL and cable Internet uses copper wires, but, comparing different types of physical media, fiber-optic cabling generally supports faster speeds for longer distances. That is, just comparing physical layer technologies across the breadth of networking, fiber-optic cabling supports longer links, and those links often run at equivalent or faster speeds.

Some ISPs now offer Internet access that goes by the name *fiber Internet*, or simply *fiber*. To make that work, some local company that owns the rights to install cabling underground in a local area (often a telephone company) installs new fiber-optic cabling. Once the cable plant is in place (a process that often takes years as well as a large budget), the fiber ISP then connects customers to the Internet using the fiber-optic cabling. Often, the fiber uses Ethernet protocols over the fiber. The end result: high-speed Internet to the home, often using Ethernet technology.

Internet VPN Fundamentals

Private WANs have some wonderful security features. In particular, the customers who send data through the WAN have good reason to believe that no attackers saw the data in transit or even changed the data to cause some harm. The private WAN service provider promises to send one customer's data to other sites owned by that customer, but not to sites owned by other customers, and vice versa.

VPNs try to provide the same secure features as a private WAN while sending data over a network that is open to other parties (such as the Internet). Compared to a private WAN, the Internet does not provide for a secure environment that protects the privacy of an enterprise's data. Internet VPNs can provide important security features, such as the following:

- **Confidentiality (privacy):** Preventing anyone in the middle of the Internet (man in the middle) from being able to read the data
- **Authentication:** Verifying that the sender of the VPN packet is a legitimate device and not a device used by an attacker
- **Data integrity:** Verifying that the packet was not changed as the packet transited the Internet
- **Anti-replay:** Preventing a man in the middle from copying and later replaying the packets sent by a legitimate user, for the purpose of appearing to be a legitimate user

To accomplish these goals, two devices near the edge of the Internet create a VPN, sometimes called a *VPN tunnel*. These devices add headers to the original packet, with these headers including fields that allow the VPN devices to make the traffic secure. The VPN devices also encrypt the original IP packet, meaning that the original packet's contents are undecipherable to anyone who happens to see a copy of the packet as it traverses the Internet.

Figure 14-20 shows the general idea of what typically occurs with a VPN tunnel. The figure shows a VPN created between a branch office router and a Cisco firewall. In this case, the VPN is called a *site-to-site VPN* because it connects two sites of a company.

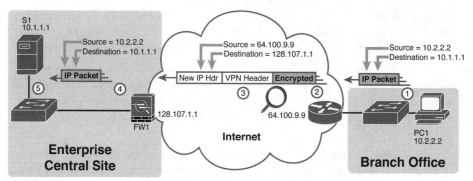

Figure 14-20 *VPN Tunnel Concepts for a Site-to-Site Intranet VPN*

The figure shows the following steps, which explain the overall flow:

1. Host PC1 (10.2.2.2) on the right sends a packet to the web server (10.1.1.1), just as it would without a VPN.

2. The router encrypts the packet, adds some VPN headers, adds another IP header (with public IP addresses), and forwards the packet.

3. An attacker in the Internet copies the packet (called a man-in-the-middle attack). However, the attacker cannot change the packet without being noticed and cannot read the contents of the original packet.

4. Firewall FW1 receives the packet, confirms the authenticity of the sender, confirms that the packet has not been changed, and then decrypts the original packet.

5. Server S1 receives the unencrypted packet.

The benefits of using an Internet-based VPN as shown in Figure 14-20 are many. The cost of a high-speed Internet access connection as discussed in the last few pages is usually much less than that of many private WAN options. The Internet is seemingly everywhere, making this kind of solution available worldwide. And by using VPN technology and protocols, the communications are secure.

> **NOTE** The term *tunnel* refers to any protocol's packet that is sent by encapsulating the packet inside another packet. The term *VPN tunnel* may or may not imply that the tunnel also uses encryption.

Site-to-Site VPNs with IPsec

A site-to-site VPN provides VPN services for the devices at two sites with a single VPN tunnel. For instance, if each site has dozens of devices that need to communicate between sites, the various devices do not have to act to create the VPN. Instead, the network engineers configure devices such as routers and firewalls (as shown in Figure 14-20) to create one VPN tunnel. The tunnel endpoints create the tunnel and leave it up and operating all the time, so that when any device at either site decides to send data, the VPN is available. All the devices at each site can communicate using the VPN, receiving all the benefits of the VPN, without requiring each device to create a VPN for themselves.

IPsec defines one popular set of rules for creating secure VPNs. IPsec is an architecture or framework for security services for IP networks. The name itself is not an acronym, but rather a name derived from the title of the RFC that defines it (RFC 4301, "Security Architecture for the Internet Protocol"), more generally called IP Security, or IPsec.

IPsec defines how two devices, both of which connect to the Internet, can achieve the main goals of a VPN as listed at the beginning of this section: confidentiality, authentication, data integrity, and anti-replay. IPsec does not define just one way to implement a VPN, instead allowing several different protocol options for each VPN feature. One of IPsec's strengths is that its role as an architecture allows it to be added to and changed over time as improvements to individual security functions are made.

The idea of IPsec encryption might sound intimidating, but if you ignore the math—and thankfully, you can—IPsec encryption is not too difficult to understand. IPsec encryption uses a pair of encryption algorithms, which are essentially math formulas, to meet a couple of requirements. First, the two math formulas are a matched set:

■ One to hide (encrypt) the data

■ Another to re-create (decrypt) the original data based on the encrypted data

Besides those somewhat obvious functions, the two math formulas were chosen so that if an attacker intercepted the encrypted text but did not have the secret password (called an *encryption key*), decrypting that one packet would be difficult. In addition, the formulas are also chosen so that if an attacker did happen to decrypt one packet, that information would not give the attacker any advantages in decrypting the other packets.

The process for encrypting data for an IPsec VPN works generally as shown in Figure 14-21. Note that the *encryption key* is also known as the *session key*, *shared key*, or *shared session key*.

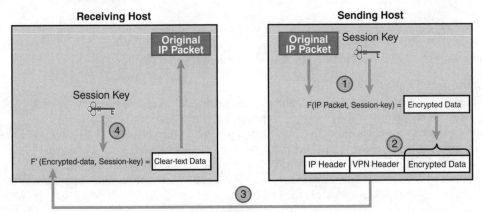

Figure 14-21 *Basic IPsec Encryption Process*

The four steps highlighted in the figure are as follows:

1. The sending VPN device (like the remote office router in Figure 14-21) feeds the original packet and the session key into the encryption formula, calculating the encrypted data.

2. The sending device encapsulates the encrypted data into a packet, which includes the new IP header and VPN header.

3. The sending device sends this new packet to the destination VPN device (FW1 back in Figure 14-21).

4. The receiving VPN device runs the corresponding decryption formula, using the encrypted data and session key—the same key value as was used on the sending VPN device—to decrypt the data.

While Figure 14-21 shows the basic encryption process, Figure 14-22 shows a broader view of IPsec VPNs in an enterprise. First, devices use some related VPN technology like Generic Routing Encapsulation (GRE) to create the concept of a tunnel (a virtual link between the routers), with three such tunnels shown in the figure. Without IPsec, each GRE tunnel could be used to forward unencrypted traffic over the Internet. IPsec adds the security features to the data that flows over the tunnel. (Note that the figure shows IPsec and GRE, but IPsec teams with other VPN technologies as well.)

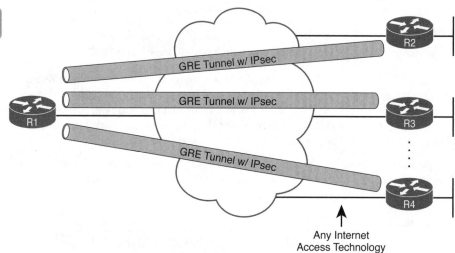

Figure 14-22 *Site-to-Site VPN Tunnels with GRE and IPsec*

Remote Access VPNs with TLS

A site-to-site VPN exists to support multiple devices at each site and is typically created by devices supported by the IT staff. In contrast, individual devices can dynamically initiate their own VPN connections in cases where a permanent site-to-site VPN does not exist. For instance, a user can walk into a coffee shop and connect to the free Wi-Fi, but that coffee shop does not have a site-to-site VPN to the user's enterprise network. Instead, the user's device creates a secure remote access VPN connection back to the enterprise network before sending any data to hosts in the enterprise.

While IPsec and GRE (or other) tunnels work well for site-to-site VPNs, remote access VPNs often use the Transport Layer Security (TLS) protocol to create a secure VPN session.

TLS has many uses today, but most commonly, TLS provides the security features of HTTP Secure (HTTPS). Today's web browsers support HTTPS (with TLS) as a way to dynamically create a secure connection from the web browser to a web server, supporting safe online access to financial transactions. To do so, the browser creates a TCP connection to server well-known port 443 (default) and then initializes a TLS session. TLS encrypts data sent between the browser and the server and authenticating the user. Then, the HTTP messages flow over the TLS VPN connection.

NOTE   In years past, Secure Sockets Layer (SSL) played the same role as TLS. SSL has been deprecated (see RFC 7568) and has been replaced by TLS.

The built-in TLS functions of a web browser create one secure web browsing session, but each session secures only the data sent in that session. This same TLS technology can be used to create a client VPN that secures all packets from the device to a site by using a *Cisco VPN client*. The Cisco AnyConnect Secure Mobility Client (or AnyConnect Client for short) is software that sits on a user's PC and uses TLS to create one end of a VPN remote-access tunnel. As a result, all the packets sent to the other end of the tunnel are encrypted, not just those sent over a single HTTP connection in a web browser.

Figure 14-23 compares the option to create a VPN remote access VPN session from a computer to a site versus for a single HTTPS session. The figure shows a VPN tunnel for PC using the AnyConnect Client to create a client VPN. The AnyConnect Client creates a TLS tunnel to the firewall that has been installed to expect VPN clients to connect to it. The tunnel encrypts all traffic so that PC A can use any application available at the enterprise network on the right.

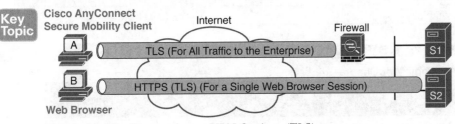

Figure 14-23   *Remote Access VPN Options (TLS)*

Note that while the figure shows a firewall used at the main enterprise site, many types of devices can be used on the server side of a TLS connection as well.

The bottom of Figure 14-23 shows a client VPN that supports a web application for a single web browser tab. The experience is much like when you connect to any other secure website today: the session uses TLS, so all traffic sent to and from that web browser tab is encrypted with TLS. Note that PC B does not use the AnyConnect Client; the user simply opens a web browser to browse to server S2.

VPN Comparisons

The CCNA 200-301 exam topics mention the terms *site-to-site* VPN and *remote access* VPN. To close the section, Table 14-4 lists several key comparison points between the two technologies for easier review and comparison.

Table 14-4 Comparisons of Site-to-Site and Remote Access VPNs

	Remote Access	Site-to-Site
Typical security protocol	TLS	IPsec
Devices supported by one VPN (one or many)	One	Many
Typical use: on-demand or permanent	On-demand	Permanent

Chapter Review

One key to doing well on the exams is to perform repetitive spaced review sessions. Review this chapter's material using either the tools in the book or interactive tools for the same material found on the book's companion website. Refer to the "Your Study Plan" element for more details. Table 14-5 outlines the key review elements and where you can find them. To better track your study progress, record when you completed these activities in the second column.

Table 14-5 Chapter Review Tracking

Review Element	Review Date(s)	Resource Used:
Review key topics		Book, website
Review key terms		Book, website
Answer DIKTA questions		Book, PTP
Review memory tables		Book, website

Review All the Key Topics

Table 14-6 Key Topics for Chapter 14

Key Topic Element	Description	Page Number
Figure 14-2	Metro Ethernet terminology in context	305
Table 14-3	MetroE service types per MEF	306
Figure 14-5	MetroE Ethernet LAN (E-LAN) service concept	309
Figure 14-6	MetroE Ethernet Tree (E-Tree) service concept	309
List	Ideas about customer Layer 3 addressing and what an MPLS VPN provider needs to know	313
Figure 14-11	MPLS terminology in context	314
List	Ideas about routing protocol neighbor relationships with MPLS VPN	316
Figure 14-22	Concepts of site-to-site VPNs with IPsec and GRE	324
Figure 14-23	Concepts of remote access VPNS with TLS	325
Table 14-4	Comparisons between site-to-site and remote access VPNs	326

Key Terms You Should Know

point-to-point, hub and spoke, partial mesh, full mesh, Ethernet WAN, Metro Ethernet, service provider (SP), point of presence (PoP), access link, E-Line, E-LAN, E-Tree, Multiprotocol Label Switching (MPLS), MPLS VPN, customer edge (CE), provider edge (PE), Multiprotocol BGP (MPBGP), IPsec, shared key, TLS, remote access VPN, site-to-site VPN, Cisco AnyConnect Secure Mobility Client

14

CHAPTER 15

Cloud Architecture

This chapter covers the following exam topics:

1.0 Network Fundamentals

1.1 Explain the role and function of network components

1.1.g Servers

1.2 Describe the characteristics of network topology architectures

1.2.f On-premises and cloud

1.12 Explain virtualization fundamentals (virtual machines)

Cloud computing is an approach to offering IT services to customers. However, cloud computing is not a product, or a set of products, a protocol, or any single thing. So, while there are accepted descriptions and definitions of cloud computing today, it takes a broad knowledge of IT beyond networking to know whether a particular IT service is or is not worthy of being called a cloud computing service.

Cloud computing, or cloud, is an approach as to how to offer services to customers. For an IT service to be considered to be cloud computing, it should have these characteristics: It can be requested on-demand; it can dynamically scale (that is, it is elastic); it uses a pool of resources; it has a variety of network access options; and it can be measured and billed back to the user based on the amount used. Cloud computing relies on data centers that can be automated. For instance, to service requests, a cloud computing system will create virtual server instances—virtual machines (VMs)—and configure the settings on each VM to provide the requested service.

This chapter gives you a general idea of the cloud services and network architecture. To do that, this chapter begins with a discussion of server virtualization basics. The next section then discusses the big ideas in cloud computing, with the final section discussing the impact of public clouds on packet flows in enterprise networks.

"Do I Know This Already?" Quiz

Take the quiz (either here or use the PTP software) if you want to use the score to help you decide how much time to spend on this chapter. The letter answers are listed at the bottom of the page following the quiz. Appendix C, found both at the end of the book as well as on the companion website, includes both the answers and explanations. You can also find both answers and explanations in the PTP testing software.

Table 15-1 "Do I Know This Already?" Foundation Topics Section-to-Question Mapping

Foundation Topics Section	Questions
Server Virtualization	1, 2
Cloud Computing Concepts	3, 4
WAN Traffic Paths to Reach Cloud Services	5, 6

1. Three virtual machines run on one physical server. Which of the following server resources are commonly virtualized so each VM can use the required amount of that resource? (Choose three answers.)

   a. NIC

   b. RAM

   c. Power

   d. Hypervisor

   e. CPU

2. Eight virtual machines run on one physical server; the server has two physical Ethernet NICs. Which answer describes a method that allows all eight VMs to communicate?

   a. The VMs must share two IP addresses and coordinate to avoid using duplicate TCP or UDP ports.

   b. The hypervisor acts as an IP router using the NICs as routed IP interfaces.

   c. Each VM uses a virtual NIC that is mapped to a physical NIC.

   d. Each VM uses a virtual NIC that logically connects to a virtual switch.

3. Which of the following cloud services is most likely to be used for software development?

   a. IaaS

   b. PaaS

   c. SaaS

   d. SLBaaS

4. Which of the following cloud services is most likely to be purchased and then used to later install your own software applications?

   a. IaaS

   b. PaaS

   c. SaaS

   d. SLBaaS

5. An enterprise plans to start using a public cloud service and is considering different WAN options. The answers list four options under consideration. Which one option has the most issues if the company chooses one cloud provider but then later wants to change to use a different cloud provider instead?

   a. Using private WAN connections directly to the cloud provider

   b. Using an Internet connection without VPN

   c. Using an intercloud exchange

   d. Using an Internet connection with VPN

6. An enterprise plans to start using a public cloud service and is considering different WAN options. The answers list four options under consideration. Which options provide good security by keeping the data private while also providing good QoS services? (Choose two answers.)

   a. Using private WAN connections directly to the cloud provider

   b. Using an Internet connection without VPN

   c. Using an intercloud exchange

   d. Using an Internet connection with VPN

Foundation Topics

Server Virtualization

When you think of a server, what comes to mind? Is it a desktop computer with a fast CPU? A desktop computer with lots of RAM? Is it hardware that would not sit upright on the floor but could be easily bolted into a rack in a data center? When you think of a server, do you not even think of hardware, but of the server operating system (OS), running somewhere as a virtual machine (VM)?

All those answers are accurate from one perspective or another, but in most every other discussion within the scope of the CCNA certification, we ignore those details. From the perspective of most CCNA discussions, a server is a place to run applications, with users connecting to those applications over the network. The book then represents the server with an icon that looks like a desktop computer (that is the standard Cisco icon for a server). This next topic breaks down some different perspectives on what it means to be a server and prepares us to then discuss cloud computing.

Cisco Server Hardware

Think about the form factor of servers for a moment—that is, the shape and size of the physical server. If you were to build a server of your own, what would it look like? How big, how wide, how tall, and so on? Even if you have never seen a device characterized as a server, consider these key facts:

No KVM: For most servers, there is no permanent user who sits near the server; all the users and administrators connect to the server over the network. As a result, there is no need for a permanent keyboard, video display, or mouse (collectively referred to as KVM).

Racks of servers in a data center: In the early years of servers, a server was any computer with relatively fast CPU, large amounts of RAM, and so on. Today, companies put many servers into one room—a data center—and one goal is to not waste space. So, making servers with a form factor that fits in a standard rack makes for more efficient use of the available space—especially when you do not expect people to be sitting in front of each server.

As an example, Figure 15-1 shows a photo of server hardware from Cisco. While you might think of Cisco as a networking company, around 2010, Cisco expanded its product line into the server market, with the Cisco Unified Computing System (UCS) product line. The photo shows a product from the UCS B-Series (Blade series) that uses a rack-mountable chassis, with slots for server blades. The product shown in the figure can be mounted in a rack—note the holes on the sides—with eight server blades (four on each side) mounted horizontally. It also has four power supplies at the bottom of the chassis.

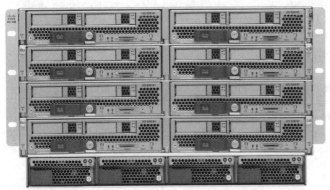

Figure 15-1   *Cisco UCS Servers: B-Series (Blade)*

No matter the form factor, server hardware today supplies some capacity of CPU chips, RAM, storage, and network interface cards (NIC). But you also have to think differently about the OS that runs on the server because of a tool called *server virtualization*.

Server Virtualization Basics

Think of a server—the hardware—as one computer. It can be one of the blades in Figure 15-1, a powerful computer you can buy at the local computer store...whatever. Traditionally, when you think of one server, that one server runs one OS. Inside, the hardware includes a CPU, some RAM, some kind of permanent storage (like disk drives), and one or more NICs. And that one OS can use all the hardware inside the server and then run one or more applications. Figure 15-2 shows those main ideas.

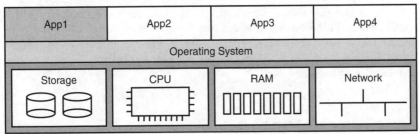

Figure 15-2   *Physical Server Model: Physical Hardware, One OS, and Applications*

With the physical server model shown in Figure 15-2, each physical server runs one OS, and that OS uses all the hardware in that one server. That was true of servers in the days before server virtualization.

Today, most companies instead create a virtualized data center. That means the company purchases server hardware, installs it in racks, and then treats all the CPU, RAM, and so on as capacity in the data center. Then, each OS instance is decoupled from the hardware and is therefore virtual (in contrast to physical). Each piece of hardware that we would formerly have thought of as a server runs multiple instances of an OS at the same time, with each virtual OS instance called a *virtual machine*, or VM.

A single physical host (server) often has more processing power than you need for one OS. Thinking about processors for a moment, modern server CPUs have multiple cores (processors) in a single CPU chip. Each core may also be able to run multiple threads with a feature called *multithreading*. So, when you read about a particular Intel processor with 8 cores and multithreading (typically two threads per core), that one CPU chip can execute 16 different programs concurrently. The hypervisor (introduced shortly) can then treat each available thread as a virtual CPU (vCPU) and give each VM a number of vCPUs, with 16 available in this example.

A VM—that is, an OS instance that is decoupled from the server hardware—still must execute on hardware. Each VM has configuration as to the minimum number of vCPUs it needs, minimum RAM, and so on. The virtualization system then starts each VM on some physical server so that enough physical server hardware capacity exists to support all the VMs running on that host. So, at any one point in time, each VM is running on a physical server, using a subset of the CPU, RAM, storage, and NICs on that server. Figure 15-3 shows a graphic of that concept, with four separate VMs running on one physical server.

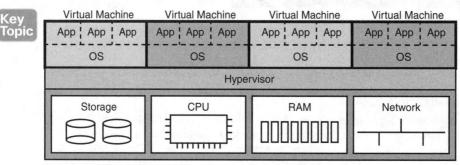

Figure 15-3 *Four VMs Running on One Host; Hypervisor Manages the Hardware*

To make server virtualization work, each physical server (called a *host* in the server virtualization world) uses a *hypervisor*. The hypervisor manages and allocates the host hardware (CPU, RAM, etc.) to each VM based on the settings for the VM. Each VM runs as if it is running on a self-contained physical server, with a specific number of virtual CPUs and NICs and a set amount of RAM and storage. For instance, if one VM happens to be configured to use four CPUs, with 8 GB of RAM, the hypervisor allocates the specific parts of the CPU and RAM that the VM actually uses.

Answers to the "Do I Know This Already?" quiz:

1 A, B, E **2** D **3** B **4** A **5** A **6** A, C

To connect the marketplace to the big ideas discussed thus far, the following list includes a few of the vendors and product family names associated with virtualized data centers:

- VMware vCenter
- Microsoft HyperV
- Citrix XenServer
- Red Hat KVM

Beyond the hypervisor, companies like those in the list (and others) sell complete virtualization systems. These systems allow virtualization engineers to dynamically create VMs, start them, move them (manually and automatically) to different servers, and stop them. For instance, when hardware maintenance needs to be performed, the virtualization engineer can move the VMs to another host (often while running) so that the maintenance can be done.

Networking with Virtual Switches on a Virtualized Host

Server virtualization tools provide a wide variety of options for how to connect VMs to networks. This book does not attempt to discuss them all, but it can help to get some of the basics down before thinking more about cloud computing.

First, what does a physical server include for networking functions? Typically it has one or more NICs, maybe as slow as 1 Gbps, often 10 Gbps today, and maybe as fast as 40 Gbps.

Next, think about the VMs. Normally, an OS has one NIC, maybe more. To make the OS work as normal, each VM has (at least) one NIC, but for a VM, it is a virtual NIC. (For instance, in VMware's virtualization systems, the VM's virtual NIC goes by the name vNIC.)

Finally, the server must combine the ideas of the physical NICs with the vNICs used by the VMs into some kind of a network. Most often, each server uses some kind of an internal Ethernet switch concept, often called (you guessed it) a virtual switch, or vSwitch. Figure 15-4 shows an example, with four VMs, each with one vNIC. The physical server has two physical NICs. The vNICs and physical NICs connect internally to a virtual switch.

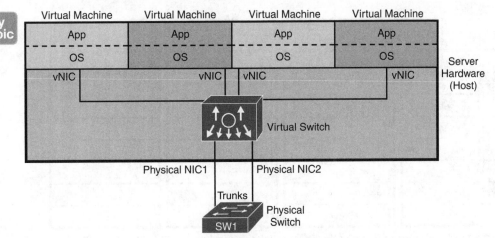

Figure 15-4 *Basic Networking in a Virtualized Host with a Virtual Switch*

Interestingly, the vSwitch can be supplied by the hypervisor vendor or by Cisco. For instance, Cisco offers the Nexus 1000VE virtual switch (which replaces the older and popular Nexus 1000V virtual switch). The Nexus 1000VE runs the NX-OS operating system found in some of the Cisco Nexus data center switch product line. Additionally, Cisco offers the Cisco ACI Virtual Edge, another virtual switch, this one following Cisco ACI networking as detailed in Chapter 16, "Introduction to Controller-Based Networking."

The vSwitch shown in Figure 15-4 uses the same networking features you now know from your CCNA studies; in fact, one big motivation to use a vSwitch from Cisco is to use the same networking features, with the same configuration, as in the rest of the network. In particular:

- **Ports connected to VMs:** The vSwitch can configure a port so that the VM will be in its own VLAN, or share the same VLAN with other VMs, or even use VLAN trunking to the VM itself.

- **Ports connected to physical NICs:** The vSwitch uses the physical NICs in the server hardware so that the switch is adjacent to the external physical LAN switch. The vSwitch can (and likely does) use VLAN trunking.

- **Automated configuration:** The configuration can be easily done from within the same virtualization software that controls the VMs. That programmability allows the virtualization software to move VMs between hosts (servers) and reprogram the vSwitches so that the VM has the same networking capabilities no matter where the VM is running.

The Physical Data Center Network

To pull these ideas together, next consider what happens with the physical network in a virtualized data center. Each host—that is, the physical host—needs a physical connection to the network. Looking again at Figure 15-4, that host, with two physical NICs, needs to connect those two physical NICs to a LAN switch in the data center.

Figure 15-5 shows the traditional cabling for a data center LAN. Each taller rectangle represents one rack inside a data center, with the tiny squares representing NIC ports, and the lines representing cables.

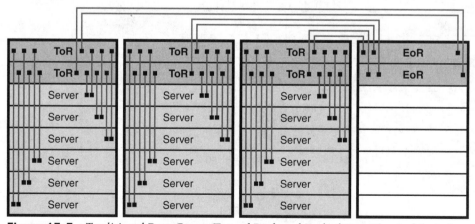

Figure 15-5 *Traditional Data Center Top-of-Rack and End-of-Row Physical Switch Topology*

Often, each host is cabled to two different switches in the top of the rack—called Top of Rack (ToR) switches—to provide redundant paths into the LAN. Each ToR switch acts as an access layer switch from a design perspective. Each ToR switch is then cabled to an End of Row (EoR) switch, which acts as a distribution switch and also connects to the rest of the network.

The design in Figure 15-5 uses a traditional data center cabling plan. Some data center technologies call for different topologies, in particular, Cisco Application Centric Infrastructure (ACI). ACI places the server and switch hardware into racks, but cables the switches with a different topology—a topology required for proper operation of the ACI fabric. Chapter 16 introduces ACI concepts.

Workflow with a Virtualized Data Center

So far, the first part of this chapter has described background information important to the upcoming discussions of cloud computing. Server virtualization has been a great improvement to the operations of many data centers, but virtualization alone does not create a cloud computing environment. Continuing the discussion of these fundamental technologies before discussing cloud computing, consider this example of a workflow through a virtualized (not cloud-based) data center.

Some of the IT staff, call them server or virtualization engineers or administrators, order and install new hosts (servers). They gather requirements, plan for the required capacity, shop for hardware, order it, and install the hardware. They play the role of long-time server administrators and engineers, but now they work with the virtualization tools as well.

For the virtualization parts of the effort, the virtualization engineers also install and customize the virtualization tools. Beyond the hypervisor on each host, many other useful tools help manage and control a virtualized data center. For instance, one tool might give the engineers a view of the data center as a whole, with all VMs running there, with the idea that one data center is just a lot of capacity to run VMs. Over time, the server/virtualization engineers add new physical servers to the data center and configure the virtualization systems to make use of the new physical servers and make sure it all works.

So far in this scenario, the work has been in preparation for providing services to some internal customer—a development team member, the operations staff, and so on. Now, a customer is requesting a "server." In truth, the customer wants a VM (or many), with certain requirements: a specific number of vCPUs, a specific amount of RAM, and so on. The customer makes a request to the virtualization/server engineer to set up the VMs, as shown in Figure 15-6.

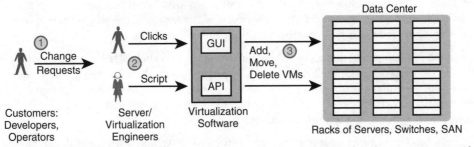

Figure 15-6 *Traditional Workflow: Customer (Human) Asks Virtualization (Human) for Service*

The figure emphasizes what happens after the customer makes a request, which flows something like this:

Step 1. The customer of the IT group, such as a developer or a member of the operations staff, wants some service, like a set of new VMs.

Step 2. The virtualization/server engineer reacts to the request from the customer. The server/virtualization engineer clicks away at the user interface, or if the number of VMs is large, she often runs a program called a script to more efficiently create the VMs.

Step 3. Regardless of whether the virtualization engineer clicked or used scripts, the virtualization software could then create a number of new VMs and start those on some hosts inside the data center.

The process shown in Figure 15-6 works great. However, that approach to providing services breaks some of the basic criteria of a cloud service. For instance, cloud computing requires self-service. For the workflow to be considered to be a cloud service, the process at step 2 should not require a human to service that request, but instead the request should be filled automatically. Want some new VMs in a cloud world? Click a user interface to ask for some new VMs, go get a cup of coffee, and your VMs will be set up and started, to your specification, in minutes.

Summarizing some of the key points about a virtualized data center made so far, which enable cloud computing:

- The OS is decoupled from the hardware on which it runs, so that the OS, as a VM, can run on any server in a data center that has enough resources to run the VM.

- The virtualization software can automatically start and move the VM between servers in the data center.

- Data center networking includes virtual switches and virtual NICs within each host (server).

- Data center networking can be programmed by the virtualization software, allowing new VMs to be configured, started, moved as needed, and stopped, with the networking details configured automatically.

Cloud Computing Services

Cloud computing is an approach to offering IT services. Cloud computing makes use of products such as the virtualization products but also uses products built specifically to enable cloud features. However, cloud computing is not just a set of products to be implemented; instead, it is a way of offering IT services. So, understanding what cloud computing is—and is not—takes a little work; this next topic introduces the basics.

From the just-completed discussions about virtualization, you already know one characteristic of a cloud service: it must allow self-service provisioning by the consumer of the service. That is, the consumer or customer of the service must be able to request the service and receive that service without the delay of waiting for a human to have time to work on it, consider the request, do the work, and so on.

To get a broader sense of what it means for a service to be a cloud service, examine this list of five criteria for a cloud computing service. The list is derived from the definition of cloud computing as put forth by the US National Institute of Standards and Technology (NIST):

On-demand self-service: The IT consumer chooses when to start and stop using the service, without any direct interaction with the provider of the service.

Broad network access: The service must be available from many types of devices and over many types of networks (including the Internet).

Resource pooling: The provider creates a pool of resources (rather than dedicating specific servers for use only by certain consumers) and dynamically allocates resources from that pool for each new request from a consumer.

Rapid elasticity: To the consumer, the resource pool appears to be unlimited (that is, it expands quickly, so it is called *elastic*), and the requests for new service are filled quickly.

Measured service: The provider can measure the usage and report that usage to the consumer, both for transparency and for billing.

Keep this list of five criteria in mind while you work through the rest of the chapter. Later parts of the chapter will refer back to the list.

To further develop this definition, the next few pages look at two branches of the cloud universe—private cloud and public cloud—also with the goal of further explaining some of the points from the NIST definition.

Private Cloud (On-Premise)

Look back to the workflow example in Figure 15-6 with a virtualized data center. Now think about the five NIST criteria for cloud computing. If you break down the list versus the example around Figure 15-6, it seems like the workflow may meet at least some of these five NIST cloud criteria, and it does. In particular, as described so far in this chapter, a virtualized data center pools resources so they can be dynamically allocated. You could argue that a virtualized data center is elastic, in that the resource pool expands. However, the process may not be rapid because the workflow requires human checks, balances, and time before provisioning new services.

Private cloud creates a service, inside a company, to internal customers, that meets the five criteria from the NIST list. To create a private cloud, an enterprise often expands its IT tools (like virtualization tools), changes internal workflow processes, adds additional tools, and so on.

NOTE The world of cloud computing has long used the terms *private cloud* and *public cloud*. In more recent years, you may also find references that instead use a different pair of terms for the same ideas, with *on-premise* meaning *private cloud*, and *cloud* meaning *public cloud*. Note that the one CCNA 200-301 exam topic that mentions cloud happens to use the newer pair of terms.

As some examples, consider what happens when an application developer at a company needs VMs to use when developing an application. With private cloud, the developer can request those VMs and those VMs automatically start and are available within minutes, with most of the time lag being the time to boot the VMs. If the developer wants many more VMs, he can assume that the private cloud will have enough capacity, and new requests are still serviced rapidly. And all parties should know that the IT group can measure the usage of the services for internal billing.

Focus on the self-service aspect of cloud for a moment. To make that happen, many cloud computing services use a *cloud services catalog*. That catalog exists for the user as a web application that lists anything that can be requested via the company's cloud infrastructure. Before using a private cloud, developers and operators who needed new services (like new VMs) sent a change request asking the virtualization team to add VMs (see Figure 15-6). With private cloud, the (internal) consumers of IT services—developers, operators, and the like—can click to choose from the cloud services catalog. And if the request is for a new set of VMs, the VMs appear and are ready for use in minutes, without human interaction for that step, as seen at step 2 of Figure 15-7.

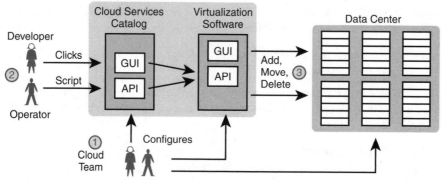

Figure 15-7 *Basic Private Cloud Workflow to Create One VM*

To make this process work, the cloud team has to add some tools and processes to its virtualized data center. For instance, it installs software to create the cloud services catalog, both with a user interface and with code that interfaces to the APIs of the virtualization systems. That services catalog software can react to consumer requests, using APIs into the virtualization software, to add, move, and create VMs, for instance. Also, the cloud team—composed of server, virtualization, network, and storage engineers—focuses on building the resource pool, testing and adding new services to the catalog, handling exceptions, and watching the reports (per the measured service requirement) to know when to add capacity to keep the resource pool ready to handle all requests.

Notably, with the cloud model, the cloud team no longer spends time handling individual requests for adding 10 VMs here, 50 there, with change requests from different groups.

Summarizing, with private cloud, you change your methods and tools to offer some of the same services. Private cloud is "private" in that one company owns the tools that create the cloud and employs the people who use the services. Even inside one company, using a cloud computing approach can improve the operational speed of deploying IT services.

Public Cloud

With a private cloud, the cloud provider and the cloud consumer are part of the same company. With public cloud, the reverse is true: a public cloud provider offers services, selling those services to consumers in other companies. In fact, if you think of Internet service providers and WAN service providers selling Internet and WAN services to many enterprises, the same general idea works here with public cloud providers selling their services to many enterprises.

The workflow in public cloud happens somewhat like private cloud when you start from the point of a consumer asking for some service (like a new VM). As shown on the right of Figure 15-8, at step 1, the consumer asks for the new service from the service catalog web page. At step 2, the virtualization tools react to the request to create the service. Once started, the services are available, but running in a data center that resides somewhere else in the world, and certainly not at the enterprise's data center (step 3).

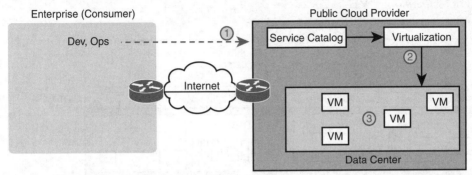

Figure 15-8 *Public Cloud Provider in the Internet*

Of course, the consumer is in a different network than the cloud provider with cloud computing, which brings up the issue of how to connect to a cloud provider. Cloud providers support multiple network options. They each connect to the Internet so that apps and users inside the consumer's network can communicate with the apps that the consumer runs in the cloud provider's network. However, one of the five NIST criteria for cloud computing is broad network access, so cloud providers offer different networking options as well, including virtual private network (VPN) and private wide-area network (WAN) connections between consumers and the cloud.

Cloud and the "As a Service" Model

So what do you get with cloud computing? So far, this chapter has just shown a VM as a service. With cloud computing, there are a variety of services, and three stand out as the most common seen in the market today.

First, a quick word about some upcoming terminology. The cloud computing world works on a services model. Instead of buying (consuming) hardware, buying or licensing software, installing it yourself, and so on, the consumer receives some service from the provider. But that idea, receiving a service, is more abstract than the idea of buying a server and installing a particular software package. So with cloud computing, instead of keeping the discussion so generic, the industry uses a variety of terms that end in "as a Service." And each "-aaS" term has a different meaning.

This next topic explains those three most common cloud services: Infrastructure as a Service, Software as a Service, and Platform as a Service.

Infrastructure as a Service

Infrastructure as a Service (IaaS) may be the easiest of the cloud computing services to understand for most people. For perspective, think about any time you have shopped for a computer. You thought about the OS to run (the latest Microsoft OS, or Linux, or macOS if shopping for a Mac). You compared prices based on the CPU and its speed, how much RAM the computer had, the size of the disk drive, and so on.

IaaS offers a similar idea, but the consumer receives the use of a VM. You specify the amount of hardware performance/capacity to allocate to the VM (number of virtual CPUs, amount of RAM, and so on), as shown in Figure 15-9. You can even pick an OS to use. Once selected, the cloud provider starts the VM, which boots the chosen OS.

NOTE   In the virtualization and cloud world, starting a VM is often called *spinning up a VM* or *instantiating a VM*.

Key Topic

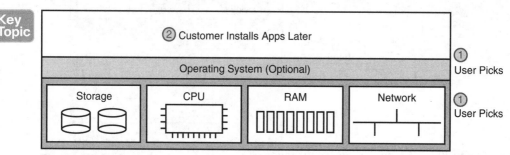

Figure 15-9 *IaaS Concept*

The provider also gives the consumer details about the VM so the consumer can connect to the OS's user interface, install more software, and customize settings. For example, imagine that the consumer wants to run a particular application on the server. If that customer wanted to use Microsoft Exchange as an email server, she would then need to connect to the VM and install Exchange.

Figure 15-10 shows a web page from Amazon Web Services (AWS), a public cloud provider, from which you could create a VM as part of its IaaS service. The screenshot shows that the user selected a small VM called "micro." If you look closely at the text, you may be able to read the heading and numbers to see that this particular VM has one vCPU and 1 GB of RAM.

Family	Type	vCPUs	Memory (GiB)	Instance Storage (GB)	EBS-Optimized Available	Network Performance
General purpose	t2.nano	1	0.5	EBS only	-	Low to Moderate
General purpose	t2.micro	1	1	EBS only	-	Low to Moderate
General purpose	t2.small	1	2	EBS only	-	Low to Moderate
General purpose	t2.medium	2	4	EBS only	-	Low to Moderate
General purpose	t2.large	2	8	EBS only	-	Low to Moderate

Figure 15-10 *AWS Screenshot—Set Up VM with Different CPU/RAM/OS*

Software as a Service

With Software as a Service (SaaS), the consumer receives a service with working software. The cloud provider may use VMs, possibly many VMs, to create the service, but those are hidden from the consumer. The cloud provider licenses, installs, and supports whatever software is required. The cloud provider then monitors performance of the application. However, the consumer chooses to use the application, signs up for the service, and starts using the application—no further installation work required. Figure 15-11 shows these main concepts.

 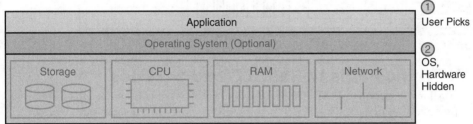

Figure 15-11 *SaaS Concept*

Many of you have probably used or at least heard of many public SaaS offerings. File storage services like Apple iCloud, Google Drive, Dropbox, and Box are all SaaS offerings. Most online email offerings can be considered SaaS services today. As another example, Microsoft offers its Exchange email server software as a service, so you can have private email services but offered as a service, along with all the other features included with Exchange—without having to license, install, and maintain the Exchange software on some VMs.

(Development) Platform as a Service

Platform as a Service (PaaS) is a development platform, prebuilt as a service. A PaaS service is like IaaS in some ways. Both supply the consumer with one or more VMs, with a configurable amount of CPU, RAM, and other resources.

The key difference between PaaS and IaaS is that PaaS includes many more software tools beyond the basic OS. Those tools are useful to a software developer during the software development process. Once the development process is complete, and the application has been rolled out in production, those tools are not needed on the servers running the application. So the development tools are particular to the work done when developing.

A PaaS offering includes a set of development tools, and each PaaS offering has a different combination of tools. PaaS VMs often include an integrated development environment (IDE), which is a set of related tools that enables the developer to write and test code easily. PaaS VMs include continuous integration tools that allow the developer to update code and have that code automatically tested and integrated into a larger software project. Examples include Google's App Engine PaaS offering (https://cloud.google.com/appengine), the Eclipse integrated development environment (see www.eclipse.org), and the Jenkins continuous integration and automation tool (see https://jenkins.io).

The primary reasons to choose one PaaS service over another, or to choose a PaaS solution instead of IaaS, is the mix of development tools. If you do not have experience as a developer, it can be difficult to tell whether one PaaS service might be better. You can still make some choices about sizing the PaaS VMs, similar to IaaS tools when setting up some PaaS services, as shown in Figure 15-12, but the developer tools included are the key to a PaaS service.

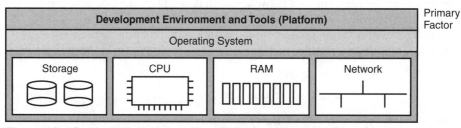

Figure 15-12 *PaaS Concept*

WAN Traffic Paths to Reach Cloud Services

This final major section of the chapter focuses on WAN options for public cloud, and the pros and cons of each. This section ignores private cloud for the most part, because using a private cloud—which is internal to an enterprise—has much less of an impact on an enterprise WAN compared to public cloud. With public cloud, the cloud services exist on the other side of some WAN connection as compared to the consumer of the services, so network engineers must think about how to best build a WAN when using public cloud services.

Enterprise WAN Connections to Public Cloud

Using the Internet to communicate between the enterprise and a public cloud provider is easy and convenient. However, it also has some negatives. This first section describes the basics and points out the issues, which then leads to some of the reasons why using other WAN connections may be preferred.

Accessing Public Cloud Services Using the Internet

Imagine an enterprise that operates its network without cloud. All the applications it uses to run its business run on servers in a data center inside the enterprise. The OS instances where those applications run can be hosted directly on physical servers or on VMs in a virtualized data center, but all the servers exist somewhere inside the enterprise.

Now imagine that the IT staff starts moving some of those applications out to a public cloud service. How do the users of the application (inside the enterprise) get to the user interface of the application (which runs at the public cloud provider's data center)? The Internet, of course. Both the enterprise and the cloud provider connect to the Internet, so using the Internet is the easy and convenient choice.

Now consider a common workflow to move an internal application to now run on the public cloud, for the purpose of making a couple of important points. First, Figure 15-13 shows the example. The cloud provider's services catalog can be reached by enterprise personnel, over the Internet, as shown at step 1. After choosing the desired services—for instance, some VMs for an IaaS service—the cloud provider (step 2) instantiates the VMs. Then, not shown as a step in the figure, the VMs are customized to now run the app that was formerly running inside the enterprise's data center.

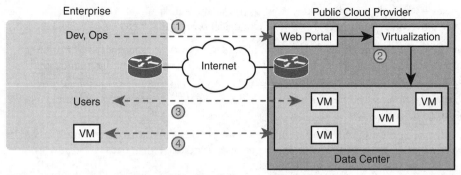

Figure 15-13   *Accessing a Public Cloud Service Using the Internet*

At this point, the new app is running in the cloud, and those services will require network bandwidth. In particular, step 3 shows users communicating with the applications, just as would happen with any other application. Additionally, most apps send much more data than just the data between the application and the end user. For instance, you might move an app to the public cloud, but you might keep authentication services on an internal server because those are used by a large number of applications—some internal and some hosted in the public cloud. So at step 4, any application communication between VMs hosted in the cloud to/from VMs hosted inside the enterprise also needs to take place.

Pros and Cons with Connecting to Public Cloud with Internet

Using the Internet to connect from the enterprise to the public cloud has several advantages. The most obvious advantage is that all companies and cloud providers already have Internet connections, so getting started using public cloud services is easy. Using the Internet works particularly well with SaaS services and a distributed workforce. For instance, maybe your sales division uses a SaaS customer contact app. Often, salespeople do not sit inside the enterprise network most of the work day. They likely connect to the Internet and use a VPN to connect to the enterprise. For apps hosted on the public cloud, with this user base, it makes perfect sense to use the Internet.

While that was just one example, the following list summarizes some good reasons to use the Internet as the WAN connection to a public cloud service:

Agility: An enterprise can get started using public cloud without having to wait to order a private WAN connection to the cloud provider because cloud providers support Internet connectivity.

Migration: An enterprise can switch its workload from one cloud provider to another more easily because cloud providers all connect to the Internet.

Distributed users: The enterprise's users are distributed and connect to the Internet with their devices (as in the sales SaaS app example).

Using the Internet as the WAN connectivity to a public cloud is both a blessing and a curse in some ways. Using the Internet can help you get started with public cloud and to get working quickly, but it also means that you do not have to do any planning before deploying a public cloud service. With a little planning, a network engineer can see some of the negatives of using the Internet—the same negatives when using the Internet for other purposes—which then might make you want to use alternative WAN connections. Those negatives for using the Internet for public cloud access are

Security: The Internet is less secure than private WAN connections in that a "man in the middle" can attempt to read the contents of data that passes to/from the public cloud.

Capacity: Moving an internal application to the public cloud increases network traffic, so the question of whether the enterprise's Internet links can handle the additional load needs to be considered.

Quality of Service (QoS): The Internet does not provide QoS, whereas private WANs can. Using the Internet may result in a worse user experience than desired because of higher delay (latency), jitter, and packet loss.

No WAN SLA: ISPs typically will not provide a service-level agreement (SLA) for WAN performance and availability to all destinations of a network. WAN service providers are much more likely to offer performance and availability SLAs.

This list of concerns does not mean that an enterprise cannot use the Internet to access its public cloud services. It does mean that it should consider the pros and cons of each WAN option.

Private WAN and Internet VPN Access to Public Cloud

The NIST definition for cloud computing lists broad network access as one of the five main criteria. In the case of public cloud, that often means supporting a variety of WAN connections, including the most common enterprise WAN technologies. Basically, an enterprise can connect to a public cloud provider with WAN technologies discussed in this book. For the sake of discussion, Figure 15-14 breaks it down into two broad categories.

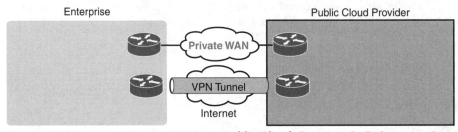

Figure 15-14 *Using Private WAN to a Public Cloud: Security, QoS, Capacity, Reporting*

To create a VPN tunnel between the enterprise and the cloud provider, you can use the same VPN features discussed earlier in Chapter 14, "WAN Architecture." The cloud provider can offer a VPN service—that is, the cloud side of the VPN tunnel is implemented by the cloud provider—and the enterprise configures the matching VPN service on one of its own routers. Or the enterprise can use its own router inside the cloud provider's network—a virtual router, running as a VM—and configure VPN services on that router. In fact, Cisco makes the *Cloud Services Router* (CSR) to do exactly that: to be a router, but a router that runs as a VM in a cloud service, controlled by the cloud consumer, to do various functions that routers do, including terminating VPNs. (Also, by running a virtual router as a VM and managing the configuration internally, the enterprise might save some of the cost of using a similar service offered by the cloud provider.)

To make a private Multiprotocol Label Switching (MPLS) VPN or Ethernet WAN connection, the enterprise needs to work with the cloud provider and the WAN provider. Because cloud providers connect to many customers with private WAN connections, they often have published set instructions to follow. In the most basic form, with MPLS, the enterprise and the cloud provider connect to the same MPLS provider, with the MPLS provider connecting the enterprise and cloud sites. The same basic process happens with Ethernet WAN services, with one or more Ethernet Virtual Connections (EVCs) created between the public WAN and the enterprise.

15

> **NOTE**   Often, the server/virtualization engineers will dictate whether the WAN connection needs to support Layer 2 or Layer 3 connectivity, depending on other factors.

Private WAN connections also require some physical planning. Each of the larger public cloud providers has a number of large data centers spread around the planet and with pre-built connection points into the major WAN services to aid the creation of private WAN connections to customers. An enterprise might then look at the cloud provider's documentation and work with that provider to choose the best place to install the private WAN connection. (Those larger public cloud companies include Amazon Web Services, Google Compute Cloud, Microsoft Azure, and Rackspace, if you would like to look at their websites for information about their locations.)

Pros and Cons of Connecting to Cloud with Private WANs

Private WANs overcome some of the issues of using the Internet without VPN, so working through those issues, consider some of the different WAN options.

First, considering the issue of security, all the private options, including adding a VPN to the existing Internet connection, improve security significantly. An Internet VPN would encrypt the data to keep it private. Private WAN connections with MPLS and Ethernet have traditionally been considered secure without encryption, but companies are sometimes encrypting data sent over private WAN connections as well to make the network more secure.

Regarding QoS, using an Internet VPN solution still fails to provide QoS because the Internet does not provide QoS. WAN services like MPLS VPN and Ethernet WANs can. As discussed in Chapter 11, "Quality of Service (QoS)," WAN providers will look at the QoS markings for frames/packets sent by the customer and apply QoS tools to the traffic as it passes through the service provider's network.

Finally, as for the capacity issue, the concern of planning network capacity exists no matter what type of WAN is used. Any plan to migrate an app away from an internal data center to instead be hosted as a public cloud provider requires extra thought and planning.

Several negatives exist for using a private WAN, as you might expect. Installing the new private WAN connections takes time, delaying when a company gets started in cloud computing. Private WANs typically cost more than using the Internet. If using a WAN connection to one cloud provider (instead of using the Internet), then migrating to a new cloud provider can require another round of private WAN installation, again delaying work projects. Using the Internet (with or without VPN) would make that migration much easier, but as shown in the next section, a strong compromise solution exists as well.

Intercloud Exchanges

Public cloud computing also introduces a whole new level of competition because a cloud consumer can move his workload from one cloud provider to another. Moving the workload takes some effort, for a variety of reasons beyond the scope of this book. (Suffice it to say that most cloud providers differ in the detail of how they implement services.) But enterprises can and do migrate their workload from one cloud provider to another, choosing a new company for a variety of reasons, including looking for a less expensive cloud provider.

Now focus on the networking connections again. The main negative with using a private WAN for the cloud is that it adds another barrier to migrating to a new public cloud provider. One solution adds easier migration to the use of a private WAN through a cloud service called an intercloud exchange (or simply an intercloud).

Generically, the term *intercloud exchange* has come to be known as a company that creates a private network as a service. First, an intercloud exchange connects to multiple cloud providers on one side. On the other side, the intercloud connects to cloud consumers. Figure 15-15 shows the idea.

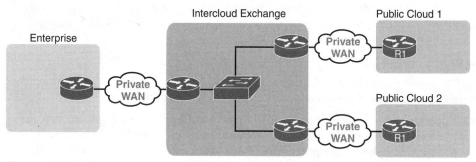

Figure 15-15 *Permanent Private WAN Connection to an Intercloud Exchange*

Once connected, the cloud consumer can be configured to communicate with one public cloud provider today, to specific cloud provider sites. Later, if the consumer wants to migrate to use another cloud provider, the consumer keeps the same private WAN links to the intercloud exchange and asks the provider to reconfigure to set up new private WAN connections to the new cloud provider.

As for pros and cons, with an intercloud exchange, you get the same benefits as when connecting with a private WAN connection to a public cloud, but with the additional pro of easier migration to a new cloud provider. The main con is that using an intercloud exchange introduces another company into the mix.

Summarizing the Pros and Cons of Public Cloud WAN Options

Table 15-2 summarizes some of these key pros and cons for the public WAN options for cloud computing, for study and reference.

Table 15-2   Comparison of Public Cloud WAN Options

	Internet	Internet VPN	MPLS VPN	Ethernet WAN	Intercloud Exchange
Makes data private	No	Yes	Yes	Yes	Yes
Supports QoS	No	No	Yes	Yes	Yes
Requires capacity planning	Yes	Yes	Yes	Yes	Yes
Eases migration to a new provider	Yes	Yes	No	No	Yes
Speeds initial installation	Yes	Yes	No	No	No

A Scenario: Branch Offices and the Public Cloud

So far in this major section about WAN design with public cloud, the enterprise has been shown as one entity, but most enterprise WANs have many sites. Those distributed enterprise sites impact some parts of WAN design for public cloud. The next discussion of WAN design issues with public cloud works through a scenario that shows an enterprise with a typical central site and branch office.

The example used in this section is a common one: the movement away from internal email servers, supported directly by the IT staff, to email delivered as a SaaS offering. Focus on the impact of the enterprise's remote sites like branch offices.

Migrating Traffic Flows When Migrating to Email SaaS

First, think of the traffic flow inside an enterprise before SaaS, when the company buys servers, licenses email server software, installs the hardware and software in an internal data center, and so on. The company may have hundreds or thousands of remote sites, like the branch office shown in Figure 15-16. To check email, an employee at the branch office sends packets back and forth with the email server at the central site, as shown.

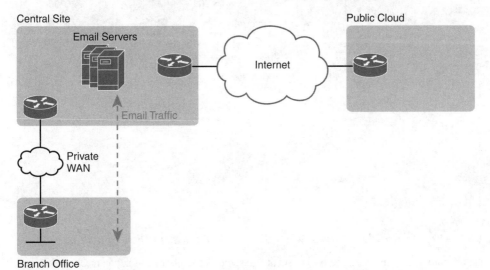

Figure 15-16   *Traffic Flow: Private WAN, Enterprise Implements Email Services*

The company then looks at the many different costs for email in this old model versus the new SaaS model. For instance, Microsoft Exchange is a very popular software package to build those enterprise email servers. Microsoft, a major player in the public cloud space with its Microsoft Azure service, offers Exchange as a SaaS service. (During the writing of this book, this particular service could be found as part of Office 365 or as "Exchange Online.") So the enterprise considers the options and chooses to migrate an email SaaS offering.

Once migrated, the email servers run in the cloud, but as a SaaS service. The enterprise IT staff, who are the customers of the SaaS service, do not have to manage the servers. Just to circle back to some big ideas, with a SaaS service, the consumer does not worry about installing VMs, sizing them, installing Exchange or some other email server software, and so on. The consumer receives email service in this case. The company does have to do some migration work to move existing email, contacts, and so on, but once completed, all users now communicate with email servers that run in the cloud as a SaaS service.

Now think about that enterprise branch office user, and the traffic flows shown in Figure 15-17, when a branch user sends or receives an email. For instance, think of an email with a large attachment, just to make the impact more dramatic. If the enterprise design connects branches to the central sites only, this is the net effect on WAN traffic:

- No reduction in private WAN traffic at all occurs because all the branch office email traffic flows to/from the central site.

- One hundred percent of the email traffic (even internal emails) that flows to/from branches now also flows over the Internet connection, consuming the bandwidth of the enterprise's Internet links.

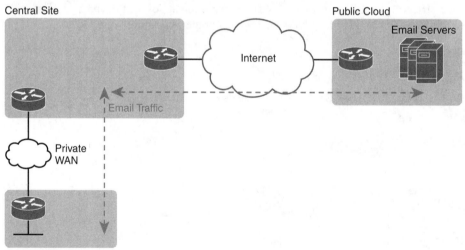

Figure 15-17 *Traffic Flow: Private WAN, Enterprise Implements Email Services*

Just to make the point, imagine two users at the same branch office. They can see each other across the room. One wants to share a file with the other, but the most convenient way they know to share a file is to email the file as an attachment. So one of them sends an email to the other, attaching the 20-MB file to the email. Before using SaaS, with an email server at the central site, that email and file would flow over the private WAN, to the email server, and then back to the second user's email client. With this new design, that email with the 20-MB attachment would flow over the private WAN, then over the Internet to the email server, and then back again over the Internet and over the private WAN when the second user downloads her email.

Branch Offices with Internet and Private WAN

For enterprises that place their Internet connections primarily at the central sites, this public cloud model can cause problems like the one just described. One way to deal with this particular challenge is to plan the right capacity for the Internet links; another is to plan capacity for some private WAN connections to the public cloud. Another option exists as well: redesign the enterprise WAN to a small degree, and consider placing direct Internet connections at the branch offices. Then all Internet traffic, including the email traffic to the new SaaS service, could be sent directly, and not consume the private WAN bandwidth or the central site Internet link bandwidth, as shown in Figure 15-18.

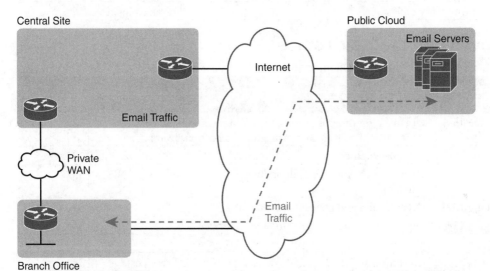

Figure 15-18   *Connecting Branches Directly to the Internet for Public Cloud Traffic*

The design in Figure 15-18 has several advantages. The traffic flows much more directly. It does not waste the WAN bandwidth for the central site. And broadband Internet connections are relatively inexpensive today compared to private WAN connections.

However, when the per-branch Internet connections are added for the first time, the new Internet links create security concerns. One of the reasons an enterprise might use only a few Internet links, located at a central site, is to focus the security efforts at those links. Using an Internet connection at each branch changes that approach. But many enterprises not only use the Internet at each site but also rely on it as their only WAN connection, as shown with Internet VPNs back in Chapter 14.

Chapter Review

One key to doing well on the exams is to perform repetitive spaced review sessions. Review this chapter's material using either the tools in the book or interactive tools for the same material found on the book's companion website. Refer to the "Your Study Plan" element for more details. Table 15-3 outlines the key review elements and where you can find them. To better track your study progress, record when you completed these activities in the second column.

Table 15-3 Chapter Review Tracking

Review Element	Review Date(s)	Resource Used
Review key topics		Book, website
Review key terms		Book, website
Answer DIKTA questions		Book, PTP
Review memory tables		Book, website

Review All the Key Topics

Table 15-4 Key Topics for Chapter 15

Key Topic Element	Description	Page Number
Figure 15-3	Organization of applications, on a VM, on an OS, with a hypervisor allocating and managing the host hardware	332
Figure 15-4	Virtual switch concept	333
List	Definition of cloud computing (paraphrased) based on the NIST standard	337
Figure 15-9	Organization and concepts for an IaaS service	340
Figure 15-11	Organization and concepts for a SaaS service	341
Figure 15-12	Organization and concepts for a PaaS service	342
List	Cons for using the Internet to access public WAN services	344
Table 15-2	Summary of pros and cons with different public cloud WAN access options	347

Key Terms You Should Know

Unified Computing System (UCS), virtual machine, virtual CPU (vCPU), hypervisor, Host (context: DC), virtual NIC (vNIC), virtual switch (vSwitch), on-demand self-service, resource pooling, rapid elasticity, cloud services catalog, public cloud, private cloud, Infrastructure as a Service (IaaS), Platform as a Service (PaaS), Software as a Service (SaaS)

Part IV Review

Keep track of your part review progress with the checklist shown in Table P4-1. Details on each task follow the table.

Table P4-1 Part IV Review Checklist

Activity	1st Date Completed	2nd Date Completed
Repeat All DIKTA Questions		
Answer Part Review Questions		
Review Key Topics		

Repeat All DIKTA Questions

For this task, use the PTP software to answer the "Do I Know This Already?" questions again for the chapters in this part of the book.

Answer Part Review Questions

For this task, use PTP to answer the Part Review questions for this part of the book.

Review Key Topics

Review all key topics in all chapters in this part, either by browsing the chapters or by using the Key Topics application on the companion website.

Part V of this book includes most of the network automation topics from the CCNA blueprint; however, the part includes as much discussion of how Cisco and others have changed the way networks work to enable better automation as it discusses tools and processes to automate networks.

Chapters 16 and 17 examine a wide range of products and architectures that also enable better operations and automation. Chapter 16 discusses how controllers can separate out part of the work formerly done by networking devices. The chapter shows the advantages of these new controller-based models and details a few examples. Chapter 17 then goes on to give more detail about Cisco Software-Defined Access (SDA), a controller-based networking approach to building enterprise campus networks.

Chapters 18 and 19 discuss a few more specific details about network automation. Controllers typically include REST APIs and often return data to automation programs in the form of formatted data like JSON. Chapter 18 introduces these concepts. Chapter 19 then moves on to discuss IT automation tools, specifically Ansible, Puppet, and Chef, with focus on how to use these tools for network automation.

Part V

Network Automation

Part V Review

CHAPTER 16

Introduction to Controller-Based Networking

This chapter covers the following exam topics:

1.0 Network Fundamentals

1.1 Explain the role and function of network components

1.1.f Endpoints

1.1.g Servers

1.2 Describe characteristics of network topology architectures

1.2.c Spine-leaf

6.0 Automation and Programmability

6.1 Explain how automation impacts network management

6.2 Compare traditional networks with controller-based networking

6.3 Describe controller-based and software defined architectures (overlay, underlay, and fabric)

6.3.a Separation of control plane and data plane

6.3.b Northbound and southbound APIs

The CCNA certification focuses on the traditional model for operating and controlling networks, a model that has existed for decades. You understand protocols that the devices use, along with the commands that can customize how those protocols operate. Then you plan and implement distributed configuration to the devices, device by device, to implement the network.

The 2010s have seen the introduction of a new network operational model: Software Defined Networking (SDN). SDN makes use of a controller that centralizes some network functions. The controller also creates many new capabilities to operate networks differently; in particular, controllers enable programs to automatically configure and operate networks through power application programming interfaces (APIs).

With traditional networking, the network engineer configured the various devices and changes requiring a long timeframe to plan and implement changes. With controller-based networking and SDN, network engineers and operators can implement changes more quickly, with better consistency, and often with better operational practices.

This chapter introduces the concepts of network programmability and SDN. Note that the topic area is large, with this chapter providing enough detail for you to understand the basics and to be ready for the other three chapters in this part.

The first major section of this chapter introduces the basic concepts of data and control planes, along with controllers and the related architecture. The second section then shows separate product examples of network programmability using controllers, all of which use different methods to implement networking features. The last section takes a little more exam-specific approach to these topics, comparing the benefits of traditional networking with the benefits of controller-based networking.

"Do I Know This Already?" Quiz

Take the quiz (either here or use the PTP software) if you want to use the score to help you decide how much time to spend on this chapter. The letter answers are listed at the bottom of the page following the quiz. Appendix C, found both at the end of the book as well as on the companion website, includes both the answers and explanations. You can also find both answers and explanations in the PTP testing software.

Table 16-1 "Do I Know This Already?" Foundation Topics Section-to-Question Mapping

Foundation Topics Section	Questions
SDN and Controller-Based Networks	1–3
Examples of Network Programmability and SDN	4–5
Comparing Traditional and Controller-Based Networks	6

1. A Layer 2 switch examines a frame's destination MAC address and chooses to forward that frame out port G0/1 only. That action occurs as part of which plane of the switch?

   a. Data plane

   b. Management plane

   c. Control plane

   d. Table plane

2. A router uses OSPF to learn routes and adds those to the IPv4 routing table. That action occurs as part of which plane of the router?

   a. Data plane

   b. Management plane

   c. Control plane

   d. Table plane

3. A network uses an SDN architecture with switches and a centralized controller. Which of the following terms describes a function or functions expected to be found on the switches but not on the controller?

   a. A northbound interface

   b. A southbound interface

   c. Data plane functions

   d. Control plane functions

4. Which of the following controllers (if any) uses a mostly centralized control plane model?

   a. OpenDaylight Controller

   b. Cisco Application Policy Infrastructure Controller (APIC)

   c. Cisco APIC Enterprise Module (APIC-EM)

   d. None of these controllers uses a mostly centralized control plane.

5. To which types of nodes should an ACI leaf switch connect in a typical single-site design? (Choose two answers.)

   a. All of the other leaf switches

   b. A subset of the spine switches

   c. All of the spine switches

   d. Some of the endpoints

   e. None of the endpoints

6. Which answers list an advantage of controller-based networks versus traditional networks? (Choose two answers.)

   a. The ability to configure the features for the network rather than per device

   b. The ability to have forwarding tables at each device

   c. Programmatic APIs available per device

   d. More consistent device configuration

Foundation Topics

SDN and Controller-Based Networks

Networking devices forward data in the form of messages, typically data-link frames like Ethernet frames. You have learned about how switches and routers do that forwarding for the entire length of preparing for the CCNA exam.

Network programmability and Software Defined Networking (SDN) take those ideas, analyze the pieces, find ways to improve them for today's needs, and reassemble those ideas into a new way of making networks work. At the end of that rearrangement, the devices in the network still forward messages, but the how and why have changed.

This first major section explains the most central concepts of SDN and network programmability. It starts by breaking down some of the components of what exists in traditional networking devices. Then this section explains how some centralized controller software, called a controller, creates an architecture for easier programmatic control of a network.

The Data, Control, and Management Planes

Stop and think about what networking devices do. What does a router do? What does a switch do?

Many ideas should come to mind. For instance, routers and switches physically connect to each other with cables, and with wireless, to create networks. They forward messages: switches forward Ethernet frames, and routers forward packets. They use many different protocols to learn useful information such as routing protocols for learning network layer routes.

Everything that networking devices do can be categorized as being in a particular plane. This section takes those familiar facts about how networking devices work and describes the three planes most often used to describe how network programmability works: the data plane, the control plane, and the management plane.

The Data Plane

The term *data plane* refers to the tasks that a networking device does to forward a message. In other words, anything to do with receiving data, processing it, and forwarding that same data—whether you call the data a frame, a packet, or, more generically, a message—is part of the data plane.

For example, think about how routers forward IP packets, as shown in Figure 16-1. If you focus on the Layer 3 logic for a moment, the host sends the packet (step 1) to its default router, R1. R1 does some processing on the received packet, makes a forwarding (routing) decision, and forwards the packet (step 2). Routers R3 and R4 also receive, process, and forward the packet (steps 3 and 4).

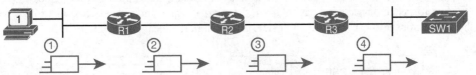

Figure 16-1   *Data Plane Processing on Routers: Basics*

Now broaden your thinking for a moment and try to think of everything a router or switch might do when receiving, processing, and forwarding a message. Of course, the forwarding decision is part of the logic; in fact, the data plane is often called the *forwarding plane*. But think beyond matching the destination address to a table. For perspective, the following list details some of the more common actions that a networking device does that fit into the data plane:

- De-encapsulating and re-encapsulating a packet in a data-link frame (routers, Layer 3 switches)

- Adding or removing an 802.1Q trunking header (routers and switches)

- Matching an Ethernet frame's destination Media Access Control (MAC) address to the MAC address table (Layer 2 switches)

- Matching an IP packet's destination IP address to the IP routing table (routers, Layer 3 switches)

- Encrypting the data and adding a new IP header (for virtual private network [VPN] processing)

- Changing the source or destination IP address (for Network Address Translation [NAT] processing)

- Discarding a message due to a filter (access control lists [ACLs], port security)

All the items in the list make up the data plane, because the data plane includes all actions done per message.

The Control Plane

Next, take a moment to ponder the kinds of information that the data plane needs to know beforehand so that it can work properly. For instance, routers need IP routes in a routing table before the data plane can forward packets. Layer 2 switches need entries in a MAC address table before they can forward Ethernet frames out the one best port to reach the destination. Switches must use Spanning Tree Protocol (STP) to limit which interfaces can be used for forwarding so that the data plane works well and does not loop frames forever.

From one perspective, the information supplied to the data plane controls what the data plane does. For instance, a router needs a route that matches a packet's destination address for the router to know how to route (forward) the packet. When a router's data plane tries to match the routing table and finds no matching route, the router discards the packet. And what controls the contents of the routing table? Various control plane processes.

The term *control plane* refers to any action that controls the data plane. Most of these actions have to do with creating the tables used by the data plane, tables like the IP routing table, an IP Address Resolution Protocol (ARP) table, a switch MAC address table, and so on. By adding to, removing, and changing entries to the tables used by the data plane, the control plane processes control what the data plane does. You already know about many control plane protocols—for instance, all the IP routing protocols.

Traditional networks use both a distributed data plane and a distributed control plane. In other words, each device has a data plane and a control plane, and the network distributes those functions into each individual device, as shown in the example in Figure 16-2.

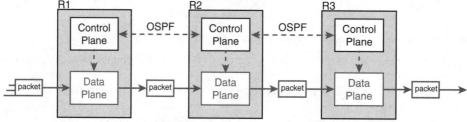

Figure 16-2 *Control and Data Planes of Routers—Conceptual*

In the figure, Open Shortest Path First (OSPF), the control plane protocol, runs on each router (that is, it is distributed among all the routers). OSPF on each router then adds to, removes from, and changes the IP routing table on each router. Once populated with useful routes, the data plane's IP routing table on each router can forward incoming packets, as shown from left to right across the bottom of the figure. The following list includes many of the more common control plane protocols:

- Routing protocols (OSPF, Enhanced Interior Gateway Routing Protocol [EIGRP], Routing Information Protocol [RIP], Border Gateway Protocol [BGP])
- IPv4 ARP
- IPv6 Neighbor Discovery Protocol (NDP)
- Switch MAC learning
- STP

Answers to the "Do I Know This Already?" quiz:

1 A **2** C **3** C **4** A **5** C, D **6** A, D

Without the protocols and activities of the control plane, the data plane of traditional networking devices would not function well. Routers would be mostly useless without routes learned by a routing protocol. Without learning MAC table entries, a switch could still forward unicasts by flooding them, but doing that for all frames would create much more load on the local-area network (LAN) compared to normal switch operations. So the data plane must rely on the control plane to provide useful information.

The Management Plane

The control plane performs overhead tasks that directly impact the behavior of the data plane. The *management plane* performs overhead work as well, but that work does not directly impact the data plane. Instead, the management plane includes protocols that allow network engineers to manage the devices.

Telnet and Secure Shell (SSH) are two of the most obvious management plane protocols. To emphasize the difference with control plane protocols, think about two routers: one configured to allow Telnet and SSH into the router and one that does not. Both could still be running a routing protocol and routing packets, whether or not they support Telnet and SSH.

Figure 16-3 extends the example shown in Figure 16-2 by now showing the management plane, with several management plane protocols.

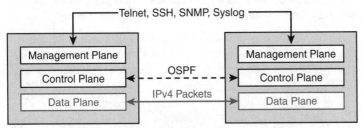

Figure 16-3   *Management Plane for Configuration of Control and Data Plane*

Cisco Switch Data Plane Internals

To better understand SDN and network programmability, it helps to think about the internals of switches. This next topic does just that.

From the very first days of devices called LAN switches, switches had to use specialized hardware to forward frames, because of the large number of frames per second (fps) required. To get a sense for the volume of frames a switch must be able to forward, consider the minimum frame size of an Ethernet frame, the number of ports on a switch, and the speeds of the ports; even low-end switches need to be able to forward millions of frames per second. For example, if a switch manufacturer wanted to figure out how fast its data plane needed to be in a new access layer switch with 24 ports, it might work through this bit of math:

- The switch has 24 ports.

- Each port runs at 1 Gbps.

- For this analysis, assume frames 125 bytes in length (to make the math easier, because each frame is 1000 bits long).

- With a 1000-bit-long frame and a speed of 1,000,000,000 bits/second, a port can send 1,000,000 frames per second (fps).

- Use full duplex on all ports, so the switch can expect to receive on all 24 ports at the same time.

- Result: Each port would be receiving 1,000,000 fps, for 24 million fps total, so the switch data plane would need to be ready to process 24 million fps.

Although 24 million fps may seem like a lot, the goal here is not to put an absolute number on how fast the data plane of a switch needs to be for any given era of switching technology. Instead, from their first introduction into the marketplace in the mid-1990s, LAN switches needed a faster data plane than a generalized CPU could process in software. As a result, hardware switches have always had specialized hardware to perform data plane processing.

First, the switching logic occurs not in the CPU with software, but in an *application-specific integrated circuit* (ASIC). An ASIC is a chip built for specific purposes, such as for message processing in a networking device.

Second, the ASIC needs to perform table lookup in the MAC address table, so for fast table lookup, the switch uses a specialized type of memory to store the equivalent of the MAC address table: *ternary content-addressable memory* (TCAM). TCAM memory does not require the ASIC to execute loops through an algorithm to search the table. Instead, the ASIC can feed the fields to be matched, like a MAC address value, into the TCAM, and the TCAM returns the matching table entry, without a need to run a search algorithm.

Note that a switch still has a general-purpose CPU and RAM as well, as shown in Figure 16-4. IOS runs in the CPU and uses RAM. Most of the control and management plane functions run in IOS. The data plane function (and the control plane function of MAC learning) happens in the ASIC.

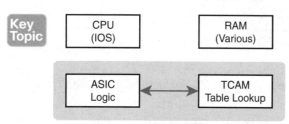

Figure 16-4 *Key Internal Processing Points in a Typical Switch*

Note that some routers also use hardware for data plane functions, for the same kinds of reasons that switches use hardware. (For instance, check out the Cisco Quantum Flow Processor for interesting reading about hardware data plane forwarding in Cisco routers.) The ideas of a hardware data plane in routers are similar to those in switches: use a purpose-built ASIC for the forwarding logic, and TCAM to store the required tables for fast table lookup.

Controllers and Software-Defined Architecture

New approaches to networking emerged in the 2010s, approaches that change where some of the control plane functions occur. Many of those approaches move parts of the control plane work into software that runs as a centralized application called a *controller*. This next topic looks at controller concepts, and the interfaces to the devices that sit below the controller and to any programs that use the controller.

NOTE The term *Software Defined Networking* (SDN) became common in the 2010s to refer to the types of controller-based networks described in the next few pages. More often today you might see terms like *software-defined architecture* or *controller-based networking*.

Controllers and Centralized Control

Most traditional control plane processes use a distributed architecture. For example, each router runs its own OSPF routing protocol process. To do their work, those distributed control plane processes use messages to communicate with each other, like OSPF protocol messages between routers. As a result, traditional networks are said to use a *distributed control plane*.

The people who created today's control plane concepts, like STP, OSPF, EIGRP, and so on, could have chosen to use a centralized control plane. That is, they could have put the logic in one place, running on one device, or on a server. Then the centralized software could have used protocol messages to learn information from the devices, but with all the processing of the information at a centralized location. But they instead chose a distributed architecture.

There are pros and cons to using distributed and centralized architectures to do any function in a network. Many control plane functions have a long history of working well with a distributed architecture. However, a centralized application can be easier to write than a distributed application, because the centralized application has all the data gathered into one place. And this emerging world of software-defined architectures often uses a centralized architecture, with a centralized control plane, with its foundations in a service called a controller.

A *controller*, or *SDN controller*, centralizes the control of the networking devices. The degree of control, and the type of control, varies widely. For instance, the controller can perform all control plane functions, replacing the devices' distributed control plane. Alternately, the controller can simply be aware of the ongoing work of the distributed data, control, and management planes on the devices, without changing how those operate. And the list goes on, with many variations.

To better understand the idea of a controller, consider one specific case as shown in Figure 16-5, in which one SDN controller centralizes all important control plane functions. First, the controller sits anywhere in the network that has IP reachability to the devices in the network. Each of the network devices still has a data plane; however, note that none of the devices has a control plane. In the variation of SDN as shown in Figure 16-5, the controller directly programs the data plane entries into each device's tables. The networking devices do not populate their forwarding tables with traditional distributed control plane processes.

NOTE Figure 16-5 shows the model used by one of the original SDN implementations that uses an industry standard called OpenFlow.

Figure 16-5 shows one model for network programmability and SDN, but not all. The figure does give us a great backdrop to discuss a few more important basic concepts; in particular, the idea of a southbound interface (SBI) and northbound interface (NBI).

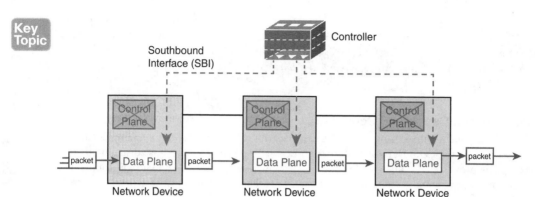

Figure 16-5 *Centralized Control Plane and a Distributed Data Plane*

The Southbound Interface

In a controller-based network architecture, the controller needs to communicate to the networking devices. In most network drawings and architecture drawings, those network devices typically sit below the controller, as shown in Figure 16-5. There is an interface between the controller and those devices, and given its location at the bottom part of drawings, the interface came to be known as the *southbound interface*, or SBI, as labeled in Figure 16-5.

NOTE In the context of this chapter's discussion of SDN, the word *interface* (including in the names of SBI, NBI, and API) refers to software interfaces unless otherwise noted.

Several different options exist for the SBI. The overall goal is network programmability, so the interface moves away from being only a protocol. An SBI often includes a protocol, so that the controller and devices can communicate, but it often includes an *application programming interface* (API). An API is a method for one application (program) to exchange data with another application. Rearranging the words to describe the idea, an API is an interface to an application program. Programs process data, so an API lets two programs exchange data. While a protocol exists as a document, often from a standards body, an API often exists as usable code—functions, variables, and data structures—that can be used by one program to communicate and copy structured data between the programs across a network.

So, back to the term *SBI*: it is an interface between a program (the controller) and a program (on the networking device) that lets the two programs communicate, with one goal being to allow the controller to program the data plane forwarding tables of the networking device.

Unsurprisingly, in a network architecture meant to enable network programmability, the capabilities of the SBIs and their APIs tell us a lot about what that particular architecture can and cannot do. For instance, some controllers might support one or a few SBIs, for a specific purpose, while others might support many more SBIs, allowing a choice of SBIs to use. The comparisons of SBIs go far beyond this chapter, but it does help to think about a few; the second major section gives three sample architectures that happen to show three separate SBIs, specifically:

- OpenFlow (from the ONF; www.opennetworking.org)
- OpFlex (from Cisco; used with ACI)

- CLI (Telnet/SSH) and SNMP (used with Cisco APIC-EM)
- CLI (Telnet/SSH) and SNMP, and NETCONF (used with Cisco Software-Defined Access)

The Northbound Interface

Think about the programming required at the controller related to the example in Figure 16-5. The figure focuses on the fact that the controller can add entries to the networking device's forwarding tables; however, how does the controller know what to add? How does it choose? What kind of information would your program need to gather before it could attempt to add something like MAC table entries or IP routes to a network? You might think of these:

- A list of all the devices in the network
- The capabilities of each devices
- The interfaces/ports on each device
- The current state of each port
- The topology—which devices connect to which, over which interfaces
- Device configuration—IP addresses, VLANs, and so on as configured on the devices

A controller does much of the work needed for the control plane in a centralized control model. It gathers all sorts of useful information about the network, like the items in the previous list. The controller itself can create a centralized repository of all this useful information about the network.

A controller's northbound interface (NBI) opens the controller so its data and functions can be used by other programs, enabling network programmability, with much quicker development. Programs can pull information from the controller, using the controller's APIs. The NBIs also enable programs to use the controller's capabilities to program flows into the devices using the controller's SBIs.

To see where the NBI resides, first think about the controller itself. The controller is software, running on some server, which can be a VM or a physical server. An application can run on the same server as the controller and use an NBI, which is an API, so that two programs can communicate.

Figure 16-6 shows just such an example. The big box in the figure represents the system where the controller software resides. This particular controller happens to be written in Java and has a Java-based native API. Anyone—the same vendor as the controller vendor, another company, or even you—can write an app that runs on this same operating system that uses the controller's Java API. By using that API to exchange data with the controller, the application can learn information about the network. The application can also program flows in the network—that is, ask the controller to add the specific match/action logic (flows) into the forwarding tables of the networking devices.

> **NOTE** The northbound interface (NBI) gets its name from its normal location as shown above the controller—that is, in what would be north on a map.

Inside the Controller

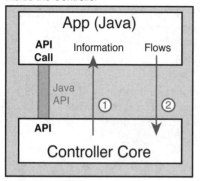

Figure 16-6 *Java API: Java Applications Communicates with Controller*

Before leaving the topic of NBIs, let me close with a brief explanation of a REST API as used for a controller. REST (*Representational State Transfer*) describes a type of API that allows applications to sit on different hosts, using HTTP messages to transfer data over the API. When you see SDN figures like Figure 16-6, with the application running on the same system as the controller, the API does not need to send messages over a network because both programs run on the same system. But when the application runs on a different system somewhere else in the network other than running on the controller, the API needs a way to send the data back and forth over an IP network, and RESTful APIs meet that need.

Figure 16-7 shows the big ideas with a REST API. The application runs on a host at the top of the figure. In this case, at step 1, it sends an HTTP GET request to a particular URI. The HTTP GET is like any other HTTP GET, even like those used to retrieve web pages. However, the URI is not for a web page, but rather identifies an object on the controller, typically a data structure that the application needs to learn and then process. For example, the URI might identify an object that is the list of physical interfaces on a specific device along with the status of each.

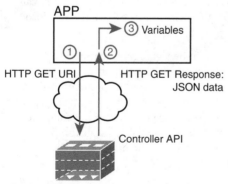

Figure 16-7 *Process Example of a GET Using a REST API*

At step 2, the controller sends back an HTTP GET response message with the object. Most REST APIs will ask for and receive structured data. That is, instead of receiving data that is a web page, like a web browser would receive, the response holds variable names and their values, in a format that can be easily used by a program. The common formats for data used for network programmability are JavaScript Object Notation (JSON) and eXtensible Markup Language (XML), shown as step 3.

Software Defined Architecture Summary

SDN and network programmability introduce a new way to build networks. The networking devices still exist and still forward data, but the control plane functions and locations can change dramatically. The centralized controller acts as the focal point, so that at least some of the control plane functions move from a distributed model to a centralized model.

However, the world of network programmability and SDN includes a wide array of options and solutions. Some options pull most control plane functions into the controller, whereas others pull only some of those functions into the controller. The next section takes a look at three different options, each of which takes a different approach to network programmability and the degree of centralized control.

Examples of Network Programmability and SDN

This second of three major sections of the chapter introduces three different SDN and network programmability solutions available from Cisco. Others exist as well. These three were chosen because they give a wide range of comparison points:

- OpenDaylight Controller
- Cisco Application Centric Infrastructure (ACI)
- Cisco APIC Enterprise Module (APIC-EM)

OpenDaylight and OpenFlow

One common form of SDN comes from the Open Networking Foundation (ONF) and is billed as Open SDN. The ONF (www.opennetworking.org) acts as a consortium of users (operators) and vendors to help establish SDN in the marketplace. Part of that work defines protocols, SBIs, NBIs, and anything that helps people implement their vision of SDN.

The ONF model of SDN features OpenFlow. OpenFlow defines the concept of a controller along with an IP-based SBI between the controller and the network devices. Just as important, OpenFlow defines a standard idea of what a switch's capabilities are, based on the ASICs and TCAMs commonly used in switches today. (That standardized idea of what a switch does is called a *switch abstraction*.) An OpenFlow switch can act as a Layer 2 switch, a Layer 3 switch, or in different ways and with great flexibility beyond the traditional model of a Layer 2/3 switch.

The Open SDN model centralizes most control plane functions, with control of the network done by the controller plus any applications that use the controller's NBIs. In fact, earlier Figure 16-5, which showed the network devices without a control plane, represents this mostly centralized OpenFlow model of SDN.

In the OpenFlow model, applications may use any APIs (NBIs) supported on the controller platform to dictate what kinds of forwarding table entries are placed into the devices; however, it calls for OpenFlow as the SBI protocol. Additionally, the networking devices need to be switches that support OpenFlow.

Because the ONF's Open SDN model has this common thread of a controller with an OpenFlow SBI, the controller plays a big role in the network. The next few pages provide a brief background about two such controllers.

16

The OpenDaylight Controller

First, if you were to look back at the history of OpenFlow, you could find information on dozens of different SDN controllers that support the OpenFlow SDN model. Some were more research oriented, during the years in which SDN was being developed and was more of an experimental idea. As time passed, more and more vendors began building their own controllers. And those controllers often had many similar features, because they were trying to accomplish many of the same goals. As you might expect, some consolidation eventually needed to happen.

The OpenDaylight open-source SDN controller is one of the more successful SDN controller platforms to emerge from the consolidation process over the 2010s. OpenDaylight took many of the same open-source principles used with Linux, with the idea that if enough vendors worked together on a common open-source controller, then all would benefit. All those vendors could then use the open-source controller as the basis for their own products, with each vendor focusing on the product differentiation part of the effort, rather than the fundamental features. The result was that back in the mid-2010s, the *OpenDaylight SDN controller* (www.opendaylight.org) was born. OpenDaylight (ODL) began as a separate project but now exists as a project managed by the Linux Foundation.

Figure 16-8 shows a generalized version of the ODL architecture. In particular, note the variety of SBIs listed in the lower part of the controller box: OpenFlow, NetConf, PCEP, BGP-LS, and OVSDB; many more exist. The ODL project has enough participants so that it includes a large variety of options, including multiple SBIs, not just OpenFlow.

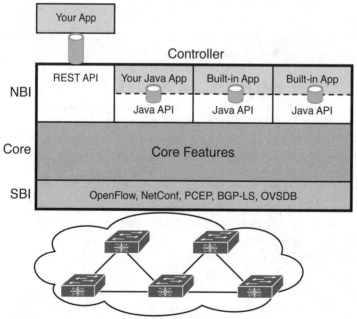

Figure 16-8 *Architecture of NBI, Controller Internals, and SBI to Network Devices*

ODL has many features, with many SBIs, and many core features. A vendor can then take ODL, use the parts that make sense for that vendor, add to it, and create a commercial ODL controller.

The Cisco Open SDN Controller (OSC)

At one point back in the 2010s, Cisco offered a commercial version of the OpenDaylight controller called the Cisco *Open SDN Controller* (OSC). That controller followed the intended model for the ODL project: Cisco and others contributed labor and money to the ODL open-source project; once a new release was completed, Cisco took that release and built new versions of their product.

Cisco no longer produces and sells the Cisco OSC, but I decided to keep a short section about OSC here in this chapter for a couple of reasons. First, if you do any of your own research, you will find mention of Cisco OSC; however, well before this chapter was written in 2019, Cisco had made a strong strategic move toward different approaches to SDN using intent-based networking (IBN). That move took Cisco away from OpenFlow-based SDN. But because you might see references to Cisco OSC online, or in the previous edition of this book, I wanted to point out this transition in Cisco's direction.

This book describes two Cisco offerings that use an IBN approach to SDN. The next topic in this chapter examines one of those: Application Centric Infrastructure (ACI), Cisco's data center SDN product. Chapter 17, "Cisco Software-Defined Access," discusses yet another Cisco SDN option that uses intent-based networking: Software-Defined Access (SDA).

Cisco Application Centric Infrastructure (ACI)

Interestingly, many SDN offerings began with research that discarded many of the old networking paradigms in an attempt to create something new and better. For instance, OpenFlow came to be from the Stanford University Clean Slate research project that had researchers reimagining (among other things) device architectures. Cisco took a similar research path, but Cisco's work happened to arise from different groups, each focused on different parts of the network: data center, campus, and WAN. That research resulted in Cisco's current SDN offerings of ACI in the data center, Software-Defined Access (SDA) in the enterprise campus, and Software-Defined WAN (SD-WAN) in the enterprise WAN.

When reimagining networking for the data center, the designers of SCI focused on the applications that run in a data center and what they need. As a result, they built networking concepts around application architectures. Cisco made the network infrastructure become application centric, hence the name of the Cisco data center SDN solution: *Application Centric Infrastructure*, or ACI.

For example, Cisco looked at the data center world beyond networking and saw lots of automation and control. As discussed in Chapter 15, "Cloud Architecture," virtualization software routinely starts, moves, and stops VMs. Additionally, cloud software enables self-service for customers so they can enable and disable highly elastic services as implemented with VMs and containers in a data center. From a networking perspective, some of those VMs need to communicate, but some do not. And those VMs can move based on the needs of the virtualization and cloud systems.

ACI set about to create data center networking with the flexibility and automation built into the operational model. Old data center networking models with a lot of per-physical-interface configuration on switches and routers were just poor models for the rapid pace of change and automated nature of modern data centers. This section looks at some of the detail of ACI to give you a sense of how ACI creates a powerful and flexible network to

16

support a modern data center in which VMs and containers are created, run, move, and are stopped dynamically as a matter of routine.

ACI Physical Design: Spine and Leaf

The Cisco ACI uses a specific physical switch topology called spine and leaf. While the other parts of a network might need to allow for many different physical topologies, the data center could be made standard and consistent. But what particular standard and consistent topology? Cisco decided on the spine and leaf design, also called a Clos network after one of its creators.

With ACI, the physical network has a number of spine switches and a number of leaf switches, as shown in Figure 16-9. The figure shows the links between switches, which can be single links or multiple parallel links. Of note in this design (assuming a single-site design):

- Each leaf switch must connect to every spine switch.
- Each spine switch must connect to every leaf switch.
- Leaf switches cannot connect to each other.
- Spine switches cannot connect to each other.
- Endpoints connect only to the leaf switches.

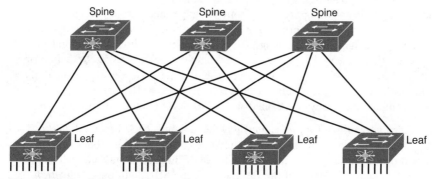

Figure 16-9 *Spine-Leaf Network Design*

Endpoints connect only to leaf switches and never to spine switches. To emphasize the point, Figure 16-10 shows a more detailed version of Figure 16-9, this time with endpoints connected to the leaf switches. None of the endpoints connect to the spine switches; they connect only to the leaf switches. The endpoints can be connections to devices outside the data center, like the router on the left. By volume, most of the endpoints will be either physical servers running a native OS or servers running virtualization software with numbers of VMs and containers as shown in the center of the figure.

Also, note that the figure shows a typical design with multiple leaf switches connecting to a single hardware endpoint like a Cisco Unified Computing System (UCS) server. Depending on the design requirements, each UCS might connect to at least two leaf switches, both for redundancy and for greater capacity to support the VMs and containers running on the UCS hardware. (In fact, in a small design with UCS or similar server hardware, every UCS might connect to every leaf switch.)

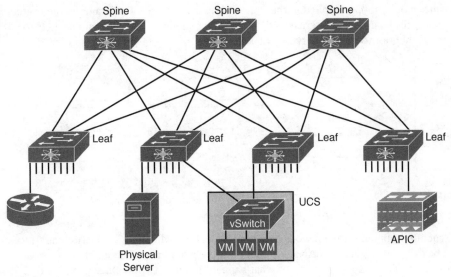

Figure 16-10 *Endpoints Found on the Leaf Switches Only*

ACI Operating Model with Intent-Based Networking

The model that Cisco defines for ACI uses a concept of endpoints and policies. The *endpoints* are the VMs, containers, or even traditional servers with the OS running directly on the hardware. ACI then uses several constructs as implemented via the Application Policy Infrastructure Controller (APIC), the software that serves as the centralized controller for ACI.

This section hopes to give you some insight into ACI, rather than touch on every feature. To do that, consider the application architecture of a typical enterprise web app for a moment. Most casual observers think of a web application as one entity, but one web app often exists as three separate servers:

■ **Web server:** Users from outside the data center connect to a web server, which sends web page content to the user.

■ **App (Application) server:** Because most web pages contain dynamic content, the app server does the processing to build the next web page for that particular user based on the user's profile and latest actions and input.

■ **DB (Database) server:** Many of the app server's actions require data; the DB server retrieves and stores the data as requested by the app server.

To accommodate those ideas, ACI uses an intent-based networking (IBN) model. With that model, the engineer, or some automation program, defines the policies and intent for which endpoints should be allowed to communicate and which should not. Then the controller determines what that means for this network at this moment in time, depending on where the endpoints are right now.

For instance, when starting the VMs for this app, the virtualization software would create (via the APIC) several endpoint groups (EPGs) as shown in Figure 16-11. The controller must also be told the access policies, which define which EPGs should be able to communicate (and which should not), as implied in the figure with arrowed lines. For example, the routers that connect to the network external to the data center should be able to send packets to all web servers, but not to the app servers or DB servers.

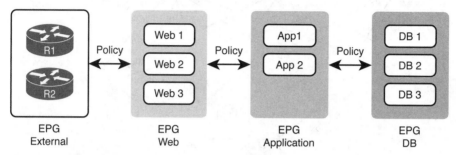

Figure 16-11 *Endpoint Groups (EPGs) and Policies*

Note that at no point did the previous paragraph talk about which physical switch interfaces should be assigned to which VLAN, or which ports are in an EtherChannel; the discussion moves to an application-centric view of what happens in the network. Once all the endpoints, policies, and related details are defined, the controller can then direct the network as to what needs to be in the forwarding tables to make it all happen—and to more easily react when the VMs start, stop, or move.

To make it all work, ACI uses a centralized controller called the *Application Policy Infrastructure Controller* (APIC), as shown in Figure 16-12. The name defines the function in this case: it is the controller that creates application policies for the data center infrastructure. The APIC takes the intent (EPGs, policies, and so on), which completely changes the operational model away from configuring VLANs, trunks, EtherChannels, ACLs, and so on.

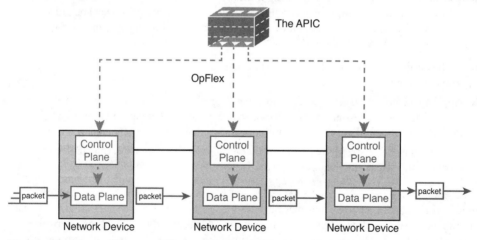

Figure 16-12 *Architectural View of ACI with APIC Pushing Intent to Switch Control Plane*

The APIC, of course, has a convenient GUI, but the power comes in software control—that is, network programmability. The same virtualization software, or cloud or automation software, even scripts written by the network engineer, can define the endpoint groups, policies, and so on to the APIC. But all these players access the ACI system by interfacing to the APIC as depicted in Figure 16-13; the network engineer no longer needs to connect to each individual switch and configure CLI commands.

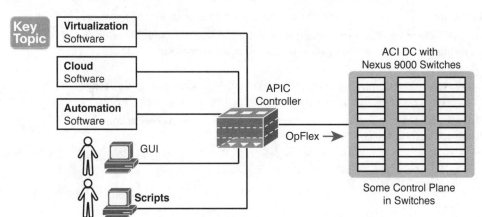

Figure 16-13 *Controlling the ACI Data Center Network Using the APIC*

For more information on Cisco ACI, go to www.cisco.com/go/aci.

Cisco APIC Enterprise Module

The next example of a Cisco SDN solution in this section, called *APIC Enterprise Module* (APIC-EM), solves a different problem. When Cisco began to reimagine networking in the enterprise, they saw a huge barrier: the installed base of their own products in most of their customer's networks. Any enterprise SDN solution that used new SBIs—SBIs that only some of the existing devices and software levels supported—would create a huge barrier to adoption.

APIC-EM Basics

Cisco came up with a couple of approaches, with one of those being APIC-EM, which Cisco released to the public around 2015.

APIC-EM assumes the use of the same traditional switches and routers with their familiar distributed data and control planes. Cisco rejected the idea that its initial enterprise-wide SDN (network programmability) solution could begin by requiring customers to replace all hardware. Instead, Cisco looked for ways to add the benefits of network programmability with a centralized controller while keeping the same traditional switches and routers in place. That approach could certainly change over time (and it has), but Cisco APIC-EM does just that: offer enterprise SDN using the same switches and routers already installed in networks.

> **NOTE** Even though APIC-EM uses the same APIC acronym used for the controller with the Cisco ACI offering, the details of how it works differ significantly.

What advantages can a controller-based architecture bring if the devices in the network have no new features? In short, adding a centralized controller does nothing in comparison with old network management offerings. Adding a centralized controller with powerful northbound APIs opens many possibilities for customers/operators, while also creating a world in which Cisco and its partners can bring new and interesting management applications to market. It includes these applications, as depicted in Figure 16-14:

- **Topology map:** The application discovers and displays the topology of the network.
- **Path Trace:** The user supplies a source and destination device, and the application shows the path through the network, along with details about the forwarding decision at each step.
- **Plug and Play:** This application provides Day 0 installation support so that you can unbox a new device and make it IP reachable through automation in the controller.
- **Easy QoS:** With a few simple decisions at the controller, you can configure complex QoS features at each device.

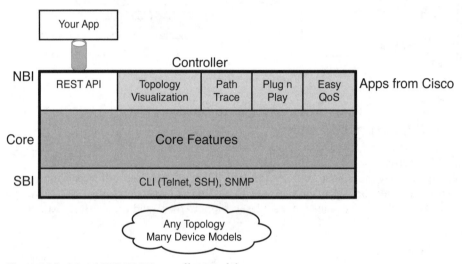

Figure 16-14 *APIC-EM Controller Model*

APIC-EM does not directly program the data or control planes, but it does interact with the management plane via Telnet, SSH, and/or SNMP; consequently, it can indirectly impact the data and control planes. The APIC-EM controller does not program flows into tables or ask the control plane in the devices to change how it operates. But it can interrogate and learn the configuration state and operational state of each device, and it can reconfigure each device, therefore changing how the distributed control and data plane operates.

APIC-EM Replacement

Cisco announced the current CCNA exam (200-301) in 2019, and around the same time Cisco announced the end of marketing for the APIC-EM product. That timing left us with a decision to make about whether to include APIC-EM in this book, and if so, to what extent. I decided to keep this small section about APIC-EM for several reasons, one reason being to give you these few closing comments about the product.

First, during the early 2020s—the years that CCNA 200-301 will likely still be the current exam—you will still see many references to APIC-EM. Cisco DevNet will likely still have many useful labs that reference and use APIC-EM, at least for a few years. Furthermore,

APIC-EM gives us a great tool to see how a controller can be used, even if the networking devices do not change their normal operation. So I think it's worth the few pages to introduces APIC-EM as done in this section.

Second, many of the functions of APIC-EM have become core features of the Cisco DNA Center (DNAC) product, which is discussed in some detail in Chapter 17. The list of applications just above this chapter's Figure 16-14 also exist as part of DNAC, for instance. So, do not look for APIC-EM version 2, but rather look for opportunities to use DNAC.

Summary of the SDN Examples

The three sample SDN architectures in this section of the book were chosen to provide a wide variety for the sake of learning. However, they differ to some degree in how much of the control plane work is centralized. Table 16-2 lists those and other comparison points taken from this section, for easy review and study.

Table 16-2   Points of Comparison: OpenFlow, ACI, and APIC Enterprise

Criteria	OpenFlow	ACI	APIC Enterprise
Changes how the device control plane works versus traditional networking	Yes	Yes	No
Creates a centralized point from which humans and automation control the network	Yes	Yes	Yes
Degree to which the architecture centralizes the control plane	Mostly	Partially	None
SBIs used	OpenFlow	OpFlex	CLI, SNMP
Controllers mentioned in this chapter	OpenDaylight	APIC	APIC-EM
Organization that is the primary definer/owner	ONF	Cisco	Cisco

If you want to learn more about the Cisco solutions, consider using both Cisco DevNet (the Cisco Developer Network) and dCloud (Demo cloud). Cisco provides its DevNet site (https://developer.cisco.com) for anyone interested in network programming, and the Demo Cloud site (https://dcloud.cisco.com) for anyone to experience or demo Cisco products. At the time this book went to press, DevNet had many APIC-EM labs, while both sites had a variety of ACI-based labs.

Comparing Traditional Versus Controller-Based Networks

Before finishing the chapter, this final topic turns directly toward the CCNA 200-301 exam. Three of the CCNA 200-301 exam topics in domain 6.0, "Automation and Programmability," ask us to compare some aspect of traditional networks versus new networking using controllers and automation. Those exam topics include

6.1: Explain how automation impacts network management

6.2: Compare traditional networks with controller-based networking

6.4: Compare traditional campus device management with Cisco DNA Center enabled device management

First, the wording in all three exam topics can be reduced to "compare and contrast." Two use the word *compare*. The other uses a longer phrase "explain how automation impacts...," which asks us to compare what was before to what happens now that automation has been added to the network.

Two exam topics (6.1 and 6.4) center on network management, so what might Cisco mean by "network management" in these exam topics? You could break that down into two aspects of network management: configuration management and operational management.

Configuration management refers to any feature that changes device configuration, with automated configuration management doing so with software (program) control. For instance, Cisco's ACI uses the APIC controller. You do not configure the devices directly, but the APIC pushes configuration down to the ACI switches that it builds based on its interpretation of the policies configured by the engineer. With ACI, the configuration management occurs as a part of the overall system. Other configuration management tools can be more focused on automating traditional configuration processes, with tools like NETCONF/RESTCONF, Ansible, Puppet, and Chef, as discussed in Chapter 18, "Understanding REST and JSON," and Chapter 19, "Understanding Ansible, Puppet, and Chef."

Operational network management includes monitoring, gathering operational data, reporting, and alerting humans to possible issues. For instance, the APIC-EM and DNA Center both have an app that checks the IOS images on Cisco devices to make sure only approved versions are used and that no changes have occurred to the images in comparison to the images created by Cisco.

The other exam topic (6.2) described in this section focuses on controller-based networking instead of network management. That exam topic includes any SDN network as characterized by the use of a controller. Today people might use that term or these other synonyms to describe some of the newer networking options that happen to use controllers:

- Software Defined Networking
- Software Defined Architecture
- Programmable Networks
- Controller-Based Networks

Table 16-3 summarizes the chapters that have content related to these three exam topics.

Table 16-3 Exam Topics and Most Relevant Chapters

Exam Topic	Exam Topic Text	Most Relevant Chapter(s)
6.1	Explain how automation impacts network management	16–19
6.2	Compare traditional networks with controller-based networking	16, 17
6.4	Compare traditional campus device management with Cisco DNA Center–enabled device management	17

How Automation Impacts Network Management

This chapter introduces many of the features that enable automation in SDNs, but so far it has not made any overt statements about how automation impacts network management. This next topic works through a couple of examples that show the power of automation as enabled through controller-based networks.

First, centralized controllers formalize and define data models for the configuration and operational data about networks. We humans might be comfortable with visually scanning the output of **show** commands to find the tidbit of information we need. Programs need to be able to identify the specific fact. To build a controller-based network with APIs, all the data about the network needs to be defined in a data model so programs can use that data via API calls. Before using controllers, automation scripts often had to begin by processing the text output of a **show** command, but with controllers and the data models behind the APIs, the data can be readily available to any automation script or vendor application through a northbound API.

For instance, Example 16-1 shows some output from a command on a switch. With a northbound API on a controller, and the data model it supplies, an automation program could issue this command and begin by parsing this text. The goal: find the configuration setting on the **switchport mode** command and the current trunking state.

Example 16-1 *Small Output from a Switch Command*

```
SW1# show interfaces gigabit 0/1 switchport
Name: Gi0/1
Switchport: Enabled
Administrative Mode: dynamic auto
Operational Mode: static access
Administrative Trunking Encapsulation: dot1q
Operational Trunking Encapsulation: native
Negotiation of Trunking: On
```

Example 16-2 shows a simple example of the starting point for a program using a controller's northbound API. Instead of asking for the text from a **show** command, the API call will result in the program having a series of variables set. In this case, there are variables for that same interface that list the trunk configuration setting and the trunk operational state.

Example 16-2 *Python Dictionary with Variables Set to Needed Values*

```
>>> interface1
{'trunk-config': 'dynamic auto', 'trunk-status': 'static access'}
>>>
```

Using a controller-based model not only supplies APIs that give us the exact same data a human could see in **show** commands, but often they also supply much more useful information. A controller collects data from the entire network, so the controller can be written so that it analyzes and presents more useful data via the API. As a result, software that uses the APIs—whether automation written by local engineers or applications written by vendors—can be written more quickly and can often create features that would have been much more difficult without a controller.

For instance, both APIC-EM and its successor DNA Center provide a path trace feature. The applications show the path of a packet from source to destination, with the forwarding logic used at each node.

Now imagine writing that application with either of these two approaches.

■ One API call that returns a list of all devices and their running configuration, with other API calls to collect each device's MAC address tables and/or their IP routing tables. Then you have to process that data to find the end-to-end path.

■ One API call to which you pass the source and destination IP addresses and TCP/UDP ports, and the API returns variables that describe the end-to-end path, including device hostnames and interfaces. The variables spell out the path the packet takes through the network.

The second option does most of the work, while the first option leaves most of the work to you and your program. But that second option becomes possible because of the centralized controller. The controller has the data if it at least collects configuration and forwarding table information. Going beyond that, these Cisco controllers analyze the data to provide much more useful data. The power of these kinds of APIs is amazing, and this is just one example.

The following list summarizes a few of the comparison points for this particular exam topic:

■ Northbound APIs and their underlying data models make it much easier to automate functions versus traditional networks.

■ The robust data created by controllers makes it possible to automate functions that were not easily automated without controllers.

■ The new reimagined software defined networks that use new operational models simplify operations, with automation resulting in more consistent configuration and less errors.

■ Centralized collection of operational data at controllers allows the application of modern data analytics to networking operational data, providing actionable insights that were likely not noticeable with the former model.

■ Time required to complete projects is reduced.

■ New operational models use external inputs, like considering time-of-day, day-of-week, and network load.

Comparing Traditional Networks with Controller-Based Networks

As for exam topic 6.2, this entire chapter begins to show the advantages created by using controller-based networks. However, this chapter only begins to describe the possibilities. By centralizing some of the functions in the network and providing robust APIs, controllers enable a large number of new operational models. Those models include the three most likely to be seen from Cisco in an enterprise: Software-Defined Access (SDA), Software-Defined WAN (SD-WAN), and Application Centric Infrastructure (ACI). (Chapter 17 introduces SDA.)

This changes the operating paradigm in many cases, with the controller determining many device-specific details:

■ The network engineer does not need to think about every command on every device.

■ The controller configures the devices with consistent and streamlined settings.

■ The result: faster and more consistent changes with fewer issues.

As another example, just consider the ACI example from earlier in the chapter. Instead of configuring each port with an access VLAN, or making it a trunk, adding routing protocol configuration, and possibly updating IP ACLs, all you had to do was create some end-point groups (EPGs) and policies. In that case, the orchestration software that started the VMs could automatically create the EPGs and policies. The new paradigm of intent-based networking was enabled through the controller-based architecture. Then the automation features enabled by the controller's northbound APIs allowed third-party applications to automatically configure the network to support the necessary changes.

Some of the advantages include the following:

- Uses new and improved operational models that allow the configuration of the network rather than per-device configuration

- Enables automation through northbound APIs that provide robust methods and model-driven data

- Configures the network devices through southbound APIs, resulting in more consistent device configuration, fewer errors, and less time spent troubleshooting the network

- Enables a DevOps approach to networks

Chapter 17 goes into some depth comparing traditional networking with controller-based networks with descriptions of Cisco Software-Defined Access (SDA). Look throughout that chapter for some of the reasons and motivations for SDA and the features enabled by using the DNA Center controller.

Chapter Review

One key to doing well on the exams is to perform repetitive spaced review sessions. Review this chapter's material using either the tools in the book or interactive tools for the same material found on the book's companion website. Refer to the "Your Study Plan" element for more details. Table 16-4 outlines the key review elements and where you can find them. To better track your study progress, record when you completed these activities in the second column.

Table 16-4   Chapter Review Tracking

Review Element	Review Date(s)	Resource Used
Review key topics		Book, website
Review key terms		Book, website
Answer DIKTA questions		Book, PTP
Review memory tables		Book, website
Watch video		Website

Review All the Key Topics

Table 16-5 Key Topics for Chapter 16

Key Topic Element	Description	Page Number
List	Sample actions of the networking device data plane	359
List	Sample actions of the networking device control plane	360
Figure 16-4	Switch internals with ASIC and TCAM	362
Figure 16-5	Basic SDN architecture, with the centralized controller programming device data planes directly	364
Paragraph	Description of the role and purpose of the NBI	365
Figure 16-7	REST API basic concepts	366
List	Spine-leaf topology requirements	370
Figure 16-10	Spine-leaf design	371
Figure 16-13	Controlling the ACI data center network using APIC	373
Table 16-2	Comparisons of Open SDN, Cisco ACI, and Cisco APIC Enterprise options	375
List	Comparisons of how automation improves network management	378
List	Comparisons of how controller-based networking works versus traditional networking	379

Key Terms You Should Know

application programming interface (API), Application Policy Infrastructure Controller (APIC), APIC Enterprise Module (APIC-EM), Application Centric Infrastructure (ACI), northbound API, southbound API, control plane, data plane, management plane, application-specific integrated circuit (ASIC), ternary content-addressable memory (TCAM), OpenFlow, Software Defined Networking (SDN), distributed control plane, centralized control plane, northbound interface (NBI), southbound interface (SBI), controller-based networking, intent-based networking (IBN), spine, leaf

Cisco Software-Defined Access (SDA)

This chapter covers the following exam topics:

1.0 Network Fundamentals

1.1 Explain the role and function of network components

1.1.e Controllers (Cisco DNA Center and WLC)

6.0 Automation and Programmability

6.1 Explain how automation impacts network management

6.2 Compare traditional networks with controller-based networking

6.3 Describe controller-based and software defined architectures (overlay, underlay, and fabric)

6.3.a Separation of control plane and data plane

6.3.b Northbound and southbound APIs

6.4 Compare traditional campus device management with Cisco DNA Center enabled device management

Cisco Software-Defined Access (SDA) uses a software defined networking approach to build a converged wired and wireless campus LAN. The word *access* in the name refers to the endpoint devices that access the network, while *software-defined* refers to many of the usual software-defined architectural features discussed in Chapter 16, "Introduction to Controller-Based Networking." Those features include a centralized controller—DNA Center—with southbound and northbound protocols. It also includes a completely different operational model inside SDA, with a network fabric composed of an underlay network and an overlay network.

SDA fills the position as Cisco's campus offering within Cisco Digital Network Architecture (DNA). Cisco DNA defines the entire architecture for the new world of software defined networks, digitization, and Cisco's reimagining of how networks should be operated in the future. This chapter introduces SDA, which exists as one implementation of Cisco DNA.

The discussion of SDA and DNA provides a great backdrop to discuss a few other topics from the CCNA blueprint: the DNA Center controller and network management. SDA uses the DNA Center controller to configure and operate SDA. However, DNA Center also acts as a complete network management platform. To understand DNA Center, you also need to understand traditional network management as well as the new management models using controllers.

"Do I Know This Already?" Quiz

Take the quiz (either here or use the PTP software) if you want to use the score to help you decide how much time to spend on this chapter. The letter answers are listed at the bottom of the page following the quiz. Appendix C, found both at the end of the book as well as on the companion website, includes both the answers and explanations. You can also find both answers and explanations in the PTP testing software.

Table 17-1 "Do I Know This Already?" Foundation Topics Section-to-Question Mapping

Foundation Topics Section	Questions
SDA Fabric, Underlay, and Overlay	1–3
DNA Center and SDA Operation	4, 5
DNA Center as a Network Management Platform	6

1. In Cisco Software-Defined Access (SDA), which term refers to the devices and cabling, along with configuration that allows the network device nodes enough IP connectivity to send IP packets to each other?

   a. Fabric

   b. Overlay

   c. Underlay

   d. VXLAN

2. In Cisco Software-Defined Access (SDA), which term refers to the functions that deliver endpoint packets across the network using tunnels between the ingress and egress fabric nodes?

   a. Fabric

   b. Overlay

   c. Underlay

   d. VXLAN

3. In Software-Defined Access (SDA), which of the answers are part of the overlay data plane?

   a. LISP

   b. GRE

   c. OSPF

   d. VXLAN

4. Which answers best describe options of how to implement security with scalable groups using DNA Center and SDA? (Choose two answers.)

   a. A human user from the DNA Center GUI

   b. An automation application using NETCONF

   c. A human user using the CLI of an SDA fabric edge node

   d. An automation application using REST

5. Which of the following protocols or tools could be used as part of the Cisco DNA Center southbound interface? (Choose three answers.)

   a. Ansible

   b. SSH

   c. NETCONF

   d. SNMP

   e. Puppet

6. Which of the following are network management features performed by both traditional network management software as well as by DNA Center? (Choose two answers.)

   a. Network device discovery

   b. Software-Defined Access configuration

   c. End-to-end path discovery with ACL analysis

   d. Device installation (day 0), configuration (day 1), and monitoring (day n) operations

Foundation Topics

SDA Fabric, Underlay, and Overlay

Cisco Software-Defined Access (SDA) creates an entirely new way to build campus LANs as compared with the traditional methods of networking discussed in most chapters of this book. In the mid 2010s, Cisco set about to reimagine campus networking, with SDA as the result.

SDA uses the software-defined architectural model introduced in Chapter 16, with a controller and various APIs. It still uses a physical network with switches and routers, cables, and various endpoints. At the center sits the Digital Network Architecture (DNA) Center controller, as shown in Figure 17-1, with human users making use of a graphical user interface (GUI) and automation using APIs. In short, DNA Center is the controller for SDA networks.

Architecturally, the southbound side of the controller contains the fabric, underlay, and overlay. By design in SDN implementations, most of the interesting new capabilities occur on the northbound side, which are examined in the second half of this chapter. This first half of the chapter examines the details south of the controller—namely, the fabric, underlay network, and overlay network.

Overlay: The mechanisms to create VXLAN tunnels between SDA switches, which are then used to transport traffic from one fabric endpoint to another over the fabric.

Underlay: The network of devices and connections (cables and wireless) to provide IP connectivity to all nodes in the fabric, with a goal to support the dynamic discovery of all SDA devices and endpoints as a part of the process to create overlay VXLAN tunnels.

Fabric: The combination of overlay and underlay, which together provide all features to deliver data across the network with the desired features and attributes.

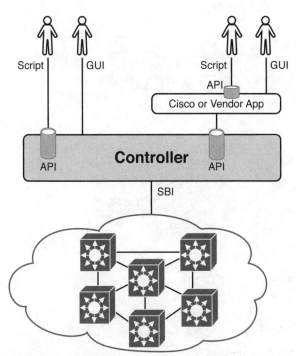

Script   GUI   Script   GUI

API

Cisco or Vendor App

API   **Controller**   API

SBI

17

Figure 17-1 *SDA Architectural Model with DNA Center*

In less formal terms, the underlay exists as multilayer switches and their links, with IP connectivity—but for a special purpose. The underlay supports some new concepts with a tunneling method called VXLAN. Traffic sent by the endpoint devices flows through VXLAN tunnels in the overlay—a completely different process than traditional LAN switching and IP routing.

For instance, think about the idea of sending packets from hosts on the left of a network, over SDA, to hosts on the right. For instance, imagine a packet enters on the left side of the physical network at the bottom of Figure 17-2 and eventually exits the campus out switch SW2 on the far right. This underlay network looks like a more traditional network drawing, with several devices and links.

The overlay drawing at the top of the figure shows only two switches—called fabric edge nodes, because they happen to be at the edges of the SDA fabric—with a tunnel labeled VXLAN connecting the two. Both concepts (underlay and overlay) together create the SDA fabric.

The next few pages explain both the underlay and overlay in a little more depth.

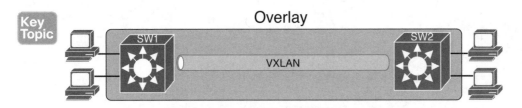

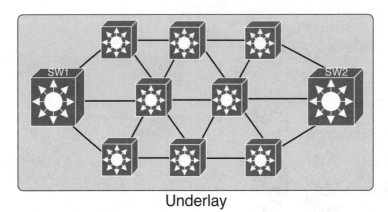

Figure 17-2 *Fabric, Underlay, and Overlay Concepts*

The SDA Underlay

With SDA, the underlay exists to provide connectivity between the nodes in the SDA environment for the purpose of supporting VXLAN tunnels in the overlay network. To do that, the underlay includes the switches, routers, cables, and wireless links used to create the physical network. It also includes the configuration and operation of the underlay so it can support the work of the overlay network.

Using Existing Gear for the SDA Underlay

To build an SDA underlay network, companies have two basic choices. They can use their existing campus network and add new configuration to create an underlay network, while still supporting their existing production traffic with traditional routing and switching. Alternately, the company can purchase some new switches and build the SDA network without concern for harming existing traffic, and migrate endpoints to the new SDA network over time.

To build SDA into an existing network, it helps to think for a moment about some typical campus network designs. The larger campus site may use either a two-tier or three-tier design as discussed in Chapter 13, "LAN Architecture." It has a cluster of wireless LAN controllers (WLCs) to support a number of lightweight APs (LWAPs). Engineers have configured VLANs, VLAN trunks, IP routing, IP routing protocols, ACLs, and so on. And the LAN connects to WAN routers.

SDA can be added into an existing campus LAN, but doing so has some risks and restrictions. First and foremost, you have to be careful not to disrupt the current network while adding the new SDA features to the network. The issues include

■ Because of the possibility of harming the existing production configuration, DNA Center should not be used to configure the underlay if the devices are currently used in production. (DNA Center will be used to configure the underlay with deployments that use all new hardware.)

■ The existing hardware must be from the SDA compatibility list, with different models supported depending on their different SDA roles (see a link at www.cisco.com/go/sda).

■ The device software levels must meet the requirements, based on their roles, as detailed in that same compatibility list.

For instance, imagine an enterprise happened to have an existing campus network that uses SDA-compatible hardware. That company might need to update the IOS versions in a few cases. Additionally, the engineers would need to configure the underlay part of the SDA devices manually rather than with DNA Center because Cisco assumes that the existing network already supports production traffic, so they want the customer directly involved in making those changes.

The SDA underlay configuration requires you to think about and choose the different SDA roles filled by each device before you can decide which devices to use and which minimum software levels each requires. If you look for the hardware compatibility list linked from www.cisco.com/go/sda, you will see different lists of supported hardware and software depending on the roles. These roles include

Fabric edge node: A switch that connects to endpoint devices (similar to traditional access switches)

Fabric border node: A switch that connects to devices outside SDA's control, for example, switches that connect to the WAN routers or to an ACI data center

Fabric control node: A switch that performs special control plane functions for the underlay (LISP), requiring more CPU and memory

For example, when I was writing this chapter back in 2019, Cisco's compatibility list included many Catalyst 9300, 9400, and 9500 switches, but also some smaller Catalyst 3850 and 3650 switches, as fabric edge nodes. However, the Catalyst 2960X or 2960XR products did not make the list as fabric edge nodes. For fabric control nodes, the list included more higher-end Catalyst switch models (which typically have more CPU and RAM), plus several router models (routers typically have much more RAM for control plane protocol storage—for instance, for routing protocols).

The beginning of an SDA project will require you to look at the existing hardware and software to begin to decide whether the existing campus might be a good candidate to build the fabric with existing gear or to upgrade hardware when building the new campus LAN.

Using New Gear for the SDA Underlay

When buying new hardware for the SDA fabric—that is, a greenfield design—you remove many of the challenges that exist when deploying SDA on existing gear. You can simply order compatible hardware and software. Once it arrives, DNA Center can then configure all the underlay features automatically.

At the same time, the usual campus LAN design decisions still need to be made. Enterprises use SDA as a better way to build and operate a campus network, but SDA is still a campus network. It needs to provide access and connectivity to all types of user devices. When planning a greenfield SDA design, plan to use SDA-compatible hardware, but also think about these traditional LAN design points:

- The number of ports needed in switches in each wiring closet
- The port speeds required
- The benefit of a switch stack in each wiring closet
- The cable length and types of cabling already installed
- The need for power (PoE/PoE+)
- The power available in each new switch versus the PoE power requirements
- Link capacity (speed and number of links) for links between switches

As far as the topology, traditional campus design does tell us how to connect devices, but SDA does not have to follow those traditional rules. To review, traditional campus LAN Layer 2 design (as discussed back in Chapter 13) tells us to connect each access switch to two different distribution layer switches, but not to other access layer switches, as shown in Figure 17-3. The access layer switch acts as a Layer 2 switch, with a VLAN limited to those three switches.

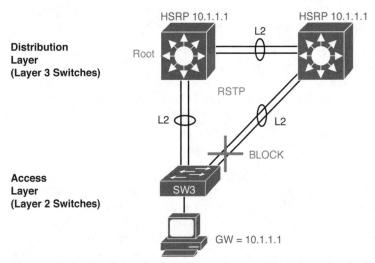

Figure 17-3 *Traditional Access Layer Design: Three Switches in STP Triangle*

Take a moment to reflect about the traditional features shown in the figure. The distribution layer switches—Layer 3 switches—act as the default gateway used by hosts and often implement HSRP for better availability. The design uses more than one uplink from the access to distribution layer switches, with Layer 2 EtherChannels, to allow balancing in addition to redundancy. And STP/RSTP manages the small amount of Layer 2 redundancy in the campus, preventing loops by blocking on some ports.

In comparison, a greenfield SDA fabric uses a *routed access layer* design. Routed access layer designs have been around long before SDA, but SDA makes good use of the design, and it works very well for the underlay with its goal to support VXLAN tunnels in the overlay network. A routed access layer design simply means that all the LAN switches are Layer 3 switches, with routing enabled, so all the links between switches operate as Layer 3 links.

With a greenfield SDA deployment—that is, all new gear that you can allow to be configured by DNA Center—DNA Center will configure the devices' underlay configuration to use a *routed access layer*. Because DNA Center knows it can configure the switches without concern of harming a production network, it chooses the best underlay configuration to support SDA. That best configuration happens to use a design called a routed access layer design, which has these features:

- All switches act as Layer 3 switches.
- The switches use the IS-IS routing protocol.
- All links between switches (single links, EtherChannels) are routed Layer 3 links (not Layer 2 links).
- As a result, STP/RSTP is not needed, with the routing protocol instead choosing which links to use based on the IP routing tables.
- The equivalent of a traditional access layer switch—an SDA edge node—acts as the default gateway for the endpoint devices, rather than distribution switches.
- As a result, HSRP (or any FHRP) is no longer needed.

Figure 17-4 repeats the same physical design as in Figure 17-3 but shows the different features with the routed access design as configured using DNA Center.

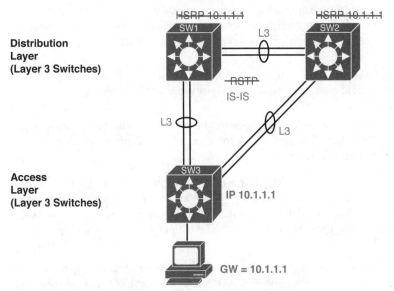

Figure 17-4 *SDA Fabric Layer 3 Access Benefits*

> **NOTE** DNA Center configures the underlay with consistent settings for each instance of DNA across an enterprise. This convention simplifies operation as an enterprise completes a migration to SDA.

The SDA Overlay

When you first think of the SDA overlay, think of this kind of sequence. First, an endpoint sends a frame that will be delivered across the SDA network. The first SDA node to receive the frame encapsulates the frame in a new message—using a tunneling specification called VXLAN—and forwards the frame into the fabric. Once the ingress node has encapsulated the original frame in VXLAN, the other SDA nodes forward the frame based on the VXLAN tunnel details. The last SDA node removes the VXLAN details, leaving the original frame, and forwards the original frame on toward the destination endpoint.

While the summary of some of SDA's overlay work in the previous paragraph may sound like a lot of work, all that work happens in each switch's ASIC. So, while it is more complex to understand, there is no performance penalty for the switches to perform the extra work.

When Cisco set about to create SDA, they saw an opportunity. Making use of VXLAN tunnels opened up the possibilities for a number of new networking features that did not exist without VXLAN. This next topic begins with a closer look at the VXLAN tunnels in the overlay, followed by a discussion of how SDA uses LISP for endpoint discovery and location needed to create the VXLAN tunnels.

VXLAN Tunnels in the Overlay (Data Plane)

SDA has many additional needs beyond the simple message delivery—needs that let it provide improved functions. To that end, SDA does not only route IP packets or switch Ethernet frames. Instead, it encapsulates incoming data link frames in a tunneling technology for delivery across the SDA network, with these goals in mind:

- The VXLAN tunneling (the encapsulation and de-encapsulation) must be performed by the ASIC on each switch so that there is no performance penalty. (That is one reason for the SDA hardware compatibility list: the switches must have ASICs that can perform the work.)

- The VXLAN encapsulation must supply header fields that SDA needs for its features, so the tunneling protocol should be flexible and extensible, while still being supported by the switch ASICs.

- The tunneling encapsulation needs to encapsulate the entire data link frame instead of encapsulating the IP packet. That allows SDA to support Layer 2 forwarding features as well as Layer 3 forwarding features.

To achieve those goals, when creating SDA, Cisco chose the *Virtual Extensible LAN* (VXLAN) protocol to create the tunnels used by SDA. When an SDA endpoint (for example, an end-user computer) sends a data link frame into an SDA edge node, the ingress edge node encapsulates the frame and sends it across a VXLAN tunnel to the egress edge node, as shown in Figure 17-5.

To support the VXLAN encapsulation, the underlay uses a separate IP address space as compared with the rest of the enterprise, including the endpoint devices that send data over the SDA network. The overlay tunnels use addresses from the enterprise address space. For instance, imagine an enterprise used these address spaces:

- 10.0.0.0/8: Entire enterprise
- 172.16.0.0/16: SDA underlay

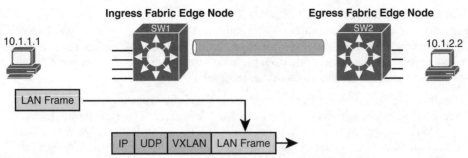

Figure 17-5 *Fundamentals of VXLAN Encapsulation in SDA*

To make that work, first the underlay would be built using the 172.16.0.0/16 IPv4 address space, with all links using addresses from that address space. As an example, Figure 17-6 shows a small SDA design, with four switches, each with one underlay IP address shown (from the 172.16.0.0/16 address space).

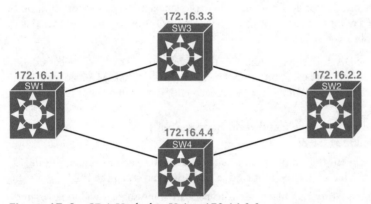

Figure 17-6 *SDA Underlay Using 172.16.0.0*

The overlay tunnel creates a path between two fabric edge nodes in the overlay IP address space—that is, in the same address space used by all the endpoints in the enterprise. Figure 17-7 emphasizes that point by showing the endpoints (PCs) on the left and right, with IP addresses in network 10.0.0.0/8, with the VXLAN overlay tunnel shown with addresses also from 10.0.0.0/8.

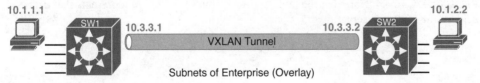

Figure 17-7 *VXLAN Tunnel and Endpoints with IPv4 Addresses in the Same IPv4 Space*

LISP for Overlay Discovery and Location (Control Plane)

Ignore SDA for a moment, and think about traditional Layer 2 switching and Layer 3 routing. How do their control planes work? In other words, how do these devices discover the possible destinations in the network, store those destinations, so that the data plane has all the data it needs when making a forwarding decision? To summarize:

■ Traditional Layer 2 switches learn possible destinations by examining the source MAC addresses of incoming frames, storing those MAC addresses as possible future destinations in the switch's MAC address table. When new frames arrive, the Layer 2 switch data plane then attempts to match the Ethernet frame's destination MAC address to an entry in its MAC address table.

■ Traditional Layer 3 routers learn destination IP subnets using routing protocols, storing routes to reach each subnet in their routing tables. When new packets arrive, the Layer 3 data plane attempts to match the IP packet's destination IP address to some entry in the IP routing table.

Nodes in the SDA network do not do these same control plane actions to support endpoint traffic. Just to provide a glimpse into the process for the purposes of CCNA, consider this sequence, which describes one scenario:

■ Fabric edge nodes—SDA nodes that connect to the edge of the SDA fabric—learn the location of possible endpoints using traditional means, based on their MAC address, individual IP address, and by subnet, identifying each endpoint with an endpoint identifier (EID).

■ The fabric edge nodes register the fact that the node can reach a given endpoint (EID) into a database called the LISP map server.

■ The LISP map server keeps the list of endpoint identifiers (EIDs) and matching routing locators (RLOCs) (which identify the fabric edge node that can reach the EID).

■ In the future, when the fabric data plane needs to forward a message, it will look for and find the destination in the LISP map server's database.

For instance, switches SW3 and SW4 in Figure 17-8 each just learned about different subnets external to the SDA fabric. As noted at step 1 in the figure, switch SW3 sent a message to the LISP map server, registering the information about subnet 10.1.3.0/24 (an EID), with its RLOC setting to identify itself as the node that can reach that subnet. Step 2 shows an equivalent registration process, this time for SW4, with EID 10.1.4.0/24, and with R4's RLOC of 172.16.4.4. Note that the table at the bottom of the figure represents that data held by the LISP map server.

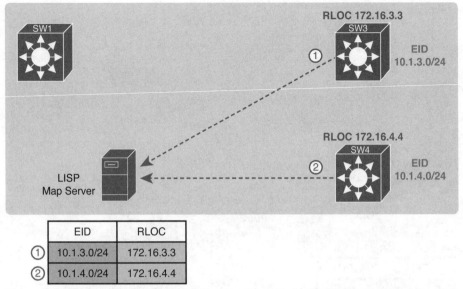

Figure 17-8 *Edge Nodes Register IPv4 Prefixes (Endpoint IDs) with LISP Map Server*

When new incoming frames arrive, the ingress tunnel router (ITR)—the SDA node that receives the new frame from outside the SDA fabric—needs some help from the control plane. To where should the ITR forward this frame? And because SDA always forwards frames in the fabric over some VXLAN tunnel, what tunnel should the ITR use when forwarding the frame? For the first frame sent to a destination, the ITR has to follow a process like the following steps. The steps begin at step 3, as a continuation of Figure 17-8, with the action referenced in Figure 17-9:

3. An Ethernet frame to a new destination arrives at ingress edge node SW1 (upper left), and the switch does not know where to forward the frame.

4. The ingress node sends a message to the LISP map server asking if the LISP server knows how to reach IP address 10.1.3.1.

5. The LISP map server looks in its database and finds the entry it built back at step 1 in the previous figure, listing SW3's RLOC of 172.16.3.3.

6. The LISP map server contacts SW3—the node listed as the RLOC—to confirm that the entry is correct.

7. SW3 completes the process of informing the ingress node (SW1) that 10.1.3.1 can be reached through SW3.

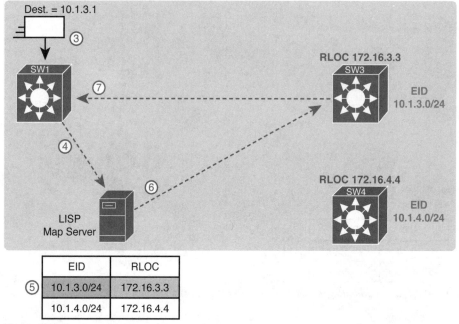

Figure 17-9 *Ingress Tunnel Router SW1 Discovers Egress Tunnel Router SW3 Using LISP*

To complete the story, now that ingress node SW1 knows that it can forward packets sent to endpoint 10.1.3.1 to the edge node with RLOC 172.16.3.3 (that is, SW3), SW1 encapsulates the original Ethernet frame as shown in Figure 17-9, with the original destination IP address of 10.1.3.1. It adds the IP, UDP, and VXLAN headers shown so it can deliver the message over the SDA network, with that outer IP header listing a destination IP address of the RLOC IP address, so that the message will arrive through the SDA fabric at SW3, as shown in Figure 17-10.

At this point, you should have a basic understanding of how the SDA fabric works. The underlay includes all the switches and links, along with IP connectivity, as a basis for forwarding data across the fabric. The overlay adds a different level of logic, with endpoint traffic flowing through VXLAN tunnels. This chapter has not mentioned any reasons that SDA might want to use these tunnels, but you will see one example by the end of the chapter. Suffice it to say that with the flexible VXLAN tunnels, SDA can encode header fields that let SDA create new networking features, all without suffering a performance penalty, as all the VXLAN processing happens in an ASIC.

This chapter next focuses on DNA Center and its role in managing and controlling SDA fabrics.

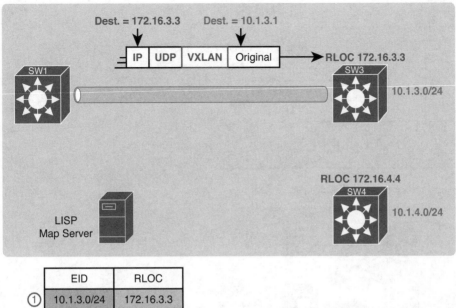

Figure 17-10 *Ingress Tunnel Router (ITR) SW1 Forwards Based on LISP Mapping to SW3*

DNA Center and SDA Operation

Cisco DNA Center (www.cisco.com/go/dnacenter) has two notable roles:

■ As the controller in a network that uses Cisco SDA

■ As a network management platform for traditional (non-SDA) network devices, with an expectation that one day DNA Center may become Cisco's primary enterprise network management platform

The first role as SDA network controller gets most of the attention and is the topic of discussion in this second of the three major sections of this chapter. SDA and DNA Center go together, work closely together, and any serious use of SDA requires the use of DNA Center. At the same time, DNA Center can manage traditional network devices; the final major section of the chapter works through some comparisons.

Cisco DNA Center

Cisco DNA Center exists as a software application that Cisco delivers pre-installed on a Cisco DNA Center appliance. The software follows the same general controller architecture concepts as described in Chapter 16. Figure 17-11 shows the general ideas.

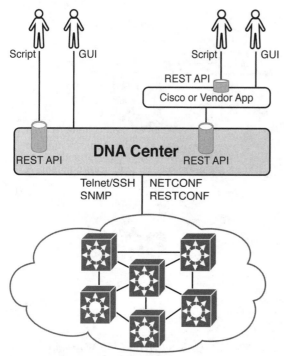

Figure 17-11 *Cisco DNA Center with Northbound and Southbound Interfaces*

Cisco DNA Center includes a robust northbound REST API along with a series of southbound APIs. For most of us, the northbound API matters most, because as the user of SDA networks, you interact with SDA using Cisco DNA Center's northbound REST API or the GUI interface. (Chapter 18, "Understanding REST and JSON," discusses the concepts behind REST APIs in more detail.)

Cisco DNA Center supports several southbound APIs so that the controller can communicate with the devices it manages. You can think of these as two categories:

- Protocols to support traditional networking devices/software versions: Telnet, SSH, SNMP

- Protocols to support more recent networking devices/software versions: NETCONF, RESTCONF

Cisco DNA Center needs the older protocols to be able to support the vast array of older Cisco devices and OS versions. Over time, Cisco has been adding support for NETCONF and RESTCONF to their more current hardware and software.

Cisco DNA Center and Scalable Groups

SDA creates many interesting new and powerful features beyond how traditional campus networks work. Cisco DNA Center not only enables an easier way to configure and operate those features, but it also completely changes the operational model. While the scope of CCNA does not allow us enough space to explore all of the features of SDA and DNA Center, this next topic looks at one feature as an example: scalable groups.

Issues with Traditional IP-Based Security

Imagine the life of one traditional IP ACL in an enterprise. Some requirements occurred, and an engineer built the first version of an ACL with three Access Control Entries (ACEs)—that is, **access-list** commands—with a **permit any** at the end of the list. Months later, the engineer added two more lines to the ACL, so the ACL has the number of ACEs shown in Figure 17-12. The figure notes the lines added for requests one and two with the circled numbers in the figure.

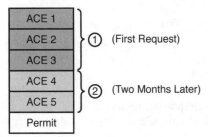

Figure 17-12   *Lines (ACEs) in an ACL after Two Changes*

Now think about that same ACL after four more requirements caused changes to the ACL, as noted in Figure 17-13. Some of the movement includes

- The ACEs for requirement two are now at the bottom of the ACL.
- Some ACEs, like ACE 5, apply to more than one of the implemented requirements.
- Some requirements, like requirement number five, required ACEs that overlap with multiple other requirements.

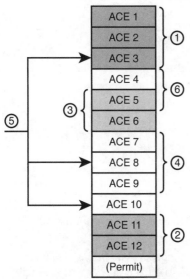

Figure 17-13   *Lines (ACEs) in an ACL after Six Changes*

Now imagine your next job is to add more ACEs for the next requirement (7). However, your boss also told you to reduce the length of the ACL, removing the ACEs from that one change made last August—you remember it, right? Such tasks are problematic at best.

With the scenario in Figure 17-13, no engineer could tell from looking at the ACL whether any lines in the ACL could be safely removed. You never know if an ACE was useful for one requirement or for many. If a requirement was removed, and you were even told which old project caused the original requirement so that you could look at your notes, you would not know if removing the ACEs would harm other requirements. Most of the time, ACL management suffers with these kinds of issues:

- ACEs cannot be removed from ACLs because of the risk of causing failures to the logic for some other past requirement.

- New changes become more and more challenging due to the length of the ACLs.

- Troubleshooting ACLs as a system—determining whether a packet would be delivered from end-to-end—becomes an even greater challenge.

SDA Security Based on User Groups

Imagine you could instead enforce security without even thinking about IP address ranges and ACLs. SDA does just that, with simple configuration, and the capability to add and remove the security policies at will.

First, for the big ideas. Imagine that over time, using SDA, six different security require-ments occurred. For each project, the engineer would define the policy with DNA Center, either with the GUI or with the API. Then, as needed, DNA Center would configure the devices in the fabric to enforce the security, as shown in Figure 17-14.

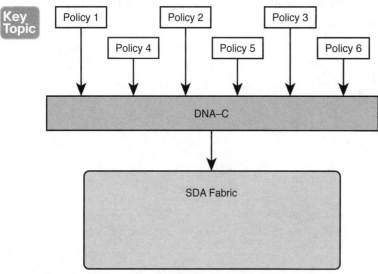

Figure 17-14 *DNA-C IP Security Policies (Northbound) to Simplify Operations*

> **NOTE** The model in Figure 17-14 helps demonstrate the concept of intent-based network-ing (IBN). The engineer configures the intent or outcome desired from the network—in this case, a set of security policies. The controller communicates with the devices in the net-work, with the devices determining exactly what configuration and behavior are necessary to achieve those intended policies.

The SDA policy model solves the configuration and operational challenges with traditional ACLs. In fact, all those real issues with managing IP ACLs on each device are no longer issues with SDA's group-based security model. For instance:

■ The engineer can consider each new security requirement separately, without analysis of an existing (possibly lengthy) ACL.

■ Each new requirement can be considered without searching for all the ACLs in the likely paths between endpoints and analyzing each and every ACL.

■ DNA Center (and related software) keeps the policies separate, with space to keep notes about the reason for the policy.

■ Each policy can be removed without fear of impacting the logic of the other policies.

SDA and Cisco DNA achieve this particular feature by tying security to groups of users, called scalable groups, with each group assigned a scalable group tag (SGT). Then the engineer configures a grid that identifies which SGTs can send packets to which other SGTs. For instance, the grid might include SGTs for an employee group, the Internet (for the Enterprise's WAN routers that lead to the Internet), partner employees, and guests, with a grid like the one shown in Table 17-2.

Table 17-2   Access Table for SDA Scalable Group Access

Dest. / Source	Employee	Internet	Partner	Guest
Employee	N/A	Permit	Permit	Deny
Internet	Permit	N/A	Permit	Permit
Partner	Permit	Permit	N/A	Deny
Guest	Deny	Permit	Deny	N/A

To link this security feature back to packet forwarding, consider when a new endpoint tries to send its first packet to a new destination. The ingress SDA node starts a process by sending messages to DNA Center. DNA Center then works with security tools in the network, like Cisco's Identity Services Engine (ISE), to identify the users and then match them to their respective SGTs. DNA Center then checks the logic similar to Table 17-2. If DNA Center sees a permit action between the source/destination pair of SGTs, DNA Center directs the edge nodes to create the VXLAN tunnel, as shown in Figure 17-15. If the security policies state that the two SGTs should not be allowed to communicate, DNA Center does not direct the fabric to create the tunnel, and the packets do not flow.

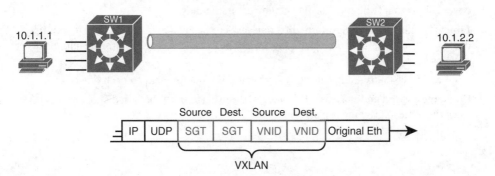

Figure 17-15   *VXLAN Header with Source and Destination SGTs and VNIDs Revealed*

> **NOTE** The figure gives a brief insight into why SDA goes to the trouble of using VXLAN encapsulation for its data plane, rather than performing traditional Layer 2 switching or Layer 3 routing. The VXLAN header has great flexibility—in this case, used to define both a source and destination SGT, matching SDA's desired logic of allowing a subset of source/destination SGTs in the SDA fabric.

The operational model with scalable groups greatly simplifies security configuration and ongoing maintenance of the security policy, while focusing on the real goal: controlling access based on user. From a controller perspective, the fact that Cisco DNA Center acts as much more than a management platform, and instead as a controller of the activities in the network, makes for a much more powerful set of features and capabilities.

DNA Center as a Network Management Platform

CCNA Exam topic 6.4 asks you to compare traditional network management with DNA Center:

> Compare traditional campus device management with Cisco DNA Center enabled device management

Note that the exam topic does not identify which traditional management product. In fact, Cisco tends to shy away from product details in most of its career certifications. So, to think through this exam topic, you need to think in general about network management products. But it also helps to think about specific products—but temper that by focusing on the more prominent features and major functions.

This section uses Cisco Prime Infrastructure (PI) (www.cisco.com/go/primeinfrastructure) as an example of a traditional enterprise network management product. For many years, Cisco Prime Infrastructure has been Cisco's primary network management product for the enterprise. It includes the following features:

- **Single-pane-of-glass:** Provides one GUI from which to launch all PI functions and features
- **Discovery, inventory, and topology:** Discovers network devices, builds an inventory, and arranges them in a topology map
- **Entire enterprise:** Provides support for traditional enterprise LAN, WAN, and data center management functions
- **Methods and protocols:** Uses SNMP, SSH, and Telnet, as well as CDP and LLDP, to discover and learn information about the devices in the network
- **Lifecycle management:** Supports different tasks to install a new device (day 0), configure it to be working in production (day 1), and perform ongoing monitoring and make changes (day *n*)
- **Application visibility:** Simplifies QoS configuration deployment to each device
- **Converged wired and wireless:** Enables you to manage both the wired and wireless LAN from the same management platform

- **Software Image Management (SWIM):** Manages software images on network devices and automates updates

- **Plug-and-Play:** Performs initial installation tasks for new network devices after you physically install the new device, connect a network cable, and power on

PI itself runs as an application on a server platform with GUI access via a web browser. The PI server can be purchased from Cisco as a software package to be installed and run on your servers, or as a physical appliance.

The next few pages now compare and contrast DNA Center to traditional management tools like PI.

DNA Center Similarities to Traditional Management

If you read the user's guide for DNA Center and look through all the features, you will find all the features just listed here as traditional management features. For instance, both can discover network devices and create a network topology map. Human operators (rather than automated processes) often start with the topology map, expecting notices (flashing lights, red colors) to denote issues in the network.

As an example, Figure 17-16 shows a topology map from DNA Center. Both PI and DNA Center can perform a discover process to find all the devices in the network and then build topology maps to show the devices. (Interestingly, DNA Center can work with PI, using the data discovered by PI rather than performing the discovery work again.)

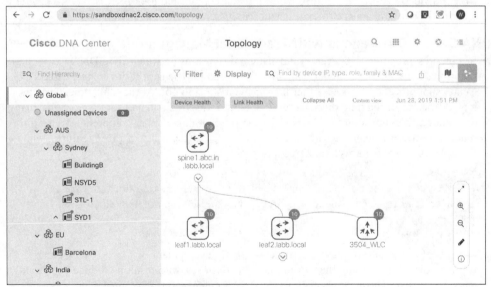

Figure 17-16 *DNA Center Topology Map*

The GUI mechanisms are relatively intuitive, with the ability to click into additional or less detail. Figure 17-17 shows a little more detail after hovering over and clicking on one of the nodes in the topology from Figure 17-16, typical actions and results in many management products.

Figure 17-17 *Hover and Click Details About One Cisco 9300 Switch from DNA Center*

I encourage you to take some time to use and watch some videos about Cisco DNA Center. The "Chapter Review" section for this chapter on the companion website lists some links for good videos. Also, start at https://developer.cisco.com and look for Cisco DNA Center sandbox labs to find a place to experiment with Cisco DNA Center.

DNA Center Differences with Traditional Management

In a broad sense, there are several fundamental differences between Cisco DNA Center and traditional network management platforms like Cisco PI. The largest difference: Cisco DNA Center supports SDA, whereas other management apps do not. At the same time, given its long history, as of the time this chapter was written, Cisco PI still had some traditional management features not found in Cisco DNA Center. So think of PI as comprehensive to traditional device management, with Cisco DNA Center having many of those features, while focusing on future features like SDA support.

> **NOTE** Cisco hopes to continue to update Cisco DNA Center's traditional network management features to be equivalent compared to Cisco PI, to the point at which DNA Center could replace PI.

In terms of intent and strategy, Cisco focuses their development of Cisco DNA Center features toward simplifying the work done by enterprises, with resulting reduced costs and much faster deployment of changes. Cisco DNA Center features help make initial installation easier, simplify the work to implement features that traditionally have challenging configuration, and use tools to help you notice issues more quickly. Some of the features unique to Cisco DNA Center include

- **EasyQoS:** Deploys QoS, one of the most complicated features to configure manually, with just a few simple choices from Cisco DNA Center
- **Encrypted traffic analysis:** Enables Cisco DNA to use algorithms to recognize security threats even in encrypted traffic

- **Device 360 and Client 360:** Gives a comprehensive (360-degree) view of the health of the device
- **Network time travel:** Shows past client performance in a timeline for comparison to current behavior
- **Path trace:** Discovers the actual path packets would take from source to destination based on current forwarding tables

Just to expound on one feature as an example, Cisco DNA Center's Path Trace feature goes far beyond a traditional management application. A typical network management app might show a map of the network and let you click through to find the configuration on each device, including ACLs. The path trace feature goes much further. The DNA user (from the GUI or the API) specifies a source and destination host and optionally transport protocol and ports. Then the path trace feature shows a map of the path through the network and shows which ACLs are in the path, and whether they would permit or deny the packet.

All of Cisco Digital Network Architecture sets about to help customers reach some big goals: reduced costs, reduced risks, better security and compliance, faster deployment of services through automation and simplified processes, and the list goes on. Cisco DNA Center plays an important role, with all the functions available through its robust northbound API, and with its intent-based networking approach for SDA. Cisco DNA Center represents the future of network management for Cisco enterprises.

Chapter Review

One key to doing well on the exams is to perform repetitive spaced review sessions. Review this chapter's material using either the tools in the book or interactive tools for the same material found on the book's companion website. Refer to the "Your Study Plan" element for more details. Table 17-3 outlines the key review elements and where you can find them. To better track your study progress, record when you completed these activities in the second column.

Table 17-3 Chapter Review Tracking

Review Element	Review Date(s)	Resource Used
Review key topics		Book, website
Review key terms		Book, website
Answer DIKTA questions		Book, PTP

Review All the Key Topics

Table 17-4 Key Topics for Chapter 17

Key Topic Element	Description	Page Number
List	Definitions for overlay, underlay, and fabric	384
Figure 17-2	SDA overlay and underlay	386
List	SDA fabric edge, fabric border, and fabric control node roles	387
List	Attributes of the SDA underlay	389
List	SDA VXLAN tunneling benefits	390
Figure 17-5	VXLAN encapsulation process with SDA	391
Figure 17-8	Registering SDA endpoint IDs (EIDs) with the map server	393
Figure 17-14	DNA Center shown controlling the fabric to implement group-based security	398
List	DNA Center features that go beyond traditional network management	400
List	Features unique to DNA Center	402

Key Terms You Should Know

Software-Defined Access, overlay, underlay, fabric, DNA Center, fabric edge node, VXLAN, LISP, scalable group tag (SGT), Cisco Prime Infrastructure (PI)

CHAPTER 18

Understanding REST and JSON

This chapter covers the following exam topics:

6.0 Automation and Programmability

6.5 Describe characteristics of REST-based APIs (CRUD, HTTP verbs, and data encoding)

6.7 Interpret JSON encoded data

To automate and program networks, some automation software does several tasks. The software analyzes data in the form of variables, makes decisions based on that analysis, and then may take action to change the configuration of network devices or report facts about the state of the network.

The different automation functions reside on different devices: the network engineer's device, a server, a controller, and the various network devices themselves. For these related automation processes to work well, all these software components need useful well-defined conventions to allow easy communication between software components.

This chapter focuses on two conventions that allow automation software to communicate. The first major section discusses application programming interfaces (APIs), specifically APIs that follow a style called REpresentational State Transfer (REST). APIs of any kind create a way for software applications to communicate, while RESTful APIs (APIs that use REST conventions) follow a particular set of software rules. Many APIs used in network automation today use REST-based APIs.

The second half of the chapter focuses on the conventions and standards for the data variables exchanged over APIs, with a focus on one: JavaScript Object Notation (JSON). If REST provides one standard method of how two automation programs should communicate over a network, JSON then defines how to communicate the variables used by a program: the variable names, their values, and the data structures of those variables.

"Do I Know This Already?" Quiz

Take the quiz (either here or use the PTP software) if you want to use the score to help you decide how much time to spend on this chapter. The letter answers are listed at the bottom of the page following the quiz. Appendix C, found both at the end of the book as well as on the companion website, includes both the answers and explanations. You can also find both answers and explanations in the PTP testing software.

Table 18-1 "Do I Know This Already?" Foundation Topics Section-to-Question Mapping

Foundation Topics Section	Questions
REST-based APIs	1–3
Data Models and JSON	4–6

1. Which of the following are required attributes of a REST-based API? (Choose two answers.)

   a. Uses HTTP

   b. Objects noted as to whether they can be cached

   c. Stateful operation

   d. Client/server architecture

2. Which answers list a matching software development CRUD action to an HTTP verb that performs that action? (Choose two answers.)

   a. CRUD create and HTTP PATCH

   b. CRUD update and HTTP PATCH

   c. CRUD delete and HTTP PUT

   d. CRUD read and HTTP GET

3. Examine the following URI that works with a Cisco DNA Controller:

   `https://dnac.example.com/dna/intent/api/v1/network-device?managementIPAddress=10.10.22.74`

   Which part of the URI, per the API documentation, is considered to identify the resource but not any parameters?

   a. https://

   b. dnac.example.com

   c. dna/intent/api/v1/network-device

   d. managementIPAddress=10.10.22.74

4. Which of the following data serialization and data modeling languages would be most likely to be used in a response from a REST-based server API used for networking applications? (Choose two answers.)

   a. JSON

   b. YAML

   c. JavaScript

   d. XML

5. Which answers correctly describe the format of the JSON text below? (Choose two answers.)

   `{ "myvariable":[1,2,3] }`

   a. One JSON object that has one key:value pair

   b. One JSON object that has three key:value pairs

   c. A JSON object whose value is a second JSON object

   d. A JSON object whose value is a JSON array

6. Which answers refer to JSON values rather than JSON keys as found in the sample
JSON data? (Choose two answers.)

```
{
    "response": {
        "type": "Cisco Catalyst 9300 Switch",
        "family": "Switches and Hubs",
        "role": "ACCESS",
        "managementIpAddress": "10.10.22.66"
    }
}
```

a. "response"

b. "type"

c. "ACCESS"

d. The entire gray area

Foundation Topics

REST-Based APIs

Applications use *application programming interfaces* (APIs) to communicate. To do so,
one program can learn the variables and data structures used by another program, making
logic choices based on those values, changing the values of those variables, creating new
variables, and deleting variables. APIs allow programs running on different computers to
work cooperatively, exchanging data to achieve some goal.

In an API software world, some applications create an API, with many other applications
using (consuming) the API. Software developers add APIs to their software so other application software can make use of the first application's features.

When writing an application, the developer will write some code, but often the developer
may do a lot of work by looking for APIs that can provide the data and functions, reducing
the amount of new code that must be written. As a result, much of modern software development centers on understanding and learning new APIs, along with the available libraries
(prebuilt software that can be used to accomplish tasks rather than writing the equivalent
from scratch).

Several types of APIs exist, each with a different set of conventions to meet a different set
of needs. The CCNA blueprint mentions one type of API—REpresentational State Transfer
(REST)—because of its popularity as a type of API in networking automation applications.
This first major section of the chapter takes a closer look at REST-based APIs.

REST-Based (RESTful) APIs

REST APIs follow a set of foundational rules about what makes a REST API and what does
not. First, from a literal perspective, REST APIs include the six attributes defined a few decades

back by its creator, Roy Fielding. (You can find a good summary at https://restfulapi.net).
Those six attributes are

- Client/server architecture
- Stateless operation
- Clear statement of cacheable/uncacheable
- Uniform interface
- Layered
- Code-on-demand

The first three of these attributes get at the heart of how a REST API works. You can more easily see those first three features at work with networking REST APIs, so the next few paragraphs give a little more explanation about those first three points.

Client/Server Architecture

Like many applications, REST applications use a client/server architectural model. First, an application developer creates a REST API, and that application, when executing, acts as a REST server. Any other application can make a REST API call (the REST client) by executing some code that causes a request to flow from the client to the server. For instance, in Figure 18-1

1. The REST client on the left executes a REST API call, which generates a message sent to the REST server.

2. The REST server on the right has API code that considers the request and decides how to reply.

3. The REST server sends back the reply message with the appropriate data variables in the reply message.

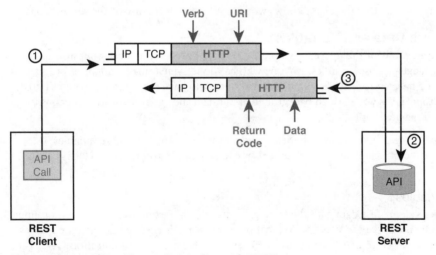

Figure 18-1   *Client/Server Operation with REST*

> **NOTE** Figure 18-1 shows the use of HTTP. While many REST APIs use HTTP, the use of HTTP is not a requirement for an API to be considered RESTful.

Stateless Operation

The stateless attribute of REST APIs means that REST does not record and use information about one API exchange for the purpose of how subsequent API exchanges are processed. In other words, each API request and reply does not use any other past history considered when processing the request.

For comparison, the TCP protocol uses a stateful approach, whereas UDP uses stateless operation. A TCP connection requires the endpoints to initialize variables on each end, with those variables updating over time, and with those variables being used for subsequent TCP messages. For instance, TCP uses sequence numbers and acknowledgment numbers to manage the flow of data in a TCP connection.

Cacheable (or Not)

To appreciate what is meant by *cacheable*, consider what happens when you browse a website. When your browser loads a new web page, the page itself contains a variety of objects (text, images, videos, audio). Some objects seldom change, so it would be better to download the object once and not download it again; in that case, the server marks that object as cacheable. For instance, a logo or other image shown on many pages of a website would almost never change and would likely be cacheable. However, the product list returned in your most recent search of the website would not be cacheable because the server would want to update and supply a new list each time you request the page.

REST APIs require that any resource requested via an API call have a clear method by which to mark the resource as cacheable or not. The goals remain the same: improve performance by retrieving resources less often (cacheable). Note that cacheable resources are marked with a timeframe so that the client knows when to ask for a new copy of the resource again.

Background: Data and Variables

To appreciate a few of the upcoming topics, it helps to have a basic idea about how programming languages use variables. Anyone who has done even a small amount of programming should have enough background, but for those who have not written programs before, this next topic gives you enough background about data and variables inside programs to understand the next topic.

If you have some programming experience and already know about simple variables, list variables, and dictionary variables, then feel free to skip ahead to the section "REST APIs and HTTP."

Simple Variables

Applications all process data with the same general actions, starting with some kind of input. The program needs data to process, so the input process reads files, sends database queries to a database server, or makes API calls to retrieve data from another application's API. The goal: gather the data that the program needs to process to do its work.

Answers to the "Do I Know This Already?" quiz:

1 B, D **2** B, D **3** C **4** A, D **5** A, D **6** C, D

Programs then process data by making comparisons, making decisions, creating new variables, and performing mathematical formulas to analyze the data. All that logic uses variables. For instance, a program might process data with the following logic:

If the router's G0/0 interface has a configuration setting of **switchport mode dynamic auto**, then gather more data to ensure that interface currently operates as a trunk rather than as an access port.

In programming, a variable is a name or label that has an assigned value. To get a general sense for programming variables, you can think of variables much like variables from algebra equations back in school. Example 18-1 shows some samples of variables of different types in a Python program (the Python language is the most popular language today for writing network automation applications). This program begins with a comment (the top three lines with triple single quotes) and then creates four variables, assigning them to different values, and prints a line of output: "The product is -12."

Example 18-1 *Simple Python Program That Shows a Product*

```
'''
Sample program to multiply two numbers and display the result
'''
x = 3
y = -4
z = 1.247
heading = "The product is "
print(heading,x*y)
```

The variables in Example 18-1 can be called *simple variables* because each variable name has a single value associated with it. Simple variables have one variable name and one associated value, so they have a simple structure.

The values of simple variables can have a variety of formats, as shown in Example 18-1. The example includes variables that contain

- Unsigned integers (x)
- Signed integers (y)
- Floating-point numbers (z)
- Text (heading)

List and Dictionary Variables

While simple variables have many great uses, programs need variables with more complex *data structures*. In programming, a data structure defines a related set of variables and values. For instance, Python uses list variables so that one variable name is assigned a value that is a list of values rather than a single value. You could imagine that a network automation program might want to have lists, such as a list of devices being managed, a list of interfaces on a device, or list of configuration settings on an interface.

First, consider the variable named list1 in Example 18-2; note that the lines that begin with a # are comment lines.

Example 18-2 *Sample List and Dictionary Variables in Python*

```
# Variable list1 is a list in Python (called an array in Java)
list1 = ["g0/0", "g0/1", "g0/2"]


# Variable dict1 is a dictionary (called an associative array in Java)
dict1 = {"config_speed":'auto', "config_duplex":"auto", "config_ip":"10.1.1.1"}
```

Even if you have never seen Python code before, you can guess at some of the meaning of the list1 variable. The code assigns variable list1 to a value that itself is a list of three text strings. Note that the list could include text, unsigned integers, signed integers, and so on.

Figure 18-2 shows the data structure behind variable list1 in Example 18-2. The variable is assigned to the list, with the list having three list elements.

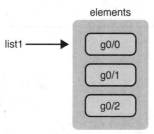

Figure 18-2 *The List Data Structure in Python*

Python supports a similar data structure called a *dictionary*. If you think of the contents of a dictionary for the English language, that dictionary lists a series of paired items: a term and a matching definition. With programming languages like Python, the dictionary data structure lists paired items as well: *keys* (like terms) and *values* (like definitions). Figure 18-3 shows the structure of that dictionary value matching the dict1 variable at the bottom of Example 18-2. Note that each key and its value is called a *key:value pair*.

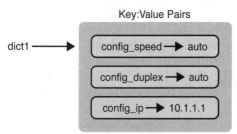

Figure 18-3 *Dictionary Data Structures in Python*

Data structures can get more complex. Additionally, the data structures can be nested. For instance, a single variable's value could be a list, with each list element being a dictionary, with the values in some key:value pairs being other lists, and so on. For now, be aware of the fact that programs use simple variables but also use list and dictionary variables to make it easier to perform different kinds of logic.

REST APIs and HTTP

APIs exist to allow two programs to exchange data. Some APIs may be designed as an interface between programs running on the same computer, so the communication between programs happens within a single operating system. Many APIs need to be available to programs that run on other computers, so the API must define the type of networking protocols supported by the API—and many REST-based APIs use the HTTP protocol.

The creators of REST-based APIs often choose HTTP because HTTP's logic matches some of the concepts defined more generally for REST APIs. HTTP uses the same principles as REST: it operates with a client/server model; it uses a stateless operational model; and it includes headers that clearly mark objects as cacheable or not cacheable. It also includes verbs—words that dictate the desired action for a pair HTTP Request and Reply—which matches how applications like to work.

This section breaks down the fundamentals of some programming terminology, how that matches HTTP verbs, and how REST APIs make use of Uniform Resource Identifiers (URIs) to specify the data desired from a RESTful API call.

Software CRUD Actions and HTTP Verbs

The software industry uses a memorable acronym—*CRUD*—for the four primary actions performed by an application. Those actions are

Create: Allows the client to create some new instances of variables and data structures at the server and initialize their values as kept at the server

Read: Allows the client to retrieve (read) the current value of variables that exist at the server, storing a copy of the variables, structures, and values at the client

Update: Allows the client to change (update) the value of variables that exist at the server

Delete: Allows the client to delete from the server different instances of data variables

For instance, if using the northbound REST API of a DNA controller, as discussed in Chapter 17, "Cisco Software-Defined Access (SDA)," you might want to create something new, like a new security policy. From a programming perspective, the security policy exists as a related set of configuration settings on the DNA controller, internally represented by variables. To do that, a REST client application would use a create action, using the DNA Center RESTful API, that created variables on the DNA Controller via the DNA Center REST API. The concept of creating new configuration at the controller is performed via the API using a create action per the CRUD generic acronym.

Other examples of CRUD actions include a check of the status of that new configuration (a read action), an update to change some specific setting in the new configuration (an update action), or an action to remove the security policy definition completely (a delete action).

HTTP uses verbs that mirror CRUD actions. HTTP defines the concept of an HTTP request and reply, with the client sending a request and with the server answering back with a reply. Each request/reply lists an action verb in the HTTP request header, which defines the HTTP action. The HTTP messages also include a URI, which identifies the resource being manipulated for this request. As always, the HTTP message is carried in IP and TCP, with headers and data, as represented in Figure 18-4.

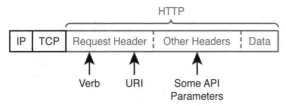

Figure 18-4 *HTTP Verb and URI in an HTTP Request Header*

To get some perspective about HTTP, ignore REST for a moment. Whenever you open a web browser and click a link, your browser generates an HTTP GET request message similar to Figure 18-4 in structure. The message includes an HTTP header with the GET verb and the URI. The resources returned in the reply are the components of a web page, like text files, image files, and video files.

HTTP works well with REST in part because HTTP has verbs that match the common program actions in the CRUD paradigm. Table 18-2 lists the HTTP verbs and CRUD terms for easy reference and study.

Table 18-2 Comparing CRUD Actions to REST Verbs

Action	CRUD Term	REST (HTTP) Verb
Create new data structures and variables	Create	POST
Read (retrieve) variable names, structures, and values	Read	GET
Update or replace values of some variable	Update	PATCH, PUT
Delete some variables and data structures	Delete	DELETE

NOTE While Table 18-2 lists HTTP POST as a create action and HTTP PATCH and PUT as CRUD update actions, all three of these HTTP verbs might be used both for create and for update actions in some cases.

Using URIs with HTTP to Specify the Resource

In addition to using HTTP verbs to perform the CRUD functions for an application, REST uses URIs to identify what resource the HTTP request acts on. For REST APIs, the resource can be any one of the many resources defined by the API. Each resource contains a set of related variables, defined by the API and identified by a URI.

For instance, imagine a user creates a REST-based API. When she does so, she creates a set of resources that she wants to make available via the API, and she also assigns a unique URI to each resource. In other words, the API creator creates a URI and a matching set of variables, and defines the actions that can be performed against those variables (read, update, and so on).

The API creator also creates API documentation that lists the resources and the URI that identifies each resource, among other details. The programmer for a REST client application can read the API documentation, build a REST API request, and ask for the specific resource, as shown in the example in Figure 18-5.

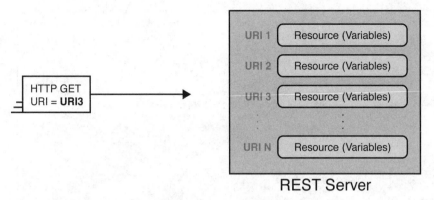

Figure 18-5 *One URI for Each API Resource—Conceptual View*

Figure 18-5 shows the URIs as generic values; however, today's network engineers need to be able to read API documentation, see URIs in that documentation, and understand the meaning of each part of the URI. Figure 18-6 shows a URI specific to the Cisco DNA Center northbound REST API as an example of some of the components of the URI.

Figure 18-6 *URI Structure for REST GET Request*

The figure shows these important values and concepts:

HTTPS: The letters before the :// identify the protocol used—in this case, HTTP Secure (which uses HTTP with SSL encryption).

Hostname or IP Address: This value sits between the // and first /, and identifies the host; if using a hostname, the REST client must perform name resolution to learn the IP address of the REST server.

Path (Resource): This value sits after the first / and finishes either at the end of the URI or before any additional fields (like a parameter query field). HTTP calls this field the path, but for use with REST, the field uniquely identifies the resource as defined by the API.

To drive home the connection between the API, URI, and resource part of the API, it can be helpful to just do a general tour of the API documentation for any REST-based API. For instance, when Cisco created DNA Center, it created the REST-based northbound interface and chose one URI as shown in Figure 18-6. Figure 18-7 shows a copy of the doc page for that particular resource for comparison. Go to https://developer.cisco.com and search for "Cisco DNA Center API documentation." Continue to search for yourself to see more examples of the resources defined by the Cisco DNA Center API.

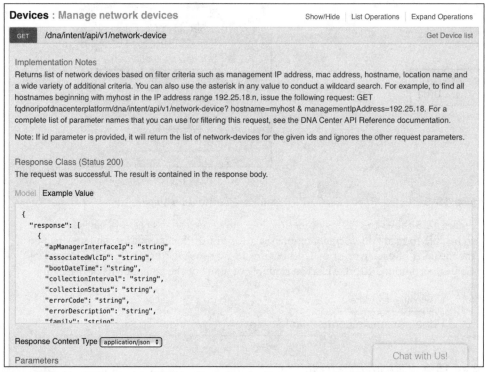

Figure 18-7 *DNA Center API Doc Page for the Network Device (List) Resource*

Many of the HTTP request messages need to pass information to the REST server beyond the API. Some of that data can be passed in header fields—for instance, REST APIs use HTTP header fields to encode much of the authentication information for REST calls. Additionally, parameters related to a REST call can be passed as parameters as part of the URI itself.

For instance, the URI in Figure 18-6 asks the Cisco DNA Center for a list of all known devices, with Cisco DNA Center returning a dictionary of values for each device. You might instead want that dictionary of values for only a single device. The Cisco DNA Center API allows for just that by tacking on the following to the end of the URI shown in Figure 18-6.

```
?managementIPAddress=10.10.22.66&macAddress=f8:7b:20:67:62:80
```

Figure 18-8 summarizes the major components of the URIs commonly used with a REST API, with the resource and parameter parts of the URI identifying specifically what the API should supply to the REST client.

Figure 18-8 *Example Components of a URI Used in a REST API Call*

Example of REST API Call to DNA Center

To pull some of the REST API concepts together, the next few pages work through a few sample API calls using a software application called an API development environment tool.

For a bit of development perspective, when working to automate some part of your network operation tasks, you would eventually use a program that made API calls. However, early in the process of developing an application, you might first focus on the data available from the API and ignore all the programming details at first. API development environments let you focus on the API calls. Later, that same tool can typically generate correct code that you can copy into your program to make the API calls.

The examples in this section use an app named Postman. Postman can be downloaded for free (www.postman.co) and used as shown in this section. Note that Cisco DevNet makes extensive use of Postman in its many labs and examples.

The first example shows a screenshot of a part of the Postman app after it sends a REST client GET request to a DNA Center REST API (see Figure 18-9). In particular, look for the following:

- The URI, near the top, lists a hostname of sandboxdnac2.cisco.com, which is an always-on DNA Center instance supplied by Cisco's DevNet site (which you can use).

- The resource part of the URI shows the same resource listed earlier in Figure 18-6, asking for a list of devices.

- The bottom center of the window shows the data returned by the DNA Center REST HTTP GET response.

- At the middle right, it lists the GET response's status code of 200, meaning "OK."

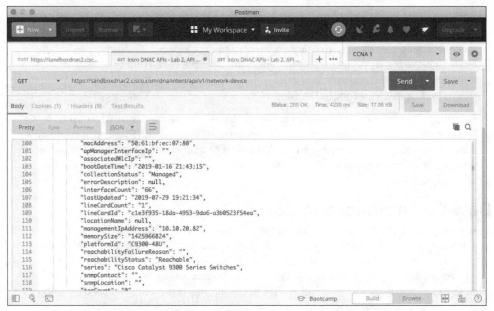

Figure 18-9 *URI Structure for REST GET Request*

Take a moment to look through the data at the bottom of the Postman window in Figure 18-9. The text follows a data modeling format called JavaScript Object Notation (JSON), which is one of the main topics for the remainder of the chapter. However, armed with just a knowledge of routers, you can find a few facts that look familiar. To help you see the text, Example 18-3 shows an edited (shortened to reduce the length) view of some of the JSON output in that window, just so you can see the format and some of the data returned in this single API call.

Example 18-3 *JSON Output from a REST API Call*

```
{
    "response": {
        "type": "Cisco Catalyst 9300 Switch",
        "family": "Switches and Hubs",
        "role": "ACCESS",
        "macAddress": "f8:7b:20:67:62:80",
        "hostname": "cat_9k_1",
        "serialNumber": "FCW2136L0AK",
        "softwareVersion": "16.6.1",
        "upTime": "17 days, 22:51:04.26",
        "interfaceCount": "41",
        "lineCardCount": "2",
        "managementIpAddress": "10.10.22.66",
        "series": "Cisco Catalyst 9300 Series Switches",
        "softwareType": "IOS-XE"
    }
}
```

API development tools like Postman help you work out the particulars of each API call, save the details, and share with other engineers and developers. Eventually, you will be ready to make the API call from a program. With a simple click from the Postman UI, Postman supplies the code to copy/paste into your program so that it returns all the output shown in the center/bottom of the window back as a variable to your program.

By now, you have a good foundational knowledge of the mechanics of REST APIs. By learning some skills, and using the API documentation for any REST API, you could now experiment with and try to make REST API calls. For many of those, the data will return to you as text, often in JSON format, so the second half of the chapter examines the meaning of that text.

Data Serialization and JSON

In your journey to become a modern network engineer with network automation skills, you will learn to understand several data serialization languages. Each data serialization language provides methods of using text to describe variables, with a goal of being able to send that text over a network or to store that text in a file. Data serialization languages give us a way to represent variables with text rather than in the internal representation used by any particular programming language.

Each data serialization language enables API servers to return data so that the API client can replicate the same variable names as well as data structures as found on the API server. To describe the data structures, the data serialization languages include special characters and conventions that communicate ideas about list variables, dictionary variables, and other more complex data structures.

This second major section of the chapter examines the concept of a data serialization language, with a focus on the one data modeling language as mentioned in the current CCNA blueprint: JavaScript Object Notation (JSON).

The Need for a Data Model with APIs

This section shows some ideas of how to move variables in a program on a server to a client program. First, Figure 18-10 and surrounding text show a nonworking example as a way to identify some of the challenges with copying variable values from one device to another. Then Figure 18-11 and its related text show how to use a data serialization language to solve the problems shown around Figure 18-10.

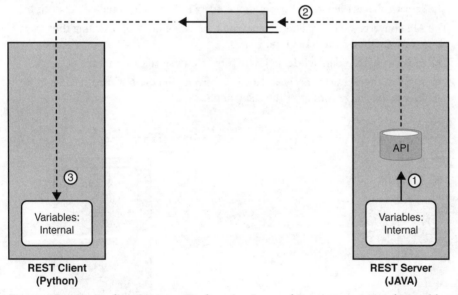

Figure 18-10 *Broken Concept: Exchanging Internal Representations of Variables*

First, for the nonworking example, consider the flow and numbered steps in Figure 18-10. A REST client sits on the left. The REST client asks for a resource, and the server needs to reply. In REST, a resource is a set of variables as defined by the API, so the REST server needs to return a set of variables to the REST client on the left. The steps in the figure run as follows:

1. The REST server (a JAVA application) takes a copy of the stored variables in RAM (step 1) in response to the REST request.

2. The REST API code creates the REST reply and sends it over the network, placing an exact replica of what the REST server had in RAM to represent the variables in that resource.

3. The REST client (a Python application) receives the REST reply message, storing the exact same bits and bytes into its RAM, in an attempt to have a copy of the variables, data, and data structures on the server.

The process shown in Figure 18-10 does not work (and is not attempted) because the REST client programs may not store variables in the same ways. First, programs written in different languages use different conventions to store their variables internally because there is no standard for internal variable storage across languages. In fact, programs written in the same language but with different versions of that language may not store all their variables with the same internal conventions.

To overcome these issues, applications need a standard method to represent variables for transmission and storage of those variables outside the program. *Data serialization languages* provide that function.

Figure 18-11 shows the correct process flow in comparison to Figure 18-10 with the data serialization process included:

1. The server collects the internally represented data and gives it to the API code.

2. The API converts the internal representation to a data model representing those variables (with JSON shown in the figure).

3. The server sends the data model in JSON format via messages across the network.

4. The REST client takes the received data and converts the JSON-formatted data into variables in the native format of the client application.

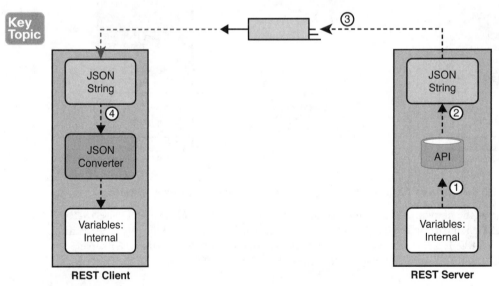

Figure 18-11 *Correct Concept: Exchanging Internal Representations of Variables*

At the end of the process, the REST client application now has equivalent variables to the ones it requested from the server in the API call. Note that the final step—to convert from the data serialization language to the native format—can be as little as a single line of code!

Finally, note that while data serialization languages like JSON enable applications to exchange variables over a network, applications can also store data in JSON format.

Data Serialization Languages

You will hear about and eventually use several data serialization and data modeling languages the more you learn about network automation. While the current CCNA blueprint mentions only JSON, learning a few facts about some of the alternatives can be helpful to add a little context to your new knowledge of JSON. These different data serialization languages exist to meet different needs that have arisen over the years. This next short section highlights four such languages.

> **NOTE** The terms *data serialization language* and *data modeling language* should be considered equivalent for the purposes of this section.

JSON

JavaScript Object Notation attempts to strike a balance between human and machine readability. Armed with a few JSON rules, most humans can read JSON data, move past simply guessing at what it means, and confidently interpret the data structures defined by the JSON data. At the same time, JSON data makes it easy for programs to convert JSON text into variables, making it very useful for data exchange between applications using APIs.

You can find the details of JSON in IETF RFC 8259 and in a number of sites found with Internet searches, including www.json.org.

XML

Back in the 1990s, when web browsers and the World Wide Web (WWW) were first created, web pages primarily used Hypertext Markup Language (HTML) to define web pages. As a markup language, HTML defined how to add the text or a web page to a file and then add "markup"—additional text to denote formatting details for the text that should be displayed. For instance, the markup included codes for headings, font types, sizes, colors, hyperlinks, and so on.

The eXtensible Markup Language (XML) came later to make some improvements for earlier markup languages. In particular, over time web pages became more and more dynamic, and to make the pages dynamic, the files needed to store variables whose values could be changed and replaced over time by the web server. To define variables to be substituted into a web page, the world needed a markup language that could define data variables. XML defines a markup language that has many features to define variables, values, and data structures.

Over time, XML has grown beyond its original use as a markup language. XML's features also make it a useful general data serialization language, and it is used as such today.

Comparing XML to JSON, both attempt to be human readable, but with XML being a little more challenging to read for the average person. For instance, like HTML, XML uses beginning and ending tags for each variable, as seen in Example 18-4. In the highlighted line in the example, the <macAddress> and </macAddress> tags denote a variable name, with the value sitting between the tags.

18

Example 18-4 *JSON Output from a REST API Call*

```
<?xml version="1.0" encoding="UTF-8"?>
<root>
   <response>
      <family>Switches and Hubs</family>
      <hostname>cat_9k_1</hostname>
      <interfaceCount>41</interfaceCount>
      <lineCardCount>2</lineCardCount>
      <macAddress>f8:7b:20:67:62:80</macAddress>
      <managementIpAddress>10.10.22.66</managementIpAddress>
      <role>ACCESS</role>
      <serialNumber>FCW2136L0AK</serialNumber>
      <series>Cisco Catalyst 9300 Series Switches</series>
      <softwareType>IOS-XE</softwareType>
      <softwareVersion>16.6.1</softwareVersion>
      <type>Cisco Catalyst 9300 Switch</type>
      <upTime>17 days, 22:51:04.26</upTime>
   </response>
</root>
```

YAML

YAML Ain't Markup Language (YAML) has a clever recursive name, but the name does tell us something. YAML does not attempt to define markup details (while XML does). Instead, YAML focuses on the data model (structure) details. YAML also strives to be clean and simple: of the data serialization/modeling languages listed here, YAML is easily the easiest to read for anyone new to data models.

Ansible, one of the topics in Chapter 19, "Understanding Ansible, Puppet, and Chef," makes extensive use of YAML files. Example 18-5 shows a brief sample. And to make the point about readability, even if you have no idea what Ansible does, you can guess at some of the functions just reading the file. (Note that YAML denotes variables in double curly brackets: {{ }}.)

Example 18-5 *YML File Used by Ansible*

```
---
# This comment line is a place to document this Playbook
- name: Get IOS Facts
  hosts: mylab
  vars:
    cli:
      host: "{{ ansible_host }}"
      username: "{{ username }}"
      password: "{{ password }}"

  tasks:
    - ios_facts:
        gather_subset: all
        provider: "{{ cli }}"
```

Summary of Data Serialization

As an easy reference, Table 18-3 summarizes the data serialization languages mentioned in this section, along with some key facts.

Table 18-3   Comparing Data Modeling Languages

Acronym	Name	Origin/Definition	Central Purpose	Common Use
JSON	JavaScript Object Notation	JavaScript (JS) language; RFC 8259	General data modeling and serialization	REST APIs
XML	eXtensible Markup Language	World Wide Web Consortium (W3C.org)	Data-focused text markup that allows data modeling	REST APIs, Web pages
YAML	YAML Ain't Markup Language	YAML.org	General data modeling	Ansible

Interpreting JSON

Cisco includes one exam topic in the current CCNA 200-301 blueprint that mentions JSON:

6.7 Interpret JSON encoded data

You can think of that skill and task with two major branches. First, even ignoring the syntax and special characters, anyone who knows the topic can probably make intelligent guesses about the meaning of many of the key:value pairs. For example, without knowing anything about JSON syntax, you could probably determine from your prior knowledge of Cisco routers and switches that the JSON in Example 18-6 lists two devices (maybe their hostnames) and a list of interfaces on each device.

Example 18-6   *Simple JSON That Lists a Router's Interfaces*

```
{
    "R1": ["GigabitEthernet0/0", "GigabitEthernet0/1", "GigabitEthernet0/2/0"],
    "R2": ["GigabitEthernet1/0", "GigabitEthernet1/1", "GigabitEthernet0/3/0"]
}
```

Honestly, you probably already know everything needed to do this kind of intelligent guessing. However, to perform the second type of task, where you analyze the JSON data to find the data structures, including objects, lists, and key:value pairs, you need to know a bit more about JSON syntax. This final topic in the chapter gives you the basic rules, with some advice on how to break down JSON data.

Interpreting JSON Key:Value Pairs

First, consider these rules about key:value pairs in JSON, which you can think of as individual variable names and their values:

- **Key:Value Pair:** Each and every colon identifies one key:value pair, with the key before the colon and the value after the colon.
- **Key:** Text, inside double quotes, before the colon, used as the name that references a value.

- **Value:** The item after the colon that represents the value of the key, which can be
  - **Text:** Listed in double quotes.
  - **Numeric:** Listed without quotes.
  - **Array:** A special value (more details later).
  - **Object:** A special value (more details later)
- **Multiple Pairs:** When listing multiple key:value pairs, separate the pairs with a comma at the end of each pair (except the last pair).

To work through some of these rules, consider Example 18-7's JSON data, focusing on the three key:value pairs. The text after the example will analyze the example.

Example 18-7 *One JSON Object (Dictionary) with Three Key:Value Pairs*

```
{
    "1stbest": "Messi",
    "2ndbest": "Ronaldo",
    "3rdbest": "Pele"
}
```

As an approach, just find each colon, and look for the quoted string just before each colon. Those are the keys ("1stbest", "2ndbest", and "3rdbest".) Then look to the right of each colon to find their matching values. You can know all three values are text values because JSON lists the values within double quotes.

As for other special characters, note the commas and the curly brackets. The first two key:value pairs end with a comma, meaning that another key:value pair should follow. The curly brackets that begin and end the JSON data denote a single JSON object (one pair of curly brackets, so one object). JSON files, and JSON data exchanged over an API, exist first as a JSON object, with an opening (left) and closing (right) curly bracket as shown.

Interpreting JSON Objects and Arrays

To communicate data structures beyond a key:value pair with a simple value, JSON uses JSON objects and JSON arrays. Objects can be somewhat flexible, but in most uses, they act like a dictionary. Arrays list a series of values.

> **NOTE** Python, the most common language to use for network automation, converts JSON objects to Python dictionaries, and JSON arrays to Python lists. For general conversation, many people refer to the JSON structures as dictionaries and lists rather than as objects and arrays.

To begin, consider this set of rules about how to interpret the syntax for JSON objects and arrays:

- **{ } - Object:** A series of key:value pairs enclosed in a matched pair of curly brackets, with an opening left curly bracket and its matching right curly bracket.
- **[ ] - Array:** A series of values (not key:value pairs) enclosed in a matched pair of square brackets, with an opening left square bracket and its matching right square bracket.

- **Key:value pairs inside objects:** All key:value pairs inside an object conform to the earlier rules for key:value pairs.
- **Values inside arrays:** All values conform to the earlier rules for formatting values (for example, double quotes around text, no quotes around numbers).

Example 18-8 shows a single array in JSON format. Notice the JSON data begins with a [and then lists three text values (the values could have been a mix of values). It then ends with a].

Example 18-8   *A JSON Snippet Showing a Single JSON Array (List)*

```
[
    "Messi",
    "Ronaldo",
    "Dybala"
]
```

While Example 18-8 shows only the array itself, JSON arrays can be used as a value in any key:value pair. Figure 18-12 does just that, shown in a graphic to allow easier highlighting of the arrays and object. The JSON text in the figure includes two arrays (lists) as values (each found just after a colon, indicating they are values).

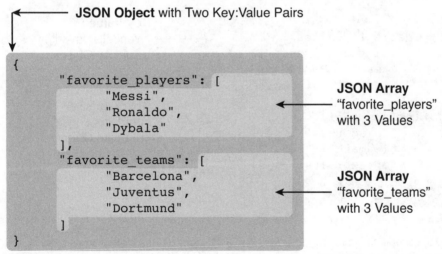

Figure 18-12   *Accurate/Complete JSON Data with One Object, Two Keys, Two JSON List Values*

Now think about the entire structure of the JSON data in Figure 18-12. It has a matched pair of curly brackets to begin and end the text, encapsulating one object. That object contains two colons, so there are two key:value pairs inside the object. When you think about the broader structure, as depicted in Figure 18-13, this JSON file has one JSON object, itself with two key:value pairs. (Note that Figure 18-13 does NOT show correct JSON syntax for the lists; it instead is intended to make sure you see the structure of the one object and its two key:value pairs.)

JSON Object

```
{
    "favorite_players": [...],          ◄─────── Key:Value

    "favorite_teams": [...]             ◄─────── Key:Value
}
```

Figure 18-13 *Structural Representation of Figure 18-13's Primary Object and Two Key:Value Pairs*

To drive home the idea of how to find JSON objects, consider the example shown in Figure 18-14. This figure shows correct JSON syntax. It has the following:

- There is one object for the entire set because it begins and ends with curly braces.
- The outer object has two keys (Wendells_favorites and interface_config).
- The value of each key:value pair is another object (each with curly braces and three key:value pairs).

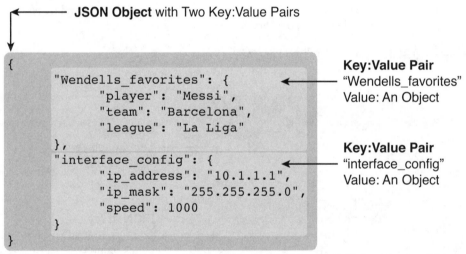

JSON Object with Two Key:Value Pairs

```
{
    "Wendells_favorites": {          ◄─────  Key:Value Pair
        "player": "Messi",                   "Wendells_favorites"
        "team": "Barcelona",                 Value: An Object
        "league": "La Liga"
    },
    "interface_config": {            ◄─────  Key:Value Pair
        "ip_address": "10.1.1.1",            "interface_config"
        "ip_mask": "255.255.255.0",          Value: An Object
        "speed": 1000
    }
}
```

Figure 18-14 *A JSON Object, with Two Key:Value Pairs, Each Value Another Object*

The JSON example in Figure 18-14 shows how JSON can nest objects and arrays; that is, JSON puts one object or array inside another. Much of the JSON output you will see as you learn more and more about network automation will include JSON data with nested arrays and objects.

Minified and Beautified JSON

So far, all the JSON examples show lots of empty space. JSON allows for whitespace, or not, depending on your needs. For humans, reading JSON can be a lot easier with the text organized with space and aligned. For instance, having the matched opening and closing brackets sit at the same left-offset makes it much easier to find which brackets go with which.

When stored in a file or sent in a network, JSON does not use whitespace. For instance, earlier in this section, Example 18-7 showed one JSON object with three key:value pairs, with whitespace, taking five lines. However, stored in a file, or sent over a network, the JSON would look like the following:

```
{"1stbest": "Messi", "2ndbest": "Ronaldo", "3rdbest": "Pele"}
```

Most of the tools you might use when working with JSON will let you toggle from a pretty format (good for humans) to a raw format (good for computers). You might see the pretty version literally called *pretty*, or *beautified*, or *spaced*, while the version with no extra whitespace might be called *minified* or *raw*.

Chapter Review

One key to doing well on the exams is to perform repetitive spaced review sessions. Review this chapter's material using either the tools in the book or interactive tools for the same material found on the book's companion website. Refer to the "Your Study Plan" element for more details. Table 18-4 outlines the key review elements and where you can find them. To better track your study progress, record when you completed these activities in the second column.

Table 18-4 Chapter Review Tracking

Review Element	Review Date(s)	Resource Used
Review key topics		Book, website
Review key terms		Book, website
Answer DIKTA questions		Book, PTP
Review memory tables		Website
Practice Editing JSON		Website

Review All the Key Topics

Table 18-5 Key Topics for Chapter 18

Key Topic Element	Description	Page Number
List	Attributes of REST APIs	409
List	The meaning of the CRUD acronym	413
Table 18-2	A comparison of CRUD actions and HTTP verbs	414
Figure 18-8	Components of a URI	416
Figure 18-11	The process of sending JSON data over a REST API	420
Table 18-3	A comparison of JSON, XML, and YAML	423
List	JSON rules related to key:value pairs	423
List	JSON rules for arrays and objects	424

Key Terms You Should Know

REpresentational State Transfer (REST), REST API, stateless, cacheable, CRUD, list variable, dictionary variable, URI path (resource), URI query (parameters), key:value pair, data serialization language, JSON (JavaScript Object Notation), XML (eXtensible Markup Language), YAML (YAML Ain't Markup Language), JSON object, JSON array

CHAPTER 19

Understanding Ansible, Puppet, and Chef

This chapter covers the following exam topics:

6.0 Automation and Programmability

6.6 Recognize the capabilities of configuration mechanisms Puppet, Chef, and Ansible

By now, you have seen how to use the IOS CLI to configure routers and switches. To configure using the CLI, you get into configuration mode, issue configuration commands (which change the running-config file), and eventually leave configuration mode. If you decide to keep those changes, you save the configuration to the startup-config file using the **copy running-config startup-config** command. Next time the router or switch boots, the device loads the startup-config file into RAM as the running-config. Simple enough.

This chapter discusses tools for configuration management that replaces that per-device configuration process. To even imagine what these tools do first requires you to make a leap of imagination to the everyday world of a network engineer at a medium to large enterprise. In a real working network, managing the configuration of the many networking devices creates challenges. Those challenges can be addressed using that same old "use configuration mode on each device" process, plus with hard work, attention to detail, and good operational practices. However, that manual per-device process becomes more and more difficult for a variety of reasons, so at some point, enterprises turn to automated configuration management tools to provide better results.

The first section of this chapter takes a generalized look at the issues of configuration management at scale along with some of the solutions to those problems. The second major section then details each of three configuration management tools—Ansible, Puppet, and Chef—to define some of the features and terms used with each. By the end of the chapter, you should be able to see some of the reasons why these automated configuration management tools have a role in modern networks and enough context to understand as you pick one to investigate for further reading.

"Do I Know This Already?" Quiz

Take the quiz (either here or use the PTP software) if you want to use the score to help you decide how much time to spend on this chapter. The letter answers are listed at the bottom of the page following the quiz. Appendix C, found both at the end of the book as well as on the companion website, includes both the answers and explanations. You can also find both answers and explanations in the PTP testing software.

Table 19-1 "Do I Know This Already?" Foundation Topics Section-to-Question Mapping

Foundation Topics Section	Questions
Device Configuration Challenges and Solutions	1–3
Ansible, Puppet, and Chef Basics	4, 5

1. Which answer best describes the meaning of the term *configuration drift*?

    a. Changes to a single device's configuration over time versus that single device's original configuration

    b. Larger and larger sections of unnecessary configuration in a device

    c. Changes to a single device's configuration over time versus other devices that have the same role

    d. Differences in device configuration versus a centralized backup copy

2. An enterprise moves away from manual configuration methods, making changes by editing centralized configuration files. Which answers list an issue solved by using a version control system with those centralized files? (Choose two answers.)

    a. The ability to find which engineer changed the central configuration file on a date/time

    b. The ability to find the details of what changed in the configuration file over time

    c. The ability to use a template with per-device variables to create configurations

    d. The ability to recognize configuration drift in a device and notify the staff

3. Configuration monitoring (also called configuration enforcement) by a configuration management tool generally solves which problem?

    a. Tracking the identity of individuals who changed files, along with which files they changed

    b. Listing differences between a former and current configuration

    c. Testing a configuration change to determine whether it will be rejected or not when implemented

    d. Finding instances of configuration drift

4. Which of the following configuration management tools uses a push model to configure network devices?

    a. Ansible

    b. Puppet

    c. Chef

    d. None use a push model

5. Which of the following answers list a correct combination of configuration management tool and the term used for one of its primary configuration files? (Choose two answers.)

   a. Ansible manifest

   b. Puppet manifest

   c. Chef recipe

   d. Ansible recipe

Foundation Topics

Device Configuration Challenges and Solutions

Think about any production network. What defines the exact intended configuration of each device in a production network? Is it the running-config as it exists right now or the startup-config before any recent changes were made or the startup-config from last month? Could one engineer change the device configuration so that it drifts away from that ideal, with the rest of the staff not knowing? What process, if any, might discover the configuration drift? And even with changes agreed upon by all, how do you know who changed the configuration, when, and specifically what changed?

Traditionally, CCNA teaches us how to configure one device using the **configure terminal** command to reach configuration mode, which changes the running-config file, and how to save that running-config file to the startup-config file. That manual process provides no means to answer any of the legitimate questions posed in the first paragraph; however, for many enterprises, those questions (and others) need answers, both consistent and accurate.

Not every company reaches the size to want to do something more with configuration management. Companies with one network engineer might do well enough managing device configurations, especially if the network device configurations do not change often. However, as a company moves to multiple network engineers and grows the numbers of devices and types of devices, with higher rates of configuration change, manual configuration management has problems.

This section begins by discussing a few of these kinds of configuration management issues so that you begin to understand why enterprises need more than good people and good practices to deal with device configuration. The rest of the section then details some of the features you can find in automated configuration management tools.

Configuration Drift

Consider the story of an enterprise of a size to need two network engineers, Alice and Bob. They both have experience and work well together. But the network configurations have grown beyond what any one person can know from memory, and with two network engineers, they may remember different details or even disagree on occasion.

One night at 1 a.m., Bob gets a call about an issue. He gets into the network from his laptop and resolves the problem with a small configuration change to branch office router BR22. Alice, the senior engineer, gets a different 4 a.m. call about another issue and makes a change to branch office router BR33.

The next day gets busy, and neither Alice nor Bob mentions the changes they made. They both follow procedures and document the changes in their change management system, which lists the details of every change. But they both get busy, the topic never comes up, and neither mentions the changes to each for months.

The story shows how configuration drift can occur—an effect in which the configuration drifts away from the intended configuration over time. Alice and Bob probably agree to what a standard branch office router configuration ought to look like, but they both made an exception to that configuration to fix a problem, causing configuration drift. Figure 19-1 shows the basic idea, with those two branch routers now with slightly different configurations than the other branch routers.

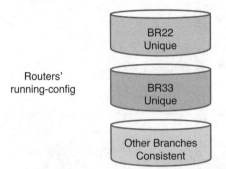

Routers' running-config

Figure 19-1 *Configuration Drift in Branch Routers BR22 and BR33*

Configuration drift becomes a much bigger problem if using only traditional manual configuration tools. For instance:

- The on-device manual configuration process does not track change history: which lines changed, what changed on each line, what old configuration was removed, who changed the configuration, when each change was made.

- External systems used by good systems management processes, like trouble ticketing and change management software, may record details. However, those sit outside the configuration and require analysis to figure out what changed. They also rely on humans to follow the operational processes consistently and correctly; otherwise, an engineer cannot find the entire history of changes to a configuration.

- Referring to historical data in change management systems works poorly if a device has gone through multiple configuration changes over a period of time.

Centralized Configuration Files and Version Control

The manual per-device configuration model makes great sense for one person managing one device. With that model, the one network engineer can use the on-device startup-config as the intended ideal configuration. If a change is needed, the engineer gets into configuration mode and updates the running-config until happy with the change. Then the engineer saves a copy to startup-config as the now-current ideal config for the device.

The per-device manual configuration model does not work as well for larger networks, with hundreds or even thousands of network devices, with multiple network engineers. For instance, if the team thinks of the startup-config of each device as the ideal configuration, if one team member changes the configuration (like Alice and Bob each did in the earlier story), no records exist about the change. The config file does not show what changed, when it changed, or who changed it, and the process does not notify the entire team about the change.

As a first step toward better configuration management, many medium to large enterprises store configurations in a central location. At first, storing files centrally may be a simple effort to keep backup copies of each device's configuration. They would, of course, place the files in a shared folder accessible to the entire network team, as shown in Figure 19-2.

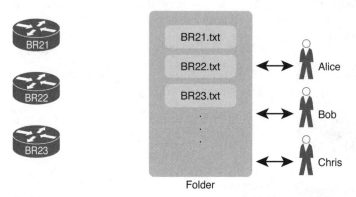

Figure 19-2 *Copying Device Configurations to a Central Location*

Which configuration file is the single source of truth in this model? The configuration files still exist on each device, but now they also exist on a centralized server, and engineers could change the on-device configuration as well as the text files on the server. For instance, if the copy of BR21's configuration on the device differs from the file on the centralized server, which should be considered as correct, ideal, the truth about what the team intends for this device?

In practice, companies take both approaches. In some cases, companies continue to use the on-device configuration files as the source of truth, with the centralized configuration files treated as backup copies in case the device fails and must be replaced. However, other enterprises make the transition to treat the files on the server as the single source of truth about each device's configuration. When using the centralized file as the source of truth, the engineers can take advantage of many configuration management tools and actually manage the configurations more easily and with more accuracy.

For example, configuration management tools use version control software to track the changes to centralized configuration files, noting who changes a file, what lines and specific characters changed, when the change occurred, and so on. The tools also allow you to compare the differences between versions of the files over time, as shown in Figure 19-3.

Answers to the "Do I Know This Already?" quiz:

1 C **2** A, B **3** D **4** A **5** B, C

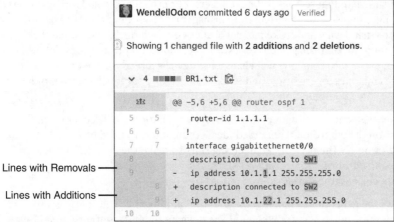

Lines with Removals ──

Lines with Additions ──

Figure 19-3 *Showing File Differences in GitHub*

The figure shows a sample of a comparison between two versions of a configuration file. The upper two highlighted lines, with the minus signs, show the lines that were changed, while the two lower highlighted lines, with the plus signs, show the new versions of each line.

Version control software solves many of the problems with the lack of change tracking within the devices themselves. Figure 19-3 shows output from a popular software-as-a-service site called GitHub (www.github.com). GitHub offers free and paid accounts, and it uses open-source software (Git) to perform the version control functions.

Configuration Monitoring and Enforcement

With a version control system and a convention of storing the configuration files in a central location, a network team can do a much better job of tracking changes and answering the who, what, and when of knowing what changed in every device's configuration. However, using that model then introduces other challenges—challenges that can be best solved by also using an automated configuration management tool.

With this new model, engineers should make changes by editing the associated configuration files in the centralized repository. The configuration management tool can then be directed to copy or apply the configuration to the device, as shown in Figure 19-4. After that process completes, the central config file and the device's running-config (and startup-config) should be identical.

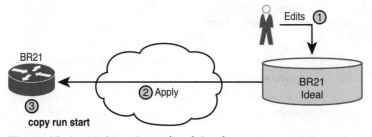

Figure 19-4 *Pushing Centralized Configuration to a Remote Device*

19

Using the model shown in Figure 19-4 still has dangers. For instance, the network engineers should make changes by using the configuration management tools, but they still have the ability to log in to each device and make manual changes on each device. So, while the idea of using a configuration management tool with a centralized repository of config files sounds appealing, eventually someone will change the devices directly. Former correct configuration changes might be overwritten, and made incorrect, by future changes. In other words, eventually, some configuration drift can occur.

Configuration management tools can monitor device configurations to discover when the device configuration differs from the intended ideal configuration, and then either reconfigure the device or notify the network engineering staff to make the change. This feature might be called *configuration monitoring* or *configuration enforcement*, particularly if the tool automatically changes the device configuration.

Figure 19-5 shows the general idea behind configuration monitoring. The automated configuration management software asks for a copy of the device's running-config file, as shown in steps 1 and 2. At step 3, the config management software compares the ideal config file with the just-arrived running-config file to check whether they have any differences (configuration drift). Per the configuration of the tool, it either fixes the configuration or notifies the staff about the configuration drift.

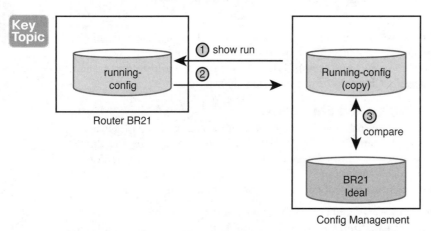

Config Management

Figure 19-5 *Configuration Monitoring*

Configuration Provisioning

Configuration provisioning refers to how to provision or deploy changes to the configuration once made by changing files in the configuration management system. As one of the primary functions of a configuration management tool, you would likely see features like these:

- The core function to implement configuration changes in one device after someone has edited the device's centralized configuration file
- The ability to choose which subset of devices to configure: all devices, types with a given attribute (such as those of a particular role), or just one device, based on attributes and logic

■ The ability to determine if each change was accepted or rejected, and to use logic to react differently in each case depending on the result

■ For each change, the ability to revert to the original configuration if even one configuration command is rejected on a device

■ The ability to validate the change now (without actually making the change) to determine whether the change will work or not when attempted

■ The ability to check the configuration after the process completes to confirm that the configuration management tool's intended configuration does match the device's configuration

■ The ability to use logic to choose whether to save the running-config to startup-config or not

■ The ability to represent configuration files as templates and variables so that devices with similar roles can use the same template but with different values

■ The ability to store the logic steps in a file, scheduled to execute, so that the changes can be implemented by the automation tool without the engineer being present

The list could go further, but these features outline some of the major features included in all of the configuration management tools discussed in this chapter. Most of the items in the list revolve around editing the central configuration file for a device. However, the tools have many more features, so you have more work to do to plan and implement how they work. The next few pages focus on giving a few more details about the last two items in the list.

Configuration Templates and Variables

Think about the roles filled by networking devices in an enterprise. Focusing on routers for a moment, routers often connect to both the WAN and one or more LANs. You might have a small number of larger routers connected to the WAN at large sites, with enough power to handle larger packet rates. Smaller sites, like branch offices, might have small routers, maybe with a single WAN interface and a single LAN interface; however, you might have a large number of those small branch routers in the network.

For any set of devices in the same role, the configurations are likely similar. For instance, a set of branch office routers might all have the exact same configuration for some IP services, like NTP or SNMP. If using OSPF interface configuration, routers in the same OSPF area and with identical interface IDs could have identical OSPF configuration.

For instance, Example 19-1 shows a configuration excerpt from a branch router, with the unique parts of the configuration highlighted. All the unhighlighted portions could be the same on all the other branch office routers of the same model (with the same interface numbers). An enterprise might have dozens or hundreds of branch routers with nearly identical configuration.

Example 19-1 *Router BR1 Configuration, with Unique Values Highlighted*

```
hostname BR1
!
interface GigabitEthernet0/0
 ip address 10.1.1.1 255.255.255.0
 ip ospf 1 area 11
```

```
!
interface GigabitEthernet0/1
!
interface GigabitEthernet0/1/0
 ip address 10.1.12.1 255.255.255.0
 ip ospf 1 area 11
!
router ospf 1
 router-id 1.1.1.1
```

Configuration management tools can separate the components of a configuration into the parts in common to all devices in that role (the template) versus the parts unique to any one device (the variables). Engineers can then edit the standard template file for a device role as a separate file than each device's variable file. The configuration management tool can then process the template and variables to create the ideal configuration file for each device, as shown in Figure 19-6, which shows the configuration files being built for branch routers BR21, BR22, and BR23.

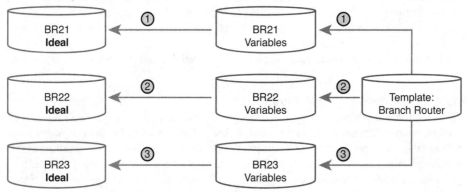

Figure 19-6 *Concept: Configuration Templates and Variables*

To give a little more insight, Example 19-2 shows a template file that could be used by Ansible for the configuration shown in Example 19-1. Each tool specifies what language to use for each type of file, with Ansible using the Jinja2 language for templates. The template mimics the configuration in Example 19-1, except for placing variable names inside sets of double curly brackets.

Example 19-2 *Jinja2 Template with Variables Based on Example 19-1*

```
hostname {{hostname}}
!
interface GigabitEthernet0/0
 ip address {{address1}} {{mask1}}
 ip ospf {{OSPF_PID}} area {{area}}
!
interface GigabitEthernet0/1
!
interface GigabitEthernet0/1/0
```

```
 ip address {{address2}} {{mask2}}
 ip ospf {{OSPF_PID}} area {{area}}
 !
router ospf {{OSPF_PID}}
 router-id {{RID}}
```

To supply the values for a device, Ansible calls for defining variable files using YAML, as shown in Example 19-3. The file shows the syntax for defining the variables shown in the complete configuration in Example 19-1, but now defined as variables.

Example 19-3 *YAML Variables File Based on Example 19-2*

```
---
hostname: BR1
address1: 10.1.1.1
mask1: 255.255.255.0
address2: 10.1.12.1
mask2: 255.255.255.0
RID: 1.1.1.1
area: '11'
OSPF_PID: '1'
```

19

The configuration management system processes a template plus all related variables to produce the intended configuration for a device. For instance, the engineer would create and edit one template file that looks like Example 19-2 and then create and edit one variable file like Example 19-3 for each branch office router. Ansible would process the files to create complete configuration files like the text shown in Example 19-1.

It might seem like extra work to separate configurations into a template and variables, but using templates has some big advantages. In particular:

- Templates increase the focus on having a standard configuration for each device role, helping to avoid snowflakes (uniquely configured devices).

- New devices with an existing role can be deployed easily by simply copying an existing per-device variable file and changing the values.

- Templates allow for easier troubleshooting because troubleshooting issues with one standard template should find and fix issues with all devices that use the same template.

- Tracking the file versions for the template versus the variables files allows for easier troubleshooting as well. Issues with a device can be investigated to find changes in the device's settings separately from the standard configuration template.

Files That Control Configuration Automation

Configuration management tools also provide different methods to define logic and processes that tell the tool what changes to make, to which devices, and when. For instance, an engineer could direct a tool to make changes during a weekend change window. That same logic could specify a subset of the devices. It could also detail steps to verify the change before and after the change is attempted, and how to notify the engineers if an issue occurs.

Interestingly, you can do a lot of the logic without knowing how to program. Each tool uses a language of some kind that engineers use to define the action steps, often a language defined by that company (a domain-specific language). But they make the languages to be straightforward, and they are generally mush easier to learn than programming languages. Configuration management tools also enable you to extend the action steps beyond what can be done in the toolset by using a general programming language. Figure 19-7 summarizes the files you could see in any of the configuration management tools.

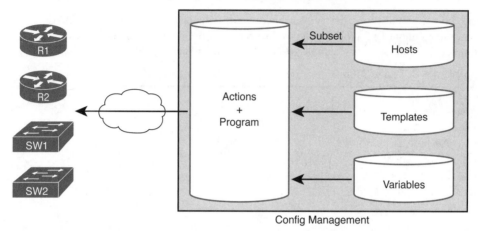

Figure 19-7 *Important Files Used by Configuration Management Tools*

Ansible, Puppet, and Chef Basics

This chapter focuses on one exam topic that asks about the capabilities of three configuration management tools: Ansible, Puppet, and Chef. The first major section of the chapter describes the capabilities of all three (and other) configuration management tools. This second major section examines a few of the features of each tool, focusing on terminology and major capabilities.

Ansible, Puppet, and Chef are software packages. You can purchase each tool, with variations on which package. However, they all also have different free options that allow you to download and learn about the tools, although you might need to run a Linux guest because some of the tools do not run in a Windows OS.

As for the names, most people use the words *Ansible*, *Puppet*, and *Chef* to refer to the companies as well as their primary configuration management products. All three emerged as part of the transition from hardware-based servers to virtualized servers, which greatly increased the number of servers and created the need for software automation to create, configure, and remove VMs. All three produce one or more configuration management software products that have become synonymous with their companies in many ways. (This chapter follows that convention, for the most part ignoring exact product names, and referring to products and software simply as Ansible, Puppet, and Chef.)

Next, on to some details about each.

Ansible

To use Ansible (www.ansible.com), you need to install Ansible on some computer: Mac, Linux, or a Linux VM on a Windows host. You can use the free open-source version or use the paid Ansible Tower server version.

Once it is installed, you create several text files, such as the following:

- **Playbooks:** These files provide actions and logic about what Ansible should do.
- **Inventory:** These files provide device hostnames along with information about each device, like device roles, so Ansible can perform functions for subsets of the inventory
- **Templates:** Using Jinja2 language, the templates represent a device's configuration but with variables (see Example 19-2).
- **Variables:** Using YAML, a file can list variables that Ansible will substitute into templates (see Example 19-3).

As far as how Ansible works for managing network devices, it uses an agentless architecture. That means Ansible does not rely on any code (agent) running on the network device. Instead, Ansible relies on features typical in network devices, namely SSH and/or NETCONF, to make changes and extract information. When using SSH, the Ansible control node actually makes changes to the device like any other SSH user would do, but doing the work with Ansible code, rather than with a human.

Ansible can be described as using a push model (per Figure 19-8) rather than a pull model (like Puppet and Chef). After installing Ansible, an engineer needs to create and edit all the various Ansible files, including an Ansible playbook. Then the engineer runs the playbook, which tells Ansible to perform the steps. Those steps can include configuring one or more devices per the various files (step 3), with the control node seen as pushing the configuration to the device.

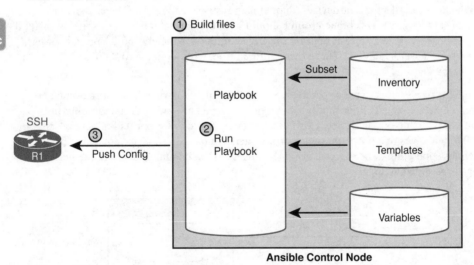

Figure 19-8 *Ansible Push Model*

As with all the tools, Ansible can do both configuration provisioning (configuring devices after changes are made in the files) and configuration monitoring (checking to find out whether the device config matches the ideal configuration on the control node). However, Ansible's architecture more naturally fits with configuration provisioning, as seen in the figure. To do configuration monitoring, Ansible uses logic modules that detect and list configuration differences, after which the playbook defines what action to take (reconfigure or notify).

Puppet

To use Puppet (www.puppet.com), like Ansible, begin by installing Puppet on a Linux host. You can install it on your own Linux host, but for production purposes, you will normally install it on a Linux server called a Puppet master. As with Ansible, you can use a free open-source version with paid versions available. You can get started learning Puppet without a separate server for learning and testing.

Once installed, Puppet also uses several important text files with different components, such as the following:

- **Manifest:** This is a human-readable text file on the Puppet master, using a language defined by Puppet, used to define the desired configuration state of a device.

- **Resource, Class, Module:** These terms refer to components of the manifest, with the largest component (module) being composed of smaller classes, which are in turn composed of resources.

- **Templates:** Using a Puppet domain-specific language, these files allow Puppet to generate manifests (and modules, classes, and resources) by substituting variables into the template.

One way to think about the differences between Ansible's versus Puppet's approach is that Ansible's playbooks use an imperative language, whereas Puppet uses a declarative language. For instance, with Ansible, the playbook will list tasks and choices based on those results, like "Configure all branch routers in these locations, and if errors occur for any device, do these extra tasks for that device." Puppet manifests instead declare the end state that a device should have: "This branch router should have the configuration in this file by the end of the process." The manifest, built by the engineer, defines the end state, and Puppet has the job to cause the device to have that configuration, without being told the specific set of steps to take.

Puppet typically uses an agent-based architecture for network device support. Some network devices enable Puppet support via an on-device agent—think of it as another feature configurable on the device. However, not every Cisco OS supports Puppet agents, so Puppet solves that problem using a proxy agent running on some external host (called agentless operation). The external agent then uses SSH to communicate with the network device, as shown in Figure 19-9.

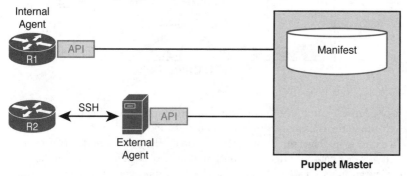

Figure 19-9 *Agent-based and Agentless Operation for Puppet*

> **NOTE** Per Puppet's website, Puppet supports both an agent-based and agentless architecture, with the agentless architecture being the case of using an agent external to the network device, as shown in the lower part of Figure 19-9.

Armed with a manifest that declares something like "This device should have this configuration state," Puppet uses a pull model to make that configuration appear in the device, as shown in Figure 19-10. Once installed, these steps occur:

Step 1. The engineer creates and edits all the files on the Puppet server.

Step 2. The engineer configures and enables the on-device agent or a proxy agent for each device.

Step 3. The agent pulls manifest details from the server, which tells the agent what its configuration should be.

Step 4. If the agent device's configuration should be updated, the Puppet agent performs additional pulls to get all required detail, with the agent updating the device configuration.

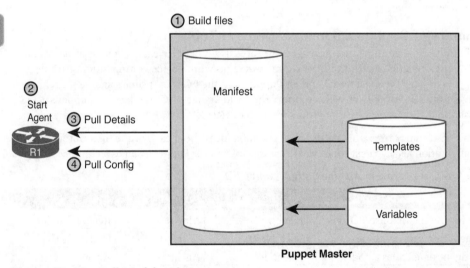

Figure 19-10 *Pull Model with Puppet*

Chef

Chef (www.chef.io), as with Ansible and Puppet, exists as software packages you install and run. Chef (the company) offers several products, with Chef Automate being the product that most people refer to simply as Chef. As with Puppet, in production you probably run Chef as a server (called server-client mode), with multiple Chef workstations used by the engineering staff to build Chef files that are stored on the Chef server. However, you can also run Chef in standalone mode (called Chef Zero), which is helpful when you're just getting started and learning in the lab.

Once Chef is installed, you create several text files with different components, like the following:

■ **Resource:** The configuration objects whose state is managed by Chef; for instance, a set of configuration commands for a network device—analogous to the ingredients in a recipe in a cookbook

■ **Recipe:** The Chef logic applied to resources to determine when, how, and whether to act against the resources—analogous to a recipe in a cookbook

■ **Cookbooks:** A set of recipes about the same kinds of work, grouped together for easier management and sharing

■ **Runlist:** An ordered list of recipes that should be run against a given device

Chef uses an architecture similar to Puppet. For network devices, each managed device (called a Chef node or Chef client) runs an agent. The agent performs configuration monitoring in that the client pulls recipes and resources from the Chef server and then adjusts its configuration to stay in sync with the details in those recipes and runlists. Note however that Chef requires on-device Chef client code, and many Cisco devices do not support a Chef client, so you will likely see more use of Ansible and Puppet for Cisco device configuration management.

Summary of Configuration Management Tools

All three of the configuration management tools listed here have a good base of users and different strengths. As for their use for managing network device configuration, Ansible appears to have the most interest, then Puppet, and then Chef. Ansible's agentless architecture and the use of SSH provides support for a wide range of Cisco devices. Puppet's agentless model also creates wide support for Cisco devices.

Table 19-2 summarizes a few of the most common ideas about each of the three automated configuration management tools. Note that the column for Puppet assumes an on-device agent.

Table 19-2 *Comparing Ansible, Puppet, and Chef*

Action	Ansible	Puppet	Chef
Term for the file that lists actions	Playbook	Manifest	Recipe, Runlist
Protocol to network device	SSH, NETCONF	HTTP (REST)	HTTP (REST)
Uses agent or agentless model	Agentless	Agent*	Agent
Push or pull model	Push	Pull	Pull

* Puppet can use an in-device agent or an external proxy agent for network devices.

Chapter Review

One key to doing well on the exams is to perform repetitive spaced review sessions. Review this chapter's material using either the tools in the book or interactive tools for the same material found on the book's companion website. Refer to the "Your Study Plan" element for more details. Table 19-3 outlines the key review elements and where you can find them. To better track your study progress, record when you completed these activities in the second column.

Table 19-3 Chapter Review Tracking

Review Element	Review Date(s)	Resource Used
Review key topics		Book, website
Review key terms		Book, website
Repeat DIKTA questions		Book, PTP
Review memory table		Book, website
Do DevNet Labs		DevNet

Review All the Key Topics

Table 19-4 Key Topics for Chapter 19

Key Topic Element	Description	Page Number
List	Issues that arise from configuration drift	431
Figure 19-3	Sample of showing router configuration file differences with GitHub	433
Figure 19-5	Basic configuration monitoring concepts.	434
List	Primary functions of a configuration management tool	434
Example 19-2	Sample Jinja2 Ansible template	436
List	Advantages of using configuration templates	437
Figure 19-8	Ansible's push model and other features	439
Figure 19-10	Puppet's pull model and other features	441
Table 19-2	Summary of configuration management features and terms	442

Key Terms You Should Know

configuration monitoring, configuration provisioning, configuration drift, configuration management tool, Git, Ansible, Puppet, Chef, configuration template, push model, pull model, agent-based architecture, agentless architecture, Ansible playbook, Puppet manifest, Chef recipe

Do DevNet Labs

Cisco's DevNet site (https://developer.cisco.com)—a free site—includes lab environments and exercises. You can learn a lot about configuration management and Ansible in particular with a few of the lab tracks on the DevNet site (at the time this book was published). Refer to the "Chapter Review" section of the companion website for links to some good labs, or just go to https://developer.cisco.com and search for learning labs about Ansible.

19

Part V Review

Keep track of your part review progress with the checklist shown in Table P5-1. Details on each task follow the table.

Table P5-1   Part V Review Checklist

Activity	1st Date Completed	2nd Date Completed
Repeat All DIKTA Questions		
Answer Part Review Questions		
Review Key Topics		

Repeat All DIKTA Questions

For this task, use the PTP software to answer the "Do I Know This Already?" questions again for the chapters in this part of the book.

Answer Part Review Questions

For this task, use PTP to answer the Part Review questions for this part of the book.

Review Key Topics

Review all key topics in all chapters in this part, either by browsing the chapters or by using the Key Topics application on the companion website.

Part VI

Final Review

Chapter 20: Final Review

CHAPTER 20

Final Review

Congratulations! You made it through the book, and now it's time to finish getting ready for the exam. This chapter helps you get ready to take and pass the exam in two ways.

First, this chapter focuses on the exam event. Now you need to think about what happens during the exam and what you need to do in these last few weeks before taking the exam. At this point, everything you do should be focused on getting ready to pass so that you can finish up this hefty task.

The second section of this chapter focuses on final content review. You should not just complete the previous chapter, which is the 48th technology chapter in the combined *CCNA 200-301 Official Cert Guide, Volume 1 and 2* books. Instead, you need to review, refine, deepen, and assess your skills. This second section of this chapter gives advice and suggestions on how to approach your final weeks of study before you take the CCNA 200-301 exam.

Advice About the Exam Event

Now that you have finished the bulk of this book, you could just register for your Cisco CCNA exam, show up, and take the exam. However, if you spend a little time thinking about the exam event itself, learning more about the user interface of the real Cisco exams and the environment at the Pearson VUE testing centers, you will be better prepared, particularly if this is your first Cisco exam.

This first of two major sections in this chapter gives some advice about the Cisco exams and the exam event itself, specifically about

- Question types
- Your time budget
- A sample time-check method
- The final week
- The 24 hours before the exam
- The final 30 minutes before the exam
- The hour after the exam

Exam Event: Learn About Question Types

In the weeks leading up to your exam, you should think more about the different types of exam questions and have a plan for how to approach those questions. One of the best ways to learn about the exam questions is to use some videos from the former Cisco Certification Exam Tutorial.

As for the backstory, Cisco formerly published a tool (the Cisco Certification Exam Tutorial) that gave anyone the ability to experience the Cisco exam user interface via an interactive flash application. Cisco has updated the real exam interface; plus, Cisco removed the exam tutorial web pages with no equivalent replacement.

However, Cisco did make videos of the exam tutorial, with someone talking through the various question types. Cisco lists the videos in a post at the Cisco Learning Network (https://learningnetwork.cisco.com), so you can start by looking for those videos as follows:

- Go to the CLN (https://learningnetwork.cisco.com) and search for the post 34312.
- Use this direct link to the same page: https://learningnetwork.cisco.com/docs/DOC-34312?dtid=osscdc000283.
- Use https://blog.certskills.com/final-review, which links to a blog post of mine that lists the above link (as well as other links useful for final review).

While watching any of the videos about the exam tutorial, pay close attention to some important behaviors. For instance, for multichoice questions, the user interface

- Identifies single-answer questions with circles beside the answers versus multiple-answer questions showing squares before the answers.
- Prevents you from choosing too many answers.
- Supplies a popup window to tell you if you have selected too few answers if you try to move to the next question, so you can stop and go back and answer with the correct number of answers.
- Does not penalize you for guessing. You should always supply the number of answers that the question asks for. There is no penalty for guessing.

Note that because there is no penalty for guessing, you should always answer every question and answer with the exact number of correct answers.

For drag-and-drop questions, the user interface lets you change your mind while you are still working on the question. The draggable items begin in one location, and you drag and drop them to answer. You can just drag them back to where they were to begin the question.

For simulation questions:

- Pay close attention to the navigation to get to the command-line interface (CLI) on one of the routers. To do so, you have to click the PC icon for a PC connected to the router console; the console cable appears as a dashed line, whereas network cables are solid lines. (You should definitely look for this interaction in the exam tutorial videos.)
- Make sure that you look at the scroll areas at the top, at the side, and in the terminal emulator window. These scrollbars let you view the entire question and scenario.
- Make sure that you can toggle between the topology window and the terminal emulator window by clicking **Show topology** and **Hide topology**. The question window can be pretty crowded for sim questions, so the user interface gives you the means to toggle between seeing different parts of the question.

Both simlet and testlet questions give you one scenario with a group of related multichoice questions. However, the behavior with this small group (usually three or four) of multiple-choice questions differs from the flow of the more common standalone multiple-choice questions. In particular:

■ You can move between the multiple-choice questions in a single simlet or testlet. You can answer one multiple-choice question, move to the second and answer it, and then move back to the first question, confirming that inside a testlet you can move around between questions.

■ You can make a big mistake by not answering all questions or by not supplying enough answers, and the user interface does not prevent you from making that mistake.

On that second point, consider this scenario with a simlet question. You see the simlet question, answer the first three multichoice questions, but forget to look at the fourth multichoice question. If you click **Next**, you will see a generic popup window that Cisco uses as a prompt to ask whether you want to move on. However, it does not tell you that you did not answer a question at all, and it does not tell you if you answered with too few answers on a multi-answer question. **So be very careful when clicking *Next* when answering simlet and testlet questions.**

Exam Event: Think About Your Time Budget

On exam day, you need to keep an eye on your speed. Going too slowly hurts you because you might not have time to answer all the questions. Going too fast can be hurtful if you are rushing because you are fearful about running out of time. So, you need to be able to somehow know whether you are moving quickly enough to answer all the questions, while not rushing.

The exam user interface shows some useful information, namely a countdown timer and a question counter. The question counter shows a question number for the question you are answering, and it shows the total number of questions on your exam.

Unfortunately, some questions require lots more time than others, and for this and other reasons, time estimating can be a challenge.

First, before you show up to take the exam, you know only a range of the number of questions for the exam; for example, the Cisco website might list the CCNA exam as having from 50 to 60 questions (the Cisco website did not list a number of questions at the time this chapter was published). You will not know how many questions are on your exam until the exam begins, when you go through the screens that lead up to the point where you click **Start Exam**, which starts your timed exam.

Next, some questions (call them *time burners*) clearly take a lot more time to answer:

Normal-time questions: Multiple-choice and drag-and-drop, approximately one minute each

Time burners: Sims, simlets, and testlets, approximately six to eight minutes each

Finally, even though testlet and simlet questions contain several multiple-choice questions, the exam software counts each testlet and simlet question as one question in the question counter. For example, if a testlet question has four embedded multiple-choice questions, in the exam software's question counter, that counts as one question. So when you start the exam, you might see that you will have 50 questions, but you don't know how many of those are time burners.

> **NOTE** Cisco does not tell us why one person taking the exam might get 50 questions while someone else taking the same exam might get 60 questions, but it seems reasonable to think that the person with 50 questions might have a few more of the time burners, making the two exams equivalent.

You need a plan for how you will check your time, a plan that does not distract you from the exam. You can ponder the facts listed here and come up with your own plan. If you want a little more guidance, the next topic shows one way to check your time that uses some simple math so that it does not take much time away from the test.

Exam Event: A Sample Time-Check Method

As a suggestion, you can use the following math to do your time-check in a way that weights the time based on those time-burner questions. You do not have to use this method. But this math uses only addition of whole numbers, to keep it simple. It gives you a pretty close time estimate, in my opinion.

The concept is simple. Just do a simple calculation that estimates the time you should have used so far. Here's the math:

> **Number of questions answered so far + 7 per time burner answered so far**

Then you check the timer to figure out how much time you have spent:

- **You have used exactly that much time or a little more time:** Your timing is perfect.
- **You have used less time:** You are ahead of schedule.
- **You have used noticeably more time:** You are behind schedule.

For example, if you have already finished 17 questions, two of which were time burners, your time estimate is $17 + 7 + 7 = 31$ minutes. If your actual time is also 31 minutes, or maybe 32 or 33 minutes, you are right on schedule. If you have spent less than 31 minutes, you are ahead of schedule.

So, the math is pretty easy: questions answered, plus 7 per time burner, is the guesstimate of how long you should have taken so far if you are right on time.

> **NOTE** This math is an estimate; I make no guarantees that the math will be an accurate predictor on every exam.

Exam Event: One Week Away

I have listed a variety of tips in the next few pages, broken down by timing versus the big exam event. First, this section discusses some items to consider when your exam is about a week away:

- **Get some earplugs:** Testing centers often have some, but if you do not want to chance it, come prepared with your own. (They will not let you bring your own noise-canceling headphones into the room if they follow the rules disallowing any user electronic devices in the room, so think low-tech disposable earplugs, or even bring a cotton ball.) The testing center is typically one room within a building of a company that does something else as well, often a training center, and almost certainly you will share the room with other test takers coming and going. So, there are people talking in nearby rooms and other office noises. Earplugs can help.

- **Create an exam-event note-taking plan:** Some people like to spend the first minute of the exam writing down some notes for reference, before actually starting the exam. For example, maybe you want to write down the table of magic numbers for finding IPv4 subnet IDs. If you plan to do that, practice making those notes between now and exam day. Before each practice exam, transcribe those lists, just like you expect to do at the real exam.

- **Plan your travel to the testing center:** Leave enough time in your schedule so that you will not be rushing to make it just in time.

- **Practice your favorite relaxation techniques for a few minutes before each practice exam:** That way you can enter the exam event and be more relaxed and have more success.

Exam Event: 24 Hours Before the Exam

After you wake up on the big day, what should you be doing and thinking? Certainly, the better prepared you are, the better chances you have on the exam. But these small tips can help you do your best on exam day:

- Rest the night before the exam rather than staying up late to study. Clarity of thought is more important than one extra fact, especially because the exam requires so much analyzing and thinking rather than just remembering facts.

- Bring as few extra items with you as possible when leaving for the exam center. You may bring personal effects into the building and testing company's space, but not into the actual room in which you take the exam. So, save a little stress and bring as little extra stuff with you as possible. If you have a safe place to leave briefcases, purses, electronics, and so on, leave them there. However, the testing center should have a place to store your things as well. Simply put, the less you bring, the less you have to worry about storing. (For example, I have been asked to remove even my analog wristwatch on more than one occasion.)

- Plan time in your schedule for the day to not rush to get there and not rush when leaving either.

- Do not drink a 64-ounce caffeinated drink on the trip to the testing center. After the exam starts, the exam timer will not stop while you go to the restroom.

- Use any relaxation techniques that you have practiced to help get your mind focused while you wait for the exam.

Exam Event: The Last 30 Minutes

It's almost time! Here are a few tips for those last moments.

- Ask the testing center personnel for earplugs if you did not bring any—even if you cannot imagine using them. You never know whether using them might help.

- Ask for extra pens and laminated note sheets. The exam center will give you a laminated sheet and dry erase pen to take notes. (Test center personnel typically do not let you bring paper and ink pen into the room, even if supplied by the testing center.) I always ask for a second pen as well.

■ Test your pens and sheets before going into the room to take the exam. Better to get a replacement pen before the clock starts.

■ Grab a few tissues from the box in the room, for two reasons. One, to avoid having to get up in the middle of the exam if you need to sneeze. Two, if you need to erase your laminated sheet, doing that with a tissue rather than your hand helps prevent the oil from your hand making the pen stop working well.

■ Find a restroom to use before going into the testing center, or just ask where one is, to avoid needing to go during the approximately two-hour exam event. Note that the exam timer does not stop if you need to go to the restroom during the exam, and you first have to find the exam center contact before just heading to the restroom, so it can cost you a few minutes.

Exam Event: Reserve the Hour After the Exam

Some people pass these exams on the first attempt, and some do not. The exams are not easy. If you fail to pass the exam that day, you will likely be disappointed. And that is understandable. But it is not a reason to give up. In fact, I added this short topic to give you a big advantage in case you do fail.

The most important study hour for your next exam attempt is the hour just after your failed attempt.

Before you take the exam, prepare for how you will react if you do not pass. That is, prepare your schedule to give yourself an hour, or at least a half an hour, immediately after the exam attempt, in case you fail. Follow these suggestions to be ready for taking notes:

■ Bring pen and paper, preferably a notebook you can write in if you have to write standing up or sitting somewhere inconvenient.

■ Make sure you know where pen and paper are so that you can take notes immediately after the exam. Keep these items in your backpack if using the train or bus, or on your car seat.

■ Install an audio recording app on your phone, and be prepared to start talking into your app when you leave the testing center.

■ Before the exam, scout the testing center, and plan the place where you will sit and take your notes, preferably somewhere quiet.

Then, once you complete the exam, if you do not pass on this attempt, use the following process when taking notes:

■ Write down anything in particular that you can recall from any question.

■ Write down details of questions you know you got right as well, because doing so may help trigger a memory of another question.

■ Draw the figures that you can remember.

■ Most importantly, write down any tidbit that might have confused you: terms, configuration commands, **show** commands, scenarios, topology drawings, anything.

■ Take at least three passes at remembering. That is, you will hit a wall where you do not remember more. So, start on your way back to the next place, and then find a place to pause and take more notes. And do it again.

■ When you have sucked your memory dry, take one more pass while thinking of the major topics in the book, to see if that triggers any other memory of a question.

Once you have collected your notes, *you cannot share the information with anyone* because doing so would break the Cisco nondisclosure agreement (NDA). Cisco considers cheating a serious offense and strongly forbids sharing this kind of information publicly. But you can use your information to study for your next attempt. Remember, anything you can do to determine what you do not know is valuable when studying for your next attempt. See the section "Exam Review: Study Suggestions for Your Second Attempt" in this chapter for the rest of the story.

Exam Review

At this point, you should have read the other chapters in both the *CCNA 200-301 Official Cert Guide, Volumes 1 and 2*, and completed the Chapter Review and Part Review tasks. Now you need to do the final study and review activities before taking the exam, as detailed in this section.

This section suggests some new activities and repeats some activities that have been previously mentioned. However, whether the activities are new or old to you, they all focus on filling in your knowledge gaps, finishing off your skills, and completing the study process. While repeating some tasks you did at Chapter Review and Part Review can help, you need to be ready to take an exam, so the Exam Review asks you to spend a lot of time answering exam questions.

The Exam Review walks you through suggestions for several types of tasks and gives you some tracking tables for each activity. The main categories are

■ Taking practice exams

■ Finding what you do not know well yet (knowledge gaps)

■ Configuring and verifying functions from the CLI

■ Repeating the Chapter Review and Part Review tasks

Exam Review: Take Practice Exams

One day soon, you need to pass a real Cisco exam at a Pearson VUE testing center. So, it's time to practice the real event as much as possible.

A practice exam using the Pearson IT Certification Practice Test (PTP) exam software lets you experience many of the same issues as when taking a real Cisco exam. When you select *practice exam* mode, the PTP software (both desktop and web) gives you a number of questions, with a countdown timer shown in the window. When using this PTP mode, after you answer a question, you cannot go back to it (yes, that's true on Cisco exams). If you run out of time, the questions you did not answer count as incorrect.

The process of taking the timed practice exams helps you prepare in three key ways:

■ To practice the exam event itself, including time pressure, the need to read carefully, and the need to concentrate for long periods

■ To build your analysis and critical thinking skills when examining the network scenario built in to many questions

■ To discover the gaps in your networking knowledge so that you can study those topics before the real exam

As much as possible, treat the practice exam events as if you were taking the real Cisco exam at a VUE testing center. The following list gives some advice on how to make your practice exam more meaningful, rather than just one more thing to do before exam day rolls around:

■ Set aside two hours for taking a 90-minute timed practice exam.

■ Make a list of what you expect to do for the 10 minutes before the real exam event. Then visualize yourself doing those things. Before taking each practice exam, practice those final 10 minutes before your exam timer starts. (The earlier section "Exam Event: The Last 30 Minutes" lists some suggestions about what to do in those last 10 minutes.)

■ You cannot bring anything with you into the VUE exam room, so remove all notes and help materials from your work area before taking a practice exam. You can use blank paper, a pen, and your brain only. Do not use calculators, notes, web browsers, or any other app on your computer.

■ Real life can get in the way, but if at all possible, ask anyone around you to leave you alone for the time you will practice. If you must do your practice exam in a distracting environment, wear headphones or earplugs to reduce distractions.

■ Do not guess, hoping to improve your score. Answer only when you have confidence in the answer. Then, if you get the question wrong, you can go back and think more about the question in a later study session.

Using the Practice CCNA Exams

The PTP questions you can access as part of this book include exam banks labeled as follows:

■ CCNA Volume 2 Exam 1

■ CCNA Volume 2 Exam 2

■ CCNA 200-301 Full Exam 1

■ CCNA 200-301 Full Exam 2

The exams whose names begin "CCNA Volume 2" have questions from this Volume 2 book only, but no questions from Volume 1. The exams titled "CCNA 200-301" (without Volume 2 in the name) include questions from the entire breadth of CCNA topics, including topics covered in both the Volume 1 and Volume 2 books.

You should do your final review with the CCNA 200-301 exams. Just select those exams and deselect the others. Then you simply need to choose the **Practice Exam** option in the upper right and start the exam.

You should plan to take between one and three practice exams with the supplied CCNA exam databases. Even people who are already well prepared should do at least one practice exam, just to experience the time pressure and the need for prolonged concentration.

Table 20-1 gives you a checklist to record your different practice exam events. Note that recording both the date and the score is helpful for some other work you will do, so note both. Also, in the Time Notes section, if you finish on time, note how much extra time you had; if you run out of time, note how many questions you did not have time to answer.

Table 20-1 CCNA Practice Exam Checklist

Exam	Date	Score	Time Notes
CCNA			
CCNA			
CCNA			

Exam Review: Advice on How to Answer Exam Questions

Our everyday habits have changed how we all read and think in front of a screen. Unfortunately, those same habits often hurt our scores when taking computer-based exams.

For example, open a web browser. Yes, take a break and open a web browser on any device. Do a quick search on a fun topic. Then, before you click a link, get ready to think about what you just did. Where did your eyes go for the first 5 to 10 seconds after you opened that web page. Now, click a link and look at the page. Where did your eyes go?

Interestingly, web browsers and the content in web pages have trained us all to scan. Web page designers actually design content expecting certain scan patterns from viewers. Regardless of the pattern, when reading a web page, almost no one reads sequentially, and no one reads entire sentences. People scan for the interesting graphics and the big words, and then scan the space around those noticeable items.

Other parts of our electronic culture have also changed how the average person reads. For example, many of you grew up using texting and social media, sifting through hundreds or thousands of messages—but each message barely fills an entire sentence. Also, we find ourselves responding to texts, tweets, and emails and later realizing we did not really understand what the other person meant.

If you use those same habits when taking the exam, you will probably make some mistakes because you missed a key fact in the question, answer, or exhibits. It helps to start at the beginning and read all the words—a process that is amazingly unnatural for many people today.

> **NOTE** I have talked to many college professors, in multiple disciplines, and Cisco Networking Academy instructors, and they consistently tell me that the number-one test-taking issue today is that people do not read the questions well enough to understand the details.

When you are taking the practice exams and answering individual questions, consider these two strategies. First, before the practice exam, think about your own personal strategy for how you will read a question. Make your approach to multiple-choice questions in particular be a conscious decision on your part. Second, if you want some suggestions on how to read an exam question, use the following strategy:

Step 1. Read the question itself, thoroughly, from start to finish.

Step 2. Scan any exhibit or figure.

Step 3. Scan the answers to look for the types of information. (Numeric? Terms? Single words? Phrases?)

Step 4. Reread the question thoroughly, from start to finish, to make sure that you understand it.

Step 5. Read each answer thoroughly, while referring to the figure/exhibit as needed. After reading each answer, before reading the next answer:

  A. If correct, select as correct.

  B. If for sure incorrect, mentally rule it out.

  C. If unsure, mentally note it as a possible correct answer.

NOTE Cisco exams will tell you the number of correct answers. The exam software also helps you finish the question with the right number of answers noted. For example, for standalone multichoice questions, the software prevents you from selecting too many or too few answers. And you should guess the answer when unsure on the actual exam; there is no penalty for guessing.

Use the practice exams as a place to practice your approach to reading. Every time you click to the next question, try to read the question following your approach. If you are feeling time pressure, that is the perfect time to keep practicing your approach, to reduce and eliminate questions you miss because of scanning the question instead of reading thoroughly.

Exam Review: Additional Exams with the Premium Edition

Many people add other practice exams and questions other than those that come with this book. Frankly, using other practice exams in addition to the questions that come with this book can be a good idea, for many reasons. The other exam questions can use different terms in different ways, emphasize different topics, and show different scenarios that make you rethink some topics.

Note that Cisco Press does sell products that include additional test questions. The *CCNA 200-301 Official Cert Guide, Volume 2, Premium Edition eBook and Practice Test* product is basically the publisher's eBook version of this book. It includes a soft copy of the book in formats you can read on your computer and on the most common book readers and tablets. The product includes all the electronic content you would normally get with the print book, including all the question databases mentioned in this chapter. Additionally, this product includes two more CCNA exam databases (plus two more CCNA Volume 2 exam databases as well).

NOTE In addition to providing the extra questions, the Premium Editions have links to every test question, including those in the print book, to the specific section of the book for further reference. This is a great learning tool if you need more detail than what you find in the question explanations. You can purchase the eBooks and additional practice exams at 70 percent off the list price using the coupon on the back of the activation code card in the cardboard sleeve, making the Premium Editions the best and most cost-efficient way to get more practice questions.

Exam Review: Find Knowledge Gaps

One of the hardest things when doing your final exam preparation is to discover gaps in your knowledge and skills. In other words, what topics and skills do you need to know that you do not know? Or what topics do you think you know, but you misunderstand about some important fact? Finding gaps in your knowledge at this late stage requires more than just your gut feeling about your strengths and weaknesses.

This next task uses a feature of PTP to help you find those gaps. The PTP software tracks each practice exam you take, remembering your answer for every question and whether you got it wrong. You can view the results and move back and forth between seeing the question and seeing the results page. To find gaps in your knowledge, follow these steps:

Step 1.   Pick and review one of your practice exams.

Step 2.   Review each incorrect question until you are satisfied that you understand the question.

Step 3.   When finished with your review for a question, mark the question.

Step 4.   Review all incorrect questions from your exam until all are marked.

Step 5.   Move on to the next practice exam.

Figure 20-1 shows a sample Question Review page, in which all the questions were answered incorrectly. The results list a Correct column, with no check mark, meaning that the answer was incorrect.

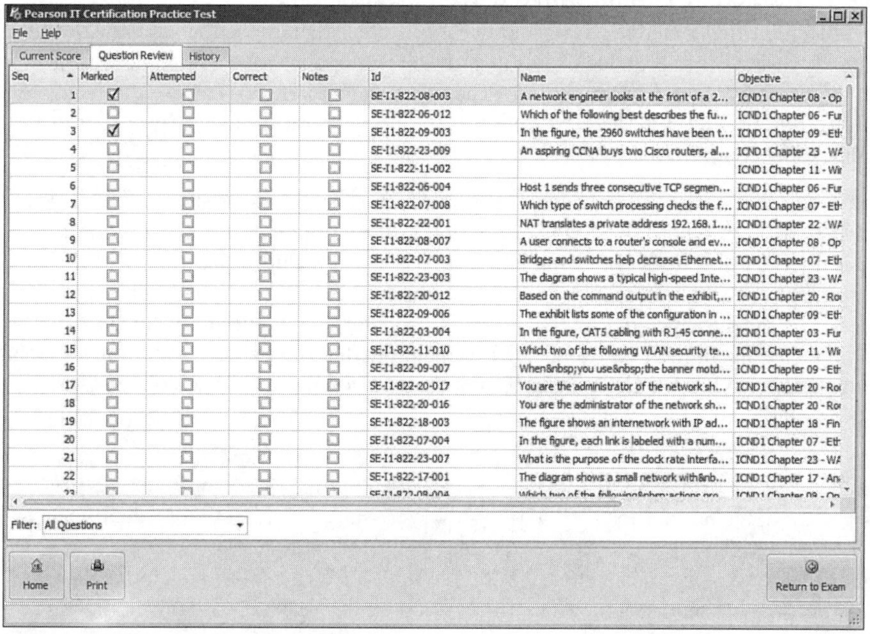

Figure 20-1   *PTP Grading Results Page*

To perform the process of reviewing questions and marking them as complete, you can move between this Question Review page and the individual questions. Just double-click a question to move back to that question. From the question, you can click **Grade Exam** to move back to the grading results and to the Question Review page shown in Figure 20-1. The question window also shows the place to mark the question, in the upper left, as shown in Figure 20-2.

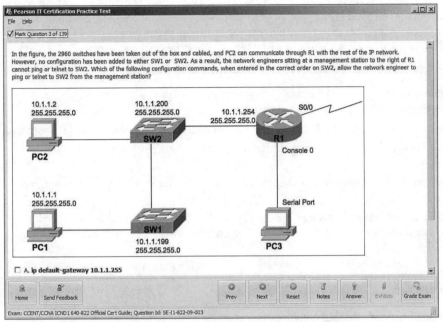

Figure 20-2 *Reviewing a Question, with the Mark Feature in the Upper Left*

If you want to come back later to look through the questions you missed from an earlier exam, start at the PTP home screen. From there, instead of clicking the Start button to start a new exam, click the **View Grade History** button to see your earlier exam attempts and work through any missed questions.

Track your progress through your gap review in Table 20-2. PTP lists your previous practice exams by date and score, so it helps to note those values in the table for comparison to the PTP menu.

Table 20-2   Tracking Checklist for Gap Review of Practice Exams

Original Practice Exam Date	Original Exam Score	Date Gap Review Was Completed

Exam Review: Practice Hands-On CLI Skills

To do well on sim and simlet questions, you need to be comfortable with many Cisco router and switch commands, and how to use them from a Cisco CLI. As described in the introduction to this book, sim questions require you to decide what configuration commands need to be configured to fix a problem or to complete a working configuration. Simlet questions require you to answer multiple-choice questions by first using the CLI to issue **show** commands to look at the status of routers and switches in a small network.

To be ready for the exam, you need to know the following kinds of information:

CLI navigation: Basic CLI mechanics of moving into and out of user, enable, and configuration modes

Individual configuration: The meaning of the parameters of each configuration command

Feature configuration: The set of configuration commands, both required and optional, for each feature

Verification of configuration: The **show** commands that directly identify the configuration settings

Verification of status: The **show** commands that list current status values and the ability to decide incorrect configuration or other problem causes of less-than-optimal status values

To help remember and review all this knowledge and skill, you can do the tasks listed in the next several pages.

CCNA Exam Topics with CLI Skill Requirements

Wondering about all the topics in CCNA 200-301 that specifically include configuration or verification skills? You can just scan the CCNA 200-301 exam topics. However, Table 20-3 and Table 20-4 summarize the topics for which you could consider practicing your CLI skills. The tables organize the topics into the same order used in the *CCNA 200-301 Official Cert Guides, Volume 1 and 2*, with chapter references.

Table 20-3 Topics with Configuration Skills in CCNA Volume 1

Topic	Volume 1 Chapter	Date You Finished Lab Review
Switch IPv4	6	
Verifying LAN switching	5	
Switch IPv4	6	
Switch passwords	6	
Switch interfaces	7	
VLANs	8	
VLAN trunking	8	
STP and RSTP	10	
Layer 2 EtherChannel	10	
Router interfaces	15	
Router IPv4 addresses and static routes	16	

Topic	Volume 1 Chapter	Date You Finished Lab Review
Router on a Stick	17	
Layer 3 switching with SVIs	17	
Layer 3 switching with routed interfaces and L3 EtherChannels	17	
OSPF fundamentals	20	
OSPF network types	21	
IPv6 addressing on routers	24	
IPv6 static routes	25	

Table 20-4   Topics with Configuration Skills in CCNA Volume 2

Topic	Volume 2 Chapter	Date You Finished Lab Review
Standard ACLs	2	
Extended ACLs	3	
Telnet and SSH Access ACLs	5	
Port Security	6	
DHCP client and DHCP relay	7	
DHCP snooping	8	
Dynamic ARP Inspection	8	
Syslog, NTP, CDP, and LLDP	9	
NAT, PAT	10	

You should research and choose your favorite methods and tools to get hands-on practice for CCNA. Those options include several that focus on giving you a specific activity to do. The options include the Pearson Network Simulator, Config Labs (on my blog), and Packet Tracer labs (on my blog).

First, one great way to practice is to use the Pearson Network Simulator (the sim) at www.pearsonitcertification.com/networksimulator. Pearson builds the sim to focus on lab exercises that help you learn and expand your skills with the topics in the CCNA exam. The sim also organizes the lab content so you can follow along with the books. You can get a sense for what the labs are like in the sim by going to the companion website for this book and downloading the Sim Lite, which uses the same core software but with a more limited number of labs compared to the full product.

Second, review the Config Checklist apps available from the book's companion website. For any configuration topics that require more than a few commands, the book collects the configuration commands into config checklists so that you can review and study in the days leading up to the exam. Take advantage of those checklists to review and remember all the required and optional configuration commands.

Finally, my blog site (https://blog.certskills.com) has informal lab exercises designed so that you can do the labs without any real gear or simulator. Config Labs list straightforward configuration requirements. Your job: configure per the requirements, writing the configuration on paper or just typing into a text document. To learn more, go to

https://blog.certskills.com/config-labs

https://blog.certskills.com/packet-tracer-labs

Exam Review: Self-Assessment Pitfalls

When you take a practice exam with PTP, PTP gives you a score, on a scale from 300 to 1000. Why? Cisco gives a score of between 300 and 1000 as well. But the similarities end there.

With PTP, the score is a basic percentage but expressed as a number from 0 to 1000. For example, answer 80 percent correct, and the score is 800; get 90 percent correct, and the score is 900. If you start a practice exam and click through it without answering a single question, you get a 0.

However, Cisco does not score exams in the same way. The following is what we do know about Cisco exam scoring:

■ Cisco uses a scoring scale from 300 to 1000.

■ Cisco tells us that it gives partial credit but provides no further details.

So, what does an 800 or a 900 mean on the actual Cisco exams? Many people think those scores mean 80 percent or 90 percent, but we don't know. Cisco doesn't reveal the details of scoring to us. It doesn't reveal the details of partial credit. It seems reasonable to expect a sim question to be worth more points than a multiple-choice, single-answer question, but we do not know.

The reason I mention all these facts to you is this:

Do not rely too much on your PTP practice exam scores to assess whether you are ready to pass. Those scores are a general indicator, in that if you make a 700 one time and a 900 a week later, you are probably now better prepared. But that 900 on your PTP practice exam does not mean you will likely make a 900 on the actual exam—because we do not know how Cisco scores the exam.

So, what can you use as a way to assess whether you are ready to pass? Unfortunately, the answer requires some extra effort, and the answer will not be some nice, convenient number that looks like an exam score. But you can self-assess your skills as follows:

1. When you do take an exam with PTP, you should understand the terms used in the questions and answers.

2. You should be able to look at the list of key topics from each chapter and explain a sentence or two about each topic to a friend.

3. You should be able to do subnetting math confidently with 100 percent accuracy at this point.

4. You should be able to do all the Config Labs, or labs of similar challenge level, and get them right consistently.

5. For chapters with **show** commands, you should understand the fields highlighted in gray in the examples spread throughout the book, and when looking at those

examples, you should know which values show configuration settings and which show status information.

6. For the key topics that list various troubleshooting root causes, when you review those lists, you should remember and understand the concept behind each item in the list without needing to look further at the chapter.

Exam Review: Adjustments for Your Second Attempt

None of us wants to take and fail any exam, but some of you will. And even if you pass the CCNA exam on your first try, if you keep going with Cisco certifications, you will probably fail some exams along the way. I mention failing an exam not to focus on the negative, but to help prepare you for how to pass the next attempt after failing an earlier attempt. This section collects some of the advice I have given to readers over the years who have contacted me after a failed attempt, asking for help about what to do next.

The single most important bit of advice is to change your mindset about Cisco exams. Cisco exams are not like high school or college exams where your failing grade matters. Instead, a Cisco exam is more like an event on the road to completing an impressive major accomplishment, one that most people have to try a few times to achieve.

For instance, achieving a Cisco certification is more like training to run a marathon in under four hours. The first time running a marathon, you may not even finish, or you may finish at 4:15 rather than under 4:00. But finishing a marathon in 4:15 means that you have prepared and are getting pretty close to your goal. Or maybe it is more like training to complete an obstacle course (for any *American Ninja Warrior* fans out there). Maybe you got past the first three obstacles today, but you couldn't climb over the 14-foot high warped wall. That just means you need to practice on that wall a little more.

So change your mindset. You're a marathon runner looking to improve your time or a Ninja Warrior looking to complete the obstacle course. And you are getting better skills every time you study, which helps you compete in the market.

With that attitude and analogy in mind, the rest of this section lists specific study steps that can help.

First, study the notes you took about your failed attempt. (See the earlier section "Exam Event: Reserve the Hour After the Exam.") Do not share that information with others, but use it to study. Before you take the exam again, you should be able to answer every actual exam question you can remember from the last attempt. Even if you never see the exact same question again, you will still get a good return for your effort.

Second, spend more time on activities that uncover your weaknesses. When doing that, you have to slow down and be more self-aware. For instance, answer practice questions in study mode, and *do not guess*. Do not click on to the next question, but pause and ask yourself if you are really sure about both the wrong and correct answers. If unsure, fantastic! You just discovered a topic for which to go back and dig in to learn it more deeply. Or when you do a lab, you may refer to your notes without thinking, so now think about it when you turn to your notes because that tells you where you are unsure. That might be a reminder that you have not mastered those commands yet.

Third, think about your time spent on the exam. Did you run out of time? Go too fast? Too slow? If too slow, were you slow on subnetting, or sims, or something else? Then make a written plan as to how you will approach time on the next attempt and how you will track time use. And if you ran out of time, practice for the things that slowed you down.

Exam Review: Other Study Tasks

If you got to this point and still feel the need to prepare some more, this last topic gives you three suggestions.

First, the Chapter Review and Part Review sections give you some useful study tasks.

Second, use more exam questions from other sources. You can always get more questions in the Cisco Press Premium Edition eBook and Practice Test products, which include an eBook copy of this book plus additional questions in additional PTP exam banks. However, you can search the Internet for questions from many sources and review those questions as well.

NOTE Some vendors claim to sell practice exams that contain the literal exam questions from the official exam. These exams, called "brain dumps," are against the Cisco testing policies. Cisco strongly discourages using any such tools for study.

Finally, join in the discussions on the Cisco Learning Network. Try to answer questions asked by other learners; the process of answering makes you think much harder about the topic. When someone posts an answer with which you disagree, think about why and talk about it online. This is a great way to both learn more and build confidence.

Final Thoughts

You have studied quite a bit, worked hard, and sacrificed time and money to be ready for the exam. I hope your exam goes well, that you pass, and that you pass because you really know your stuff and will do well in your IT and networking career.

I encourage you to celebrate when you pass and ask advice when you do not. The Cisco Learning Network is a great place to make posts to celebrate and to ask advice for the next time around. I personally would love to hear about your progress through Twitter (@wendellodom) or my Facebook page (www.facebook.com/wendellodom). I wish you well, and congratulations for working through the entire book!

Part VII

Appendixes

Numeric Reference Tables

This appendix provides several useful reference tables that list numbers used throughout this book. Specifically:

Table A-1: A decimal-binary cross reference, useful when converting from decimal to binary and vice versa.

Table A-1   Decimal-Binary Cross Reference, Decimal Values 0–255

Decimal Value	Binary Value	Decimal Value	Binary Value	Decimal Value	Binary Value	Decimal Value	Binary Value
0	00000000	32	00100000	64	01000000	96	01100000
1	00000001	33	00100001	65	01000001	97	01100001
2	00000010	34	00100010	66	01000010	98	01100010
3	00000011	35	00100011	67	01000011	99	01100011
4	00000100	36	00100100	68	01000100	100	01100100
5	00000101	37	00100101	69	01000101	101	01100101
6	00000110	38	00100110	70	01000110	102	01100110
7	00000111	39	00100111	71	01000111	103	01100111
8	00001000	40	00101000	72	01001000	104	01101000
9	00001001	41	00101001	73	01001001	105	01101001
10	00001010	42	00101010	74	01001010	106	01101010
11	00001011	43	00101011	75	01001011	107	01101011
12	00001100	44	00101100	76	01001100	108	01101100
13	00001101	45	00101101	77	01001101	109	01101101
14	00001110	46	00101110	78	01001110	110	01101110
15	00001111	47	00101111	79	01001111	111	01101111
16	00010000	48	00110000	80	01010000	112	01110000
17	00010001	49	00110001	81	01010001	113	01110001
18	00010010	50	00110010	82	01010010	114	01110010
19	00010011	51	00110011	83	01010011	115	01110011
20	00010100	52	00110100	84	01010100	116	01110100
21	00010101	53	00110101	85	01010101	117	01110101
22	00010110	54	00110110	86	01010110	118	01110110
23	00010111	55	00110111	87	01010111	119	01110111
24	00011000	56	00111000	88	01011000	120	01111000
25	00011001	57	00111001	89	01011001	121	01111001
26	00011010	58	00111010	90	01011010	122	01111010
27	00011011	59	00111011	91	01011011	123	01111011
28	00011100	60	00111100	92	01011100	124	01111100
29	00011101	61	00111101	93	01011101	125	01111101
30	00011110	62	00111110	94	01011110	126	01111110
31	00011111	63	00111111	95	01011111	127	01111111

Decimal Value	Binary Value	Decimal Value	Binary Value	Decimal Value	Binary Value	Decimal Value	Binary Value
128	10000000	160	10100000	192	11000000	224	11100000
129	10000001	161	10100001	193	11000001	225	11100001
130	10000010	162	10100010	194	11000010	226	11100010
131	10000011	163	10100011	195	11000011	227	11100011
132	10000100	164	10100100	196	11000100	228	11100100
133	10000101	165	10100101	197	11000101	229	11100101
134	10000110	166	10100110	198	11000110	230	11100110
135	10000111	167	10100111	199	11000111	231	11100111
136	10001000	168	10101000	200	11001000	232	11101000
137	10001001	169	10101001	201	11001001	233	11101001
138	10001010	170	10101010	202	11001010	234	11101010
139	10001011	171	10101011	203	11001011	235	11101011
140	10001100	172	10101100	204	11001100	236	11101100
141	10001101	173	10101101	205	11001101	237	11101101
142	10001110	174	10101110	206	11001110	238	11101110
143	10001111	175	10101111	207	11001111	239	11101111
144	10010000	176	10110000	208	11010000	240	11110000
145	10010001	177	10110001	209	11010001	241	11110001
146	10010010	178	10110010	210	11010010	242	11110010
147	10010011	179	10110011	211	11010011	243	11110011
148	10010100	180	10110100	212	11010100	244	11110100
149	10010101	181	10110101	213	11010101	245	11110101
150	10010110	182	10110110	214	11010110	246	11110110
151	10010111	183	10110111	215	11010111	247	11110111
152	10011000	184	10111000	216	11011000	248	11111000
153	10011001	185	10111001	217	11011001	249	11111001
154	10011010	186	10111010	218	11011010	250	11111010
155	10011011	187	10111011	219	11011011	251	11111011
156	10011100	188	10111100	220	11011100	252	11111100
157	10011101	189	10111101	221	11011101	253	11111101
158	10011110	190	10111110	222	11011110	254	11111110
159	10011111	191	10111111	223	11011111	255	11111111

A

Table A-2: A hexadecimal-binary cross reference, useful when converting from hex to binary and vice versa.

Table A-2   Hex-Binary Cross Reference

Hex	4-Bit Binary
0	0000
1	0001
2	0010
3	0011
4	0100
5	0101
6	0110
7	0111
8	1000
9	1001
A	1010
B	1011
C	1100
D	1101
E	1110
F	1111

Table A-3: Powers of 2, from 2^1 through 2^{32}.

Table A-3   Powers of 2

X	2^X	X	2^X
1	2	17	131,072
2	4	18	262,144
3	8	19	524,288
4	16	20	1,048,576
5	32	21	2,097,152
6	64	22	4,194,304
7	128	23	8,388,608
8	256	24	16,777,216
9	512	25	33,554,432
10	1024	26	67,108,864
11	2048	27	134,217,728
12	4096	28	268,435,456
13	8192	29	536,870,912
14	16,384	30	1,073,741,824
15	32,768	31	2,147,483,648
16	65,536	32	4,294,967,296

A

Table A-4: Table of all 33 possible subnet masks, in all three formats.

Table A-4 All Subnet Masks

Decimal	Prefix	Binary
0.0.0.0	/0	00000000 00000000 00000000 00000000
128.0.0.0	/1	10000000 00000000 00000000 00000000
192.0.0.0	/2	11000000 00000000 00000000 00000000
224.0.0.0	/3	11100000 00000000 00000000 00000000
240.0.0.0	/4	11110000 00000000 00000000 00000000
248.0.0.0	/5	11111000 00000000 00000000 00000000
252.0.0.0	/6	11111100 00000000 00000000 00000000
254.0.0.0	/7	11111110 00000000 00000000 00000000
255.0.0.0	/8	11111111 00000000 00000000 00000000
255.128.0.0	/9	11111111 10000000 00000000 00000000
255.192.0.0	/10	11111111 11000000 00000000 00000000
255.224.0.0	/11	11111111 11100000 00000000 00000000
255.240.0.0	/12	11111111 11110000 00000000 00000000
255.248.0.0	/13	11111111 11111000 00000000 00000000
255.252.0.0	/14	11111111 11111100 00000000 00000000
255.254.0.0	/15	11111111 11111110 00000000 00000000
255.255.0.0	/16	11111111 11111111 00000000 00000000
255.255.128.0	/17	11111111 11111111 10000000 00000000
255.255.192.0	/18	11111111 11111111 11000000 00000000
255.255.224.0	/19	11111111 11111111 11100000 00000000
255.255.240.0	/20	11111111 11111111 11110000 00000000
255.255.248.0	/21	11111111 11111111 11111000 00000000
255.255.252.0	/22	11111111 11111111 11111100 00000000
255.255.254.0	/23	11111111 11111111 11111110 00000000
255.255.255.0	/24	11111111 11111111 11111111 00000000
255.255.255.128	/25	11111111 11111111 11111111 10000000
255.255.255.192	/26	11111111 11111111 11111111 11000000
255.255.255.224	/27	11111111 11111111 11111111 11100000
255.255.255.240	/28	11111111 11111111 11111111 11110000
255.255.255.248	/29	11111111 11111111 11111111 11111000
255.255.255.252	/30	11111111 11111111 11111111 11111100
255.255.255.254	/31	11111111 11111111 11111111 11111110
255.255.255.255	/32	11111111 11111111 11111111 11111111

CCNA 200-301, Volume 2 Exam Updates

Over time, reader feedback allows Pearson to gauge which topics give our readers the most problems when taking the exams. To assist readers with those topics, the authors create new materials clarifying and expanding on those troublesome exam topics. As mentioned in the Introduction, the additional content about the exam is contained in a PDF on this book's companion website, at www.ciscopress.com/title/9781587147135.

This appendix provides you with updated information if Cisco makes minor modifications to the exam topics during the life of the 200-301 exam. In particular, this appendix does the following:

- Mentions technical items that might not have been mentioned elsewhere in the book
- Covers new topics if Cisco adds new content to the exam over time
- Provides a way to get up-to-the-minute current information about content for the exam

Note that this appendix shows updated information related to the subset of CCNA 200-301 exam topics covered in this book. Refer also to the *CCNA 200-301 Official Cert Guide, Volume 1*, for more details about the rest of the exam topics and for an Appendix B similar to that of this book.

Always Get the Latest at the Book's Product Page

Many of you are reading the version of this appendix that was available when your book was printed or when you downloaded the e-book. However, given that the main purpose of this appendix is to be a living, changing document, it is important that you look for the latest version online at the book's companion website. To do so, follow these steps:

Step 1. Browse to www.ciscopress.com/title/9781587147135.

Step 2. Click the **Updates** tab.

Step 3. If there is a new Appendix B document on the page, download the latest Appendix B document.

> **NOTE** The downloaded document has a version number. Comparing the version of the print Appendix B (**Version 1.0**) with the latest downloadable version of this appendix, you should do the following:
>
> - **Same version:** Ignore the PDF that you downloaded from the companion website.
>
> - **Website has a later version:** Ignore this Appendix B in your book and read only the latest version that you downloaded from the companion website.

Technical Content

The current **Version 1.0** of this appendix does not contain additional technical coverage.

Answers to the "Do I Know This Already?" Quizzes

Chapter 1

1. D and E. Many headers include a field that identifies the next header that follows inside a message. Ethernet uses the Ethernet Type field, and the IP header uses the Protocol field. The TCP and UDP headers identify the application that should receive the data that follows the TCP or UDP header by using the port number field in the TCP and UDP headers, respectively.

2. A, B, C, and F. IP, not TCP, defines routing. Many other protocols define encryption, but TCP does not. The correct answers simply list various TCP features.

3. C. TCP, not UDP, performs windowing, error recovery, and ordered data transfer. Neither performs routing or encryption.

4. C and F. The terms *packet* and *L3PDU* refer to the header plus data encapsulated by Layer 3. *Frame* and *L2PDU* refer to the header (and trailer), plus the data encapsulated by Layer 2. *Segment* and *L4PDU* refer to the header and data encapsulated by the transport layer protocol.

5. B. Note that the hostname is all the text between the // and the /. The text before the // identifies the application layer protocol, and the text after the / represents the name of the web page.

6. C and D. Web traffic uses TCP as the transport protocol, with HTTP as the application protocol. As a result, the web server typically uses well-known TCP port 80, which is the well-known port for HTTP traffic. Messages flowing to the web server would have a destination TCP port of 80, and messages flowing from the server would have a source TCP port of 80.

Chapter 2

1. A and C. Standard ACLs check the source IP address. The address range 10.1.1.1–10.1.1.4 can be matched by an ACL, but it requires multiple **access-list** commands. Matching all hosts in Barney's subnet can be accomplished with the **access-list 1 permit 10.1.1.0 0.0.0.255** command.

2. A and D. The range of valid ACL numbers for standard numbered IP ACLs is 1–99 and 1300–1999, inclusive.

3. D. 0.0.0.255 matches all packets that have the same first three octets. This is useful when you want to match a subnet in which the subnet part comprises the first three octets, as in this case.

4. E. 0.0.15.255 matches all packets with the same first 20 bits. This is useful when you want to match a subnet in which the subnet part comprises the first 20 bits, as in this case.

5. A. The router always searches the ACL statements in order, and stops trying to match ACL statements after a statement is matched. In other words, it uses first-match logic. A packet with source IP address 1.1.1.1 would match any of the three explicitly configured commands described in the question. As a result, the first statement will be used.

6. B. One wrong answer, with wildcard mask 0.0.255.0, matches all packets that begin with 172.16, with a 5 in the last octet. One wrong answer matches only specific IP address 172.16.5.0. One wrong answer uses a wildcard mask of 0.0.0.128, which has only one wildcard bit (in binary), and happens to only match addresses 172.16.5.0 and 172.16.5.128. The correct answer matches the range of addresses 172.16.4.0–172.16.5.255.

Chapter 3

1. E and F. Extended ACLs can look at the Layer 3 (IP) and Layer 4 (TCP, UDP) headers and a few others, but not any application layer information. Named extended ACLs can look for the same fields as numbered extended ACLs.

2. A and E. The correct range of ACL numbers for extended IP access lists is 100 to 199 and 2000 to 2699. The answers that list the **eq www** parameter after 10.1.1.1 match the source port number, and the packets are going toward the web server, not away from it.

3. E. Because the packet is going toward any web client, you need to check for the web server's port number as a source port. The client IP address range is not specified in the question, but the servers are, so the source address beginning with 172.16.5 is the correct answer.

4. A and C. Before IOS 12.3, numbered ACLs must be removed and then reconfigured to remove a line from the ACL. As of IOS 12.3, you can also use ACL configuration mode and sequence numbers to delete one ACL line at a time.

5. C and D. In the command output, line number 10 references a permit command that matches addresses in subnet 172.16.1.0/24. The question stem identifies the subnet, so it indirectly asks about line 10 of the ACL. Any specific Access Control Entry (ACE) in ACL can be deleted in ACL config mode. Two methods can be used: the short **no** *line-number*, where line-number is the ACE's line number, or by issuing a **no** version of the **permit** or **deny** command, as shown in one of the correct answers. The three incorrect answers show correct commands but incorrect modes in which to use the commands.

6. C and D. The **show ip access-lists** and **show access-lists** commands both display the configuration of IPv4 access lists, including ACL line numbers. Neither the **show running-config** nor **show startup-config** commands list the ACL line numbers; in this case, the startup-config file would not contain the ACL configuration at all.

Chapter 4

1. **B.** A vulnerability is a weakness that can be exploited. Attack is not correct because it is a threat that is taking place.

2. **D.** When a vulnerability can be exploited, a threat is possible.

3. **A and B.** Attackers usually spoof the source IP address in packets they send in order to disguise themselves and make the actual IP address owner into a victim of the attack. MAC addresses can also be spoofed in ARP replies to confuse other hosts and routers on the local network. Destination IP addresses are not normally spoofed because packets used in the attack would go to unknown or nonexistent hosts. Finally, ARP address is not correct because it is not a legitimate term.

4. **D.** A denial-of-service attack is likely occurring because the attacker is trying to exhaust the target's TCP connection table with embryonic or incomplete TCP connections.

5. **C.** In a reflection attack, the goal is to force one host (the reflector) to reflect the packets toward a victim. Therefore, the spoofed source address contains the address of the victim and not the reflector.

6. **A and C.** Once an attacker is in position in a man-in-the-middle attack, traffic between hosts can be passively inspected and actively modified. This type of attack does not lend itself to inducing buffer overflows or using sweeps and scans.

7. **B.** In a brute-force attack, an attacker's software tries every combination of letters, numbers, and special characters to eventually find a string that matches a user's password.

8. **D.** The Cisco ISE platform provides the AAA services needed for authentication, authorization, and accounting. DHCP does not perform AAA but leases IP addresses to hosts instead. DNS resolves hostnames to IP addresses. SNMP is used for network management functions.

9. **C.** Physical access control is a necessary element of a security program that keeps sensitive locations like data centers and network closets locked and inaccessible, except to authorized personnel.

Chapter 5

1. **B.** If both commands are configured, IOS accepts only the password as configured in the **enable secret** command

2. **A.** The **service password-encryption** command encrypts passwords on a router or switch that would otherwise be shown in clear text. While a great idea in concept, the algorithm can be easily broken using websites found in the Internet. Cisco long ago provided replacements for commands that store passwords as clear text, instead using hashes—commands like **enable secret** and **username secret**. These commands are preferred in part because they avoid the issues of clear-text passwords and easily decrypted passwords.

3. **B.** The **enable secret** command stores an MD5 hash of the password. It is unaffected by the **service password-encryption** command. The router does not unhash the value back to the clear-text password. Instead, when the user types her clear-text password,

the router also hashes that password and compares that hashed value with the hashed value as listed in the configuration.

4.   A. The **ip access-class 1 in** command enables ACL 1 for processing inbound Telnet and SSH connections into that router, based on the source IP address of those incoming packets. It has no impact on Telnet or SSH attempts from the router to some other host. It has no impact on a user later reaching enable mode. It also has nothing to do with filtering packets that would otherwise be routed through the router. Note that the ACL matches all packets whose source IP address is in subnet 172.16.4.0/23, which includes the range of numbers from 172.16.4.0 to 172.16.5.255.

5.   B. Traditional and next-generation firewalls can check TCP and UDP port numbers, but next-generation firewalls are generally characterized as being able to also check application data beyond the Transport layer header. An NGFW would look into the application data, identifying messages that contain data structures used by Telnet, instead of matching with port numbers. This matching can catch attacks that seek to use port numbers that the firewall allows while using those ports to send data from applications that do not normally use those ports.

For the other answers, a traditional firewall would likely match based on destination port 23, which is the well-known port for Telnet. IP protocol number has nothing to do with Telnet.

6.   A and D. Both traditional and next-generation IPSs (NGIPSs) use a signature database, with each signature listing details of what fields would be in a series of messages to identify those messages as part of some exploit. They both also generate events for review by the security team.

NGIPS devices add features that go beyond using a signature database, including gathering contextual information from hosts, like the OS used, currently running apps, open ports, and so on, so that the NGIPS does not have to log events if the hosts could not possibly be affected. Additionally, an NGIPS can use a list of reputation scores about IP addresses, domain names, and URIs of known bad actors, filtering traffic for sources that have a configured poor reputation level.

Chapter 6

1.   B. The setting for the maximum number of MAC addresses has a default of 1, so the **switchport port-security maximum** command does not have to be configured. With sticky learning, you do not need to predefine the specific MAC addresses either. However, you must enable port security, which requires the **switchport port-security** interface subcommand.

2.   B and D. First, about the sticky parameter...this command causes the switch to learn the source MAC and to add it to a **switchport port-security mac-address** *address* interface subcommand. However, port security adds that command to the running-config file; the network engineer must also issue a **copy running-config startup-config** EXEC command to save that configuration.

About the other correct answer, users can connect a switch to the end of the cable, with multiple devices connected to that switch. That happens in real networks when users decide they need more ports at their desk. However, the default setting of

switchport port-security maximum 1 means that a frame from the second unique source MAC address would cause a violation, and with the default violation action, to err-disable the port.

For the other incorrect answer, the configuration does not prevent unknown MAC addresses from accessing the port because the configuration does not predefine any MAC address.

3. B and C. IOS adds MAC addresses configured by the port security feature as static MAC addresses, so they do not show up in the output of the **show mac address-table dynamic** command. **show mac address-table port-security** is not a valid command.

4. B. The question states that the port security status is secure-shutdown. This state is used only by the shutdown port security mode, and when used, it means that the interface has been placed into an err-disabled state. Those facts explain why the correct answer is correct and two of the incorrect answers are incorrect.

   The incorrect answer that mentions the violation counter is incorrect because in shutdown mode, the counter no longer increments once the interface is placed into secure-shutdown mode.

5. B and C. First, about the two incorrect answers: In restrict mode, the arrival of a frame that violates the port security policy does not cause the switch to put the interface into err-disabled state. It does cause the switch to discard any frames that violate the policy, but it leaves the interface up and does not discard frames that do not violate the security policy, like the second frame that arrives.

   Regarding the two correct answers, a port in port security restrict does cause the switch to issue log messages for a violating frame, send SNMP traps about that same event (if SNMP is configured), and increment the counter of violating frames.

Chapter 7

1. B and D. The client sends a Discover message, with the server returning an Offer message. The client then sends a Request, with the server sending back the IP address in the Acknowledgment message.

2. A and B. The two correct answers list the two primary facts that impact which IP addresses the server will lease to clients. For the incorrect answer about DNS servers, the DHCP server does supply the IP address of the DNS servers, but not the hostnames of the DNS servers. Also, the DHCP server supplies the IP address (but not the MAC address) of the default gateway in each subnet.

3. A and C. A router needs act as a DHCP relay agent if DHCP clients exist on the connected subnet and there is no DHCP server in that subnet. If a DHCP exists in the subnet, the router does not need to forward DHCP messages to a remote DHCP server (which is the function of a DHCP relay agent). The answer that mentions the **ip address dhcp** command makes the router interface act as a DHCP client and has nothing to do with DHCP relay agent.

4. D. The **ip address dhcp** command tells the router to obtain its address using DHCP. The router learns all the same information that a normal DHCP client would learn. The router uses the address listed as the default gateway to build a default route, using the

default gateway IP address as the next-hop address. The router continues to work like a router always does, forwarding packets based on its IP routing table.

5. B and C. The output shows the MAC address, IP address, subnet mask (in hex format), and the subnet broadcast address. Of those, the DHCP server supplies the information in the two correct answers. The two incorrect answers mention the MAC address (not supplied by DHCP, but known to the device's NIC) and the subnet broadcast address (calculated by the host).

6. D. Windows supports both **ipconfig** and **ipconfig /all** commands, but the **ipconfig** command does not mention the DNS servers. Note that the **ifconfig** command works on Linux and macOS, and the **ifconfig /all** command is an invalid command.

Chapter 8

1. A and C. DHCP Snooping must be implemented on a device that performs Layer 2 switching. The DHCP Snooping function needs to examine DHCP messages that flow between devices within the same broadcast domain (VLAN). Layer 2 switches, as well as multilayer switches, perform that function. Because a router performs only Layer 3 forwarding (that is, routing) and does not forward messages between devices in the same VLAN, a router does not provide a good platform to implement DHCP Snooping (and is not even a feature of Cisco IOS on routers). End-user devices would be a poor choice as a platform for DHCP Snooping because they would not receive all the DHCP messages, nor would they be able to prevent frames from flowing should an attack occur.

2. B and C. Switch ports connected to IT-controlled devices from which DHCP server messages may be received should be trusted by the DHCP Snooping function. Those devices include IT-controlled DHCP servers and IT-controlled routers and switches. All devices that are expected to be DHCP client devices (like PCs) are then treated as untrusted, because DHCP Snooping cannot know beforehand from which ports a DHCP-based attack will be launched. In this case, the ports connected to all three PCs will be treated as untrusted by DHCP Snooping.

3. C and D. Because of a default setting of untrusted, the switch does not need any configuration commands to cause a port to be untrusted. Of the two (incorrect) answers that related to the trust state, **no ip dhcp snooping trust**, in interface config mode, would revert from a trust configuration state to an untrusted state. The other answer, **ip dhcp snooping untrusted**, is not a valid command.

   The two correct answers list a pair of configuration commands that both must be included to enable DHCP Snooping (**ip dhcp snooping**) and to specify the VLAN list on which DHCP Snooping should operate (**ip dhcp snooping vlan 5**).

4. A. All the answers list commands with correct syntax that are useful for DHCP Snooping; however, the correct answer, **no ip dhcp snooping information**, disables DHCP Snooping's feature of adding DHCP Option 82 fields to DHCP messages. This setting is useful if the switch does not act as a DHCP relay agent. The opposite setting (without the **no** to begin the command) works when the multilayer switch acts as a DHCP relay agent.

5. B. DAI always uses a core function that examines incoming ARP messages, specifi-cally the ARP message origin hardware and origin IP address fields, versus tables of data in the switch about correct pairs of MAC and IP addresses. DAI on a switch can use DHCP Snooping's binding table as the table of data with valid MAC/IP address pairs or use the logic in configured ARP ACLs. The question stem states that DAI uses DHCP Snooping, so the correct answer notes that the switch will compare the ARP message's origin hardware address to the switch's DHCP Snooping binding table.

One incorrect answer mentions a comparison of the message's ARP origin MAC (hard-ware) address with the message's Ethernet source MAC address. DAI can perform that check, but that feature can be configured to be enabled or disabled, so DAI would not always perform this comparison. The other incorrect answers list logic never per-formed by DAI.

6. B and D. Because of a default setting of untrusted, the switch must be configured so DAI trusts that one port. To add that configuration, the switch needs the **ip arp inspection trust** command in interface config mode. The similar (incorrect) answer of **no ip arp inspection untrust** is not a valid command.

To enable DAI for operation on a VLAN, the configuration needs one command: the **ip arp inspection vlan 6** command. This command both enables DAI and does so specifically for VLAN 6 alone. The answer **ip arp inspection** shows a command that would be rejected by the switch as needing more parameters.

7. C and D. With DAI, you can set a limit on the number of received ARP messages with a default burst interval of 1 second, or you can configure the burst interval. Once con-figured, DAI allows the configured number of ARP messages over the burst interval number of seconds. With the two correct answers, one shows 16 ARP messages, with a 4-second interval, for an average of 4 per second. The other correct answer shows a limit of 4, with the default burst interval of 1 second, for an average of 4. The two incorrect answers result in averages of 2 per second and 5 per second.

Chapter 9

1. D. By default, all message levels are logged to the console on a Cisco device. To do so, IOS uses logging level 7 (debugging), which causes IOS to send severity level 7, and levels below 7, to the console. All the incorrect answers list levels below level 7.

2. C. The **logging trap 4** command limits those messages sent to a syslog server (configured with the **logging host** *ip-address* command) to levels 4 and below, thus 0 through 4.

3. A. NTP uses protocol messages between clients and servers so that the clients can adjust their time-of-day clock to match the server. NTP is totally unrelated to serial line clocking. It also does not count CPU cycles, instead relying on messages from the NTP server. Also, the client defines the IP address of the server and does not have to be in the same subnet.

4. C. The **ntp server 10.1.1.1** command tells the router to be both an NTP server and cli-ent. However, the router first acts as an NTP client to synchronize its time with NTP server 10.1.1.1. Once synchronized, R1 knows the time to supply and can act as an NTP server.

5. E and F. CDP discovers information about neighbors. **show cdp** gives you several options that display more or less information, depending on the parameters used.

6. E and F. LLDP lists the neighbors enabled capabilities in the output of the **show lldp neighbors** command, and both the enabled and possible (system) capabilities in the output of the **show lldp entry** *hostname* command.

Chapter 10

1. D. CIDR's original intent was to allow the summarization of multiple Class A, B, and C networks to reduce the size of Internet routing tables. Of the answers, only 200.1.0.0 255.255.0.0 summarizes multiple networks.

2. B and E. RFC 1918 identifies private network numbers. It includes Class A network 10.0.0.0, Class B networks 172.16.0.0 through 172.31.0.0, and Class C networks 192.168.0.0 through 192.168.255.0.

3. C. With static NAT, the entries are statically configured. Because the question mentions translation for inside addresses, the **inside** keyword is needed in the command.

4. A. With dynamic NAT, the entries are created as a result of the first packet flow from the inside network.

5. A. The **list 1** parameter references an IP ACL, which matches packets, identifying the inside local addresses.

6. A and C. The configuration is missing the **overload** keyword in the **ip nat inside source** command and in the **ip nat outside** interface subcommand on the serial interface.

7. B. The last line mentions that the pool has seven addresses, with all seven allocated, with the misses counter close to 1000—meaning that close to 1000 new flows were rejected because of insufficient space in the NAT pool

Chapter 11

1. A, B, and E. QoS tools manage bandwidth, delay, jitter, and loss.

2. B and C. The Class of Service (CoS) field exists in the 802.1Q header, so it would be used only on trunks, and it would be stripped of the incoming data-link header by any router in the path. The MPLS EXP bits exist as the packet crosses the MPLS network only. The other two fields, IP Precedence (IPP) and Differentiated Services Code Point (DSCP), exist in the IP header and would flow from source host to destination host.

3. A, B, and C. In general, matching a packet with DiffServ relies on a comparison to something inside the message itself. The 802.1p CoS field exists in the data-link header on VLAN trunks; the IP DSCP field exists in the IP header; and extended ACLs check fields in message headers. The SNMP Location variable does not flow inside individual packets but is a value that can be requested from a device.

4. B and C. Low Latency Queuing (LLQ) applies priority queue scheduling, always taking the next packet from the LLQ if a packet is in that queue. To prevent queue starvation of the other queues, IOS also applies policing to the LLQ. However, applying shaping

C

to an LLQ slows the traffic, which makes no sense with the presence of a policing function already.

5. A and D. Policers monitor the bit rate and take action if the bit rate exceeds the policing rate. However, the action can be to discard some packets, or to re-mark some packets, or even to do nothing to the packets, simply measuring the rate for later reporting. For shaping, when a shaper is enabled because the traffic has exceeded the shaping rate, the shaper always queues packets and slows the traffic. There is no option to re-mark the packets or to bypass the shaping function.

6. C and D. Drop management relies on the behavior of TCP, in that TCP connections slow down sending packets due to the TCP congestion window calculation. Voice traffic uses UDP, and the question states that queue 1 uses UDP. So, queues 2 and 3 are reasonable candidates for using a congestion management tool.

Chapter 12

1. D. With this design but no FHRP, host A can send packets off-subnet as long as connectivity exists from host A to R1. Similarly, host B can send packets off-subnet as long as host B has connectivity to router R2. Both routers can attach to the same LAN subnet and basically ignore each other in relation to their roles as default router because they do not use an FHRP option. When either router fails, the hosts using that router as default router have no means by which to fail over.

2. C. The use of an FHRP in this design purposefully allows either router to fail and still support off-subnet traffic from all hosts in the subnet. Both routers can attach to the same LAN subnet per IPv4 addressing rules.

3. C. HSRP uses a virtual IP address. The virtual IP address comes from the same subnet as the routers' LAN interfaces but is a different IP address than the router addresses configured with the **ip address** interface subcommand. As a result, the hosts will not point to 10.1.19.1 or 10.1.19.2 in this design. The other wrong answer lists an idea of using the Domain Name System (DNS) to direct hosts to the right default router; although this idea exists in some other forms of network load balancing, it is not a part of any of the three FHRP protocols.

4. B. SNMPv1 and SNMPv2c use community strings to authenticate Get and Set messages from an NMS. The agent defines a read-only community and can define a read-write community as well. Get requests, which read information, will be accepted if the NMS sends either the read-only or the read-write community with those requests.

5. A and C. SNMP agents reside on a device being managed. When an event happens about which the device wants to inform the SNMP manager, the agent sends either an SNMP Trap or SNMP Inform to the SNMP manager. The SNMP manager normally sends an SNMP Get Request message to an agent to retrieve MIB variables or an SNMP Set Request to change an MIB variable on the agent.

6. A. FTP uses both a control connection and a data connection. The FTP client initiates the control connection. However, in active mode, the FTP server initiates the data connection. Also, note that FTP does not use TLS, while FTP Secure (FTPS) does use TLS.

7. B and D. TFTP supports fewer functions than FTP as a protocol. For instance, the client cannot change the current directory on the server, add directories, remove directories, or list the files in the directory. Both TFTP and FTP support the ability to transfer files in either direction.

Chapter 13

1. B and D. The access layer switches play the role of connecting to the endpoint devices, whether they are end-user devices or servers. Then, from the access to the distribution layer, each access layer connects to two distribution switches typically, but with no direct connections between access layer switches, creating a mesh (but a partial mesh). A two-tier design, also called a collapsed core, does not use core switches at all.

2. A and C. The access layer switches, not the distribution layer switches, play the role of connecting to the endpoint devices, whether they are end-user devices or servers. Then, from the access to the distribution layer, each access layer connects to two distribution switches typically, but with no direct connections between access layer switches, creating a mesh (but a partial mesh). A three-tier design, also called a core design, does use core switches, with a partial mesh of links between the distribution and core switches. Basically, each distribution switch connects to multiple core switches but often does not connect directly to other distribution switches.

3. D. The access layer uses access switches, which connect to endpoint devices. A single access switch with its endpoint devices looks like a star topology. The distribution layer creates a partial mesh of links between the distribution switches and access switches, so it is neither a full mesh nor a hybrid.

4. A and C. With a SOHO LAN, one integrated device typically supplies all the necessary functions, including routing, switching, wireless access point (AP), and firewall. The AP uses standalone mode, without a wireless LAN controller (WLC), and without a need to encapsulate frames in CAPWAP.

5. A. First, the switch does not supply power based on a configured value to avoid the unfortunate case of supplying power over the cable to a device that does not support the circuitry to receive the power, because doing so will likely harm the electronics on the connected device.

   If configured to use PoE, the switch begins with IEEE autonegotiation messages while sensing the load on the circuit, which indicates whether the device desires to receive power, and indicates the power class desired (which dictates the amount of power to initially deliver). Note that once the attached device (called the powered device, or PD) boots, the PD can request additional power using CDP and/or LLDP.

6. B and D. Universal Power over Ethernet (UPoE) and the enhanced UPoE Plus (UPoE+) supply power over all four pairs of the cable. Note that 1000BASE-T and faster UTP-based Ethernet standards often require four pair, whereas earlier/slower standards did not, and UPoE/UPoE+ take advantage of the existence of four pairs to supply power over all four pairs. Power over Ethernet (PoE) and PoE+ use two pairs for power and therefore work with Ethernet standards like 10BASE-T and 100BASE-T that use two pairs only.

C

Chapter 14

1. **B and C.** A Metro Ethernet E-Tree service uses a rooted point-to-multipoint Ethernet Virtual Connection (EVC), which means that one site connected to the service (the root) can communicate directly with each of the remote (leaf) sites. However, the leaf sites cannot send frames directly to each other; they can only send frames to the root site. Topology design like this that allows some but not all pairs of devices in the group to communicate is called a partial mesh, or hub and spoke, or in some cases a multipoint or point-to-multipoint topology.

   Of the incorrect answers, the *full mesh* term refers to topology designs in which each pair in the group can send data directly to each other, which is typical of a MetroE E-LAN service. The term *point-to-point* refers to topologies with only two nodes in the design, and they can send directly to each other, typical of a MetroE E-Line service.

2. **A.** Metro Ethernet uses Ethernet access links of various types. Time-division multiplexing (TDM) links such as serial links, even higher-speed links like T3 and E3, do not use Ethernet protocols, and are less likely to be used. MPLS is a WAN technology that creates a Layer 3 service.

   Two answers refer to Ethernet standards usable as the physical access link for a Metro Ethernet service. However, 100BASE-T supports cable lengths of only 100 meters, so it is less likely to be used as a Metro Ethernet access link in comparison to 100BASE-LX10, which supports lengths of 10 km.

3. **A and D.** An E-LAN service is one in which the Metro Ethernet service acts as if the WAN were a single Ethernet switch so that each device can communicate directly to every other device. As a result, the routers sit in the same subnet. With one headquarters router and 10 remote sites, each router will have 10 OSPF neighbors.

4. **B and C.** A Layer 3 MPLS VPN creates an IP service with a different subnet on each access link. With one headquarters router and 10 remote sites, 11 access links exist, so 11 subnets are used.

   As for the OSPF neighbor relationships, each enterprise router has a neighbor relationship with the MPLS provider edge (PE) router, but not with any of the other enterprise (customer edge) routers. So each remote site router would have only one OSPF neighbor relationship.

5. **D.** Architecturally, MPLS allows for a wide variety of access technologies. Those include TDM (that is, serial links), Frame Relay, ATM, Metro Ethernet, and traditional Internet access technologies such as DSL and cable.

6. **A.** The PE-CE link is the link between the customer edge (CE) router and the MPLS provider's provider edge (PE) router. When using OSPF, that link will be configured to be in some area. OSPF design allows for that link to be in the backbone area, or not, through the use of the OSPF super backbone, which exists between all the PE routers.

7. **A.** The term *remote access* VPN, or *client* VPN, typically refers to a VPN for which one endpoint is a user device, such as a phone, tablet, or PC. In those cases, TLS is the more likely protocol to use. TLS is included in browsers, and is commonly used to connect securely to websites. GRE along with IPsec is more likely to be used to create a site-to-site VPN connection. FTPS refers to FTP Secure, which uses TLS to secure FTP sessions.

Chapter 15

1. A, B, and E. The hypervisor will virtualize RAM, CPU, NICs, and storage for each VM. The hypervisor itself is not virtualized, but rather does the work to virtualize other resources. Also, as virtual machines, the VMs do not use power, so the power is not virtualized.

2. D. Hypervisors create a virtual equivalent of Ethernet switching and cabling between the VMs and the physical NICs. The VMs use a virtual NIC (vNIC). The hypervisor uses a virtual switch (vswitch), which includes the concept of a link between a vswitch port and each VM's vNIC. The vswitch also connects to both physical NICs. The switch can then be configured to create VLANs and trunks as needed.

3. B. Platform as a Service (PaaS) supplies one or more virtual machines (VMs) that have a working operating system (OS) as well as a predefined set of software development tools.

   As for the wrong answers, Software as a Service (SaaS) supplies a predefined software application, but typically with no ability to then later install your own applications. Infrastructure as a Service (IaaS) supplies one or more working VMs, optionally with an OS installed, so it could be used for software development, but the developer would have to install a variety of development tools, making IaaS less useful than a PaaS service. Finally, Server Load Balancing as a Service (SLBaaS) can be offered as a cloud service, but it is not a general service in which customers get access to VMs on which they can then install their own applications.

4. A. Infrastructure as a Service (IaaS) supplies one or more working virtual machines (VMs), optionally with an OS installed, as a place where you can then customize the systems by installing your own applications.

   Software as a Service (SaaS) supplies a predefined software application, but typically with no ability to then later install your own applications. Platform as a Service (PaaS) could be used to install your own application, because PaaS does supply one or more VMs, but it is most likely used as a software development environment, a service designed specifically to be used for development, with VMs that include various tools that are useful for software development. Finally, Server Load Balancing as a Service (SLBaaS) can be offered as a cloud service, but it is not a general service in which customers get access to VMs on which they can then install their own applications.

5. A. Both options that use the Internet allow for easier migration because public cloud providers typically provide easy access over the Internet. An intercloud exchange is a purpose-built WAN service that connects to enterprises as well as most public cloud providers, with the advantage of making the cloud migration process easier. The one correct answer—the worst option in terms of being prepared for migrating to a new cloud provider—is to use a private WAN connection to one cloud provider. While useful in other ways, migrating when using this strategy would require installing a new private WAN connection to the new cloud provider.

6. A and C. Private WAN options use technologies like Ethernet WAN and MPLS, both of which keep data private by their nature and which include QoS services. An intercloud exchange is a purpose-built WAN service that connects to enterprises as well as

most public cloud providers, using the same kinds of private WAN technology with those same benefits.

For the two incorrect answers, both use the Internet, so both cannot provide QoS services. The Internet VPN option does encrypt the data to keep it private.

Chapter 16

1. A. The *data plane* includes all networking device actions related to the receipt, processing, and forwarding of each message, as in the case described in the question. The term *table plane* is not used in networking. The *management plane* and *control plane* are not concerned with the per-message forwarding actions.

2. C. The *control plane* includes all networking device actions that create the information used by the data plane when processing messages. The control plane includes functions like IP routing protocols and Spanning Tree Protocol (STP).

    The term *table plane* is not used in networking. The *management plane* and *data plane* are not concerned with collecting the information that the data plane then uses.

3. C. Although many variations of SDN architectures exist, they typically use a centralized controller. That controller may centralize some or even all control plane functions in the controller. However, the data plane function of receiving messages, matching them based on header fields, taking actions (like making a forwarding decision), and forwarding the message still happens on the network elements (switches) and not on the controller.

    For the incorrect answers, the control plane functions may all happen on the controller, or some may happen on the controller, and some on the switches. The northbound and southbound interfaces are API interfaces on the controller, not on the switches.

4. A. The OpenDaylight Controller uses an Open SDN model with an OpenFlow southbound interface as defined by the Open Networking Foundation (ONF). The ONF SDN model centralizes most control plane functions. The APIC model for data centers partially centralizes control plane functions. The APIC-EM controller (as of time of publication) makes no changes to the control plane of routers and switches, leaving those to run with a completely distributed control plane.

5. C and D. ACI uses a spine-leaf topology. With a single-site topology, leaf switches must connect to all spine switches, and leaf switches must not connect to other leaf switches. Additionally, a leaf switch connects to some endpoints, with the endpoints being spread across the ports on all the leaf switches. (In some designs, two or more leaf switches connect to the same endpoints for redundancy and more capacity.)

6. A and D. Controller-based networks use a controller that communicates with each network device using a southbound interface (an API and protocol). By gathering network information into one central device, the controller can then allow for different operational models. The models often let the operator think in terms of enabling features in the network, rather than thinking about the particulars of each device and command on each device. The controller then configures the specific commands, resulting in more consistent device configuration.

For the incorrect answers, both the old and new models use forwarding tables on each device. Also, controllers do not add to or remove from the programmatic interfaces on each device, some of which existed before controllers, but rather supply useful and powerful northbound APIs.

Chapter 17

1. C. The SDA underlay consists of the network devices and connections, along with configuration that allows IP connectivity between the SDA nodes, for the purpose of supporting overlay VXLAN tunnels. The fabric includes both the underlay and overlay, while VXLAN refers to the protocol used to create the tunnels used by the overlay.

2. B. The overlay includes the control plane and data plane features to locate the endpoints, decide to which fabric node a VXLAN tunnel should connect, direct the frames into the tunnel, and perform VXLAN tunnel encapsulation and de-encapsulation. The SDA underlay exists as network devices, links, and a separate IP network to provide connectivity between nodes to support the VXLAN tunnels.

The fabric includes both the underlay and overlay, while VXLAN refers to the protocol used to create the tunnels used by the overlay.

3. D. The SDA overlay creates VXLAN tunnels between SDA edge nodes. Edge nodes then create a data plane by forwarding frames sent by endpoints over the VXLAN tunnels. LISP plays a role in the overlay as the control plane, which learns the identifiers of each endpoint, matching the endpoint to the fabric node that can teach the endpoint, so that the overlay knows where to create VXLAN tunnels.

For the other incorrect answers, note that while GRE is a tunneling protocol, SDA uses VXLAN for tunneling, and not GRE. Finally, OSPF acts as a control plane routing protocol, rather than a data plane protocol for SDA.

4. A and D. As with any SDA feature, the configuration model is to configure the feature using DNA Center, with DNA Center using southbound APIs to communicate the intent to the devices. The methods to configure the feature using DNA Center include using the GUI or using the northbound REST-based API.

Of the incorrect answers, you would not normally configure any of the SDA devices directly. Also, while DNA Center can use NETCONF as a southbound protocol to communicate with the SDA fabric nodes, it does not use NETCONF as a northbound API for configuration of features.

5. B, C, and D. Cisco DNA Center manages traditional network devices with traditional protocols like Telnet, SSH, and SNMP. DNA Center can also use NETCONF and RESTCONF if supported by the device. Note that while useful tools, Ansible and Puppet are not used by DNA Center.

6. A and D. Traditional network management platforms can do a large number of functions related to managing traditional networks and network devices, including the items listed in the two correct answers. However, when using Cisco's Prime Infrastructure as a traditional network management platform for comparison, it does not support SDA configuration, nor does it find the end-to-end path between two endpoints and analyze the ACLs in the path. Note that the two incorrect answers reference features available in DNA Center.

Chapter 18

1. B and D. The six primary required features of REST-based APIs include three features mentioned in the answers: a client/server architecture, stateless operation, notation of whether each object is cacheable. Two items from these three REST attributes are the correct answers. Of the incorrect answers, stateful operation is the opposite of the REST-based API feature of classless operation. For the other incorrect answer, although many REST-based APIs happen to use HTTP, REST APIs do not have to use HTTP.

2. B and D. In the CRUD software development acronym, the matching terms (create, read, update, delete) match one or more HTTP verbs. While the HTTP verbs can sometimes be used for multiple CRUD actions, the following are the general rules: create performed by HTTP POST; read by HTTP GET; update by HTTP PATCH, PUT (and sometimes POST); delete by HTTP DELETE.

3. C. The URI for a REST API call uses a format of protocol://hostname/resource?parameters. The API documentation details the resource part of the URI, as well as any optional parameters. For instance, in this case, the resource section is /dna/intent/api/v1/network-device. Additionally, the API documentation for this resource details optional parameters in the query field as listed after the ? in the URI.

4. A and D. Of the four answers, two happen to be most commonly used to format and serialize data returned from a REST API: JSON and XML. For the incorrect answers, JavaScript is a programming language that first defined JSON as a data serialization language. YAML is a data serialization/modeling language and can be found most often in configuration management tools like Ansible.

5. A and D. JSON defines variables as key:value pairs, with the key on the left of the colon (:) and always enclosed in double quotation marks, with the value on the right. The value can be a simple value or an object or array with additional complexity. The number of objects is defined by the number of matched curly brackets ({ and }), so this example shows a single JSON object.

   The one JSON object shown here includes one key and one :, so it has a single key:value pair (making one answer correct). The value in that key:value pair itself is a JSON array (a list in Python) that lists numbers 1, 2, and 3. The fact that the list is enclosed in square brackets defines it as a JSON array.

6. C and D. To interpret this JSON data, first look for the innermost pairing of either curly brackets { }, which denote one object, or square brackets [ ], which denote one array. In this case, the gray highlighted area is one JSON object, enclosed with { } and no other brackets of either type inside. That makes the gray area one object, which itself holds key:value pairs.

   Inside that one object, four key:value pairs exist, with the key before each colon and the value after each colon. That means "type" is a key, and "ACCESS" is one of the values.

   If you look at the other pair of curly brackets that begin and end the JSON data, that pair defines an object. That object has a key of "response" (making one answer incorrect). The "response" key then has a value equal to the entire inner object (the gray highlighted part), confirming one of the correct answers.

Chapter 19

1. C. Devices with the same role in an enterprise should have a very similar configuration. When engineers make unique changes on individual devices—different changes from those made in the majority of devices with that same role—those devices' configurations become different than the intended ideal configuration for every device with that role. This effect is known as configuration drift. Configuration management tools can monitor a device's configuration versus a file that shows the intended ideal configuration for devices in that role, noting when the device configuration drifts away from that ideal configuration.

2. A and B. The version control system, applied to the centralized text files that contain the device configurations, automatically tracks changes. That means the system can see which user edited the file, when, and exactly what change was made, with the ability to make comparisons between different versions of the files.

   The two incorrect answers list very useful features of a configuration management tool, but those answers list features typically found in the configuration management tool itself rather than in the version control tool.

3. D. Configuration monitoring (a generic description) refers to a process of checking the device's actual configuration versus the configuration management system's intended configuration for the device. If the actual configuration has moved away from the intended configuration—that is, if configuration drift has occurred—configuration monitoring can either reconfigure the device or notify the engineering staff.

   For the other answers, two refer to features of the associated version control software typically used along with the configuration management tool. Version control software will track the identity of each user who changes files and track the differences in files over time. The other incorrect answer is a useful feature of many configuration management tools, in which the tool verifies that the configuration will be accepted when attempted (or not). However, that useful feature is not part of what is called configuration monitoring.

4. A. Ansible uses a push model, in which the Ansible control node decides when to configure a device based on the instructions in a playbook. Puppet and Chef use pull models, in which an agent asks for information from a server, with the agent then making the decision of whether it needs to pull configuration data to itself and reconfigure itself.

5. B and C. Of the terms *manifest* and *recipe*, both refer to files that define the actions to take and/or the end state desired when taking action in one of the configuration management tools. These files go by the names Ansible playbook, Puppet manifest, and Chef recipe.

C

GLOSSARY

NUMERICS

3G/4G Internet   An Internet access technology that uses wireless radio signals to communicate through mobile phone towers, most often used by mobile phones, tablets, and some other mobile devices.

802.1 Q   The IEEE standardized protocol for VLAN trunking.

A

AAA   Authentication, authorization, and accounting. Authentication confirms the identity of the user or device. Authorization determines what the user or device is allowed to do. Accounting records information about access attempts, including inappropriate requests.

AAA server   *See* authentication, authorization, and accounting (AAA) server.

Access Control Entry (ACE)   One line in an access control list (ACL).

access interface   A LAN network design term that refers to a switch interface connected to end-user devices, configured so that it does not use VLAN trunking.

access layer   In a campus LAN design, the switches that connect directly to endpoint devices (servers, user devices), and also connect into the distribution layer switches.

access link   In Frame Relay, the physical serial link that connects a Frame Relay DTE device, usually a router, to a Frame Relay switch. The access link uses the same physical layer standards as do point-to-point leased lines.

access link (WAN)   A physical link between a service provider and its customer that provides access to the SP's network from that customer site.

access rate   The speed at which bits are sent over an access link.

accounting   In security, the recording of access attempts. *See also* AAA.

ACI   *See* Application Centric Infrastructure (ACI).

ACL   Access control list. A list configured on a router to control packet flow through the router, such as to prevent packets with a certain IP address from leaving a particular interface on the router.

Active Directory   A popular set of identity and directory services from Microsoft, used in part to authenticate users.

administrative distance   In Cisco routers, a means for one router to choose between multiple routes to reach the same subnet when those routes are learned by different routing protocols. The lower the administrative distance, the more preferred the source of the routing information.

agent   Generally, an additional software process or component running in a computing device for some specific purpose; a small and specific software service.

agent-based architecture   With configuration management tools, an architecture that uses a software agent inside the device being managed as part of the functions to manage the configuration.

agentless architecture   With configuration management tools, an architecture that does not need a software agent inside the device being managed as part of the functions to manage the configuration, instead using other mainstream methods like SSH and NETCONF.

amplification attack   A reflection attack that leverages a service on the reflector to generate and reflect huge volumes of reply traffic to the victim.

analog modem   *See* modem.

Ansible   A popular configuration management application, which can be used with or without a server, using a push model to move configurations into devices, with strong capabilities to manage network device configurations.

Ansible inventory   Device host names along with information about each device, like device roles, so Ansible can perform functions for subsets of the inventory.

Ansible playbook   Files with actions and logic about what Ansible should do.

Ansible template   A text file, written in Jinja2 language, that lists configuration but with variable names substituted for values, so that Ansible can create standard configurations for multiple devices from the same template.

anti-replay   Preventing a man in the middle from copying and later replaying the packets sent by a legitimate user, for the purpose of appearing to be a legitimate user.

antivirus   Software that monitors files transferred by any means, for example, web or email, to look for content that can be used to place a virus into a computer.

APIC   *See* Application Policy Infrastructure Controller.

APIC-EM   *See* Application Policy Infrastructure Controller—Enterprise Module.

Application Centric Infrastructure (ACI)   Cisco's data center SDN solution, the concepts of defining policies that the APIC controller then pushes to the switches in the network using the OpFlex protocol, with the partially distributed control plane in each switch building the forwarding table entries to support the policies learned from the controller. It also supports a GUI, a CLI, and APIs.

Application Policy Infrastructure Controller—Enterprise Module (APIC-EM)   The software that plays the role of controller in an enterprise network of Cisco devices, in its first version as of the publication of this book, which leaves the distributed routing and switching control plane as is, instead acting as a management and automation platform. It provides robust APIs for network automation and uses CLI (Telnet and SSH) plus SNMP southbound to control the existing routers and switches in an enterprise network.

Application Policy Infrastructure Controller (APIC)   The software that plays the role of controller, controlling the flows that the switches create to define where frames are forwarded, in a Cisco data center that uses the Application Centric Infrastructure (ACI) approach, switches, and software.

application programming interface (API)   A software mechanism that enables software components to communicate with each other.

application signature   With Network Based Application Recognition (NBAR), the definition of a combination of matchable fields that Cisco has identified as being characteristic of a specific application, so that NBAR can be configured by the customer to match an application, while IOS then defines the particulars of that matching.

Application Visibility and Control (AVC)   A firewall device with advanced features, including the ability to run many related security features in the same firewall device (IPS, malware detection, VPN termination), along with deep packet inspection with Application Visibility and Control (AVC) and the ability to perform URL filtering versus data collected about the reliability and risk associated with every domain name.

application-specific integrated circuit (ASIC)   An integrated circuit (computer chip) designed for a specific purpose or application, often used to implement the functions of a networking device rather than running a software process as part of the device's OS that runs on a general-purpose processor.

AR   *See* access rate.

ARP   Address Resolution Protocol. An Internet protocol used to map an IP address to a MAC address. Defined in RFC 826.

ARP ACL   A configuration feature on Cisco LAN switches that define MAC and IP address pairs that can be used directly for filtering, as well as to be referenced by the Dynamic ARP Inspection feature.

ARP reply   An ARP message used to supply information about the sending (origin) host's hardware (Ethernet) and IP addresses as listed in the origin hardware and origin IP address fields. Typically sent in reaction to receipt of an ARP request message.

ARP request   An ARP message used to request information from another host located on the same data link, typically listing a known target IP address but an all-zero target hardware address, to ask the host with that target IP address to identify its hardware address in an ARP reply message.

ARP table   A list of IP addresses of neighbors on the same VLAN, along with their MAC addresses, as kept in memory by hosts and routers.

ASAv   A Cisco ASA firewall software image that runs as a virtual machine rather than on Cisco hardware, intended to be used as a consumer-controlled firewall in a cloud service or in other virtualized environments.

ASIC   *See* application-specific integrated circuit.

Assured Forwarding (AF)   The name of a grid of 12 DSCP values and a matching grid of per-hop behavior as defined by DiffServ. AF defines four queuing classes and three packet drop priorities within each queuing class. The text names of the 12 DSCP values follow a format of AFXY, where X is the queuing class, and Y is the drop priority.

authentication   In security, the verification of the identity of a person or a process. *See also* AAA.

authentication, authorization, and accounting (AAA) server   A server that holds security information and provides services related to user login, particularly authentication (is the user who he says he is), authorization (once authenticated, what do we allow the user to do), and accounting (tracking the user).

Authoritative DNS server   The DNS server with the record that lists the address that corresponds to a domain name (the A Record) for that domain.

authorization   In security, the determination of the rights allowed for a particular user or device. *See also* AAA.

autonomous system (AS)   An internetwork that is managed by one organization.

autonomous system number (ASN)   A number used by BGP to identify a routing domain, often a single enterprise or organization. As used with EIGRP, a number that identifies the routing processes on routers that are willing to exchange EIGRP routing information with each other.

AutoQoS   In Cisco switches and routers, an IOS feature that configures a variety of QoS features with useful settings as defined by the Cisco reference design guide documents.

B

bandwidth   The speed at which bits can be sent and received over a link.

bandwidth profile   In Metro Ethernet, a contractual definition of the amount of traffic that the customer can send into the service and receive out of the service. Includes a concept called the committed information rate (CIR), which defines the minimum amount of bandwidth (bits per second) the SP will deliver with the service.

Brownfield   A term that refers to the choice to add new configuration to hardware and software that are already in use, rather that adding new hardware and software specifically for a new project.

brute-force attack   An attack where a malicious user runs software that tries every possible combination of letters, numbers, and special characters to guess a user's password. Attacks of this scale are usually run offline, where more computing resources and time are available.

buffer overflow attack   An attack meant to exploit a vulnerability in processing inbound traffic such that the target system's buffers overflow; the target system can end up crashing or inadvertently running malicious code injected by the attacker.

C

cable Internet   An Internet access technology that uses a cable TV (CATV) cable, normally used for video, to send and receive data.

cacheable   For resources that might be repeatedly requested over time, an attribute that means that the requesting host can keep in storage (cache) a copy of the resource for a specified amount of time.

candidate config   With configuration management tools like Ansible, Puppet, and Chef, an updated configuration for a device as it exists in the management tool before the tool has moved the configuration into the device.

carrier Ethernet   Per MEF documents, the term for what was formerly called Metro Ethernet, generally referring to any WAN service that uses Ethernet links as the access link between the customer and the service provider.

CDP   Cisco Discovery Protocol. A media- and protocol-independent device-discovery protocol that runs on most Cisco-manufactured equipment, including routers, access servers, and switches. Using CDP, a device can advertise its existence to other devices and receive information about other devices on the same LAN or on the remote side of a WAN.

CDP neighbor   A device on the other end of some communications cable that is advertising CDP updates.

central office (CO)   A term used by telcos to refer to a building that holds switching equipment, into which the telco's cable plant runs so that the telco has cabling from each home and business into that building.

centralized control plane   An approach to architecting network protocols and products that places the control plane functions into a centralized function rather than distributing the function across the networking devices.

Chef   A popular configuration management application, which uses a server and a pull model with in-device agents.

Chef client   Any device whose configuration is being managed by Chef.

Chef Cookbook   A set of recipes about the same kinds of work, grouped together for easier management and sharing.

Chef Recipe   The Chef logic applied to resources to determine when, how, and whether to act against the resources—analogous to a recipe in a cookbook.

Chef Runlist   An ordered list of recipes that should be run against a given device.

Chef server   The Chef software that collects all the configuration files and other files used by Chef from different Chef users and then communicates with Chef clients (devices) so that the Chef clients can synchronize their configurations.

CIDR   Classless interdomain routing. An RFC-standard tool for global IP address range assignment. CIDR reduces the size of Internet routers' IP routing tables, helping deal with the rapid growth of the Internet. The term *classless* refers to the fact that the summarized groups of networks represent a group of addresses that do not conform to IPv4 classful (Class A, B, and C) grouping rules.

Cisco Access Control Server (ACS)   A legacy Cisco product that acts as a AAA server.

Cisco AnyConnect Secure Mobility Client   Cisco software product used as client software on user devices to create a client VPN. Commonly referred to as the Cisco VPN client.

Cisco Open SDN Controller (OSC)   A former commercial SDN controller from Cisco that is based on the OpenDaylight controller.

Cisco Prime   Graphical user interface (GUI) software that utilizes SNMP and can be used to manage your Cisco network devices. The term *Cisco Prime* is an umbrella term that encompasses many different individual software products.

Cisco Prime Infrastructure (PI)   The name of Cisco's long-time enterprise network management application.

Cisco Talos Intelligence Group   A part of the Cisco Systems company that works to perform security research on an ongoing basis, in part to supply up-to-date data, like virus signatures, that Cisco security products can frequently download.

Cisco VPN client   *See* Cisco AnyConnect Secure Mobility Client.

Class of Service (CoS)   The informal term for the 3-bit field in the 802.IQ header intended for marking and classifying Ethernet frames for the purposes of applying QoS actions. Another term for Priority Code Point (PCP).

Class Selector (CS)   The name of eight DSCP values that all end with binary 000, for the purpose of having eight identifiable DSCP values whose first 3 bits match the eight values used for the older IP Precedence field. Originally used for backward compatibility with IP Precedence, but today the values are often used as just more values to use for packet marking.

classification   The process of examining various fields in networking messages in an effort to identify which messages fit into certain predetermined groups (classes).

classless addressing   A concept in IPv4 addressing that defines a subnetted IP address as having two parts: a prefix (or subnet) and a host.

client VPN   A VPN for which one endpoint is a user device, like a phone, tablet, or PC. Also called a remote access VPN.

clock rate   The speed at which a serial link encodes bits on the transmission medium.

clock source   On serial links, the device to which the other devices on the link adjust their speed when using synchronous links. With NTP, the external device or NTP server on which a device bases its time.

clocking   The process of supplying a signal over a cable, either on a separate pin on a serial cable or as part of the signal transitions in the transmitted signal, so that the receiving device can keep synchronization with the sending device.

Clos network   A term for network topology that represents an ideal for a switch fabric and named after Charles Clos, who formalized the definition. Also called a spine-leaf network.

cloud services catalog   A listing of the services available in a cloud computing service.

Cloud Services Router (CSR)   A Cisco router software image that runs as a virtual machine rather than on Cisco hardware, intended to be used as a consumer-controlled router in a cloud service or in other virtualized environments.

code integrity   A software security term that refers to how likely that the software (code) being used is the software supplied by the vendor, unchanged, with no viruses or other changes made to the software.

collapsed core design   A campus LAN design in which the design does not use a separate set of core switches in addition to the distribution switches—in effect collapsing the core into the distribution switches.

confidentiality (privacy)   Preventing anyone in the middle of the Internet (a.k.a. man in the middle) from being able to read the data.

configuration drift   A phenomenon that begins with the idea that devices with similar roles can and should have a similar standard configuration, so when one device's configuration is changed to be different, its configuration is considered to have moved away (drifted) from the standard configuration for a device in that role.

configuration enforcement   Another term for configuration monitoring.

configuration management   A component of network management focused on creating, changing, removing, and monitoring device configuration.

configuration management tool   A class of application that manages data about the configuration of servers, network devices, and other computing nodes, providing consistent means of describing the configurations, moving the configurations into the devices, noticing unintended changes to the configurations, and troubleshooting by easily identifying changes to the configuration files over time.

configuration monitoring   With configuration management tools like Ansible, Puppet, and Chef, a process of comparing over time a device's on-device configuration (running-config) versus the text file showing the ideal device configuration listed in the tool's centralized configuration repository. If different, the process can either change the device's configuration or report the issue.

configuration provisioning   With configuration management tools like Ansible, Puppet, and Chef, the process of configuring a device to match the configuration as held in the configuration management tool.

configuration template   With configuration management tools like Ansible, Puppet, and Chef, a file with variables, for the purpose of having the tool substitute different variable values to create the configuration for a device.

congestion window   With TCP, a calculation each TCP receiver does that limits the window it grants to the receiver by shrinking the window in response to the loss of TCP segments.

connection establishment   The process by which a connection-oriented protocol creates a connection. With TCP, a connection is established by a three-way transmission of TCP segments.

control plane   Functions in networking devices and controllers that directly control how devices perform data plane forwarding, but excluding the data plane processes that work to forward each message in the network.

controller-based networking   A style of building computer networks that use a controller that centralizes some features and provides application programming interfaces (APIs) that allow for software interactions between applications and the controller (northbound APIs) and between the controller and the network devices (southbound APIs).

core   In computer architecture, an individual processing unit that can execute instructions of a CPU; modern server processors typically have multiple cores, each capable of concurrent execution of instructions.

core design   A campus LAN design that connects each access switch to distribution switches, and distribution switches into core switches, to provide a path between all LAN devices.

core layer   In a campus LAN design, the switches that connect the distribution layer switches, and to each other, to provide connectivity between the various distribution layer switches.

CRUD   In software development, an acronym that refers to the four most common actions taken by a program: Create, Read, Update, and Delete.

customer edge (CE)   A term used by service providers, both generally and also specifically in MPLS VPN networks, to refer to the customer device that connects to the SP's network and therefore sits at the edge of the SP's network.

customer premises equipment (CPE)   A telco term that refers to equipment on site at the telco customer site (the enterprise's site) that connects to the WAN service provided by the telco.

D

data integrity   Verifying that the packet was not changed as the packet transited the Internet.

data model   A set of variables and their structures, like lists and dictionaries.

data modeling language   Another term for data serialization language.

data plane   Functions in networking devices that are part of the process of receiving a message, processing the message, and forwarding the message.

data serialization language   A language that includes syntax and rules that provides a means to describes the variables inside applications in a text format, for the purpose of sending that text between applications over a network or storing the data models in a file.

data structure   Another term for data model.

declarative policy model   A term that describes the approach in an intent-based network (IBN) in which the engineer chooses settings that describe the intended network behavior (the declared policy) but does not command the network with specific configuration commands for each protocol (as would be the case with an imperative policy model).

decrypt/decryption   The ability to receive encrypted data and process it to derive the original unencrypted data.

default gateway/default router   On an IP host, the IP address of some router to which the host sends packets when the packet's destination address is on a subnet.

delay   In QoS, the amount of time it takes for a message to cross a network. Delay can refer to one-way delay (the time required for the message to be sent from the source host to the destination host) or two-way delay (the delay from the source to the destination host and then back again).

demilitarized zone (DMZ)   In an Internet edge design at an enterprise, one or more subnets set aside as a place to locate servers that should allow users in the Internet to initiate connections to those servers. The devices in the DMZ typically sit behind a firewall.

denial-of-service (DoS) attack   An attack that tries to deplete a system resource so that systems and services crash or become unavailable.

deny   An action taken with an ACL that implies that the packet is discarded.

DevNet   Cisco's community and resource site for software developers, open to all, with many great learning resources; https://developer.cisco.com.

DHCP   Dynamic Host Configuration Protocol. A protocol used by hosts to dynamically discover and lease an IP address, and learn the correct subnet mask, default gateway, and DNS server IP addresses.

DHCP attack   Any attack that takes advantage of DHCP protocol messages.

DHCP binding table   A table built by the DHCP snooping feature on a switch when it sees messages about a new DHCP lease, with the table holding information about legitimate successful DHCP leases, including the device's IP address, MAC address, switch port, and VLAN.

DHCP chaddr   Client hardware address. The original DHCP header field used to identify the DHCP clients; typically includes the client MAC address.

DHCP client   Any device that uses DHCP protocols to ask to lease an IP address from a DHCP server or to learn any IP settings from that server.

DHCP client identifier   A DHCP header field used to identify a DHCP client, used as a more flexible alternative to the DHCP chaddr field.

DHCP giaddr   Gateway IP address. In DHCP, a header field used to identify a router on a subnet, typically an IP address on the DHCP relay agent, so that the DHCP server knows an address to which to send messages in reply to the client.

DHCP option 82   Optional DHCP header fields, as defined in RFC 3046, that provide useful features of use to a device that acts as a DHCP relay agent. The fields allow better relay agent operation and also help prevent various types of DHCP-based attacks.

DHCP relay agent   The name of the router IOS feature that forwards DHCP messages from client to servers by changing the destination IP address from 255.255.255.255 to the IP address of the DHCP server.

DHCP server   Software that waits for DHCP clients to request to lease IP addresses, with the server assigning a lease of an IP address as well as listing other important IP settings for the client.

DHCP Snooping   A switch security feature in which the switch examines incoming DHCP messages and chooses to filter messages that are abnormal and therefore might be part of a DHCP attack.

DHCP Snooping binding table   When using DHCP Snooping, a table that the switch dynamically builds by analyzing the DHCP messages that flow through the switch. DHCP Snooping can use the table for part of its filtering logic, with other features, such as Dynamic ARP Inspection and IP Source Guard also using the table.

dictionary attack   An attack where a malicious user runs software that attempts to guess a user's password by trying words from a dictionary or word list.

dictionary variable   In applications, a single variable whose value is a list of other variables with values, known as key:value pairs.

Differentiated Services (DiffServ)   An approach to QoS, originally defined in RFC 2475, that uses a model of applying QoS per classification, with planning of which applications and other traffic types are assigned to each class, with each class given different QoS per-hop behaviors at each networking device in the path.

Differentiated Services Code Point (DSCP)   A field existing as the first 6 bits of the ToS byte, as defined by RFC 2474, which redefined the original IP RFC's definition for the IP header ToS byte. The field is used to mark a value in the header for the purpose of performing later QoS actions on the packet.

Digital Subscriber Line (DSL)   A public network technology that delivers high bandwidth over conventional telco local-loop copper wiring at limited distances. Typically used as an Internet access technology, connecting a user to an ISP.

distributed control plane   An approach to architecting network protocols and products that places some control plane functions into each networking device rather than centralizing the control plane functions in one or a few devices. An example is the use of routing protocols on each router which then work together so that each router learns Layer 3 routes.

distributed denial-of-service (DDoS) attack   A DoS attack that is distributed across many hosts under centralized control of an attacker, all targeting the same victim.

distribution layer   In a campus LAN design, the switches that connect to access layer switches as the most efficient means to provide connectivity from the access layer into the other parts of the LAN.

DNA   Digital Network Architecture—Cisco's software-oriented approach to networking and intent-based networking products and services.

DNA Center   Cisco software, delivered by Cisco on a server appliance, that acts as a network management application as well as a being the control for Cisco's software-defined access (SDA) offering.

DNS Domain Name System. An application layer protocol used throughout the Internet for translating host names into their associated IP addresses.

DNS reply In the Domain Name System (DNS), a message sent by a DNS server to a DNS client in response to a DNS request, identifying the IP address assigned to a particular hostname or fully qualified domain name (FQDN).

DNS request In the Domain Name System (DNS), a message sent by a DNS client to a DNS server, listing a hostname or fully qualified domain name (FQDN), asking the server to discover and reply with the IP address associated with that host name or FQDN.

DNS server An application acting as a server for the purpose of providing name resolution services per the Domain Name System (DNS) protocol and worldwide system.

domain-specific language A generic term that refers to an attribute of different languages within computing, for languages created for a specific purpose (domain) rather than a general-purpose language like Python or JavaScript.

DSL Digital subscriber line. Public network technology that delivers high bandwidth over conventional telco local-loop copper wiring at limited distances. Usually used as an Internet access technology connecting a user to an ISP.

DSL modem A device that connects to a telephone line and uses DSL standards to transmit and receive data to/from a telco using DSL.

Dynamic ARP Inspection (DAI) A security feature in which a LAN switch filters a subset of incoming ARP messages on untrusted ports, based on a comparison of ARP, Ethernet, and IP header fields to data gathered in the IP DHCP Snooping binding table and found in any configured ARP ACLs.

E

egress tunnel router (ETR) With LISP, a node at the end of a tunnel that receives an encapsulated message and then de-encapsulates the message.

E-LAN A specific carrier/Metro Ethernet service defined by MEF (MEF.net) that provides a service much like a LAN, with two or more customer sites connected to one E-LAN service in a full mesh so that each device in the E-LAN can send Ethernet frames directly to every other device.

E-Line A specific carrier/metro Ethernet service defined by MEF (MEF.net) that provides a point-to-point topology between two customer devices, much as if the two devices were connected using an Ethernet crossover cable.

enable mode A part of the Cisco IOS CLI in which the user can use the most powerful and potentially disruptive commands on a router or switch, including the ability to then reach configuration mode and reconfigure the router.

enable password A reference to the password configured on the **enable password** *pass-value* command, which defines the password required to reach enable (privileged) mode if the **enable secret** *pass-value* command does not exist.

enable secret   A reference to the password configured on the **enable secret** *pass-value* command, which defines the password required to reach enable (privileged) mode.

encrypt/encryption   The ability to take data and send the data in a form that is not readable by someone who intercepts this data.

encryption key   A secret value used as input to the math formulas used by an encryption process.

End of Row (EoR) switch   In a traditional data center design with servers in multiple racks and the racks in multiple rows, a switch placed in a rack at the end of the row, intended to be cabled to all the Top of Rack (ToR) switches in the same row, to act as a distribution layer switch for the switches in that row.

endpoint group   In ACI, a set (group) of VMs, containers, physical servers, or other endpoints in an ACI data center that should receive the same policy treatment.

Endpoint ID (EID)   With LISP, a number that identifies the endpoint.

err-disable recovery   Cisco switches can place ports in a nonworking state called "err-disabled" in reaction to a variety of events, and by default, to leave the port in the nonworking err-disabled state until the engineer takes action to recover from the issue. The err-disable recovery configuration feature includes settings to direct the switch to automatically revert away from the err-disabled state, back to a working state, after a period of time.

error detection   The process of discovering whether a data-link level frame was changed during transmission. This process typically uses a Frame Check Sequence (FCS) field in the data-link trailer.

error disabled (err-disable)   An interface state on LAN switches that can be the result of one of many security violations.

error recovery   The process of noticing when some transmitted data was not successfully received and resending the data until it is successfully received.

Ethernet access link   A WAN access link (a physical link between a service provider and its customer) that happens to use Ethernet.

Ethernet LAN Service   Another term for E-LAN; *see also* E-LAN.

Ethernet Line Service   Another term for E-Line; *see also* E-Line.

Ethernet Tree Service   Another term for E-Tree; *see also* E-Tree.

Ethernet Virtual Connection (EVC)   A concept in carrier/Metro Ethernet that defines which customer devices can send frames to each other over the Ethernet WAN service; includes E-Line, E-LAN, and E-Tree EVCs.

Ethernet WAN   A general and informal term for any WAN service that uses Ethernet links as the access link between the customer and the service provider.

E-Tree   A specific carrier/metro Ethernet service defined by MEF (MEF.net) that provides a rooted multipoint service, in which the root site can send frames directly to all leaves, but the leaf sites can send only to the root site.

Expedited Forwarding (EF)   The name of a particular DSCP value, as well as the term for one per-hop behavior as defined by DiffServ. The value, decimal 46, is marked for packets to which the networking devices should apply certain per-hop behaviors, like priority queuing.

exploit   A means of taking advantage of a vulnerability to compromise something.

extended access list   A list of IOS access-list global configuration commands that can match multiple parts of an IP packet, including the source and destination IP address and TCP/UDP ports, for the purpose of deciding which packets to discard and which to allow through the router.

F

fabric   In SDA, the combination of overlay and underlay that together provide all features to deliver data across the network with the desired features and attributes.

fabric border node   In SDA, a switch that connects to devices outside SDA's control—for example, switches that connect to the WAN routers or to an ACI data center.

fabric control node   In SDA, a switch that performs special functions for the underlay (LISP), requiring more CPU and memory.

fabric edge node   In SDA, a switch that connects to endpoint devices.

fiber Internet   A general term for any Internet access technology that happens to use fiber-optic cabling. It often uses Ethernet protocols on the fiber link.

filter   Generally, a process or a device that screens network traffic for certain characteristics, such as source address, destination address, or protocol. This process determines whether to forward or discard that traffic based on the established criteria.

firewall   A device that forwards packets between the less secure and more secure parts of the network, applying rules that determine which packets are allowed to pass and which are not.

First Hop Redundancy Protocol (FHRP)   A class of protocols that includes HSRP, VRRP, and GLBP, which allows multiple redundant routers on the same subnet to act as a single default router (first-hop router).

flash memory   A type of read/write permanent memory that retains its contents even with no power applied to the memory, and uses no moving parts, making the memory less likely to fail over time.

flow control   The process of regulating the amount of data sent by a sending computer toward a receiving computer. Several flow control mechanisms exist, including TCP flow control, which uses windowing.

forward acknowledgment   A process used by protocols that do error recovery, in which the number that acknowledges data lists the next data that should be sent, not the last data that was successfully received.

forwarding plane   A synonym for data plane. *See also* data plane.

FTP   File Transfer Protocol. An application protocol, part of the TCP/IP protocol stack, used to transfer files between network nodes. FTP is defined in RFC 959.

FTP active mode   One of two modes of operation for FTP connections (the other being passive mode) that dictates how the FTP data mode connection is established. In active mode, the FTP client listens on a port, it identifies that port to the server, and the server initiates the TCP connection.

FTP client   An application that can connect to an FTP server for the purpose of transferring copies of files to and from the server.

FTP control connection   A TCP connection initiated by an FTP client to an FTP server for the purpose of sending FTP commands that direct the activities of the connection.

FTP data connection   A TCP connection created by an FTP client and server for the purpose of transferring data.

FTP over TLS   An FTP standard defined by RFC 4217, also known as FTP Secure (FTPS), which adds a variety of security features to the somewhat insecure original FTP standard (RFC 957), including the addition of the encryption of all data as well as username/password information using Transport Layer Security (TLS).

FTP passive mode   One of two modes of operation for FTP connections (the other being active mode) that dictates how the FTP data mode connection is established. In passive mode, the FTP client declares the use of passive mode, causing the server to choose and identify a new listening port, with the client establishing a TCP connection to that port.

FTP server   An application that runs and waits for FTP clients to connect to it over TCP port 21 to support the client's commands to transfer copies of files to and from the server.

FTPS   FTP Secure. Common term for FTP over TLS.

full mesh   From a topology perspective, any topology that has two or more devices, with each device being able to send frames to every other device.

G

Gateway Load Balancing Protocol (GLBP)   A Cisco-proprietary protocol that allows two (or more) routers to share the duties of being the default router on a subnet, with an active/active model, with all routers actively forwarding off-subnet traffic for some hosts in the subnet.

Generic Routing Encapsulation (GRE)   A protocol, defined in RFC 2784, that defines the headers used when creating a site-to-site VPN tunnel. The protocol defines the use of a normal IP header, called the Delivery Header, and a GRE header that the endpoints use to create and manage traffic over the GRE tunnel.

Git   An open-source version control application, widely popular for version control in software development and for other uses, like managing network device configurations.

GitHub   A software-as-a-service application that implements Git.

gratuitous ARP   An ARP Reply not sent as a reaction to an ARP request message, but rather as a general announcement informing other hosts of the values of the sending (origin) host's addresses.

GRE tunnel   A site-to-site VPN idea, in which the endpoints act as if a point-to-point link (the tunnel) exists between the sites, while actually encapsulating packets using GRE standards.

greenfield   A term that refers to the installation of new equipment for a project rather than adding configuration to existing in-use hardware and software.

H

host (context: DC)   In a virtualized server environment, the term used to refer to one physical server that is running a hypervisor to create multiple virtual machines.

Hot Standby Router Protocol (HSRP)   A Cisco-proprietary protocol that allows two (or more) routers to share the duties of being the default router on a subnet, with an active/standby model, with one router acting as the default router and the other sitting by waiting to take over that role if the first router fails.

HSRP active   A Hot Standby Router Protocol (HSRP) state in which the router actively supports the forwarding of off-subnet packets for hosts in that subnet.

HSRP standby   A Hot Standby Router Protocol (HSRP) state in which the router does not currently support the forwarding of off-subnet packets for hosts in that subnet, instead waiting for the currently active router to fail before taking over that role.

HTML   Hypertext Markup Language. A simple document-formatting language that uses tags to indicate how a given part of a document should be interpreted by a viewing application, such as a web browser.

HTTP   Hypertext Transfer Protocol. The protocol used by web browsers and web servers to transfer files, such as text and graphic files.

HTTP verb   The action defined in an HTTP request message.

hub and spoke   From a topology perspective, any topology that has a device that can send messages to all other devices (the hub), with one or more spoke devices that can send messages only to the hub. Also called point-to-multipoint.

hyperthreading   The name of Intel's multithreading technology.

hypervisor   Software that runs on server hardware to create the foundations of a virtualized server environment primarily by allocating server hardware components like CPU core/threads, RAM, disk, and network to the VMs running on the server.

I

IANA   The Internet Assigned Numbers Authority. An organization that owns the rights to assign many operating numbers and facts about how the global Internet works, including public IPv4 and IPv6 addresses. *See also* ICANN.

ICANN   The Internet Corporation for Assigned Names and Numbers. An organization appointed by IANA to oversee the distributed process of assigning public IPv4 and IPv6 addresses across the globe.

imperative policy model   A term that describes the approach in traditional networks in which the engineer chooses configuration settings for each control and data plane protocol (the imperative commands) that dictate specifically how the devices act. This model acts in contrast to the newer declarative policy model and intent-based networking (IBN).

Infrastructure as a Service (IaaS)   A cloud service in which the service consists of a virtual machine that has defined computing resources (CPUs, RAM, disk, and network) and may or may not be provided with an installed OS.

ingress tunnel router (ITR)   With LISP, the node that receives an unencapsulated message and encapsulates the message.

inside global   For packets sent to and from a host that resides inside the trusted part of a network that uses NAT, a term referring to the IP address used in the headers of those packets when those packets traverse the global (public) Internet.

inside local   For packets sent to and from a host that resides inside the trusted part of a network that uses NAT, a term referring to the IP address used in the headers of those packets when those packets traverse the enterprise (private) part of the network.

integrity   In data transfers, means that the network administrator can determine that the information has not been tampered with in transit.

intent-based networking (IBN)   An approach to networking in which the system gives the operator the means to express business intent, with the networking system then determining what should be done by the network, activating the appropriate configuration, and monitoring (assuring) the results.

intercloud exchange   A WAN service that provides connectivity between public cloud providers and their customers so that customers can install and keep the WAN connections, even when migrating from one cloud provider to another.

Internet access technology   Any technology that an ISP offers that allows its customers to send and receive data to/from the ISP, including serial links, Frame Relay, MPLS, Metro Ethernet, DSL, cable, and fiber Internet.

Internet edge   The part of the topology of the Internet that sits between an ISP and the ISP's customer.

Internet service provider   A company or organization that provides Internet services to customers; the company may have a heritage as a telco, WAN service provider, or cable company.

internetwork operating system (IOS)   *See* IOS.

intrusion detection system (IDS)   A security function that examines more complex traffic patterns against a list of both known attack signatures and general characteristics of how attacks can be carried out, rating each perceived threat and reporting the threats.

intrusion prevention system (IPS)   A security function that examines more complex traffic patterns against a list of both known attack signatures and general characteristics of how attacks can be carried out, rating each perceived threat, and reacting to prevent the more significant threats. *See also* IPS.

IOS   Cisco operating system software that provides the majority of a router's or switch's features, with the hardware providing the remaining features.

IOS feature set   A set of related features that can be enabled on a router to enable certain functionality. For example, the Security feature set would enable the ability to have the router act as a firewall in the network.

IOS File System (IFS)   A file system created by a Cisco device that uses IOS.

IOS image   A file that contains the IOS.

IP Precedence (IPP)   In the original definition of the IP header's Type of Service (ToS) byte, the first 3 bits of the ToS byte, used for marking IP packets for the purpose of applying QoS actions.

IPS   *See* intrusion prevention system.

IPsec   The term referring to the IP Security protocols, which is an architecture for providing encryption and authentication services, usually when creating VPN services through an IP network.

ISDN   Integrated Services Digital Network. A communication protocol offered by telephone companies that permits telephone networks to carry data, voice, and video.

Iterative DNS server   A DNS server that will answer DNS requests directly but will not take on the extra work to recursively send other DNS messages to find the answer.

J

JavaScript   A programming language popular for building dynamic web pages, commonly used to run scripts on a web client.

Jinja2   A text-based language used to define templates, with text plus variables; used by Ansible for templates.

jitter   The variation in delay experienced by successive packets in a single application flow.

JSON (JavaScript Object Notation)   A popular data serialization language, originally used with the JavaScript programming language, and popular for use with REST APIs.

JSON array   A part of a set of JSON text that begins and ends with a matched set of square brackets that contain a list of values.

JSON object   A part of a set of JSON text that begins and ends with a matched set of curly brackets that contain a set of key:value pairs.

K–L

key:value pair   In software, one variable name (key) and its value, separated by a colon in some languages and data serialization languages.

keyboard, video, mouse (KVM)   Three components of a typical desktop computer that are typically not included in a modern server because the server is installed and managed remotely.

KVM (Red Hat)   Kernel-Based Virtual Machine (KVM), a server virtualization/hypervisor product from the Red Hat company.

leaf   In an ACI network design, a switch that connects to spine switches and to endpoints, but not to other leaf switches, so that the leaf can forward frames from an endpoint to a spine, which then delivers the frame to some other leaf switch.

library   In software, a collection of programs packaged so that it can be posted as available in a software repository, found by others, and installed as one entity, as a means to make it easier to share code.

LISP   Locator/ID Separation Protocol. A protocol, defined in RFC 6830, that separates the concepts and numbers used to identify an endpoint (the endpoint identifier) versus identifying the location of the endpoint (routing locator).

LISP mapping database   With LISP, the table that contains mapped pairs of endpoint identifiers and routing locators.

LISP Routing Locator (RLOC)   With LISP, a value that identifies the location of an endpoint, typically the address of the egress device.

list variable   In applications, a single variable whose value is a list of values, rather than a simple value.

LLDP   Link Layer Discovery Protocol. An IEEE standard protocol (IEEE 802.1AB) that defines messages, encapsulated directly in Ethernet frames so they do not rely on a working IPv4 or IPv6 network, for the purpose of giving devices a means of announcing basic device information to other devices on the LAN. It is a standardized protocol similar to Cisco Discovery Protocol (CDP).

local loop   A line from the premises of a telephone subscriber to the telephone company CO.

local username   A username (with matching password), configured on a router or switch. It is considered local because it exists on the router or switch, and not on a remote server.

log message   A message generated by any computer, but including Cisco routers and switches, for which the device OS wants to notify the owner or administrator of the device about some event.

loss   A reference to packets in a network that are sent but do not reach the destination host.

low latency queue   In Cisco queuing systems, a queue from which the queue scheduling algorithm always takes packets next if the queue holds any packets. This scheduling choice means that packets in this queue spend little time in the queue, achieving low delay (latency) as well as low jitter.

Low Latency Queuing (LLQ)   The name of a queuing system that can be enabled on Cisco routers and switches by which messages sensitive to latency and jitter are placed in a queue that is always serviced first, resulting in low latency and jitter for those messages.

LTE   Literally, Long Term Evolution, but this term is used as a word itself to represent the type of wireless 4G technology that allows faster speeds than the original 4G specifications.

M

malware   Malicious software.

Management Information Base (MIB)   The data structures defined by SNMP to define a hierarchy (tree) structure with variables at the leaves of the tree, so that SNMP messages can reference the variables.

management plane   Functions in networking devices and controllers that control the devices themselves but that do not impact the forwarding behavior of the devices like control plane protocols do.

man-in-the-middle attack   An attack where an attacker manages to position a machine on the network such that it is able to intercept traffic passing between target hosts.

marking   The process of changing one of a small set of fields in various network protocol headers, including the IP header's DSCP field, for the purpose of later classifying a message based on that marked value.

markup language   A language that provides conventions to tag text to identify the type of text, which allows application of different treatments to different types of text.

match/action logic   The basic logic done by a networking element: to receive incoming messages, to match fields in the message, to then use logic based on those matches to take action against the message, and to then forward the message.

MD5 hash   A specific mathematical algorithm intended for use in various security protocols. In the context of Cisco routers and switches, the devices store the MD5 hash of certain passwords, rather than the passwords themselves, in an effort to make the device more secure.

Metro Ethernet   The original term used for WAN service that used Ethernet links as the access link between the customer and the service provider.

MIB   *See* Management Information Base.

MIB view   A concept in SNMPv3 that identifies a subset of an SNMP agent's MIB for the purpose of limiting access to some parts of the MIB to certain SNMP managers.

mitigation technique   A method to counteract or prevent threats and malicious activity.

modem   Modulator-demodulator. A device that converts between digital and analog signals so that a computer may send data to another computer using analog telephone lines. At the source, a modem converts digital signals to a form suitable for transmission over analog communication facilities. At the destination, the analog signals are returned to their digital form.

MPLS   *See* Multiprotocol Label Switching.

MPLS experimental bits   A 3-bit field in the MPLS label used for QoS marking.

MPLS VPN   A WAN service that uses MPLS technology, with many customers connecting to the same MPLS network, but with the VPN features keeping each customer's traffic separate from others.

MTU   Maximum transmission unit. The maximum packet size, in bytes, that a particular interface can handle.

multifactor authentication   A technique that uses more than one type of credential to authenticate users.

multipoint   A topology with more than two devices in it (in contrast to a point-to-point topology, which has exactly two devices). Without any further context, the term *multipoint* does not define whether all devices in the topology can send messages directly to each other (full mesh) or not (partial mesh).

Multiprotocol BGP (MPBGP)   A particular set of BGP extensions that allows BGP to support multiple address families, which when used to create an MPLS VPN service gives the SP the method to advertise the IPv4 routes of many customers while keeping those route advertisements logically separated.

Multiprotocol Label Switching (MPLS)   A WAN technology used to create an IP-based service for customers, with the service provider's internal network performing forwarding based on an MPLS label rather than the destination IP address.

multithreading   In computer architecture, a process of maximizing the use of a processor core by sharing an individual core among multiple programs, taking advantage of the typical idle times for the core while it waits on various other tasks like memory reads and writes.

N

name resolution   The process by which an IP host discovers the IP address associated with a host name, often involving sending a DNS request to a DNS server, with the server supplying the IP address used by a host with the listed host name.

name server   A server connected to a network that resolves network names into network addresses.

named access list   An ACL that identifies the various statements in the ACL based on a name rather than a number.

NAT   Network Address Translation. A mechanism for reducing the need for globally unique IP addresses. NAT allows an organization with addresses that are not globally unique to connect to the Internet, by translating those addresses into public addresses in the globally routable address space.

NAT overload   Another term for Port Address Translation (PAT). One of several methods of configuring NAT, in this case translating TCP and UDP flows based on port numbers in addition to using one or only a few inside global addresses.

National Institute of Standards and Technology (NIST)   A U.S. federal agency that develops national standards, including standards for cloud computing.

NBI   *See* northbound API.

Nest   In JSON, the concept that values can contain objects and arrays so that each object can contain other objects and arrays in a myriad of combinations.

Network Based Application Recognition (NBAR)   A Cisco router feature that looks at message details beyond the Layer 2, 3, and 4 headers to identify over 1000 different classifications of packets from different applications.

Network Management System (NMS)   Software that manages the network, often using SNMP and other protocols.

Network Time Protocol (NTP)   A protocol used to synchronize time-of-day clocks so that multiple devices use the same time of day, which allows log messages to be more easily matched based on their timestamps.

Next-generation firewall (NGFW)   A firewall device with advanced features, including the ability to run many related security features in the same firewall device (IPS, malware detection, VPN termination), along with deep packet inspection with Application Visibility and Control (AVC) and the ability to perform URL filtering versus data collected about the reliability and risk associated with every domain name.

Next-generation IPS (NGIPS)   An IPS device with advanced features, including the capability to go beyond a comparison to known attack signatures to also look at contextual data, including the vulnerabilities in the current network, the capability to monitor for new zero-day threats, with frequent updates of signatures from the Cisco Talos security research group.

Nexus 1000v   A Cisco Nexus data center switch that runs as a software-only virtual switch inside one host (one hardware server), to provide switching features to the virtual machines running on that host.

NMS   Network Management Station. The device that runs network management software to manage network devices. SNMP is often the network management protocol used between the NMS and the managed device.

northbound API   In the area of SDN, a reference to the APIs that a controller supports that gives outside programs access to the services of the controller; for instance, to supply information about the network or to program flows into the network. Also called a northbound interface.

northbound interface   Another term for northbound API. *See also* northbound API.

notification community   An SNMP community (a value that acts as a password), defined on an SNMP manager, which then must be supplied by any SNMP agent that that sends the manager any unsolicited SNMP notifications (like SNMP Trap and Notify requests).

NTP client   Any device that attempts to use the Network Time Protocol (NTP) to synchronize its time by adjusting the local device's time based on NTP messages received from a server.

NTP client/server mode   A mode of operation with the Network Time Protocol (NTP) in which the device acts as both an NTP client, synchronizing its time with some servers, and as an NTP server, supplying time information to clients.

NTP primary server   A term defined in NTP RFCs 1305 and 5905 to refer to devices that act as NTP servers alone, with a stratum 1 external clock source.

NTP secondary server   A term defined in NTP RFCs 1305 and 5905 to refer to devices that act as NTP clients and servers, synchronizing as a client to some NTP server, and then acting as an NTP server for other NTP clients.

NTP server   Any device that uses Network Time Protocol (NTP) to help synchronize time-of-day clocks for other devices by telling other devices its current time.

NTP synchronization   The process with the Network Time Protocol (NTP) by which different devices send messages, exchanging the devices' current time-of-day clock information and other data, so that some devices adjust their clocks to the point that the time-of-day clocks list the same time (often accurate to at least the same second).

NVRAM   Nonvolatile RAM. A type of random-access memory (RAM) that retains its contents when a unit is powered off.

O

ODL   *See* OpenDaylight.

OID   Object identifier. Used to uniquely describe an MIB variable in the SNMP database. This is a numeric string that identifies the variable uniquely and also describes where the variable exists in the MIB tree structure.

on-demand self-service   One of the five key attributes of a cloud computing service as defined by NIST, referring to the fact that the consumer of the server can request the service, with the service being created without any significant delay and without waiting on human intervention.

one-way delay   The elapsed time from sending the first bit of data at the sending device until the last bit of that data is received on the destination device.

ONF   *See* Open Networking Foundation.

on-premises   An alternate term for private cloud. *See also* private cloud.

Open Networking Foundation   A consortium of SDN users and vendors who work together to foster the adoption of open SDN in the marketplace.

OpenDaylight   An open-source SDN controller, created by an open-source effort of the OpenDaylight project under the Linux foundation, built with the intent to have a common SDN controller code base from which vendors could then take the code and add further features and support to create SDN controller products.

OpenFlow   The open standard for Software-Defined Networking (SDN) as defined by the Open Networking Foundation (ONF), which defines the OpenFlow protocol as well as the concept of an abstracted OpenFlow virtual switch.

operational management   A component of network management focused on extracting data about the network from the network devices, analyzing that data, and providing the data to operations staff.

OpFlex   The southbound protocol used by the Cisco ACI controller and the switches it controls.

ordered data transfer   A networking function, included in TCP, in which the protocol defines how the sending host should number the data transmitted, defines how the receiving device should attempt to reorder the data if it arrives out of order, and specifies to discard the data if it cannot be delivered in order.

origin hardware address   In both an ARP request and reply message, the field intended to be used to list the sender (origin) device's hardware address, typically an Ethernet LAN address.

origin IP address   In both an ARP request and reply message, the field intended to be used to list the sender (origin) device's IP address.

outside global   With source NAT, the one address used by the host that resides outside the enterprise, which NAT does not change, so there is no need for a contrasting term.

overlay   In SDA, the combination of VXLAN tunnels between fabric edge nodes as a data plane for forwarding frames, plus LISP for the control plane for the discovery and registration of endpoint identifiers.

P

partial mesh   A network topology in which more than two devices could physically communicate, but by choice, only a subset of the pairs of devices connected to the network is allowed to communicate directly.

password guessing   An attack where a malicious user simply makes repeated attempts to guess a user's password.

per-hop behavior (PHB)   The general term used to describe the set of QoS actions a device can apply to a message from the time it enters a networking device until the device forwards the message. PHBs include classification, marking, queuing, shaping, policing, and congestion avoidance.

permit   An action taken with an ACL that implies that the packet is allowed to proceed through the router and be forwarded.

pharming   An attack that compromises name services to silently redirect users toward a malicious site.

phishing   An attack technique that sends specially crafted emails to victims in the hope that the users will follow links to malicious websites.

Platform as a Service (PaaS)   A cloud service intended for software developers as a development platform, with a variety of tools useful to developers already installed so that developers can focus on developing software rather than on creating a good development environment.

PoE   Power over Ethernet. Both a generalized term for any of the standards that supply power over an Ethernet link, as well as a specific PoE standard as defined in the IEEE 802.3af amendment to the 802.3 standard.

point of presence (PoP)   A term used for a service provider's (SP) perspective to refer to a service provider's installation that is purposefully located relatively near to customers, with several spread around major cities, so that the distance from each customer site to one of the SP's PoPs is short.

point-to-multipoint   *See* hub and spoke.

point-to-point   From a topology perspective, any topology that has two and only two devices that can send messages directly to each other.

policing   A QoS tool that monitors the bit rate of the messages passing some point in the processing of a networking device, so that if the bit rate exceeds the policing rate for a period of time, the policer can discard excess packets to lower the rate.

policing rate   The bit rate at which a policer compares the bit rate of packets passing through a policing function, for the purpose of taking a different action against packets that conform (are under) to the rate versus those that exceed (go over) the rate.

policy model   In both ACI and other intent-based networks (IBNs), the operational conventions (model) that combine policies of what the network will provide to grouped sets of network endpoints (endpoint groups) to create a contract for what the network will provide.

port   (Multiple definitions) (1) In TCP and UDP, a number that is used to uniquely identify the application process that either sent (source port) or should receive (destination port) data. (2) In LAN switching, another term for switch interface.

Port Address Translation (PAT)   A NAT feature in which one inside global IP address supports over 65,000 concurrent TCP and UDP connections.

port number   A field in a TCP or UDP header that identifies the application that either sent (source port) or should receive (destination port) the data inside the data segment.

port security   A Cisco switch feature in which the switch watches Ethernet frames that come in an interface (a port), tracks the source MAC addresses of all such frames, and takes a security action if the number of different such MAC addresses is exceeded.

port-scanner   Jargon that refers to a security vulnerability during the time between the day in which the vulnerability was discovered, until the vendor or open-source group responsible for that software can develop a fix and make it public.

power budget   With PoE, data and calculations about the amount of power expected to be used by the various powered devices (PDs), the numbers of devices expected to connect to each switch, versus the amount of power available to PoE based on the capacity of the power supplies in the switches.

power class   In various PoE standards, a designation that can be sensed/identified via different discovery processes, with the class defining the maximum amount of power the powered device (PD) would like to receive over the Ethernet link.

Power over Ethernet (PoE)   Both a generalized term for any of the standards that supply power over an Ethernet link and a specific PoE standard as defined in the IEEE 802.3af amendment to the 802.3 standard.

Power over Ethernet Plus (PoE+)   A specific PoE standard as defined in the IEEE 802.3at amendment to the 802.3 standard, which uses two wire pairs to supply power with a maximum of 30 watts as supplied by the PSE.

power sourcing equipment (PSE)   With any Power over Ethernet standard, a term that refers to the device supplying the power over the cable, which is then used by the powered device (PD) on the other end of the cable.

powered device (PD)   With any Power over Ethernet standard, a term that refers to the device that receives or draws its power over the Ethernet cable, with the power being supplied by the power sourcing equipment (PSE) on the other end of the cable.

Priority Code Point (PCP)   The formal term for the 3-bit field in the 802.IQ header intended for marking and classifying Ethernet frames for the purposes of applying QoS actions. Another term for Class of Service (CoS).

priority queue   In Cisco queuing systems, another term for a low latency queue (LLQ).

private cloud   A cloud computing service in which a company provides its own IT services to internal customers inside the same company but by following the practices defined as cloud computing.

private IP network   Any of the IPv4 Class A, B, or C networks as defined by RFC 1918, intended for use inside a company but not used as public IP networks.

private key   A secret value used in public/private key encryption systems. Either encrypts a value that can then be decrypted using the matching public key, or decrypts a value that was previously encrypted with the matching public key.

programmable network   A computer network which provides programmatic interfaces that allow automation applications to change and interrogate the configuration of network devices.

provider edge (PE)   A term used by service providers, both generally and also specifically in MPLS VPN networks, to refer to the SP device in a point of presence (PoP) that connects to the customer's network and therefore sits at the edge of the SP's network.

public cloud   A cloud computing service in which the cloud provider is a different company than the cloud consumer.

public key   A publicly available value used in public/private key encryption systems. Either encrypts a value that can then be decrypted using the matching private key, or decrypts a value that was previously encrypted with the matching private key.

pull model   With configuration management tools, a practice by which an agent representing the device requests configuration data from the centralized configuration management tool, in effect pulling the configuration to the device.

Puppet   A popular configuration management application, which can be used with or without a server, using a pull model in which agents request details and pull configuration into devices, with the capability to manage network device configurations.

Puppet manifest   A human-readable text file on the Puppet master, using a language defined by Puppet, used to define the desired configuration state of a device.

Puppet master   Another term for Puppet server. *See also* Puppet server.

Puppet server   The Puppet software that collects all the configuration files and other files used by Puppet from different Chef users and then communicates with Puppet agents (devices) so that the agents can synchronize their configurations.

Push model   With configuration management tools, a practice by which the centralized configuration management tool software initiates the movement of configuration from that node to the device that will be configured, in effect pushing the configuration to the device.

Python   A programming language popular as a first language to learn and also popular for network automation tasks.

Python dictionary   A Python variable like a JSON dictionary, containing a set of key:value pairs.

Python list   A Python variable like a JSON array, containing a list of values.

Q–R

Quality of Experience (QoE)   The users' perception of the quality of their experience in using applications in the network.

Quality of Service (QoS)   The performance of a message, or the messages sent by an application, in regard to the bandwidth, delay, jitter, or loss characteristics experienced by the message(s).

queuing   The process by which networking devices hold packets in memory while waiting on some constrained resource; for example, when waiting for the outgoing interface to become available when too many packets arrive in a short period of time.

RADIUS   A security protocol often used for user authentication, including being used as part of the IEEE 802.lx messages between an 802.lx authenticator (typically a LAN switch) and a AAA server.

RAM   Random-access memory. A type of volatile memory that can be read and written by a microprocessor.

rapid elasticity   One of the five key attributes of a cloud computing service as defined by NIST, referring to the fact that the cloud service reacts to requests for new services quickly, and it expands (is elastic) to the point of appearing to be a limitless resource.

read-only community   An SNMP community (a value that acts as a password), defined on an SNMP agent, which then must be supplied by any SNMP manager that sends the agent any messages asking to learn the value of a variable (like SNMP Get and GetNext requests).

read-write community   An SNMP community (a value that acts as a password), defined on an SNMP agent, which then must be supplied by any SNMP manager that sends the agent any messages asking to set the value of a variable (like SNMP Set requests).

reconnaissance attack   An attack crafted to discover as much information about a target organization as possible; the attack can involve domain discovery, ping sweeps, port scans, and so on.

recursive DNS server   A DNS server that, when asked for information it does not have, performs a repetitive (recursive) process to ask other DNS servers in sequence, hoping to find the DNS server that knows the information.

reflection attack   An attack that uses spoofed source addresses so that a destination machine will reflect return traffic to the attack's target; the destination machine is known as the reflector.

remote access VPN   A VPN for which one endpoint is a user device, such as a phone, tablet, or PC, typically created dynamically, and often using TLS. Also called a client VPN.

Representational State Transfer (REST)   A type of API that allows two programs that reside on separate computers to communicate, with a set of six primary API attributes as defined early in this century by its creator, Roy Fielding. The attributes include client/server architecture, stateless operation, cachability, uniform interfaces, layered, and code-on-demand.

resource pooling   One of the five key attributes of a cloud computing service as defined by NIST, referring to the fact that the cloud provider treats its resources as a large group (pool) of resources that its cloud management systems then allocate dynamically based on self-service requests by its customers.

REST   *See* Representational State Transfer.

REST API   Any API that uses the rules of Representational State Transfer (REST).

RESTful API   A turn of phrase that means that the API uses REST rules.

RFC   Request For Comments. A document used as the primary means for communicating information about the TCP/IP protocols. Some RFCs are designated by the Internet Architecture Board (IAB) as Internet standards, and others are informational. RFCs are available online from numerous sources, including www.rfc-editor.org.

root DNS server   A small number of DNS servers worldwide that provide name resolution for the root zone of DNS, providing information about servers that know details about top-level domains (TLDs) such as .com, .org, .edu, and so on.

round robin   A queue scheduling algorithm in which the scheduling algorithm services one queue, then the next, then the next, and so on, working through the queues in sequence.

Round Trip Time (RTT)   The time it takes a message to go from the original sender to the receiver, plus the time for the response to that message to be sent back.

round-trip delay   The elapsed time from sending the first bit of data at the sending device until the last bit of that data is received on the destination device, plus the time waiting for the destination device to form a reply, plus the elapsed time for that reply message to arrive back to the original sender.

route redistribution   A method by which two routing protocol processes running in the same device can exchange routing information, thereby causing a route learned by one routing protocol to then be advertised by another.

routed access layer   A design choice in which all the switches, including the access layer switches that connect directly to endpoint devices, all use Layer 3 switching so that they route packets.

Router on a Stick (ROAS)   Jargon to refer to the Cisco router feature of using VLAN trunking on an Ethernet interface, which then allows the router to route packets that happen to enter the router on that trunk and then exit the router on that same trunk, just on a different VLAN.

S

SBI   *See* Southbound API.

scalable group   In SDA, the concept of a set of related users that should have the equivalent security access.

scalable group tag (SGT)   In SDA, a value assigned to the users in the same security group.

Secure Shell (SSH)   A TCP/IP application layer protocol that supports terminal emulation between a client and server, using dynamic key exchange and encryption to keep the communications private.

Secure Sockets Layer (SSL)   A deprecated security protocol that was formerly used to secure networks and was commonly integrated into web browsers to provide encryption and authentication services between the browser and a website.

segment   (Multiple definitions) (1) In TCP, a term used to describe a TCP header and its encapsulated data (also called an L4PDU). (2) Also in TCP, the set of bytes formed when TCP breaks a large chunk of data given to it by the application layer into smaller pieces that fit into TCP segments. (3) In Ethernet, either a single Ethernet cable or a single collision domain (no matter how many cables are used).

service provider (SP)   A company that provides a service to multiple customers. Used most often to refer to providers of private WAN services and Internet services. *See also* Internet service provider.

session key   With encryption, a secret value that is known to both parties in a communication, used for a period of time, which the endpoints use when encrypting and decrypting data.

SFTP   SSH File Transfer Protocol. A file transfer protocol that assumes a secure channel, such as an encrypted SSH connection, which then provides the means to transfer files over the secure channel.

shaping   A QoS tool that monitors the bit rate of the messages exiting networking devices, so that if the bit rate exceeds the shaping rate for a period of time, the shaper can queue the packets, effectively slowing down the sending rate to match the shaping rate.

shaping rate   The bit rate at which a shaper compares the bit rate of packets passing through the shaping function, so that when the rate is exceeded, the shaper enables the queuing of packets, resulting in slowing the bit rate of the collective packets that pass through the shaper, so the rate of bits getting through the shaper does not exceed the shaping rate.

shared key   A reference to a security key whose value is known (shared) by both the sender and receiver.

shared port   With 802.lw RSTP, a port type that is determined by the fact that the port uses half duplex, which could then imply a shared LAN as created by a LAN hub.

Simple Network Management Protocol (SNMP)   An Internet standard protocol for managing devices on IP networks. It is used mostly in network management systems to monitor network-attached devices for conditions that warrant administrative attention.

simple variable   In applications, a variable that has a single value of a simple type, such as text and integer or floating-point numbers.

single point of failure   In a network, a single device or link that, if it fails, causes an outage for a given population of users.

site-to-site VPN   The mechanism that allows all devices at two different sites to communicate securely over some unsecure network like the Internet, by having one device at each site perform encryption/decryption and forwarding for all the packets sent between the sites.

sliding windows   For protocols such as TCP that allow the receiving device to dictate the amount of data the sender can send before receiving an acknowledgment—a concept called a *window*—a reference to the fact that the mechanism to grant future windows is typically just a number that grows upward slowly after each acknowledgment, sliding upward.

SNMP   *See* Simple Network Management Protocol.

SNMP agent   Software that resides on the managed device and processes the SNMP messages sent by the Network Management Station (NMS).

SNMP community   A simple password mechanism in SNMP in which either the SNMP agent or manager defines a community string (password), and the other device must send that same password value in SNMP messages, or the messages are ignored. *See also* read-only community, read-write community, and notification community.

SNMP Get   Message used by SNMP to read from variables in the MIB.

SNMP Inform   An unsolicited SNMP message like a Trap message, except that the protocol requires that the Inform message needs to be acknowledged by the SNMP manager.

SNMP manager   Typically a Network Management System (NMS), with this term specifically referring to the use of SNMP and the typical role of the manager, which retrieves status information with SNMP Get requests, sets variables with the SNMP Set requests, and receives unsolicited notifications from SNMP agents by listening for SNMP Trap and Notify messages.

SNMP Set   SNMP message to set the value in variables of the MIB. These messages are the key to an administrator configuring the managed device using SNMP.

SNMP Trap   An unsolicited SNMP message generated by the managed device, and sent to the SNMP manager, to give information to the manager about some event or because a measurement threshold has been passed.

SNMPv2c   A variation of the second version of SNMP. SNMP Version 2 did not originally support communities; the term *SNMPv2c* refers to SNMP version 2 with support added for SNMP communities (which were part of SNMPvl).

SNMPv3   The third version of SNMP, with the notable addition of several security features as compared to SNMPv2c, specifically message integrity, authentication, and encryption.

social engineering   Attacks that leverage human trust and social behaviors to divulge sensitive information.

Software as a Service (SaaS)   A cloud service in which the service consists of access to working software, without the need to be concerned about the details of installing and maintaining the software or the servers on which it runs.

Software-Defined Access   Cisco's intent-based networking (IBN) offering for enterprise networks.

software-defined architecture   In computer networking, any architecture that provides mechanisms for automated software control of the network components, typically using a controller. Any architecture that leads to a Software-Defined Network (SDN).

Software-Defined Networking (SDN)   A branch of networking that emerged in the marketplace in the 2010s characterized by the use of a centralized software controller that takes over varying amounts of the control plane processing formerly done inside networking devices, with the controller directing the networking elements as to what forwarding table entries to put into their forwarding tables.

SOHO   A classification of a business site with a relatively small number of devices, sometimes in an employee office in their home.

Source NAT   The type of Network Address Translation (NAT) used most commonly in networks (as compared to destination NAT), in which the source IP address of packets entering an inside interface is translated.

southbound API   In the area of SDN, a reference to the APIs used between a controller and the network elements for the purpose of learning information from the elements and for programming (controlling) the forwarding behavior of the elements. Also called a southbound interface.

southbound interface   Another term for southbound API. *See also* southbound API.

spear phishing   Phishing that targets a group of users who share a common interest or connection.

spine   In an ACI network design for a single site, a switch that connects to leaf switches only, for the purpose of receiving frames from one leaf switch and then forwarding the frame to some other leaf switch.

spine-leaf network   A single-site network topology in which endpoints connect to leaf switches, leaf switches connect to all spine switches (but not to other leaf switches), and spine switches connect to all leaf switches (but not to other spine switches). The resulting topology results in predictable switching paths with three switches between any two endpoints that connect to different leaf switches.

spoofing attack   A type of attack in which parameters such as IP and MAC addresses are spoofed with fake values to disguise the sender.

spurious DHCP server   A DHCP server that is used by an attacker for attacks that take advantage of DHCP protocol messages.

SSL   *See* Secure Sockets Layer.

standard access list   A list of IOS global configuration commands that can match only a packet's source IP address for the purpose of deciding which packets to discard and which to allow through the router.

star topology   A network topology in which endpoints on a network are connected to a common central device by point-to-point links.

stateful   A protocol or process that requires information stored from previous transactions to perform the current transaction.

stateless   A protocol or process that does not use information stored from previous transactions to perform the current transaction.

subinterface   One of the virtual interfaces on a single physical interface.

switch abstraction   The fundamental idea of what a switch does, in generalized form, so that standards protocols and APIs can be defined that then program a standard switch abstraction; a key part of the OpenFlow standard.

syslog   A server that takes system messages from network devices and stores them in a database. The syslog server also provides reporting capabilities on these system messages. Some syslog servers can even respond to select system messages with certain actions such as emailing and paging.

syslog server   A server application that collects syslog messages from many devices over the network and provides a user interface so that IT administrators can view the log messages to troubleshoot problems.

T

T1   A line from the telco that allows transmission of data at 1.544 Mbps, with the capability to treat the line as 24 different 64-Kbps DSO channels (plus 8 Kbps of overhead).

T3   A line from the telco that allows transmission of data at 44.736 Mbps, with the capability to treat the line as 28 different 1.544-Mbps DS1 (Tl) channels, plus overhead.

TACACS+   A security protocol often used for user authentication as well as authorization and accounting, often used to authenticate users who log in to Cisco routers and switches.

tail drop   Packet drops that occur when a queue fills, another message arrives that needs to be placed into the queue, and the networking device tries to add the new message to the tail of the queue but finds no room in the queue, resulting in a dropped packet.

target hardware address   In both an ARP request and reply message, the field intended to be used to list the destination (target) device's hardware address, typically an Ethernet LAN address. This field is left as all binary 0s for typical ARP request messages.

target IP address   In both an ARP request and reply message, the field intended to be used to list the destination (target) device's IP address.

TCAM   *See* ternary content-addressable memory.

TCP   Transmission Control Protocol. A connection-oriented transport layer TCP/IP protocol that provides reliable data transmission.

TCP window   The mechanism in a TCP connection used by each host to manage how much data the receiver allows the sender to send to the receiver.

TCP/IP   Transmission Control Protocol/Internet Protocol. A common name for the suite of protocols developed by the U.S. Department of Defense in the 1970s to support the construction of worldwide internetworks. TCP and IP are the two best-known protocols in the suite.

telco   A common abbreviation for telephone company.

ternary content-addressable memory (TCAM)   A type of physical memory, either in a separate integrated circuit or built into an ASIC, that can store tables and then be searched against a key, such that the search time happens quickly and does not increase as the size of the table increases. TCAMs are used extensively in higher-performance networking devices as the means to store and search forwarding tables in Ethernet switches and higher-performance routers.

TFTP   Trivial File Transfer Protocol. An application protocol that allows files to be transferred from one computer to another over a network, but with only a few features, making the software require little storage space.

TFTP client   An application that can connect to a TFTP server for the purpose of transferring copies of files to and from the server.

TFTP server   An application that runs and waits for TFTP clients to connect to it over UDP port 69 to support the client's commands to transfer copies of files to and from the server.

threat   An actual potential to use an exploit to take advantage of a vulnerability.

three-tier design   *See* core design.

time interval (shaper)   Part of the internal logic used by a traffic shaping function, which defines a short time period in which the shaper sends packets until a number of bytes are sent, and then the shaper stops sending for the rest of the time interval, with a goal of averaging a defined bit rate of sending data.

TLD DNS server   A DNS server with the role of identifying the IP address of the authoritative DNS server for a domain that resides within its top-level domain.

Top of Rack (ToR) switch   In a traditional data center design with servers in multiple racks and the racks in multiple rows, a switch placed in the top of the rack for the purpose of providing physical connectivity to the servers (hosts) in that rack.

top-level domain (TLD)   With DNS name services, the top-level domain is the most significant (rightmost) of the period-separated values in a DNS host name—for example, the .com within host name www.example.com.

Transport Layer Security (TLS)   A security standard that replaced the older Secure Sockets Layer (SSL) protocol, providing functions such as authentication, confidentiality, and message integrity over reliable in-order data streams like TCP.

trojan horse   Malware that is hidden and packaged inside other legitimate software.

trust boundary   When thinking about a message as it flows from the source device to the destination device, the trust boundary is the first device the message reaches for which the QoS markings in the message's various headers can be trusted as having an accurate value, allowing the device to apply the correct QoS actions to the message based on the marking.

trusted port   With both the DHCP snooping and Dynamic ARP Inspection (DAI) switch features, the concept and configuration setting that tells the switch to allow all incoming messages of that respective type, rather than to consider the incoming messages (DHCP and ARP, respectively) for filtering.

tunnel interface   A virtual interface in a Cisco router used to configure a variety of features, including Generic Routing Encapsulation (GRE), which encapsulates IP packets into other IP packets for the purpose of creating VPNs.

two-tier design   *See* collapsed core design.

Type of Service (ToS)   In the original definition of the IP header, a byte reserved for the purpose of QoS functions, including holding the IP Precedence field. The ToS byte was later repurposed to hold the DSCP field.

U

UDP   User Datagram Protocol. Connectionless transport layer protocol in the TCP/IP protocol stack. UDP is a simple protocol that exchanges datagrams without acknowledgments or guaranteed delivery.

uncacheable   For resources that might be repeatedly requested over time, an attribute that means that the requesting host should not use its local copy of the resource, but instead ask for a new copy every time the resource is required.

underlay   In SDA, the network devices and links that create basic IP connectivity to support the creation of VXLAN tunnels for the overlay.

Unified Computing System (UCS)   The Cisco brand name for its server hardware products.

Universal Power over Ethernet (UPoE)   A specific PoE standard as defined in the IEEE 802.3bt amendment to the 802.3 standard, which uses four wire pairs to supply power with a maximum of 60 watts as supplied by the PSE.

Universal Power over Ethernet Plus (UPoE+)   A specific PoE standard as defined in the IEEE 802.3bt amendment to the 802.3 standard, which uses four wire pairs to supply power with a maximum of 100 watts as supplied by the PSE.

untrusted port   With both the DHCP snooping and Dynamic ARP Inspection (DAI) switch features, the concept and configuration setting that tells the switch to analyze each incoming message of that respective type (DHCP and ARP) and apply some rules to decide whether to discard the message.

UPoE   Universal Power over Ethernet. A specific PoE standard as defined in IEEE 802.3bt amendment to the 802.3 standard, which uses four wire pairs to supply power with a maximum of 60 watts as supplied by the PSE.

URI   Uniform Resource Identifier. The formal and correct term for the formatted text used to refer to objects in an IP network. This text is commonly called a URL or a web address. For example, http://www.certskills.com/blog is a URI that identifies the protocol (HTTP), host name (www.certskills.com), and web page (blog).

URI parameters   *See* URI query (parameters).

URI path (resource)   In a URI, the part that follows the first /, up to the query field (which begins with a ?), which identifies the resource in the context of a server.

URI query (parameters)   In a URI, the part that follows the first ?, which provides a place to list variable names and values as parameters.

URI resource   *See* URI path (resource).

URL   Uniform Resource Locator. The widely popular terms for the formatted text used to refer to objects in an IP network. For example, http://www.certskills.com/blog is a URL that identifies the protocol (HTTP), host name (www.certskills.com), and web page (blog).

user network interface (UNI)   A term used in a variety of WAN standards, including carrier/Metro Ethernet, that defines the standards for how a customer device communicates with a service provider's device over an access link.

username secret   A reference to the password configured on the **username** *name* **secret** *pass-value* command, which defines a username and an encoded password, used to build a local username/password list on the router or switch.

V

variable   In applications, a method to assign a name to a value so that the application can refer to the value, change it, compare it to other values, apply logic, and perform other actions typical of software applications.

version control software   Applications that monitor files for changes, tracking each specific change, the user, the date/time, with tools so that users can compare versions of each file through its history to see the differences.

violation mode   In port security, a configuration setting that defines the specific set of actions to take on a port when a port security violation occurs. The modes are shutdown, restrict, and protect.

virtual CPU (vCPU)   In a virtualized server environment, a CPU (processor) core or thread allocated to a virtual machine (VM) by the hypervisor.

virtual IP address   For any FHRP protocol, an IP address that the FHRP shares between multiple routers so that they appear as a single default router to hosts on that subnet.

virtual MAC address (vMAC)   For any FHRP protocol, a MAC address that the FHRP uses to receive frames from hosts.

virtual machine   An instance of an operating system, running on server hardware that uses a hypervisor to allocate a subset of the server hardware (CPU, RAM, disk, and network) to that VM.

virtual network function (VNF)   Any function done within a network (for example, router, switch, firewall) that is implemented not as a physical device but as an OS running in a virtualized system (for instance, a VM).

virtual network identifier (VNID)   In SDA and VXLAN, the identifier for a separate routing and switching instance. All devices in the same VNID are considered to be allowed to send data to each other unless prevented from doing so by other security mechanisms.

virtual NIC (vNIC)   In a virtualized server environment, a network interface card (NIC) used by a virtual machine, which then connects to some virtual switch (vSwitch) running on that same host, which in turn connects to a physical NIC on the host.

virtual private network (VPN)   A set of security protocols that, when implemented by two devices on either side of an unsecure network such as the Internet, can allow the devices to send data securely. VPNs provide privacy, device authentication, anti-replay services, and data integrity services.

Virtual Router Redundancy Protocol (VRRP)   A TCP/IP RFC protocol that allows two (or more) routers to share the duties of being the default router on a subnet, with an active/standby model, with one router acting as the default router and the other sitting by waiting to take over that role if the first router fails.

virtual switch (vSwitch)   A software-only virtual switch inside one host (one hardware server), to provide switching features to the virtual machines running on that host.

virus   Malware that injects itself into other applications and then propagates through user intervention.

VPN   *See* virtual private network.

VPN client   Software that resides on a PC, often a laptop, so that the host can implement the protocols required to be an endpoint of a VPN.

vulnerability   A weakness that can be used to compromise security.

VXLAN   Virtual Extensible LAN. A flexible encapsulation protocol used for creating tunnels (overlays).

W

WAN edge   The device (typically a router) at enterprise sites that connects to private WAN links, therefore sitting at the edge of the WAN.

WAN link   Another term for leased line.

WAN service provider   A company that provides private WAN services to customers; the company may have a heritage as a telco or cable company.

watering hole attack   An attack where a site frequently visited by a group of users is compromised; when the target users visit the site, they will be infected with malware, but other users will not.

web server   Software, running on a computer, that stores web pages and sends those web pages to web clients (web browsers) that request the web pages.

well-known port   A TCP or UDP port number reserved for use by a particular application. The use of well-known ports allows a client to send a TCP or UDP segment to a server, to the correct destination port for that application.

whaling   A phishing technique that targets high-profile individuals to follow links to malicious sites.

wildcard mask   The mask used in Cisco IOS ACL commands and OSPF and EIGRP **network** commands.

window   Represents the number of bytes that can be sent without receiving an acknowledgment.

worm   Malware that propagates from one system to another, infecting as it goes, all autonomously.

write community   *See* read-write community.

X–Y–Z

XML (eXtensible Markup Language)   A markup language that helps enable dynamic web pages; also useful as a data serialization language.

YAML (YAML Ain't Markup Language)   A data serialization language that can be easily read by humans; used by Ansible.

zero-day vulnerability   Jargon that refers to a security vulnerability during the time between the day in which the vulnerability was discovered, until the vendor or open-source group responsible for that software can develop a fix and make it public.

Index

B

N

Q

S

REGISTER YOUR PRODUCT at CiscoPress.com/register

Access Additional Benefits and SAVE 35% on Your Next Purchase

- Download available product updates.
- Access bonus material when applicable.
- Receive exclusive offers on new editions and related products.
  (Just check the box to hear from us when setting up your account.)
- Get a coupon for 35% for your next purchase, valid for 30 days.
  Your code will be available in your Cisco Press cart. (You will also find
  it in the Manage Codes section of your account page.)

Registration benefits vary by product. Benefits will be listed on your account page under Registered Products.

CiscoPress.com – Learning Solutions for Self-Paced Study, Enterprise, and the Classroom
Cisco Press is the Cisco Systems authorized book publisher of Cisco networking technology, Cisco certification self-study, and Cisco Networking Academy Program materials.

At **CiscoPress.com** you can
- Shop our books, eBooks, software, and video training.
- Take advantage of our special offers and promotions (ciscopress.com/promotions).
- Sign up for special offers and content newsletters (ciscopress.com/newsletters).
- Read free articles, exam profiles, and blogs by information technology experts.
- Access thousands of free chapters and video lessons.

Connect with Cisco Press – Visit CiscoPress.com/community
Learn about Cisco Press community events and programs.

Cisco Press

ALWAYS LEARNING   PEARSON